The Festivals of Opet, the Valley, and the New Year

The Festivals of Opet, the Valley, and the New Year

Their socio-religious functions

Masashi Fukaya

Archaeopress Egyptology 28

Archaeopress Publishing Ltd
Summertown Pavilion
18-24 Middle Way
Summertown
Oxford OX2 7LG

www.archaeopress.com

ISBN 978-1-78969-595-3
ISBN 978-1-78969-596-0 (e-Pdf)

Cover image: The portable shrine of the goddess Mut at the Opet Festival, represented at Luxor temple and drawn by Howard Carter during 1916–17 (Gardiner MS 11.02), reproduced with permission of the Griffith Institute, University of Oxford.

Printed in England by Severn, Glocester

This book is available direct from Archaeopress or from our website www.archaeopress.com

For my parents

F

Contents

Acknowledgements

This monograph is a revised and extended version of my doctoral thesis submitted to the University of Oxford in 2014.

I would like to express my deepest gratitude to my supervisor Professor Mark Smith at Oxford University for his substantial support and all-embracing supervision for many years. He has always been enlightening and patient with my slow progress.

My thanks are also sent to those who have provided me with invaluable assistance over many years since I moved into Oxford in 2006. I am grateful to the now retired Professor John Baines for having me as a member of the Queen's College, to which the pleasant Peet Library belong, to the then Lecturer Elizabeth Frood and Doctor Martin Bommas for their useful suggestions and information during my confirmation examination, and to Professor Mark Collier and again Associate Professor Frood for being the examiners for my viva and encouraging me to carry on.

I am also indebted to the experienced staff of the Griffith Institute, who always provided me with valuable sources. Most unpublished materials included in this study were collected from the magnificent archives under the expert guidance of the warm-hearted staff.

It was fortunate for me to have many nice fellow students who have been inspiring by drawing my attention to their fresh topics and sharing the same general interests and experience. All those days with them are now cherished memories and will remain so for the rest of my life. Much is lightly referenced, but Christina Adams is the one to whom I should express my gratitude for the hospitality, generosity, and support that she offered me when I had difficulties.

Finally, my special thanks are sent to Andrew Knight for his friendly and encouraging support since we met in Portsmouth in 1999, when we were still in our early twenties, and to my parents Tokiko and Kazunari for enlightening me on histories and cultures in general with great respect. I perhaps began this exploration partly from self-asking how to view my grandparents' lives, who had an extremely difficult time during the World War II, as all people across the continents were irrationally forced to do so in the negligent and devastating age. There are, I believe, many that we could learn from Egyptians who remarkably sustained their fairly stable culture over three millennia from the very beginning of the written human history.

List of Figures, Tables and Text

Abbreviations

Below are listed abbreviations to be used in this study, other than those listed in *Lexikon der Ägyptologie*, which was edited by Otto and Helck (1975). Numbers in bold refer to the dated records presented at the end of this study as Appendix 1. References to museum collections are indicated in abbreviated forms for the sake of the page limitation. In particular, those in possession of the Cairo Museum are to be understood as belonging to either Journal d'Entrée (JE) or Catalogue General (CG).

2PA: second-priest of Amun
A: Amenhotep
Abusir: Abusir series published by the Czech Institute of Egyptology, 1977–, Praha.
App.: Appendix
DB: Deir el-Bahari
DeM: Deir el-Medina
Epag.: Epagomenal Days
F.: Festival
Façade: Epigraphic Survey, *The façade, portals, upper register scenes, columns, marginalia, and statuary in the colonnade hall*, OIP 116, Chicago, 1998.
HP: high-priest
HPA: high-priest of Amun
Khonsu: Epigraphic Survey, *The temple of Khonsu*, OIP 100–, Chicago, 1979–.
KRI: K. Kitchen, *Ramesside inscriptions*, 8 vols, Oxford, 1975.
Kheruef: Epigraphic Survey, *The tomb of Kheruef*, OIP 102, Chicago, 1980.
LD: R. Lepsius, *Denkmaeler aus Aegypten und Aethiopien*, 12 vols, Berlin, 1849.
MH: Medinet Habu
MH: Epigraphic Survey, *Medinet Habu*, OIP 8–, Chicago, 1930–.
MHC: Medinet Habu calendar
NY: New Year
Opet: Epigraphic Survey, *The festival procession of Opet in the colonnade hall*, OIP 112, Chicago, 1994.
R: Ramses
RIK: Epigraphic Survey, *Reliefs and inscriptions at Karnak*, OIP 25–, Chicago, 1936–.
T: Thutmose
TIP: Third Intermediate Period
Wb: A. Erman and H. Grapow, *Wörterbuch der aegyptischen Sprache*, 7 vols, Leipzig, 1926.

Chapter 1

Introduction

1.1. Introduction

1.1.1. Aim

This study will focus on and examine three Theban festivals in the New Kingdom. In doing so, I aim to shed additional light both on the dynamics of the interaction between the god, king, and those present, and on religious and social benefits that the festival participants gained from these celebrations. The processional appearance of the god, made by both land and river, was one of the main features of Egyptian celebrations. It was when an ostentatious journey was taking place, including royal excursions, expeditions, and the transport of magnificent monumental objects, that a wider audience than that usually limited to designated individuals could witness and access to the divine and/or the royal; a spectacle and public ceremony being performed in a broader arena.[1]

Looking at public display, I will begin my exploration with the Opet Feast because it involved the barque processions of the Theban triad on both the paved street and the Nile between the temples of Karnak and Luxor. These temples were located in the residential area of Thebes, and the processions appeared in a setting accessible to any who sought the earthly image of Amun. Reciprocal relations between the god/king and people were more clearly visible at public celebrations. The underlying purpose was to distribute benefaction from the divine/royal to the subjects, often expressed in the forms of *ꜥnḫ* 'life' and *ṯꜣw n ꜥnḫ* the 'breath of life',[2] in order to promulgate the legitimacy of their authority as a world ruler.[3] People were requested to follow the world order Maat,[4] which had been established since time immemorial and maintained in the succession of rulers by upholding piety, allegiance, social responsibilities, and goodness. This was partly achieved through oracular sessions during the Opet Festival in order to deliver the divine power by more effective means through lego-judicial process.

Such a socio-religious function may argue for the possibility that other celebrations also incorporated divine-human reciprocity, but in different forms. Hence, for reasons presented in 1.1.3, I select both the Festivals of the Valley and the New Year to compare their performative and theoretical domains with those of the Opet Feast. The former two celebrations are particularly significant regarding the mortuary cult that also encompasses the realm of the dead, and broader geographical locations including western Thebes, thus providing more idealized and theoretically all-embracing contexts.

1.1.2. Research background

The mythological, theological, and ideological aspects of formal Egyptian religion have long drawn attention not only from scholars, but also from the general public. However, our knowledge of social, economic, and public sides of religiosity is limited.[5] Studies of the characteristics of festivals witnessed by a wider audience are few; Černý's (1927) work on the cult of Amenhotep I at western Thebes, and more recently Jauhiainen's (2009) on those celebrated at Ramesside Deir el-Medina. Despite a narrow range of corpus included, the latter work is significant in focusing on the functions, rather than the meanings, of celebrations.

Some textual evidence bears witness to larger celebrations that took place not only within a single community, but also inter-communally, involving different social, ideological strata, ranging from the divine and crown to the dead. Gods and the king revealed themselves from temples or the palace. Hence, P. BM 10059 (recto, XVI, 1–4), an Eighteenth Dynasty prophylactic document, described a person wishing to attend festive excitement at Thebes, where Amun, the king, and people were all present.[6] By involving people in acting as part of normative occasions, festivals functioned as a vehicle for converging and consolidating society. In particular, official celebrations embodied social order in their modality, periodicity, and publicness. These characteristics enhanced commitment and participation on the part of the general public to affirm self-identification as social and

1 Baines 2006: 271–6; Stadler 2008: 3.

2 Assmann 1983b: 178–80.

3 Assmann (1983b: 250–63) also proposes that the god embodied three essential elements of light, water, and air. This triad of divine nature was also evident in the descriptions of the king's role in the Middle Kingdom, but its canonical formulation was completed in the Twentieth Dynasty, when each element was equated to heaven, the underworld, and earth.

4 Teeter 1997: 89–90.

5 Studies of popular religion, for example, broadly began in 1960s, one of the major works being Fecht's (1965), and have since made some progress in certain areas, such as votive objects, magical practices, pilgrimages, oracles, and prophylaxes. See Baines and Frood 2011: 1–3, and Baines 1991: 184–5, n. 163 for references to earlier works. Among the earliest authors, who explored the popular aspect of religion, were Erman (1911), who first coined the term 'persönliche Frömmigkeit', Breasted (1912: 344–70), and Gunn (1916). Also see Sadek (1987) for a more recent and general study of popular religion.

6 Leitz 1999: 82, pl. 41.

cultural beings. This is what Baines and Yoffee (1998: 236) defines as one of the components of 'high cultures' that were essential to civilizations but possessed by the elite only. They (ibid., 234) stress the inequality and exclusiveness of the high culture that overrode the 'moral economy' sustained only in small communities.[7] Quite differently, Richards (2000: 39 and 43–5) demonstrates that the high culture was emulated and exploited by non-elites by the Middle Kingdom, when they benefited from its accessibility and participation in the system that was geared to the moral economy.

Despite the significance of religious celebrations with regard to their public aspects and functions as a social bond, few studies have explored Egyptian festivals individually. Some major scholarly works on certain celebrations are still referred to on a frequent basis, but most of them are now almost half a century old, and seem to require some revision, further supplementation with recent discoveries, and new interpretations (see the research history section of each following chapter). New Kingdom Theban festivals can be explored in far greater details than those celebrated at other cities of any period. This owes a lot to the geographical extent of Thebes defined by intact large temple remains and still visible processional routes, coupled with considerable progress in documentation of temple reliefs and tomb paintings in recent years.

Due to the lack of archaeological and textual evidence related to the general public as is the case for other ancient cultures, my exploration confines itself largely to examining elite performances. When 'people' are refereed to, I use the word to designate social classes belonging not only the inner elite group, which is a decision-making body, but also broader and more marginal groups including lower elites, such as local officials, lay priests, and scribes, as well as those who do not own an official title but belong to the machine of state administration, such as soldiers, workmen, and perhaps skilled foreigners.[8] The peculiar absence of, or little attention to, burials for non-elites in Egyptological literatures is coined by Richards (2005: 51–3) as the 'Tomb Problem', largely resulting from (the) negligence on the part of scholars. She argues for a possibility to obtain more insight into, for instance, the middle class in the Middle Kingdom by integrating archaeological and textual evidence more extensively. My theoretical approach does not rule out this possibility, and in some cases 'people' may broadly mean non-divine beings encompassing the royal to the lowest classes of society. This is my hypothesis and a possible area for future research to seek that all the populace had access to the divine to variable extent and was part of the mortuary landscape; ritual performances and the ownership of burials.

1.1.3. Selection of the festivals to be examined in this study

One might gain the impression that the Egyptians were fond of having many religious celebrations performed throughout the year. The classic image of a pious people, portrayed for example by Herodotus (*Histories* II, 58–9), may or may not represent reality.

The incomplete yet most detailed Medinet Habu calendar lists eight monthly festivals and, at least, 25 annual ones (Appendix 1). This shows that out of 365 days, more than 180 days were spent for celebrations during the reign of Ramses III, if eight monthly feasts are also taken in consideration (8x12=96). Given that these festivals lasted more than one day, the Egyptian year was undoubtedly awash with religious events. One may wonder whether or not these feasts involved the majority of society in merrymaking, bringing other economic and social activities to a halt.

If the number of consumed divine offerings is taken as an indicator of the scale of each festival, several festivals recorded in the Medinet Habu calendar can be considered to be important occasions. The number of major feasts can be narrowed down to six as listed below when those commemorating historical achievements made by Ramses III are excluded, and some performances are considered part of a series of rituals comprising a single feast.

1. Opet Festival (II Akhet–III Akhet);
2. Khoiak Festival (IV Akhet–I Peret);
3. Festival of the Two Goddesses (I Peret);
4. Festival of Lifting-Up the Sky (II Peret–III Peret);
5. Festival of Entering the Sky (III Peret–IV Peret);
6. Valley Festival (II Shemu).

Comparing the offering quantities and durations, the Festivals of Opet and Khoiak stand out. P. Harris I (XVIIa, 3–5) records that Ramses III established new endowments for 'monthly and annual festivals' at Thebes. However, only the Opet Festival and the celebration of his accession anniversary are specified.[9]

Other significant evidence for the Theban celebrations is a private statue of a Horsaaset, dated to the Twenty-Second or Twenty-Third Dynasty, found at Karnak temple.[10] The text carved on this statue is of a unique

[7] Also see Baines 2013: 7–8 for the limitation and exclusiveness of the high culture.

[8] For a brief summary of social hierarchies, see Frood 2010b: 476.

[9] Erichsen 1933: 21; Grandet 1994, vol. 1, 246.

[10] Statue Cairo 42210 discovered from the cachette of Court I at Karnak (PM II², 150; Jansen-Winkeln 1985, vol. 1, 63–82, vol. 2, 462–69; *idem* 2007, vol. 2, 234; Spalinger 1996, 74).

nature because it includes some festivals that are not normally included in private festival lists. It records:

1. His Beautiful Festival of *wp nṯr* the 'Opening of the God' (error for *wpy-rnp.t* ?);
2. His Beautiful Festival at *ip.t rsy.t* 'Southern Opet';
3. His Beautiful Festival of *nḥb-k3.w* 'Nehebkau';
4. His Beautiful Festival of *nb w3ḥ n nn nsw.t* (reading uncertain);
5. His Beautiful Festival of *ḥb Ḫnsw* the 'Khonsu Festival';
6. His Beautiful Festival of *ḥb in.t* the 'Valley Festival';
7. His Beautiful Festival of *ip(.t) ḥm.t=s* 'Ipe(t), Her Mistress'.

These seven festivals, when the statue of Horsaaset received divine offerings originating from Amun of Karnak, seem to be listed in calendrical order, roughly corresponding to:

1. I Akhet;
2. II Akhet–III Akhet;
3. IV Akhet–I Peret;
4. III Peret ? (Festival of Amenhotep I ?);
5. I Shemu;
6. II Shemu;
7. IV Shemu.

The Festivals of Opet and Khoiak were still of some importance in the Ptolemaic Period. The geographical list carved on the sanctuary of Edfu temple, dated to the time of Ptolemy VI, records all the Egyptian nomes as well as their principal towns and representative local festivals. For the Theban nome,[11] four celebrations are specified: the Festivals of Opet, Khoiak, I Shemu, and II Shemu, the last two of which are likely to be associated with the Feasts of Khonsu and the Valley.[12] A geographical list parallel to this is attested from scattered hieratic papyri discovered at Tebtynis, where the Theban festivals are written as: 'II Akhet, Amenopet, II Shemu, Khoiak.'[13] At face value, four festivals are referred to here. However, they are not listed in chronological order and the first two entries might represent one and the same event. Thus, it cannot be securely confirmed how many celebrations are recorded here. Be that as it may, 'II Akhet' and 'II Shemu' most probably represent the Festivals of Opet and the Valley.

Hence, Thebes was traditionally regarded as embracing at most four feasts by later times. This was perhaps the case for the New Kingdom, including the Festivals of Opet and the Valley. These celebrations were considered to be a pair, as seen in some textual and pictorial evidence that records them in remarkable juxtaposition (1.3.3).[14] From the New Kingdom onwards, the civil months in which the two festivals fell were named after these festivals—*p3-n-ip.t* 'the (month) of Opet' and *p3-n-in.t* 'the (month) of the Valley'—and, despite their later emergence and local origins, these designations survived in the Coptic month names, Phaophi and Payni. These two festivals represented life and death respectively, and had inverse characteristics in some respects, particularly in the orientations of their processional routes (south and west) and associations with the seasonal cycle (the Nile's increase and recession).[15] The significance of the Festivals of Opet and the Valley is also indicated by the larger amount of evidence relating to them, compared with other festivals.

Lastly, the New Year celebration will be included in this volume, instead of the Festivals of Khoiak and I Shemu, for the following four reasons. First, abundant evidence is available to explore this celebration of the New Kingdom although only the Ptolemaic-Roman Period has been a focus of scholarly works. Second, it is manifest that the New Year Feast embraced rituals parallel to those performed at the Sed Festival and the Khoiak Festival, both of which celebrated the renewal of the kingship and were so deeply embedded in Egyptian ideology that they were ubiquitously referred to in literature and representations.[16] Therefore, it is not surprising to find many characteristics of the New Year in association with these age-old royal celebrations (4.2.1.2 and 4.3.3). Third, fiscal functions of the New Year are evident and it boasted about a wider range of activities than the Khoiak Feast, to which several studies have already been devoted.[17] Fourth, unlike the Khoiak

[11] *Edfou* I, 338: 5–9, XV, pl. 9, b. Spalinger (1992, 14) maintains that the entries may represent month names, rather than festivals.
[12] Klotz 2012, 39, n. k.
[13] PSI inv. I 2+P. Carlsberg 54+P. Tebt. Tait Add. 1 a–f+P. Berlin 14412i (Osing and Rosati 1998, 33; Osing 1998, 268; Klotz 2012, 34).

[14] Red Chapel (Lacau and Chevrier 1977, vol. 1, 154–204, vol. 2, pl. 7; Burgos and Larché 2006, vol. 1, 43–53, 59–65, 95–9, and 108–14); Great Hypostyle Hall at Karnak (Nelson 1981, pls 258–9 and 262–3); Medinet Habu (*MH* III, pl. 138, col. 36; Nelson and Hölscher 1934, 12 for translation). Also see the southern interior wall in the first court of the temple of Medinet Habu, where we find the 'window of appearance' sandwiched between two doorways, each depicting the Valley Festival and the Opet Festival (*MH* II, pl. 239; *MH* IV, pl. 237). In a text from the tomb of Amenemheb (TT 85), who was in charge of the royal barge, he is referred to as taking part in the Festivals of the Valley and Opet (PM I-1², 172 (7)).
[15] Fukaya 2007, 99–104.
[16] Leitz 1994a, 428; Spalinger 1994b, 303–4.
[17] Loret (1882, 1883, and 1884) published three articles on this feast. He essentially focused on translating inscriptions accompanying the scenes of the Osiride rituals at Dendera. This text was later compiled with other parallels from different Ptolemaic temples by Junker (1910). The first attempt to explore the Khoiak Festival in its own right was made by Wohlgemuth (1957). Chassinat (1966) examined mythical rituals performed at Dendera. Following this, Gaballa and Kitchen (1969) primarily investigated the Medinet Habu reliefs depicting the Sokar Festival and covered principal, but not all, textual and pictorial evidence from the Old Kingdom to the New Kingdom to delineate the sequence of this festival. Mikhail (1983) devotes his thesis to liturgical texts with regard to the sacred performances of the festival. His overview of the relation between the myth and ritual is particularly useful. More recently, Graindorge-Héreil (1992, 1994,

celebrations, the Festival of I Shemu is far less attested (to) and difficult to catch a glimpse.[18] A difficulty lies in singling out this feast from surviving evidence. There was more than one celebration that fell in I Shemu: the Festivals of Min (**966**, **987**, **1041**, and **1060**), of Amun (**979**, **986**, and **1037**), of Renenutet (**961–2** and **966**), and of Khonsu (**1014**). The first two feasts were probably one and the same event, and called the 'Festival of I Shemu' because both were associated with the new moon. However, another issue remains regarding the recondite identities of Amun and the ithyphallic god Min. It is only Gauthier (1931) and Bleeker (1956) who endeavored to examine the Min Festival, but many difficulties still lie in the highly theological association of Amun with Min and their numerous representations, which often alternate in consecutive scenes.[19] Whether Min was worshipped in his own right or possessed a distinctive form of cult at Thebes also remains in the realm of conjecture, although Ricke (1954) identified a remain to the north of the Mut precinct of Karnak with a temple devoted to Min.[20] The festival of the goddess Renenutet was associated with the harvest and, according to the Medinet Habu calendar, fixed to I Shemu 1 (**962**). The cult of Khonsu is far more elusive. Although I Shemu was called *pꜣ-n-ḫnsw* 'the (month) of Khonsu', a feast celebrated exclusively for this moon god is hardly attested in texts (the aforementioned statue of Horsaaset and **1014**, both dating from after the New Kingdom). It cannot be ruled out that his festival overlapped with the Min Feast in their lunar natures. However, full moon festivals, which are, unlike new moon celebrations, hardly attested with a specific date, are also known to have fallen in I Shemu from two sources of the Ptolemaic Period (**1063–4**). Hence, it is difficult to conclude whether these celebrations were associated with one another and, if so, in what way.

1.1.4. Material evidence and methodological approaches

In search of surviving evidence of the Festivals of Opet, the Valley, and the New Year, three large corpora are essential to this study. First, temple reliefs and inscriptions are the main sources of information about official rituals pertaining to the cults of Amun and the kingship. In particular, Karnak is of prime importance because the three celebrations took place there, but each perhaps in a distinctive precinct. Processions departed this temple for Luxor to the south at the Opet Feast, and for Deir el-Bahari to the west at the Valley Feast. This is represented in the distribution and orientations of reliefs depicting the two celebrations within Karnak (1.3.3). This also proves true for New Year representations and textual references located in the northern area of Karnak. Their locations, which may represent the direction of Heliopolis seen from Thebes, are corroborated by certain Heliopolitan traits of this celebration (4.3.5.1). By combining various characteristics underlying ritual performances, myth, ideology, and ideals with archaeological evidence, such as temple sites and processional routes, more secure evidence can be obtained in order to locate a hitherto unspecified depiction representing a given celebration. I will use this approach in the hope that further insights into other celebrations may be gained for future research.

Second, representations in the Theban private tombs are related to mortuary cults and several of them are relevant to the Festivals of the Valley and the New Year, when a banquet was performed by a family for the dead. Iconographic features and phraseology are relatively uniform and it is difficult but not impossible to locate representations depicting these festivals. Unlike spacious temples, tombs had only a limited space and thus representations were often amalgamated or highly standardized. Their orientations alone, for example, can hardly signify a subject depicted. My approach towards the tomb representations of the Festivals of the Valley and the New Year is therefore based on weighing the occurrence of certain characteristics against one another rather than seeking exclusive elements. Hence, I attempt to tabulate them to see which element is more attested for which festival. This is only possible for Thebes, where more than 400 private tombs survive in a limited area.

Third, further insights can be given by compiling dated records of religious events together with other different sources, including work journals. Such a scholarly attempt was previously made by Schott (1950), who collected 160 textual records. One can draw more accurate pictures by developing his method. Hence, my examination will broadly count on my own concordance (Appendix 1), which contains about 1400 dated records listed in chronological order. This approach enables us, for example, to identify a cluster of events that fall within a particular time of the year with a festival which is known only from temple calendars. By combining several isolated texts in this way, one can first glimpse a wider context of a given

and 1996) has published a few works on subjects relating to this feast. She places her emphasis broadly on the theological aspects of the god Sokar and the relevant Osiride myth and rituals, performed not only in IV Akhet, but also in other months. Finally, Klotz (2012, 392–98) explores this celebration at Roman Thebes, focusing on a significant role played by Mentu of Armant.

[18] Following Legrain (1900), Kruchten (1989) compiles graffiti left at the Akh-menu, most of which are dated to the Third Intermediate Period, and demonstrates that the appointment of priests and officials took place at Karnak temple during this festival.

[19] Other minor studies on the Min Feast are: Müller (1906), Lacau (1953), Wessetzky (1984), and Feder (1998) on the ritual of the *sꜥḥꜥ sḥn.t* 'erecting the *sḥn.t*-pole', a characteristic of the cult of this god; Jacobson (1939, 28–40) on the relation between Min and the kingship; Munro (1983) on the tent sanctuary of Min; Moens (1985) on the origin and meaning of Min's stairway; Defossez (1985) on lettuces figured beside Min.

[20] PM II^2, 275–6.

celebration. This is particularly useful for locating celebrations associated with the lunar cycle, whose dates were usually not recorded because they varied from year to year. The popular and functional aspects of the Theban festivals are evidenced by short accounts of a number of ostraca and graffiti chiefly discovered on the West Bank of Thebes. They record, for instance, visits of high officials, reward givings, and deliveries of divine offerings at festivals, and thus bear witness to an administrative and social link between a community and the state, plus an ideological link between the god and people.

1.2. Overview of Egyptian calendrical systems and festivals

Just as in our own time, Egyptians had various designations for festivals, depending on their nature, location, scale, significance, etc. The word *ḥb* was usually used in texts, but *wp* could also mean 'festival' from the New Kingdom onwards.[21] Wilson (1997, 224) says that *wp* had originally denoted *wpy-rnp.t* the 'New Year' and later became a verb 'to celebrate (a festival)', development akin to *sd* which derived from *ḥb sd* the 'Sed Festival' but came to denote 'to celebrate' as a verb (ibid., 973). However, one may bear in mind that *wp* was used to denote the beginning of each civil month in accounting texts in the Old and Middle Kingdoms.[22] While *ḥb* was used to refer to a specific festival in its own right, *wp* was perhaps a term for regular celebrations in general, or their recurrence. Hence, a *wp* is rarely attested with a specific date, except O. Ashmolean 70, dated to I Peret 1 in the time of Ramses IV (**570**). It may refer to the Khoiak Feast, but it is not impossible that it simply marks the beginning of the month, when a festival usually took place.

Festivals that were celebrated on a large scale were called *ḥb.w n p.t n t3 tp rnp.t* 'annual festivals of the sky and of the land'[23] or *ḥb m t3 ḏr=f* the 'festival in its entire land'.[24] The conceptualization of the entire world involved in these festivals gives rise to another category of celebrations that are smaller in scale and designated differently. Due to the limitation of sources, little is known about such festivals, particularly local ones.[25] Even major sites, such as Memphis, Heliopolis, Asyut, and those in the Delta, have been severely reduced by environmental changes and urban development.[26] As a result, apart from the Medinet Habu calendar, temple calendars survive mainly from the Ptolemaic-Roman Period. These later sources tell us that the festival calendar was called either *rn n ḥb.w* the 'name of the festivals' or *rḫ ḥb.w* the 'list of the festivals'.[27]

During the Old Kingdom, some celebrations took place at the interval of several years, such as the Sokar Festival celebrated every six years,[28] and the less-known 'Festival of *ḏ.t*' at the interval of an unspecified period.[29] The former feast later came to be performed annually. Hence, the Sed Festival remained the only celebration that had a long cycle of 30 years.[30] Little is known of festivals celebrated at the interval of less than a year, apart from the Decade Ritual celebrated every ten days (3.2.2) and a few monthly festivals based on the lunar cycle. In the Medinet Habu calendar, lunar festivals are listed first, followed by civil-based celebrations. The former are called *ḥb.w n p.t ḫpr* the 'festivals of the sky that occur' and the latter *ḥb.w tp tri* the 'seasonal festivals'.[31]

1.2.1. Monthly festivals

The earliest surviving lunar celebration is the one that took place on day 6, which is recorded on the Palermo Stone.[32] The Pyramid Texts mention the 1st, 2nd, 6th, 7th, and 15th lunar days, on which rituals were performed.[33] The private offering formulae appear to attest the 1st and 15th days more often than other lunar celebrations.[34]

The number of lunar days recorded in the Lahun papyri of the Middle Kingdom is limited. The most often recorded are the 1st, 2nd, and 15th days, as well as the less frequent 4th day.[35] Spell 557 of the Coffin Texts is

[21] *Wb* I, 304, 12–3; Jauhiainen 2009, 243–6.

[22] For the Old Kingdom, see Abusir X, 127 and 151 (Reneferef archive) and Posener-Kriéger and de Cenival 1968, pls 36, 40, 50, and 84 (Neferirkare archive). For the Middle Kingdom, see James 1962, pl. 17 A (a papyrus from Deir el-Bahari). In one of the Heqanakht papyri, *wp* 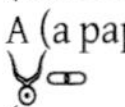 appears as a regular supply at the beginning of each decade (James 1962, 33, pl. 6 A, col. 32; Allen 2002b, 17, pl. 30, l. 32). For other references, see Dunham 1938, 5, n. 9.

[23] First attested in the Second Intermediate Period (Hannig 2006, vol. 2, 1642, 20076).

[24] **190, 753, 1063–4, 1416,** etc. P. Leiden I 344 (recto, XIV, 4), dated to the Nineteenth Dynasty, includes unclear signs that may be read as *hrw ḥb t3* (Enmarch 2005, 55 for transcription and photograph; *idem* 2008, 238 for transliteration and translation).

[25] Some local festivals are known, such as the '*ḏsr-t3* Festival' evidenced by two Old Kingdom graffiti at el-Kab (Vandekerckhove and Müller-Wollermann 2001, vol. 1, 41 and 47; Strudwick 2005, 162). The festival of the god Dewen-Anwy (*Dwn-ʿnwy*) is attested in a letter to the dead (P. MFA 04.2059), dated to the First Intermediate Period, from Naga ed-Deir (Simpson 1999, 393–4).

[26] Minor festival lists are known for the cities of: Buto under Thutmose III (Bedier 1994a); Sais under Ptolemy III (Grenfell and Hunt 1906, vol. 1, 138–57); Tanis, dated to the first century AD (Griffith and Petrie 1889, 21–5, pls 9–15); Abydos under Thutmose III and Ramses II; Tod perhaps under Ramses III; Armant possibly under Thutmose III; Elephantine under Thutmose III (see el-Sabban 2000 for these last calendars). Also see 1.1.3, for geographical lists of later periods which include local celebrations.

[27] Grimm 1994a, 18.

[28] Gaballa and Kitchen 1969, 15, n. 1.

[29] Wilkinson 2000, 102.

[30] Hornung and Staehelin 2006, 39–40.

[31] *MH* III, pls 148 and 152.

[32] Wilkinson 2000, 153; Krauss 2006, 386.

[33] PT 373, Pyr. 657b–c; 408, Pyr. 716a–b; 437, Pyr. 794a–b; 552, Pyr. 1260a; 610, Pyr. 1711b; and 684, Pyr. 2056c.

[34] Barta 1968, 10.

[35] Luft 1992, 27, 37, 40, 45, 52–3, 59, 112, etc. The significance of the

unique in nature because it specifies 'six festivals of eternity' to be performed for the deceased, namely, the 4th day, 8th day, *msy.t*, *w3g*, *iḥhy*, and the Sokar Feast.[36] A list from the tomb of Khnumhotep at Beni Hasan records the 1st, 2nd, 4th, 5th, 6th, 15th, and 29th lunar celebrations.[37]

The Medinet Habu calendar attests the 1st, 2nd, 4th, 6th, 10th, 15th, 29th, and 30th days.[38] Stela Cairo 34002, dated to the time of Ahmes, records the 1st, 4th, 5th, and 6th lunar festivals, as well as the *h3k*-Festival, Wag Festival, and Thoth Festival to be celebrated *m tp tri rʿ nb* 'seasonally, every day'.[39] The idiom *tp tri* was probably a general term for feasts that were regularly celebrated in accordance with any calendrical cycle.[40]

It is evident that the 1st and 6th remained the most significant days in the New Kingdom. Thutmose III specifies only them for his new endowments to Karnak.[41] Scenes of these celebrations were represented in the Great Hypostyle Hall of Karnak.[42] The new moon celebration seems to have been the most important of all lunar celebrations. It was documented not only in liturgical literature but also in administrative and calendrical records as corresponding to the Festivals of Mentu (2.2.1) and Min (**987**). The 6th festival is attested in the Pyramid Texts[43] and the Coffin Texts[44] as taking place at *ẖr-ʿḥ3*, a location identified by Jacq (1993, 20) with the old city of Cairo.[45] Our knowledge of full moon celebrations before the Greek-Roman Period is very limited.[46] There are only two dated historical accounts attesting a ceremony on a full-moon day: a contract-making between the god Min and a member of the *pat* on IV Akhet 25 in the First Intermediate Period among the Koptos Decrees (**513**), and an oath-taking before Khonsu on II Shemu 13 in year 12 of Amasis (**1105**).

It is hardly surprising to find in texts many references to the four consecutive days (29th, 30th, 1st, and 2nd) over the transition of the month, because a religious celebration usually took place on these days. Hence, every beginning of the month was prognosticated to be 'good, good, good' in the calendars of lucky and unlucky days.[47] Among such striding celebrations are the well-known Festival of Lifting-Up the Sky from II Peret 29 to III Peret 1 (**775**, **781**, and **788**), and the Festival of Entering the Sky from III Peret 29 to IV Peret 1 (**868**, **874**, and **887**), both from the New Kingdom onwards. Festivals of this type often entailed the symbolism of death and resurrection. For instance, the Sokar Festival took place from the end of IV Akhet, followed by the *k3-ḥr-k3* celebration on I Peret 1, when Horus was considered to succeed his dead father Osiris.[48] Such symbolism appears not only at the turn of months, but also over the transition from one year, season, or week to another, and perhaps even within a single festival.

Remnants of lunar time-reckoning within the civil calendar may also be seen in the sitting of the Wag and Thoth Festivals in the middle of I Akhet (4.2.3.1 and 4.2.3.2). They are thought to have originally been feasts for the lunar New Year. The arbitrary use of the lunar cycle for the civil one is visible in some civil-based celebrations, which always fall in a particular civil month but begin on a specific lunar day. For example, the Opet Feast evidently began on a new moon day under Thutmose III (2.2.2).

1.2.2. Annual festivals

Apart from temple calendars and mortuary texts, Old-Kingdom accounting papyri may be of some interest regarding rituals that were actually performed. The Abusir archives attest the Wag-, Thoth-,[49] Sokar-,[50] Sed-,[51] Min-,[52] and new moon celebrations.[53]

Among Middle-Kingdom sources, Hepdjef, count of Asyut in the time of Senusret I, was particularly eager to address his contracts with his local temple in order to request that festival offerings be duly delivered to his tomb. This noble man, therefore, stressed upon *hrw.w 22 ḥw.t-nṯr* '22 days of the temple', which most probably refers to the number of festivals.[54] Amenhotep I's fragment from Karnak describes the sums of offerings that were dedicated to Amun as amounting to 50.[55] This may also represent the number of festivals because each celebration appears to have been given one offering. The fragmentary offering list of Thutmose III, located to the south of the granite sanctuary at Karnak, records 60 festivals or festival days, 28 of which

4th day remains unclear, but it is known that the *mnḫ.t* took place on that day (Spalinger 1992, 7).

36 *CT* VI, 158m–159a.

37 Newberry 1898, pl. 24.

38 *MH* III, pls 148–50; Parker 1950, 11–2; Spalinger 1998a, 242.

39 *Urk.* IV, 27: 4–7; Spalinger 1996, 11.

40 Gardiner 1952, 21, n. 2.

41 A passage to the south of the sanctuary (PM II², 106 (329); *Urk.* IV, 177; el-Sabban 2000, 19) and his annals (*Urk.* IV, 747: 7).

42 Nelson 1949, 333; *idem* 1981, pls 206 bottom and 228.

43 PT 493, Pyr. 1062.

44 *CT* VII, 221m–n [1004].

45 For the significance of the 6th day feast, see Barta 1969.

46 Note that strictly speaking, the full moon varies from 13.73 to 15.80 after the conjunction because of the elliptic orbit of the moon (Parker 1950, 6). This may explain the significance of the new moon as a more reliable marker. For demotic sources containing references to full moon festivals, see M. Smith 1993, 54, n. c.

47 Porceddu, Jetsu, Markkanen, and Toivari-Viitala 2008, 329.

48 Gaballa and Kitchen 1969, 57–74.

49 Abusir X, pls 11–2.

50 P. Louvre E 25416, C, verso (Posener-Kriéger and de Cenival 1968, pl. 13).

51 P. Berlin 15726, verso (Posener-Kriéger and de Cenival 1968, pl. 88, B).

52 P. Berlin 15723, recto (Posener-Kriéger and de Cenival 1968, pl. 82, col. b).

53 P. Louvre E 25279, recto (Posener-Kriéger and de Cenival 1968, pl. 5, col. f).

54 PM IV, 26 (10-11); Griffith 1889, pl. 7, col. 284.

55 Spalinger 1992, 22, pl. IV.

are associated with lunar festivals.[56] Another list of the same king, located at the Akh-menu, includes 54 seasonal celebrations.[57] The incomplete Medinet Habu calendar lists eight monthly festivals and more than 25 annual festivals (Appendix 1). In the time of Psametik I, the total number of festivals or festival days was 50.[58]

1.2.3. Designation and structure of festivals

The phrase *ḥb nfr n nṯr* is attested in the Old Kingdom, but it seems to be a term denoting celebrations in general.[59] The new expression  *ḥb=f nfr n X* 'his beautiful festival of X' came to be used for standardizing the designation of festivals by the Twelfth Dynasty and continued into the Ptolemaic-Roman Period.[60] The stela of Sehetepibre, deputy overseer of the seal in the time of Amenemhat III, originating from Abydos, refers to Osiris and Upwaut, for each of whom are performed 'his first beautiful festivals of Akhet' (*ḥb.w=f nfr.w tpy.w ꜣḫ.t*).[61] A theophoric designation associated with Amun is known from a graffito of Neferabed, a wab-priest of Amun, and a stela of Mentuhotep, a wab-priest of Bastet, both dated to the Twelfth Dynasty (3.2.1). The former refers to a river journey of Amun to the 'valley of Nebhepetre (Mentuhotep II)' and reads: *ḥb.w=f tpy.w šmw* 'his first festivals of Shemu'. All these Middle Kingdom records have  and refer to more than one celebration performed for a specific god. This may argue for the existence of *ḥb.w=f nfr.w tpy.w pr.t*, which however is hitherto unknown. The earliest theophoric designation of a single event is attested on a stela of Iutjeni, chief of the ten of Upper Egypt, also dating from the Middle Kingdom, recording *ḥb=f nfr n ḫn.t* 'His (Amun's) Beautiful Festival of Procession' (3.2.1). In all probability, such was applied to other gods in different cities, although surviving evidence is too little to produce a general picture.

The full designation of the Opet Festival *ḥb=f nfr n ip.t* is first evidenced in Hatshepsut's Red Chapel.[62] It is not uncommon to observe that this format was employed for celebrations of Mut and Khonsu, who formed the Theban triad with Amun. Hence, the Opet Feast was also called 'Her (Mut's) Festival'.[63] In addition, the stela of Merimaat, dated to the time of Ramses VI, refers to the goddess Maat, for whom the Opet Feast was celebrated, as: *Mꜣꜥ.t sꜣ.t Rꜥ ḥry-ib wꜣs.t ir[.t] Rꜥ ḥkꜣ idb.wy m ḥb=s nfr n ip.t* 'Maat, daughter of Re, who dwells in Thebes, ey[e] of Re, ruler of the Two Banks, at Her Beautiful Festival of Opet'.[64] Likewise, the Valley Feast came to be called *ḥb=f nfr n in.t* perhaps by the Eighteenth Dynasty or earlier although the oldest surviving evidence is dated to the times of Ramses I and Seti I.[65]

Egyptian festivals had a standard structure from the Old Kingdom. They consisted of an evening event and a morning event following it (Table 1).[66] However, quite to the contrary of what we might expect, the Pyramid Texts[67] and the Coffin Texts[68] describe the 6th and 7th day lunar festivals as a setting for a morning meal (*iꜥw*) and an evening one (*msy.t*) respectively, not *vice versa*.[69] The aforementioned Middle-Kingdom tomb of Hepdjef at Asyut, first attests the night (*grḥ*) of the Wag Feast, followed by the main celebration next day (**86** and **96**). P. UC 32191, discovered in Middle-Kingdom Lahun, records some instances of *iḫ.t ḫꜣwy* the 'offering of the night' for the celebration of the *šsp-itrw* (**421**). *iḫ.t ḫꜣwy* or *iḫ.t ḥr ḫꜣw.t* the 'offering on the altar' was also the designation of the 5th lunar day.[70] A stone fragment discovered at Karnak, apparently Amenhotep I's copy of a Middle-Kingdom festival list, refers to a performance called *ḫꜣw.t n.t ḥb=f* [...] the 'altar of His Festival of [ ]' ahead of the 'His Festival of the First Month [of Shemu]' (**1048**). Thutmose III's list at Karnak counts eleven occurrences of *iḫ.t ḫꜣwy n.t ḥb.w Imn* the 'evening offering of the festivals of Amun,' corresponding to the number of Amun's annual festivals.[71] These festivals apparently included the Festivals of the New Year (4.5.1), Wag (**86** and **90**), and Opet (**233**), whose evening events are elsewhere known. Because the Medinet Habu calendar contains separate entries for an evening ritual at some celebrations, they are likely to have required a distinct setting. It is not impossible that the evening ritual was identical with a drinking party, which also took place within the temple (4.6.1). P. Berlin 3115 (Text A, II, 1–18), dated to IV Peret 10 in year 8(?) of Ptolemy IX, lists fifteen different occasions throughout the year and those celebrated every ten days as *hrw.w n swr* the 'days of drinking', perhaps taking place at Medinet Habu (**904**).

---

56 *Urk.* IV, 176–7; Spalinger 1996, 4; el-Sabban 2000, 17–9.

57 PM I-1², 126 (462); Gardiner 1952, 21, pl. 9 (gg).

58 A lost text in TT 390 (PM I-1², 441 (4); Champollion, *Not. descr.* I, 512 upper).

59 Coffins of Nefertjentet (Kanawati 1980, vol. 6, 63–4, pl. 16, fig. 32, e), of Ankhnes (Kanawati 1980, vol. 7, 53, pl. 12, fig. 41, a), of Qeri (Kanawati 1980, vol. 7, 53–4, pl. 14, b, fig. 41, c), all originating from Akhmim.

60 See Jauhiainen (2009, 246–54) for the use of *ḥb=f* and *pꜣy=f ḥb* to designate personal festivals performed at Deir el-Medina.

61 Stela Cairo 20538, sides III and IV (PM V, 45; Lange and Schäfer 1902, vol. 2, 150; Lichtheim 1973, vol. 1, 127 for partial translation and reference).

62 Burgos and Larché 2006, vol. 1, 47, Block 169, a.

63 *Opet*, 29.

64 Vernus 1975, 106.

65 Tomb of Amenmes (TT 19): PM I-1², 33 (3); Foucart 1935, pl. 6; Figure 16.

66 For a brief summary of the eve of feast, see Sayed Mohamed 2004, 139–46.

67 PT 408, Pyr. 716a–b.

68 *CT* III, 158c–159a [207].

69 Spalinger (1993b, 164 (10)) argues that the sixth lunar festival took place in I Akhet and the seventh in II Akhet.

70 *Urk.* IV, 27: 5; Parker 1950, 11. The *ḫꜣwy* and *ḫꜣw.t* perhaps had the same implications and were sometimes used alternately because the Medinet Habu calendar attests *ḫꜣw.t* with the determinative of , which is usually employed for the *ḫꜣwy* (*MH* III, pl. 154, list 28).

71 PM II², 106 (329); *Urk.* IV, 177; el-Sabban 2000, 19.

It was at this evening-morning transition that festivals played out the mythological death and resurrection of the world. This was evidently the case for the Festivals of Opet, the Valley, and the New Year.

1.2.4. Synchronicity of the civil calendar with the seasonal cycle in the New Kingdom

The Egyptian civil calendar did not accord with the natural cycle throughout most of its history—their perfect symphony occurred only twice in the native dynastic period of three thousand years. Detailed discussion on the complex calendrical systems is beyond the scope of this study, but it is useful to delineate how the natural cycle was in harmony with the civil calendar in the New Kingdom.[72] Various documents attest natural phenomena, including the heliacal rising of Sothis and precipitation. In particular, those recording the dates of the Nile's inundation at Thebes are of significant value.

According to Peden (2001, 170, n. 217), there are 11 fully dated texts attesting the high-rise of the Nile (*h3y n p3 mw n ḥꜥpy ꜥ3*), mostly originating from western Thebes of the Ramesside Period. The number is, in fact, 14 with additional evidence: seven cases in II Akhet and seven in III Akhet (Table 2). Two of them are securely dated to years 1 and 2 of Merenptah, each falling on III Akhet 3 (**303**) and II Akhet 3 (**155**). Thus, Janssen (1987, 136) suggests that dates that fall in II Akhet are likely to belong to the time of Ramses II, while those in III Akhet belong to the late Nineteenth Dynasty and later.

Thanks to observations of the Nile during about thirty years from 1873 before the Aswan Dam was completed in 1901, it is possible to determine when the inundation used to begin and culminate.[73] At Aswan the average day of the Nile's minimum level was 2 June (all dates refer to the Gregorian calendar hereafter unless otherwise indicated) and that of the culmination 6 September (Table 3). The flow of the Nile takes six to twelve days, depending on the quantity of the water (the more water, the faster the speed), to run from Aswan to Cairo,[74] thus approximately one to two days between Aswan and Thebes. As of 1300 BC (corresponding to −1299 astronomical),[75] the heliacal rising of Sothis is calculated to have taken place on 18 July (Julian)/7 July (Gregorian) in the Memphite area and on 14 July (Julian)/3 July (Gregorian) in the Theban area. Given that in ideal terms the heliacal rising of Sothis occurred on I Akhet 1, at Thebes the Nile marked its minimum level on *ca.* IV Shemu 8, and the maximum level on *ca.* III Akhet 6. These dates were heralded by the Festivals of the Valley (3.2.3) and Opet (2.2.2) respectively. III Akhet 6, in particular, fell within the period of the Opet Feast, which was celebrated from II Akhet 19 to III Akhet 15 in the time of Ramses III (**237**).

This picture roughly agrees with a series of observations on the nilometer at medieval Cairo over 1200 years from the seventh century, which are meticulously studied by Popper (1951). In Cairo the Nile reached its maximum water level on 30 September on average, but could be varied between 8 September and 19 October.[76] Hence, at Thebes the maximum occurred on 22 September on average, but could be as early as 31 August. On the other hand, the Nile's minimum was observed on 8 June on average in Cairo.[77] Hence, it took place on about 1 June at Thebes.

Regarding the two aforementioned graffiti dated to the time of Merenptah, the Nile's water was supposed to increase in the first half of IV Shemu, and reach its maximum in the first half of III Akhet at Thebes in his time. This assumption does not contradict one of the graffiti dated to III Akhet 3 in year 1, whereas the other one dated to II Akhet 3 in year 2 may refer to an early arrival of the high-rise. It may be of some interest that some rock inscriptions at the West Bank of Gebel Silsila, 65 km north of Aswan, attest two dates pertaining to the Nile in the times of Ramses II (year 1), Merenptah (year 1), and Ramses III (year 6). They invariably refer to I Akhet 15 and III Shemu 15, when an offering ritual was performed for Hapi (**78** and **1243**). These dates may refer to the Nile's movements at Gebel Silsila in year 1 of Ramses II. It is likely that Merenptah and Ramses III simply copied Ramses II's original text.

In conclusion, the civil calendar accorded with the natural cycle at the beginning of the Nineteenth Dynasty.[78] This is also backed by the observation on the length of the day and night recorded in P. Cairo 86637 (verso, XIV), which is dated to the beginning of the Nineteenth Dynasty.[79] The civil calendar could be

[72] To justify this fact, it would be sufficient to refer to Parker 1950, 51 and Depuydt 1997, 17 for the heliacal rising of Sothis. In the Egyptian time-reckoning, it was expected to occur on the civil New Year's Day. This ideal coincidence took place on 21 July (Julian) in AD 140, corresponding to 20 July (Gregorian) in AD 139. Taking this date as a cornerstone, *ca.* 1320 BC and 2780 BC are calculated to be the years of the beginning of the Sothic cycle (see Krauss 2006c, 445 for a slightly different result and a useful table of records). The present examination concerns 1320 BC only, which corresponds to the beginning of the Nineteenth Dynasty. Insofar as the New Kingdom is concerned, the heliacal rising of Sothis should have occurred between the first half of III Shemu and the beginning of III Akhet.

[73] Willcocks and Craig 1913, vol. 1, 184; Janssen 1987, 133.

[74] Willcocks and Craig 1913, vol. 1, 144, Table 70.

[75] Given that the *arcus visionis* of Sirius is 10° and the altitude of this star above the horizon is 3° (Gautschy 2011, 117–8).

[76] Popper 1951, 87–8.

[77] Popper 1951, 220. The Copts regarded 20 June (Julian) as the day of the beginning of the Nile's inundation, regardless of when it was actually observed (ibid., 64–6). On that day the official measurement of the height of water level took place and the result was subsequently announced.

[78] Rose 1999, 89.

[79] Bakir 1966, pl. 44; Leitz 1989, 22–3; *idem* 1994a, vol. 2, pl. 44.

used within the minimal discrepancy of less than two months during the whole New Kingdom. This seasonal agreement provided religious celebrations with proper settings within the liturgical calendar. This must have had a considerable impact particularly on festivals associated with seasonal changes. Indeed, at the Opet Festival great emphasis was placed on the renewal of the kingship to be secured by the recurrent inundation. The New Kingdom might have seen a revision of old celebrations, which had been dislocated from the seasonal cycle over 1000 years, in order to re-locate them into the original contexts but in new forms.

1.3. Theban religiosity

1.3.1. Visits to Thebes of the king, vizier, and high officials

1.3.1.1. King and prince

It is well known that kings visited Thebes to celebrate major festivals (2.4.3). In particular, they were required to participate in the Opet Feast every year, as stated in Horemheb's decree.[80] In the chronicle of Osorkon (III), he is said to have visited Thebes three times a year, perhaps including a sojourn to perform this celebration.[81] A key religious role played by the king is evident in the very common epithet *nb ir.t iḫ.t* the 'lord of the ritual', known from the Old Kingdom.[82] In addition, *sšm ḥb* 'festival leader'[83] and *nb ḥb* the 'lord of the festival'[84] came to be used as part of royal epithets. The king's attendance to the festivals, however, could not always be coordinated particularly when he was in a remote place. Hence, members of the royal family or high officials would be sent to act on his behalf. When Osorkon (III) was a prince, he visited Thebes to participate in the Festival of I Shemu on I Shemu 11 in year 11 of his father Takelot II (**988**). He also bore the titles of the high-priest of Amun-Re and the general (*imy-r mšꜥ.w wr*).

1.3.1.2. Vizier and royal butler

Among high officials who acted on behalf of the king, the vizier was undoubtedly a key figure. His duties covered a wide range of state affairs from provision supplies and juridical decision-making to organizing the army.[85] These tasks were primarily administrative, but did not exclude religious missions. For example, Paser under Seti I and Ramses II,[86] Rahotep under Ramses II,[87] Panehesy under Merenptah,[88] and Pinedjem II (**925**) held the office of the festival leader among other titles.[89]

A letter written on O. Nash 11 (BM 65933), dated to the time of Ramses III, describes the workmen on the West Bank as expecting their lord (vizier) to come in order to perform a celebration, as follows:[90]

> *pꜣy=f ii r di.t ḫꜥy ꞽmn m pꜣ* [two groups lost]
>
> His visit to cause Amun to appear at the [ ].

This account is unique in its clear reference to a religious ceremony.[91] Viziers usually appeared in connection with the supervision of the work force serving the construction of royal monuments. The earliest evidence of such is O. MMA 23001.51, dated to year 45 of Thutmose III, discovered at Deir el-Bahari,[92] but vizier's visits are chiefly attested in Ramesside ostraca from Deir el-Medina and the Valley of the Kings. Some documents record their administrative and religious tasks together.

O. Cairo 25538 (**1117**), dated to year 6 of Seti II, tells us that the vizier Pareemheb visited the Valley of the Kings:

> *ḥꜣ.t-sp 6 ꜣbd 2-nw šmw sw 16 hrw n ii ir.n imy-r niw.t ṯꜣty Pꜣ-rꜥ-m-ḥb r sḫ.t ꜣbd 2-nw šmw sw 25 hrw n ḏꜣj n ꞽmn r niw.t iw ṯꜣty ḥr ḫd*
>
> Year 6, II Shemu 16: The day of a visit made by the city governor and vizier, Pareemheb, to the Field. II Shemu 25: The day of the river journey of Amun to the Town when the vizier travelled downstream.

Significantly, the reason of Pareemheb's visit to the West Bank is documented elsewhere on O. Cairo 25515 (**1116**). He is described as 'having ordered a scribe to

[80] Pflüger 1946, 263. For the royal attendance to the Opet Feast, see Fukaya 2012, 203. Exell (2009, 69–72) argues that Ramses II visited Thebes to attend the Valley Feast in an unknown year.

[81] Caminos 1958, 78 and 117–8.

[82] Hannig 2003, 612, 15234. For a detailed examination of the royal epithet *nb ir.t iḫ.t*, see Routledge 2001, 162–305.

[83] Seti I before he succeeded the throne (*KRI* II, 288: 8); Ramses III (*MH* III, pl. 138, col. 38; *MH* V, pl. 331, col. 6).

[84] Ramses II (*KRI* III, 106: 10; Schulman 1988, 35, fig. 18). Horemheb was called *tp ḥb=f* the 'head of his festival' (*Opet*, 35, pl. 94). Their prime religious role was reminiscent of the lector-priest, who was called *sšm ḥb.t* the 'leader of the festival proceedings' (*Wb.* III, 61, 4).

[85] Boorn 1988, 218, 250, and 283.

[86] *KRI* I, 298: 11.

[87] *KRI* I, 54: 13.

[88] *KRI* IV, 85: 10.

[89] Note that the first three viziers bore the title of the 'fan-bearer on the right of the king'. This title was not exclusively possessed by high-ranking individuals but could be given to lesser officials within the royal court (Eichler 2000, 126, n. 569). Two 'fan-bearers on the right of the king' are known to have had the title of the festival leader: Suemniut under Amenhotep II (*Urk.* IV, 1452: 5) and Maya under Horemheb (*Urk.* IV, 2163: 16).

[90] *KRI* V, 584: 1–2; Wente 1990, 50.

[91] O. Turin 57168 also refers to an unnamed vizier in association with a festival (Lopez 1978, 31, pl. 75).

[92] Hayes 1960, 44–5.

commission (*sḥn.t*) the workmen' on the very same date of II Shemu 16.[93] The 'river journey of Amun to the Town' most probably refers to the return travel to the East Bank of this god at the Valley Festival.

Tasks assigned to the vizier may be encapsulated in a series of journeys made by Neferrenpet, the well-documented vizier under Ramses IV. For instance, O. BM 50744 reads (**939**):

> *ḥ3.t-sp 5 3bd 4-nw pr.t sw 26 hrw pn ii in imy-r niw.t ṯ3ty Nfr-rnp.t r w3ḥ mw iw=f rsi p3 sḥn*
>
> Year 5, IV Peret 26: This day of a visit by the city governor and vizier Neferrenpet to offer a libation when he inspects the assignment.

Some other evidence attests that the rite of *w3ḥ-mw* is associated with a mortuary cult on the West Bank but took place on different days throughout the year (3.2.2). In addition, O. DeM 45, dated three years earlier, describes those who accompanied this vizier as (**227** and **230**):

> *sw 17 K3-r3 s3* [a few groups lost] *spr ir.n imy-r niw.t ṯ3ty Nfr-rnp.t r niw.t mit.t wdpw nsw.t Ḥri wdpw nsw.t ʾImn-ḫʿw s3 Tḫj sw 18 iw=w ṯs r sḫ[.t] r gmgm sp-sn s.t sd.t ḫr n Wsr-m3.ʿt-(rʿ)-stp-n-im[n]*
>
> (Year 2, II Akhet) 17: Karo, son of [ ]. The city governor and vizier Neferrenpet arrived at the Town, and so did the royal butler Hori and the royal butler Amenkhau, son of Tekhy. Day 18: they went up to the Fie[ld] really to discover the place and (to) cut the tomb of Wesermaat(re)-setepename[n].

The vizier's presence was required to make such an important decision on locating the future tomb of the reigning king. McDowell (1999, 207) regards the presence of the royal butlers as an indication of an attempt to maintain political power balance, because the king, whose residence was in the Delta at that time, was very mindful of the powerful counterpart in the south, a stronghold of the vizier and the priests of Amun. Royal butlers were often portrayed close to the king, holding fans for him at ceremonies.[94] When Ramses IV died four years later, Neferrenpet together with four royal butlers and the high-priest of Amun supervised the final preparation for the burial of this king (**1085**).[95] Indeed, the date of our ostracon may refer to a ceremonial occasion, which they participated in. If Ramses IV maintained the same tradition as Ramses III's, the eve of the Opet Festival would have taken place on II Akhet 18 (**233**). It is likely that the officials in question were sent on behalf of the king to attend the festival. It is also not impossible that they came to accompany the king who stayed elsewhere in the city.

Additional information is obtained from P. Turin 1891. It documented that Neferrenpet together with the royal butler Sethherwenemyef, the overseer of the treasury Mentuemtauy, and the butler Hori gave instructions to increase the workforce for the construction of the royal tomb according to a royal command, and that it took place on III Akhet 28 in the same year of Ramses IV (**404**). The date is shortly after the Opet Festival, which, according to P. Harris I, ends on III Akhet 15 under Ramses III (**359**). Hence, Neferrenpet seems to have stayed at Thebes over a month.

Neferrenpet and Sethherwenemyef are attested together in other documents, all dated to year 6 (Table 4). Graffito 790, located in a mountain at western Thebes, records that Neferrenpet visited 'the Town' on I Akhet 9 and 'the Enclosure of the Necropolis (*p3 ḫtm n p3 ḫr*)' next day (**59**).[96] Sethherwenemyef accompanied the vizier on the first day, but the purpose of their visit was not specified. These two individuals are also attested in O. Cairo 25274 with the date I Akhet 12, on which they supervised works (**68**). Sethherwenemyef alone remained at Thebes, as evidenced by Graffito 2056, dated to II Akhet 7 (**169**). In addition, he is referred to in O. Cairo 25277, dated to II Akhet 19 (**238**). This time his physical presence is not entirely clear, but he sent a message (*h3b*) concerning two wooden chests. Yet, he is likely to have stayed in Thebes because he is reported in O. Cairo 25283 as having departed for the north on IV Akhet 21 (**490**). In the mean time, Neferrenpet sent his

[93] This text does not explain the detail of this commission but the death of Seti (II) nine months later on I Peret 19 is referred to on the other side of this ostracon (**650**). This may rather argue for an urgent situation that the tomb of that king was to be completed as soon as possible in anticipation of his death.

[94] *MH* IV, pls 238, B and 240, A.

[95] Our knowledge is limited as to how many royal butlers concurrently served the king and where their bureau was located. Three royal butlers are portrayed accompanying Ramses IX at Karnak (PM II^2, 172 (505)). Their key roles are attested in P. Abbott (BM 10221), which records that the royal butler Nesamen acted as a superior judge to tackle the Great Robbery issue in the time of the same king (McDowell 1999, 195–8). He seems to have possessed a position higher than the city governors of Thebes and of western Thebes but less than the vizier. In principle, the vizier was the supreme judge when a regular juridical court was not able to settle a lawsuit and decided to hand it over to him (O. BM 65930 (**1225**); O. DeM 663 (*KRI* IV, 160–1); P. BM 10055 (*KRI* IV, 408–14); P. Geneva D 409+P. Turin 2021 (*KRI* VI, 738–42)).

[96] For a general introduction to the Enclosure of the Necropolis, see Ventura 1986, 83–106; *idem* 1987; Sturtewagen 1990, 938; McDowell 1990, 93–105; Burkard 2006. Koh (2005/2006) locates this building on the northeastern edge of Qurnet Murai, facing the Ramesseum. Similarly, Eyre (2009, 110) suggests its location at the northern entrance to Deir el-Medina.

message (*ḥ3b*) to the workmen on I Peret 19, according to O. Cairo 25287 (**651**).[97]

The tour of Neferrenpet and Sethherwenemyef in year 6 shows a pattern typical of high officials visiting Thebes. They travelled to Thebes during the Akhet season, particularly in II–III Akhet (Table 5). O. Cairo 25565 records that Sethherwenemyef visited western Thebes to reward the workmen on III Akhet 21 in year 5, followed by Neferrenpet's visit on IV Akhet 7 (**456**). As will be described in 2.5.5, reward-givings required a ceremonial setting. Such is represented in the tomb of Neferhotep, a divine father of Amun (TT 50), where the deceased is portrayed receiving a reward from the king Horemheb who is accompanied by the southern and northern viziers, the overseer of the treasury, and two royal butlers.[98]

The Akhet season was also significant in the case of the previous vizier Ta, who served from year 16 to 32 of Ramses III. Dated records of his official visits to western Thebes are fourteen in number, including four ambiguous ones (Table 6).[99] Eight of them convey dates within either II Akhet or III Akhet. According to O. Berlin P 10633, he was promoted to be the vizier of Upper and Lower Egypt on II Akhet 23 in year 29, perhaps during the Opet Festival (2.5.3).

Remarkably, like II–III Akhet, many visits of high officials were made at the end of the year. They are not explicitly associated with a particular celebration, but rather linked to the investigation of tomb robberies that incessantly happened at the end of the Twentieth Dynasty. It is, however, not impossible that those officials visited Thebes to carry out various other tasks, perhaps including participation in the New Year Feast.[100]

1.3.2. Historical development of the religious city Thebes

The temple complex of Karnak dominates at the northeastern corner of the huge rectangular area of Thebes. This urban area was apparently defined by three processional routes, apart from the western border delimited by the barren mountains lying from the north to south.[101]

The earliest border probably appeared between Karnak and the corresponding position on the West Bank. Some tombs of the Old Kingdom are located at el-Tarif and those of the First Intermediate Period at el-Khokha (TT 185, 186, and 405).[102] A small temple, dated to the early dynastic period, is also known to have stood on top of the so-called Thoth Hill, two kilometers north of the Valley of the Kings.[103] Intef I, II, and III of the Eleventh Dynasty were the first rulers who were interred at Thebes. By the time of Intef II, Amun of Karnak was already associated with the cult of Re.[104] At the same time, Hathor came to be worshipped as Re's consort, as evidenced by a text of that king's tomb.[105] It was by the time of Mentuhotep II that Karnak and the West Bank was visibly connected beyond the river. He built his funerary temple, Akhsut, at Deir el-Bahari and its causeway running towards Karnak.[106]

Thebes expanded from this northern line towards the south during the following dynasties.[107] It was this east-west axis that defined the route of the Valley Festival. In contrast, the southern boundary extended between the temples of Luxor and Medinet Habu. Our knowledge of the history of these two sites before the New Kingdom is very limited.[108] The queen Hatshepsut is known to have

[97] Neferrenpet is also recorded in O. Cairo 25300 and O. Cairo 25303 for day 17 and 22 in unknown months of Peret (*KRI* VII, 454: 14 and 455: 2).

[98] PM I-1², 95 (2, I); Hari 1985, 16–9, pl. 6.

[99] In a chapel near the Queen's Valley, he is portrayed adoring Meretseger, Ptah, and Amenhotep I (PM I-2², 707, Chapel A; Sadek 1987, 72).

[100] High officials rarely visited Thebes in the Peret season. It may be of some interest to point out that the Medinet Habu calendar records eight celebrations for that month but only the *nḥb-k3.w* Festival stands out in its large number of offerings (Appendix 1). It is difficult to confirm whether the particular inactivity in this season resulted from seasonal/agricultural patterns, which may have halted social and religious activities to some extent. The workforce at Deir el-Medina seems not to have been influenced by any of these patterns (Eyre 1987b, 176). However, the Peret season featured another aspect regarding mining expeditions. Many expeditions took place in the Shemu season during the Sixth Dynasty (Eichler 1993, 152). According to Eyre (1987b, 181), the Shemu season in that time roughly corresponded to the winter season, when there were precipitation in Syria and Palestine, and hence overseas campaigns had to cease.

[101] Kemp 1989, 203, fig. 71.

[102] Arnold 1976. For potteries discovered in these areas predating the Old Kingdom, see Ginter and Kammer-Grothaus 1998. For the origin and landscape of the city Thebes, see Nims 1955; Vandorpe 1995, 219–20. Gabolde (1998, 159–62) suggests that the processional route between Karnak and Luxor existed in the time of Senusret I, based on the orientation of a restored relief of the Middle Kingdom court erected by that king at Karnak. Likewise, Hirsch (2004, 49) concludes that Senusret I had a complete plan of the city of Thebes, an idea followed by Gundlach (2010, 88–9), who proposes that the Theban quadrangle, formed by Karnak, Deir el-Bahari, Luxor, and Medinet Habu, existed in the Eleventh Dynasty, and that when Amun took over the role of Re at Thebes, the axis between Karnak and Deir el-Bahari emerged to bear resemblance to the geographical location between Heliopolis and Giza.

[103] Vörös 1998; *idem* 2003; Weeks 2000, fig. 1.

[104] The compound form Amun-Re is attested on a polygonal pillar of Intef II discovered at Karnak (Sethe 1929a, 11; Morenz 2003b; Ullmann 2005).

[105] Gundlach 2010, 88.

[106] Arnold 1974.

[107] Kondo 1999.

[108] Two Thirteenth Dynasty architrave fragments from the reign of Sobekhotep I may attest to the existence of a building at the site of Luxor temple before the New Kingdom (PM II², 338; Daressy 1926, 8). Ryholt (1997, 336, n. 1), however, maintains that these stone fragments do not testify to an earlier origin of that temple, but were transported from Karnak to be reused for a statue base (see Pamminger 1992, 129, n. 201 for evidence from before the reign of Amenhotep III). Likewise, an altar of Senusret III discovered at Luxor is considered to

erected temples on these two sites, but it was only from the Ramesside Period onwards that the two sites were figuratively connected by the Decade Ritual (3.2.2).

The Opet Festival is first attested in the reign of Hatshepsut.[109] This festival linked Karnak to Luxor with a stone-paved processional street, aligned with six barque-stations, stretching over 2.5 kilometers, and defined the north-south axis of eastern Thebes. It is possible that this axis existed before the New Kingdom and extended (or emulated) later, because a procession took place between Karnak and Medamud, five kilometers northeast, at the Mentu Festival during the Second Intermediate Period (2.2.1). This earlier axis seems to have remained during the New Kingdom and might have been regarded as a bearing on Heliopolis (4.3.5.1). In fact, north Karnak was a setting for the New Year celebrations, whose association with the Heliopolitan cult was evident (4.5.2).

1.3.3. Orientations of reliefs depicting the Festivals of Opet and the Valley at Karnak

These axial components saw completion when Amenhotep III erected the temple of Luxor in its present form. He probably decided to locate this temple as a focal site connected to Karnak to the north and his own memorial temple on the West Bank. His building projects finally formed the Theban city area, perhaps first defined by Senusret I. Amenhotep III seems to have been well aware of the upcoming synchronization of the civil calendar with the natural cycle in a few generations for the first time in the past 1460 years (1.2.4). In anticipation that seasonal festivals would once again be celebrated in their original contexts, he established new religious foundations, resulted in the creation of some enormous temple structures. The temple of Karnak itself extended on these east-west and north-south axes during the Eighteenth Dynasty. Kings continued to add a new pylon to those built by their predecessors. Each space between the pylons was enclosed by walls and called *wsḫ.t.* As a result, the unique appearance of the vast temple complex of Karnak was created by two series of open-air courts, extending towards the west and south.[110]

The two axes partly represented the Festivals of Opet and the Valley because temple reliefs depicting these festivals seem to have borne the same orientations as them. This conforms to the textual juxtaposition of these celebrations and is particularly true for the Great Hypostyle Hall of Karnak, where the two axes meet. In this hall, the scenes of the Opet Feast are carved on the west wall and those of the Valley Feast on the south and perhaps north walls (Figures 1–2).[111] This hall functioned as an entrance to Karnak in the times of Seti I and his son Ramses II. This was also the case with the Colonnade Hall of Luxor temple, where the Opet Feast had been represented on a grand scale (2.4.1), before Ramses II added the outer court to the then entrance to this temple. The easily accessible, prominent position of the representations of the feasts suggests an intention to appeal to wider audiences visiting the temples.[112]

originate from elsewhere (Hirsch 2004, 92). Regarding the foundation date of Karnak, scholars' opinions have been divided between the Old Kingdom and the reign of Senusret I, depending on how one interprets the statuettes representing Old Kingdom rulers that were discovered at that temple (Daumas 1967; Wildung 1969; Habachi 1974, 214). For general discussions on the foundation of Karnak temple, see Le Saout 1987; Franke 1990; Gabolde, Carlotti, and Czerny 1999; and Blyth 2006, 7–9.

[109] Callender (2002, 38–9) explains that Hatshepsut set up new religious foundations for the Festivals of Opet and the Valley, if not their origins. Keller (2005, 97) also posits that the queen took initiatives to restore religious festivals after the Hyksos age of 'Re's absence', as recorded at Speos Artemidos (*Urk.* IV, 390: 9). Allen (2002, 17), however, takes that account not as evidence of a historical event, but as a statement of the queen's accomplishment in removing the last traces of the devastation. It is clear that some new aspects of the royal cult were highlighted during the time of Hatshepsut and Thutmose III, when the former gained power over the latter and took the throne as a female king. She probably needed to promote the legitimacy of her succession to the throne and to propagandize it through various religious and architectural schemes (O'Connor 1998, 138; Teeter 1997, 14, n. 61).

[110] Graindorge-Héreil (2002, 86) proposes that the north-south axis of Karnak already existed under Amenhotep I.

[111] Gaballa (1976, 153, n. 82) first presented a list of temple reliefs that depicts the Opet Festival. By revising Gaballa's work, Murnane (1982, 577, n. 15) located ten groups of representations at the temples of Karnak, Luxor, and Deir el-Bahari.

[112] Baines (2006, 276–87) cautions that only limited individuals entitled to enter temples were allowed to witness rituals therein, and that one should not interpret pictorial evidence and the size of buildings too literally to argue for any broad public participating in temples.

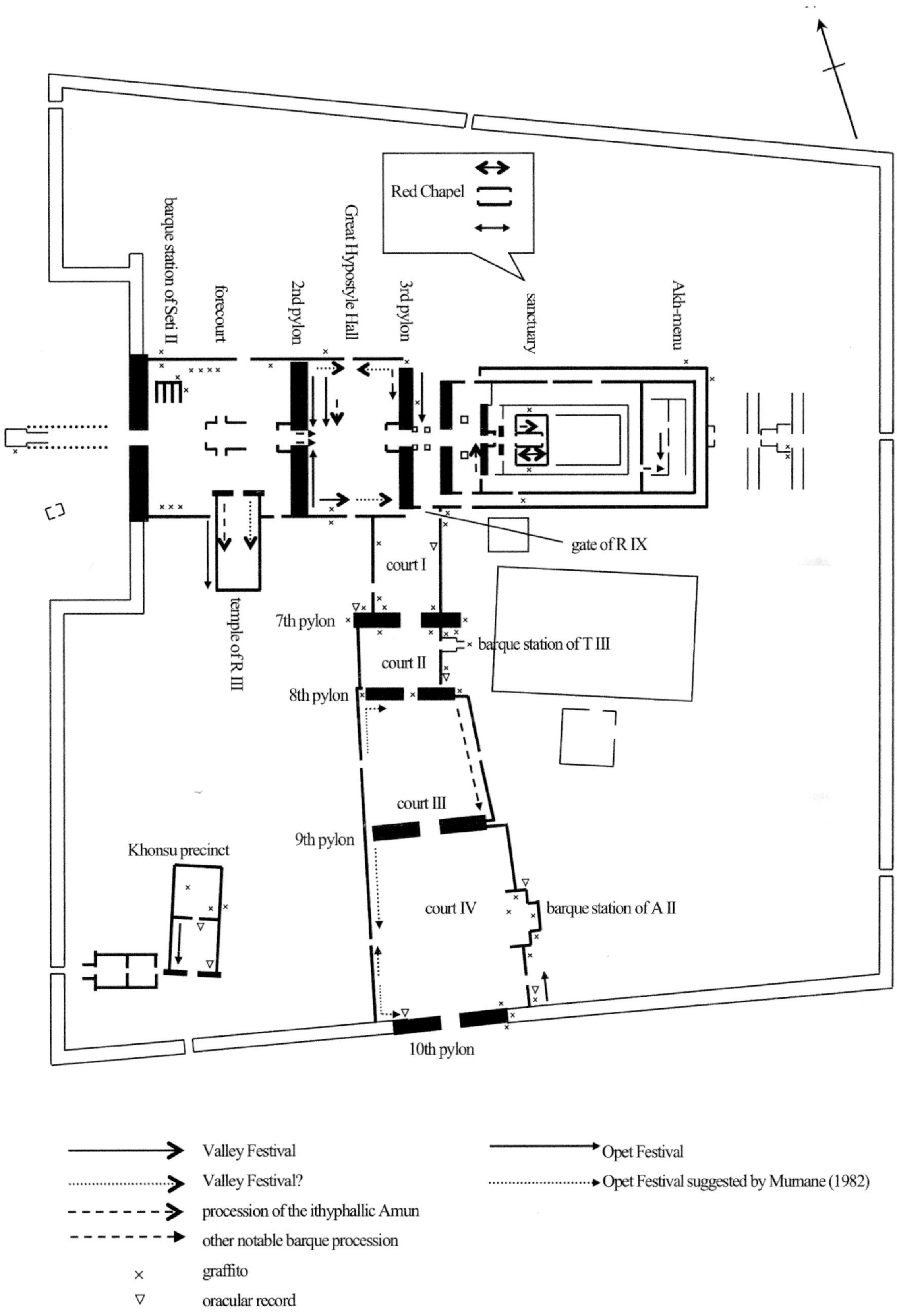

Figure 1. Locations of festival reliefs and graffiti within the Karnak temple.

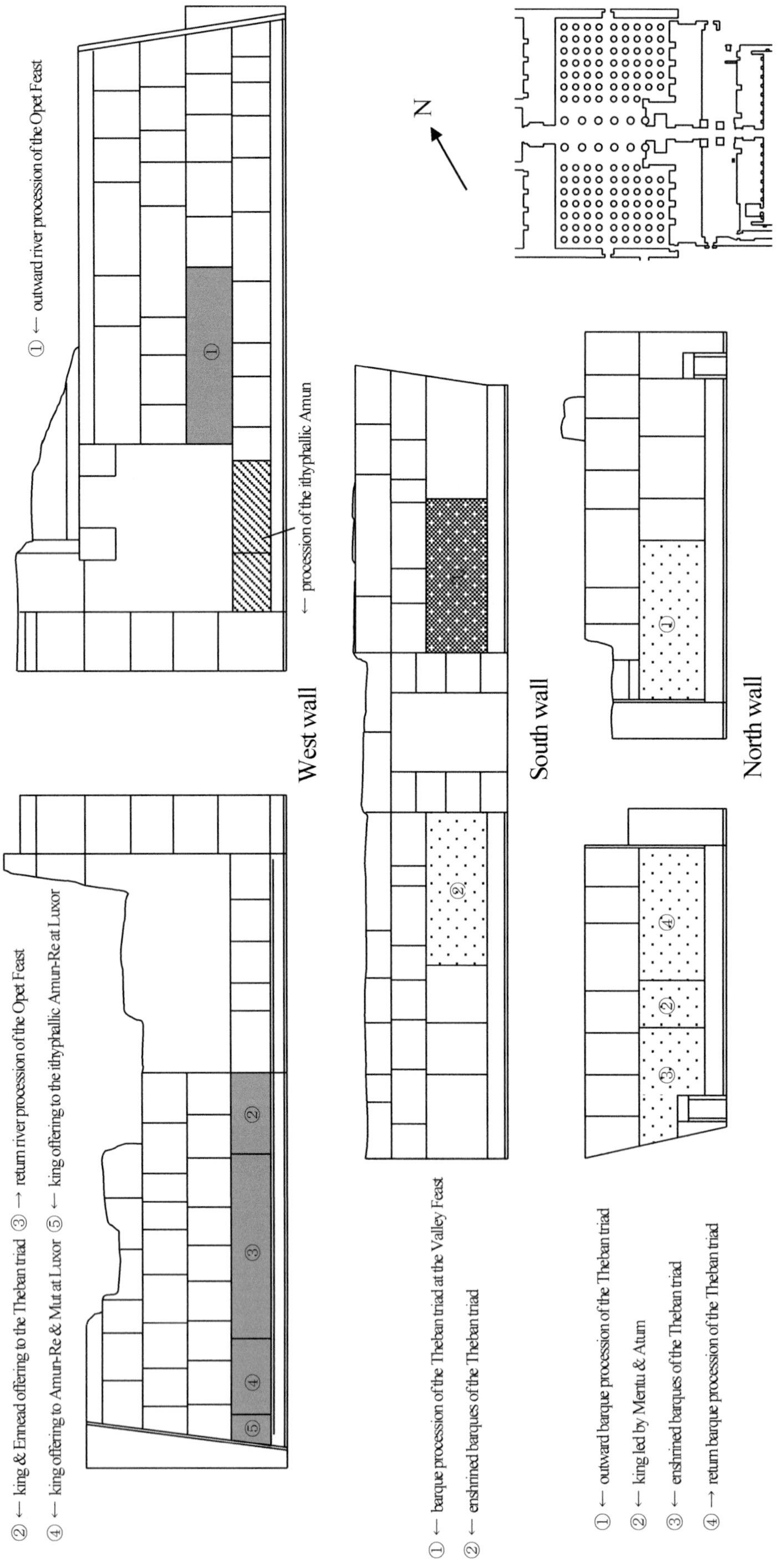
① ← outward river procession of the Opet Feast
← procession of the ithyphallic Amun
② ← king & Ennead offering to the Theban triad ③ → return river procession of the Opet Feast
④ ← king offering to Amun-Re & Mut at Luxor ⑤ ← king offering to the ithyphallic Amun-Re at Luxor
West wall
① ← barque procession of the Theban triad at the Valley Feast
② ← enshrined barques of the Theban triad
South wall
① ← outward barque procession of the Theban triad
② ← king led by Mentu & Atum
③ ← enshrined barques of the Theban triad
④ → return barque procession of the Theban triad
North wall
N

Figure 2. Elevation of the Great Hypostyle Hall at Karnak.

Chapter 2

Opet Festival

2.1. Research history

The Opet Festival is referred to on a frequent basis in Egyptological literature, but its religious and social functions have rarely been discussed in detail. This is partly because less attention has been paid to the destination of this celebration, the temple of Luxor. Compared with the gigantic architectures of Karnak and the picturesque memorial temples on the West Bank, comprehensive studies on Luxor temple and the publication of the reliefs and inscriptions have regrettably been delayed. The then half-buried temple was first excavated by Maspero in 1881 and followed by Daressy in 1885. Two reports published by Daressy (1892 and 1893) provided new information. In particular, the former publication first brought to light the reliefs depicting the Opet Festival. This was, however, no more than a simple description of the reliefs. In the course of sporadic excavations at the site until the 1960s, Howard Carter created drawings of part of the Opet scenes during 1916–1917 by Alan Gardiner's commission, but they were never completed and published, now in possession of the Griffith Institute, University of Oxford. Wreszinski (1923) also reproduced the reliefs, but it was Wolf (1931) who examined the reliefs for the sake of this festival. His work has been regarded as standard to consult on the festival since then.

The reliefs in discussion spread over the interior sidewalls of the Colonnade Hall to the full extent of about 50 meters in length, depicting for the most part the river processions of the Theban triad. The walls are thought to have once been 15 meters high, comprising four registers of reliefs, only the lowest one being extant. The Colonnade Hall itself, including its decorative scheme, was first created by Amenhotep III. Most of the decoration was executed by short-lived Tutankhamen, and he is thought to have died before completion. His successor Ay took over the project only to add some reliefs on the north wall. Subsequently, Horemheb usurped the cartouches of his predecessors. Finally, the enterprise was completed when Seti I furnished the southern part with his own reliefs. Later, the wall decoration received minor additions by the following Ramesside rulers.

The representations of the Opet Festival are also located in various temples within Thebes. Gaballa (1976, 153, n. 82) and Murnane (1982, 577, n. 15) presented a list of those temple reliefs. It was Bell (1985) who developed an ideological analysis of this celebration by associating Luxor temple with the royal cults. He presented a supplementary report (1987) on the representation of the Opet Festival at this temple and a chapter (1998) on the cultic aspects of the same temple. In the meantime, Murnane (1986) published a short article on this feast. The latest research by these American scholars was done in line with the then on-going conservation project of the Colonnade Hall at Luxor temple conducted by the Oriental Institute, University of Chicago. The results brought by the Epigraphic Survey (1994 and 1998) were published meticulously with translations and commentaries in *The festival procession of Opet in the Colonnade Hall*, OIP 112, 1994 (*Opet* hereafter) and *The façade, portals, upper register scenes, columns, marginalia, and statuary in the Colonnade Hall*, OIP 116, 1998 (*Façade* hereafter). More recently, Klotz (2008, 574–8 and 2012, 386–8) and Jauhiainen (2009, 92–103) devote some pages to this celebration in their theses, focusing on Roman Thebes and on popular festivals at Deir el-Medina respectively. Finally, Darnell (2010a) publishes an article dedicated to this feast, which is going to be part of the UCLA encyclopedia of Egyptology, edited by the University of California. His work is valuable especially for the updated discussion and references to recent authors.

2.2. Chronological study

2.2.1. Early attestations and precursors

The Opet Festival is first attested in Hatshepsut's the Red Chapel at Karnak. Bell (1997, 161) retains a possibility that the festival came to be celebrated earlier than her reign. According to the Tombos Stela, Thutmose I celebrated his accession anniversary on II Akhet 15 in year 2 (**212**), while a later record from Elephantine documents that the Opet Feast took place from II Akhet 15–25 for eleven days in an unknown year of his grandson Thutmose III (**213**). The actual accession of Thutmose I is elsewhere known as having taken place on III Peret 21 (**843**). As Spalinger (1995a, 279) rightly points out, it appears from the context that Thutmose I co-celebrated his accession with the Opet Feast approximately six months after his enthronement. Less direct evidence for the feast may be a Karnak stela of the king Ahmes mentioning the construction of Amun's river barge Userhat the 'Mighty of Prow'.

The Opet Festival was associated with specific areas and a seasonal cycle. It took place within the residential area of Thebes between the temples of Karnak and Luxor, respectively called *ip.t-s.wt* 'Opet of the Seats' and *ip.t-rsy.t* 'Southern Opet', from which the designation of 'Opet' derived. This celebration marked the high-rise of the Nile in the Akhet season (1.2.4) and perhaps developed during the Eighteen Dynasty as the natural cycle and the civil calendar began to come more into synchronization. Insofar as surviving records are concerned, this feast is not attested in its own name before the New Kingdom. Evidence is too scarce to define the temples of Karnak and Luxor as a co-operative set before that time (1.3.2). However, this festival could have been an echo of pre-existing celebrations before the New Kingdom. There are three possible candidates.

The first is the *šsp-itrw*, tentatively rendered as the 'Taking of the River', which is associated with the mortuary cult from the Middle Kingdom. The dates of this event are recorded mostly in the Lahun papyri. Their occurrence clearly indicates that the *šsp-itrw* was not fixed to a particular civil date but fell in a period of time from the last half of III Akhet to the first half of IV Akhet (Table 8, a). This reveals the lunar nature of this celebration, taking place in the third lunar cycle from the beginning of the civil calendar. Little is known of this festival, but the denotation including 'river' and its celebration date in the inundation season may explain the *šsp-itrw* as a seasonal festival that was celebrated for the flooding of the Nile. In P. UC 32191 (**421**), *ḫ.t ḫ3wy n.t šsp-itrw* the 'Eve of the Taking of the River' and *šsp-itrw* are recorded together for III Akhet.

Remarkably, three Middle Kingdom coffins, all from Upper Egypt, depict this celebration. Their representations parallel one another, showing an elevated river, on which a ship floats, and a row of human figures facing towards it. Among them, two women with raised arms are in all probability Isis and Nephtys on account of their label as the 'two kites'. Willems (1996, 217–21) relates these depictions to the navigation of Sais, a tradition from the Old Kingdom, and to the Osiride myth. Luft (1992, 185–7) translates the *šsp-itrw* as 'Leine der Nilmeile' and associates it with the measuring of newly created cultivation lands after the Nile's inundation, an interpretation opposed by Willems.

It should, however, be noted that the seasonal cycle during the Twelfth Dynasty was not at all in harmony with the civil calendar—it was rather reverse. The Nile reached the maximum level roughly from the end of IV Peret to the beginning of I Shemu during the reign of Amenemhat III. This prompted Willems to relate the *šsp-itrw* to the deterioration of the divine power of Osiris and his resurrection. Indeed, the stela of Sobekhotep VIII of the Sixteenth Dynasty records that Karnak was overflowed with the Nile's water during (or prior to) the epagomenal days (**1436**). The *šsp-itrw* is commonly referred to with other mortuary festivals in the Theban private tombs belonging to the New Kingdom, but none of them are accompanied with a specific date.

Two other religious events that we might regard as more relevant to Thebes are the Festival of Mentu and the *ḫnp-šꜥ* the 'Poring of the Sand'. Mentu was a major deity in the Theban area from before the New Kingdom, but the details of his festival are still far from clear, apart from his journey between Medamud and Karnak in one instance (**268**), and between Tod, Karnak, and Armant in another. It fell in either II Akhet or III Akhet, whereas the *ḫnp-šꜥ* took place exclusively in II Akhet (Table 8, b–c). Their occurrence on different days within the same month suggests their lunar nature. Strikingly, P. Berlin 10282 and 10130 record the Mentu Festival and the *ḫnp-šꜥ* that occur on one and the same day, corresponding to the second lunar day, a date of the first crescent (**197**). Moreover, their mortuary nature is suggested by the fact that the *mnḫ.t* the 'Clothing' took place after the *ḫnp-šꜥ*. P. Berlin 10248 records *ḫnp-šꜥ n ꞽnpw* the 'Pouring of the Sand of Anubis' falling on II Akhet 18, corresponding to the second lunar day (**229**). This was followed by *mnḫ.t ꞽnpw* the 'Clothing of Anubis' two days later, and the both rituals took place at the mortuary temple of Senusret III. In New Kingdom Thebes, the seemingly parallel event of *wš3-šꜥ* the 'Dispersing of the Sand' took place together with *sfḫ.t-ḏb3.t* the 'Removing of the Garment'.

It may be of some interest that before II Akhet was given the eponym of *p3-n-ip.t*, it had been called *mnḫ.t*, as evidenced by P. Ebers, dated to Amenhotep I. Remarkably, the Medinet Habu calendar records *hrw pn n mnḫ.t* 'this day of the Clothing' for the eighth day of the Opet Festival, corresponding to II Akhet 26 (**269**). Earlier during the Thirteenth Dynasty, the Mentu Festival is known to have taken place on the same day (**268**). The significance of the 'Clothing' in the context of the Opet Feast is not clear, but it may be associated with a ritual of adorning Amun's statue when the god underwent renewal. Alternatively, the *mnḫ.t* for the Opet Feast could refer to banners tied to the flagstaffs of the temple pylon, marking a crucial moment of the celebration. Elsewhere in P. Berlin 10092, dated to the Middle Kingdom, the 'Clothing' is recorded for II Akhet 27

(**270**). These facts may point to an age-old tradition associated with the mortuary cult that had taken place in II Akhet since the Middle Kingdom and was eventually transformed anew into the Opet Feast in the New Kingdom.

It is noteworthy that the temple of Mentuhotep II at Deir el-Bahari was at times called the 'Mentu temple of Khakaure (Senusret III)' beside its more popular name Akhsut 'Glorious are the Seats (of Amun)'. Amun's cult emerged in Thebes in the Eleventh Dynasty, but it had not attained great importance until Amenemhat I founded the Twelfth Dynasty. Mentu remained one of presiding deities at Thebes in the New Kingdom and later, but there is no evidence attesting a festival solely dedicated to this god after the Second Intermediate Period. Hence, it cannot be ruled out that the Mentu Festival was replaced or subsumed by the Opet Feast.

2.2.2. Date and duration (Table 9)

A few texts carved on the Red Chapel and at Luxor temple refer to the Opet Festival as an annual (*tp rnp.t*) festival. The festival started in II Akhet, the eponym of which was *pꜣ-n-ip.t* 'the (month) of Opet' and Phaophi in Coptic. Thutmose III celebrated this festival from II Akhet 15 to 25 for eleven days in an unknown year (**213**). Another record at Karnak attests the different date II Akhet 14 in year 23 of that king (**199**). According to the annals of Thutmose III elsewhere within Karnak, he celebrated *ḫꜥ.t nsw.t* the 'royal appearance' on I Shemu 21 in year 23, corresponding to a new moon day, while he was at Megiddo during his Asian war campaign (**1021**). This proves that II Akhet 14 in the same year corresponded to a new moon day.

I Shemu 21: II Akhet 14 (148 tropical days in between)≈5.012 lunar months

(148/29.530589=5.0117524)

Borchardt (1936, 55, n. 8) first drew attention to the association of the new moon with this feast but somehow regarded II Akhet 14 as the end of the festival. Because this date is close to Thutmose I's accession anniversary celebrated on II Akhet 15 in year 2 (**212**), presumably in harmony with the Opet Festival, II Akhet 14 of Thutmose III is likely to have been an echo of the earlier tradition. These two dates of Thutmose I and Thutmose III theoretically postdated the Nile's culmination and were rather in proximity to the autumnal equinox in their times (Table 3). Hence, on the one hand the civil calendar was used to follow traditions, the lunar cycle was employed to determine the specific date of a given celebration on the other, particularly when the dislocation of the civil calendar from the natural cycle was not minor enough to disregard. This was clearly the case for the aforementioned 'royal appearance' of Thutmose III celebrated on I Shemu 21, a new moon day, at Megiddo, whereas four other documents confirm that his accession day was I Shemu 4 as a historical matter of fact (**972–5**). It appears that in the time of Thutmose III the lunar cycle had still played a key role in determining festival dates as a more reliable marker than later times, when the civil calendar came into harmony with the seasonal cycle, and thus some celebrations became fixed to a specific date in the civil calendar.

It may be that II Akhet 14 was the eve of the Opet Festival. In the Medinet Habu calendar (Figure 10), the 'eve (*ḫꜣw.t*) of Amun's festival at the Festival of Opet' is recorded for II Akhet 18, followed by the first day of this celebration next day (**233**). It is also recorded that the festival lasted 24 days from II Akhet 19 to III Akhet 12 (**236**). On the other hand, P. Harris I (XVIIa, 5–6) attests the duration of 27 days from II Akhet 19 to III Akhet 15 (**237**). The discrepancy between the Medinet Habu calendar and P. Harris I may be explained by the fact that the former is likely to be a copy of a now lost calendar at the Ramesseum of Ramses II, apart from the first five lists mentioning new endowments of Ramses III. Hence, the duration of 24 days perhaps belongs not to the Opet Festival under Ramses III, but to that under Ramses II. Indeed, P. Harris I specifies that this feast was invariably celebrated for 27 days from year 1 to 31 of Ramses III, namely, during his whole reign. This explains that the festival extended into mid III Akhet in the Ramesside Period. At Thebes in 1300 BC, the Nile theoretically reached the maximum level on III Akhet 6 (1.2.4). Thus, it took place on *ca.* II Akhet 1 in mid Thutmose III's reign, on *ca.* III Akhet 11 at the beginning of Ramses II' reign, and on ca. IV Akhet 11 in the last half of Ramses III's time. It is possible that Ramses II and Ramses III attempted not only to fix the beginning of the Opet Feast to the civil date of II Akhet 19, but also to accord this celebration with the ever-delaying occurrence of the Nile's peak within the civil calendar by extending the festival duration.

It is not known why these Ramesside rulers maintained the date of II Akhet 19 that preceded the high rise of the Nile by dozens of days. One possibility is that it might have been the day of measuring the Nile. It was the tradition in medieval Cairo that the plenitude of Nile at sixteen cubits high, the same height as stated by Herodotus (*Histories* II, 13), was recorded and celebrated before the highest level of the year was marked. The plenitude could take a few weeks before the maximum. In fact, the significance of II Akhet 19 remained as the day of the Opet Feast after the Ramesside Period. The tomb of Irterau (TT 390), a female scribe and the chief attendant of the divine adoratice of Nitocris in the time of Psametik I, records thirteen festival days for II Akhet, the same number as recorded in the Medinet Habu calendar. If these days are all to be assigned to the Opet Feast including its eve, II Akhet 19 is taken as the initial day. Sources from the Roman Period are not few and they all attest this particular day (**240–3**).

It might be that day 19 was first standardized during the time of Amenhotep III. Theoretically, the Nile's high-rise is likely to have corresponded to II Akhet 19 in his reign. This king was perhaps responsible for many new religious foundations, including the temple of Luxor and the third pylon of Karnak, at both of which the Opet Festival was the main focus (1.3.2). It is also not impossible that day 19 was a suitable holiday for people to spend a weekend. The Opet Festival was undoubtedly the largest Egyptian festival with respect to the long duration, only after the Sed Festival that could have lasted for more than a few months (**937**) and the reunion of Horus with Hathor that was celebrated at Ptolemaic Edfu and Dendera (**1306–7**).

2.2.3. Later attestations

It is beyond the scope of the present study to examine all later records arguably associated with the Opet Feast. Although dated documents are not few, our knowledge of this celebration after the New Kingdom is limited. Thus, this section is given only to conclude that the Opet Feast is not securely attested in historical records after the Twenty-Sixth Dynasty, and that later references to this feast may only be liturgical. A fragmentary stela, dated to the Twenty-Second Dynasty or the Twenty-Third Dynasty, says: *iw=i ḥr (s)ḫnty Ỉmn [r] ip.t* 'I escorted Amun upstream [to] Opet.' Stela Cairo 48862, originating from Gebel Barkal, records a return journey of Amun to Karnak on III Akhet 2 in year 21(?) of Piankhi. An autobiographical account carved on a statue of Ibi, chief steward of the divine adoratice Nitocris, dated to the Twenty-Sixth Dynasty, records: *[s3i]=s [wi3]=f ḫft wḏ it=s Ỉmn r ip.t=f [ḥ]n(ꜥ) ḫnr.wt=f wn ḥn(ꜥ)=s m ḥb=f* 'she (Nitocris) [satisfies(?)] his [barge(?)] when her father Amun proceeds to his Opet [together] with his singers, who accompany her at his festival'.

A very short account of the calendar at Esna temple is the only non-liturgical source that clearly attests the Opet Festival in the Ptolemaic-Roman Period (**242**). It gives the date of II Akhet 19. The calendar at the temple of Kom Ombo, dated to the time of Ptolemy VI, may also refer to this feast in some more detail, but the dates that it records differ from the Esna calendar (**152**). Klotz (2012, 386) associates these texts with the Opet Feast, but they do not explicitly have Theban traits. Other accounts relevant to the present examination are attested in two mortuary texts, dated to the Roman Period: the Book of the Traversing Eternity (P. Leiden T 32) and the Book of Embalmment (P. Boulaq III), both of which refer to the Opet Feast celebrated on II Akhet 19 (**241** and **243**).

These later documents cannot be taken as historical accounts, and thus it is difficult to confirm that the Opet Festival survived after the Twenty-Sixth Dynasty.

2.3. Designation of the Opet Festival

As the name of the festival derives from *ip.t* designating the temples of Karnak and Luxor, called *ip.t-s.wt* 'Opet of the Seats' and *ip.t-rsy.t* 'Southern Opet' respectively, a series of rituals took place in these two temples. Although often translated a 'harem' in connection with the assumed ritual of sacred marriage between a pair of Amun and the royal consort, or between the king and Hathor (2.4.10), Opet was a general term denoting a confined space or container. When it refers to temples, it is best rendered a 'sanctuary'. Accordingly, *ḥb ip.t* can be translated as the 'Festival of the Sanctuary(-ries)'. Of the two temples involved, *ip.t* is more likely to refer to the temple of Luxor when its referent is not explicitly expressed. In the coronation text of Horemheb, this celebration is unusually called *ḥb=f nfr ḫnty ip.t-rsy.t* 'His Beautiful Festival of Going Up Stream (to) Southern Opet', while Karnak is referred to as 'Waset'. A text accompanying the river-procession scene in the Khonsu temple at Karnak explains that the party moves to Luxor in the name of *ip.t*, while Karnak is separately referred to as 'it' by the singular feminine pronoun *s*. The statue of Horsaaset records this celebration as 'His Beautiful Festival at Southern Opet' (1.1.3). Thus, a translation as the 'Festival of Luxor temple' is also possible because the designation of celebration was taken after the name of the destination in the cases of the Valley Festival and the Behedet Festival at Edfu, during the latter of which Horus and Hathor visited Behedet, a necropolis to the southwest of Edfu.

It is self-evident from several representations that the greatest moment of the Opet Festival was the river-journey to Luxor of the Theban triad. The trip of the god from one temple to another was a distinctive feature of many Egyptian festivals, but it is with the Opet Festival that we can best illustrate a ceremonial route. The location of Luxor 2.5 kilometers to the south of Karnak had an ideological significance. A text accompanying the relief of Luxor temple reads:

> *t3 r [ḏr=f] m rš.wt r spr r ip.t špsy s.t=f n sp tpy di=f ꜥnḫ w3s n s3=f Ḏsr-ḫpr.w-rꜥ-stp-n-rꜥ s3 3ḫ n ms sw mi ḫni.n=f it Ỉmn r ir.t hrr.t k3=f*

> The land in [its entirety] is in joy on the arrival at noble Opet, his (Amun-Re's) seat of the first time, where he gives life and dominion to his son Djoserkheperure-setepenre, son who is beneficial to the one who begot him, as he has navigated the father Amun in order to cause his ka to be pleased.

Likewise, a legend in the Opet Feast reliefs of Ramses III's temple at Karnak also refers to Southern Opet as a primordial site where the sun rises (2.4.6).

The Great Hypostyle Hall at Karnak contains a unique representation of Luxor temple also as a primeval site (2.4.6). Water is depicted overflowing from under the legs of Amun-Re and running through the river-procession scene. Above the prow of the Userhat barge is a text referring to Amun-Re as being 'in the primeval water (*nnw*)'. The association of Amun with the *nnw* is an echo of the old creation myth that the demiurge Atum emerged in the form of the primordial hill from the *nnw*. It was this hill that Luxor was identified with and that the freshly delivered Nile's water originated from. The Egyptians traditionally located the source of fresh water at Elephantine. In a similar manner, the Thebans looked for it at the southern end of the city. Hence, the location of Luxor temple to the south of Karnak temple is not accidental but deliberate, and embedded in the mythology.

2.4. Sequence of the Opet Festival

2.4.1. Overview of the Colonnade Hall at Luxor temple

According to Hatshepsut's Red Chapel, the outward trip of Amun from Karnak took a land route, whereas the return trip was on the river. The land route was furnished with six repository barque-chapels (*w3ḥ.t*), the first and sixth of which survive today. The Luxor reliefs, on the other hand, represent both trips by water. They are deployed in juxtaposition on the west and east walls and divided into 14 episodes:

1. Emergence of the king from the palace;
2. Ritual at Karnak;
3. Departure from Karnak;
4. Outward river procession;
5. Arrival at Luxor;
6. Ritual at Luxor;
7. Offering to Amun and (Mut?);
8. Offering to Amun and (Amenet?)
9. Ritual at Luxor;
10. Departure from Luxor;
11. Return river procession;
12. Return to Karnak;
13. Ritual at Karnak;
14. Return of the king to the palace.

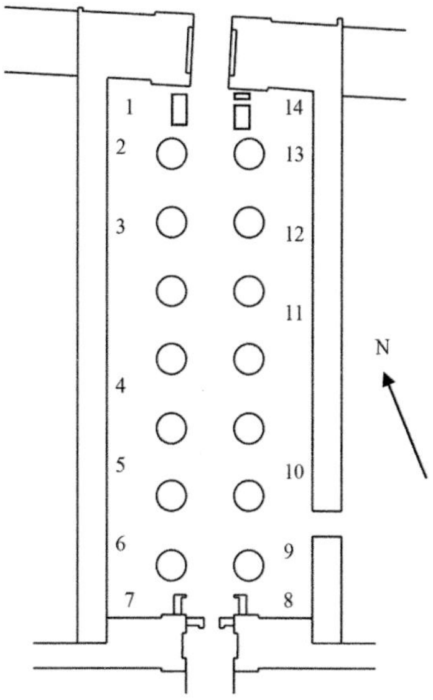

Colonnade Hall at Luxor

In each of the following sections, the west and east walls will be examined together to complement missing parts one another.

2.4.2. Eve

As described in 2.2.2, the eve of the Opet Festival may be recorded for year 23 of Thutmose III. The only unequivocal evidence for the evening rite, however, is the Medinet Habu calendar, which records *hrw n iḫ.t ḫ3w.t n ḥb 'Imn m ḥb=f n ip.t* the 'day of the evening meal of Amun's festival at His Festival of Opet' for II Akhet 18 (**233**). The number of divine offerings (*ḥtp-nṯr*) consumed on this day was 295, whereas that on the following day, i.e. the first day of the festival, was 355. The consumption on the eve is not significantly less than that of the first day, but appears humble for a major celebration, compared with 285 offerings for the eve of the Wag Festival (**99**).

In P. Bibliothèque Nationale 237, a work journal dated to year 3 of Ramses VI, three subjects are documented for II Akhet 18: 1) painters and metal workers inscribed the king's name in the granary of the Enclosure (*p3 ḫtm*); 2) the high-priest of Amun (probably Ramsesnakht) and the royal butler Qedren as well as the overseer of the treasury Mentuemtauy visited Thebes (*niw.t*); 3) the appearance of an unidentified god and his oracular session concerning a royal document (**234**).[1] Although not explicitly reported, these events are highly likely

[1] Černý (1952b, 29), Borghouts (1982, 25), and Jauhiainen (2009, 98) identify the god in question with the deified king Amenhotep I.

to have been associated with the Opet Feast because of the presence of the high-ranking individuals (1.3.1.2).

2.4.3. Emergence of the king from the palace[2]

It is postulated that the rulers of the later Eighteenth Dynasty resided mostly in Memphis.[3] Apart from the Malkata palace of Amenhotep III, which was built in his later years at western Thebes and used until the time of Horemheb,[4] and a part of the temple of Medinet Habu,[5] no sites have been archaeologically located as a royal dwelling in Thebes.[6] It is generally accepted by scholars that whether ceremonial or residential, the main palace of Thebes stood to the northwest of Karnak temple.[7] The Luxor relief is reticent about the episode of the king's departure from the palace. This scene portrays Horemheb, who usurped Tutankhamen's cartouche, led by Amun and an unidentified goddess. The preserved part shows only a regular formula promising the king many jubilees. A relief at the temple of Medinet Habu also bears witness to this episode. Ramses III follows two fan-bearers, the legend of which reads:[8]

> *ḫʿy ḥm=f m sfy nṯry mi Rʿ psḏ n km.t ib nb mḥ m nfr.w=f bʿḥi.n mr.wt=f t3.wy r m3 it=f Imn-rʿ m ḥb=f tpy n ip.t di=f ḥb.w sd ʿš3.w wr.w n s3=f nb t3.wy Wsr-m3ʿ.t-rʿ-mry-imn nb ḫʿ.w Rʿ-ms-sw-ḥk3-iwn di ʿnḫ ḏ.t*
>
> Appearance of his person as a divine child like Re, light for Egypt, every heart being filled with his beauty, whose love has flooded the Two Lands, in order to see his father Amun-Re at his first Festival of Opet. May he give very many jubilees to his son, lord of the Two Lands, Usermaatre-meryamen, lord of the diadems, Ramses-heqaiun, given life forever.

It is remarkable that the festival is referred to as the 'first' one. Such specification is not attested elsewhere. This may signify the king's attendance at the first Opet Festival shortly after he assumed the throne.

Visits to Thebes paid by two other Ramesside kings are also known. Ramses II left this city for the north on III Akhet 23 in year 1 after celebrating the Opet Feast (**389**).[9]

Seti I probably visited Karnak in year 1.[10] He also took on a national tour in year 2 and was present at Thebes in II Akhet.[11] Seti II too 'came to the Southern City' (*mni r niw.t rsy.t*) on II Akhet 10 in year 1 and sojourned there for four or more days (**178**). An account of P. Turin 2044 may argue for the possibility that Ramses VI or his delegation visited Thebes in year 1.[12]

As described in 1.3.1.1, the king was theoretically required to attend the Opet Feast every year. It probably became a practice for the king to visit Thebes in the first year in order to participate in this celebration. Concomitantly, his first visit was aimed at co-celebrating the accession, which may have been repeated in Heliopolis and Memphis too.[13] By doing so, the king reported his enthronement to each patron deity at these cities. Indeed, it is well known that Horemheb performed the Opet Feast and his accession anniversary together at Thebes.[14]

It may also be of some interest that some royal decrees concerning exemptions from tax were issued in the first year of reign and at the Sed Festival. Galán (2000) proposes a possibility of royal decrees renewed at the beginning of each reign in order to re-confirm official edicts passed down from earlier generations. Such was possibly the case for major festivals, where a ceremonial setting for divine approval was coordinated. This forms a model for reward ceremonies and the appointment of officials (2.5.2 and 2.5.3).

[2] *Opet*, 1, pl. 3.
[3] O'Connor and Cline 1998, 15.
[4] Stadelmann 1994, 314.
[5] Stadelmann 1996, 230
[6] O'Connor (1989, 81) and Stadelmann (1994, 311–2) conclude that it was from the Ramesside Period that a temporal royal palace was constructed within the memorial temple of each king on the West Bank and that these palaces were used only for the cult of the dead king. O'Connor (2012, 228–32) adds that the memorial temple of Ay and Horemheb had a palace attached to it, but maintains his view on the temple palace to be only ceremonial by comparison with the larger palaces of Amenhotep IV at Amarna and of Merenptah at Memphis.
[7] Gitton 1974; O'Connor 1989, 79–80; Stadelmann 1996, 226.
[8] PM II², 495 (77, c); *MH* IV, pl. 237, A.

[9] Pi-Ramses was not yet completed in his early years, but it is speculated that Ramses II resided either in Memphis or Heliopolis (Redford 1971, 111, n. 4). His accession date has not been confirmed by direct evidence, but scholars seem to agree that it took place on III Shemu 27 (**1280**). If the body of his father Seti I had undergone seventy-day embalmment, his funeral must have fallen after II Akhet 2. Redford (1971, 110) posits that Ramses II attended his father's funeral, based on an inscription at Abu Simbel dated to II Akhet 25 in year 1 (**260**). For many other records dated to year 1 of Ramses II, see Schmidt 1973, 22–5.
[10] PM II², 198 (8); *KRI* I, 41: 4.
[11] P. Bibliothèque Nationale 206, II, 12 (*KRI* I, 247: 10). Merenptah likewise visited Thebes in year 2 'in order to see his father Amun-Re, king of the gods' (*KRI* IV, 25: 8).
[12] *KRI* VI, 341: 13–6. Amer (1985b, 66) associates the recorded event with the Valley Feast, but it predates I Peret, suggesting a reference to the Opet Festival.
[13] Hatshepsut's coronation text at Deir el-Bahari narrates that she travelled to the north with her father Thutmose I accompanied by all gods in Egypt, who approved her succession to the throne (*Urk.* IV, 246: 12; Naville 1895, vol. 3, pl. 57, cols 4–5). According to a dedicatory inscription at Karnak, Ramses IV repeated the ritual of 'writing the royal name on the *išd*-tree' in year 1 at Heliopolis, Memphis, and Thebes (*KRI* VI, 5: 10–8: 5; Peden 1994a, 137–43 for translation). These three cities are also referred to in a similar context in the coronation text of Horemheb (Gardiner 1953, 15, l. 18).
[14] Gardiner 1953.

2.4.4. *Rituals at Karnak*[15]

It is not entirely sure where Mut and Khonsu joined the procession of Amun.[16] The Luxor reliefs depict them brought together behind a Karnak pylon. The king censes and pours water over offerings piled up in front of the barques of the Theban triad, with an offering list for each god. The triad is attended by the royal barque facing towards them.

Hatshepsut's Red Chapel also attests this episode in an abridged fashion with Amun's barque only.[17] The figure of the queen, now destroyed, censes to the barque, which is placed on the 'great seat (*s.t wr.t*) at Karnak'. The fact that the Opet Festival is represented in the Great Hypostyle Hall and on the third pylon at Karnak explains the significance of these precincts once as a temple entrance, where visitors could see elaborate and colorful representations carved on them (1.3.3). The processional barques perhaps gathered around this area, where the two temple axes, namely, the east-west and north-south ones, converged. This is also where the portal of Ramses IX opens, which, according to Amer (1999, 32), can be associated with the Festivals of Opet and the Valley.

It may be of some interest to remark on the king's barque. When Horemheb visited Thebes from the north to celebrate his accession anniversary at the Opet Festival, a statue of Horakhety accompanied the king.[18] As a father of the king this statue appears to have played an intermediary role between Amun and the king. In the Luxor reliefs the king's barque is represented up to the point when it reached Luxor, but not in the ritual scenes within the temple.[19] More significantly, when the royal barque is represented, it is usually positioned separately to the divine barques. It faces towards Amun's barque as if it officiates in servicing the god.[20] The subsidiary role of the royal barque invites comparison with the barque of Ahmes-Nefertari and the portable image of the reigning king, each represented on board of Amun's barge in Seti I's reliefs at the Great Hypostyle Hall of Karnak[21] and in Herihor's reliefs at the Khonsu temple[22]. They had a role more aligned with the king than the gods and could be invested with a patronage function within the royal court.

Johnson (1994, 138–9) assumes that a standing figure of Amenhotep III behind the cabin of each divine barge in the Luxor reliefs is a statue of the deified king. According to him, when Tutankhamen completed the scene, which was originally planned for Amenhotep III, he paid a special homage to his predecessor by representing him, who theologically manifested not only himself, but also all the past rulers as well as the reigning king.

2.4.5. *Departure from/arriving at Karnak*[23]

The Luxor reliefs depict the barques of the Theban triad and of the king departing from a large pylon to the quay, where their river barges await. Based on the eight flagstaffs, this pylon is thought to be the third one of Karnak.[24] Unlike other parallels, Amun's barque is followed first by that of Khonsu, rather than that of Mut. The king is represented behind Amun's barque, while a group of priests and musicians proceeds before it. One of them sprinkles milk on the ground. The Red Chapel portrays Hatshepsut and Thutmose III leading Amun's barque.[25] There are two possibilities regarding where the Theban triad embarked on their river barges. Karnak temple had its own quay at the western end of the east-west axis. If this quay was used, it is likely that the Theban triad gathered within Karnak temple proper. The other quay may have been located to the west of the Mut precinct. The existence of this site is evidenced by the extension of the processional way with some chapels leading from the Mut temple towards the Nile. Nims (1965, 122) and Bell (1997, 160) were inclined to the latter possibility and assumed that when Amun departed Karnak, he first turned to the south to visit Khonsu and Mut at their precincts. However, the extension of the processional way from the Mut precinct to the Nile is securely attested only from the Third Intermediate Period onwards.[26]

[15] *Opet*, 1–5, pl. 5.

[16] Ricke1954, 41. Dégardin (1984, 194) assumes that the barques of Amun and Mut met that of Khonsu at the Khonsu temple.

[17] Lacau and Chevrier 1977, vol. 1, 157, vol. 2, pl. 7 (Block 226); Burgos and Larché 2006, vol. 1, 53.

[18] Gardiner 1953, 15, l. 22. Elsewhere in the same text, this god is called 'Horus, lord of *ḥw.t-nsw.t*'. Gardiner (1953, 16, n. b and 21–2) identified *ḥw.t-nsw.t* with a site near Sharuna, where Horemheb was born.

[19] The royal barque is first attested in the time of Amenhotep III (Bell 1985, 261). Bell (1997, 158) asserted that the king's barque resided at the Akh-menu of Karnak. Contrary to the representations of the Luxor reliefs, he (1985, 262–3 and 280, n. 146) supposed that the royal barque accompanied the king into Luxor temple proper and rested in Room VI.

[20] For other examples of the king's barque facing Amun, see the scene of an unknown Amun's festival at Medinet Habu (PM II^2, 499–500 (96–8, II-1); *MH* IV, pls 229–35) and Stela Cairo JE 45548, dated to the Ramesside Period (Schulman 1980, pl. 2).

[21] PM II^2, 44 (152, III-1); Nelson 1981, pl. 152. There may have been a chapel for her cult within Karnak (Larché 2009, 168). Her barque is also represented in the processional scene of the Valley Festival at the temple of Qurna (PM II^2, 408 (6)).

[22] PM II^2, 230 (17–8, III); *Khonsu* I, pl. 21, col. 37.

[23] *Opet*, 5–7, pl. 14.

[24] *Opet*, 38, n. 129.

[25] Lacau and Chevrier 1977, vol. 1, 158, vol. 2, pl. 7 (Blocks 226 and 300); Burgos and Larché 2006, vol. 1, 52–3.

[26] Cabrol 2001, 32–4. A unique topographical representation of the Mut precinct, together with a processional way extending in front of it and the barge of Mut floating on the temple lake, is attested in the tomb of Khabekhenet (TT 2), dated to the time of Ramses II (PM I-1^2, 6 (5, I); Cabrol 1995, pl. 5). Exell (2009, 87, n. 26) associates this scene with the Opet Feast.

2.4.6. River procession[27]

The river procession was regarded as an epitome of the whole proceedings of the Opet Festival. Not a few kings selected this episode to be represented on a far larger scale than other events surrounding this celebration.

Hatshepsut, for example, carved the festival at two sites, where mush is focused on the scenes of the river journeys. left us two representations. The Red Chapel depicts both the outward and return journeys, of which the former was made by land through six way-stations.[28] When returning, Amun's barge was towed by the king's vessel. The return journey is also represented on the southern half of the eastern interior wall belonging to the upper terrace of her Deir el-Bahari temple.[29] Only the lower register, which depicts a river-procession scene, remains today (Figure 6). A legend says: [unknown groups lost] *ḥḳ3 s3 ỉmn ỉw=f ḥr ẖn.t=f m ỉp.t r ỉp.t-s.wt* '[ ] ruler, son of Amun, when he navigates him from Opet to Karnak'.[30] Some features, such as ships towing the royal barge, officials, and soldiers figured in a long band below the river-procession, parallel later representations. Hatshepsut's reliefs portray Amun only. This style continued until Amenhotep III's reign. Murnane (1979, 19) speculated that Mut and Khonsu did not yet possess their own river barges in the early Eighteenth Dynasty.[31] The upper part of the Deir el-Bahari reliefs has been restored only in a tiny portion. According to Karkowski (1976, fig. 2), the first episode to the left end portrays the king offering to the Theban triad at Karnak, a representation parallel to the one in the lower register. The last episode to the right end represents the king servicing Amun's barque, which is placed on a pedestal at Luxor. He (2001, 132) adds that six way-stations were originally depicted in between, but later reduced to two in number.

The reliefs in the Great Hypostyle Hall at Karnak, executed by Seti I and his son Ramses II, represent river processions in a fashion similar to those of Hatshepsut. It was, however, Horemheb who first conceived an idea to represent the Opet Feast in this hall. Traces of Horemheb's reliefs, which were originally designed on a grand scale but replaced with a smaller-scale scheme by the Ramesside rulers, are still visible today partially on the western interior wall.[32] They are very poorly preserved but recognizable enough to grasp the overall layout. On the north half, Amun's barge is towed by the royal vessel towards the south. There is a row of divinities depicted above this scene. On the south half, little remains. Priests carry two barques, perhaps of Mut and Khonsu, towards the north. It may be that the representations on both sides of the wall were juxtaposed, depicting a return trip of the Opet Feast. Horemheb probably developed his idea from the reliefs of Amenhotep III on the third pylon of Karnak and those of Tutankhamen at Luxor.[33] He perhaps died before the completion of his own reliefs.

Subsequently, Seti I decided to finish the decoration but on a much smaller scale by adding a number of minor ritual scenes, including a procession of the ithyphallic Amun.[34] As a result of this reduction, Amun's river barge had to accommodate not only his barque but also those of Mut, Khonsu, and Ahmes-Nefertari altogether. On the towing boat are depicted the king together with Southern-Upwaut-Ruler-of-the-Two-Lands (*Wp-w3.wt-šmʿw-sẖm-t3.wy*), Khnum-Lord-of-the-Cool-Water (*Ḫnm-nb-ḳbḥ*), and Horus-Foremost-of-the-Cool-Water (*Ḥr-ḫnty-ḳbḥ*). Seti I's scheme was ultimately finished off by his son Ramses II, who decorated the south half of the hall.[35] Ramses introduced some changes—for example, Horus-Lord-of-the-Cool-Water (*Ḥr-nb-ḳbḥ*) was added to the towing boat and the barque of Ahmes-Nefertari disappeared from Amun's barge.[36]

At Luxor the river-procession scene is most detailed and largest in scale. Amun's barque is represented on board of the Userhat, an earliest surviving example that unveils a divine barque within a cabin. The barque of the king accompanies that of Amun. The Userhat is towed by the king's vessel named *sḥtp-nṯr.w* the 'One-Who-Satisfies-the-Gods'. The royal vessel is tied to

[27] *Opet*, 7–17, pls 17 and 68.

[28] Lacau and Chevrier 1977, vol. 1, 161–73, vol. 2, pl. 7 (Blocks 300, 26, 305, 135, 169, and 170); Burgos and Larché 2006, vol. 1, 46–52; Arnold 2004, 15. For the six barque-stations, see Cabrol 2001, 528–42. Nims (1965, 122) proposed that this processional route was built on an old canal connecting the temples of Karnak and Luxor.

[29] PM II², 357–8 (79–80).

[30] Naville 1895, vol. 5, pl. 124. Werbrouck (1949, 88–9) regarded each half of the eastern wall as representing a journey at the Valley Feast, symbolizing Upper and Lower Egypt, whereas Gaballa (1976, 153, n. 82) attributed both of them to the Opet Festival.

[31] Dolińska (1994, 35) argues that Mut and Khonsu came to be represented after the time of Hatshepsut, when the figures of the triad became more common, probably reflecting the conceptual development of the theology of the Theban triad. The earliest representation of the Theban triad in a procession is carved on the eighth pylon of Karnak, constructed by Hatshepsut and Thutmose III (PM II², 174 (517)). The goddess Mut is first referred to in a text in the Second Intermediate Period, but Theban sources attest her name only from the time of Amenhotep I onwards (te Velde 1982, 246, n. 5). The earliest evidence for the Mut precinct is dated to the reign of Hatshepsut (F. Arnold 2004, 19).

[32] Nelson 1981, pls 266–7. These traces might be dated neither to Horemheb nor to Ramses I, as has conventionally been accepted. Brand (2000, 201) explains that the construction of the Great Hypostyle Hall began under Seti I, and that the remains of early reliefs in honour of Ramses I were only posthumous. This means that Seti I changed his own decoration plan to downsize the river procession scenes considerably.

[33] For Amenhotep III's relief, see PM II², 61 (183); Foucart 1924, pls I–III. Murnane (1979, 14) dated this relief to the later reign of that king, long after the pylon had been completed.

[34] Foucart (1924, 65) cautioned that the representations of the west wall did not belong to one particular feast but were ensembles of some ceremonies.

[35] Murnane 1977, 76–8.

[36] PM II², 46 (157, IV-3); Nelson 1981, pls 37–8.

ten small towing boats running before it. Behind the Userhat are the barges of Mut and Khonsu, represented in two separate registers.[37] Each barge appears to be towed by two ships. One of the ships towing Mut's barge parallels the king's vessel towing the Userhat, and thus it is another royal vessel perhaps belonging to the queen. On the eastern wall, none of the divine barges is pulled by people on the riverbank. This reflects the fact that the return journey did not require much force to go down the Nile. Apart from these people, there are soldiers, standard bearers, musicians, and singers as well as Nubians and Libyans. Conquered foreigners are repeatedly referred to in legends, normally spoken by the Theban triad, praising the king's achievements. Contrary to these accounts, foreigners portrayed in the reliefs were probably sent as peaceful representatives of their lands to participate in the great festival in order to pay homage to Amun and the Egyptian ruler. They were an essential part of the Egyptian cosmography, embodying the extension of the Egyptian territory and prosperity.[38]

The river-procession scene carved at Luxor has close parallels at Karnak: the reliefs of Ramses III and of Herihor, both of which depict the outward journey only. These later representations also include two royal vessels, implying the presence not only of the king, but also of other royal family members, the queen in particular. Indeed, a vertical text above the royal vessel towing Mut's barge on the eastern wall at Luxor proves the queen's attendance:[39]

> *r-pꜥ.t.t w*[*r*]*.t nb.t im3*[*.t*] *nḏm mr.t* [*ḫ*]*nw.t šmꜥw mḥw wꜥb.t* [*ꜥ.wy*] *ḥr sšš* [one group lost] *nṯr m ḫr.w*[*=s*] *nb.t f3w* [*wr.t*] *mr.wt ḥnw.t idb*[*.wy Ḥr*] *wbn Mw.t r di.t n=s* [*ḥs*]*.wt r k3b mr*[*.wt n*] *ḥm.t nsw.t wr.t mr*[*=f*] *ḫ*[*nw.t*] *t3.wy tm*[*=w*] *nb.t ḥs.wt Mw.t-nḏm.t* [one group lost] *ḥr ḫn*[*.t Mw.t*] *nb.t p.t m ḥb=s nfr n ip.t*
>
> Gre[at] female member of the *pat*, lady of char[m], sweet of love, [mi]stress of Upper and Lower Egypt, pure [of arms] with a sistrum [ ] the god with [her] voice, lady of splendor, [great of] love, mistress of the [two] banks of Horus. Mut rises to give [praise]s to her in order to double love [for] the great royal wife, beloved [of him], mist[ress] of the Two Lands in [their] entirety, lady of praises, Mutnedjemet [ ], who is at row[ing Mut], lady of sky, at Her Beautiful Festival of Opet.

In the relief of Ramses III at Karnak, the king appears on both the Userhat and the king's vessel, the latter of which is named the *ꜥ3 mr Imn* 'Amun's-Love-Is-Great'. There is no royal figure on the towing vessel of Mut but, seven female members of some importance and several singers are represented above the king's vessel. The first figure, who is portrayed slightly larger than the others, wears the Nekhbet headdress, typical of the royal consort.

A figure similar to this is represented in Herihor's reliefs, not in the river-procession scene but in the register below it (Figure 3). The register in question is divided into two smaller registers, depicting 19 princes, four princesses, and 15 singers.[40] The row of the royal members is headed by the queen, 'great royal wife, beloved of him, Nedjemet'. Because this scene moves towards the north, in the opposite direction to the river-procession scene above, it seems to continue to the adjacent scene on the north wall. The latter scene represents land processions of the Theban triad and of Amenet moving towards the east.[41] Amun-Re visited Khonsu at this temple, as the text accompanying the barque of the former reads: *sḫꜥ ḥm nṯr pn šps Imn-rꜥ nb ns.wt* [*t3.wy*] *ḫn.ty ip.t-s.wt r ḥ*[*tp*] *m* [*pr*] *Ḫnsw m* [*w3s.t*] *nfr-ḥtp r šsp*(*.t*) *m*[*nw*] [*p*]*n nfr wꜥb rwḏ mnḫ ir n*[*=f* one group lost] *Ḥry-ḥr-s3-imn* 'The appearance of the majesty of this august god Amun-Re, lord of the thrones of [the Two Lands], foremost of Karnak, to re[st] in [the house] of Khonsu in [Thebes], Neferhotep, in order to receive [th]is beautiful, pure, permanent, and excellent monu[ment], which [ ] Herihor-siamen made for [him].' The association of the west scene with the north one may also be suggested by the fact that two princes who are portrayed in the former scene appear in the latter as sem-priests accompanying the barques of Mut and Khonsu.[42]

The attendance of the queen is also indicated by two chariots depicted behind a group of soldiers in the Luxor reliefs—probably one for the king and the other for the queen, although each is accompanied by a caption *ḥtri ꜥ3 n ḥm=f* the 'great span of horses of his person'.[43] The hymn carved in front of the soldiers refers to the dedication of offerings from foreign lands to Amun:[44]

[37] The barge of Khonsu was called *wsḫ-nmt.wt* the 'Broad-of-Stride' (*Opet*, 33, n. c).

[38] *Opet*, 36, n. 123. Darnell and Manassa (2007, 206) and Darnell (2010a, 8–9) propose that the presence of Nubians and Libyans symbolizes a terrestrial domain of the raged goddess, who returns from the south every year.

[39] *Opet*, 30, pl. 83.

[40] *Khonsu* I, 11, pl. 26.

[41] *Khonsu* I, 22, pl. 44.

[42] Dégardin (1984, 193–4) seems to attribute all the representations of divine barques in this temple to the Opet Feast.

[43] *Opet*, 10–1, n. 28, pl. 22. Also see *Opet*, 28–9, nn. 86–8 for a silver dish (Berlin 14117) depicting a river procession accompanied by chariots. A corresponding scene at Deir el-Bahari represents only a single palanquin carried by 12 men (Naville 1895, vol. 5, pl. 125). See Champdor 1955, 143 for a photograph in the present condition.

[44] *Opet*, 9, pl. 18.

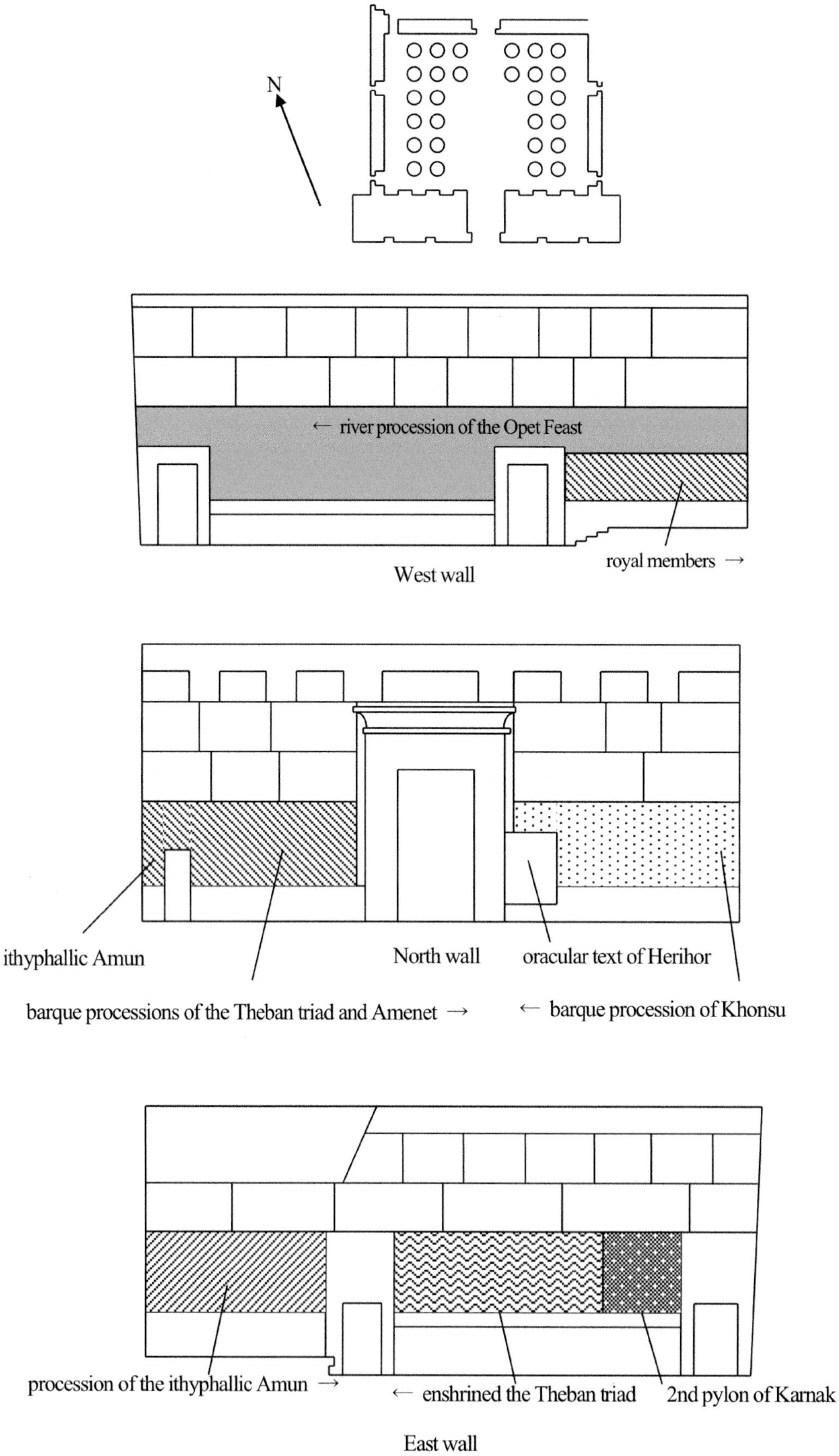

Figure 3. Elevation of the court of Herihor, Khonsu temple at Karnak.

> *iw n=k* [one group lost] *bš.t ꜣtp.w ḥr psd=sn* [*ḥr*] *in.w=sn* [*iḫ*].*wt nb.t m stp n iḫ.(w)t=sn ḥ*[*rp=w m ḥtp-nṯr m iwꜣ.w wnḏ*].*w gḥs.w mꜣ.w-ḥḏ.w ir*[*p dkr.w m*]*i nw ꜣpd.w nn ḏr wdn=sn sꜣ=k ir-*[*iḫ.t*] *m ḥb=k n ip.t nḏm ib=tn pꜣ tꜣ n* [*km.t* one or two groups lost *ḥr m*]*ꜣꜣ Imn ḥtp m ip.t=f* [rest of the column lost]
>
> Rebellious [foreign lands?] come to you (with) loads on their backs [with] their tributes, (consisting of) every[th]ing, namely, the choicest of their goods, which are de[dicated as a divine offering, consisting of the *iwꜣ*-bulls, *wnḏ*]-cattle, gazelles, oryxes, w[ine, and fruits l]ike water, as well as birds without limit. Your son, ritual conductor, offers them at Your Festival of Opet. May your hearts be pleased. O the land of [Egypt at se]eing Amun resting in his Opet [...

In a horizontal text below the Userhat in the same relief, people pulling the barge with a rope sing:[45]

> *sꜣ s.w ḫnw.w n.ty ḥr itḥ pꜣ wiꜣ ḥn nhm.w r ḏd=sn* [two groups lost] *ḫꜥ.w m wiꜣ=f mi Rꜥ m-ḫnw* [*p*].*t tꜣ r-ḏr=f twt ḥr nhm.w ḥr mꜣꜣ nꜣy=f* [*mnḫ.w*]*t m wiꜣ=f n* [*ḥr*] *itr mi Rꜥ m-ḫnw mskt.t ꜥḥ*[*ꜥ* five or more groups lost] *nhm.w tꜣ r*[*-ḏr=f*] *m ršw r spr r ip.t šps s.t=f n sp tpy di=f* [one group lost] *m ꜥnḫ wꜣs n sꜣ=f Ḏsr-ḫpr.w-rꜥ-stp-n-rꜥ sꜣ ꜣḫ n ms sw mi ḫn=f it Imn r ir.t hrr.t kꜣ=f*
>
> The company of sailors who pull a rope of the vessel. The song of joy that they sing: '[ ] of the diadems is in his barque like Re in [he]aven. The land in its entirety is united in jubilation at seeing his [excellen]ce in his barque [on] the river like Re in the night-barque [ ] jubilating. The land in [its entirety] is in joy at arriving at august Opet, his primordial site. May he (Amun-Re) gives [ ] with life and dominion to his son Djedkheperure-setepenre (Horemheb), son who is beneficial to the one who bore him, as he navigates the father Amun to perform what pleases his ka.'

A similar account describing Amun-Re as the rising sun emerging from the temple of Luxor, which is liken to a primeval site, is also attested in Ramses III' reliefs at Karnak:[46]

> *sḥb.n=k wꜣs.t m mꜣw.t m sn r ꜣḫ.t n.t p.t ḫꜥꜥ=i im=s r ip.t-rsy.t s.t=i n sp tpy r ir(.t) ḫn.t=i nfr n tp rnp.t sꜣ=i ḥr ḥꜣ.t=i šsp.n=f wsr ḥr ḫn ḫry it=i*[sic] *šps r ḥtp=f m ip.t-rsy.t mi Rꜥ m wbn=f*
>
> You have made Thebes festive anew in passing to the horizon of the sky. I (Amun-Re) shall appear from it (Karnak) to Southern Opet, my primordial site, in order to perform my good navigation annually. My son, who is before me, has taken an oar at navigating down his august father to satiate him at Southern Opet like Re as he rises.

The reference to Luxor as where the sun rises invites comparison with the description of Amun (or the king) as being carried on Mesketet, the night-barque of Re. An analogy between Amun's barge and the night-barque is attested in association with the Opet Feast in the Book of the Traversing Eternity.[47] The stela of Piankhi from Gebel Barkal also describes Amun's appearance at Luxor as taking place in *grḥ m ḥb mn m wꜣs.t ir n=f Rꜥ m sp tpy* the 'night at the festival established in Thebes, which Re created for him (Amun) in the first time'.[48] These accounts metaphorically locate Karnak in west and Luxor in east. Unlike the Valley Festival, when the journey of Amun from Karnak to the West Bank was likened to the circuit of the sun (3.4.1), the east-west symbolism was difficult to be applied to the Opet Feast, which bore a north-south axis. Hence, the Egyptians seemed to have solved the problem by associating each of the cardinal points to another, namely, north-west-right and south-east-left.[49] According to Meyer-Dietrich (2010, 127), the four cardinal points as well as the sky and earth are associated one another in a musical formula carved in the Opet reliefs (2.4.10).

Furthermore, Luxor temple as the primordial place is visually represented in Ramses II's relief in the Great Hypostyle Hall of Karnak.[50] The first episode portrays

[45] Wolf 1931, 56; *Opet*, 7, pl. 17.

[46] *RIK* II, pl. 90, cols 3–6. This text has a close parallel in Herihor's reliefs (*Khonsu* I, 7, pl. 21, cols 17–24).

[47] P. Leiden T 32, III, 5, dated to the Roman Period (Herbin 1994, 439; Klotz 2008, 576; *idem* 2012, 387 for translation).

[48] Stela Cairo 48862 (*Urk.* III, 14: 17–15: 1; Grimal 1981a, 15*; Jansen-Winkeln 2007, vol. 2, 341).

[49] These notional combinations are most visible in temple decorations, where Lower and Upper Egypt are represented in half along a north-south axis. On the base of the sanctuary of Edfu temple are represented the Egyptian nomes, of which the northern ones appear on the west side (right when seen from the god) and the southern ones on the east (left) (PM VI, 146–7 (219–26)). Note that this principle usually applies only to temples located on the east bank of the Nile, and that those on the west bank have the reverse combinations: south-west-right and north-east-left. This means that Edfu temple is an exceptional case (Cauville 1983, 52).

[50] PM II^2, 46 (157, IV, 2–3); Nelson 1981, pls 36–8; M. Gabolde 1995, 236. A striking feature, which is not reported by Nelson, is that there are some peg holes around the figure of Amun-Re. Brand (2004, 263–4) proposes that these holes were used to hide the representation of Amun by means of a veil, which was removed only on special

the king and the Great Ennead adoring the Theban triad. This scene is very unusual that Amun holds a *w3s*-scepter topped with an *ꜥnḫ*-sign, whish is encircled by an undulant water stream running towards the feet of Amun. The Ennead says:

> *pr mw ẖr rd.wy=k di=k ḥw [n] k3 n s3=k Rꜥ-ms-sw-mri-imn di ꜥnḫ*
>
> Water comes out from under your legs,[51] and you give nourishment [to] the ka of your son Ramses-meriamen, given life.

In another caption carved above the prow of the Userhat, Amun-Re replies to the king and the Ennead, the latter of which is described as *imy.t nw Gb* 'being in the primeval water of Geb'. According to a hymn to Amun-Re, dated to the time of Ramses II, the sun god was the one who created himself first of all from *nw* in the primordial time.[52] There must have been some sort of theological renovation to the myth of Amun in order to replace the role of the old demiurge Atum.[53] The texts of the Opet Feast evidently show that the old creation myth was adapted to the narrative of this celebration. The water coming from Amun runs all the way through the river-procession scene and becomes the Nile itself, on which the divine vessels float. The primeval water is also signaled by the representations of Khnum-Lord-of-the-Cool-Water, Horus-Foremost-of-the-Cool-Water, and Horus-Lord-of-the-Cool-Water on the boat towing the Amun's barge.[54] By representing Amun as the origin of the Nile and his emission of the power of life, the overall iconographic description is a clear illustration of the annual inundation of the Nile. By the same token, this image overlaps with the renewal of kingship, which was performed at this celebration in the inundation season.

This association with the natural cycle embraces two key ideological aspects of the Opet Festival. First, it is the essential reason for this festival to be celebrated in the Akhet season, when the Nile reached its maximum water level during the New Kingdom (1.2.4). The transfer from one year to another and from a low water level to a high one concomitantly marked the renewal of the king's power. The emphasis on the succession of kingship from the dead ancestors at the Opet Festival was not as clearly evident as at the Valley Festival, but what was consistently stressed is the theological father–son relationship between the god and the ruling king. Hence, another passage in Ramses II's relief reads:[55]

> *ity n ḫpr mit.t=f mw nṯry pr m [ḥ]ꜥ[.w] nṯr km3.n nsw.t nṯr.w Imn sw iw=f m swḥ.t r ir.t nsy.t=f*
>
> Sovereign, unequaled one, divine semen, which comes from the god's fl[esh]. The king of the gods Amun has created him, who was in an egg, to make his kingship.

Second, the sun is explained to rise from south in the accounts of the Opet Feast. The above-mentioned text of Ramses III contains the passage, '(the king) satiates him at Southern Opet like Re as he rises'. This markedly contrasts with the Valley Feast, where the sun was regarded as coming from Karnak. At the Opet Festival the sun and Nile were ideologically identical and seen as a manifestation of the new world order, which brought the life force. The association of this celebration with the Nile was so prominent that it was referred to in texts many times, particularly when Luxor temple was described as the origin of the primeval water.

2.4.7. Arrival at/departure from Luxor[56]

After disembarkation from their river barges, the portable barques make a progress proceed to the temple of Luxor. Just as they depart Karnak, the barque of Amun is followed by those of Khonsu, Mut, and the king. A band of male musicians with clappers in their hands are portrayed leading processions together with priests. Female musicians and acrobatic dancers are also shown in the lower register. The processional way is lined up with eight small booths, each of which is filled with various offerings and attended by a priest. The register above represents eight bulls that are being dismembered and probably brought to the booths subsequently. A butchery scene is also attested in the

occasions, such as the Opet Festival. This is one of rare examples found on interior, rather than exterior, temple walls, where such cavities are normally observed. It is not easy to confirm when the holes were driven in this scene, but perhaps during the late Twentieth Dynasty or the early Twenty-First Dynasty.

51 There is no parallel representation of water coming out under the feet of a god, apart from literary descriptions: P. Leiden I 350 (V, 18: stanza 600), dated to the time of Ramses II, where Amun is referred to as the origin of the Nile (Gardiner 1905, 38–9; Zandee 1947, 98); P. MMA 35.9.21, dated to the Ptolemaic Period, describing water as coming from beneath the soles of Osiris in association with the Khoiak Feast (Goyon 2006, 19; M. Smith 2009, 144); the Famine Stela on the Sehel Island, dated to the Ptolemaic Period, portraying Khnum with his sandals resting on flooding water and his town (i.e. Elephantine) being *ṯs n t3 gy gb.ty* the 'earthly elevation and celestial hill' (Barguet 1953, 19, pl. 3; Lichtheim 1973, vol. 3, 97, col. 9 for translation); a text from Edfu temple describing the primeval water as coming from the leg (*si3ty* probably referring to the legs of Osiris) in association with the New Year (PM VI, 138 (126, g); *Edfou* II, 232: 7; Traunecker 1972, 233 and Germond 1981, 328–9 for translation).

52 P. Leiden I 350, IV, 3 and 14, and V, 3 (Gardiner 1905, 31–7; Zandee 1947, 68, 79, and 92; Assmann 1983b, 141 for partial translation and other parallels).

53 Bickel 1998, 167. Atum is referred to several times in the speech of Amun in the Luxor reliefs, such as 'you (king) having appeared on the throne of Atum', 'the years of Atum', 'the excellent office of Atum', etc. (*Opet*, 20, 22–3, pls 46, 58–9).

54 Nelson 1981, pls 151 and 37.

55 Nelson 1981, pl. 37, cols 15–20.

56 *Opet*, 17, pls 35 and 63.

Deir el-Bahari reliefs.[57] These booths were perhaps temporal buildings erected by the river, rather than within the temple, because they are located outside of what appears to be the main gateway to Luxor temple.[58] The processions enter this gate, where high-ranking officials and priests await.[59]

A long procession entering this temple is represented elsewhere in Ramses II's reliefs carved on the southwestern corner of the forecourt.[60] This pompous procession is formed by 17 princes of Ramses II, 11 fat bulls, and one calf, which may continue onto the northwestern wall depicting the queen, three princes, and 17 princesses.[61] These fat bulls are decorated on their horns, ears, and necks, in a fashion similar to those depicted in the Colonnade Hall. On the buttocks of the fifth to ninth bulls is carved *ḥb ip.t* the 'Opet Festival'. More explicit evidence is attested in the horizontal text above the sixth bull, where one can read *[ḥ]b=f [n]fr [n i]p.t* 'His [Beau]tiful [Fes]tival [of O]pet' (Figure 5). The fact that the triple shrine of Ramses II is located within this court suggests that the barque procession was brought to at least one halt after entering the temple.[62] This was probably also the case for the Eighteenth Dynasty. On the restored west wall of Amenhotep III's court, Amun's barque is represented resting and receiving offerings from the king.[63] Meticulously restored by Johnson (1990, 30) from a numerous small pieces of fragments, it is now visible that this barque faces towards the inner part of the temple, which may bear witness to its temporal station outside of the temple proper, rather than a repository in the sanctuary. It has also been speculated that a small chapel was erected between the temple and the Nile bank in the time of Ramses III.[64]

It was perhaps at these stations that people were able to catch sight of the gods before they disappeared into the inner precinct. It is, however, difficult to conclude to what extent the general public could obtain access to rituals that took place in the temple vicinity and courts.[65]

2.4.8. Rituals at Luxor[66]

This scene, completed by Seti I, represents the barques of the Theban triad enshrined at the final destination, Luxor, in the same manner as at Karnak. There is, however, a significant difference: the absence of the king's barque. It is not certain whether this reflected the actual disappearance of the royal barque while rituals were taking place within the temple proper, or Seti I omitted it from the relief for the sake of space on the wall. It is unlikely that the king did not use his barque at festivals because it also appeared in the scene of the Valley Festival at his Qurna temple.[67] Each portable shrine of the Theban triad received a substantial amount of offerings from the king, whose figure survives only on the eastern wall today.

The repositories of the divine barques within the inner temple cannot securely be located, but there must have been some spaces to the north of the innermost sanctuary, where divine statues could have been taken out of their portable shrines and underwent hidden rituals. This is corroborated by the fact that the above-mentioned representations of the enshrined barques are followed by two episodes parallel one another, which are carved on both sides of the south wall. On the badly damaged right half, Seti I holding a *sḫm*-scepter proceeds to the seated Amun-Foremost-of-His-Opet and an unidentified goddess, presumably Mut, behind him.[68] Four priests stand in front of the king and pour unknown fluids for the gods from large amphora-type jars. On the better-preserved left half, the goddess behind Amun can be identified with Amenet on account of her common red headdress.[69] The king offers a large bouquet to the god and goddess with the Ennead behind him. These two episodes are thought to

[57] Naville 1895, vol. 5, pls 124 and 126.

[58] For other instances of booths depicted in private tombs, see Barthelmess 1992, 85.

[59] This gate appears to be connected to a smaller portal. The former probably represents the northern entrance to the Colonnade Hall, the then entrance of the temple itself until the time of Seti I (*Opet*, 19, nn. 60–1). The smaller gate is perhaps located within the temple precinct. Darnell (2010a, 4) proposes that processions entered the western gate to Ramses II's forecourt from the Ramesside Period onwards.

[60] PM II^{2}, 308 (29–30, II).

[61] PM II^{2}, 308 (28, III). Xekalaki and el-Khodary (2011, 567–8) reserve a non-specific context for the representations of the female royal members. Some scenes and texts in this court are clearly associated with specific celebrations and historical accounts. The Opet Feast is also referred to together with the Decade Ritual in a band of text carved on the other side of the court (PM II^{2}, 307 (27, between II and III); *KRI* II, 607: 13–4; Abd el-Razik 1974, 147, col. 11 for facsimile; *idem* 1975, 128 for translation).

[62] This shrine was erected on the site of the once sixth way-station of Hatshepsut (Habachi 1965a, 94). Stone blocks belonging to the older building are still visible on the ground today.

[63] PM II^{2}, 317 (95).

[64] PM II^{2}, 312 (68); *KRI* V, 292: 3–5; Cabrol 2001, 527–8.

[65] Thutmose III's chronicle narrates how he was selected by Amun as the future king: *sḥb.n=f p.t tꜣ m nfr.w=f šsp.n=f biꜣy.t ꜥꜣ.t stw.t=f m ir.ty pꜥ.t [nb.t mi] pr.t Ḥr-ꜣḫ.ty* 'He (Amun) has made the heaven and land festive with his beauty. He performed a great revelation, his rays being in the eyes of [every] member of the *pat* [like] the coming-forth of Horakhety' (*Urk.* IV, 157: 15–158: 1). At this oracular session, only certain individuals belonging to the *pat*-class witnessed the divine appearance in the Hypostyle Hall at Karnak. In a fashion similar to this, Horemheb in his coronation text narrated how he was selected by Amun but with extended audiences: *nṯr pn ḥr sṯn sꜣ=f m ḥr tꜣ tm.w* 'this god elevated his son before the entire land' (Gardiner 1953, 14, l. 5). As a designation of part of population, the *pat* is construed to refer to an elite component of society, whereas its counterpart the *rḫy.t* is generally understood as the common folk. Based on the distribution of the *rḫy.t*-signs within Ramses II's forecourt of Luxor temple, Bell (1997, 164–7) demonstrated that the folk could enter the eastern half of the court when a divine procession appeared in the western half, a supposition opposed by Baines (2006, 279).

[66] *Opet*, 19, pl. 43.

[67] PM II^{2}, 408 (6).

[68] *Opet*, 21, pl. 52.

[69] *Opet*, 22, pl. 54.

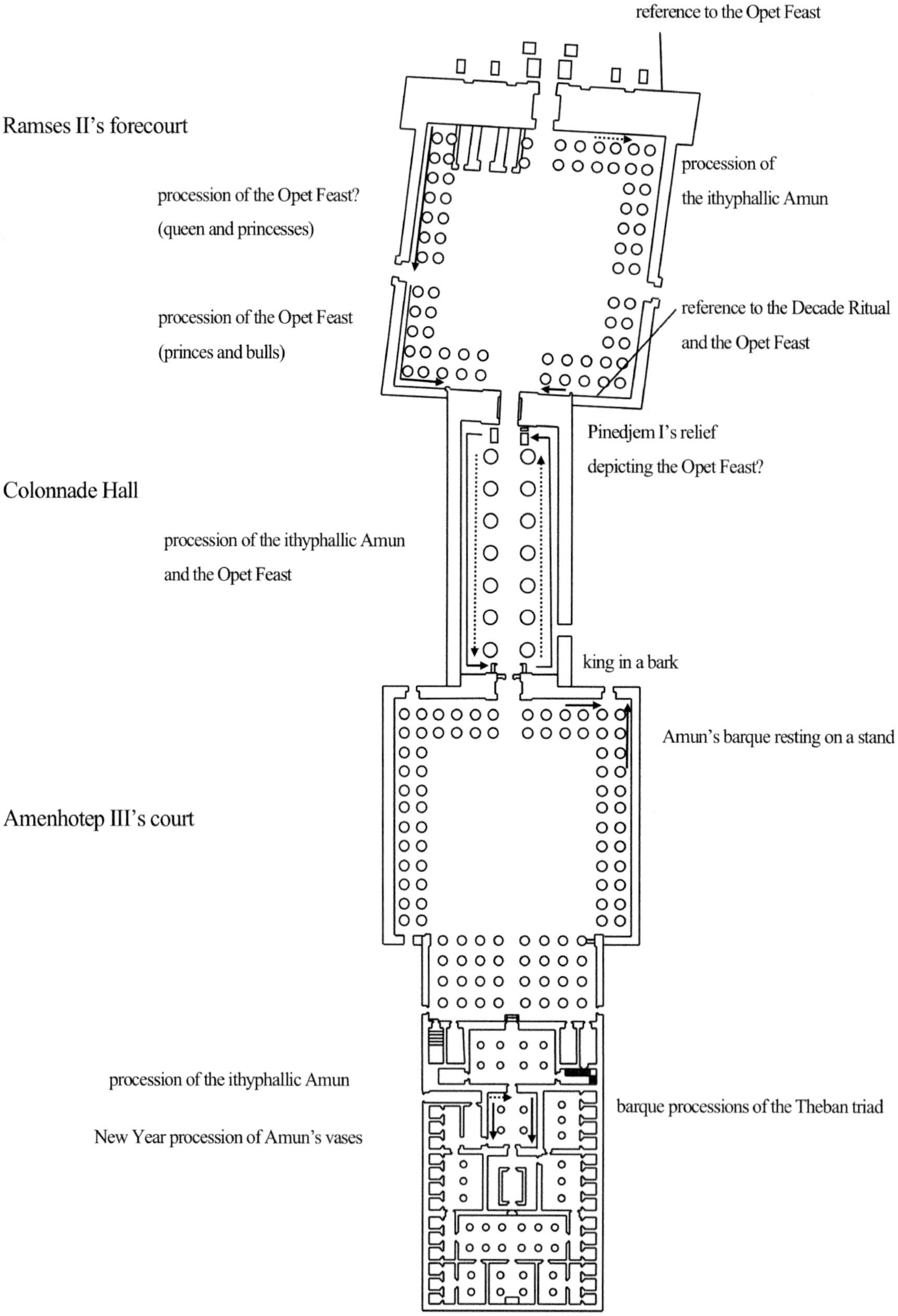

Figure 4. Locations of references to and representations of festivals at the Luxor temple.

Figure 5. Procession of bulls moving towards the Luxor temple at the Opet Festival, represented on the western wall of Ramses II's forecourt at Luxor. (This photograph shows the sixth bull, on whose buttocks are carved the two signs [hieroglyphs] the 'Festival of Opet'. The broken bandeau text above this bull can read [hieroglyphs] '[...] at His Beautiful Festival [of] Opet [...] with [...]' Photograph taken by the author).

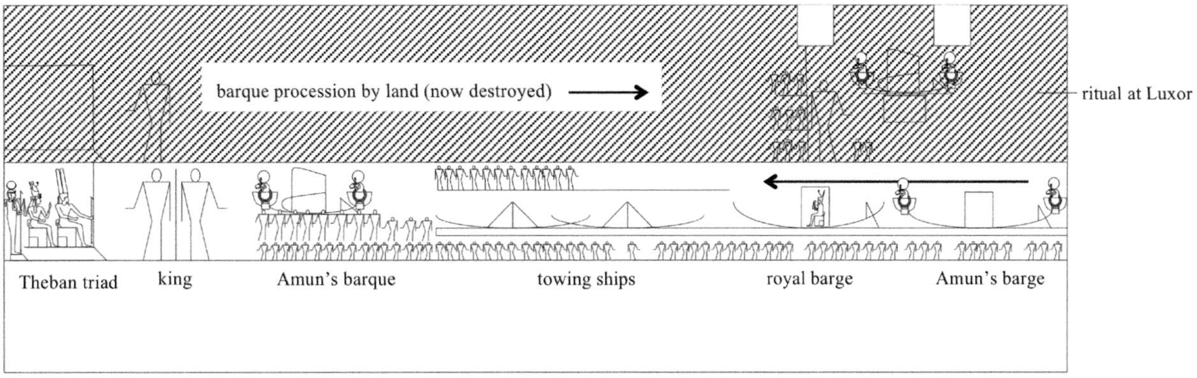

Figure 6. Elevation of the southern wing of the eastern wall, upper terrace, Hatshepsut's temple at Deir el-Bahari (based on Naville 1985, vol. 5, pls 123–6; Karkowski 1976, fig. 2; *idem* 2001, 132).*
*Several fragments have been found for the upper register to occupy only 10 % of it: an unidentified episode (Karkowski 1990, fig. 7); Amun's barque procession with royal statues (Kwaśnica 2001, 86, fig. 2); Amun's barque resting at Luxor (ibid., fig. 3 right).

have taken place in the innermost area of the temple, but any further insight into these rites is not provided.

Ramses II's relief at Karnak is a little more eloquent about these abstruse episodes. It also comprises two parts following the river-procession scene.[70] In the first scene, the king consecrates a large pile of the *ꜥ3b.t*-offerings to Amun-Re-Foremost-of-[His]-Opet and Mut-Who-Dwells-in-Southern-Opet seated in a shrine. The king is explained as *ḫꜥw m pr it Ỉmn-rꜥ ḥr smꜣꜥ ꜥ3b[.t ꜥ3.t n] k3=f* 'appearing in the house of the father Amun-Re at consecrating the [great] *ꜥ3b[.t*-offerings to] his ka'. In the second scene he offers smaller offerings to 'Amun-Re-Foremost-of-His-Opet, great god [on] the great seat'. Unlike the previous scene, the god here takes an ithyphallic form. Larger in scale but less revealing is Ramses III's reliefs at Karnak, where the king offers the 'great *ꜥ3b.t*-offerings' to the Theban triad of Karnak, rather than Amun of Luxor.[71]

This scene parallels representations carved by Amenhotep III on the third pylon of Karnak.[72] In this scene, the king, preceded by a goddess, offers the 'great *ꜥ3b.t*-offerings' to Amun and Mut, perhaps belonging to Karnak. It is noteworthy that all the instances of the *ꜥ3b.t*-offerings in these scenes include slaughtered bulls, which bears witness to the significance of cattle offerings at the Opet Feast (2.5.4).

Horemheb's coronation text records the proceedings of his accession anniversary, coupled by the Opet Festival, which broadly consisted of two parts. The last half of the celebration took place at a 'palace', referred to as either *pr-nsw.t* or *ꜥḥ*. After the crowning ceremonies were performed at *pr-wr* and *pr-nsr*, symbolizing Upper and Lower Egypt respectively, the royal titulary was recorded, both in Amun's company. Thereafter, Amun and the king emerged from the palace before the 'entire land (*t3 tm.w*)'. Gardiner (1953, 24–5) regarded the 'palace' as referring to the temple of Luxor, rather than the royal residence.[73] It is not easy to conclude for sure whether these crowning ceremonies were the same as those performed at accession anniversaries that were repeated during the reign of a given ruler, but it was likely the case. The renewal of the kingship perhaps took a very similar form at the Opet Festival too.[74]

Aforementioned Ramses II's relief at Karnak, where two Amuns are represented, provides a further insight into the highly ideological aspects of this god, who often changes his form with an erected phallus.[75] How the encounter of Amun of Karnak with that of Luxor was performed remains in the realm of conjecture. However, it is not too daring briefly to explore what theological doctrines underpinned the complex identity of Amun in order to encapsulate the significance of Luxor temple, which is repeatedly referred to as a primordial site at the Opet Festival.

2.4.9. Rituals of the divine ka

From the Ramesside Period onwards, Amun had double origin at Thebes. While Luxor temple was regarded as a primordial site, where Amun of Karnak would go back every year, a mythological mound called Djeme at Medinet Habu came to gain great significance as a destination for Amenopet to reach every ten days (3.2.2). The two sites for the destination of Amun within one city are difficult to comprehend. Additionally, the god Min shared the name of Kamutef with Amuns worshipped at Karnak and Luxor.[76]

As Bell (1997, 179) pointed out, it is not unreasonable to regard Luxor temple as two dwellings in one, for Amun-Re of Karnak and Amenopet of Luxor. The prime importance was given to a ritual of mystical unification of these two deities during the Opet Festival in order for Amun-Re to gain the regenerative power from Amenopet who resides on the primordial site. There is no father–son relationship between them, while it is documented in association with the Decade Ritual that Amenopet is Kamutef as well as 'Horus, upraised of arm', 'Horus, son of Isis', 'Horus, heir of Osiris',[77] and more explicitly *ḥwn* a 'child'.[78] In these texts he is also called the 'creator of the Ogdoad' and 'creator of the gods'.[79] This indicates the double nature of Amenopet as a cosmogonic and young god. This god appears to have had an isolated personality—no consort deity was known—and been a focal point in the Theban theology, from which his different manifestations were issued for Karnak and Djeme from his primeval life

[70] Nelson 1981, pls 39–40.

[71] *RIK* II, pl. 94.

[72] PM II^{2}, 61 (183).

[73] Luxor temple is referred to as the *ꜥḥ* in an inscription carved on an architrave at Amenhotep III's court (Bell 1985, 254 and 273–4). Bell (1997, 154) also proposed the existence of a small mud-brick palace accessible through the door on the east side of the hypostyle hall (PM II^{2}, 318 (105)).

[74] It was also during the Opet Festival that the kingship was decreed for the ruler by Amun (*Opet*, 35, pl. 91). Bell (1985, 289 and 1997, 182) suggested a connection between the Opet and Sed Festivals, at both of which rites to bestow a new royal name to the king were performed.

[75] A representation similar to Ramses II's scene is attested in Pinedjem's relief in the forecourt of Luxor temple (PM II^{2}, 307 (27, III-2); *Façade*, 52, pl. 200; Frood 2013). He, accompanied by his daughters, is portrayed fumigating four deities: the seated Amun-Re, ithyphallic Amun-Re-Kamutef of Luxor, Mut, and Khonsu.

[76] For example, epithets of the ithyphallic Amun recorded on a column at the Colonnade Hall of Luxor reads: *Ỉmn-rꜥ-k3-mw.t=f nb p.t ḥk3 ip.t-s.wt ḫnty ip.t=f* 'Amun-Re-Kamutef, lord of sky, ruler of Karnak, foremost of his Opet' (*Façade*, pl. 186, cols 2–4). Even when the god was not in his ithyphallic form, he was called 'Amun-Re, lord of the thrones of the Two Lands, foremost of Karnak, lord of eternity, he who dwells in his Opet, lord of sky, ruler of Thebes' (*Façade*, pl. 188, cols 2–5). The identification of Amun of Karnak with Amun of Luxor was not uncommon (*Façade*, 53, n. b).

[77] Doresse 1971, 126.

[78] Doresse 1973, 97–8.

[79] Doresse 1973, 132.

force. Hence, it is not surprising to find Amun-Re of Karnak not only embodying a solar power in the first instance but also possessing an ithyphallic form, when his regenerative aspect was pronounced. By extension, Amuns worshipped at Karnak and Luxor can be seen as ideologically identical rather than different deities.[80] All the Kamutef deities had an ithyphallic form, except when Amenopet was represented squatting and half-veiled on his palanquin at the Decade Ritual. The shared form is to be understood as a manifestation of the regenerative force, namely, the divine ka, as evidenced by some representations.[81]

An emphasis should be placed on the time-bound state of Amun-Re of Karnak like the Nile—he progressively experienced the deterioration of power while he was away from Amenopet. In other words, Amun-Re was always conditional on Amenopet. This may be explained by the fact that oracular sessions are attested only after Amun left the temple of Luxor so that his decrees could have full divine authority (2.5.1). Presumably, the royal power was also subject to the same temporal cycle as Amun's. This is the reason why he was officially required to attend the Opet Festival every year (1.3.1.1). Later in the Ptolemaic Period, Diodorus Siculus (I, 15) describes the temples of Karnak and Luxor as two golden chapels dedicated to Zeus, of which 'the larger one (is) to him as god of heaven (and) the smaller one to him as former king and father of the Egyptians'.[82] Ostensibly, Karnak temple was the *de facto* head office of Egyptian religion on account of its physical size and powerful influence. Theoretically, however, Luxor temple presided over Karnak.[83]

2.4.10. Debate on the hierogamy and Hathoric celebrations

The marriage between the divine and royal has been one of foci when it comes to the Opet Festival. It is because the temple of Luxor contains a series of scenes representing the divine birth of the king Amenhotep III.[84] However, in Egyptological literature today, the existence of the sacred marriage in Egyptian religion, particularly before the Ptolemaic Period, is not widely accepted.[85] There are two good reasons for this. First, the notion of the sacred marriage was introduced from outside Egyptian contexts. In Mesopotamian religions, ritualistic marriages between a god and one of the royal family members can be attested to in liturgical literature.[86] By performing this, the rebirth of the ruler and, by extension, of the world was secured. The idea of the sacred marriage drew attention from the school of Myth and Ritual and, as a result, highly structuralistic approaches to liturgical texts were adopted for other cultures as a means to examine rituals and festivals, especially those which involved cultic death and resurrection.[87] Second, although some Egyptian festivals, such as the Sed Feast and New Year celebrations, have been explored with regard to the sacred marriage, there is no direct evidence that attests it.

The conceptual divine origin of the king was an essential ideology in Egypt. It is most evident in the cult of the goddess Hathor, who is portrayed suckling, for example, the queen Hatshepsut at her Deir el-Bahari temple. There are three recent advocates for the sacred marriage performed at the Opet Festival—Barta, Altenmüller, and Darnell—and they all associate the sacred marriage with the goddess Hathor. However, her role is not prominent at the Opet Feast and rather scarce when compared to the Valley Fesival.

Barta (1975, 112) associates the annual fecundity brought by the Nile with the sacred marriage on the basis of a sailors' song documented at Luxor temple and elsewhere. It was first examined by Sethe (1929b), who named the song die 'Lieder von der Trinkstätte'. Three texts survive from the New Kingdom, two of which accompany the river-procession scene of the Opet Festival:[88]

> *mswr ḳd n mr nt(y) m wiꜣ n wiꜣ.w wꜣ.wt r ꜣkr.w mr n=k ḥꜥpy wr ꜥẖi sḥtp=k nb.ty nb n.t/ḥḏ.t Ḥr ṯmꜣ-ꜥ ẖn=t(w) nṯr ẖr nfr.t nṯr pꜣ.n Ḥw.t-ḥr ir(.t) nfr.t nfr.wt n Ḏsr-ẖpr.w-rꜥ-stp-n-rꜥ mry ꞽImn ḥsy nṯr.w i N.t*
>
> 'A drinking place[89] is built for the party which is on the ship of ships. Paths to the Akeru are hacked for you. A great inundation is raised up. May you pacify the Two Ladies. O lord of the red/white crown, Horus strong of arm.

[80] Bell 1985, 259; Quaegebeur 1986, 104–5.

[81] For example, one scene containing an image of the ithyphallic Amun-Re is described as *ir.t sntr n ḥr=k nfr n kꜣ nb ḏ.t* 'Making incense to your beautiful face of the ka, lord of everlastingness' (*Façade*, pl. 145).

[82] Oldfather 1933, 51.

[83] Bell 1985, 289.

[84] PM II², 326 (152).

[85] Versnel (1970, 230, n. 1) does not observe the Egyptian sacred marriage in comparison with the Mesopotamian tradition. Bell (1985, 289) stressed on the rebirth of the king as a process to re-legitimate his kingship, rather than the sacred marriage as a ritualistic objective. Brunner (1964, 194–203 and 233–8) regards the scene of the royal birth at Luxor temple as representing a visualized myth, rather than a cult performance.

[86] Black 1981, 40 and 47–8.

[87] See Mikhail 1983, 35–50 for a summary of the assertion of this school.

[88] Akh-menu of Thutmose III (PM II², 110 (336); Barguet 1962, 175–6; Carlotti 2001, pl. 17); Red Chapel of Hatshepsut (Lacau and Chevrier 1979, vol. 1, 187, vol. 2, pl. 9 (Blocks 104 and 171); Burgos and Larché 2006, vol. 1, 60–1); Colonnade Hall at Luxor (*Opet*, 12–4, pls 26 and 97; Altenmüller 1998, 764). For more recent studies, see Meyer 1998, 135–42; Darnell 2010a, 8 and 2010b, 124; Meyer-Dietrich 2010.

[89] A festival booth and a beer hut at a feast are referred to in a love song, dated to the Twentieth Dynasty (P. Turin 1966: Fox 1985, 46, 49, n. q). Also see Darnell 1995, 59–62 for a Hathoric intoxication setting in front of Karnak temple.

> One navigates the god with the beauty of the god. Hathor has done the best of good deeds[90] for Djeserkheperure-setepenre (Horemheb), beloved of Amun, praised of the gods' says Neith.[91]

Barta (1983, 102–3) also draws attention to the 'House of Love' of Hathor known from the Old Kingdom in his attempt to find the origin of the sacred marriage in much earlier times.

Altenmüller (1994, 357) stands in the same line. By cautiously referring to the festival of Horus and Hathor at Edfu, which Kurth regards as a funerary ritual, Altenmüller (1998a, 764) concludes that the Osiride myth played a key role in crystallizing the sacred marriage between Horus and Hathor. He further presents an analogy between the bed chamber in Old Kingdom private tombs, where the sexual unification of the deceased with his wife is implicitly represented,[92] and the pilgrimage to Abydos, a popular subject depicted in later private tombs, and, by extension, makes comparison with the Opet Festival.

Darnell (1995, 59; 2007, 204; and 2010a, 5–8) associates other songs in the Luxor reliefs to a ritual of a sexual union at the Opet Feast. By citing some New Kingdom love poems and parallel literature from earlier periods, he (2010b, 125) explains that Hathoric sexual performances represented the circuit of the sun and the returning goddess from the south in the inundation season.

The cult of Hathor evidently had sexual connotations, but her cult was rather pronounced at celebrations other than the Opet Feast. Egberts (1995, 406–9), for instance, associates the representation of the divine birth at Luxor temple with the Festival of I Shemu. It is also undoubted that people visited Deir el-Bahari to address to Hathor during the Valley Feast (3.6.5). In fact, like the Opet Festival and the Sed Festival,[93] the presence of royal consorts and daughters is also recorded for the Valley Feast (3.7). If one is prone to the idea of sacred marriage, it may be more desirable to look at the Hathor Feast, which was celebrated on IV Akhet 1 (**427**, **433–4**, **437**, and **441**). The divine birth scenes represented at Luxor includes some Hathoric rituals including a river procession to the temple of Hathor (*wd r tꜣ r ḥw.t-nṯr n Ḥw.t-ḥr* 'landing to the temple of Hathor').[94] A scene parallel to this is attested in the Hathor shrine at Deir el-Bahari, where 'an annual festival' of Hathor is represented.[95]

In conclusion, the scholarly argument for the association of the Opet Feast with the sacred marriage is broadly based on either earlier or later sources, which cannot satisfactorily explain the situation in the New Kingdom. Moreover, the surviving New Kingdom evidence may be best explored in contexts other than this celebration.

2.4.11. Rituals back at Karnak[96]

The Luxor reliefs show a slight difference between the western and eastern walls. While the king offers incense and a libation to the Theban triad at the outset of the outward journey, he purifies Amun's barque on returning to Karnak.

In the Opet Festival scenes at Hatshepsut's Deir el-Bahari temple, the north end of the lower register corresponds to this episode (Figure 6).[97] This largely damaged scene represents a barque procession, undoubtedly of Amun, followed by another scene, which portrays the king adoring the Theban triad, seated in a shrine.

The surviving part of the Red Chapel, also erected by Hatshepsut, attests three episodes after the return journey from Luxor.[98] In the first episode Hatshepsut stands with four *mr.t*-chests in front of her and welcomes the barque procession of Amun, which is captioned as *sḫꜥ.t m wsḫ.t ḥby.t* 'appearing in the festival hall'. The second episode portrays the queen driving the Apis bull (*pḥrr ḥpw*) towards a chapel containing Amun's portable shrine and called *Mn-mnw-Ỉmn* 'Established is the monument of Amun'. This building has been identified with the restored barque shrine of Amenhotep I, now displayed in the Open-Air Museum of Karnak, the original location of which is not known.[99] The queen is accompanied by musicians and female dancers. Thereafter, Amun's barque proceeds *r ḥtp m ḥw.t ꜥꜣ Ỉmn-rꜥ nb p.t* 'to rest in the great house of Amun-Re, lord of sky', being led by a group of priests.

The Red Chapel represents identical episodes for the Valley Festival (3.4.5). The ritual of driving the Apis bull is widely attested in association with a variety of events from the Old Kingdom.[100] Instead of the Apis bull, driving four calves combined with the rite of

[90] An expression parallel to this is attested in many graffiti at Thutmose III's temple at Deir el-Bahari, including prayers to Hathor (Marciniak 1974), and in a love poem recorded in P. Harris 500 (=BM 10060: Fox 1985, 22–3).

[91] For the association between the goddess Neith, inundation, and inebriation, see Žabkar 1988, 107, fig. 8 and 181, n. 25.

[92] For example, the mastaba of Mereruka at Saqqara attests a passage parallel to our sailors' song (*nfr.t nṯr*) in association with a Hathoric river journey (The Sakkarah Expedition 1938, vol. 2, pl. 141).

[93] *Kheruef*, pls 26, 32, 42, 49, and 57.

[94] PM II², 327 (153, II, 2); Gayet 1894, pl. 68, fig. 211.

[95] PM II², 350 (30); Naville 1895, vol. 4, pls 88–91.

[96] *Opet*, 39, pl. 108.

[97] Naville 1895, vol. 5, pl. 123; Karkowski 1976, figs 1–2 for additional restorations.

[98] Lacau and Chevrier 1977, vol. 1, 192–203, vol. 2, pl. 9 (Blocks 176, 102, 66, and 130); Burgos and Larché 2006, vol. 1, 62–5.

[99] Cabrol 2001, 504–7.

[100] Wilkinson 2000, 117–8.

the *mr.t*-chests is attested elsewhere in proximity to the representations of the Opet Festival.[101] Egberts (1995, 348 and 401–4) associates the combined scene of the *mr.t*-chests and the driving of calves with certain mortuary festivals, such as the Festivals of Sokar, Min, and Behedet. The two rituals were certainly relevant to the cult of Osiris,[102] but it should be questioned that they constituted a nucleus of the Festivals of Opet and the Valley. In the case of the former celebration, in particular, the cult of Osiris was not at all prominent.

2.4.12. Return to the palace of the king[103]

As is the case for the departure of the king from the palace at the beginning of the festival, two modest reliefs at Luxor and Medinet Habu are again the only representations attesting the return of the king. The one at Luxor is much the same as the departure scene carved on the other side of the doorway, but with a better-preserved inscription. It describes the king as *tꞽ.t Rꜥ ḫnty tꜣ.wy stp.n ꞽImn ḏs=f* the 'figure of Re, foremost of the Two Lands, one whom Amun himself selected', and Amun-Re as *nsw.t nṯr.w ḫnty ip.t-s.wt ḥry-ꞽb ip.t=f šps.t nṯr ꜥꜣ nb p.t* the 'king of the gods, foremost of Karnak, one who dwells in his august Opet, great god, lord of sky'.

The other relief located at the temple of Medinet Habu displays a remarkable difference in the king's costume.[104] He wears a wig with the Uraeus serpent on his forehead on entering the temple, whereas his headdress on leaving is an unusual combination of the blue crown with two horns, two uraei, and two plumes attached to the side of the crown.[105] The plumes hold a sun-disk between them. The accompanying legend says:

> *ꞽꞽ.tꞽ m ḥtp nṯr pn nfr Ḥr-wsr-rnp.wt ꞽb=k ꜣw sšp tw ꞽt=f*[sic]*=k ꞽImn nb nṯr.w swḏ=f n=k šn n ꞽtn smn=f tw m nsw.t šmꜣw mḥw nsw.t sꜣ ꞽImn-rꜥ pr ḥꜥ.w=f ṯnr ꜥšꜣ.t mnw m wꜣs.t nḫt.t sḥtp nb r-ḏr [m] nꜣy=f ꜣḫ.w ḳꜣb rsf.w ḏfꜣ.w ḥr wn m-bꜣḥ*
>
> Come in peace, O this good god, Horus-mighty-of-years! Your heart is happy for your father Amun, lord of the gods, accepts you. May he assign to you the circle of the sun-disc. May he establish you as the king of Upper and Lower Egypt. King, son of Amun-Re, one who came forth from his flesh, hero (with) a multitude of monuments at Thebes, the strong, one who satisfies all [with] his benefactions, one who doubles birds, fish, and sustenance before the one who is in front.

This is not merely a eulogy on the king who was given the kingship from the supreme god. Neither Amun nor the king speaks in the first person here, which gives readers a third person's view as though they are witnessing the king's emergence from the temple. Indeed, in this scene the king is represented being accompanied by some fan-bearers, who were in all probability court officials, rather than priests. It is likely that within the temple proper they appeared before a broader audience awaiting to catch sight of the the king's rejuvenated appearance. While this was taking place behind the temple walls, the general public probably gathered, or was even called on, to see the 'new' god and king. Such was seen in the entire formal attire of the king, duly changing through each phase of rituals that he would undergo. Both at Luxor and Medinet Habu Amun is described as selecting the king. The king was a recipient of authority from Amun-Re, borrowing his divine solar manifestation. This explains the transformation of the king's headdress. The king's new form is best described as being 'in praise' in the tomb of Nebwenenef, high-priest of Amun in the reign of Ramses II (2.5.2). Unlike gods who usually veiled themselves in a closed shrine, the king in new dress was a good physical sign that the rituals were all done, the god was renewed, and ultimately the world order was re-established.

---

101 The north wing of the west wall belonging to the Great Hypostyle Hall at Karnak (Nelson 1981, pl. 146) and the register above the Opet Festival reliefs at Luxor (Egberts 1995, 403–4).

102 A set of four *mr.t*-chests are generally regarded as having contained four coloured cloths to be used for mummy bandages of Osiris (Berlandini-Grenier 1982, 92). Egberts (1995, 436) also explains that these chests symbolized four cardinal points. Goebs (2011, 62, n. 34) places stress on their rejuvenating function in association with the daily cult.

103 *Opet*, 42–3, pl. 119.

104 PM II^2, 495 (77, c); *MH* IV, pl. 237, B; K*RI* V, 190: 9–12.

105 One of the earliest representations of this headdress is found at Seti I's temple at Abydos (PM VI, 7 (74); Calverley 1933, vol. 4, pl. 44). The significance of this particular type of crown is not clear. Collier (1996, 111, fig. 53 and 127) proposes that the *ḫprš*-crown was worn by the king as a new heir to the throne that is bestowed by Amun. Other examples are attested elsewhere in the same temple (PM II^2, 497 (87, c) and 508 (136, g); *MH* V, pls 254 and 335) and at Luxor (PM II^2, 310 (41); Bell 1985, 267, fig. 5).

2.5. Events associated with the Opet Festival

2.5.1. Oracular session

There are three records that securely attest oracular sessions at the Opet Feast, all from the Twentieth Dynasty and later. They are all dated to III Akhet, which suggests that oracular sessions took place during the last half of this celebration.[1] The examination in this section will be limited mostly to the dates of these sessions in order to demonstrate that divine verdicts gained full effect only after the god completed rituals at the temple of Luxor. In addition, a text of Herihor, dated to the time of Ramses XI, is included here because its subject possibly bears witness to the Opet Feast.

The account of P. BM10335, provenance unknown but likely discovered somewhere in western Thebes, begins with an appeal of the servant Amenemwia to Amun-of-Pakhenty on III Akhet 1 in year 2 of Ramses IV during the Opet Feast (**291**). His petition was concerned with a theft, and the god replied that it had been done by the farmer Pachauemdiamen. After denying this sentence, Pachauemdiamen went before Amun-of-Tashenyt and then Amun-of-Buqenen, and finally came back to Amun-of-Pakhenty during the Khoiak Feast for his 'third' defense appeal. After all, his petitions were rejected in the presence of witnesses, and he was sentenced to a hundred blows. It is remarkable that he addressed at least three times, two of which took place during the Feasts of Opet and Khoiak. This suggests that some major celebrations functioned as a provider of juridical sessions. Little is known of the three local forms of Amun, but Amun-of-Pakhenty is likely to have been worshipped on the West Bank.[2]

On the other hand, the subject of an oracular session recorded in the stela of Merimaat, a wab-priest of Maat, is not known. It was unearthed within the Mentu precinct of Karnak, and dated to III Akhet 8 in year 7 of Ramses VI (**331**). Given the commemorative nature of stelae in general, his petition to Amun-Re is best understood in a ceremonial context, rather than in a juridical one. He is represented raising his arms upright and being vested or anointed by an assistant behind him, a typical gesture of a person at a reward ceremony. It is therefore plausible that he received a reward in the name of Amun-Re, probably a return for his successful service either in the form of material goods or promotion to a higher rank.[3]

The text of Djehutymes, chief chamberlain, is located on the outer wall at the southeastern corner of Court IV at Karnak (**321**). This document is dated to the time of Pinedjem II, but it provides a better insight into New Kingdom texts and hence is examined here. In the upper part the barque processions of the Theban triad are represented moving towards the north, a direction that suggests their return to Karnak. The legend above a priest offering incense to Amun's barque is written in vertical columns and begins:

> *hrw pn m pr ỉmn-rˁ nsw.t nṯr.w mḥ hrw.w 13 n ḫˁ n nṯr pn šps nb nṯr.w ỉmn-rˁ nsw.t nṯr.w Mw.t wr.t nb.t išrw Ḫnsw m w3s.t nfr-ḥtp ḥr n p3 t3 n ḥḏ n pr ỉmn m pḥ-nṯr in ḥm nṯr tpy n ỉmn-rˁ nsw.t nṯr.w imy-r mšˁ wr ḥ3wty P3-nḏm m3ˁ ḫrw s3 Mn-ḫpr-rˁ m3ˁ ḫrw nḏnḏ ḥr.w t3 pn m-b3ḥ p3 nṯr ˁ3 mḥ 3bd.w 2 hrw.w 5* [one group lost] *p3 nṯr ˁ3 w3w r šp.t n sḫnti.n=f r ip.t m ḥb=f n ip.t m rnp.t tn is.t smn p3 nṯr ˁ3 r n3 sš.w rwḏ.w ḫnty.w i-ir=w sp.w n grg m-ḫnw niw.t p3y=f dmi ˁḥˁ.n p3 nṯr ˁ3 ḥr n3 sš.w rwḏ.w ḫnty.w ḥr n3 sp.w n grg i-ir.n=w sḥˁ in p3 nṯr ˁ3 ḥr n p3 t3 n ḥḏ n pr ỉmn m tri n dw3.t ii in ḥm nṯr tpy n ỉmn-rˁ nsw.t nṯr.w P3-nḏm m3ˁ ḫrw m-b3ḥ p3 nṯr ˁ3*
>
> On this day in the temple of Amun-Re, king of the gods, completing 13 days[4] of the appearance of this august god, lord of the

[1] For oracles in general, see Černý 1962, 43–5. For discussion on earlier evidence for oracles, see Baines and Parkinson 1997, and Kammerzell 2001 for the Old Kingdom, and see Anthes 1928, 42, pl. 18; Posener 1963; Blumenthal 1976; and Kruchten 2001, 609 for the Middle Kingdom. There are only four texts that unequivocally record oracular ceremonies in the Eighteenth Dynasty: 1) Hatshepsut: The queen visited the 'stair of the lord of the gods' to make a decision (*wḏ, nḏw.t-r3*) on a campaign to Punt (PM II², 347 (14); *Urk.* IV, 342: 10; Shirun-Grumach 1993, 69 and 72); 2) Thutmose III: Oracular appointment (*bi3y.t, wḏ*) of the young prince Thutmose as the future king when a divine procession of Amun took place in the Hypostyle Hall at Karnak (PM II², 106–7 (328–30); *Urk.* IV, 156–8); 3) Thutmose III: The Extension-of-the-Cord ritual at Karnak during an Amun festival on II Peret 30 in year 24, when Amun responded (*bi3y.t, nḏw.t-r3*) and desired to extend a cord himself (**780**); 4) Thutmose IV: The king visited Amun at Karnak and asked (*nḏ*) for a decision on his Nubian campaign on III Peret 2 in year 8 (**798**). Oracles concerning non-royal affairs are attested in the Ramesside Period, mostly by Deir el-Medina ostraca (Černý 1927 and 1942a; Kruchten 2000). Direct material evidence, such as speaking statues and the related architectural structures, is known from later periods (Loukianoff 1936; Habachi 1947; Brunton 1947; Fakhry 1971), except an arguable pre-dynastic example of a nodding statue of the seated Horus from Hierakonpolis (Simpson 1971, 161, fig. 10). A few sets of two oracular questionnaires have also been discovered elsewhere in some places (Ryholt 1993; Fischer-Elfert 1996; Kruchten 2000).

[2] Leitz 2002a, vol. 1, 315, 336, and 316. Jauhiainen (2009, 96, n. 3) posits that Amun-of-Pakhenty was worshipped at western Thebes.

[3] The latter possibility is suggested by another source: a small relief of Nesamen, a scribe of the storehouse of Amun's temple, carved on an outer wall of Amenhotep II's chapel in Court IV of Karnak. This graffiti-like relief was made by a skilled hand on the bottom surface of the chapel. Here Nesamen is portrayed in the same gesture as Merimaat, and described as being promoted to an office of his fathers' through an oracle of Amun-Re at the Feast of Ipet on III Shemu 28 in renaissance year 7 of Ramses XI (**1286**).

[4] *mḥ hrw.w 13* is understood either as the thirteenth or fourteenth day from the beginning of a given event. The reading for the thirteenth day is supported by the Medinet Habu calendar (Kruchten 1986, 59). The latter reading is evident in P. Louvre 3129 (K, 49) and P. BM 10252 (12, 27–33), dated to the time of Nectanebo I, which record *hrw mḥ 3.t* as a fourth day (*Urk.* VI, 143: 17).

source	reign	year	date	location	remark	App. 1
Story of Pachauemdiamen (P. BM10335)	Ramses IV	2	III Akhet 1	West Thebes?	Amun-of-Pakhenty	**291**
Stela of Merimaat (Cairo 91927)	Ramses VI	7	III Akhet 8	Karnak	at the Silver Floor	**331**
Text of Djehutymes, Karnak	Pinedjem II	2?	III Akhet 6?	Karnak	at the Silver Floor	**321**
Text of Herihor	Ramses XI	–	–	Karnak	Khonsu temple	–

> gods[5], Amun-Re, king of the gods, Mut the great, lady of Isheru, and Khonsu in Thebes, Neferhotep, at the Silver Floor of the temple of Amun, at reaching the god (*pḥ-nṯr*) by the high-priest of Amun-Re, king of the gods, general, chief(?), Pinedjem, true of voice, son of Menkheperre, true of voice, inquiring about matters of this land in front of the great god. Completing two months and five days (i.e. III Akhet 6?)[6] [ ] the great god, who is distant from evil. He has not travelled upstream to Opet[7] at His Festival of Opet in this year. Now the great god stopped at the scribes, agents, and officers, who did evil acts in the city, his town. The great god condemned (*ḫr*) the scribes, agents, and officers for the evil acts that they had done. The great god appeared at the Silver Floor of the temple of Amun in the time of morning.[8] The high-priest of Amun-Re, king of the gods, Pinedjem, true of voice, came before the great god.

This account is remarkable for three respects: the detailed description of an oracular session, the references to dates, and more significantly the extreme delay or cancellation of Amun's visit to the temple of Luxor. Theoretically, divine decrees were issued with full effect only after the god underwent renewal rituals at Luxor temple, his primordial site. Hence, the two New Kingdom texts, presented in the table above, attest III Akhet, in which the latter half of the Opet Festival most probably fell. Piankhi's stela, originating from Gebel Barkal, tells us that the return journey took place on III Akhet 2 (**300**). Elsewhere in our text of Djehutymes, it is recorded that the Theban triad appeared at Luxor on II Akhet 27 in year 5 of Pinedjem II (**271**). Hence, Amun's oracle-giving without his visit to Luxor proves to be very unusual. This may explain the reason why our text emphasizes that 'Amun-Re has not travelled upstream to Opet' in a specific year, perhaps year 2 of Pinedjem II.

Lastly, among these texts is Herihor's account that is worth mentioning for its characteristic description. It is dated to the time of Ramses XI and located in the forecourt of the Khonsu temple at Karnak.[9] Above the text Khonsu's barque is depicted being carried by priests. Unfortunately, more than half of the text is damaged and the date in the heading is missing. It records an oracular session of Khonsu concerning an honorific appeal from Herihor as the high-priest of Amun-Re, who wished another ten years of priesthood to be added to his twenty-year service, which Amun-Re had previously granted him. Although this text was dedicated to Khonsu in the first instance, it appears that Amun-Re played a main role to issue a divine decree to Herihor.[10] After the god's consent (*hn tp r wr wr* 'nodding very much'), the passage in line 13 reads: [half of the line lost *Ἰ*]*mn-rˁ nsw.t nṯr.w iw=f di.t ḥr=f m ḫd r ip.t-s.wt ˁḥˁ=f spr r pꜣ wbꜣ* [more than half of the following line lost] '[... A]mun-Re, king of the gods, turned his face northwards to Karnak. Then he arrived at the court [...]'. If this text is to be associated with the Opet Feast, the oracular session must have taken place on the return journey to Karnak.

[5] Kruchten (1991, 186) associates one of Amun's epithets *nb nṯr.w* with his oracular processional image, a hypothesis followed by Exell (2009, 34). Exell also suggests that *nṯr šps* can be applied to any god in the same way.

[6] Naville (1883, 4) interpreted this date as II Akhet 5 and placed this oracular session before the Opet Feast. Kruchten (1985, 20) suggests that this text refers to three different events, respectively falling on II Akhet 5, II Akhet 19, and IV Akhet 23, and that the first unknown event took place 13 days before the second one dated to II Akhet 19, a traditional day of the Opet Festival. Therefrom he adds 65 days (two months and five days) to II Akhet 19, which corresponds to IV Akhet 23 on which our oracular session falls. It is, however, an anomaly to have an unknown event that is never referred to in the text (note that there is not a space large enough to include an account of such an event in this relief). It is more likely that 'completing 65 days' means III Akhet 6 by counting from New Year's Day although such a way to count days is not attested elsewhere. The 'fourteenth day' is perhaps referred to as III Akhet 6. If this assumption is correct, this celebration is meant to have begun on II Akhet 23.

[7] 'Opet' here means Luxor temple. This invites comparison with the dedication text of Ramses II at Abydos, which records the king's journey from Thebes to Abydos *ḥr sꜣ sḫnti Ἰmn r ip.t* 'after Amun travels upstream to Opet' (PM VI, 3 (34–7); *KRI* II, 325: 6).

[8] The appearance of the god in the morning is evidenced by other sources: stela of Merimaat (**331**); oracular inscription concerning Henuttauy (north face of the tenth pylon of Karnak: Gardiner 1962, 58; Winand 2003, 638–9); oracular text of Nesamen (**1286**).

[9] PM II², 231 (22, III-2); *Khonsu* II, 14–7, pl. 132.

[10] A joint oracular session of Amun-Re with Khonsu is also attested in the oracular text of the high-priest of Amun Menkheperre, located in the same court (PM II², 232; *Khonsu* II, 17–20, pl. 133).

2.5.2. Reward ceremony

In the Luxor reliefs, it is referred to several times that the god rewarded the king for his excellent monuments and sovereignty on earth.[11] A song sung by soldiers, for example, includes the word *mtn* 'to reward':[12]

> *ḥn nhm.w ḏd=sn Ḏsr-ḫpr.w-rꜥ-stp-n-rꜥ m tp ḥb=f ḥr ḫn.t ms sw wḏ n=f nsy.t m šꜣ ꜥḥꜥ n Rꜥ m p.t mtn.tw=f m ḳn.t nḫt r ḫꜣs.t nb* [*pḥ*] *sw wḏ ỉmn nḫt n Ḏsr-ḫpr.w-rꜥ-stp-n-rꜥ ỉmn pꜣ nṯr wḏ sw pꜣ nḫt pꜣ ḥḳꜣ nsw.t nḫt mry.t ḥr ḫn*[*.t*] *ỉmn di.t* [two or more groups lost]
>
> The song of jubilation which they sing: 'Djeserkheperure-setepenre (Horemheb) at the head of his festival navigates the one who bore him. The kingship has been decreed (*wḏ*) for him in equivalence to the lifetime of Re in the sky. He was rewarded (*mtn*) with valour and victory against every foreign land [which attacks] him. Amun decrees the victory for Djeserkheperure-setepenre. Amun is the god who decrees (*wḏ*) it. The victorious one is the ruler! The victorious and beloved king navigates Amun, [ ] may give [ ].'

In this and other texts accompanying the Luxor reliefs, *mtn* and *wḏ* 'to decree' are alternately used. Divine decrees are referred to as such in temple representations, usually when the king is praised for his successful campaigns and abundant dedications to the god. This forms theoretical reciprocity between the god and king. It was modeled on this divine-royal mutual relationship that the king rewarded his subordinates: priests, officials, and soldiers.[13] The royal reward was often referred to as the *ḥs.t* 'praise'.[14]

The high-priest of Amun-Re Amenhotep, for example, is portrayed receiving rewards before the king. This representation is located on the exterior wall of Court II of Karnak and dated to III Akhet 19 in year 10 of Ramses IX (**371**). The king praises Amenhotep for monuments that he made for Amun-Re in the name of the king. The king orders:

> *imy ḥs.w ḳn.w fḳꜣ.w ꜥšꜣ.w m nb.w nfr*(*.w*) *ḥḏ.w ḥḥ.w m ḫ.t nb*(*.t*) *nfr*(*.t*) *n ḥm nṯr tpy n ỉmn-rꜥ nsw.t nṯr.w ỉmn-ḥtp mꜣꜥ ḫrw*
>
> Give many praises and numerous rewards[15] consisting of fine gold, silver, and millions of every good thing to the high-priest of Amun-Re, king of the gods, Amenhotep, true of voice.

This ceremony took place in *pꜣ wbꜣ ꜥꜣ n ỉmn m hrw pn iw.tw rdi.t ir.tw ḥs.w r tnw rnp.t nb* 'the great court of Amun on this day, when one (king) caused that praises be made every year.' This text does not specify the setting of this ceremony but a link to the Opet Feast is suggested by the dating. If the tradition of Ramses III still continued in the reign of Ramses IX, III Akhet 19 was four days after the Opet Festival concluded. This date was rather close to the 'Amun Festival after the Opet Festival' that, according to the Medinet Habu calendar, was celebrated on III Akhet 17 (**363**). Such a 'post-festival festival' is not elsewhere known and its significance is not entirely clear.[16] It is not impossible to assume that Amenhotep as the high-priest achieved a great service at the Opet Festival, and the Amun Festival later on III Akhet 17 was deemed a fitting occasion to reward those who contributed to a great deal of logistics required for the Opet Feast.

Another high-priest of Amun in the time of Ramses II also received a great favour at or after the Opet Festival. In the tomb of Nebwenenef (TT 157), he is represented proceeding to the royal couple at a window of appearance (**423**). He is followed by fan-bearers and priests with a legend that reads:

> *ḥꜣ.t-sp 1 ꜣbd 3-nw ꜣḫ.t m-ḫt ḥd ḥm=f m niw.t rsy.t ḥr ir.t ḥs.wt it=f ỉmn-rꜥ nb ns.wt tꜣ.wy kꜣ wr ḥry-tp psḏ.t Mw.t wr.*[*t*] *nb.t išrw Ḫnsw m wꜣs.t nfr-ḥtp psḏ.t imy wꜣs.t m ḥb=f nfr n ip.t ii.w im m ḥs.t* [*šs*]*p.tw ḥs.w ḥr-tp ꜥnḫ wḏꜣ snb n nsw.t-bi.ty Wsr-mꜣꜥ.t-rꜥ-stp-n-rꜥ ꜥnḫ ḏ.t di r tꜣ r tꜣ-wr sṯꜣ ḥm nṯr tpy n ỉmn Nb-wnn=f mꜣꜥ ḫrw m-bꜣḥ ḥm=f is.t sw m ḥm nṯr tpy n ỉn-ḥr m ḥm nṯr tpy n Ḥwt-ḥr nb.t iwn.t imy-r ḥm.w nṯr n nṯr.w nb.w rsy.t=f r ḥr=i-ḥr-imn mḥy. t=f r tnw ḏd in n=f ḥm=f tw=k m ḥm nṯr tpy n ỉmn pr.wy-ḥḏ=f šnw.t=f ḥr ḏbꜥ.t=k*

[11] *Opet*, 2, 3, 9, 35, 39, and 45.

[12] *Opet*, 35, pls 94–6. See Jansen-Winkeln (1989, 237–8) for the verb *mtn/mty* 'to reward'.

[13] Schulman 1988, 118. In the scene of a royal reward ceremony represented in the tomb of Neferhotep (TT 50), dated to the time of Horemheb, Neferhotep speaks: *wḏ nb=i ỉmn rdi ḥs.tw=i m-bꜣḥ* 'My lord Amun decrees to cause one (king) to praise me in front (PM I-1², 95 (2); Hari 1985, 18, pl. 6, cols 11–3).

[14] For example, Iahhotep's decree concerning rewards to be given to one of her officials on I Shemu 1 in year 10 of Amenhotep I (**959**); Ramses III's decree to reward an official with a land property (Stela Cairo 88879: *KRI* V, 395: 5).

[15] *ḥs* and *fḳꜣ* are also attested together in the dedication text of Ramses II, which describes the king as receiving rewards from Amun at the Opet Festival (*KRI* II, 325: 6–7). O. Cairo 25552 records that *fḳꜣ.w* were given by the king to the workmen(?) on I Peret 17 in year 3, perhaps of Merenptah (*KRI* IV, 154: 2–3). These rewards were also called *pꜣ snḏm ib* 'the sweetener of heart' elsewhere in the same text.

[16] It is known that Amenhotep III rewarded Amenhotep, son of Hapu, on III Shemu 2 after his first Sed Festival in year 30 (**1193**). The reward was given for the considerable contribution of this official to the preparation for the jubilee (O'Connor and Cline 2001, 70).

Year 1, III Akhet, when his person sailed northwards from the southern city, having performed the praises of his father Amun-Re, lord of the thrones of the Two Lands, great bull, foremost of the Ennead, Mut the grea[t], lady of Isheru, Khonsu in Thebes, Neferhotep, and the Ennead in Thebes at His Beautiful Festival of Opet, therefrom he came in praise. Praises were [rece]ived on behalf of the life, prosperity, and health of the king of Upper and Lower Egypt, Usermaatre-setepenre, living forever, who disembarked at Tawer (Thinis). The high-priest of Amun, Nebwenenef, true of voice, was brought before his person. Now he was the high-priest of Onuris, the high-priest of Hathor, lady of Dendera, and the overseer of the priests of all the gods, his south being as far as Heriheramen and his north being as far as Thinis. Then, his person said to him: 'You are the high-priest of Amun! His double-treasury and his granary are under your seal'.

This personal account is supplemented by Ramses II's inscription at the temple of Seti I in Abydos. It records that the king left Thebes on III Akhet 23 in year 1 after celebrating the Opet Feast and subsequently issued a decree to complete that temple (**389**). This trip is referred to as *wḏy.t=f tpy.t r w3s.t* 'his first travel to Thebes'. By combining these two texts, one can explain that Nebwenenef accompanied Ramses II during his official tour within Upper Egypt in year 1. The aim of their journey was to proclaim Ramses II's enthronement and his newly established government (2.4.3). It may be that other high officials and priests also participated in this journey and some were appointed in that year.[17] The expression *st3 m-b3h ḥm=f* 'to bring before his person' undoubtedly refers to a ceremonial nomination of the priest, because the same cliché is employed to describe the installation of the vizier Useramen on the New Year's Day in year 5 of Thutmose III (**4**). Nebwenenef was appointed the high-priest of Amun at, or prior to the journey to, Abydos, while his son succeeded the office of the high-priest of Hathor. Is it logical for Nebwenenef to be appointed as the high-priest of Amun at Abydos? Provided that he accompanied the king at Thebes during the Opet Feast, it is more likely that he was given that office at Thebes and subsequently introduced to the board of priests at Abydos.

The ideological mechanism of the distribution of Amun's favours to the king thus provided a model for that of the king's to his subordinates. Undoubtedly, this model was applied further to lower stratum of society, namely, the common folk. In most of ostraca from the Theban West, a reward was referred to as the *mk*, which formed provisions of special nature, rather than the ordinary supply of commodities for daily use.[18] In many cases provisions of this type were given to people, regardless of their official ranks, who were employed by the royal administration. According to Janssen (1975a, 489–90), the *mk* can be distinguished from the usual salary *ḥtri*. Hence, it is not surprising to find the *mk* that includes meat, as evidenced by O. Cairo 25504, O. DeM 353, and O. DeM 46. In particular, O. DeM 46, dated to year 2 perhaps of Ramses IV, records that the workmen at Deir el-Medina received a seemingly large portion of meat (**349**):

> *hrw 11 ... iw.tw in t3 is.wt r mk m dbḥ*[one group lost]*sy n p3-n-ip.t k3 šꜥd 11 k3 iwf 9* [a lacuna?] *dḥri*
>
> Day 11 (of III Akhet) ... One brought the workmen to reward with necessi[ties] of the (month) of Opet. Butchered oxen 11 and meat oxen 9 [ ] leather.

Meat products were usually not included in the workmen's regular salary. *p3-n-ip.t* is more likely to denote the month name of II Akhet, rather than the name of the Opet Feast per se. The reason why the meat of the previous month was delivered in III Akhet is best explained in association with the Opet Festival, when divine offerings were consumed and subsequently apportioned to the workmen.

O. Cairo 25504, dated to the time of Merenptah, records three occasions for rewarding (*mk*) the workmen for their work on a final preparation for the burial of Merenptah. These occasions took place at *p3 ḫtm n p3 ḫr* 'the Enclosure of the Necropolis'. The first reward was given by the overseer of the double-treasury Tjay on III Akhet 11 in year 7 (**346**). The second one was granted by the royal butler Ramesemper, the scribe Pamer, and the vizier and city governor Panehesy on IV Shemu 19 in the same year (**1356**). The final one was given on II Akhet 20 next year by the overseer of craftsmen (**246**). Based on the dates, the first and third occasions probably took place during the Opet Festival.[19] On the other hand, it is difficult to associate the second occasion with any known celebration. Note that the work for which the last reward was given was achieved in the presence of the vizier Pensekhmet, the overseer of the double-treasury Meryptah, and the scribe of the house of gold Huy, who brought a king's letter concerning

[17] The vizierate of Paser, who had served under Seti I, was probably renewed by Ramses II in year 1 (*KRI* III, 9: 6–7; Brand 2000, 341).

[18] *mk* has both verbal and nominal forms as is clearly attested in O. Cairo 25504 recto, col. II, l. 2, where the overseer of the treasury is described as: *iw=f ḥr mk t3 is.wt* (*ḥr*) *rdi.t n=sn mk* 'he rewarded the workmen, giving rewards to them' (*KRI* IV, 155: 9).

[19] Jauhiainen 2009, 101.

rewards to be given to the workmen. This suggests that Pensekhmet was the northern counterpart to the well-known southern vizier Panehesy, and the former repaid the workmen on behalf of the king.

A reward-giving postdating the Opet Festival is attested in O. Cairo 25565, dated to III Akhet 21 in year 5 of Ramses IV (**383**). It records that the royal butler Sethherwenemyef *ii r di.t tꜣ ḥs.t* 'came to give the praise' to the workmen.

2.5.3. Appointment of priests and officials

Like Nebwenenef, who was appointed the high-priest of Amun in year 1 of Ramses II, other offices were also conferred during the Opet Festival. The accession anniversary of Horemheb and official visits to Thebes of some Ramesside rulers in year 1 are best described as the most conventional version of status confirmation through Amun's approval (2.4.3).[20] In previous sections was demonstrated that festivals functioned as a means to distribute gods' power through the king in the forms of oracle and reward, and that the ceremonies of their reception usually took place during the latter half of or shortly after the Opet Feast. Rewards were awarded for one's services, and official titles themselves did not guarantee a reward. There seems to have been clear distinction between a reward and an office. With regard to dates, the appointment of officials represents a different picture from oracle- and reward-givings. It bears witness to a pre-festival ceremony, rather than a post-festival one.

There are two New Kingdom examples to be considered here. First, a statue of Nebnefer, discovered in the temple of Wadjmes at western Thebes, records a royal decree concerning the inheritance of an office from his father in year 20 of Amenhotep III (**283**). The text on the back of the statue reads:

> *[ḥꜣ.t-sp] 20 ꜣbd 2-nw ꜣḫ.t [ḫr] ḥm n nsw.t-bi.ty Nb-mꜣꜥ.t-rꜥ sꜣ-rꜥ Ỉmn-ḥtp-ḥkꜣ-wꜣs.t ꜥnḫ ḏ.t mry Ỉmn nb [ns.wt] tꜣ.wy ḫnty ipt-s.wt ḫꜥ.w ḥr s.t Ḥr n.t ꜥnḫ.w mi Rꜥ rꜥ nb hrw pn is.t [ḥm=f m ḥw.t-kꜣ-ptḥ m pr] Ptḥ inb-rsy.t=f nb ꜥnḫ-tꜣ.wy wp.t ii ḥr=s sš nsw.t imy-r pr Ḫꜥ-m-p.t n sḏꜣw bi.ty ḥm nṯr tpy n [Ỉmn Mry-ptḥ wḏ] m pr-ꜥꜣ ꜥ.w.s. imy mn.tw ḥry ḫꜣy.t n šnw.t ḥtp-nṯr Nb-nfr m ḥr it.w [m iwꜥw n it ḥry ḫꜣy.t Ḥw]y di r s.t=f m šnw.t ḥtp-nṯr n Ỉmn*
>
> [Year] 20, II Akhet [under] the person of the king of Upper and Lower Egypt, Nebmaatre, son of Re, Amenhotep-heqawaset, living forever, beloved of Amun, lord of the [thrones] of the Two Lands, foremost of Karnak, when he appeared on the throne of Horus of the living like Re every day. On this day, when [his person was in the house of the ka of Ptah in the temple of] Ptah-South-of-His-Wall, lord of Life-of-the-Two-Lands. A messenger came concerning it, the royal scribe, steward, Khaempet, to the seal-bearer of the king of Lower Egypt, high-priest of [Amun, Meryptah. Decree] from the pharaoh, l.p.h., 'Let the chief measurer of the granary of divine offerings Nebnefer be established in the presence of the fathers [as an heir to the father, chief measurer, Hu]y, being promoted to his office in the granary of the divine offerings of Amun.'

The following passage names some witnesses to his promotion. It appears that Amenhotep III was at Memphis. Thebes is also not impossible because there was a temple dedicated to Ptah in that city too. Regardless of where the king was, Nebnefer seems to have been promoted at Thebes because the letter was sent to the high-priest of Amun. Although the date may refer to the day of the royal decree, rather than the day of the assumption of the office, the context seems to be religious and ceremonial, and suggests a link to the Opet Festival.

Second, the vizierate of Ta during the reign of Ramses III might bring a slightly clearer picture of the conferment of an office. He is first attested in year 16 of Ramses III as a vizier in charge of either Upper or Lower Egypt (Table 6). On the basis that three stelae name certain individuals as accompanying him to Thebes in years 15 and 16, Exell (2009, 81–2) supposes that he was appointed a vizier in those years and paid a visit to Thebes. He is known to have assigned some individuals for a work on the West Bank during his stay in Thebes (**328** and **424**). It is probable that when he first became a vizier, he established a new set of officials at his disposal in year 16. As described in 1.3.1.2, he visited Thebes in III Akhet that year, probably to attend the Opet Feast. Ta was later promoted to the office of the 'vizier of the Two Lands' on II Akhet 23 in year 29 of Ramses III (**251**). Whether or not he was installed in Thebes is again a matter of speculation. He is elsewhere attested to have remained in Upper Egypt at least until III Peret 28 that year (**864**). Is II Akhet 23 the day of his appointment or a report to Thebes? This is not easily answered. It would be natural for Ta to be appointed the vizier in the north, where his head office and the royal residence were located. His visits to Thebes were probably aimed at confirming his new office in the presence of Amun. Like the royal accession anniversary, visiting major

[20] Appointments of the ruler through Amun's oracle in the Ramesside Period and later are attested in P. Turin 1882, dated to the time of Ramses IV (Gardiner 1955a; *idem* 1956, 10; Jansen-Winkeln 1999, 54) and in Stela Cairo 48866, dated to II Peret 15 in year 1 of Aspelta (**728**).

religious cities was a prerequisite for confirming a new status through divine approval. Thebes was only one of them. Hence, it is not impossible that II Akhet 23 was the day of confirmation of his vizierate with Amun's consent.

II Akhet recorded for the cases of Nebnefer and Ta suggests that their ceremonies took place at the beginning of the Opet Feast and that a setting different from reward ceremonies was required.[21] This may be evident in the installation of the divine wife (*ḥm.t nṯr*) of Amun Nitocris (I), the eldest daughter of Psametik I. She was sent from Sais and arrived in Thebes on II Akhet 14 in year 9 of Psametik I (**206**). Thebans welcomed her in joy on her arrival at Karnak, followed by reception rituals, in which Amun received 'what the king made for him', namely his daughter and her dowry. She was adopted by the incumbent foremost priestess of Amun (*dwꜣ.t nṯr* 'divine adoratice') Shepenwepet (II), a sister of Taharqa, and by the second priestess (*ḏr.t nṯr* 'divine hand') Amenirdis (II), a daughter of Taharqa.[22] Properties possessed by Shepenwepet and Amenirdis were transferred to Nitocris by handing over a property document (*imy-pr*), which the parent of Shepenwepet, Piankhi, had created for his daughter. According to Caminos (1964, 99), this property transaction appears to have been authorized with divine approval through an oracular ritual of Amun. The final confirmation was most probably provided at the Opet Feast to begin shortly.[23]

This pre-festival ceremony was a practice continued from the Middle Kingdom. P. UC 32037, discovered at Lahun, reports on an office transferred from a father to his son, which was promised with an *imy.t-pr* document on IV Akhet 29 (**542**). More significantly, Stela Cairo 52453 records that the mayor of el-Kab, Kebsi, sold his office to his relative on IV Akhet 30 in year 1 of the Seventeenth Dynasty ruler Nebiryaut (**547**). This transaction was made again with an *imy.t-pr* document and approved by witnesses the next day, which correspond to the day of Nehebkau. The final confirmation was probably provided at Karnak because the stela was discovered in that temple.

The situation akin to this is recorded for the queen Ahmes-Nefertari, whose promotion to the divine wife was approved on IV Akhet 7 by order of her husband, king Ahmes (**455**). This decision was also made with an *imy.t-pr* document and subsequently confirmed in the presence of Amun and the king at the Khoiak Feast. It was perhaps an age-old tradition that the transaction of offices was executed at the Khoiak Festival that echoed the myth of Horus succeeding his dead father Osiris (4.2.1.2).

This practice later extended over to other festivals. In fact, P. Bibliothèque Nationale 237 records an oracular session of an unnamed god on II Akhet 18 in year 3 of Ramses VI (**234**). This document is docketed as an '*imy-pr* document made by the king', which suggests the significance of this session, perhaps associated with a high-ranking individual, whose office was presumably confirmed during the Opet Feast.

2.5.4. Bull at the Opet Festival

As described in 2.4.7, the presence of fat bulls is a feature prominent in the representations of the Opet Feast. P. Bournemouth 17/1931, a fragmentary letter written by a woman in the late Twentieth Dynasty, concerns oxen to be sacrificed for Amun presumably during the Opet Feast (**239**):

> ...] *tw=i tꜣ md.t nꜣ kꜣ.w m-bꜣḥ 'Im[n* half of the line lost] *r tꜣy ry.t m ꜣbd 2-nw ꜣḫ.t sw 19*

> ... I (speak of) the matter of the oxen before Amu[n] to this side on II Akhet 19.

This correspondence apparently speaks of bulls to be sacrificed before the god. Animal victims were probably collected from several sources, not one agent. It must have required an enormous amount of preparatory work to put together not only duly deliveries of divine offerings, but also the allocation of thousands of human resources, maintenance of a busy schedule, deployment of security forces, looking after the royal party, polishing ritual paraphernalia, etc. Our letter is only a tiny part of enormous logistic correspondence.

It is remarkable that a representation of a 'blessed bull of the Opet Festival (*iwꜣ ḥs n ḥb ip.t*)' is found not only at Thebes but also in the temple of Seti I at Abydos.[24] How can we understand the bull of the Opet Feast to be

[21] There are later cases that cannot be explained for the sake of this hypothesis. P. Berlin 3048, for example, lists some priests of Amun-Re who entered (*ꜥḳ*) a temple (probably Karnak) on various days. Among them is the entry: *hrw pn ꜥḳ r pr n ḥm-nṯr n 'Imn-rꜥ nsw.t nṯr.w imy-r niw.t ṯꜣty Ḥri* 'this day of entering the temple of the priest of Amun-Re, king of the gods, overseer of the town, vizier Hori' on III Akhet 6 in year 14 of Takelot II (**322**).

[22] The functional distinction between 'divine wife' and 'divine adoratice' is not as clear-cut as has generally been accepted because there are examples that one person held the two titles at the same time (Dodson 2002, 181).

[23] The divine adoratice Isis, a daughter of Ramses VI, appears to have been appointed at the Valley Feast (3.7). Also Ankhnesneferibre, a daughter of the king Psametik II and an heiress to Nitocris, was first sent to Thebes on III Shemu 29 in year 1 of Psametik II (**1292**). Her adoption ceremony perhaps took place at the Ipet Festival, for which concentration of some religious events is observed at the turn of III Shemu to IV Shemu.

[24] PM IV, 27 (245–6); Cabrol 1999, fig. 7. A chapel located to the northeast of the enclosure wall of Deir el-Medina attests parallel representations of fat bulls (PM I-2[2], 691; Bruyère 1924, *Rapport (1934–1935)*, 37–9). Valbelle (1985, 326) associated them with the Opet Feast, questioned by Bomann (1991, 69). Also see Jauhiainen 2009, 94.

depicted outside of Thebes? A key to the answer may be found in another representation of five large bulls in the tomb of Amenhotep (TT 73) on the West Bank (4.5.12). They are included in the New Year gifts dedicated to the queen Hatshepsut. The legend reads: [*ẖr*]*p iwȝ.w n ḥb n ip.t ḥr-tp ꜥnḫ wḏȝ snb nsw.t-bi.ty nb*[*.t*] *tȝ.wy* [*Mȝꜥ.t-kȝ-rꜥ*] *di ꜥnḫ ir ẖr ꜥ n r-pꜥ.t* '[leadin]g(?) the bulls of the Opet Festival on behalf of the life, prosperity, and health of the king of Upper and Lower Egypt, Lad[y] of the Two Lands, [Maatkare], given life, done under the supervision of a member of the *pat*'. These oxen were registered at the New Year for the Opet Feast to come within a given year, rather than were slaughtered and consumed at the New Year.

In Tutankhamen's reliefs are depicted a number of bulls slaughtered before a gate of Luxor temple and subsequently deposited in several small shrines lined up in front of it.[25] Yet, they were not all killed at once because five adorned bulls appear at the third pylon of Karnak on the return journey.[26] They were presumably going to be kept at Karnak as a manifestation of the renewed divine power in order to serve subsequent rituals. After a short period of time, the bulls were selected for different purposes, probably some to be delivered to other major temples, some to be kept for other religious celebrations, and others to be slaughtered. A slaughtered bull depicted at Abydos is perhaps one of these bulls, which was brought from Thebes initially to distribute the divine power of Amun-Re and secondly to be used for rituals that paralleled the Opet Festival, or to be kept for different occasions.[27] It is also not impossible that some local temples were requested to deliver a bull to Thebes for the occasion.

Another representation of fat bulls is carved on the north interior wall of Court III at Karnak, dated to the time of Horemheb.[28] The association of this relief with the Opet Festival is not clear, but it closely parallels the Luxor reliefs.[29] Three bulls with adorned horns are shown proceeding to a pylon of Karnak. On the body of one of these bulls is written the 'high-priest of Amun Meryamen'.

It is of some interest that the Medinet Habu calendar records that a drinking party took place at that temple every day during the Opet Festival but did not consume the meat that was listed for the main celebration.[30] This was also the case for the post-festival meal of Ramses III's accession anniversary.[31] After being offered to the god, some meat was apparently not subject to immediate consumption within the temple but may have been stored or delivered to the outside of the temple, perhaps to the general public.[32]

[25] *Opet*, 17, pl. 36.
[26] *Opet*, 38, pl. 101.
[27] Cabrol (1999, 26, n. 43) argues that nationwide festivals were performed at Abydos, at least, on a smaller scale.
[28] PM II², 178 (532); Pillet 1939, figs1–2. For identification of this pylon with the third one of Karnak, see *Opet*, 38, n. 129.
[29] Nims (1965, 105) and Murnane (1982, 578) related this relief to the Opet Festival.
[30] *MH* III, pl. 156, list 37.
[31] *MH* III, pl. 152, list 22.
[32] Ikram (1995, 219) also proposes that the surplus of meat could be sold by a temple to merchants or householders.

Chapter 3

Valley Festival

3.1. Research history

When Jean-François Champollion visited Egypt from 1828 to 1829, he was well aware of the mortuary nature of the royal temples at western Thebes. Brugsch (1862, vol. 1, 65) probably first acknowledged the existence of the Valley Festival. He (1879, vol. 2, 1103–4) later described that river journeys took place over the Nile at this celebration. Subsequently, Renouf (1880, 224) introduced this feast in his lecture in 1879, and then Tiele (1882, 169–20) referred to it in his monograph. It was, however, not until Foucart (1924) published his long article that a thorough examination of evidence relevant to this festival was carried out. His work encompassed then available evidence that attests Amun's Userhat barge and river processions. Accordingly, he collected documents recording other festivals, during which the Userhat was also used. As a result, his study revealed that the Valley Festival and Opet Festival were often referred to together in texts. However, Foucart disregarded a large corpus of additional texts and representations from private tombs at western Thebes. Finally, S. Schott (1953) published a monograph that was solely dedicated to the Valley Festival, which added to what had escaped from Foucart's survey. Schott's comprehensive study is particularly useful for containing texts that have hitherto been unpublished and are severely damaged now.

Since then, only three articles have been published in an attempt to shed light on the Valley Festival in its own right. Wiebach (1986) explores the ideological aspects of this celebration, based on textual records from private tombs and an etymological analysis of specific terms that frequently appear in these texts. It seems beyond the frame of her study, however, to cover all evidence available at the moment and to reconstruct the whole proceedings of this festival. Subsequently, two articles have been presented by two Polish scholars Karkowski (1992) and Dolińska (2007). Karkowski's study is significant in his attempt to examine, for the first time, the unpublished representations on the northern wall belonging to the upper terrace of Hatshepsut's temple at Deir el-Bahari, and to present a study of rituals that were performed inside this temple at the Valley Festival. Dolińska endeavours to reconstruct the sequence of this feast from wider perspectives by taking in consideration not only the valley temples at Deir el-Bahari but also the memorial temples located on the edge of the cultivation area. She carries out some calendrical analyses regarding the dates and duration of the Valley Festival. The contributions made by the last two authors broadly resulted from the conservation project at Hatshepsut's temple, which had been completed by the Polish-Egyptian team in 2000.

In addition, recent publications have provided a wealth of information. A series of the Archaeologische Veröffentlichungen (AVDAIK) since 1970 and the volumes of Theban Series since 1983, both of which have been published by the Deutschen Archäologisches Institut Kairo, include documentation about many Theban private tombs. These volumes complement a series of publications produced by Norman de Garis Davies and his wife Nina between 1913 and 1963. Based on all these publications, I undertake an analogical study between the Festivals of the Valley and Opet by examining the distribution of the divine life force.[1] More recently, Klotz (2008, 578–82 and 2012, 389–391) and Jauhiainen (2009, 147–52) devote some pages to the Valley Feast in their theses, the former focusing on Roman Thebes and the latter on popular cults at Deir el-Medina.

As described in the previous chapter, studies of the Opet Festival have seen some improvement in the last two decades. It is, therefore, desirable to bring together this celebration and the Valley Festival in order to carry out a comparative study in search of a better insight into their religious meanings and functions, more than half a century after Schott's monograph.

3.2. Chronological study

3.2.1. Early attestations and precursors

Like the Opet Festival, the historical development of the Valley Festival from before the New Kingdom remains conjectural. The apt designation *ḥb in.t* is securely attested from the time of Hatshepsut onwards.[2] However, mortuary celebrations are known to have

[1] Fukaya 2007.

[2] Dolińska (2007, 72) associates Amenhotep I's brick building, located in the second court of Hatshepsut's temple at Deir el-Bahari, with the Valley Festival.

taken place in the Middle Kingdom at western Thebes. Winlock (1947, 88–90) proposed the possibility that the Valley Feast was founded in a different name by Amenemhat I, who inaugurated the Twelfth Dynasty perhaps by promoting Amun's cult as a major religio-political vehicle. There are four pre-New Kingdom texts, which are all from Twelfth Dynasty Thebes and might be relevant to the present examination. On a cliff in West Thebes is a graffito written by Neferabed, a wab-priest of Amun who was contemporary with Amenemhat I. It reads:[3]

> *wʿb Nfr-ꜣbd rdi.t iꜣw n Imn sni tꜣ n nb nṯr.w m ḥb.w=f tpy.w šmw wbn=f hrw n ẖni r in.t Nb-ḥpt-rʿ in wʿb Imn Nfr-ꜣbd*
>
> The wab-priest Neferabed, giving adoration to Amun and kissing the ground for the lord of the gods at his first festivals[4] of Shemu, when he rises (on) the day of the navigation to the valley of Nebhepetre (Mentuhotep II), by the wab-priest of Amun Neferabed.

In a fashion similar to this, Stela Louvre C 200, belonging to a Mentuhotep, a wab-priest of Bastet who, according to Vernus (1987, 166), lived at the beginning of the Twelfth Dynasty, reads:[5]

> *iw rmn.n=i nb nṯr.w m wiꜣ=f wṯs nfr.w pẖr=f wꜣ.w(t) mr.t n=f m ḥb.w=f tpy.w šmw*
>
> I shouldered the lord of the gods in his barque *wṯs nfr.w* when he went around the ways that he desired at his first festivals of Shemu.

In which month of the Shemu season these 'festivals' fell is not entirely clear from these texts, but I Shemu is likely to be referred to here because two early New Kingdom texts attest *ḥb=f nfr n tpy šmw* 'His Beautiful Festival of I Shemu', which is probably a copy of a Middle Kingdom text (see the next paragraph). The significance of I Shemu may also be evident in an elaborate rock graffito at Wadi el-Hôl located in the western desert near modern Luxor. It was carved by the priest of priests Dedsobek, who lived under Amenemhat III (**862**):

> *ḥꜣ.t-sp 30 ꜣbd 3-nw pr.t sw 28 sḥtp nsw.t mr(y) nb=f ḫr ḥm n nsw.t-bi.ty Ny-mꜣʿ.t-rʿ ʿnḫ ḏ.t n[sic] r nḥḥ ḏ(.t) mry=f[sic] nb=f mꜣʿ n(y) s.t ib=f irr ḥss(.t)=f nb.t m hr.t hrw n.t rʿ nb ḥm-nṯr n ḥm(.w)-nṯr Dd-sbk nb imꜣḫ ir.n=f m mnw=f ḫft iw.t=f m Tꜣ-wr r ir.t iḫ.wt n Mntw-ḥtp*
>
> Year 30, III Peret 28: the one who satisfies the king, beloved of his lord, under the person of the king of Upper and Lower Egypt Nymaatre, may he live everlastingly, forever and ev(er), the truly beloved of his lord, his favorite, who performs all his praises every day, priest of priest(s) Dedsobek, possessor of veneration. He made (this) as his monument at the time of his coming from the Thinite nome to make offerings to Mentuhotep.

It seems that Dedsobek stayed at Thebes for more than one month to attend the 'first festivals of Shemu'.[6] Finally, the Middle Kingdom stela of Iutjeni, chief of the ten of Upper Egypt, discovered in el-Tarif or Dra Abu el-Naga, records a *ḥtp-di-nsw.t* formula preceded by a short account: *šsp=k sny n Imn m ḥb=f nfr n ẖn.t* 'May you receive the offerings of Amun at His Beautiful Festival of the Navigation'.[7]

The earliest surviving evidence for the 'Festival of I Shemu' from the New Kingdom is a stone fragment of Amenhotep I's calendar, discovered at Karnak (**1048**). It records 'His Festival of I [Shemu]' and its evening celebration. The other entries in this calendar suggest that this record was a copy of a Middle Kingdom document.[8] The significance of this celebration as a mortuary celebration appears to have remained because it is referred to together with the Valley Festival in the relief depicting the latter feast at Hatshepsut's Deir el-Bahari temple (3.4.4).

While the Festival of I Shemu was local to Thebes, there might have been another precursor of the Valley Feast, which had been non-Theban in origin, namely, the Wag Festival. According to Posener-Kriéger (1986, 1137) and Luft (1992, 151), there were two kinds of the Wag Festival during the Middle Kingdom: one fixed to I Akhet 18 and the other movable within the Shemu season. The movable version is documented in five

[3] Winlock 1947, 84, pl. 40, 1.

[4] Dolińska (2007, 68) explains that  refers to several rites performed at this festival, whereas Egberts (1995, 407) regards the plural sign as indicating more than one festival, such as the Festivals of the Valley and I Shemu. Where the third Sed Festival of Amenhotep III is referred to in the tomb of Kheruef (TT 192),  also appears with the plural strokes (*Kheruef*, pls 51 and 56), which, according to *Opet* 1994, 28, n. a, suggests the multiplicity of rituals comprising that specific jubilee. Winlock translated *tpy.w šmw* as the 'first day of Shomu', which cannot be corroborated. See 1.2.3 for standardized designations of festivals.

[5] Vernus 1987 for photograph and facsimile; Egberts 1995, vol. 1, 407 for partial translation; Ullmann 2007, 8 for partial transliteration and translation. Ullmann maintains that this stela is dated to the end of the Eleventh Dynasty.

[6] Darnell (2002, 129–38, esp. 137) also presents four Middle Kingdom graffiti at Wadi el-Hôl as related to visits to this area of some individuals, who participated in festivals.

[7] Stela Cairo 20476 (PM I-2², 598; Lange and Schäfer 1902, vol. 2, 73–4, vol. 4, pl. 33).

[8] Grimm 1994b, 74.

papyri from Lahun, dated to the Middle Kingdom (Table 12). All the instances fell on different dates in either II or III Shemu, which bears witness to the lunar cycle and parallels the occurrence of the Valley Festival. In fact, two texts attest to a link to the full moon. First, a passage recorded in P. Berlin 10016 reads: *wꜢgi r ḫpr m ḥꜢ.t-sp 18 Ꜣbd 2-nw šmw sw 17 snw n smd.t* 'Wag to occur in year 18, II Shemu 17, the second of the full moon' (**1121**). Second, P. Berlin 10165 records II Shemu 22 (**1139**). Because this entry is preceded by a reference to the full moon that took place on day 19 of an unknown month, the proximity of the Wag Festival to the full moon is implied.[9] Based on the latter evidence, Luft (1994, 41) relates the wandering Wag Festival to the 18th lunar day that fell in the second lunar month after the heliacal rising of Sothis.[10] Posener-Kriéger (1985, 42) noted the fact that the 18th lunar day was called *iꜥḥ* the 'moon' and associated the waning moon with the mortuary cult.

Given that II Shemu 1 was roughly three months after the heliacal rising of Sothis was observed at the beginning of the Twelfth Dynasty, these Middle Kingdom sources could be associated with the high-rise of the Nile, a result that contradicts the proposed association of the Valley Feast with the falling level of the Nile (Table 3). Hence, it is difficult to support for sure a relation between the Festivals of Wag and the Valley, and it should be left to future research.

3.2.2. Later attestations

As described in the preceding section, the Festival of I Shemu is likely to have developed into, or at least provided some grounds for establishing, the Valley Festival in the New Kingdom. Both of them appear to have been reshaped over time but continued as distinctive celebrations into the Ptolemaic-Roman Period—the Festival of I Shemu came to be associated with the Min Festival, while the Valley Festival was radically reformed by the Ramesside Period (1.1.3).

This reform presumably resulted from the introduction of a new mortuary celebration to Thebes, namely, the Decade Ritual. The earliest evidence that attests this ceremony as a distinctive festival is thought to date from the time of Ramses II,[11] but a ritual service performed at memorial temples is known to have taken place every ten days in the reign of Thutmose II[12] and Hatshepsut.[13] As Gabolde (1989, 151) rightly points out, this religious service was not a 'festival' in a strict sense because it always appeared without the sign 𓎰 in texts (hence, it is called the Decade 'Ritual' in this book).[14] This ritual was performed primarily at the temples of Luxor and Medinet Habu, and entailed a divine journey between these two sites.

While the increasing importance of the Decade Ritual was observed, the Valley Feast is less attested in Ramesside sources (Table 18). It is impossible to explain well the situation in which the Festival of I Shemu, the Valley Feast, and the Decade Ritual co-existed and were all associated with the mortuary cult on the West Bank of Thebes. We can produce only speculative scenarios by delineating the history of Deir el-Bahari from the late Eighteenth Dynasty onwards.[15] To what extent Akhenaten abandoned the Theban festivals is broadly unknown,[16] but Tutankhamen evidently resumed mortuary celebrations on the West Bank although he did not possess his own memorial temple.[17] However, we know no textual evidence for the Valley Festival from the time of Akhenaten to Horemheb, apart from the tomb of Neferhotep (TT 49), dated to the reign of Ay.[18] Merenptah restored the temple of Mentuhotep II, called *Ꜣḫ-s.wt*, when Deir el-Bahari still attracted visitors for the cult of the Theban triad and Hathor. Yet, a significant reform might have taken place by the Twentieth Dynasty. Traunecker, Le Saout, and Masson (1981, 134–7) explain that the Valley Feast was absorbed in the Decade Ritual, the latter of which, according to them, was first attested in the Twenty-Fifth Dynasty. Traunecker (1995, 193–4) further concludes that the focal point of the Theban mortuary cult on the West Bank shifted from the north to the south.[19] Indeed,

[9] Winter 1951, 65.

[10] Parker (1950, 57) and Krauss (1998, 53) believe an association of the Wag Feast with the 13th and 17th lunar day respectively, but their assumptions cannot be corroborated. Rose (1999, 242) cautions that the movable Wag Feast was celebrated 16 days after the new crescent, which usually takes place on lunar day 2 but can theoretically occur as late as on day 4.

[11] Doresse 1979, 37–8.

[12] A stone block discovered at Karnak (Gabolde 1989, 150, pl. 16).

[13] Statue of Senmut (Cairo 579) from the Mut precinct of Karnak (PM II^2, 262; *Urk.* IV, 411: 10).

[14] The supply of mortuary offerings at the interval of ten days was an echo of earlier traditions, the earliest surviving evidence being from the Fourth Dynasty (Barta 1968, 10). The Pyramid Texts (PT 497, Pyr. 1067 c) describes the dead king as receiving the eye of Horus every ten days (*m tp sw 10*). The partially preserved calendar of Niuserre's solar temple records two oxen to be offered *hrw n di.t tp sw 10 n ḥb wr* 'on the day of the supply every ten days of the Great Festival (Helck 1977, 70, pl. 3, col. 10). The Coffin Texts include two references to offerings to be supplied to the dead every ten days (*CT* I, 189b [44] and II, 106e [102]). Private festival lists also attest such a practice (for example, mastaba of Idu at Giza (G 7102: PM III-1^2, 185–6 (1, a–b); Simpson 1976, 21, fig. 33); mastaba of Sabu at Saqqara (E 1, Cairo 1565: PM III-2^2, 460 (4); Borchardt 1937, vol. 2, 31); a lintel belonging to the tomb of an unknown individual (Cairo 1434: Borchardt 1937, vol. 1, 114–5, pl. 28). It is evident from these texts that the decade service formed part of the sequence of mortuary performances, which took place, in ideal, every year, season, month, and day.

[15] Łajtar 2006, 3–11.

[16] Amenhotep III's memorial temple remained in service during the Amarna Period (Ullmann 2002, 171, n. 632). Ockinga (2004, 127) argues that the Valley Feast as one of Amun's major religious celebrations was refused in that period, based on the fact that a text referring to this feast is carefully erased in TT 147 (2).

[17] Ullmann 2002, 196.

[18] PM I-1^2, 92 (23 and C, c).

[19] According to Exell (2009, 70), the cult of Hathor was imported from Deir el-Bahari to the temple at Deir el-Medina, probably in the time

such a transition seems to have been an aspect of the Ramesseum. The disposition of this temple was largely skewed, a feature that parallels the Forecourt of Luxor temple, also built by Ramses II. As a result, these two temples retained the unusual form of a parallelogram to the same angle, and thus facing each other. This bears witness to increasing emphasis on the axis between the temple of Luxor and the West Bank, unlike Ramses II's father Seti I who erected his memorial temple at Qurna, a site right across the Nile from the temple of Karnak. M. Smith (2009, 183–4) observes the Osirianized nature of the Valley Feast, a character comparable with the Decade Ritual. Haikal (1970, vol. 2, 13–4) argued for an earlier transition after the Amarna Period, when representations of the Valley Festival disappeared and the cult of Amun-Re was replaced by that of Ptah-Sokar-Osiris. She also explained that Amun's cult and his celebrations, including the Valley Festival, did not fully recover their previous status after the Amarna Period. The last textual reference to Hatshepsut's temple is attested in the tomb of Imiseba (TT 65), dating from the time of Ramses IX. Djeser-akhet (Thutmose III's temple at Deir el-Bahari) was also still functioning during the latter half of the Twentieth Dynasty on account of many hieratic graffiti written by pilgrims to the site in that period (3.2.3). The population of Deir el-Medina began moving close to the green area at Medinet Habu no later than the time of Ramses IX.[20] Eventually, Deir el-Bahari appears to have been abandoned at the end of that dynasty after a landslide, which caused a fatal damage to this site. The rulers after Ramses III were not able to make their own memorial temples complete.[21]

The last secure 'historical' evidence of *ḥb=f nfr in.t* is attested in Graffito DB 31, which Krauss (2006b, 416) dates to the time of Ramses XI (**1141**). The cult at Deir el-Bahari saw a revival to some extent from the Twenty-Fifth to Twenty-Sixth Dynasty, when some large tombs were built by the causeway to Deir el-Bahari.[22] This fact prompted Bietak and Reisner-Haslauer (1978, 29) to assume that the Valley Festival was still celebrated at Deir el-Bahari in that time. Indeed, the tomb of Ibi (TT 36), dated to the time of Psametik I, attests a banal reference to this celebration.[23] Elsewhere on one of Ibi's statues (Cairo 36158, exact provenance unknown), the divine adoratice Nitocris is described as acting at the Festivals of Opet and I Shemu.[24] As I concluded that the Opet Festival probably continued into the Saite Dynasty (2.2.3), the Valley Festival may have survived until that period. However, it is very doubtful that the latter celebration maintained the same appearance as in the New Kingdom because Deir el-Bahari was probably not fully restored, whereas the Decade Ritual came to play a key role on the West Bank. More significantly, kings were no longer buried in the Valley of the Kings after the Ramesside Period, a fact that must have caused a major reform of the Valley Feast, which originally embraced the royal ancestral cult (3.4.3).

Like the Opet Feast, references to the Valley Festival were not uncommon in later sources. However, it is difficult to regard them exclusively as historical accounts.[25] A wealth of information provides details rather on the 'Festival of II Shemu'. This celebration is likely to have echoed the Valley Feast but was never referred to as such in texts. For example, about 300 graffiti carved on the roof of the Khonsu temple at Karnak may bear witness to the Valley Feast after it had radically been reformed. They were written by low-ranking priests, mostly wab-priests or divine-fathers exclusively associated with the cult of Khonsu from the Twenty-Second Dynasty to the Twenty-Third Dynasty. Out of 12 dated texts, nine are dated to either II or III Shemu (Table 13). Because divine images, particularly of the ithyphallic Amun, and barges of different gods, are included among these graffiti, it may be that the priests came up to the roof to make a signal for their patron god Khonsu to reveal himself from the temple and join the processions of Amun and Mut, or they simply looked on grandiose moments of some celebrations. Jacquet-Gordon (2004, 5–6) associates these graffiti with the Festivals of Min and Opet, but their dates may argue for the Valley Festival.

The festival of the Theban West was widely acknowledged by the Greek writers, such as Eustathius

of Ramses II. Whether this attests to the geographical shift of her cult or simply its expansion is uncertain.

[20] Janssen 1992, 13.

[21] Ramses IV, for example, inaugurated the construction of his own memorial temple but could not complete it before his death (Polz 1998, 279–80). The cult of Ramses V and VI seems to have been established together in the temple of Ramses IV after it was completed.

[22] Ćwiek 2008, 58.

[23] PM I-1², 67 (23); Kuhlmann and Schenkel 1983, vol. 2, pl. 70, a.

[24] Graefe 1994, 88, col. 25.

[25] Various Ptolemaic-Roman documents refer to the Valley Feast. Two are from Theban temples: the calendar carved on the propylon of the Mut precinct at Karnak (PM II², 256 (1, f); Sauneron 1983, pl. 9, l. 34) and an inscription at the northern chapel of the Deir el-Medina temple (PM II², 406 (30, d); Klotz 2008, 86). Also see Statue Cairo 36576, dating from the Thirtieth Dynasty to the beginning of the Ptolemaic Period (PM II², 284; Guermeur 2004, 256). Mortuary papyri are also abundant, such as the Book of the Valley Festival (P. BM 10209, I, 19: Haikal 1970, vol. 2, 11–7); the Book of Embalmment (P. Boulaq III, 4, 1: Sauneron 1952, 10 for transcription; Goyon 1972b, 52–3 for translation), note that *in.t* is referred to in association not with the Valley Feast but with the cult of Amenhotep and Imhotep; the Book of Traversing Eternity (P. Leiden T 32, II, 21: Stricker 1950, 57; M. Smith 2009, 411 for translation; Klotz 2012, 390 for transliteration and translation); the Book of Breathing (P. BM 10124: Herbin 2008, 104–5); P. Berlin 3162, III, 6–7 (von Frank-Kamenetzky 1914, 150; Kaplony-Heckel 1971, vol. 3, 45). Haikal (1970, vol. 2, 16) explained that Amun-Re of Karnak no longer visited Deir el-Bahari but travelled to Medinet Habu by the Macedonian Period, based on contemporary evidence, including the relief of the sanctuary of Karnak, erected by Philip Arrhidaeus. The association of Amun of Karnak with the Decade Ritual is attested in the building of Taharqa (PM II², 220 (16, a–b); Parker, Leclant, and Goyon 1979, 65, pl. 25, col. 21; Cooney 2000, 34–7) and the chapel of Akoris (PM II², 23; Traunecker, Le Saout, and Masson 1981, vol. 1, 109). Łajtar (2006, 65) also disagrees with the idea that the Valley Festival survived in later times.

of Thessaloniki, a codex writer to Homer's Iliad, who annotated that it lasted 12 days in 'Libya',[26] and Diodorus Siculus (I, 97), who likewise described Zeus as visiting 'Libya' every year.[27] A decree stela of Ptolemy V or VIII, erected on the dromos of Karnak, refers to the 'navigation' of Amun 'to the Memnonia'.[28] It is also known that an epistrategos visited Thebes on behalf of the king to participate in the navigation of great Amun in II Shemu.[29] According to Wilcken (1927, vol. 2, 39 and 86), the choachytes (the *w3ḥ-mw* priests, who performed mortuary rituals) were appointed during this festival. If his hypothesis is correct, it may argue for close association with the Decade Ritual, when the ritual of *w3ḥ-mw* 'presenting a libation' was performed for the gods on the West Bank.[30] Finally, a Greek graffito at Hatshepsut's temple at Deir el-Bahari attests a visit to the god Amenophis of pilgrims on II Shemu 12 in year 3 of Hadrian (**1103**). Klotz (2012, 390–1) identifies this god with Amenopet of Luxor temple in association with the Valley Festival, but Amenophis here is most likely to have been the deified Amenhotep, son of Hapu, who was worshipped at Deir el-Bahari.[31]

3.2.3. *Date and duration*

Our knowledge of the date and duration of the Valley Feast is very limited although there are several texts pertaining to mortuary rituals performed in the Shemu season on the West Bank. As listed in Table 11, they are all originating from the West Bank and dated to the Ramesside Period. These documents refer either to a river procession (*d3y*) or a visit to western Thebes of Amun, including Graffito DB 31, which clearly records the 'Valley Festival' (**1141**). Their dates falling in II Shemu or III Shemu but on different days suggest a link to the lunar cycle.

The Medinet Habu calendar records II Shemu for this feast but no specific date is given (**1171–2**). The same holds for the Festival of the Going-Forth of Min, which was also a lunar feast celebrated in I Shemu. The association of this celebration with the new moon is evident in some records (**987** and **1060**). Likewise, the Valley Festival has also been associated with the new moon by scholars. However, because the Medinet Habu calendar is the only surviving evidence and contains illegible signs, the link to the new moon cannot be securely confirmed. The passage in question reads (Figure 7):

> *m3ʿ n ỉmn-rʿ nsw.t nṯr[.w m ḥby.t n ḥb=f n in.t ḫpr].w m 3bd 2-nw šmw [i(?)]-n-p-[s]-rʿ nb(?) in m hrw tpy n ḥtp n nṯr pn šps ỉmn-rʿ nsw.t nṯr.w m t3 ḥw.t n.t ḥḥ m [rnp.wt]*
>
> Presentation to Amun-Re, king of the god[s, as the festival offering of His Festival of the Valley, which occurs] in II Shemu, [*i*(?)]-*n*-*p*-[*s*]-*rʿ nb*(?), brought on the first day of resting of this august god Amun-Re, king of the gods, in the house of millions of [years].

Schott (1934, 74; 1950, 107; and 1953, 40) read the signs that are carved over a gap between two stone blocks as the logogram of *psḏntyw* .[32] However, the following entry for the second day reads with no doubt *m 3bd 2-nw šmw rʿ nb ḫpr.w* 'in II Shemu, any day that appears'. Hence, what has traditionally been rendered *psḏntyw* may actually be written *rʿ nb*, and the rest of the signs above still does not make sense. It is, therefore, not safely concluded that the Valley Festival was celebrated on a new moon day.

Dolińska (2007, 70) associates this celebration with a certain seasonal/astronomical marker that fell in April in order to explain its occurrence from I Shemu to III Shemu over time. Although her argument is broadly in line with Krauss, who maintains the new moon connection, she does not rule out associations with three seasonal and astronomical events: the vernal equinox, resumption of inundation, and summer solstice, which took place on approximately I Shemu 22, IV Shemu 9, and IV Shemu 26 respectively at the beginning of the Nineteenth Dynasty (Table 3). These events moved within the civil calendar by roughly 50 days during the Ramesside Period over 200 years. Therefore, the vernal equinox took place between I Shemu 22 and III Shemu 12, the resumption of inundation between IV Shemu 9 and I Akhet 24, and the summer solstice between IV Shemu 26 and II Akhet 11. In particular, the range generated by the vernal equinox appears to accord with the dates of the Valley Feast (Table 11).

Two other groups of evidence have a pattern similar to this seasonal cycle. First, the *w3ḥ-mw*, briefly mentioned at the end of the preceding section, is attested in association with a specific genre of mortuary cult, which may have required the attendance of high officials from the north in the Ramesside Period.[33] Out of 11 dated texts, six fall between II Shemu and IV Shemu 1 (Table

---

[26] van der Valk 1971, vol. 1, 196, l. 28.

[27] Oldfather 1933, 335; Burton 1972, 281–2. Bataille (1952, 91) regarded the account of Diodorus as only retrospective and second-hand, and thus not reflecting the reality at his time.

[28] Bataille 1952, 89; Wagner 1971, 12, l. 3 and 14, ll. 1–2; Klotz 2012, 390, n. 52.

[29] Pestman 1992, 184, n. a; Vandorpe 1995, 218.

[30] Doresse 1979, 61–2.

[31] The cult of Amenhotep, son of Hapu, was introduced to Hatshepsut's temple at Deir el-Bahari at the beginning of the Ptolemaic Period and was known for his oracular performance (Łajtar 2006, 22–3). Ptolemy VIII dedicated the innermost chapel of this temple to this sage together with the Old Kingdom legend Imhotep.

[32] This translation is followed by Kitchen (*KRI translations* V, 123: 5), el-Sabban (2000, 67), and Krauss (1981, 28 and 1985, 136).

[33] Donker van Heel 1992.

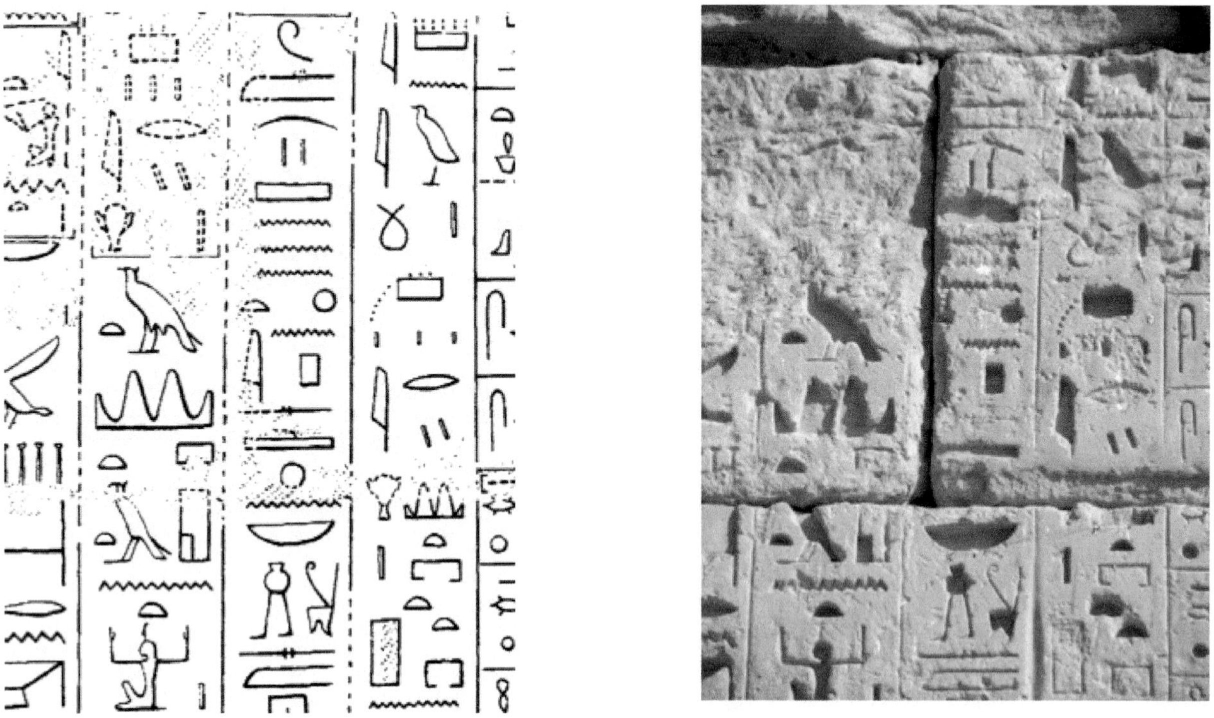

a. Day 1 of the Valley Festival (facsimile from *MH* III, pl. 142, list 2, by courtesy of the Oriental Institute, University of Chicago, and photograph taken by the author).

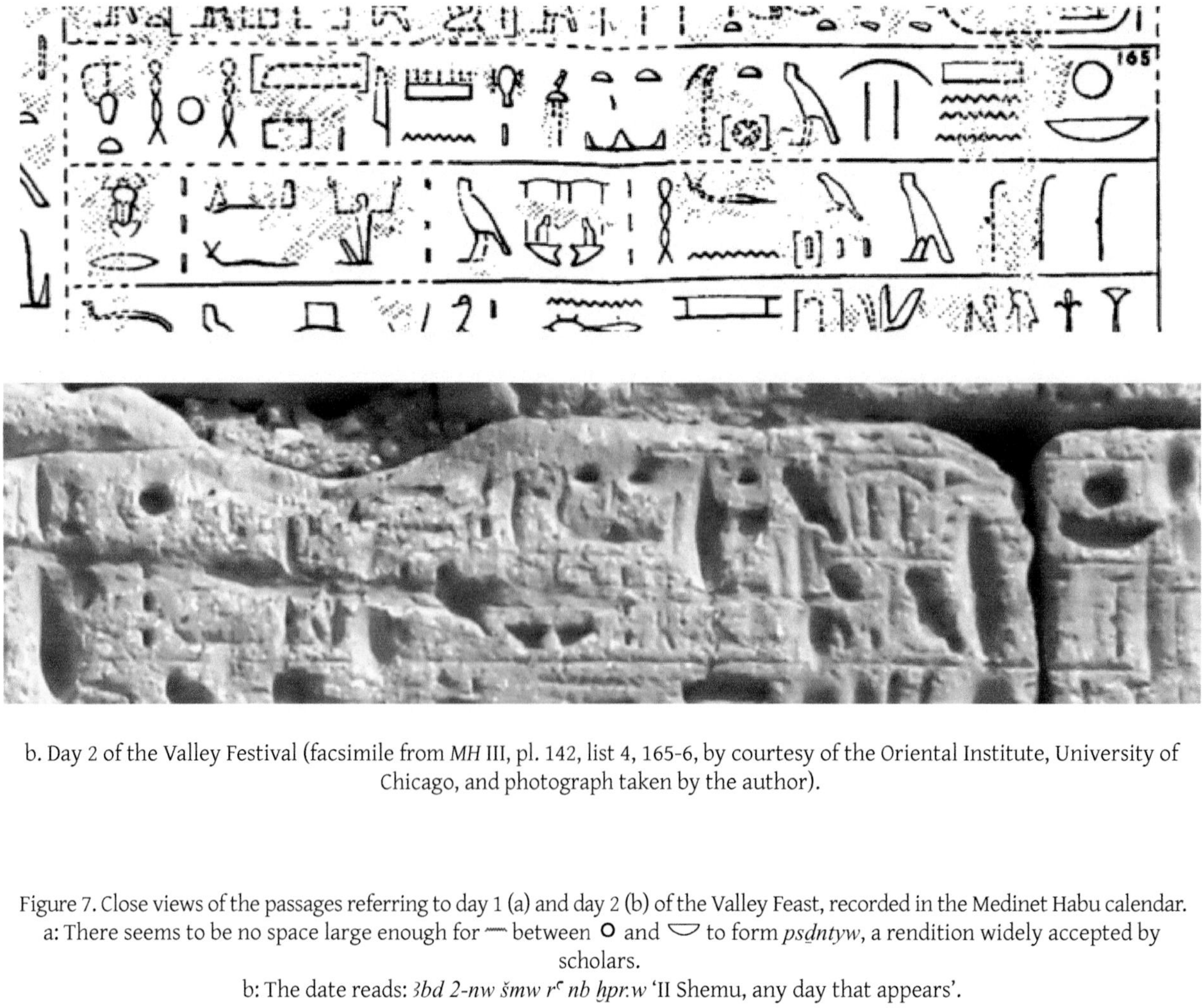

b. Day 2 of the Valley Festival (facsimile from *MH* III, pl. 142, list 4, 165-6, by courtesy of the Oriental Institute, University of Chicago, and photograph taken by the author).

Figure 7. Close views of the passages referring to day 1 (a) and day 2 (b) of the Valley Feast, recorded in the Medinet Habu calendar.
a: There seems to be no space large enough for — between O and ◡ to form *psḏntyw*, a rendition widely accepted by scholars.
b: The date reads: *ꜣbd 2-nw šmw rꜥ nb ḫpr.w* 'II Shemu, any day that appears'.

14). O. Cairo 25290, dated to the reign of Ramses IV and discovered in the Valley of the Kings, says (**1249**):

> *ḥ3.t-sp 6 3bd 3-nw šmw sw 16 ii pw in imy-r niw.t ṯ3ty Nfr-rnp.t r ir(.t?) p3 sḥn iw=f w3ḥ mw p3 m3ḥw ḥr* [two groups lost[34]]*y.t nb.t w3s.t*
>
> Year 6, III Shemu 16: the city governor, vizier, Neferrenpet came to make the order when he offered water and the garland on [ ]yt, lady of Thebes.

P. Geneva MAH 15274+P. Turin 54063, also dated to III Shemu 16 in year 6 of the same king, includes a short reference to *w3ḥ mw n n3 nsw.t-bi.ty.w* 'presenting a libation to the kings' (**1248**). This was probably one and the same ceremony as recorded in O. Cairo 25290. Two other sources, O. DeM 39 and P. Turin 1946+1949, attest the same date of III Shemu 16, but in year 32 of Ramses IV's predecessor Ramses III (**1247**). These texts record that the death of Ramses III was reported to the workmen that day. The *w3ḥ-mw* and past kings are also referred to in O. Cairo 25265, dated to IV Shemu 1, year 5 perhaps of Ramses IV, when Amun-Re crossed the river to the Wes Bank (**1311**). O. Turin 57034, dating from the time of Ramses III, records the *w3ḥ-mw* for II Shemu 8 (**1088**), four days before *p3 ḏ3y* 'the river procession' on II Shemu 12 (**1099**). The *w3ḥ-mw* could have been performed by a private person. O. BM 5634, dated to the reign of Ramses II, records that a workman performed it on II Shemu 8, following a mummification or burial rite (*wt*) of his brother on II Shemu 7 (**1087**). There were probably two types of the *w3ḥ-mw* ritual: one performed for the royal ancestors and the other for dead private individuals.[35]

Second, the Ramesside graffiti left at Thutmose III's temple at Deir el-Bahari attest pilgrimages to this site of various individuals from various places all over Egypt, and some from Nubia. Out of about 500 graffiti, 142 have been published by Marciniak (1974). A large proportion of them include a petitionary formula dedicated to Hathor, which typically begins with *ir nfr ir nfr* 'Make good! Make good!' Out of 30 dated texts, 16, including three less convincing documents, fall either in II Shemu or III Shemu and eight in IV Akhet (Table 15). Those dated to IV Akhet are most probably associated with the Hathor Festival, which was celebrated at the beginning of that month (**427**, **433–7**, **441**, and **446**). Those dated to II Shemu or III Shemu fall on various dates, which suggests their lunar nature.

It is remarkable that at the temple of Edfu the Valley Festival was celebrated on II Shemu 9, corresponding to the sixth lunar day ( *snw.t*), in year 30 of Ptolemy VIII (**1093**). Although the text seems to be specific and historical, caution must be required for taking it as echoing precisely the age-old tradition of this feast from the New Kingdom. As presented earlier in 3.2.2, the nature of the Valley Festival had been exclusively local to Thebes, and after the New Kingdom, was considerably reduced to a canonical reference, at the most a minor ritual remaining in liturgical literature and performed within the small part of a temple, perhaps like our case at Edfu.

Unlike the Opet Festival, the duration of the Valley Festival is not securely attested to in any record, except the Medinet Habu calendar, which records a two-day duration (**1171–2**). Krauss (1985, 136) regards this calendar as referring to ceremonies performed on the West Bank only and suggests a duration longer than three days (at least one day on the East Bank). By examining the aforementioned Deir el-Bahari graffiti, Marciniak (1974, 33) explains that the Valley Festival could have lasted from II Shemu to III Shemu. However, the duration of only a few days may be evidenced by O. Turin 57034, which records *p3 ḏ3y* 'the river procession' taking place on II Shemu 12 in year 22, perhaps of Ramses III (**1099**). Three consecutive days from II Shemu 11 to 13 that year were probably non-working days.[36] Two other Ramesside ostraca, O. Turin 57044 (**1161**) and O. Gardiner 11 (**1150**), record a work free day only for the day of a river procession.

In conclusion, the Valley Festival is very elusive with regard to its date and duration. Available information is too scarce to answer any of our questions. The festival was undoubtedly associated with the lunar year, but which phase of the moon determined its celebration day remains open to question. Regarding the duration, no source attests to a long one like the Opet Feast. This come as no surprise because the Valley Festival is not so far known for a time-consuming ritual like oracular sessions.

[34] *Ḥw.t-ḥr ḥry-tp smy.t*(?), as recorded on the statue of the royal butler Neferrenpet (3.4.4).

[35] It may be of some interest that a celebration took place in honour of Amenhotep I on III Shemu 11, 12, and 13 (**1228**, **1231** and **1236**), of Seti I on III Shemu 24 (**1272**), of Ramses II on III Shemu 27 (**1278** and **1280–1**), and of the queen Nefertari on II Shemu 14 and 15 (**1107** and **1111**). The *w3ḥ-mw* is not recorded for these occasions and it is difficult to confirm what they commemorated, apart from III Shemu 27 associated with Ramses II, which Helck (1959, 119), Krauss (1977, 147), and Kitchen (1982, 43) regard as the accession day of that king, a hypothesis opposed by Murnane (1975/6, 25). If this hypothesis is correct, then III Shemu 24, when a celebration was performed for Seti I, might be associated with the death of this king (for the debate on his accession date, see Hornung 2006, 210).

[36] Jauhiainen (2009, 151) regards this non-business period as beginning from II Shemu 8.

3.3. Designation of the Valley Festival

The Valley Festival was one of celebrations that took place exclusively at Thebes. Despite its local nature, this feast enjoyed a prominent position for its setting at the centre of Amun's cult and in association with the royal cult. Hence, II Shemu, in which this festival took place, was called *pꜣ-n-in.t* 'the (month) of the Valley' in Egyptian and Payni in Coptic.

The topographical constituent the 'Valley' denotes the widely open wadi at Deir el-Bahari on the West Bank. The terraced temple of Hatshepsut, called *ḏsr-ḏsr.w-imn* the 'Holy of the Holies of Amun', dominates a large part of the basin below the escarpments at this site. Like other festivals (1.2.3), the standard format *ḥb=f nfr* was employed for the Valley Festival to be called *ḥb=f nfr n in.t*, which is recorded on the north wall of the upper terrace belonging to Hatshepsut's temple (Figure 10, col. 1). However, this part of the wall was restored after the Amarna Period and thus we cannot confirm that this celebration was designated as such when Hatshepsut was in power. In fact, two other sources from her time attest *ḥb=f n ḏsr-ḏsr.w r mnw* [*Mꜣꜥ.t-kꜣ-rꜥ*] 'His Festival of Djeser-djeseru to the monument of [Maatkare]' (another part of the temple of Deir el-Bahari temple: 3.4.2) and *ẖn.t n.t ḏsr-ḏsr(.w)* the 'Navigation of Djeser-djeser(u)' (Red Chapel),[37] an emphasis placed on her own monument.

When only *ḏsr(.w)* appears in texts, it may or may not refer to the Valley Feast, but can also be used as a more general term for the 'necropolis' on the West Bank and celebrations that took place there (3.5.1). Such broad usage of term was also the case for *imnt.t* the 'West'. It hardly appeared independently but in conjunction with the *in.t* when referring to the Valley Feast. Hence, *ḥb=f n in.t imnt.t* is attested in the tomb of Userhat (TT 56), dating from the time of Thutmose III to Thutmose IV (3.5.2.2) and in the tomb of an unknown individual (TT 129), dating from the time of Thutmose III to Amenhotep II.[38] The more elaborate expression *ḥb=f nfr in.t m ẖn.t n.t imnt.t* 'His Beautiful Festival of the Valley at the Navigation of the West' is documented in the tomb of Neferrenpet (TT 147), dating from the reign of Thutmose IV to Amenhotep III.[39] There is one instance from the tomb of Kaemheribsen (TT 98), dating from the time of Amenhotep II to Thutmose IV, where the *imnt.t* is the only main constituent as *ḥb=f nfr n imnt.t* and seems to refer to the Valley Feast.[40]

Royal monuments also show some variations of the designation. For example, Amenhotep III's building stela includes two references to this feast: *ḥb=f n in.t m ẖn.t ꞽImn n.t imnt.t* 'His Festival of the Valley at the Navigation of Amun of the West' and *ẖn.t=f n.t imnt.t* 'His Navigation of the West'.[41]

It should be born in mind, however, that the Hathor Feast, which was celebrated on IV Akhet 1, was referred to as *ḥb n imnt.t* in one text (**437**). Thus, the *imnt.t* alone cannot be regarded as bearing witness to one specific celebration.

3.4. Sequence of the Valley Festival at the temple

The aforementioned Red Chapel and Deir el-Bahari temple, both built by Hatshepsut, are the sources of the earliest evidence for the Valley Festival from royal monuments. It is only possible with these two monuments to reconstruct the general sequence of this celebration. At the upper terrace of the temple of Deir el-Bahari, the scenes in question extend on the northern half of the eastern wall and the whole northern wall.[42] These walls are, in most part, destroyed in their upper registers, especially in the eastern section. As a whole they represent a return travel of the Theban triad: the outward journey in the lower register and the return journey in the upper register. The poor state of preservation today and alterations to the decorations after the reign of Hatshepsut make it difficult to obtain a clear picture of the sequence of rituals. Naville (1895, vol. 5, pl. 122) published only the northern half of the lower register belonging to the eastern wall, where Amun's river procession is depicted. After a long time, Dąbrowska-Smektała and Gartkiewicz (1968, pl. 1) edited the south half of this wall, which represents two episodes before Amun sets for the river journey.[43] Subsequently, Karkowski (1976, fig. 1) published additional fragments, which belong to Amun's barque procession moving towards a quay. The conservation work on these walls was completed by the Polish-Egyptian team in the 1986/1987 season, but only a tiny proportion of the upper register of the north wall, which represents episodes on the West Bank, has so far been published by Karkowski (1992, 160–2, figs 3–4) and Kwaśnica (2001, 91, fig. 3, left). Hence, the representations on the north wall are roughly reproduced in Figure 8. It is possible to divide the Valley Festival into seventeen episodes by adding other sources to the Deir el-Bahari reliefs (see the table below). In the following sections, these episodes will be explored in five groups for convenience.

---

37 Burgos and Larché 2006, vol. 1, 98, Block 40.

38 PM I-1², 244 (1, I).

39 PM I-1², 258 (8); Ockinga 2004, 127. Phraseology similar to this is attested in the tomb of Tjanuny (TT 74), dating from the time of Thutmose III to Thutmose IV (3.5.2.1) and in the tomb of Heqaerneheh (TT 64), dating from the time of Thutmose IV to Amenhotep III (PM I-1², 128 (2); *Urk.* IV, 1573: 16).

40 PM I-1², 204 (1, 2); *Urk.* IV, 1500: 5. This text accompanies a scene representing the deceased couple receiving Amun's bouquet from two daughters, who carry a sistrum and a menit respectively.

41 Cairo 34025 recto (PM II², 447–8; *Urk.* IV, 1650: 7–8 and 1653: 16; Petrie 1897, 24–5, pl. 12, ll. 9 and 20).

42 PM II², 358 (81–3). According to Wiercińska (1990, 68 and 2006, 308), the same decorative arrangement was employed for the valley temple of Thutmose III, where many fragments of scenes depicting a river procession of Amun were uncovered.

43 A slightly better edition of the identical plate was published in the same year by Dabrowska-Smektała (1968, pl. 1).

section		Episode		main source
3.4.1	rituals at and departure from Karnak	1	offering to the Theban triad at Karnak	East wall, upper terrace, Deir el-Bahari
		2	procession departing Karnak	Block 40 of the Red Chapel; Hypostyle Hall of Karnak
3.4.2	river procession to the West Bank	3	outward river procession	East wall, upper terrace, Deir el-Bahari
3.4.3	tour on the West Bank	4	arrival on the West Bank	North wall, upper terrace, Deir el-Bahari; Stela Cairo 43591; TT 19 (3)
		5	divine barques at way-stations	North wall, upper terrace, Deir el-Bahari; portico of Seti I's temple at Qurna
3.4.4	rituals at Deir el-Bahari	6	arrival at Deir el-Bahari	North wall, upper terrace at Deir el-Bahari; Block 273 of the Red Chapel
		7	offering to the Theban triad	North wall, upper terrace, Deir el-Bahari
		8	king taken before Werethekau by two gods	North wall, upper terrace, Deir el-Bahari
		9	king taken before Amun by a goddess	North wall, upper terrace, Deir el-Bahari
		10	procession departing Deir el-Bahari	North wall, upper terrace, Deir el-Bahari
3.4.5	return journey and rituals back at Karnak	11	divine barques at way-stations	North wall, upper terrace, Deir el-Bahari
		12	departure from the West Bank	Block 126 of the Red Chapel
		13	return river procession	Blocks 279 and 291 of the Red Chapel; sanctuary of Karnak
		14	arrival at Karnak	Block 303 of the Red Chapel; Court 1 of Medinet Habu
		15	presenting four *mr.t*-boxes to Amun's barque	Block 303 of the Red Chapel
		16	driving the Apis bull before Amun	Block 128 of the Red Chapel
		17	musical play and dance	Block 61 of the Red Chapel

Sequence of the Valley Festival.

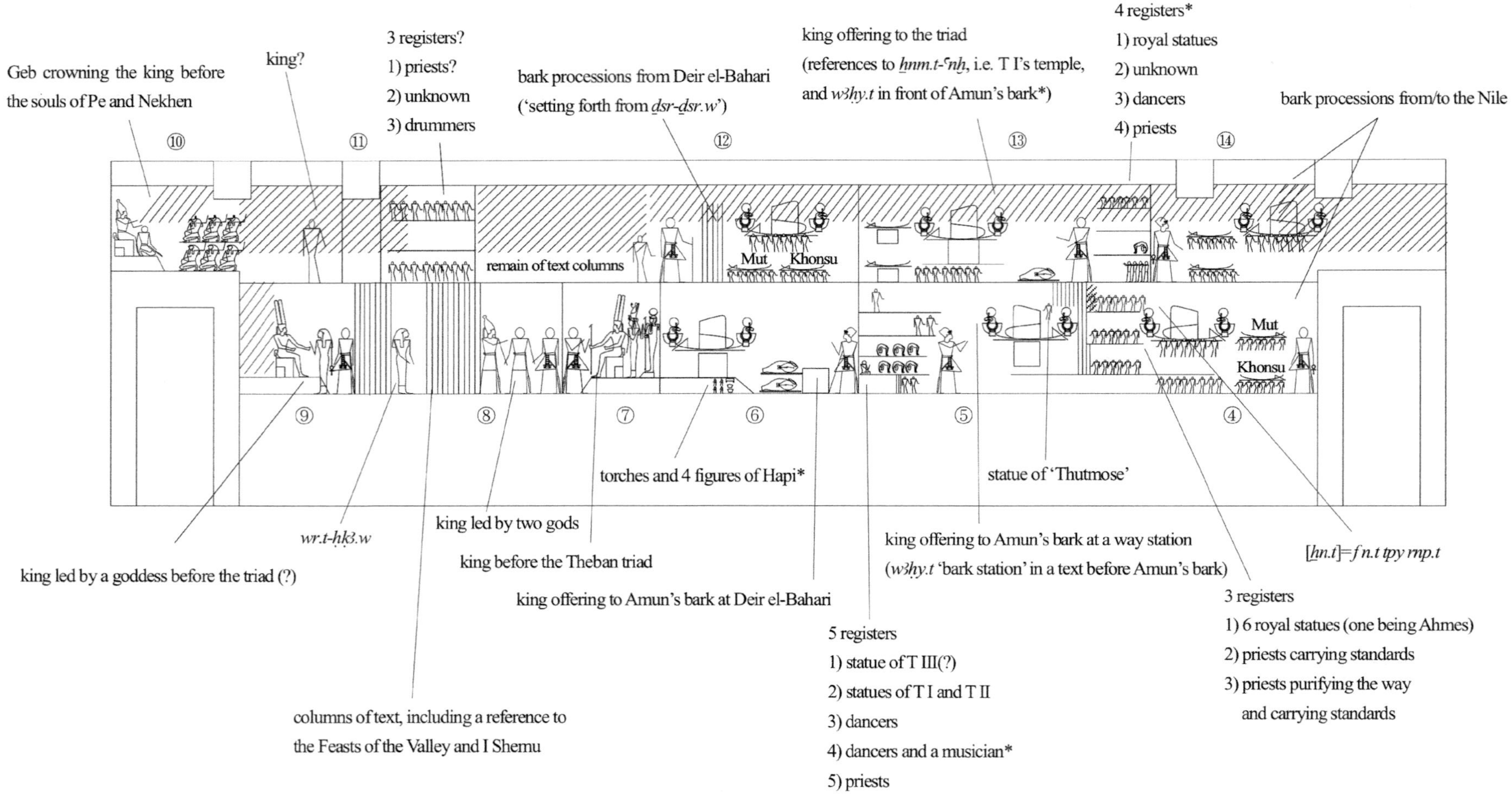

Figure 8. Elevation of the northern wall of the upper terrace depicting the Valley Festival at Hatshepsut's temple at Deir el-Bahari.

* These scenes are partially published by Karkowski (1992, 160–2, figs 3–5) and Kwaśnica (2001, 91, fig. 3, left).

3.4.1. *Rituals at and departure from Karnak*

In the Deir el-Bahari reliefs the first ceremony performed at Karnak is represented at the right end of the lower register belonging to the eastern wall. Thutmose III is portrayed presenting offerings to the Theban triad. In the original decoration Hatshepsut had been represented together with Thutmose III, but her figure was later replaced by piled offerings. Such an alteration was made in all the following scenes, in each of which Thutmose III appears alone today, and therefore will not be noted unless a special remark is necessary. Thutmose III wears the elaborate Atef-crown combined with two spiral ram horns, two cow horns, and a sun disk. The king wearing this crown appears in five other instances in association with the Valley Feast: Hatshepsut leading Amun's barque;[44] Seti I kneeling before Amun-Re;[45] the dead Seti I following the barques of the Theban triad[46]; Ramses I being anointed by Seti I;[47] Ramses II being led by gods and crowned by Amun.[48] All these representations are likely to portray the deified king, whether he is reigning or dead. According to Collier (1996, 68), the Atef-crown symbolized the renewed kingship over Egypt in the other world, an opposite function from the Double-crown that displayed the earthly sovereignty.

The fact that Thutmose III wears this crown at the very beginning of the festival shows that the king had already embodied a solar character before the divine procession set forth from Karnak to the West Bank. In the scene of Seti I at Karnak, Amun-Re says: *smn(=i)* [*n=*]*k ḫ*ʿ*.w ḥr tp=k ḫkr n R*ʿ *ḥr wp.t*[*=k*] '(I) place [for] you the crowns on your head and the ornament of Re on [your] forehead.' This scene is preceded by two episodes of purification and induction of the king, who is described as *bsi r ḥw.t-nṯr n it*[*=k*] 'inducted into the temple of [your] father' and *r s.t wr.t* [*r*] *m33 it=k* [*Imn-r*ʿ] 'to the great seat [to] see your father [Amun-Re].' This suggests that like at the Opet Festival the king came out from the palace to Karnak.[49]

A series of episodes parallel to this are carved on the barque sanctuary of Karnak, which was erected by Philip Arrhidaeus.[50] They too include rites of purification and induction of the king, plus another scene of vesting the king in between. In the last scene, the king is crowned by Amun-Re, behind whom Amenet is portrayed suckling the young king. Unlike the Deir el-Bahari relief, his headdress is not the Atef-crown but the White-crown. Because Amun's return journey at the Valley Festival is represented in two registers below, it is not impossible that the representations of the top register can also be associated with this festival.[51]

The rituals that had been performed in the precinct of Karnak were followed by a barque procession to the Nile. This is represented on the Red Chapel and at Deir el-Bahari, both depicting Amun's barque only. The latter, despite its poor state today, preserves more details: priests and a statue of the reigning king lead the divine barque.[52] The northern wall of the Great Hypostyle Hall of Karnak, dated to the time of Seti I, represents the same episode, including the barques of Mut and Khonsu.[53] It, however, does not show notable characteristics.

Amun-Re revealed himself from Karnak in the morning. Two reliefs at the temple of Medinet Habu portray Ramses III appearing from the palace:[54]

> *ḫ*ʿ*.w nsw.t mi.ty R*ʿ *m* ʿ*ḥ.t n ḥw.t=f šps.t r sḫ*ʿ *it=f Imn m ḥb=f n in.t ḥk3* ʿ*n m pr=f mi nsw.t m ḫ*ʿʿ*=f m ḥry.t ḥr tp dw3y.t m* ʿ*ḥ.t=f šps(.t) n.ty mi 3ḫ.t n R*ʿ *psḏ=f m p.t r*ʿ *nb Imn-r*ʿ *ḥ*ʿ*.w ḥr ḥw.t=f psḏ.t=f ḥtp(.w) m k3ri=sn sr=w ḥb.w ḥḥ n rnp.wt ḏ.t m ḳn nḫt n s3=sn nb t3.wy Wsr-m3*ʿ*.t-r*ʿ*-mry-imn*
>
> Appearance of the king, who is like Re, from the palace of his august house to cause his father Amun to appear at His Festival of the Valley! The beautiful rulership comes forth like the king at his rising in the sky in the morning from his augus(t) palace, which is like the horizon of Re when he shines in the sky every day, when Amun-Re rejoices on his house and his Ennead are contente(d) in their chapel. They foresee festivals (for) a million of years and everlastingness in valour and strength for their son, lord of the Two Lands, Usermaatre-meryamen.

---

[44] Red Chapel (Lacau and Chevrier 1977, vol. 1, 192–4, vol. 2, pl. 9 (Block 303); Burgos and Larché 2006, vol. 1, 111).

[45] North wall of the Great Hypostyle Hall (PM II², 45 (154, III-4); Nelson 1981, pl. 200).

[46] Two scenes on the south wall of the Great Hypostyle Hall (PM II², 47 (158, III-2) and 48 (159, III-1); Nelson 1981, pls 53 and 76.

[47] Room XXIX of the temple of Qurna (PM II², 418 (106–7)).

[48] Room XXVIII of the temple of Qurna (PM II², 417 (101–2, I-1, II-2); *KRI* I, 221–2 and II, 641–2).

[49] O'Connor 1989, 82.

[50] Uppermost register of the south exterior wall (PM II², 100 (291, I); Gardiner 1950, pl. 2).

[51] Philip Arrhidaeus, according to his inscription, replaced Thutmose III's barque sanctuary, which had once stood on the site of Hatshepsut's Red Chapel since, at least, year 46 of Thutmose III (van Siclen 1984). Fragmentary blocks belonging to Thutmose III's sanctuary, uncovered at Karnak, display a style parallel to Hatshepsut's building (Legrain 1917, pl. 7 (1–3); *idem* 1929, fig. 96; Foucart 1924, pl. 7).

[52] Dąbrowska-Smektała and Gartkiewicz 1968, pl. 1; Karkowski 1976, fig. 1. One of the earliest attestations of a statue of the living king that followed Amun of Karnak is found in the annals of Amenemhat II, discovered at Memphis (Altenmüller and Moussa 1991, 21). However, the context, in which the statue was used, is not specified.

[53] PM II², 45 (154, III-1); Nelson 1981, pl. 197.

[54] PM II², 495 (78, c); *MH* IV, pl. 239, A; *KRI* V, 226: 11–3.

Amun's journey was analogous to travelling on the day-barque. On the entrance thickness of the tomb of Tjanuny (TT 74), dating from the time of Thutmose IV to Amenhotep III, the deceased couple is depicted in adoration and the legend, which is mostly damaged, reads:[55]

> *[dwꜣ Rꜥ m wbn=f m ꜣḫ.t iꜣbt.t n.t p.t in sš nsw.t mꜣꜥ mr=f imy-r sš.w mšꜥ Ṯꜣ-n-ny mꜣꜥ ḫrw ḏd=f inḏ ḥr=k Rꜥ m wbn=k Ꞽmn sḫm nṯr.w m wbn=k sḥḏ=k tꜣ.wy ḏꜣi=k ḥry.t m ḥtp.w ib=k ꜣw.w] m mꜥnḏ.t [swꜣy]=k [ḥr ṯsw n mr nḫꜣ.wy] sḫr ḫfty.w=k iw=k ḫꜥ.ti m [ḥw.t] šw ḥtp.ti m [ꜣḫ.t imnt.t šsp.n ḥm=k imꜣḫy ꜥ.wy mw.t=k m ḥꜣ=k ẖr.t hrw n.t rꜥ nb mꜣ(=i) tw m ḥb=k nfr m ẖn.t=k n ḏsr-ḏsr.w] di=k ḥtp=i m ḥr.t ir.t.n(=i) m ḥs.wt n.(w)t nṯr nfr mi irr.wt n mꜣꜥ tp tꜣ*
>
> [Adoring Re at his rising from the eastern horizon of the sky by the true royal scribe, his beloved, and overseer of the army scribes, Tjanuny, true of voice. He says: 'Hail to you, Re at your rising and Amun, mighty one of the gods, at your rising. You illuminate the Two Lands and cross over the sky in satisfaction with your heart being extended] on the day-barque. You [pass on the sandbank of the sea of the two swords] with your enemies being overthrown, when you appear from [the house] of the sun and are satisfied in [the western horizon for your person has received veneration so that your mother's arms are around you daily and everyday. May (I) witness you at Your Beautiful Festival at your navigation to Djeser-djeseru.] May you let me rest in the tomb, which (I) made with praises of the good god like what is done for the righteous on earth.'

The reference to the sandbank of the sea of the two swords is particularly significant because it connotes the mid-day, when the enemy of the sun is defeated, as evidenced by the Book of the Day.[56] Contrary to the Opet Festival, when Amun's barge was likened to *mskt.t* the 'night-barque', his journey at the Valley Festival accorded with its geographical orientation from Karnak to Deir el-Bahari and the circuit of the sun. Later evidence also refers to the day-barque in association with the Theban West.[57] Note that the king is referred to as a 'good god', an epithet often used in association with the god Osiris. Here the king is figuratively deified as a supreme one in the netherworld. Like the king, Amun-Re was already an embodiment of the full divine force when he departed Karnak. This is a marked difference from the Opet Feast, when the regeneration of Amun's deteriorated power was performed at the temple of Luxor (2.4.9). The distribution of his power started from the very beginning of the Valley Festival because elsewhere in the same tomb it is recorded that a divine bouquet was delivered from the Theban triad and *Ꞽmn.t ḥry.t-ib ip.t-s.wt* 'Amenet-who-dwells-in-Karnak' to the deceased on the West Bank, probably directly from the temple of Karnak, rather than from one of the memorial temples (3.6.5).[58]

It is remarkable that Amenet accompanied the Theban triad on this occasion. This is evident from a barque procession scene in Ramses III's temple at Karnak, which may represent the Valley Festival.[59] In this scene the barques of the Theban triad are followed by those of Amenet-who-dwells-in-Karnak and *Ꞽmn ẖnm.t-nḥḥ* 'Amun-of-Khenemet-neheh', who was worshipped at Ramses III's memorial temple at Medinet Habu.[60] This relief has not so far been attributed to an episode of a specific occasion. However, we may witness a historical account here because the long dedication text carved on the same wall begins with the date *ḥꜣ.t-sp 22 ꜣbd 2-nw* [one or two groups lost *ḥr*] *ḥm* ... 'Year 22, the second month of [under] the person of ...'[61] This date marked Ramses III's endowment to Karnak in that year, by which this temple was supposedly completed.[62] Such a dedication rite is likely to have taken place in a ceremonial setting, probably at his accession anniversary celebrated from I Shemu 26 to II Shemu 15

[55] PM I-1², 144 (1); Brack and Brack 1977, 23–4, pl. 19, a.
[56] Piankoff 1942, 18–9; Assmann 1969, 296–7 and 1983b, 77–80.
[57] One in association with the Decade Ritual and Amenopet (barque shrine at Medinet Habu from the Ptolemaic Period: PM II², 470 (47); Dümichen 1869, pl. 36, e) and another with Medinet Habu (propylon of the Khonsu temple: PM II², 225 (1-2, lintel); *Urk.* VIII, 59, k; Clère 1961, pl. 14; Klotz 2012, 387, n. 37).

[58] Our knowledge of Amenet, a female counterpart to Amun, is very limited. She appears to have possessed her own priesthood in later periods. The earliest surviving evidence is from the Twenty-Sixth Dynasty (Leitz 2002a, vol. 1, 358, L). See Fairman 1934 for attestations of her priesthood; Guermeur 2004, 271 and Klotz 2012, 70, n. 193 for her cult place. She is associated with Neith and her priesthood is attested in the title *ḥm-nṯr n N.t-Ꞽmn.t*, dated to the Ptolemaic Period (Sackho-Autissier 2003, 575, n. d). Neith-Amenet is also referred to at Deir el-Bahari, dated to the time of Ptolemy VIII (PM II², 367 (146)).
[59] PM II², 28 (51–3); *RIK* I, pl. 17, A.
[60] Contrary to the legend, the aegis of this barque represents a human head, rather than a ram's head, which clearly displays its identity as a royal portable shrine. Such a royal barque and a statue contained inside most probably belonged to each of the royal memorial temples on the West Bank. *ẖnm.t-nḥḥ* was not only used to designate Ramses III's temple but could also be associated with a deified form of any ruler, who was worshipped on the West Bank. The Ramesseum, for example, was called *s.t=f wr.t [m] ḥw.t[-nṯr] Rꜥ-ms-sw-mry-imn ẖnm.t-nḥḥ m pr Ꞽmn* 'his (Amun-Re) western/great seat [in] the tem[ple] of Ramses-meryamen, united with eternity, in the domain of Amun' (triple shrine at Luxor: PM II², 310 (43); K*RI* II, 615: 1–2). Also see Teeter 2012, 51 for the Osirianization of Amun and the king in the Ramesside Period.
[61] *RIK* I, pl. 23; K*RI* V 221: 5; Seele 1935, 224–41.
[62] Haring 1997, 89. The vizier Ta was certainly active at Thebes in year 22 (Table 6). In addition, P. Harris I (XVIIa: 3–4) records the accession anniversary of Ramses III only for year 22 onwards (**1033**).

(**1033**) or at the Valley Feast. Hence, it is not too daring to restore the missing season in the text as *šmw*.

As described in 2.4.6, the Opet Festival is magnificently represented on the whole western exterior wall of this temple, while there is no single representation of the Valley Festival executed by Ramses III at Karnak. His predecessors, Seti I and Ramses II, depicted this celebration together with the Opet Feast in the Great Hypostyle Hall. Given that Ramses III was keen on following the styles of Ramses II in many respects, it is not surprising that Ramses III would have desired to represent the Valley Festival somewhere at Karnak. The fact that his temple once stood as an isolated building before the then main entrance to Karnak (second pylon today) underlines its function as a way-station used for divine processions.[63] This recalls the triple shrine of Seti II, which was located to the northwest in the same area and undoubtedly used as a barque chapel.[64]

Amenet's barque is also included in a processional scene at the Ramesseum, which probably represents the Valley Festival.[65] The barque processions of the Theban triad, of which that of Amun is missing today, are followed by those of Amenet, Ahmes-Nefertari, and Ramses II. This parallels the southern portico of Seti I's memorial temple at Qurna, where the barque processions of Seti I and Ahmes-Nefertari are added to those of the Theban triad.[66] Two identical bandeau texts carved on both halves of the portico include a reference to 'His Valley Feast' among building works completed by Ramses II in honour of his father Seti I.[67] It is, therefore, plausible that the representations on both halves of the portico as well as the rooms behind the portico are associated with this celebration.[68]

At Hatshepsut's Deir el-Bahari temple portable statues of Thutmose III are represented in the scenes of the Valley Festival. Seti I's statue is likewise carved in the Great Hypostyle Hall at Karnak.[69] They accompany Amun's barque when the god was present at Karnak. What does the presence of these royal statues and the divine barques of Amenet and Amun-of-Khenemet-neheh at Karnak mean? Karkowski (1992, 162) explains that the royal statues were collected from royal memorial temples in advance to participate in Amun's journey from Karnak and then returned to their home on the West Bank at the end of the festival before Amun crossed the Nile back to the East Bank. This assumption can be corroborated by the fact that several royal statues of predecessors disappear from the last episode on the West Bank in the Deir el-Bahari reliefs (Figure 8, Episode 14).

The collection of royal statues at Karnak may represent a distinctive feature of the Valley Festival, when the divine power appears to have accumulated at Karnak and then been delivered to Deir el-Bahari and the royal memorial temples by means of divine and royal portable images.

3.4.2. River procession to the West Bank

Both outward and return river processions will be examined together in this section because they are almost identical each other when depicted together. Representations of the return procession from the West Bank survive on the Red Chapel of Hatshepsut and on the Karnak sanctuary of Philip Arrhidaeus in a parallel fashion, both depicting Amun's journey only. In the latter example a feeble legend remains in front of a figure of the king, who is aboard the royal vessel and pulls a rope tied to Amun's barge on his way back to Karnak. It reads: *ḥtp nsw.t m wiꜣ m ḥꜣ.t ii m ḥtp m* [*imn*] *t.t* 'The king rests on the barge in advance, coming in peace from the [Wes]t.'[70]

The outward journey is preserved at Hatshepsut's Deir el-Bahari temple. This scene is apparently juxtaposed with the return journey of the Opet Festival, which is represented in a parallel fashion on the other half of the wall (2.4.6). Thus, detailed description of it is not essential here, apart from some accompanying texts.[71]

The caption above the prow of the first crew ship reads: *wḏ r tꜣ r imnt.t m ꜣw.t-ib tꜣ r-ḏr=f m ḥꜥꜥ.wt m ḥb pn nfr n nṯr pn nhm=sn dd=sn iꜣw.w swꜣš=sn* [*Mꜣꜥ.t-kꜣ-rꜥ*] 'Landing at the land to the West in delight. The entire land is in jubilations at this beautiful festival of this god. They jubilate. They praise. They applaud [Maatkare].'[72]

[63] Mojsov 2012, 286.

[64] These buildings at Karnak were called *ḥw.t-nṯr n.t ḥḥ m rnp.wt* the 'temple of millions of years' (Rondot 1997, 144). The Great Hypostyle Hall of Karnak was also described as standing: *m pr Ỉmn m-ḫft ḥr n ip.t-s.wt m inr ḥḏ rwḏ.t s.t ḥtp n nb nṯr.w* 'in the domain of Amun in front of Karnak, (built) in white hard stones (as) a resting place for the lord of the gods' (Rondot 1997, 17, 139). Significantly, the memorial temples were also called the *s.t ḥtp* in association with the Valley Festival: the temples of Amenhotep III (*Urk.* IV, 1650: 7), of Seti I (PM II², 410; *KRI* I, 214: 12), of Ramses II (*KRI* II, 650: 2), and of an unknown ruler (a reused block: PM II², 237 (47, b); Schwaller de Lubicz 1982, vol. 2, pl. 267).

[65] The southern wall of the so-called astronomical room, where eight barques are carved (incorrect entries in PM II² (439 (22–3), which are to be amended as: (22) I, 1, barques of Khonsu, 2, of Amenet, II, 1, of Mut, 2, of Ramses II; (23) I, 1, barque of Khonsu, 2, of Ahmes-Nefertari, II, 1, of Mut, 2, of Ramses II). *KRI* II, 652–4.

[66] PM II², 408 (6–7).

[67] North half (PM II², 409 (below 12); *LD* III, pl. 152, a; *KRI* II, 636, 4–5) and south half (PM II², 409 (below 6); *KRI* II, 637, 5).

[68] Unfortunately, these representations have not yet been fully published. This is also the case for the scenes in the neighboring Hypostyle Hall behind the portico. This hall was undoubtedly used at the Valley Feast, which is referred to on the architraves (PM II², 410 (16–26), 417–9 (98–116); *KRI* I, 214: 12).

[69] PM II², 47 (158, III); Nelson 1981, pl. 53, col. 53. Note that Amun's barque is carried by the Souls of Pe and Nekhen, which is also represented at the Akh-menu (PM II², 112 (348)).

[70] PM II², 100 (290, II); Legrain 1917, pl. 4; Bothmer 1952, fig. 7.

[71] For detailed description of the scene see Karkowski 1992, 156–9.

[72] Naville 1895, vol. 5, pl. 122; Werbrouck 1949, 89; *Urk.* IV, 309: 5–10.

Another legend accompanying the second galley describes a man at the prow as: *ꜥš ḥ3.t imy wr.t [mni].t nfr.t n ity[.t] ḫr it Ỉm[n] r ḥb=f n ḏsr-ḏsr.w r mnw [M3ꜥ.t-k3-rꜥ]* 'A pilot on the starboard side (says): "Good [moor]ing for the sovereign with the father Amu[n] at His Festival of Djeser-djeseru to the monument of [Maatkare]!"'[73] Between these texts is located another caption, which contains cartouches of Thutmose II and III. If we take the reference to Thutmose II as part of the name of the royal barge, this text can be read:

> *ir.t hnw.w in is.wt wi3 n nsw.t ꜥ3-ḫpr-n-rꜥ-dw3-t3.wy ḏd=sn p3 ḥb nfr n p3 ḥk3 ḫꜥ Ỉmn im=f ḥr sw3ḥ rnp.wt s3=f nsw.t-bi.ty Mn-ḫpr-rꜥ ḥr s.t Ḥr n.t ꜥnḫ.w mi Rꜥ ḏ.t*
>
> Making jubilation by the crews of the royal ship 'Aakheperenre (Thutmose II)-is-the-one-who-adores-the-Two-Lands.' They say: 'The beautiful festival for the ruler! May Amun appear therein, establishing the years of his son, the king of Upper and Lower Egypt, Menkheperre (Thutmose III) on the throne of Horus of the living like Re, forever!'

This text was probably added to an older text when Thutmose III began the proscription of Hatshepsut in year 43. Therefore, his royal vessel was named after not the queen but his father. The ascendance to the seat of Horus of this king points to the renewal of the kingship, the same ideological orientation as the Opet Festival. An expression parallel to this is attested in a broken relief of Mentuhotep II from his temple at Deir el-Bahari.[74] This relief portrays Mentuhotep rowing a boat and wearing the White-crown. The first of the two episodes preceding this scene represents Amun embracing the king. The god says: *di.n(=i) n=k Ḥr ḥr s.t=f mi wḏ.t.n(=i) ꜥnḫ.ti ḏ.t* '(I) gave you (as) Horus on his throne according to what (I) decreed. Live forever!' Portraying the king rowing a boat is reminiscent of another Middle Kingdom example discovered in Senusret I's court at Karnak, where he is depicted rowing towards the ithyphallic Amun, who stands on stairs.[75] It is, however, difficult to conclude whether these Middle Kingdom representations can be associated with the Valley Feast.

The outward journey is also painted in the tomb of Amenmes (TT 19), dating from the time of Ramses I to Ramses II (Figure 16).[76] This is the only private tomb that illustrates a river procession of the Valley Festival. The scene includes the barges of the Theban triad, of which that of Khonsu is missing today, and continues onto the adjacent wall, which represents ceremonies performed on the West Bank. Amun's barge arrives at an elevated platform and is greeted by a portable image of the seated Amenhotep I. It is one of various forms of this deified king worshipped at western Thebes. The legend reads: *Ỉmn-ḥtp n p3 wb3 nty ḥr m3 it=f Ỉmn-rꜥ nsw.t nṯr.w m ḥb=f nfr n in.t* 'Amenhotep-of-the-Forecourt, who sees his father Amun-Re, king of the gods, at His Beautiful Festival of the Valley.' The inclusion of his image in this scene is explained by the fact that Amenmes was the 'high-priest of Amenhotep-of-the-Forecourt'. The stela of Ameneminet (Cairo 43591), another private monument from the Nineteenth Dynasty, also represents Amun's arrival at the West Bank.[77] In the lower register Ameneminet is portrayed kneeling and adoring Amun's barge. The legend reads:

> *ḏd=f my n=i Ỉmn ḳn mni di=k pḥ=i p3 ꜥḏ my n=i Ỉmn p3 šd bg3w di=k pḥ=i t3 rwḏ my n=i Ỉmn mḫnw di=k pḥ=i imnt.t r pḥ.tw im3ḫ m ḥtp m dd (n)=i nb w3s.t*
>
> He says: 'Come to me Amun, mighty herdsman! May you cause me to reach the shore. Come to me Amun, the saviour of the shipwrecked! May you cause me to reach the firm ground. Come to me Amun, ferryman! May you cause me to reach the West in order to reach you, the venerable one, in peace with what the lord of Thebes gives me'.

In the upper register Amun's portable barque is depicted led by a king, probably Ramses II, from Seti I's memorial temple at Qurna. In front of the temple pylon Paser, who was the vizier from the time of Seti I to Ramses II, stands in adoration.[78]

It was from the time of Hatshepsut onwards that Karnak and the West Bank were referred to by using the topographical name *ḫft.t-ḥr-nb=s* 'she who is before her lord'.[79] This phrase was later transformed into a goddess of the same name.[80] The memorial temples of Seti I and Ramses IV were regarded as

This part of the original relief has been removed and possessed by the Berlin Museum (Berlin 1636: Karkowski 1997, 106–7 for photograph).

[73] Naville 1895, vol. 5, pl. 122; *Urk.* IV, 310: 2–5.

[74] Arnold 1974, vol. 2, pl. 22.

[75] Gabolde 1998, 49–51, pls 9–10.

[76] PM I-1², 33 (3, I); Foucart 1928, pls 2–8. A scene similar to this is attested in TT 217 (2, IV), but its association with a specific celebration is uncertain.

[77] PM I-2², 699; *KRI* I, 403: 9–11; Foucart 1924, 67, 123, pl. 11; Bruyère, *Deir el-Médineh (1935–40)*, vol. 2, 7–8, fig. 76. Also see ibid., 44–5, fig. 127 (no. 157) for a stone fragment depicting a part of Amun's barge.

[78] The vizier Paser, owner of TT 106, restored Djeser-djeseru after it was damaged during the Amarna Period (Pinch 1993, 9). It was for this achievement that he was remembered together with Ramses II by the Deir el-Medina workmen, as evidenced by many stelae and tomb representations (TT 4 (6), TT 7 (9), and TT 10 (6)). Exell (2009, 90–1) relates some of these monuments to the Valley Feast.

[79] *Urk* IV, 312: 10.

[80] Leitz 2002a, vol. 5, 725.

located *ḫft-ḥr n ip.t-s.wt* 'before Karnak' over the river.[81] The river procession perhaps arrived at a site close to these temples or to the memorial temple dedicated to Amenhotep I and Ahmes-Nefertari, the latter of which was called *mn-s.t* and located between Qurna and the mouth of the causeway to Deir el-Bahari. This may explain the presence of the portable images of the early Eighteenth Dynasty figures in some of our sources.

After the procession crossed the river, it probably took a canal way to a certain point before reaching Deir el-Bahari.[82] The Red Chapel of Hatshepsut attests three canals in the following order: [*mr nsw.t*] *M3ˁ.t-k3-*[*rˁ*] the 'royal canal of Maatka[re]'; *mr nsw.t ˁ3-ḫpr-k3-rˁ* the 'royal canal of Aakheperkare (Thutmose I)'; *mr nsw.t Mn-ḫpr-rˁ s.t-ib-nnw* the 'royal canal of Menkheperre (Thutmose III), Seat-of-the-Heart-of-Nun'.[83] Because each of these canals appears to follow an entry for the memorial temple of each ruler, it unequivocally designates a waterway leading to the temple. In particular, the temples of Thutmose I and Thutmose III are thought to have stood next to each other on the desert edge. It may be that the three canals converged near these temples.

3.4.3. *Tour on the West Bank*

This section will include both outbound and return land journeys to present an overall picture of the itinerancy of divine processions. At the temple of Deir el-Bahari, all these scenes move onto the north wall, where the journey of the Theban triad begins from the extreme right in the lower register (Figure 8, Episode 4). Note that the barques of Mut and Khonsu first appear here as the result of a post-Amarna restoration. The processions were led by statues of four kings and two queens, the latter two being Ahmes, a consort of Thutmose I, and perhaps Mutneferet, another consort of that king, who is also portrayed in the Opet Feast scene at this temple (Figure 9, a). In a sub-register below Amun's barque, priests carry poles, which support one long strip of cloth. The legend reads: *ir.t ḥbs ỉmn ḫr ḥ3.t nṯr pn šps* 'presenting the *ḥbs*-cloth of Amun before this august god'.[84]

The party moves towards *w3ḥy.t* a 'station', the same designation as those erected by Hatshepsut between Karnak and Luxor for the Opet Festival. This barque station represented in Episode 5 is most likely to have been one of the royal memorial temples on the basis of the corresponding episode of the return journey, which includes partial references to *ḫnm.t-ˁnḫ* (memorial temple of Thutmose I) and the [*w3ḥy*].*t*.[85] Thutmose I's temple has not yet been located but stood on the site of the temple of Wadjmes, according to Quirke (1990b, 174).[86] The tomb of Iamnedjeh records that a bouquet of Amun was delivered from this temple (3.6.5).[87] The memorial temple of Thutmose III is also attested elsewhere in the same tomb.[88] Because the construction of the latter temple began in the time of Hatshepsut's co-regency[89] and Iamnedjeh's tomb is dated to the last years of Thutmose III[90], it is possible that Amun could visit both the memorial temples of Thutmose I and Thutmose III at the Valley Festival during the later reign of Thutmose III.

In the time of Hatshepsut, the memorial temples of Thutmose I and Thutmose II would have functioned as a way-station. Although we know very little about the latter temple, the cult of these kings is evident from Hatshepsut's monuments, including her Deir el-Bahari temple.[91] In fact, two statues of Thutmose I and Thutmose II are depicted in our episode (Figure 9, b). It is, therefore, more likely that during her reign Amun visited the memorial temple of Thutmose II on the journey to Deir el-Bahari, and that of Thutmose I on the way back to Karnak. Given that Thutmose II's temple was located between Qurnet Murai and Medinet Habu,[92] the whole tour on the West Bank may have taken more time to complete. Interpretation of the episode in question depends on whether one sees it as a version of Hatshepsut or Thutmose III. Among other buildings in the vicinity of Deir el-Bahari, one temple was erected by Hatshepsut at the entrance of a causeway, to which a kiosk was added on its way.[93] It is not surprising that these buildings were also used at the Valley Feast, but all way-stations could not have been represented in the Deir el-Bahari reliefs as a result of the space limitation, particularly after the figures of Mut and Khonsu were

[81] Seti I (PM II², 409, (8–13); *LD* III, pl. 152, a); Ramses IV (P. Turin 1882 recto, IV, 1; *KRI* VI, 74: 2–3). *ḫft-ḥr-nb=s* could be associated with any temple axis and thus used to refer to buildings located to the east of Karnak temple (*Urk.* IV, 834: 4) and in front of Luxor temple (Manniche 1982, 273). The temple of Medinet Habu was also described as standing *n ḫft-ḥr=k* 'before you', a connotation of its location against Luxor temple (P. Harris I, III, 11). The location of the Theban private tombs was likewise described in, for example, TT 183 (19), TT 259 (2, I and II), and TT 390 (4). In particular, the tomb of Paser (TT 106) attests *ḫft-ḥr-nb=s* in association with the Valley Feast (3.6.2). For other references to *ḫft-ḥr-nb=s*, see Otto 1952, 49 and Nims 1955, 118.

[82] Schott 1953, 6; Kemp 1989, 210; Karkowski 2001, 101.

[83] Nims 1955, 114–5; Burgos and Larché 2006, vol. 1, 19, Block 290.

[84] Karkowski 1992, 159.

[85] Karkowski 1992, 162, fig. 5.

[86] Also see Haring 1997, 419, n. 4 for references to the memorial temple of Thutmose I.

[87] TT 84 (PM I-1², 168–9 (7) and (14)).

[88] TT 84 (PM I-1², 169 (10)).

[89] Ullmann 2002, 87.

[90] Davies 1941, 96.

[91] The cult of Thutmose I and Thutmose II in her time is manifest in their figures represented in the sanctuary of Djeser-djeseru (PM II², 366 (133, 2)). A small chapel to the south of the upper terrace was also dedicated to the cult of Thutmose I (PM II², 361, Room IV).

[92] Haring 1997, 419; Wilkinson 2000, 191.

[93] PM II², 423–4. Archaeological evidence testifies the presence of a kiosk on the causeways to both Hatshepsut's and Thutmose III's temples at Deir el-Bahari. Cabrol (2001, 550–3) regards O. BM 41228, which depicts the ground plan of a repository, as evidence for such a kiosk (Glanville 1930).

a. Six royal statues portrayed in Episode 4. Four kings, the first of which has been hacked out, and two queens are portrayed above priests, all leading the barque procession of Amun. The first of the two queens is Ahmes, wife of Thutmose I, and the second perhaps Mutneferet, another consort of that king.

b. A statue of an unidentified king in the upper register and two statues of Thutmose I and Thutmose II in the lower register, in Episode 5.

c. A statue of 'Thutmose' represented behind the cabin of Amun's portable barque in Episode 5.

Figure 9. Royal figures in the Valley Festival scenes at Hatshepsut's temple at Deir el-Bahari (photographs taken by the author).

added to that of Amun in the post-Amarna Period, and thus the entire representation was crammed into the small room.

When the barque procession first took a rest, purification ceremonies were performed with musicians and dancers at the first station. As represented on the stela of Ameneminet (3.4.2), Amun visited the memorial temple of the reigning king Seti I.[94] Bietak and Reisner-Haslauer (1978, vol. 1, 19) assume that all the memorial temples on the West Bank had a sanctuary for Amun-Re, who visited from Karnak and used it as a way-station at the Valley Festival. Dolińska (2007, 75) posits that the gods visited all these temples at once, which was, however, unlikely because the two-day duration of this celebration was too brief to cover the whole area on the West Bank (3.2.3). Be that as it may, Amun was, in ideal, expected to visit all deities worshipped on the West Bank. The building stela of Amenhotep III refers to 'His Festival of the Valley at the navigation of Amun of the West for seeing the gods of the West'.[95]

According to textual evidence, primarily from private tombs, Amun visited one or more of the memorial temples at the Valley Feast. However, sources from these tombs are limited to a very short period from Thutmose III to Thutmose IV, except some sporadic examples up to the reign of Ramses II (Table 16). These texts refer to the distribution of divine offerings to dead tomb owners from the temples, where Amun had received the offerings in the first instance. The offerings were normally referred to as *iḫ.t nb.t ḥr ḫ3w.t n.t Ỉmn ḫft ḥtp=f m* 'everything on the altar of Amun when he rests at (the such-and-such temple)'. When specified, they commonly form bouquets, which were delivered from a limited number of temples, usually those of the reigning or directly preceding king.

This does not necessarily mean that other temples were left out from festivities, but representatives on behalf of Amun-Re might have been dispatched to each mortuary institution. These representatives were possibly royal statues that accompanied Amun from the beginning of this celebration at Karnak.

After the Amarna Period, emphasis was not exclusively placed on the temple of the reigning king.[96] For instance, only the memorial temples of Thutmose I and Thutmose III are referred to in the tomb of Neferhotep (TT 49), dating from the time of Tutankhamen to Horemheb (Table 16, no. 15). This may be explained by the fact that the memorial temples of Thutmose IV and Ay were possibly not yet completed at the time of record. However, the tombs of Djeserkareseneb (TT 38) and of Amenhotep-Sise (TT 75), both dated to the time of Thutmose IV, refer to Djeser-djeseru only. The aforementioned tomb of Amenmes (TT 19) (3.4.2 and Figure 16), dated to the time of Ramses II, represents none of the Ramesside memorial temples but a ritualistic combat before the barque of Thutmose III, which is enshrined in the memorial temple of that king.[97] Ramses IV erected his own memorial temple at the mouth of Deir el-Bahari, but by doing so disturbed the causeways to the temples of Mentuhotep II and Thutmose III.[98] Hence, processions were no longer able to take their way on these causeways, apart from that of Hatshepsut.[99]

Our knowledge of rituals performed at the memorial temples is very limited. Strangely enough, there is no representation of the Valley Festival at the best-preserved temple of Medinet Habu, except the small reliefs mentioned in 3.4.1. The lack of a grand-scale representation cannot satisfactorily be explained.[100] Evidence relevant to our interest is provided only by Seti I's temple at Qurna, the portico of which depicts this festival. As already described in 3.4.1, the southern half of the portico represents the barque processions of the Theban triad, Seti I, and Ahmes-Nefertari. This scene was completed by Ramses II in honour of his dead father Seti I. The processions are led by Ramses II himself and enter this temple with a figure of Seti I standing in front of it. The columns of text in front of Seti I document his wish to let his son Ramses II become the king according to what he decreed at Thebes.[101]

As the counterpart to the southern portico, the northern half appears to represent five episodes after the processions enter this temple.[102] In the first three episodes, Ramses II presents offerings to different gods, including the deified Seti I. The fourth episode portrays the king running with a *ḥs*-vase towards the ithyphallic Amun-Re-Kamutef. In the last episode the king offers incense and a libation to the Theban triad and a figure

[94] Primary emphasis placed on the memorial temples of reigning kings is manifest in the case of the queen Tausret. Amun visited her memorial temple on II Shemu 28 in year 7 (**1160**), when the construction of that temple must have just begun, given that Siptah died in year 6 or 7 (Hornung 2006, 213). Ullmann (2002, 436) explains that a temporal architecture (or a tent-like shrine) was used during the festival. That temple services commenced shortly after the beginning of construction is also evidenced by Ramses IV's memorial temple that began to deliver divine offerings in year 1 (*KRI* VI, 8: 39 and 61; Peden 1994, 133 and 144–7 for translation).

[95] Stela Cairo 34025 recto, l. 9 (PM II^2, 447; *Urk.* IV, 1650: 8).

[96] Krauss 1985, 136.

[97] For the ritualistic fighting at festivals, see *Opet*, 16, n. 46. Darnell and Manassa (2007, 204–5) explain that the combatants of ceremonial fighting were warriors, the history of which was very ancient, probably dating from before the Old Kingdom.

[98] Bietak and Reiser-Haslauer 1978, vol. 1, 28.

[99] Dolińska 2007, 80.

[100] The north interior wall of the second court at the temple of Medinet Habu represents an unspecified celebration of Amun (PM II^2, 500 (96–8, II)). It is difficult securely to associate this representation with the Valley Feast without an unequivocal reference to it in the accompanying texts.

[101] *KRI* II, 637: 12–3.

[102] PM II^2, 409 (8–13).

of the king himself standing behind them. Like other representations similar to these, there is no specific feature that draws our attention. They seem to be an ordinary series of rituals, which do not significantly differ from the daily temple cult.

Seti I first began the construction of this temple for his own cult and that of his father Ramses I. A group of rooms at the southeast corner behind the portico (Rooms XXVIII–XXXI) were dedicated to the cult of Ramses I.[103] Remaining reliefs in these rooms do not bear witness to rituals specific to the Valley Festival. The Ramesseum must also have had representations akin to those at Seti's temple, but only barque procession scenes remain today. With regard to the king's role as a mortuary priest, one may draw attention to the tomb of Amenemheb (TT 85), where Amenhotep II is portrayed clad in a panther skin and proceeding to Osiris, who is seated in a naos. The text on the naos includes the Horus- and Nebty-names of Amenhotep II himself.[104] A scene comparable with this is attested in the tomb of Nakhtamen (TT 341).[105] The deceased is portrayed presenting offerings to the composite deity Ptah-Sokar-Osiris, behind whom Ramses II stands. Ptah-Sokar-Osiris is not clad in a commonly attested shroud but vested like a king with the *nms*-headdress. Because Nakhtamen was a priest belonging to the Ramesseum, it may be that the deified Ramses II is portrayed in two hypostases here.

It is not easy to explore cult practices at these memorial temples any further without referring to a wealth of information from the private tombs, which may argue for a huge amount of offerings to be consecrated to Amun and then distributed to people. This will be examined in 3.6.5.

3.4.4. *Rituals at Deir el-Bahari*

When the divine barques reached the temple of Hatshepsut at Deir el-Bahari, they probably stopped at two T-shaped ponds located at the foot of the lower ramp and went through some rituals.[106] Thereafter, they ascended to the upper court, where the representations of this celebration are carved. After Thutmose III completed his own valley temple in a later year, it was no longer possible for processions to pass the narrow passage into the upper court of Hatshepsut's temple due to his enlargement of the width of divine barques by adding two more carrying poles.[107] This resulted in five poles altogether and explains the enlargement of doorways at his temple with the width of 4.60 meters, whereas that of Hatshepsut's temple remained 2.78 meters (Lipińska 1968, 89).

The Theban triad is likely to have spent a night at Deir el-Bahari.[108] Like other Egyptian festivals, mortuary celebrations performed on the West Bank culminated in the morning, when the sun appeared from the eastern horizon (1.2.3). Hence, it is often the case that the hymn to Re is carved on the entrance of the Theban tombs (3.6.1). Amun probably reached Deir el-Bahari before the dawn and then saw the sun coming up from the eastern horizon over the Nile.

Rituals performed at this temple are represented on the Red Chapel, at the temple of Deir el-Bahari, and possibly on the north and south walls of the Great Hypostyle Hall at Karnak. On the Red Chapel Hatshepsut, together with Thutmose III, is portrayed presenting the *ꜥ3b.t*-offerings to Amun-Re's barque, which is described as:[109]

> *ḥtp ḥr s.t wr.t m ḏsr-ḏsr.w-imn m mnw M3ꜥ.t-k3-rꜥ Ḥr-wsr.t-k3.w s.t=f 3ḫ.t n.t ḏ.t*
>
> Resting on the great seat in Djeser-djeseru-Amun as the monument of Maatkare, Horus-Useretkau, his glorious seat of everlastingness.

An Osiride statue of Hatshepsut, who is called *M3ꜥ.t-k3-rꜥ mry.t Ỉmn* 'Maatkare, beloved of Amun', stands in front of this building, a reminiscence of the figures of the deified kings, described in the preceding section.

On the other hand, the Deir el-Bahari reliefs comprise four episodes. In the first episode (Figure 8, Episode 6), the king offers large offerings to Amun's barque resting in a shrine, while the barques of Mut and Khonsu disappear. Some scholars have paid attention to four figures of Hapi and three unique containers, which are represented on the base of the shrine.[110] Two of the three containers are in the shape of a trapezium topped with ten torches. Schott (1937, 17–25) associated these objects with a nocturnal ritual by referring to parallel representations. He rightly regarded the four figures of Hapi as symbolizing the seas of the four cardinal points, on which a divine barque floated. These objects were not exclusively related to a specific festival but any ceremony, when the rebirth of the sun was celebrated. Hence, they are also attested in association with the New Year celebrations (4.3.4).

[103] PM II², 417–9 (98–116); Ullmann 2002, 286.
[104] PM I-1², 172 (16, I); Virey 1891, 247, fig. 4; Radwan 1969, 43, pl. 5.
[105] PM I-1², 408 (5–7); Davies 1948, pl. 23.
[106] Karkowski 2001, 106–7.
[107] Legrain 1917, 13; Dolińska 2007, 73, n. 43. See Carlotti 2003 for more recent discussion on this topic.
[108] Haikal 1972, vol. 2, 13. Dolińska (2007, 72 and 75) inclines to the idea that they spent a night at either a way-station or the memorial temple of the reigning king, if available. However, it is more plausible that they stayed overnight at Deir el-Bahari, provided that the duration of the feast was only two days.
[109] Chevrier and Lacau 1979, vol. 1, 172, vol. 2, pl. 19 (Block 273); Burgos and Larché 2006, vol. 1, 99.
[110] Schott 1937, pl. 4, a; Karkowski 1992, 161, fig. 4.

Episodes thereafter are poorly preserved and their details are difficult to observe. They can be summarized as follows: in Episode 7 the king presents offerings to the Theban triad; in Episode 8 two unidentified gods bring the king before the goddess Werethekau, who makes the *nyny*-gesture. Very fragmentary twenty-three columns of text accompany the latter episode (Figure 10). This text begins with a reference to year 3 or 4 but probably underwent alterations twice during Thutmose III's sole reign and after the Amarna Period.[111] These changes and the poor preservation state make it extremely difficult to understand the text as a whole. Therefore, it would be sufficient to present the first two columns containing references to the Festivals of the Valley and I Shemu.

> *ḥ3.t*[*-sp*] *3* [two or three groups lost] *ḫpr* [unknown groups lost *m*] *ḥb=f nfr n in.t* [two or three groups lost] *nsw.t-bi.ty Mn-ḫpr-rʿ di ʿnḫ* [one or two groups lost] *sḫʿ.t* [three groups lost] *m r*[three groups lost] *m ḥb nfr n tpy šmw t3 r-ḏr=f m ḥʿ*[*ʿ* three groups lost] *m* ...

> Yea[r] 3 [ ] appear [at] His Beautiful Festival of the Valley [ ] the king of Upper and Lower Egypt Menkheperre, given life [ ] causing [ ] at(?) [ ] at His Beautiful Festival of I Shemu. The entire land is in joy [ ] at ...

As Karkowski points out, this part of the text may be Thutmose III's version because a reference to the 'Festival of the Valley' is not attested elsewhere in surviving records from the time of Hatshepsut, when that celebration was called the 'Festival of Djeser-djeseru' (3.3).

Episode 9 was considerably altered after the time of Hatshepsut. In the original design, she had been portrayed kneeling before Amun with the goddess Werethekau behind him, a gesture characteristic of the coronation rite.[112] The renewed version represents Thutmose III introduced by Werethekau before Amun and one or two more deities.[113] The surviving part shows only the upper part of the seated Amun, who is perhaps *Ỉmn-rʿ m ḏsr-ḏsr.w* 'Amun-Re-in-Djeser-djeseru', the colour of his body being entirely black.[114]

Seti I's relief on the north wall of the Great Hypostyle Hall at Karnak may also depict a sequence of rituals comparable to Hatshepsut's at Deir el-Bahari, on account of its orientation and juxtaposition with the Opet Festival scene (1.3.3). The episode to the extreme left could be identified with a ritual performed at the destination of the Valley Feast.[115] Ramses II appears to have desired to execute his own version on the other side. Strangely enough, this counterpart is oriented in the reverse direction. In an episode to the left, where we usually expect a ritual performed at Karnak, Ramses II offers a libation and a bouquet to the barques of the Theban triad resting in a shrine.[116] Behind this shrine stands a statue of Seti I, who is described as: [*wnn nsw.t*] *nb t3.wy Mn-m3ʿ.t-rʿ m3ʿ ḫrw ḥr šms it=f Ỉmn m ḥw.t-nṯr 3ḫ Sṯḫy-mry-n-ptḥ m pr Ỉmn ḥr šsp snw* [one or two groups lost] *ḫr.t hrw n.t* [*rʿ nb*] '[The king], lord of the Two Lands, Menmaatre, true of voice, follows his father Amun in the glorious temple of Setekhy-meryenptah in the domain of Amun, and receives provisions [ ] everyday'. This scene depicts an episode at Seti I's memorial temple at Qurna. On the other hand, an episode to the right describes the same king as: *wnn nsw.t nb t3.wy nb ir.t iḫ.t Mn-m3ʿ.t-rʿ ḥr šms it Ỉmn-rʿ m ḥb=f nfr n in.t ḫnm ḥʿ.w=f m ṯ3w=f* 'The king, lord of the Two Lands, lord of rituals, Menmaatre, follows the father Amun-Re at His Beautiful Festival of the Valley. He himself unites with his breath'. Because Ramses II's relief has an indication of some alterations from the original design, it is difficult to understand the consistency of the ritual sequence (2.4.6).

Although Hathor's key role at the Valley Festival has generally been accepted,[117] no official and temple sources explicitly attest the goddess in association with this celebration. The paucity of evidence might have resulted from the decorum characteristic of Egyptian art, which did not overtly express rituals performed in the innermost part of temples. There were three shrines that were dedicated to Hathor at Deir el-Bahari by the end of the Eighteenth Dynasty, each at Mentuhotep II's Akh-sut, Hatshepsut's Djeser-djeseru, and Thutmose III's Djeser-akhet.[118] The cult of Hathor at Thebes had an old history from the end of the Old Kingdom.[119] Its popular aspect is manifest in a number of Ramesside graffiti left at Djeser-akhet (3.2.3 and Table 15). In

[111] Karkowski 1992, 163.

[112] Karkowski 1992, 163–4.

[113] It may be that the goddess Hathor is seated behind Amun, as represented in the corresponding part of the valley temple of Thutmose III (Dolińska 1994, 44, fig. 5).

[114] Leitz 2002a, vol. 1, 332 and 339. Barwik (2010, 7) demonstrates that Amun's sacred statue placed in the sanctuary of Hatshepsut's temple was an enthroned figure, on account of the dimension of the sanctuary and its naos. Amun-who-dwells-in-Djeser-akhet worshipped at the valley temple of Thutmose III is known to have been black in colour (Gawlikowski 2001, 26, fig. 9; Aksamit 2007, 9, fig. 3).

[115] PM II^2, 44 (153, III-3); Nelson 1981, pl. 178.

[116] PM II^2, 48 (159, III-1); Nelson 1981, pl. 76.

[117] Wente 1962, 121.

[118] Although whether or not Akh-sut itself was fully in function is not sure, Hathor's cult there seems to have continued into the end of the Eighteenth Dynasty (Pinch 1993, 5). Her cult at Djeser-djeseru survived during the Third Intermediate Period, while that at Djeser-akhet ceased when the whole temple was destroyed by a rock-fall happened at the end of the Twentieth Dynasty (the last attestation of this temple is a text in TT 65 (9), dating from the time of Ramses IX).

[119] Allam 1963, 58. A limestone stela of the king Wahankh-Intef II of the Eleventh Dynasty, originating from his tomb at el-Tarif, attests to Hathoric celebrations at Thebes (Stela MMA 13.182.3; Lichtheim 1973, vol. 1, 94–6 for translation).

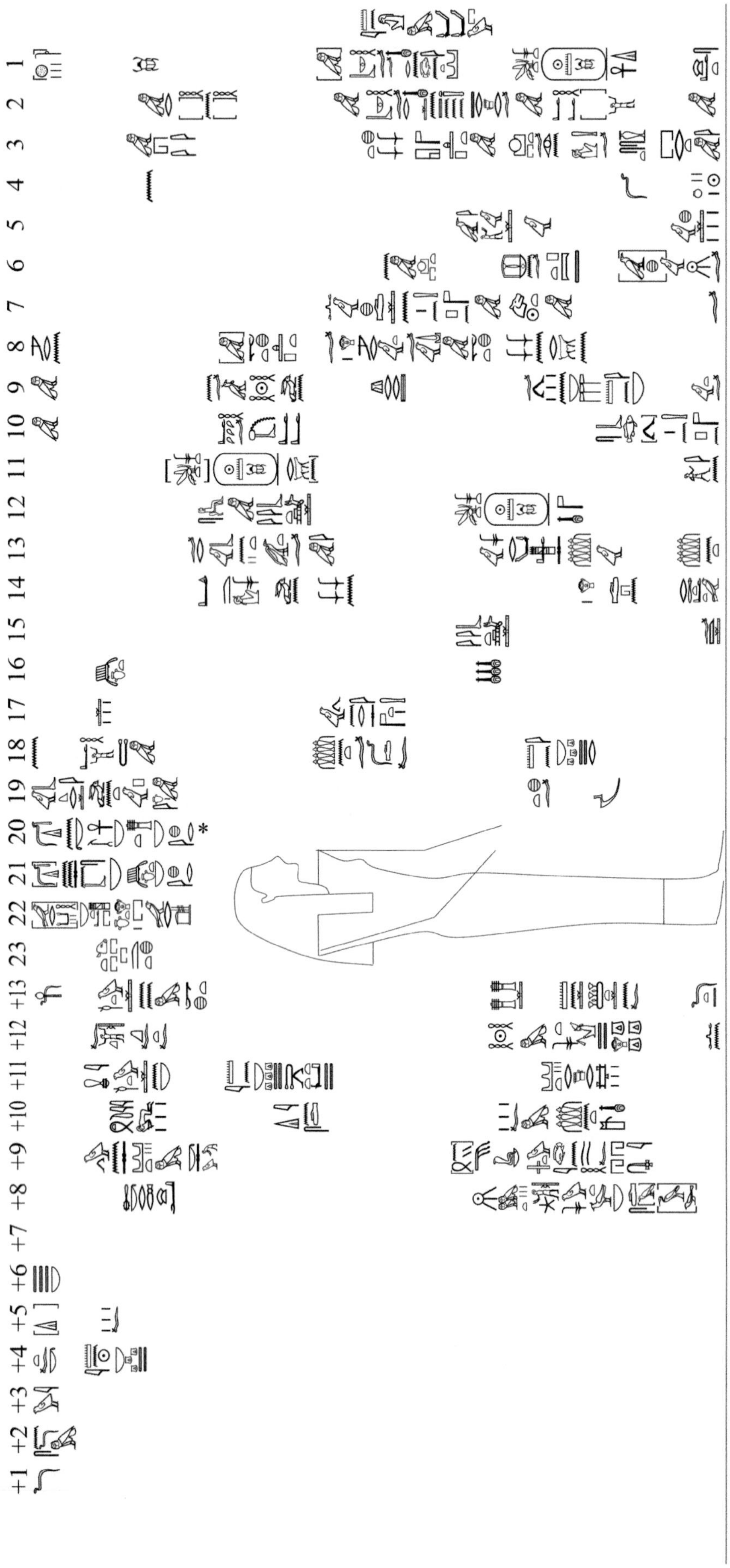

* Originally written as [hieroglyph].

Figure 10. Episode 8 and the column texts in the Valley Festival scenes at Deir el-Bahari (PM II², (83, II)).

addition, a statue of Neferrenpet, a royal butler under Amenhotep III, bears witness to Hathor for the Valley Festival.[120] The text carved on the back reads:

> *ḥtp di nsw.t ỉmn ḫnty ḏsrw.t Ḥw.t-ḥr ḥry-tp smy.t(?) di=sn d3.t(=i) r t3 m ip.t-s.wt r t[s.t] iḫ.wt hrw nb pr.t m t3 r m3 ỉmn m ḥb=f nfr n in.t šsp wꜥb.w ḥnꜥ ꜥḳw bꜥḥ im m p3.t n k3 n wb3 nsw.t imy-r pr Nfr-rnp.t m3ꜥ ḫrw*
>
> Offering that the king gives. May Amun-foremost-of-Djeserut and Hathor-who-dwells-in-the-West(?),[121] cause (my) river journey to the land from Karnak to par[take] offerings every day, namely, what comes forth on earth, in order to see Amun at His Beautiful Festival of the Valley, receiving pure cloths with provisions of the flooding therein as offerings. For the ka of the royal butler, steward, Neferrenpet, true of voice.

The same sentiment but without referring to Hathor is found on a stela of the wab-priest Nia, dating from the end of the Eighteenth to the Nineteenth Dynasty.[122] The standard *ḥtp-di-nsw.t* formula includes the passage: *šsp=f snw.w m ḏsr.w m ḥb in(.t) m-b3ḥ nb.w nḥḥ* 'May he receive provisions at Djeseru at the Festival of the Vall(ey) before the lords of eternity.' It was not exclusively for Amun and Hathor worshipped on the West Bank, that the Valley Feast was celebrated, but all gods and dead beings at western Theban were theoretically addressed, whether deified kings or private individuals.

It is probable that the official cult of Hathor was also performed at the Valley Feast. Karkowski (1992, 164) postulates that a statue of Hathor was carried out of her shrine to meet the Theban triad, and then ascended to the upper terrace of Djeser-djeseru with them. O'Connor (2012, 211 and 215) advances that a sacred marriage was performed between Amun and Hathor. Pinch (1993, 244) also hypothesizes that Amun-Re in his ithyphallic form slept with Hathor. Alternatively, Dolińska (1994, 36–7) suggests the union of the king with Amun. These consequences were not impossible but highly speculative.

Dolińska (2007, 73) further explains that after leaving Djeser-djeseru the procession made a progress to the Hathor shrine of Thutmose III and the neighboring temple of Mentuhotep II in the time of the former king and his successor Amenhotep II, on account of the distribution of votive offerings dedicated to Hathor and of her priesthood at Hatshepsut's temple in the time of Amenhotep II.[123] In addition, the last episodes at Deir el-Bahari may be represented on a stela in the tomb of Ramose (TT 7), dating from the first half of Ramses II's reign (Figure 17).[124] Three registers portray: 1) Ramses II, the vizier Paser, and the deceased offering incense to the Theban triad in a mountain; 2) the deceased and his family adoring Osiris, Ptah, Horus, Isis, and Min-Kamutef; 3) the deceased and his family adoring Anubis, Isis, Nephtys, and two Hathor-cows in a mountain. Because Amun here is not the one worshiped on the West Bank, but 'Amun-Re, lord of the thrones of the Two Lands, foremost of Karnak', it is very likely that these deities assembled somewhere at Deir el-Bahari on the occasion of the Valley Festival.

Finally, it may be of some interest to refer to the tomb of Imiseba (TT 65), dated to the time of Ramses IX. On the eastern wall of the antechamber, the king is portrayed censing towards the barque procession of *ỉmn-rꜥ nsw.t nṯr.w p3w.ty ḥry-ib m3nw nb ꜥnḫ.t ḫnty msḳ.t* 'Amun-Re, king of the gods, primeval one, who resides in the western mountains, lord of the West, foremost of the Milky Way'.[125] This barque is followed by a figure of the goddess Hathor. Other parts of the legends give no clue to understand this scene in a specific context. See 4.3.5.1 for other elaborate representations in this remarkable tomb, one of which can be associated with the New Year celebrations.

3.4.5. Return journey and rituals back at Karnak

This section will only outline the return journey, which did not considerably differ from the outward journey in representations. The river-procession scenes carved on the Red Chapel and the barque sanctuary of Philip Arrhidaeus at Karnak as well as the north and south walls of the Great Hypostyle Hall of Karnak all provide insignificant information. In addition, major part of upper register of the Deir el-Bahari reliefs is missing today and thus difficult to be reconstructed in detail.

[120] Statue Louvre E 14241 (Boreux 1933, 22–3 for transcription and translation; Schott 1953, 95, 6 for partial translation).

[121]  This reading is uncertain (Leitz 2002a, vol. 5, 85).

[122] Stela Turin 1585 (Habachi 1972, 73, fig. 3). A *ḥtp-di-nsw.t* formula in the tomb of Neferhotep (TT 49) reads: *ḥtp di nsw.t Ḥr-3ḫ.ty Wsir ḫnty imnt.t Ptḥ-skr nb šty.t ḥry-ib ḥw.t-ꜥ3 ỉnpw nb r3-st3.w Ḥw.t-ḥr ḥry.t-ib ḏsr.t nṯr.w nb.w imnt.t di=sn m33=i itn ḫꜥꜥ=f r r3 n is=i šms=i nṯr r nmt.t=f m ḥb=f n in.t ḫnm snṯr šsp iḫ.wt it.wt m ḫnm.t-ꜥnḫ* 'Offerings that the king gives. Horakhety, Osiris, foremost of the West, Ptah-Sokar, lord of the *šty.t*-sanctuary, who dwells in the great house, Anubis, lord of Rasetau, Hathor, who dwells in Djeseret, and all the gods of the West. May they let me see the sun disk when it appears to the entrance of my tomb, follow the god at his procession at His Festival of the Valley, smelling incense and receiving things that come from Khenemet-ankh (Thutmose I's memorial temple)' (PM I-1², 94 (23); Davies 1933a, vol. 1, 65, pl. 55, A).

[123] A graffito depicting Amun's barque is found at Mentuhotep II's temple, which may argue for Amun's visit to this temple (Naville 1907, vol. 1, 24, pl. 8, fig. 6).

[124] PM I-1², 16 (9); *KRI* III, 613–4. A scene parallel to this is attested on a stela of Didia (BM 706: Naville 1907, vol. 3, 4, pl. 8 (C, a–c); Lowle 1976, 94–5 for translation).

[125] PM I-1², 130 (3); Bács 2001, fig. 2 for photograph.

They can be divided into roughly five episodes (10 to 14) until the divine barques reach back to the Nile.

At Deir el-Bahari Episode 10 is located to the left end of the wall above a doorway and portrays Geb placing the White-crown on the kneeling king before the souls of Pe and Nekhen.[126] In Episode 11, a large figure, probably of Thutmose III, is preceded by priests and musicians. Episode 12 depicts the king following the barque processions of the Theban triad with no remarkable feature, apart from a text in front of the king. This text is carved to replace a figure of Hatshepsut and includes a passage: [unknown groups lost] *wḏ3 m ḏsr-ḏsr.w r ḥtp m* '[ ] going out from Djeser-djeseru to rest in [ ]'. Episode 13 depicts the three divine barques resting at the memorial temple of Thutmose I, as described earlier in 3.4.3. Finally, Episode 14 represents the barque processions reaching the Nile, the journey of which continues onto the adjacent east wall.

Ceremonies at the final destination, Karnak, are largely unknown. At Deir el-Bahari Amun is depicted retiring to the sanctuary of Karnak.[127] On the Red Chapel the king is portrayed performing the rituals of four *meret*-boxes and driving a calf, and accompanied by musicians and singers, representations parallel to those of the Opet Festival (2.4.11).[128] Here again, they seem to have been performed as an essential constituent of a major festival, not exclusively for the Valley Festival. The barque sanctuary of Philip Arrhidaeus depicts Amun's barque carried by priests and then undergone a purification ritual in his sanctuary.[129]

The most revealing representation attesting the last moment of the Valley Feast is a small relief at the temple of Medinet Habu.[130] This relief is carved on the other side of the doorway thickness depicting the beginning of this celebration (3.4.1). The king reveals himself from the temple as a divine manifestation, the legend of which reads:

> *Ḥr nb 3bw.t mi nsw.t ẖʿʿ=f m* [*ḥw.t-nṯr mit.t*] *Rʿ wn=f r3=f ẖr ṯ3.w n rẖy.t r sʿnẖ idb.wy m t3y=f rr* [two groups lost]*y n* [one group lost] *n tm.w ʿ.wy=f m i3w mi Ḥr-3ẖ.ty* [one group lost]
>
> Horus, lord of the form like the king, who appears from [the temple like] Re and opens his mouth with breath to people to cause the Two Banks to live with his words(?) [ ] to [ ] entire land. His arms are in adoration like Horakhety [ ].

The king's appearance is nothing more than common investiture with the Blue-crown, but this short text tells us how he was transfigured and presented a new form to his subjects at the end of the festival. The presence of people at this celebration is also manifest in representations in private tombs. In the following chapter, the way that private individuals presented themselves and how they participated in the Valley Festival will be examined.

3.5. Valley Festival as a popular celebration

3.5.1. Methodological problems in examining the private tomb

When examining Egyptian representations, we are constantly confronted with a major problem regarding their specific/non-specific contexts. In particular, various mortuary ceremonies that are described in Theban private tombs cannot carefully be examined without comparing with a huge number of other cultic and secular subjects. It is hardly possible to draw a clear line between cultic and secular scenes. Where a dead tomb owner is portrayed carrying out his official job, it may be understood as a pictorial historical account of his lifetime. However, scenes are normally not attributed to a specific moment by texts, and hence it is not necessarily always possible to consider them a biography in a strict sense. The lack of temporal emphasis was also the case for temple reliefs, where the indefinite repetition of ritual performances was emphasised, whether a king is dead or alive. Dated scenes and texts are scarcely attested in the private tombs but they do have historical significance among other 'eternal' representations.[131] With regard to festivals, datings without a year cannot be regarded as a purely historical account because it is apparent that religious celebrations were also what the deceased desired to repeat in the hereafter.

Even historical narratives may be taken as a constituent of non-historical accounts when they are to be seen as part of neighbouring timeless representations. This is manifest, for example, in the New Year scenes, some of which are undoubtedly allied to adjacent scenes on the same wall or on a consecutive wall. They as a whole represent a sequence of seasonal events from harvesting through the registration of products to a final delivery to a temple. Only the last episode is sometimes labelled the New Year but the rest consists of what one may call idealized afterlife scenes, such as fishing, fowling,

126 This episode may not directly be associated with the Valley Feast because it is also represented above the corresponding doorway in the south wall.

127 Karkowski 2001, 131.

128 Burgos and Larché 2006, vol. 1, 109–11 (Blocks 61, 128, and 303).

129 PM II^2, 100 (291, II).

130 PM II^2, 495 (78, d); *MH* IV, pl. 239, B; *KRI* V, 226: 15–6. For other minor representations of the Valley Festival in this temple, see PM II^2, 493 (65) and 494 (71); *MH* II, pls 60 and 123.

131 For instance, TT 57 (11 and 15) and TT 192 (5–8) represent the Sed Festival in year 30 of Amenhotep III.

hunting, and reaping (4.6.1). Thus, the representations of the private tombs are defined as a uniform series of memories, consisting of both historical and non-historical accounts. Festival scenes, of course, have this double nature. As a result, an argument regarding whether a given scene is historical or idealized proves to be impotent.

Undoubtedly, the Valley Festival was one of the most popular subjects represented in these tombs. It was the most distinctive feature of this celebration that the state/royal cult was performed at temples on one hand and the private one at individual tombs on the other. The voyage to the West Bank of Amun can be reconstructed in more detail by sources from private tombs than by those from royal memorial temples. Schott (1953, 94–133) presented 148 textual sources as relating to this celebration. However, many of them cannot securely be associated with the Valley Feast. In fact, only eight private tombs are presented as textual evidence when only uncontested references to this celebration are taken into consideration.[132]

The number of sources relevant to the present study varies, depending on what criteria are applied to identify them. For instance, Schott's list includes the tomb of Piay (TT 263), dating from the early years of Ramses II. A text on the entrance to the inner-room reads:[133]

> *di=f šsp=i mnḫ.t sfḫ=i ky ḥr šms nṯr pn m wḏꜣ=f r ḏsr.w m ḥb=f n tpy-rnp.t*
>
> May he let me receive one cloth and remove another at following this god at his advance to Djeseru[134] at his festival of *tpy-rnp.t*.

Topographical Bibliography assigns this text to the Valley Feast.[135] Unfortunately, this identification is dubious for two reasons. First, this text seems to be juxtaposed with the one carved on the other jamb, which refers to the Khoiak Feast.[136] As will be described shortly, the New Year celebration, rather than the Valley Festival, was regularly mentioned together with the Khoiak Feast in the Ramesside tombs. Second, the renewal of a cloth is mostly, if not exclusively, attested in association with the New Year (Table 19, no. 30).

A difficulty lies in how many times Amun frequented the West Bank within the year and where he visited. Amenopet travelled from Luxor to the West at the Decade Ritual. The Festival of I Shemu might have embraced Amun's visit from Karnak during the Middle Kingdom (3.2.1). The Khoiak Festival is another popular subject depicted in the private tombs, particularly in the Ramesside Period. Amun's role played at this feast is evident, but whether or not he crossed the river remains conjectural.[137] A part of the New Year celebrations is known to have taken place at the 'palace' on the West Bank when the king sojourned there, but whether or not Amun of Karnak accompanied him is again not concluded for sure (4.3.5.2). It is often documented that while mortuary ceremonies took place in the private tombs, Amun 'rested at (*ḥtp=f m*)' one of the memorial temples. However, this characteristic expression does not necessarily signal only the Valley Feast but also the New Year celebration (Table 19, no. 18).[138]

It is, therefore, desirable to present an overview of general scenes of the private tombs, particularly those in the antechamber, before starting to examine the private cult performed at the Valley Feast. The architectural structure and decorations of the antechamber are closely linked to one another and display distinctive features, compared with those in the inner-room, which places more emphasis on otherworldly/ideal aspects than earthly/secular images.[139] The presence of personal representations in the antechamber can be seen as an element essential for evoking the deceased to mingle with his living relatives on certain occasions.[140]

[132] Schott 1953, 94–6.

[133] PM I-1², 345 (7); *KRI* III, 382: 10–11.

[134] For *ḏsr.w*, *ḏsr.t*, or *ḏsr* as topographical names for the site of Deir el-Bahari, see Pinch (1993, 3), who explains that the area was so called after Hatshepsut erected her temple *ḏsr-ḏsr.w-imn*. It is evident that *ꞽImn-rꜥ m ḏsr.t* 'Amun-Re-in-Djeseret' was a different hypostasis from those worshipped at Djeser-djeseru, Djeser-akhet, and Akh-sut, as attested in TT 65 (PM I-1², 130 (9); *KRI* VI, 549: 14; Leitz 2002a, vol. 1, 332).

[135] PM I-1², 345 (7).

[136] *KRI* III, 383: 5.

[137] The Bubastite gate at Karnak, for example, records that a procession and oracular session of Amun-Re took place at the Nehebkau Festival, when the high-priest of Amun Osorkon III issued two decrees in year 2 of Takelot II (Caminos 1958, 34–5, 54, and 57–8; Jansen-Winkeln 2007, vol. 2, 161–8). For other instances of Amun's presence at this festival, see Fukaya 2012, 193 and 198.

[138] Valley Feast (TT 49 (C, c); TT 55 (5); TT 106 (D, d); TT 129 (1); Graffiti DB 3 and 10); New Year celebration (TT 76 (3); TT 343 (11 and 13)).

[139] Hermann (1940, 26) explained that the west and the east walls of the antechamber depict official and private activities respectively. Fitzenreiter (1995, 115) views that a collective cult place is located in the south half of the chamber, while presentations of official works are found in the north half. For the tomb of Amenmes (TT 89), Shaw (2006, 209) observes a symmetrical decorative scheme: 'a temple style' in the north and 'a court style' in the south. Classification of tomb scenes on a temporal basis is proposed by Schulman (1984, 170), who presents three categories: general, repetitive, and timeless scenes; historical scenes; and otherworldly scenes. On the other hand, the inner-chamber represents a highly standardized style with limited subjects, mostly a funeral procession and the pilgrimage to Abydos (Engelmann-von Carnap 1999, 229). This contrast is generally present in tombs dated to the Eighteenth Dynasty, rather than those to the Ramesside Period, when the functional dichotomy between the antechamber and the inner-room seems to have collapsed, or even reversed in some examples, such as TT 41 and TT 178. When compared with the inner-room, which is predominantly funerary in nature, the antechamber is regarded as a gathering place for the deceased's family to perform rituals. The distinctive functions of the inner-room and the antechamber parallel the royal mortuary cult, where the royal tombs were completely separated from the memorial temples for the sake of security as well as ritual purposes (Bács 2001, 95).

[140] Hermann 1940, 132.

As will be described in the next chapter, the New Year celebrations embraced mortuary rituals similar to those performed at the Valley Festival. For instance, offering scenes belonging to both feasts are represented within the same room in some tombs (Table 18). However, it is often difficult to distinguish between them, as Schott (1953, 7) admitted that depictions in the private tombs were generally not clearly labelled by texts.

Moreover, serious confusion is caused by the terms *tp rnp.t* and *ḏsr* (or *ḏsr.t*), the meaning of which can vary depending on contexts. *tp rnp.t* can mean either the 'beginning of the year' (originally *tpy-rnp.t*) or 'annual'. Rondot (1997, 51, n. d) argues that *ḥb(.w) tp rnp.t* can imply three different meanings: more than one feast in the same place or of the same god, the repetition of the same feast, and feasts of more than one god. When referring to the Valley Festival, it should exclusively denote 'annual', but in the case of the New Year celebrations it can also mean the 'beginning of the year'. *ḏsr* is understood as a general designation of a western district or necropolis, but can also denote a specific site, particularly Deir el-Bahari, in Theban contexts.

Multiple mortuary festivals appear to be referenced to in some tombs. On the entrance of the tomb of Amenhotep (TT 345), the deceased with his wife is portrayed pouring incense on braziers, the legend of which reads: *snm ꜥḥ.wy m ꜥntyw [snṯ]r n [Imn] m ḥb.w nb.w* [one group lost *m*] *ḫn.t dp.t=f nfr.t n.t tp rnp.t* 'Supplying two brazier-cups with frankincense and [incen]se for [Amun] at all festivals [at] the beautiful annual navigation of his ship'.[141] Likewise, on a pillar near the entrance of the tomb of Tjenna (TT 76), the deceased couple is represented adoring with a hymn, which reads: [*ca.* four groups lost] *nṯr m ḫn.t=f tp rnp.wt m ḥb.w=f nfr(.w) n ḏsr* '[ ] god at his annual navigation at his beautif(ul) festivals to Djeser'.[142] While these two cases seem to bear witness to more than one river journey of Amun that take place every year, the Valley Festival per se is also referred to in expressions similar to them, such as *ḥb=f nfr n ḏsr-ḏsr.w* 'His Beautiful Festival of Djeser-djeseru' (3.4.2). We cannot, therefore, count exclusively on these designations for distinguishing between references to different festivals, but have to understand contexts that scenes and legends provide.

Among religious events depicted in the private tombs, the most common were: the celebrations of the New Year, harvest, Valley, Khoiak, and the king Amenhotep I. As is shown in Table 18, the first three feasts were represented mostly in tombs dating from Thutmose III to Thutmose IV, and tended to disappear from those belonging to the Ramesside Period.[143] During the latter period, Sokar's barque, often associated with the Khoiak Feast, came to be represented more frequently, while the Valley Feast was reduced to such an extent that it was only referred to in frieze texts in some tombs.[144]

3.5.2. Examination of tomb scenes

The following examination will mainly focus on the below-listed tombs, which contain representations relevant to this study. The New Year Feast will be treated in detail in the next chapter but will be cited in this chapter too when a comparative analysis with the Valley Feast is necessary. Like the Festivals of Opet and the Valley, which were often represented in juxtaposition in temple reliefs and inscriptions, the Festivals of the Valley and the New Year had a similar but less conspicuous relative positioning within tomb decorations. The Khoiak Feast will also be mentioned briefly to demonstrate the transition of the decorative scheme between the Eighteenth Dynasty and the Ramesside Period. The number of sources available to us is limited when uncontested textual references only are taken in consideration as a definite criterion to identify the subject of a scene. There are 12 representations for the Valley Feast, whereas those for the New Year celebrations are 26. The New Year scene in TT 131 (8–9) may be an exceptional case, where secure textual evidence is missing. It portrays Useramen appointed a vizier in the time of Thutmose III. However, this appointment is elsewhere recorded in P. Turin 1878 to have taken place on I Akhet 1 in year 5.

Valley Festival (12 examples): 19 (3–4, I); 36 (23); 49 (3 and C, c); 56 (5); 64 (2); 69 (8); 74 (2); 106 (D, d); 129 (1, I); 147 (2 and 8).

New Year Festival (26 examples): 2 (10, III); 4 (5, II); 9 (6, I–II); 23 (8, II); 39 (14); 46 (1); 50 (9–10, I, IV); 60 (11); 61 (7); 73 (2–3); 82 (5 and 17); 85 (C, a); 86 (8); 93 (9 and G, d); 96 (6); 99 (A, a); 107 (2, I–II); 112 (6, I–III); 127 (5, II); 131 (8–9); 172 (9); 345 (3 and 5); 415 (1, II).

Khoiak Festival (12 or possibly more examples)[145]*: 2 (9, II); 9 (6, I); 23 (31–2); 41 (16); 50 (9–10, I–III); 65 (11); 148 (2, I); 157 (6); 158 (3); 219 (5, II); 296 (4, I); 341 (8–9, I).*

In order to examine Valley Festival scenes in detail and delineate their characteristics, four tombs are selected here as model cases. They cover the period between Thutmose III and Amenhotep III. Three of them had a T-shape ground plan typical of that time before

[141] PM I-1², 413 (1); *LD* III, pl. 9, d.

[142] PM I-1², 150 (B, b); Bouriant 1889, 158 (h).

[143] Wente 1962, 121.

[144] TT 183 (18) (*KRI* III, 185: 6) and TT 184 (10–11) (*KRI* III, 163: 6; Lichtheim 1992, 178 for translation).

[145] There are ample instances of Sokar's barque depicted in the Ramesside tombs, but most of them seem to be part of mortuary texts or of mere decorative motifs. Hence, representations that can be interpreted in a festival context are small in number.

later tombs were generally remodeled in shape and decoration as the result of a change in the mortuary cult during the Ramesside Period or a slightly earlier time. These four tombs do not appear to have suffered major usurpation in subsequent times.

3.5.2.1. Case 1. Tomb of Tjanuny (TT 74)

The Festivals of the Valley and the New Year are likely to be deliberately juxtaposed in the tomb of Tjanuny, a royal scribe under Thutmose IV. It used to have a T-shape ground plan but only the antechamber has remained (Figure 11). A reference to *[ḫn.t]=f n.t imnt.* *[t]* 'His [Navigation] of the Wes[t]' is found on the right thickness of the entrance.[146] Tjanuny is portrayed entering the tomb but the legend describes him as coming out and in the tomb. The other thickness represents the same subject if Brack and Brack (1977, 23–4, pl. 19, a) have correctly restored part of the legend as *[ḥb=k nfr m ḫn.t=k n ḏsr-ḏsr.w]*, which is entirely missing today. Tjanuny here adores with his arms being upraised towards the outside of the tomb, and is accompanied by his wife Mutiry, who holds a sistrum and a menit in each hand. Each of these scenes seems to represent the tomb owner coming in and out of his tomb. This type of scene at the entrance is categorized as Type A hereafter (Figure 15).

The representation on the left thickness continues onto the southeast wall, which depicts two scenes. In the first one (wall 2) the deceased couple offers on braziers and is followed by offering bringers (Type B).[147] A small butchery scene is included below, as is often the case for this genre of scene. Like other parallels, this scene is accompanied by a hymn to Horakhety, probably as an episode continuing from Type A scene. The hymn reads:[148]

> *wdn iḫ.t nb.t nfr.t wꜥb.t n=k Imn nb ns.wt tꜣ.wy [Ḥr-ꜣḫ.]ty [m] ḫn.t=f n.t imnt.t m ḥb=f nfr [n (i)n.t]*
>
> Offering every good and pure thing to you, Amun, lord of the thrones of the Two Lands, and [Horakhe]ty[149] [at] his navigation of the West at His Beautiful Festival [of the Valley].

In the next scene (wall 3), the deceased couple receives a bouquet from a man with a woman behind him, presumably their son and daughter. The son is described as:[150]

> *rdi.t ꜥnḫ n Imn-rꜥ nsw.t nṯr.w n Mw.t nb.t [i]š[rw] n Imn.t ḥry.t-ib ip.t-s.wt n Ḫnsw m wꜣs.t nb ꜣw.t-ib ḥs=sn tw mry=sn tw di=sn kꜣ ḥs.wt=k*
>
> Presenting a bouquet of Amun-Re, king of the gods, of Mut, lady of [I]she[ru], of Amenet-who-dwells-in-Karnak, and of Khonsu in Thebes, lord of exaltation. May they bless you. May they love you. May they elevate your praises.

It may be that the successive walls 1 to 3 are all dedicated to the Valley Feast scenes. While scene 3 depicts a banquet held *m pr=k* 'in your house (i.e. tomb)',[151] the setting of scene 2 is not clear. Type B (=scene 2 here) often precedes a banqueting scene and portrays the deceased taking an active role in offering on braziers, contrary to his passive role of seating and receiving gifts at a banquet. This composition is widely attested in many tombs.

The deceased depicted as a celebrant is perhaps part of a dichotomy, reflecting two major parts of proceedings on the part of people at this festival, namely, a ritual outside of a tomb (at a temple) and a gathering at a tomb, regardless of whether or not the tomb owner is dead. In a parallel scene in the tomb of the vizier Amenopet (TT 29), offerings on braziers appear to be presented for the ka of the king Amenhotep II by the tomb owner.[152] This may refer to rituals taking place at the memorial temple of that king.

To the north of the entrance, another Type B scene is followed by that portraying the deceased couple offering to Osiris (walls 7 and 8).[153] The less-preserved west walls (5–6 and 10–11) appear to represent secular aspects of Tjanuny's life. On the southern half, military processions are represented. Among the standards carried by the soldiers, two are annotated as 'Thutmose IV, the Festival [of the Victory]', which suggests a return from a campaign.[154] They move towards Tjanuny, who then turns to a kiosk where the king sits. The northern half portrays Tjanuny assessing recruits, cattle, and horses, and then turning to the seated king. He plays an

[146] PM I-1², 144 (1); *Urk.* IV, 1009: 15–7; Brack and Brack 1977, 25–6, pl. 19, b.

[147] For the typology of Type B scenes, see Engelmann-von Carnap 1999, 331–8.

[148] *Urk.* IV, 1008: 12–4; Brack and Brack 1977, 30, pls 20, a and 22, a.

[149] As will be described in 4.5.11, Horakhety here seems to be a hypostasis of Amun, whose solar aspect is stressed.

[150] *Urk.* IV, 1012: 5–6; Brack and Brack 1977, 33, pls 21, a and 24, a.

[151] *Urk.* IV, 1012: 2.

[152] PM I-1², 45 (2); Schott 1953, 100 (32). A text parallel to this is attested in TT 109 (3).

[153] Brack and Brack (1977, 30) relate scene 7 only to the Valley Feast, leaving scene 8 unspecified. The frieze text above these two scenes is a *ḥtp-di-nsw.t* formula addressing Amun-Re, Mut, Amenet, and Khonsu (*idem* 1977, 36–7). The Valley Feast depicted on both wings of the east wall is also attested in TT 147 (2 and 8) (Ockinga 2004, 127, pl. 10; Parkinson 2008, 61, fig. 72) and perhaps in TT 295 (1 and 4).

[154] Brack and Brack 1977, 42, pls 28 and 35.

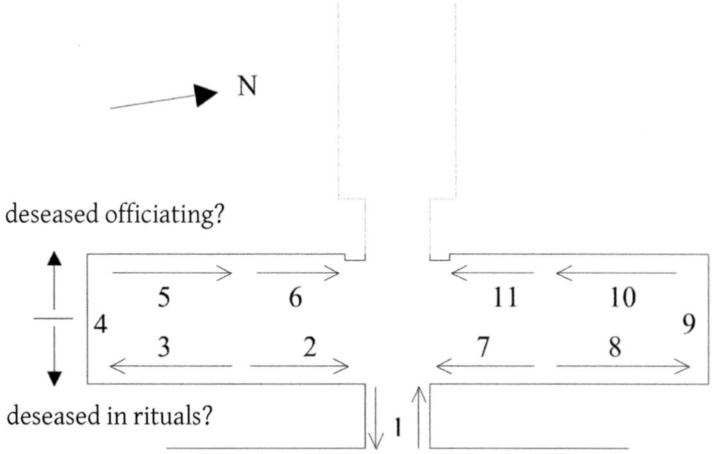

1. deceased couple adoring (south) deceased coming in and out the tomb (north)
2. deceased couple offering on brazier at the Valley Feast
3. deceased couple receiving a bouquet of Amun
4. false door
5. military parade including Nubian soldiers
6. deceased offering a bouquet of Amun to Thutmose IV
7. deceased couple offering on braziers
8. deceased couple offering to Osiris
9. stela
10. deceased inspecting recruits, bulls, and horses
11. deceased offering to Thutmose IV with Syrian vases

Figure 11. Tomb of Tjanuny (TT 74).

intermediary role between soldiers and the king in his official capacities of a royal scribe and the overseer of the army scribes. It is probable that the western walls are entirely dedicated to his biographical account.[155] Kings are portrayed in many tombs belonging to the Eighteenth Dynasty.[156] Particularly, the appearance of the king (*ḫʿ.t-nsw.t*) in an elaborate kiosk was one of popular subjects (Table 21). This characteristic representation is associated with various occasions, such as reward ceremonies, promotions, foreign delegations, and gift deliveries. Because all these would have required ceremonial settings, a link between the *ḫʿ.t-nsw.t* and religious celebrations cannot be ruled out. Indeed, the Sed Festival and the New Year Festival were sometimes associated with the *ḫʿ.t-nsw.t* scene.

3.5.2.2. Case 2. Tomb of Userhat (TT 56)

The Valley Feast and the *ḫʿ.t-nsw.t* are also juxtaposed but in a different layout in the tomb of Userhat, a royal scribe under Amenhotep II. This monument remains intact and has a T-shape ground plan (Figure 12). Unlike Tjanuny's tomb, Type B and a banqueting scene are represented on separate walls in the antechamber. While the former is located right next to the tomb entrance (wall 2), the latter is painted on opposing wall 5. In this banqueting scene, two daughters and a son are portrayed offering to the deceased couple. The legend reads:[157]

> *n kꜣ=k ir hrw nfr m pr=k nfr n nḥḥ s.t=k n.t ḏ.t ḥms=k im=f ib=k nḏm ḥr šms nṯr pn nfr Wsir ḥḳꜣ ḏ.t di=f šsp=k snw.w m-bꜣḥ=f m ḫr.t hrw n.t rʿ nb sꜣ.t=k mry.t=k ḫkr nsw.t ḥsy.t n nṯr nfr Ḥnw.t-nfrt.t sꜣ.t=f mry.t=f Nb.t-tꜣ.wy ḥsy=f tw n Ỉmn-rʿ ḫft ḥtp=f m ʿb-ꜣḫ.t m ḥb=f n in.t imnt.t in sꜣ=k mry=k wʿb Ptḥ* [name lost]

> For your ka—Make a good day in your good house of eternity, your seat of everlastingness. May you sit therein, your heart being content at following this good god, Osiris, ruler of everlastingness. May he let you receive provisions before him every day. Your beloved daughter, royal concubine, blessed one of the good god, Henutneferet. His beloved daughter Nebettauy. May he, namely, Amun-Re praise you when he rests at Ab-akhet (the memorial temple of Amenhotep II) at His Festival of the Western Valley—by your beloved son, wab-priest of Ptah, [.........].

A text parallel to this is attested in a small scene accompanying the false-door on wall 4, where a couple

[155] The same decorative scheme is attested in TT 63 (Dziobek and Abd el-Razik 1990).
[156] Brock and Shaw 1997, 173, n. 61 and 175, n. 82.

[157] PM I-1², 112 (5); *Urk.* IV, 1479: 8–9; Beinlich-Seeber 1987, 53–6, pls 1 and 40.

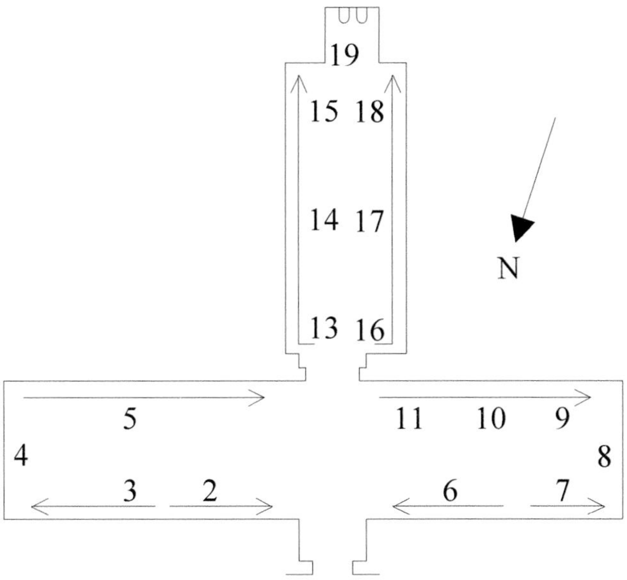

2. deceased couple with mother offering on braziers
3. deceased inspecting cattle and agriculture
4. false-door
5. deceased couple receiving offerings at the Valley Feast
6. deceased couple offering on braziers
7. couple receiving offerings and banqueting
8. stela
9–11. deceased offering to Amenhotep II with storehouse men and recruits
13–5. deceased hunting, fishing, and fowling, and the harvest celebrations
16–8. funeral procession
19. statue of the deceased couple

Figure 12. Tomb of Userhat (TT 56).

is portrayed receiving offerings with a reference to Henqet-ankh, rather than Ab-akhet:[158]

> *n k3=k ꜥnḫ n Ỉmn-rꜥ [ḥs]y=f tw mry=f tw ḫft ḥtp=f m ḥnk.t-ꜥnḫ m ḥb=f nfr n [in.t imnt.t]*
>
> For your ka. A bouquet of Amun-Re. May he [prai]se you and love you when he rests at Henqet-ankh (the memorial temple of Thutmose III) at His Beautiful Festival of [the Western Valley].

The 'provisions' and 'bouquet', which are referred to in these texts, originated from two royal memorial temples. Significantly, the phraseology *šms nṯr* is attested only for a limited number of festivals, including the Valley Feast, but not the New Year Feast (Table 19, no. 77).

The *ḫꜥ.t-nsw.t* scene is represented on walls 9 to 10. This scene is unusual for its orientation not towards the doorway and continuation onto part of wall 8. The deceased is depicted offering to the king Amenhotep II, who sits in a kiosk. On wall 11 scenes of inspecting recruits and supplying provisions to storehouses are represented.

3.5.2.3. Case 3. Tomb of Amenemheb (TT 85)

The Valley Festival and the New Year celebration could be represented on a small surface of pillars, which stand next to each other and exemplify a juxtaposition of these celebrations. This is manifest in the tomb of Amenemheb, lieutenant-commander of soldiers under Thutmose III and Amenhotep II (Figure 13). On pillar D the deceased is portrayed entering his tomb with a girl, who holds a menit in his front. The legend reads:[159]

> *ꜥḳ m-ḫt pr.t r ḥtp m ḫr.t-[nṯr] ḫnm tpḥ.t imy.t nḥḥ m-b3ḥ ꜥ n Wn-nfr ḫft i.t ḥr m33 Ỉmn m [ḥb]=f n ḏsr-ḏsr.w*
>
> Entering after going out to rest in the Necro[polis], uniting with the grotto, which is in eternity in front of Wennefer when coming at seeing Amun at His [Festival] of Djeser-djeseru.

The New Year celebration is represented on pillar C.[160] The deceased offers a bouquet of Amun to his wife, who suckles a young prince, a representation commonly attested in the mid-Eighteenth Dynasty. The short legend reads:

> *i.t ḫr [ꜥnḫ n Ỉmn]-Rꜥ m ḥb=f n wpy-rnp.t*
>
> Coming with [a bouquet of Amun]-Re at His Festival of the New Year.

[158] *Urk.* IV, 1479: 14–5; Beinlich-Seeber 1987, 72–3, pl. 8.

[159] PM I-1^{2}, 173 (D, d); *Urk.* IV, 919: 10–2; Schott 1953, 108 (67).

[160] PM I-1^{2}, 173 (C, a); *Urk.* IV, 925: 13–4.

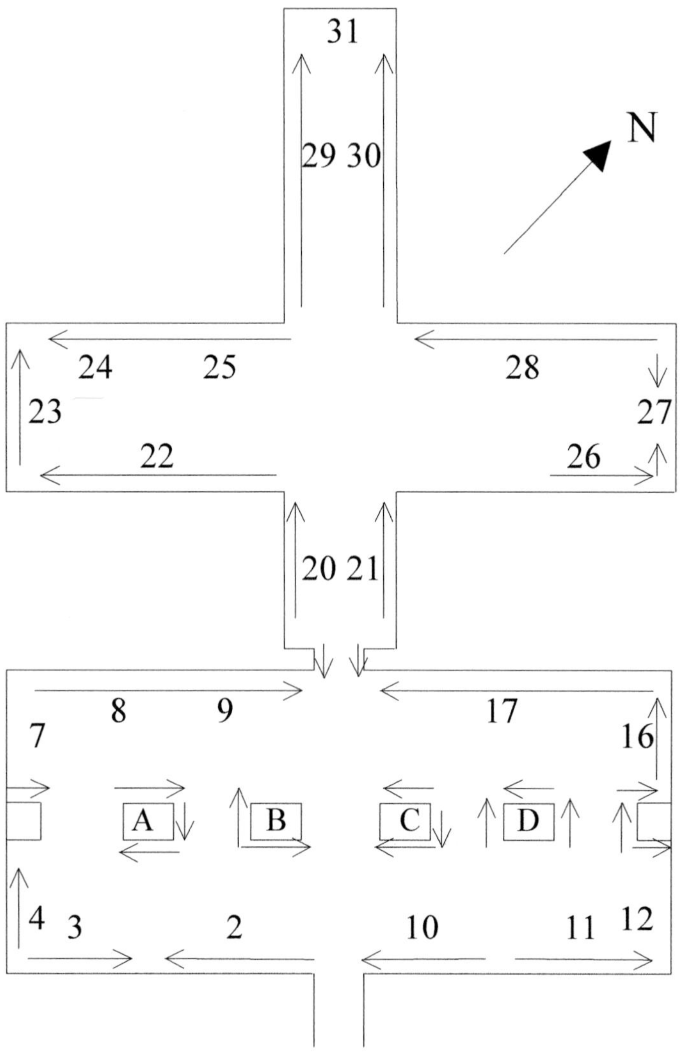

2. deceased registering troops in front of the storehouse of Amenhotep II
3. deceased inspecting provisions
4. deceased at rest
7. false-door
8. officers and recruits
9. wife offering a bouquet of Amun to Amenhotep II
10. deceased couple offering on braziers
11. deceased couple receiving a bouquet of Amun, accompanied by musicians and guests
12. stela
16. Amenhotep II as a sem-priest offering to Osiris
17. deceased before Thutmose III and the Syrian tributes
20. deceased family inspecting
21. sem-priest dedicating an offering list to the deceased couple
22. funeral procession to the West
23. deceased couple offering to Osiris
24. deceased spearing a hippopotamus
25. deceased with his wife
26–7. fishing and fowling
28. deceased couple receiving offerings at a banquet
29. funeral rituals
30. deceased couple inspecting a garden
31. Anubis and Osiris

Figure 13. Tomb of Amenemheb (TT 85).

It is remarkable that Amun's bouquet was also distributed at the New Year (4.5.11). Wall 9 attests another instance of divine bouquet, which is presented to the king Amenhotep II by Amenemheb's wife.[161] The beginning of the legend has been restored as: *i*[.*t*] *ẖr* [*ꜥnḫ n Ꞽmn nb ns.wt tꜣ*].*wy* [*ḫnty ip.t-s.wt*] 'Co[ming] with [a bouquet of Amun, lord of the thrones of the Two La] nds, [foremost of Karnak]'. Because this scene parallels one in the tomb of Menkheperreseneb, high-priest of Amun under Thutmose III, which possibly represents the New Year (TT 86),[162] it may be associated with that celebration (4.3.5.2).

3.5.2.4. Case 4. Tomb of Menna (TT 69)

Lastly, the tomb of Menna, a scribe of the fields of the lord of the Two Lands of Upper and Lower Egypt, dating from the time of Thutmose IV to Amenhotep III, is analysed here as an example where a context cannot be confirmed by a text but by iconography only. This tomb also has a T-shape form (Figure 14). A sequence of scenes belonging to Types A and B is visible from the entrance to the south half of the northeast wall.[163] On the north half a man is portrayed offering a bouquet to the deceased couple. Several offering bringers and singers are also represented in these scenes. Hartwig (2001, 402 and 2013, 45–53, figs 2.8a–b) regards these scenes as representing the Valley Feast. Her hypothesis

[161] *Urk.* IV, 923: 7–8; Radwan 1969, pl. 6.
[162] PM I-1², 177 (8).
[163] Hartwig 2013, figs 2.1a–b and 2.8a–b.

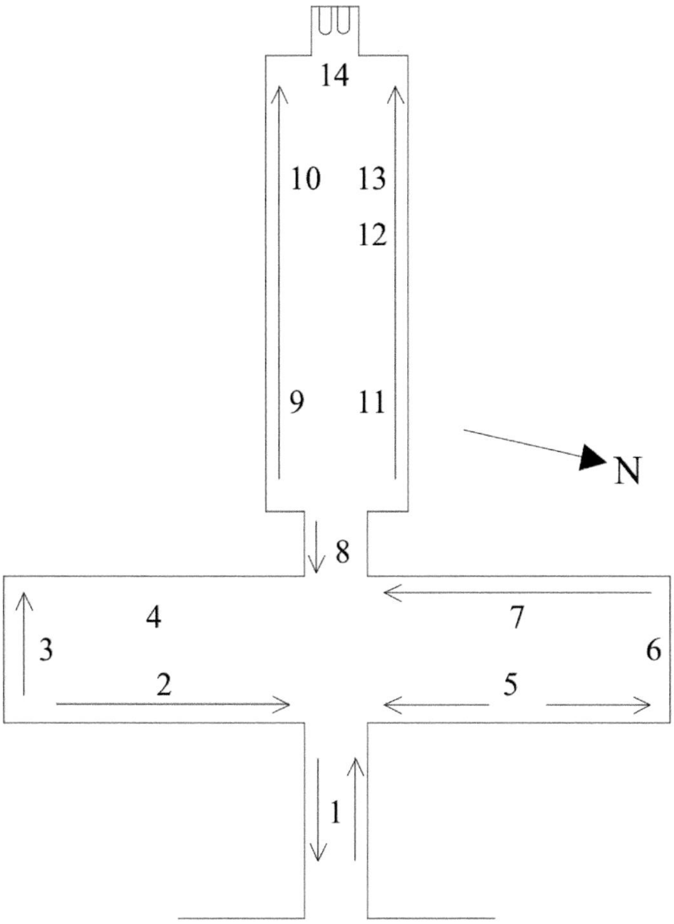

1. deceased couple and their daughter adoring with the hymn to Re at the Valley Feast?
2. deceased inspecting agriculture
3. deceased couple adoring Osiris
4. remains of banqueting
5. deceased offering on braziers and deceased couple receiving a bouquet at the Valley Feast?
6. stela
7. deceased couple receiving offerings at the New Year Feast?
8. deceased couple leaving the tomb at the Valley Feast
9–10. journey to the West
11. Abydos pilgrimage
12. deceased family fishing and fowling
13. deceased couple receiving offerings
14. statue of the deceased couple

Figure 14. Tomb of Menna (TT 69).

may be corroborated by the fact that Djeser-djeseru is referred to in the hymn to Re, which is written on the entrance (3.6.1).

In the upper register of the northwest wall, a lively episode of a banquet is painted.[164] To the left extreme a man clad in a short skirt offers a bouquet to the seated deceased couple. Two rows of seated guests follow to the right. A shrine-like structure stands to the extreme right of the upper row. It contains some offerings in the upper half. The identity of this structure is not known. It can be a false-door within the tomb, but is more likely to be a building, from which offerings were delivered to the dead.[165] A small shrine akin to this is represented standing in front of a temple pylon in the tomb of Khonsu, high-priest of (the cult of) Thutmose III under Ramses II (TT 31).[166] Hence, a distribution of temple offerings may be illustrated here.

In the lower register, the deceased couple receives an offering list from a man clad in a panther skin. To the extreme right the same couple appears again and receives vases and candles, objects typical of the New Year celebrations.

At face value, the two registers on this wall appear to depict different occasions, but they probably represent different episodes at the New Year Festival. The same-wall-single-event principle is not unusual in tombs belonging to the Eighteenth Dynasty (Table 20). For example, in the tomb of Ramose, vizier under Amenhotep IV (TT 55), a Type B scene continues into two registers (Figure 15 A).[167] In the upper register the deceased couple receives a menit and two sistra 'of

[164] Hartwig 2013, figs 2.11a–b.

[165] Hartwig (2013, 63, nn. 147–8) describes this as comprising a shrine-like structure placed on top of a fire altar with five round peaks.

[166] PM I-1², 48 (8, I); Davies 1948, pl. 15. It can be an altar-like one represented in the Khonsu temple (*Khonsu* I, pl. 34).

[167] PM I-1², 109 (8–10); Davies 1941, pls 13–21.

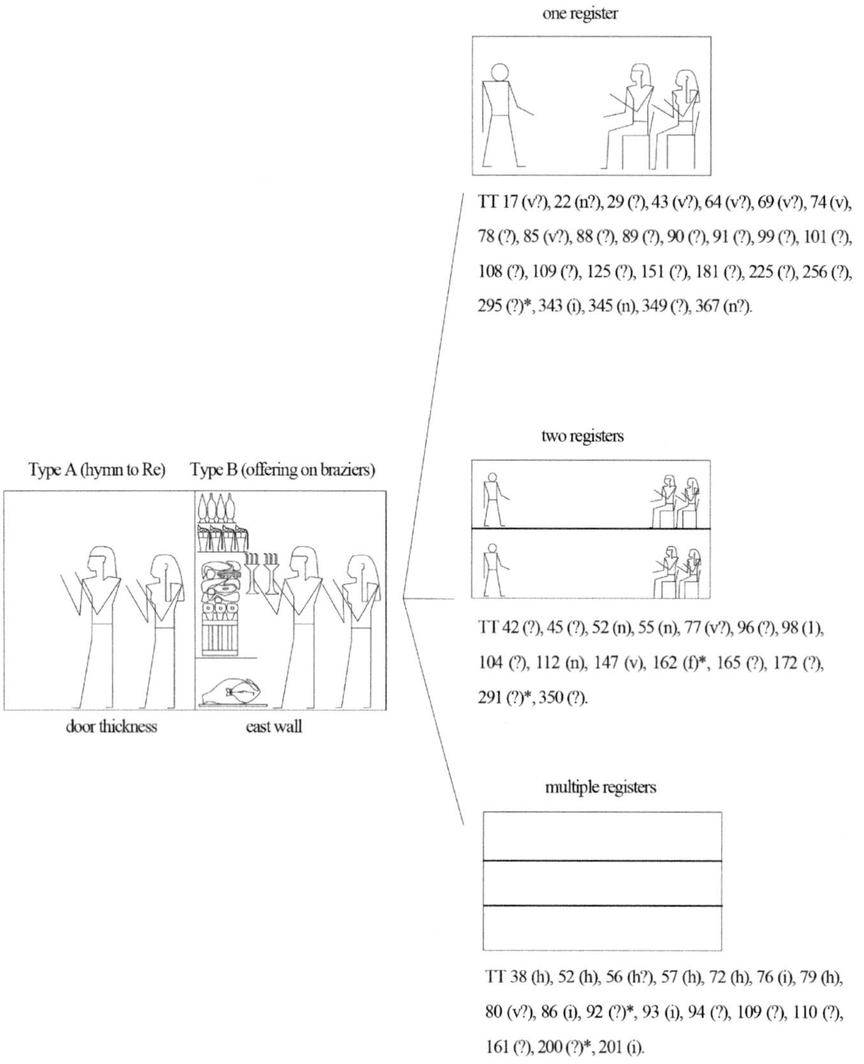

Figure 15. Schematic sequence of Type A and B scenes in the private tomb (v=Valley Feast, n=New Year Feast, h=Harvest Feast, i=inspection, f=foreigners, *=Type B integrated into one of its following registers).

Amun-Re' from three girls. This episode is followed by another one, where the deceased couple and his parents are portrayed approached by two rows of priests carrying ointment jars and cloths, which suggest a connection with the New Year. In the lower register priests purify a statue of Ramose. The next episode portrays Ramose, his wife, his brother (or cousin?) Amenhotep, and Amenhotep's wife receiving a large offering list. This list is presented by the wab-priest of Maat Pawahy, who is clad in a panther skin. It is probable that the lower register represents the Opening-of-the-Mouth ritual, a characteristic of the New Year scenes (4.5.3). Since Pawahy appears in the upper register too, both the upper and lower registers are likely to represent the New Year celebrations.[168]

However, a new style was introduced to the Ramesside tombs. New Year episodes came to be represented together with other Osiride celebrations, such as the Festivals of Khoiak, of the Two Goddesses celebrated on I Peret 22 (**665–7**), and of Bastet celebrated on IV Peret 4 (**894–7**), on the same wall (Table 20). In the tomb of Khabekhenet, a servant in the Necropolis who lived in the second half of Ramses II's reign (TT 2), the Feasts of the Two Goddesses and the New Year occupy two of the four registers on the north wall, the former being in the second register and the latter in the third register (**666** and **895**). An example parallel to this is attested in the largely unpublished tomb of Qen (TT 4), a chiseller of Amun in the Necropolis who lived in the first half of Ramses II's reign (Figure 31 and **1397**). On the north wall a banquet performed on IV Shemu 30 is represented in the much-damaged lower register. To

[168] Assmann (2005, 343–4) relates the upper scenes to the Valley Feast.

Figure 15 A. Northeast wall of the tomb of Ramose (TT 55 (8–10)), after Davies 1941, pls 13–21.

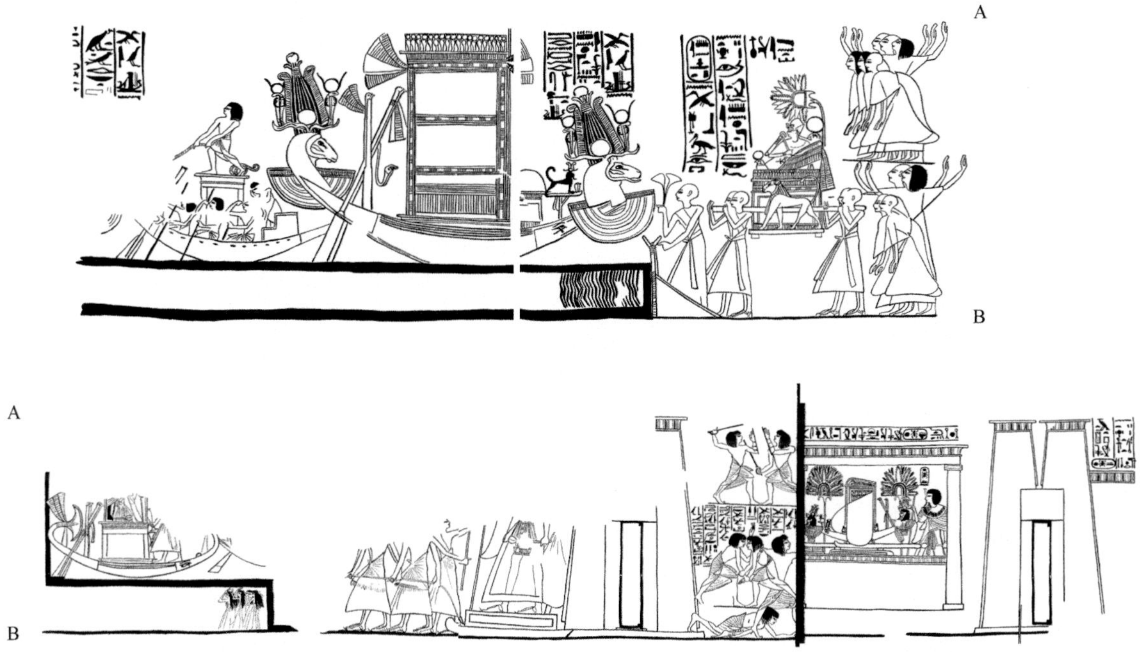

Figure 16. Valley Festival represented in the tomb of Amenmes (TT 19 (3–4, I)), after Foucart 1928, pls 6–8, 13–4, and 16.

the left Qen and his wife Nefertari are served by their daughter. Likewise, Qen and his other wife Henutmehyt are portrayed in the middle, being visited by their three sons, of whom only the last figure remains. In the upper register Qen and his family visit the god Ptah and the goddess Maat. Although the legend does not specify the subject of this scene, it is most likely to represent the Feast of the Two Goddesses on account of the iconographical resemblance to the contemporaneous tomb of Khabekhenet (TT 2).

The separation between two registers may reflect family structures. For instance, in the tomb of Djehutymes (TT 295), head of the secrets of the chest of Anubis from the time of Thutmose IV to Amenhotep III, his son Huy is portrayed presenting floral offerings to Djehutymes and his wife in each of two registers on the southwest wall.[169] Djehutymes had two wives Nefertiry and Renenutet, of whom the former is depicted in the upper register and the latter in the lower register. Significantly, in the lower register he receives two bouquets—one already in his hand and the other to be given by his son. The one in his hand appears to represent the bouquet that he has received in the upper register. Hence, a temporal sequence from the top register to the bottom one can be seen here. The first bouquet in the lower register was probably given in honour not only of Djehutymes but also of Nefertiry. On the other hand, the second one, described as originating from Amun, was presented to Renenutet by Huy and his stepsister(?), of whom the latter is portrayed in the lower register only and thus

[169] PM I-1², 377 (1); Hegazy and Tosi 1983, 12, pl. 4.

thought to have been a daughter of Renenutet. The subject of these scenes cannot be confirmed, but it may possibly be either the Valley Feast or the New Year celebration.

3.6. Sequence of the Valley Festival at the private tomb

It is evident from the four tombs examined in the preceding section that the Festivals of the Valley and the New Year were major subjects depicted in the Theban private tombs, particularly of the Eighteenth Dynasty. That the number of sources relating to the Valley Feast is considerably less than that of the New Year may be explained by two facts. First, the former celebration is generally less attested in the Ramesside tombs. Second and more significantly, there are not phraseology or representations that are exclusively characteristic of the Valley Festival. The re-distribution of temple offerings, such as bouquets of Amun, sistra, and menits was also evident in other celebrations. It is probable that a great number of unspecified representations in the private tombs include yet-unknown scenes of this feast.

3.6.1. The deceased coming in and out of the tomb, and hymn to Re

As described earlier, the hymn to Re is generally written on the tomb entrance, or sometimes on the doorway to the inner-room.[170] The deceased tomb owner, often with his wife following him, is portrayed coming out and in his tomb. In ideal, his appearance was repeated on various occasions throughout the year. Assmann (2005, 379) explains that the New Year is not specifically referred to in the hymn to Re. Similarly, only a few examples are explicitly associated with the Valley Feast. For instance, two scenes in the aforementioned tomb of Menna (TT 69), on the entrance to the antechamber and on that to the inner-room, portray the deceased and his wife in adoration of Re (Figure 14).[171] While the former includes a reference to *[ḥb=k nfr m] ḫn.t[=k n] ḏsr-ḏsr.w* '[your beautiful festival at your] navigation [to] Djeser-djeseru',[172] the more specific designation 'His Beautiful Festival of the Valley of the West' is written on the latter.[173] The same phraseology is attested in the text on the right thickness of the entrance to the inner-room in the tomb of Amenhotep-Sise, second-priest of Amun under Thutmose IV (TT 75), which reads:[174]

> *pr.[t] m dw3.[t m] i[m]ḫ.t r m3 'Imn ḫft ḫʿ=f m ḏsr-ḏsr[.w]*
>
> Com[ing] out in the mornin[g from the t]omb in order to see Amun when he appears at Djeser-djeser[u].

These texts place emphasis on the solar aspect of Amun, but it is apparently not a result of stressing his function exclusively at the Valley Feast but of identifying him with Re, a transfiguration that fits decorations on the entrance, which generally faces towards the east. In addition to Re's principal character, Amun played another key role as Osiris at the Valley Feast. In the previously mentioned tomb of Userhat (TT 56), Amun worshipped on the West Bank appears to be analogous to *nṯr pn nfr Wsir ḥk3 ḏ.t* 'this good god, Osiris, ruler of everlastingness' (3.5.2.2). This may explain the otherwise inexplicable representation of Osiris in the tomb of Tjanuny (TT 74), described earlier in 3.5.2.1.[175] In the hymn to Re, the deceased was described as if he were alive, being able to move in and out of his tomb. He came out to witness Amun, who visited the West Bank. This was not only a canonical expression but an echo of the actual cult performance, in which statues of the deceased were used and possibly taken out from their tombs.

3.6.2. Participation in Amun's procession

Participation in a divine procession is attested in many celebrations. It is expressed in the standard phraseology *šms nṯr* 'to follow the god', which was almost exclusively used for the Valley Feast (Table 19, no. 77). At this celebration it was Amun of Karnak who was to be witnessed and followed. Hence, a text from the tomb of Paser, vizier and festival leader of Amun under Seti I and Ramses II (TT 106), reads:[176]

> *ḏd=f i nb=i nṯr=i niw.t=i 'Imn nb ns.wt t3.wy di=k wn=i m-m tpy.w-ʿ šps.w 3ḫ.w iḳr.w dw3w=i ḥm=k ḫnm=k sp3.t imnt.t ḫft-ḥr-nb=s iw=i m tp n nty m šms.w[=k] m ḥb=k nfr n in.t [šsp]=i wʿb sfḫ=i ky mi ḥsy=k nb*
>
> He (Paser) says 'O my lord, my god of my town, Amun, lord of the thrones of the Two Lands. May you cause me to be among the august ancestors, excellent spirits. I will adore your majesty when you are united

[170] Assmann 1983a.

[171] PM I-1², 134–7 (1 and 8); Hartwig 2013, figs 2.2a–b and 2.12 a–b.

[172] Assmann 1983a, 138.

[173] Schott 1952, 109 (71). The hymn to Re in association with the Valley Feast is also found on a pillar in TT 106 (PM I-1², 223 (D, d); Schott 1952, 95–6 (10)).

[174] PM I-1², 149 (7); *Urk.* IV, 1216: 5–6; Davies 1923, 18.

[175] TT 98 (1–2) has a parallel sequence of two scenes, in the last of which is portrayed the deceased adoring Osiris at 'His Beautiful Festival of the West'. Ptah-Sokar is also referred to in association with the Valley Feast in some tombs, such as TT 49 (3), TT 51 (1), and TT 263 (7). In TT 138 (8) the deceased couple adores Osiris with a text referring to Amun's sojourn at the mortuary temple of Thutmose I (Feucht 2006, 41, pl. 9, d).

[176] PM I-1², 223 (D, d); *KRI* III, 6: 9–12; Schott 1953, 96 (10) for translation.

> with the western district, Khefet-her-nebes. I am the first of those who are at [your] following at Your Beautiful Festival of the Valley. May I [receive] one clean cloth and remove another like all your blessed ones.

A hymn to Amun in the tomb of Neferhotep, chief scribe of Amun (TT 49), dating from the time of Tutankhamen to Horemheb, more clearly specifies where and what the deceased desired to witness:[177]

> *šms=i ḥm nṯr pn šps ỉmn nb ns.wt tȝ.wy m ḥb=f nfr n in.t šsp(=i) sn.w pr m-bȝḥ=f ḥr ḫȝ n nb nḥḥ ḫnm(=i) snṯr n wdn iḫ.wt iw=w m ḥnkt-ʿnḫ wʿb ḥʿ=i šsp sfḫ mȝ Ptḥ-skr*
>
> May I follow the majesty of this august god, Amun, lord of the thrones of the Two Lands, at His Beautiful Festival of the Valley, receive offerings that come out before him on the altar of the lord of eternity, and smell incense for offering goods, which were (offered) in Henqet-ankh (memorial temple of Thutmose III). My body is pure (for) receiving a removed cloth and seeing Ptah-Sokar.

Elsewhere in this tomb, Khenemet-ankh (the memorial temple of Thutmose I) is also referred to as where Amun took a rest.[178]

Schott (1953, 32–3) explained that statues of the deceased actually participated in Amun's procession. The inability of the deceased to take part in a divine procession was otherwise expressed on a stela in the tomb of Nebamen, a steward of the royal wife Nebtu under under Thutmose II and Thutmose III (TT 24). He is described as 'following the god' on one hand but someone else is expected to visit his tomb in order to deliver a bouquet to him on the other hand:[179]

> *ḫnm=i snṯr n rȝ.w-pr.w šms=i nṯr=i imy niw.t=i r ḏsr.w r ȝḫ.t imnt.t pr=tw n=i ḥr ʿnḫ nṯr pn ḥtp m ȝḫ.t =f*
>
> I shall smell the incense of temples. I shall follow my god, who is in my town, to Djeseru,[180] to the western horizon. One shall come forth to me with a bouquet of this god when (he) rests on his horizon.

Also in the tomb of Nebsumenu (TT 183), chief steward and festival leader of Amun in the time of Ramses II, the deceased appealed to the living regarding the Valley Feast:[181]

> *ḏd=f i ḥm.w-nṯr it.w-nṯr wʿb.w ḫry-ḥb.w nty nb ḥr ir.t ḥn.wt=sn m-ḫnw pr ỉmn šms ḥr tȝ r mȝȝ ỉmn m ḥb=f nfr m*[sic] *in.t stwt ib=sn m in.t šps.t r-gs w ḏ.t irr.t n sḳd* [unknown groups lost]
>
> He says 'O priests, divine-fathers, wab-priests, lector-priests, and all who do their tasks within the temple of Amun and follow on earth to see Amun at His Beautiful Festival of the Valley, with their heart proceeding in the august valley beside the everlasting district, which is made for the draughtsman [ ]'.

Hence, participation in festivals was guaranteed for the deceased by partaking of offerings that were distributed from temples or simply by addressing the living.

3.6.3. Changing cloth

Temple offerings were brought by living family members in order for the deceased to secure a link between a temple and the tomb. As will be described in 4.5.5, it was an essential part of the New Year celebrations that tomb statues were adorned with a new cloth. This practice was also referred to in association with the Valley Feast, as evidenced by the aforementioned texts of Neferhotep (TT 49) and Paser (TT 106) (3.6.2).

In the tomb of Piay (TT 263), a scribe of the granary in Amun's temple, dating from the first half of Ramses II's reign, references to the Festivals of the Valley and Sokar appear to be juxtaposed on each of the jambs of the entrance to the inner-room.[182] The text on the left jamb reads:

> *di=f šsp=i wʿb sfḫ=i ky ḥr šms nṯr pn m wḏ=f r ḏsr.w m ḥb=f n tp rnp.t*
>
> May he let me receive one clean cloth and remove another at following this god at his journey to Djeseru at his annual festival.

It should be noted that these references to a new garment in association with the Valley Feast date only from the end of the Eighteenth Dynasty and later, when this celebration came to be less attested in the

[177] PM I-1², 91 (3); Davies 1933a, 53, pl. 36; Assmann 1983a, 86–7 for transliteration and translation.
[178] PM I-1², 94 (23 and C, c).
[179] PM I-1², 42 (9); *Urk.* IV, 150: 7–10.
[180] Sethe (*Urk.* IV, *Übersetzung*, 73), Schott (1953, 94 (3)), and Assmann (2005, 248) translated *ḏsr.w* as 'Deir el-Bahari'.
[181] PM I-1², 290 (18); *KRI* III, 185: 5–7. A text parallel to this is attested in TT 184 (PM I-1², 291 (10–1); *KRI* III, 163: 5–7; Lichtheim 1992, 178 for translation).
[182] PM I-1², 345 (7); *KRI* III, 382: 10–11 and 383: 5.

private tombs (Table 19, no. 30). This may argue for the appropriation of specific formulae, which had been used only for a celebration other than the Valley Feast, most probably the New Year Festival.

3.6.4. Banqueting at the private tomb

Among many participants, a male singer is portrayed in the Valley Feast scene in the aforementioned tomb of Tjanuny (TT 74). His song describes the opening of the tomb as a result of the deceased's worthiness, as follows: *wdn.n=k sbꜣ.w wn iw šsp ir.t n=k ꜥ.wy=k wꜥb ḥr ir.t iḫ.wt Imn ḥr šsp st* 'You have offered. The doors are open when what has been made for you is received because your arms are pure at making offerings of Amun and receiving them.'[183] Songs and musicians appear in various banqueting representations but they do not bear any sorrow. Unlike the scenes of a funeral journey to the west, lamenting women are usually absent from these scenes.

By observing soot marks remained on some tomb walls at regular intervals, Schott (1953, 67, n. 2) speculated that they were generated by torches that were burnt in those tombs when a banquet took place. Each tomb was perhaps furnished with mats, chairs, and tables for temporary use. It would have been rather natural to spread stools in an open-air area outside a tomb in order to accommodate more attendants.[184] The banqueting scene in the previously mentioned tomb of Userhat (TT 56) portrays two daughters serving their parents (3.5.2.2). Elsewhere in the same scene, these daughters are seated on chairs, while others sit on the floor. Leading family members were probably invited into the tomb and sat there at a banquet, while others remained outside. As the text of Amenhotep-Sise (TT 75) tells us (3.6.1), the deceased desired to witness Amun in the morning, when the god appeared at Djeser-djeseru. Banqueting at the tomb is likely to have continued overnight until temple rituals marked the culmination.

Singers and musicians performed on various occasions (Table 19, no. 55). They visited tombs to recite musical spells in order to deliver the divine power through their performance.[185] On a pillar in the inner-room of the tomb of Neferhotep (TT 49), chief scribe of Amun from the time of Tutankhamen to Horemheb, he is portrayed going out at the Valley Feast, the legend of which reads:[186]

> *ḏd=f wꜣḏ.wy šmsw Imn m ḥb=f n in.t hrw nfr ꜥḥꜥ nfr ptri ir.ty=i nfr Imn ḥtp m ḫnm.t-ꜥnḫ mi sḫr.w=f n imy ḥꜣ.t iw pr.[tw] n=i ḫr [ꜥ]nḫ m* [unknown groups lost]
>
> He says: 'How refreshing it is to follow Amun at His Festival of the Valley! Good day, Good life. My eyes see the beauty of Amun when (he) rests at Khenemet-ankh (memorial temple of Thutmose I) in accordance with his ancient traditions when [one] comes to me with a [b]ouquet from [ ]'

hrw nfr was phraseology characteristic of any festive occasion.[187] There are two other instances where a banqueting scene at the Valley Feast is labelled *ir hrw nfr* 'making a good day'.[188] Many examples of *ir hrw nfr* appear in a musical formula played by harpers, which Lichtheim (1945, 183) classified as the 'make-holiday' song. Wente (1962, 120) and Assmann (2005, 345–6) associate this song with the Valley Feast, but its exclusive use only for this celebration cannot be corroborated.

3.6.5. Distribution of Amun's offerings from temples: bouquets, sistra, and menits

As described in 3.4.3, various divine offerings were delivered from memorial temples, normally of the reigning monarch. Among these offerings, bouquets, sistra, and menits were most frequently documented in texts. In particular, bouquets (*ꜥnḫ*) were considered highly significant, bearing the same phonetic value as 'life'.[189] The presentation of a bouquet to the dead was an old practice dating back to the Middle Kingdom and probably much earlier.[190] Offerings were first presented *ḥr ḫꜣw.t n Imn* 'on the altar of Amun' when he visited one or more of the memorial temples on the West Bank, except the tomb of Ipuy (TT 217), a sculptor under Ramses II, which records a bouquet delivered from Karnak on an unspecified occasion (Table 16, no. 19). Bouquets were collected at these temples and then infused with the divine power of Amun through rituals (p. 296, n. 241). They functioned as a means to distribute the divine power of the supreme god.[191]

183 PM I-1², 144 (2); Brack and Brack 1977, 31, pl. 23, b.
184 Hartwig 2004, 12–3.
185 Manniche 1991, 72.
186 PM I-1², 94 (C, c); Davies 1933a, vol. 1, 62, pl. 53 (c).

187 Darnell (2002, 130–5) associates this phraseology with the Hathoric cult.
188 TT 56 (PM I-1², 112 (5); *Urk.* IV, 1479: 2; Beinlich-Seeber 1987, 56, pl. 1) and TT 129 (PM I-1², 244 (1, I)).
189 Dittmar 1986, 119.
190 On a Middle Kingdom torch-stand, discovered in the valley temple of Sneferu at Dahshur, the chief sculptor Seshenu is portrayed receiving a bouquet (*ꜥnḫ*) of Ptah (PM III-2², 880; Fakhry 1959, vol. 2, II, fig. 388).
191 In the tomb of Khabekhenet (TT 2), for example, bouquets are described as: *ḥꜣ.w nb(.w) nḏm-sty ꜥnḫ nṯr im=sn* 'all flowers, sweet of scent, in which the god lives' (PM I-1², 7 (8, II); Černý 1949, 14). The ideological function of bouquets is encapsulated in a representation in the tomb of Djehut (TT 110), where an *ankh*-sign with arms is depicted hanging over a tall bouquet and presenting a smaller bouquet before the queen Hatshepsut (PM I-1², 228 (9); Davies 1932, pl. 40). A representation reminiscent of this is attested in the tomb of

Floral offerings, which were usually called *ꜥnḫ* and *rnpi*, were essential to rituals and celebrations.[192] However, in tomb decorations the occurrence of bouquets 'of Amun' appears to be limited to the Festivals of the Valley and the New Year (Table 19, no. 24). They originated from a temple to which an offering bringer belonged as a priest, who was normally a male family member. For example, the tomb of the first royal herald Iamnedjeh (TT 84), dated to the last years of Thutmose III, attests Amun's bouquets in two different scenes (Table 16, no. 2). The legends in these scenes refer to *ꜥnḫ n Ỉmn ꜥꜣ-ḫpr-kꜣ-rꜥ m ḫnm.t-ꜥnḫ* a 'bouquet of Amun of Aakheperkare (Thutmose I) from Khenemet-ankh (memorial temple of Thutmose I)'.[193] The bouquet was offered by the deceased's brother Kaemwaset, who was the 'fourth lector-priest of the temple of Aakheperkare'. Another offering scene elsewhere in this tomb includes the legend: *prr.t nb.t ḥr ḫꜣ.t n.t [Ỉmn] ḫft ḥtp=f m ḥnk.t-ꜥnḫ* 'All that comes forth on the altar of [Amun] when he rests at Henqet-ankh (memorial temple of Thutmose III).'[194] Unfortunately, the figure of the offering presenter is missing. He was probably a person different from Khaemwaset and may have belonged to a different temple, probably the memorial temple of Thutmose III.

Those who did not have priestly titles but were rather close to the royal court, such as the vizier and royal nurse, received bouquets mostly from the temple of Karnak. They are often portrayed presenting a bouquet to the king in the *ḥꜥ.t-nsw.t* scenes. In these scenes, a bouquet is described as having belonged to Amun who was considered the 'father' of the king (*ꜥnḫ n it=k Ỉmn*). As will be described in 4.5.12, this particular genre of scene is sometimes associated with the New Year celebration, when officials visited the king to salute (*inḏ ḥr*) and dedicate annual gifts (Table 21). It is remarkable that when an offering was transferred between a husband and his wife, it was exclusively associated with the New Year, as evidenced in the tomb of Ramose, a royal scribe during or after the Amarna Period (TT 46),[195] the tomb of Amenemheb, lieutenant-commander of soldiers under Thutmose III and Amenhotep II (TT 85)[196], the tomb of Qenamen, chief royal steward under Amenhotep II (TT 93),[197] and the tomb of Sennefer, overseer of the seal in the time of Thutmose III (TT 99).[198] Amenemheb's wife Baki was the chief royal nurse, who was portrayed suckling a young prince, and Qenamen's mother Amenemopet was a royal nurse. Hence, the association of the New Year celebrations with the royal circle was more evident than the Valley Feast. In addition, it appears that while representations of the Valley Feast were essentially posthumous, those of the New Year were contemporary in nature.

Young female relatives also played a key role as a songstress, who could have obtained a sistrum and menit from Hathoric institutions. However, the use of these cultic objects at the Valley Feast is only indirectly known—no representations of sistra and menits that are securely associated with this celebration have survived in the private tombs. In the unpublished tomb of an unknown person (TT 129), for example, his daughter is portrayed servicing her parents at the Valley Feast.[199] She extends the right hand over an offering table and holds a vase in the left hand, but a sistrum or menit is not represented. The text over the offering table reads:

> *n kꜣ=k m pr=k nfr wn dwꜣy.t šsp sn.w Ỉmn-rꜥ ḫft ḥt[p]=f m ḥnk.t-ꜥnḫ m [ḥ]b=f n [i]n.t imnt.t ir hrw nfr m dd n=k sꜣ.t=k mr.t=k*
>
> For your ka in your good house when it is morning. Receive the offerings of Amun-Re when he rest[s] at Henqet-ankh (memorial temple of Thutmose III) at His [Fe]stival of the Western [Va]lley. Make a good day with what your beloved daughter gives you.

In the tomb of Userhat (TT 56), examined in 3.5.2.2, his two daughters, Henutneferet and Nebettauy, are also chief offering presenters at the Valley Feast.[200] They hold a broad collar and a drinking bowl towards their parents. Henutneferet has the title of *ḥsy.t n(.t) Ḥw.t-ḥr nb.t iwn.t* the 'praised one of Hathor, lady of Dendera', but is not carrying a sistra or menit.[201] The best example of Hathoric objects carried by female attendants is attested in the tomb of Menkheperreseneb (TT 112), high-priest of Amun under Thutmose III. Four females are portrayed behind a man, who offers a bouquet of Amun to the deceased couple. The legend reads:[202]

> *n kꜣ=k ꜥnḫ n Ỉmn nb ns.wt tꜣ.wy ḫnty ip.t-s.wt niw.t ḫft ḥtp=f m ḥnk.t-ꜥnḫ ḥs=f tw swꜣḥ=f tw n kꜣ=k sš.wt mni.wt n.wt Ỉmn m*

Nakht (TT 161), a bearer of the floral offerings of Amun (PM I-1^2, 269 (6, I); Schott 1953, 55, fig. 15).

192 A substantial number of plant offerings are recorded in P. Harris I (XXIa, 2–XXIb, 10) as part of oblation consumed during the accession anniversary and the Opet Feast in the time of Ramses III (Erichsen 1933, 24–5; Grandet 1994, vol. 1, 251). Amun's bouquets are also associated with lunar celebrations, such as of the new moon (Nelson 1981, pl. 228) and of the sixth lunar day (P. Chester Beatty IX (BM 10589), recto, XIV, 9–11: Gardiner 1935, vol. 1, 97, vol. 2, pl. 56; Dittmar 1986, 120 for translation). For bouquets originating from other deities, see Dittmar 1986, 126.

193 *Urk.* IV, 136: 8 and 14.

194 PM I-1^2, 169 (10); *Urk.* IV, 955: 8.

195 PM I-1^2, 86 (1); Kawai 2010, 215, fig. 5.

196 PM I-1^2, 173 (C, a).The wife is portrayed suckling a young prince in her capacity as the chief royal nurse. Elsewhere within the same tomb she is likewise portrayed, which may also be associated with the New Year (PM I-1^2, 172 (16, II), unpublished).

197 PM I-1^2, 193 (G, d).

198 PM I-1^2, 205 (A, a).

199 PM I-1^2, 244 (1).

200 PM I-1^2, 112 (5); Beinlich-Seeber 1987, pl. 1.

201 PM I-1^2, 111 (2); Beinlich-Seeber 1987, 43–4, pl. 3.

202 PM I-1^2, 229 (3, I); Davies 1933b, 21, pl. 24.

> *ḏsr-ḏsr.w šsp n=k st di=w r fnd=k wn.ti n ḥḥ.w m s3[.t]=f snḫ[ḫ]=f ṯ3w r fnd=k m ḫr.t hrw n.t rꜥ nb*
>
> For your ka. Bouquet of Amun, lord of the thrones of the Two Lands, foremost of Karnak of Thebes, when he rests at Henqet-ankh (memorial temple of Thutmose III). May he praise you. May he make you endure. For your ka. Sistra and menits of Amun from Djeser-djeseru. Take them for yourself that are given to your nostril. Be of millions in his neighbour[hood]. May he give breath to your nostril every day.

Neither the personal relationship of these females with the deceased nor their priestly titles are known. It is, however, significant that the sistra and menits were brought from Deir el-Bahari, while Amun's bouquet originated from the memorial temple of Thutmose III. The other tomb belonging to this Menkheperreseneb (TT 86) includes a scene similar to this, and the legend refers to sistra and menits that were delivered from Djeser-akhet, the valley temple of Thutmose III.[203] It is probable that sistra and menits derived only from Deir el-Bahari, a focus of the Hathoric cult.[204] Pinch (1993, 280) explains that these instruments bore the same function as bouquets to convey the divine power and that female attendants at a banquet played a role of Hathor, who emanated the life-giving force to the king.

The significance of Deir el-Bahari as a focal point of Hathor's cult is evidenced by a number of graffiti discovered at Thutmose III's valley temple (3.2.3). People visited this site to worship Hathor on certain occasions, including the Valley Festival. In particular, a graffito numbered DB 31 is of great significance since it includes a reference to this Festival. It was written by a scribe named Ashaikhet, who lived in the Ramesside Period, and reads (**1141**):

> *ḥ3.t-sp 22 3bd 2-nw šmw sw 22 hrw n iy.t ir n sš ꜥ3-iḫ.t n pr Ḫnsw-n-Ỉmn-n-ip.t irm šmꜥy(.t) n Ỉmn T3y-nḏm r sm3ꜥ n nb.t Ḥw.t-ḥr.t nb.t ḏsr.t m ḥb nfr in.t n Ỉmn-rꜥ nsw.t nṯr.w Mw.t Ḫn[sw] imy n=i* [four or five groups illegible] *ink wꜥb [n] pr* [a few groups lost] *m* [one group lost] *p3 nṯr n ḥw.t nsw.t* [three groups lost *n*] *ḥry.t m hrw nb n ꜥnḫ* [one group lost] *m* [one group lost] *Ḫnsw-n-[Ỉ]mn-n-ip.t*
>
> Year 22, II Shemu 22: day of a visit paid by the scribe Ashaikhet of the temple of Khonsu-of-Amenopet with the songster(ss) of Amun Taynedjem to make an offering to the lady Hathor, lady of Djeseret, at the Beautiful Festival of the Valley of Amun-Re, king of the gods, Mut, and Khon[su]. Give me [ ] I am a wab-priest [of] the temple of [ ] in [ ] the god to the temple of the king, upper [ ] on the day. The lord of life [ ] in [ ] Khonsu-of-[A]menopet.

If Ashaikhet's family was of Theban origin, he would have visited his family tomb after the visit to Deir el-Bahari. It was probably at this point that his wife Taynedjem, in her capacity as a songstress of Amun, could have received Hathoric instruments to be delivered to the family tomb. A visit to Deir el-Bahari of a couple as such may be illustrated in the tomb of Panehesy, a priest of Amenhotep-of-the-forecourt under Ramses II (TT 16).[205] The deceased couple is portrayed adoring the Hathor-cow 'lady of the West, khefet-her-nebes' in a mountain. A menit-necklace hangs over the cow's neck towards the couple. His wife Tarenu, a songstress of Amun, holds a tall bouquet in one hand.[206]

With regard to the physical quantity of divine offerings, one may ask how many were consumed at the Valley Feast. Bouquets, sistra, and menits were only an epitome of all that was distributed from temples. It is not impossible that broader terms, such as *prr.t nb.t ḥr k3w.t n Ỉmn* 'all that comes on the altar of Amun' and *iḫ.t nb.t nfr.t wꜥb.t* 'every good pure thing', might have included offerings that met people's daily needs. Even so, it is difficult to conclude whether such a distribution system at the Valley Feast functioned as part of the mass production and consumption of provisions on a regular basis, or was only symbolic and minimal to circulate Amun's power.[207] The fiscal functions of festival were more evident in the New Year celebrations, when state incomes were collected and registered (4.6.1).

The Valley Festival stands out in that ordinary people worshipped their ancestors when the royal family performed a parallel celebration under the same roof of the mortuary cult. The cult of Amun, in the guise of or associated with Osiris, connected the memorial temples and the private tombs by delivering divine offerings from the former to the latter. This, at least on an ideological level, functioned as a very expansive and systematic vehicle for sharing the divine force with all strata of

[203] PM I-1², 175 (1); Davies 1933b, 14, pl. 17.

[204] The latest evidence for a sistrum that was delivered from Djeser-djeseru is attested in the tomb of Sheshonq (TT 27), dated to the Twenty-Sixth Dynasty (Sist 1976, fig. 6, b).

[205] PM I-1², 28 (5, I); Baud and Drioton 1932b, fig. 17. This genre of scene could be an isolated subject depicted on stelae in the Nineteenth Dynasty (Exell 2009, 52–9).

[206] Visits of couples may be interpreted in a sexual context. Based on the fact that small phallic votive objects were discovered in the Hathor chapel belonging to the valley temple of Thutmose III, Pinch (1993, 244) proposes that people visited this site at the Valley Feast to pray for good sex lives.

[207] A workshop attached to Djeser-djeseru is known to have produced beads and perhaps textiles for popular votive offerings (Pinch 1993, 327).

society, including the dead.[208] Since the Valley Festival centred on the royal memorial temples and the Hathoric cult at Deir el-Bahari, it was purely Theban in nature and no other cities could have had grounds for creating a local version of this celebration. In other words, the Valley Feast was destined for a radical reform when the kings were no longer buried at Thebes and the royal residence moved to the north.[209] This may explain the lack of evidence that securely attests this celebration to have continued into the Third Intermediate Period and later, apart from highly liturgical and canonical literature.

3.7. Excursus: appointment of the divine wife Isis, a daughter of Ramses VI

No surviving evidence securely attests an oracular session performed during the Valley Festival. This is probably not accidental and conforms to the short duration of this celebration (3.2.3). However, this feast may have also provided a setting for appointing high-ranking officials and priests like other celebrations (2.5.3 and 4.4.2). This is evidenced by a fragmentary relief dated to the time of Ramses VI. It originated from an unknown monument at Deir el-Bakhit in western Thebes, now lost of its location, and the relief itself is also missing.[210] The upper part of Amun-Re's barque is represented on two stone blocks. Three lines of text run over the barque and read:

> [unknown groups lost *ḫr ḥm=f nsw.t*]-*bi͗.ty* [*nb*] *tꜣ.wy* [*Wsr-m*]*ꜣꜥ.t-rꜥ*-[*stp-n-i͗*]*mn* [*sꜣ*] *Rꜥ* [*nb*] *ḫꜥ.w* [*R*]*ꜥ*-[*ms-sw*]-*nṯr-ḥḳꜣ-i͗wn h*]*rw* [*p*]*n* [two groups lost] *n ẖ.t=f m-bꜣḥ ḥm nṯr pn* [unknown groups lost *m ḥb=f nf*]*r n i͗n.t i͗w.tw m wbꜣ ꜥꜣ n ꞽImn r smn rn n ḥm.t nṯr wꜥb.t ꜥ.wy n ꞽImn-rꜥ nsw.t nṯr.w sꜣ.t nsw.t nb.t tꜣ.wy dwꜣ.t nṯr ꜣs.t* [unknown groups lost] *ḥnꜥ mw.t nsw.t Ḥm-ḏry*[*.t*] *i͗my-r ni͗w.t ṯꜣty Nḥy* [*mꜣꜥ*] *ḫrw i͗w ꞽImn-rꜥ nsw.t nṯr.w Mw.t Ḫnsw wšd=s* [one sign lost?] *i͗w=w sr n=s nfr.w r šꜣꜥ*
>
> [Under his person, the king of Upper and] Lower Egypt, [lord] of the Two Lands, [Userm]aatre-[setepena]men,[211] [son] of Re, [lord] of the diadems, [R]a[mses]-netjerheqaiun. On [th]is day [ ] born of him, before the majesty of this god [at His Beauti]ful [Festival] of the Valley. One was in the great audience hall of Amun in order to establish the name of the divine wife, pure of arms, of Amun-Re, king of the gods, royal daughter, lady of the Two Lands, divine adoratice Isis [ ] with the royal mother Hemdjere[t] and the mayor and vizier Nehy,[212] [true] of voice. Amun-Re, king of the gods, Mut, and Khonsu saluted her and foretold her good things until [...

It is difficult to conclude whether this event took place during, before, or after the Valley Festival. Four centuries later at the beginning of the Saite Period, when Nitocris I, a daughter of Psametik I, was sent from Sais in order to Thebes to become the divine wife, she was accompanied by dignitaries, but not a royal mother and the king. As described in 2.5.3, Nitocris' ordination took place at Karnak on II Akhet 14, a day perhaps before the Opet Festival (**206**). It is probable that Isis was likewise appointed at the temple of Karnak, not on the Theban West, where our relief originally came from. The visit with the royal mother from the northern capital city may argue for her role to convey a royal message on behalf of the king and more importantly to witness Isis' debut ceremony.[213] Since Nitocris is likely to have acted a newly appointed priestess at the Opet Festival shortly after her debut, such was probably also the case for Isis at the Valley Feast.

---

[208] Hence, a text in the tomb of Ibi, chief steward of the divine adoratice Nitocris I under Psametik I (TT 36 (23): Kuhlmann and Schenkel 1983, 209, pl. 70) reads: *ḏd=f i͗ ꜥnḫ.w tp.w tꜣ ms nty r ms š*[*m*]*=sn ḥr swḏꜣ i͗b ḥr i͗mnt.t wꜣs.t i͗w.t=sn m šms.w n ꞽImn m i͗p.t-s.wt m ḥb=f nfr n i͗n.t i͗r.t=sn swꜣ ḥr* [two groups lost *=s*]*n ꜥḳ.t=sn r i͗s pn mꜣ=sn nty i͗m=f* 'He says: O the livings on earth and the one who was born and will be born. They wen[t] in delight on the West of Thebes. They came at the followings of Amun from Karnak at His Beautiful Festival of the Valley. They passed [ ]. They entered this tomb and saw the one who was in it'.

[209] Traunecker, Le Saout, and Masson 1981, 135.

[210] *LD* III, pl. 218, a–b (better configured in *LD text* III, 101); *KRI* VI, 321–2; Kitchen 1972, 190; Černý 1958b, 32; Seele 1960, 195.

[211] The prenomen here clearly indicates usurpation of a name belonging to a predecessor, probably Ramses III (Černý 1958b, 32, n. 3) or Ramses IV (Seele 1960, 194). Ramses VI seems to have changed the royal names only, which left this account alien to historical facts. Seele (1960, 196), however, explained that the original text partially fitted Ramses VI's biography because he had a daughter with the same name Isis. As a result, Seele suggested two different women with the same name and title, daughters of Ramses IV and Ramses VI. The daughter of the latter is described on a stela, discovered at Koptos, as born of that king and the queen Nebkhesbed (Petrie 1986, pl. 19). Kitchen (1972, 191) concluded that the usurpation did not happen at all and our text belonged solely to Ramses VI. For the queen mother Hemdjeret, see Černý (1958b, 33) who maintained that she was a grand mother of Ramses VI and a mother-in-law of Ramses III, a hypothesis opposed by Seele (1960, 204) who considered her one of Ramses III's wives. Murnane (1971/1972, 131) identified a few royal women of the same name Hemdjeret in the genealogy in the first half of the Twentieth Dynasty.

[212] Dresbach (2012, 88) dates this vizier to the time of Ramses VI.

[213] Amer (1985b, 66, n. 4) argues that Ramses VI himself visited Thebes for this occasion.

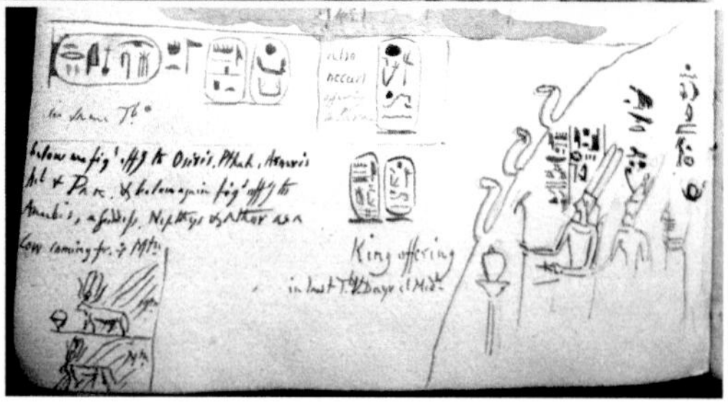

Figure 17. Stela in the tomb of Ramose (TT 7 (9)).
Above: Griffith Institute photograph no. 2016, by courtesy of the Griffith Institute, Oxford.
Right: Some details drawn by Gardner Wilkinson in the mid Nineteenth century (from his notebook numbered MSS. Wilkinson dep. e. 59), by courtesy of the Bodleian Library, Oxford.
The top register represents Ramses II offering incense to the Theban triad in the western moutain, the ridge line of which extends from the king's feet over the double plumes of Amun-Re (note that Amun-Re here is not one of those worshipped on the West Bank, but the one resided at Karnak). The vizier Paser and Ramose stand behind the king. The second register portrays Ramose and his family adoring Osiris, Ptah, Horus, Isis, and Min-Kamutef. He and his family appear again in the third register, and adore Anubis, Isis, and Nephtys, as well as two Hathor cows emerging from a mountain, likely the same location as that represented in the first register.

Chapter 4

New Year Festival

4.1. Research history

Although the New Year Festival is not always given a prominent position in festival lists, it had been a traditional celebration since the Old Kingdom. The occasion embraced various events, from the erection of obelisks at temples to evening meals at private tombs.

The frequent visits to Thebes of the vizier and high officials at this time of the year are known from Ramesside texts, mostly ostraca from Deir el-Medina (Table 7). Despite the absence of any mention of a particular religious ceremony, the concentration of their visits at the end of the year stands out. Some visits appear to have been occasioned by the tomb robberies that were a constant feature of the later Twentieth Dynasty. However, some visits were followed by juridical sessions which required the attendance of high officials from the state administration in the north. It is hardly surprising that these officials also participated in the New Year celebrations and the Opet Feast, possibly on the king's request (1.3.1.2).

Quite a few scholars have explored the New Year celebrations but most attention has been paid to the Ptolemaic-Roman Period because intact sources survive from major temples in Upper Egypt, most notably at Edfu and Dendera. Relevant works have been published at some length by: Alliot (1949, vol. 1, 303–433); Fairman (1954/1955); Goyon (1972a and 2006); Daumas (1980); Germond (1981, 194–224 and 1986); Cauville (2002, 35–49, 121–40); Corthals (2004); and Coppens (2008 and 2010).

The exploration of earlier times, on the other hand, is sparse as Waitkus (2008, 278) justifiably points out. For instance, *ẖnm itn* the 'uniting of the sun-disk', is attested in Ptolemaic-Roman temples as an essential component of the New Year Feast, but there is only scarce and indirect evidence for this taking place in the New Kingdom. However, Barguet (1962, 291) was well aware of the significance of this ceremony when it was performed at the Akh-menu, Thutmose III's festival complex located to the east of Karnak temple. No work exists that has been solely dedicated to the New Year Festival during that period other than Aldred's (1969) short article on New Year gift scenes in Theban private tombs and Jauhiainen's thesis (2009, 74–84), a section of which is dedicated to the popular characteristics of this feast when it was celebrated at Deir el-Medina. Ancillary works pertinent to the present research do exist: Davies (1924) collected representations of large candles from those tombs. Although he confined himself to examining their physical form, some were undoubtedly associated with the New Year. E. Schott (1970) and Traunecker (1972) examined a ceremony relating to a libation ritual at this celebration. Finally, Stricker (1948) and Bommas (1999) examined the highly significant liturgical text P. Leiden I 346, which gives a valuable insight into rites performed at the end of the year in the Eighteenth Dynasty.

Additionally, one may want to refer to Versnel (1970, 201–35), who compared the Egyptian and Mesopotamian New Year celebrations by focusing largely on the Sed Festival.

4.2. Chronological study

4.2.1. Designations, precursors, and historical development

4.2.1.1. pr.t-spd.t, wpy-rnp.t, tpy-rnp.t, and msw.t-Rꜥ: calendrical designations

A chronological, calendrical analysis of the New Year Festival cannot be separated from an examination of the terminology and phraseology associated with it. Therefore, this section opens with a presentation of different designations associated with the beginning of the year. There were four characteristic designations: *pr.t-spd.t* 'coming-out of Sothis'; *wpy-rnp.t* 'opening of the year'; *tpy-rnp.t* 'beginning of the year'; and *msw.t-Rꜥ* 'birth of Re'. These terms appear to have been linked to four distinctive moments regarded by Egyptians as important calendrical markers: the heliacal rising of Sothis (natural year cycle); the beginning of the civil calendar (I Akhet 1), the beginning of the lunar calendar (any day falling within I Akhet), and the intercalary lunar month (to be inserted between civil IV Shemu and I Akhet every two or three years). However, it is difficult to confirm whether these designations all explain the complexity of the Egyptian calendrical systems; and, if they do, which designation is employed in which system. Since the terms were probably used differently from time to time, it is safer to limit the present examination to their occurrence in surviving texts, and to the ideological, rather than the functional, connotation that each of them evokes.

It is logical that the heliacal rising of Sothis was celebrated because it was the most important astronomical event for Egyptians.[1] However, it is not securely attested before the Middle Kingdom but may be represented on an ivory tablet dating from the First Dynasty.[2] P. Berlin 10007 and P. Berlin 10012 B from Lahun record that festival offerings (*ḥby.t*) were brought to a temple for the day of *pr.t-spd.t*.[3] Other than these, little evidence attests a heliacal celebration before the Ptolemaic Period. The decree of Canopus records *pr.t-spd.t* as being *wpy-rnp.t* but fixed to II Shemu 1 in year 9 of Ptolemy III (**1073**). The festival celebrated for this astronomical event lasted five days.

Unlike the other three, *wpy-rnp.t* normally appears with the determinative , either following or combined with it. The implication of this designation is straightforward, denoting the civil New Year on I Akhet 1 and its celebrations.[4] This was the only designation which could be modified as *ḥb=f n wpy-rnp.t*, defining the association with Amun as a local Theban feast.[5] According to Parker (1950, 58), both *wpy-rnp.t* and *msw.t-Rᶜ* originally meant the heliacal rising of Sothis and were ultimately employed as the designation of the last civil month (IV Shemu). By the Ramesside time *msw.t-Rᶜ* presided over *wpy-rnp.t* and it had become the Coptic month known as Mesore.[6] Both could also be used as a designation of the civil New Year's Day. The former was a cosmogonical term referring to the renewal of the cosmic power, while the latter was functional and pertinent to the operation of the civil calendar.

A distinction between *wpy-rnp.t* and *tpy-rnp.t* is hard to draw. From the Old Kingdom they normally appeared separately in festival lists, the earliest evidence dating to the Fourth Dynasty.[7] Parker (1950, 31 and 62) proposed that *tpy-rnp.t* was originally the first day of the original lunar year, and later came to denote the day of the beginning of the regnal year on a mythological level, particularly in association with I Peret 1, the day on which Horus ascended to the throne. Perhaps in line with this, the temple calendar at Edfu records *ḥb wpy-rnp.t* for I Peret 1.[8] According to Parker (1950, 62), followed by Spalinger (1990, 290), there were two kinds of the orthography for *tpy-rnp.t* and their usage was apparently distinct. The one beginning with was associated with the beginning of the year, whereas the other, with , was equated with I Peret 1. However, there is no justification for such a clear distinction because, as Spalinger (1996, 36, n. 18) later admits, they alternate in passages where I Akhet 1 is intended.[9] Insofar as the New Kingdom sources are concerned, it is safe to define *tpy-rnp.t* with not strictly in a calendrical, but in a semantic context, as an expression emphasizing the recurrence of a given event. This naturally recalls the general translation of *tpy rnp.t* as 'annual' (3.5.1).

4.2.1.2. *nḥb-kꜣ.w*: mythological aspect of the New Year

The mythological implications signified by I Akhet 1 and I Peret 1 is most evident from *nḥb-kꜣ.w*, a designation shared by both and tentatively rendered the 'unification of the kas'.[10] On these days, the Festivals of the New Year and Khoiak saw the culmination and renewal of the world, when the kingship was accomplished.[11] According to Corthals (2004, 8), each celebration was characterized by a solar nature (Heliopolitan) and a

[1] Note the scientific fact that the heliacal rising of Sothis corresponded to the summer solstice in around 2500 BC but was dislocated from it by *ca.* ten days by 1300 BC (1.2.4).

[2] Parker 1950, 34.

[3] Luft 1992, 45 and 58.

[4] However, later in the Ptolemaic-Roman Period, *wpy-rnp.t* had three different meanings, as seen in the Canopus decree: the beginning of the civil year, the heliacal rising of Sothis, and the birthday of rulers (Depuydt 2003, 58–9). It also referred to three different events at Esna, celebrated on I Akhet 1, I Akhet 9, and II Shemu 26 (Spalinger 1992, 51–9; Depuydt 2003, 60–7).

[5] TT 85 (PM I-1^2, 173 (C, a); *Urk.* IV, 925: 13).

[6] It may be worth noting that 1 Thoth of the Coptic calendar corresponds to 29 August (Julian) and to 11 September (Gregorian), not to the heliacal rise of Sothis. This modification alludes to a link to the culmination of the Nile's inundation. Indeed, the Coptic New Year's Day is celebrated as the Festival of Neyrouz, which has its etymological origin in *nꜣ-itrw* 'the rivers', coupled with confusion with the Persian designation of the New Year 'Nowruz' (Popper 1951, 123–30).

[7] For example, the mastabas of the queen Meresankh III (Simpson 1974, vol. 1, 15, pl. 7 a, fig. 7); of Nensedjerkai (PM III-1^2, 72 (1–2); Junker 1929, vol. 2, 115, fig. 7); of Werptah (PM III-1^2, 140; Junker 1929, vol. 6, 242). The very fragmentary calendars of Sahure's valley temple (Borchardt 1910, vol. 2, pl. 72) and of the valley temple of Niuserre's solar temple (Helck 1977, pl. 2, cols 1 and 4) contains a reference to *tpy-rnp.t* (and to *wpy-rnp.t* too in the latter temple). The pyramid temple of Pepi II perhaps includes the only surviving relief depicting the celebration of *tpy-rnp.t* (Jéquier 1936, vol. 2, pl. 50). It represents a gathering of gods from all over Egypt, according to Arnold (1997, 68–9, fig. 29), for the Sed Festival.

[8] *Edfou* V, 399: 7. The calendar at the Mut precinct of Karnak, records *ḥb kꜣ-ḥr-[kꜣ]* and *wpy-rnp.t* in the same context (Sauneron 1983, pl. 9, ll. 20–1 for facsimile; Spalinger 1993b, 169–9 for translation). The Legend of the Winged Disk recorded at Edfu speaks of Horus as a son of Re, defeating his enemies from the south to the north of Egypt. Rites related to this story were performed on I Akhet 1–2, IV Akhet 24, I Peret 7, and II Peret 21 (Fairman 1935, 33–4).

[9] For example, two texts each from TT 99 (*Urk.* IV, 538: 12) and TT 46 (Kawai 2010, fig. 5) include identical phraseology regarding I Akhet 1, but and alternate.

[10] For evidence from New Kingdom Thebes, see *MH* III, pl. 163, list 52; TT 50 (9–10, I); TT 341 (8–9); TT 46 (1); TT 93 (G, a); and TT 345 (3 and 5).

[11] For the significance of I Akhet 1 and I Peret 1 as the days of the accession and the Sed Feast, see Parker 1950, 62; Bleeker 1967, 109; Spalinger 1990, 293, n. 1 for references. Also see Białostocka 2010, 19, n. 36 for more references.

chthonic nature. It was only for the Khoiak Feast that *nḥb-kꜣ.w* could be replaced with the designation *kꜣ-ḥr-kꜣ* the 'ka on the ka'.[12] This designation remained in use and eventually became the Coptic month-name Khoiak. In the Medinet Habu calendar, the day of *nḥb-kꜣ(.w)* is recorded for I Peret 1 with *ḫꜥ-nsw.t* the 'appearance of the king', which does not appear for the New Year (**568**).

Whatever the exact translation of *nḥb-kꜣ.w* may be, it is associated with the renewal of the old regime, of which the Osiride myth is a part. The word is attested in the Pyramid Texts as the name of a mythological serpent, manifesting the sun. Shorter (1935) rendered *nḥb-kꜣ.w* as a 'bestower of dignities' or 'he who appoints the positions'. Subsequently, some gods, such as Ptah and Horus, came to carry this name.[13] The term seems to be used to stress the youthfulness of an heir and the orthodoxy given to him by the dead father. The earliest evidence of the words *nḥb* and *kꜣ.w* in association with a mortuary cult practice is attested in the Middle Kingdom tomb of Khnumnefer, count of the Hypselite nome, at Deir Rifeh, where one of the prayers of the deceased is expressed as: *nḥb=f kꜣ.w šps.w* 'May he unite with the august kas.'[14]

Whether *nḥb-kꜣ.w* as a feast name was transferred from the Khoiak Feast to the New Year celebration (or *vice versa*), or it was shared from the beginning, cannot be confirmed.[15] Spalinger (1994b, 303) seems to indicate that *nḥb-kꜣ.w* of I Akhet 1 was secondary by referring to P. Cairo 86637 (recto I, 2), which records *wpy-rnp.t sn-nw* the 'second Opening of the Year' as corresponding to *nḥb-kꜣ.w* of I Akhet 1 (**17**). The earliest evidence of *nḥb-kꜣ.w* as a distinctive ceremony dates to the Twelfth Dynasty and was celebrated on I Peret 1 (**563**), whereas that of I Akhet 1 may have been first attested as late as the time of Thutmose I to Thutmose III.[16] In a scene in the tomb of Sennefer, overseer of the seal (TT 99) dating to the time of Thutmose III, the presentation of the New Year gifts is described as taking place *hrw wpy-rnp.t nḥb-kꜣ.w hrw tpy-rnp.t pr.t-spd.t* 'on the day of the Opening of the Year, Nehebkau, the day of the Beginning of the Year, the Appearance of Sothis'.[17] Phraseology parallel to this is attested in the tomb of Ramose (TT 46), a royal scribe under Amenhotep III or later, as: *msw n Rꜥ wpy-rnp.t hrw nḥb-kꜣ.w hrw tpy-rnp.t hrw pr.t-spd.t* the 'Birth of Re, the Opening of the Year, the day of Nehebkau, the day of the Beginning of the Year, the day of the Appearance of Sothis'.[18]

4.2.1.3. *ḥꜣ.t rnp.t and ihhy: beginning of the ideological regnal year*

There are other ancillary expressions associated with the New Year. First, *ḥꜣ.t rnp.t* the 'front of the year' may be restored in P. UC 32191 discovered in Lahun, where *ḥꜣ.t* [...] is written next to *wpy-rnp.t*, but this restoration is not secure.[19] Regardless of whether or not it was directly associated with the civil New Year, the usage of *ḥꜣ.t rnp.t* was essentially ideological in the early Eighteenth Dynasty, evoking the earlier tradition of starting the regnal year at the New Year during the Old and Middle Kingdoms.[20] This phrase disappeared during the Ramesside Period and later. Then, it re-appeared in the Ptolemaic-Roman time. In the Canopus decree, the sign of *wpy-rnp.t* is replaced with that of *ḥꜣ.t rnp.t* in the demotic version.[21] Some magical texts of the Eighteenth Dynasty and later, known as the 'Book of the Year', include the 'Book of the End of the Year (*mḏꜣ.t n.t ꜥrḳy rnp.t*) and the 'Book of the Front of the Year (*mḏꜣ.t n.t ḥꜣ.t rnp.t*)' as a counterpart to each other.[22] It is probable that *ḥꜣ.t rnp.t* here does not bear any specific meaning but simply denotes the start of the year. On the other hand, *hrw tpy n [ḥb] ihy ẖr ḥꜣ.t rnp.t* the 'first day of [the festival of] *ihy* every front of the year', recorded in the Edfu calendar, is associated with the specific day of I Akhet 13 (**73**).

It is significant to see the association of *ḥꜣ.t rnp.t* with *ihy*. The latter word as an expression of delighted

[12] The rite of *kꜣ-ḥr-kꜣ* is only attested for I Peret 2 (**590**), 4 (**601**), and 5 (**606**).

[13] Leitz 2002a, vol. 4, 274.

[14] PM V, 3; Griffith 1889, pl. 16, middle, l. 9; Montet 1936, 139–40.

[15] The Sokar Festival is recorded in one of the Abusir accounting papyri as taking place on IV Akhet 25 (**512**). To date, this is the only Old Kingdom celebration whose date is fixed to a specific civil day.

[16] The tomb of Amenhotep, TT 345 (PM I-1^2, 414 (5); *Urk.* IV, 107: 7).

[17] PM I-1^2, 205 (pillar A, a); *Urk.* IV, 538: 12.

[18] PM I-1^2, 86 (1); Kawai 2010, 215, fig. 5 for photograph.

[19] Spalinger (1992, 24, a) and Collier and Quirke (2006, 94 and an unnumbered plate at the end) reconstructed the passage as *ḥꜣ.t [rnp.t]*. Luft (1992, fig. 2 on the opposite side of p. 140) also publishes a configuration of the text.

[20] Counting the regnal year of each king from New Year's Day was a practice, dating unbroken from the Old Kingdom up to the Second Intermediate Period (Gardiner 1945; Ryholt 1997, 321). This recalls the regnal year ideogram 𓆳𓊗, whose reading has long been debated. Based on texts from Edfu temple, the reading *ḥꜣ.t-sp* as the 'front of the occasion' was first proposed by Sethe (1905, 94–7) and followed by Gardiner (1945, 14). Sethe further remarked that this reading eventually underwent consonantal modification to *ḥsp*, which also meant the fraction 1/4, the implication being that an intercalary day was inserted every four years. This reading was first challenged by Mattha (1962, 18–9) who read the ideogram, on the basis of parallels in Coptic, as *ḥsb.t-sp* 'reckoning/dating the year of the occasion', a participle form of the verb *ḥsb* 'divide'. He further maintained that when 𓊗 was replaced by 𓇳 (or remained only as a traditional component or was completely dropped), the reading *ḥsb.t* was the most appropriate. Also rejecting Sethe's view, Edel (1949) retained the reading *rnp.t-sp*, based on an examination of the Coptic parallels, which has been accepted by Fecht (1985). Caminos (1958, 76–7) drew attention to another orthography 𓆳𓊗. For references to other general discussions on this issue, see Vinson 2009, 151, n. 2.

[21] Spiegelberg 1922, 18 and 22; Depuydt 2003, 59.

[22] For instance, P. Leiden I 346, dating from the Eighteenth Dynasty, is entitled as *mḏꜣ.t n.t ꜥrḳy rnp.t* the 'Book of the End of the Year', and *mḏꜣ.t n.t hrw.w 5 ḥr.w rnp.t* the 'Book of the Five Epagomenal Days' (Stricker 1948; Bommas 1999). The Book of the End of the Year, together with the 'Book of the Front of the Year (*mḏꜣ.t ḥꜣ.t rnp.t*)', appears to be a harmful agent among major gods, against which divine amuletic decrees were issued to protect petitioners during the Third Intermediate Period (Edwards 1960). The nature of these scrolls is unknown, but they might have been issued at the turn of the year to make a new wish for both evil and good purposes.

laudation appears in the Pyramid Texts several times when the king is described as returning from the dead,[23] but it is only from the Middle Kingdom that the doubling of the *h*-sign appeared as *ihhy* and became the name of feasts with the sign of .[24] The Coffin Texts specifies the *ihhy* as one of six mortuary celebrations to be performed for the deceased.[25] Given that it comes after *msy.t* the 'Supper' and the Wag Feast but before the Sokar Feast, the *ihhy* seems to have fallen in the Akhet season. In fact, there are several texts attesting this celebration taking place on various dates falling in I Akhet (Table 22). There is only one New Kingdom pictorial source representing a procession of royal statues moving towards a god on the occasion of *ihhy n ḥꜣ.t rnp.t* at the Akh-menu of Thutmose III in Karnak (4.3.4).

At face value, the *ihhy* seems to have been governed by the movement of the moon, as the various dates of its occurrence suggest. By analyzing P. Berlin 10001, Luft (1992, 26–30 and 148–9) relates it to a new moon day that falls between the civil New Year's Day and the heliacal rising of Sothis. However, the word *ihhy* and semantically similar expressions are attested in conjunction with the civil New Year and the Wag Feast. Hence, the Medinet Habu calendar records the eve of the Wag Feast (I Akhet 17) as *hrw ꜣꜥꜥ n wꜣg* the 'day of the laudation of the Wag Festival'.[26] The surviving texts suggest that *ihhy* was not a distinctive event but an expression applied to any event that celebrated the 'beginning' in general and, by extension, a series of celebrations for the New Year, including an unknown ceremony performed on IV Shemu 21, evidenced by an Abusir papyrus.[27]

It is also noteworthy that the date of I Akhet 13 in the aforementioned Edfu text, may not be a coincidence but an echo of an earlier tradition, as Grimm (1994b, 74) proposes. An unnumbered stone fragment discovered at Karnak witnesses *ihhy n ḥꜣ.t rnp.t* as taking place on the same date in the time of Amenhotep I. In addition, the fragmentary calendar of Thutmose III at the Akh-menu records one other instance of I Akhet 13 as the day of an unspecified seasonal festival (**69**).

4.2.1.4. *ḥꜣ.t nḥḥ*

An expression similar to *ḥꜣ.t rnp.t* but somewhat different in nature is *ḥꜣ.t nḥḥ* the 'front of eternity'.[28] Sethe (1930, 2–3) related it to the renewal of the Sothic cycle that, he believed, took place during the reign of Seti I. However, as Gardiner (1952, 21–2) and Černý (1961, 150–1) questioned, *ḥꜣ.t nḥḥ* was only a flowery phrase for the king to wish many more years of his reign because it is used for later rulers, as well.[29] Spalinger (1990, 291) associated *ḥꜣ.t nḥḥ* and *tpy-rnp.t* with I Akhet 1 and I Peret 1, on the latter of which Horus succeeded his dead father Osiris, coupled by the ideological accession of the king at the Sed Feast.

The New Year is described as *ḥꜣ.t n nḥḥ pḥ ḏ.t* the 'front of eternity and the end of everlastingness' in the tomb of Sennefer (TT 96), mayor of the Southern City under Amenhotep II (4.5.12). The earliest evidence is attested in the festival list of Thutmose III at the Akh-menu, dated to 'year after 23', an expression reminiscent of the year-counting system of the Old Kingdom (Table 23). It records *wpy[-rnp.t] ḥꜣ.t nḥḥ* for I Akhet 1. The Nauri Stela of Seti I employs the phrase for I Peret 1, as follows:[30]

> *ḥꜣ.t-sp 4 tpy pr.t sw 1 ḥꜣ.t nḥḥ šsp ꜣw.t ib ḥfn.w m rnp.wt ḥtp.wt ḥḥ.w m ḥb.w sd ḥr s.t ꜣḫ.ty ḏ.t m nswy.t Itm*
>
> Year 4, I Peret 1, front of eternity, receiving joy, hundreds of thousands of peaceful years, millions of jubilees on the seat of the two horizons, everlastingness in the kingship of Atum.

Phraseology parallel to this is found in a text at Speos Artemidos recording Seti I's first year, with a date missing.[31] However, *ḥꜣ.t nḥḥ* does appear in association with dates other than I Akhet 1 and I Peret 1. For instance, a statue of Ramose, a scribe in the Necropolis, originating from Deir el-Medina (Cairo 72000) records a royal decree to dedicate offerings to the statue in the temple of Hathor-Dweller-of-Thebes. It is dated to III Akhet 8 (or 7) in year 9 of Ramses II, which is expressed as *[ḥꜣ.t n]ḥḥ* (**330**). Another instance from the same reign attests III Shemu in year 40 (**1301**), which Spalinger (1990, 292) explains in association with the accession of Ramses II by following Helck's hypothesis (1959, 119) that it took place on III Shemu 27.[32]

23 PT 438, Pyr. 809b; 604, Pyr. 1680d; etc.

24 In P. Edwin Smith (XX, 3), there is one example that comes with the determinative (Breasted 1930, 484). It is a prescription for warding off diseases emanating from the followers of Sekhmet, against whom a petitioner identifies himself with Horus as well as *ihhy* 'one who jubilates'.

25 *CT* VI, 159a [557].

26 *MH* III, pl. 152, list 24.

27 Also see the tomb of Min (TT 109: PM I-1², 226 (3, II); *Urk.* IV, 978: 10), where he is portrayed offering at Amun's temple in *ihhy ḥt [tꜣ p] n* 'jubilation through [th]is [land]'; Ramses IV's inscription at Karnak, which records *hrw nfr ihꜣhꜣy* the 'good day of *ihꜣhꜣy*' in association with the king's accession (*KRI* VI, 5: 3; Peden 1994a, 134–5 for transliteration and translation).

28 Leitz 1994a, 11, n. b.

29 Gardiner (1952, 21) suggested treating the phrase *tpy rnpw.t ḥtp.wt* the 'first of peaceful years' in the same way. Such is attested for the accession of Hatshepsut on New Year's Day (*Urk.* IV, 262: 7).

30 *KRI* I, 46: 2–3.

31 *KRI* I, 41: 10.

32 Helck's dating has been accepted by Krauss (1977, 147) and Kitchen (1982, 43). For more information, see Hornung 2006, 211.

Hence, it seems that *ḥ3.t nḥḥ* marked both the ceremonial and actual anniversary of royal accessions.[33] It comes as no surprise to find this expression for the civil calendar, the beginning of which corresponded to the commencement of the regnal year during the Old and Middle Kingdoms.[34] Although the significance of III Akhet 8 of Ramses II is not clear, it may signify an unidentified celebration relating to the renewal of Ramses' kingship. If so, the Opet Feast is the one that comes to mind.

4.2.1.5. sp tpy: the New Year as an epitome of recurring occasions

The expression *sp tpy* had a cosmogonical implication, indicating the first time, when the world was created. It also represented the New Year, as witnessed in two Theban private tombs. In the tomb of Qenamen, chief royal steward (TT 93), the beginning of a text accompanying the figure of Amenhotep II, who receives New Year gifts from the deceased, reads: *sp tpy ir.t bw nfr m ꜥḥ wr m ms inḏ-ḥr n wpy-rnp.t* The 'first occasion of making the good thing in the great palace on bringing the salutation of the New Year'.[35] The second example is found in the tomb of Amenhotep, overseer of carpenters of Amun under Amenhotep III (TT 415), who is represented with his wife receiving offerings from a sem-priest.[36] Behind the priest follow two sub-registers, depicting the Opening-of-the-Mouth ritual and New Year offerings, respectively (Figure 30). In the upper register, the legend reads: *sn=f wꜥb n Ptḥ Dw3 šsp nw Inpw m sp tpy wp r3 n wsir Imn-ḥtp* 'His brother, wab-priest of Ptah, Dua. Take the *nw*-adze of Anubis on the first occasion of the Opening-of-the-Mouth for Osiris, Amenhotep.' In the lower register, which will be examined in detail in 4.5.3, some men carry *tk3.w n wpy-rnp.t* 'candles of the New Year' and linen. The association of the Opening-of-the-Mouth ritual with the New Year is remarkable, but it is also natural to speculate that *sp tpy* evoked the first occasion that a performance of any kind took place, whether religious or secular. In fact, it was used as a starting point to count a sequence of rites as: 'First (*sp tpy*), such and such should be done. Second (*sp sn*), such and such should be done.'[37]

It perhaps derived from this ordinal use of the *tp* that *ḥb tpy* the 'First Festival' came in use to denote the New Year Feast, first attested in the time of Ramses III and widely employed later in the Ptolemaic-Roman Period (4.3.4). This is likely to have developed from the festival counting system first used by Thutmose III. In his annals at Karnak, Amun's festivals are numbered from one to five.[38] According to the annals, the first victory feast was celebrated at the 'first Amun Festival' after the king had returned from his first war campaign to Thebes, between I Shemu 21 and II Akhet 14 in year 23. This probably corresponded to the New Year celebration. The evening meal and Opening-of-the-Mouth ritual performed in private tombs at the New Year were likewise called the first one (of the year) (4.5.1). This conforms to the fact that offerings dedicated for this celebration were often modified by *tp*, which should be interpreted not only in the qualitative sense of 'finest' but also in the temporal sense of 'first'. In all likelihood, the New Year was regarded as the first of a cycle of repeating rituals throughout the year.

4.2.1.6. Others

There are also other less familiar literary variants. In the Coffin Texts, the New Year's Eve is called *grḥ ḫnty rnp.t* the 'night of the head of the year'.[39] At Dendera *ḥb=s nfr n ms Rꜥ* 'Her Beautiful Festival of the Birth of Re' is attested.[40] P. Leiden T 32, dated to the Roman Period, rephrases the New Year variously as *hrw n wn tr.w* the 'day of opening the seasons', *ḥb nḥḥ* the 'feast of eternity', and *ḥb ḏ.t* the 'feast of everlastingness'.[41]

4.2.2. Date and duration of the New Year Festival in the New Kingdom

Given that the New Year Festival was a nationwide celebration, its humble treatment in the Medinet Habu calendar is odd (**12**). The festival is not called *wpy-rnp.t* but *pr.t-spd.t*.[42] Unlike the Festivals of Opet, the Valley, and Khoiak, the duration of this event is not specified. Moreover, the number of divine offerings (*ḥtp-nṯr*) consumed at this feast is remarkably small, a mere 112, compared to 11,341 at the Opet Festival, 1150 at the Valley Festival, and more than 9000 at the Khoiak Festival. The small number may be the result of the complete absence of sections recording the second half of IV Shemu in this calendar. The Buto Stela of Thutmose III records the largest number of offerings for New Year's Day among the others listed on it (**8**).

[33] Aldred 1969, 78.
[34] Leitz 1994a, 11, n. b.
[35] PM I-1², 191 (9); Davies 1930, 24, pl. 11.
[36] PM I-1², 456 (1, II); Loret 1889, 31.
[37] Two variants of the Opening-of-the-Mouth ritual, described within the tomb of the king Seti I (Otto 1960, vol. 1, 79, Szene 32 (a, 2)) and on the coffin of Butehamen, a royal scribe of the Necropolis in the Twenty-First Dynasty, from Thebes (Turin 2237: Otto 1960, vol. 1, 104, Szene 46 (a, 4)). The expression *sp tpy* is also attested in a temple ritual (Parker 1979, 64, pl. 25).
[38] Sixth pylon of Karnak (Redford 2003, 137–8). Stela Cairo 34013 testifies to 12 festivals of Amun, each perhaps representing a celebration performed in each month (*Urk.* IV, 768: 7–8; Klug 2002, 140 for transliteration and translation).
[39] *CT* V, 94e [397].
[40] *Dendara* VIII, 32: 5.
[41] The Book of Traversing Eternity, IV, 30 to V, 1 (Stricker 1953, 22 for transcription; Herbin 1994, 192–4 for full publication; M. Smith 2009, 418 for translation).
[42] The equation of *wpy-rnp.t* to *pr.t-spd.t* is seen in TT 99 (PM I-1², 205, A, a).

According to a stone fragment of Thutmose III's festival list from Elephantine, a Khnum Festival (**7**) and an Amun Festival (**6**) were celebrated at Elephantine over the first three days of I Akhet (Table 24).[43] The work journals from Deir el-Medina illustrate when the workmen had a day's holiday.[44] O. DeM 209, dated to year 2 perhaps of Amenmes, records that the entire community of Deir el-Medina did not work for ten days from IV Shemu 29 to I Akhet 3 'on the days of the New Year Festival (*m hrw n wpy-rnp.t*)' (**1389**). O. Cairo 25539, dated to year 3 of Merenptah,[45] and O. Cairo 25266, dated to year 3 of Ramses IV,[46] may also indicate the same time span because those days are left blank.[47] O. Cairo 25515, dated to year 6 of Seti II, attests 13 non-working days (*wsf*) beginning on IV Shemu 26 until I Akhet 3 (**1379**). O. Turin 57032, dated to an unknown year of Ramses III, specifies the first four days of the year as inactive days (**13**). It is likely that the first three days of the year, at least, were *de facto* public holidays in the New Kingdom.

Additionally, there is earlier evidence that bears witnesses to ceremonies taking place before New Year's Day. A reference to the epagomenal days is attested in one of the Abusir accounting documents, but without an explicit connection with festival activities.[48] P. Berlin 10007 from Lahun records festival offerings dedicated on IV Shemu 30.[49] The tomb of Hepdjef, count of Asyut under Senusret I, witnesses a nocturnal ritual involving kindling fires on the fifth epagomenal day and New Year's Day.[50] That there was an evening meal (*msy*) on IV Shemu 30 is known from some New Kingdom tombs (4.5.1). Hence, by the New Kingdom, the New Year Feast seems to have had a nine-day duration from IV Shemu 30 to I Akhet 3 by default.[51]

Moreover, some subsidiary ceremonies were performed before IV Shemu 30 as part of the mortuary cult. The tomb of Neferhotep, a divine father of Amun-Re in the time of Horemheb or later (TT 50) attests 'making the offerings and moistening the barley for Osiris (the deceased tomb owner)' from IV Shemu 23 to IV Shemu 30 (**1370**). A parallel to this is also known for IV Akhet 18 to 25, obviously pertaining to the Khoiak Festival, in the same tomb (**479**). During this period of time, the 'coming-out of the bed (*sšm ḥnky.t*)', i.e. the germination of the grain, was performed.[52]

The doubling up of the Osiride cult that took place at the New Year and Khoiak Festivals is striking. Interestingly, another longer cycle existed for these two celebrations. According to the mythological account recorded in P. Cairo 86637 (recto, XI, 3–4) and P. Sallier IV (recto, VI, 2–4), both dated to the Ramesside Period, the god Seth began his campaign against Osiris on II Akhet 20. Leitz (1994a, 91) proposes that Osiris was killed on that day and began to undergo a 70-day embalmment process from then until IV Akhet 30. A cycle parallel to this started from II Shemu 21 which, according to P. Cairo 86637 (verso, IV, 5), was *hrw pwy n wʿr.ty ʿnḫ ms.w Nw.t* 'that day of the thighs, when the children of Nut lived'.[53] This conforms to the Book of Nut recorded in P. Carlsberg I (IV, 35–7 and V, 31–VI, 23), which was found at Tebtynis and dated to the second century AD. Stars, including Sothis, are described as being swallowed up in the mouth of the goddess Nut and staying in the house of Geb, i.e. the Duat, for 70 days, during which time impurity was imposed on earth.[54] Beyond doubt this bears witness to the disappearance of sidereal bodies for 70 days, when they move behind the sun and become invisible. Goyon (1987, 62–4) defines the significance of the number seven and its multiplied numerals in mortuary cults associated with the reunion of Re with Geb.

Ultimately, a far longer version of the periodic cycle was formulated. By examining P. Cairo 86637, Leitz (1994a, 474–5) successfully tabulates an identical sequence of entries for two different periods of time, one starting from I Akhet 9 to IV Peret 30 and the other from I Shemu (a scribal error for Peret?) 9 to IV Shemu 30, each lasting 232 days. However, it is hard to know what exactly the period of 232 days signifies. Various elements were incorporated into the mythological stories, resulting in the creation of more than one cycle of ritual performances. At least, it is likely that the Osiride cult and the Heliopolitan mythology were interwoven for the New Year.

Later in the Ptolemaic-Roman Period, the New Year Feast seems to have been extended beyond I Akhet 3. The calendar of Kom Ombo, dated to the time of

[43] *Urk.* IV, 823: 13 and 824: 9; Bommas 2000, 468 and 493.
[44] Jauhiainen 2009, 74–84.
[45] *KRI* IV, 171: 9.
[46] Helck 2002, 384–5.
[47] O. Ashmolean (= O. Gardiner 11), dated to year 2 of Ramses III, likewise omits days from IV Shemu 29 to I Akhet 2 (*KRI* VI, 249: 9). O. Cairo 25533, dated to the time of Ramses IV, refers to I Akhet 3, when an unspecified 11-day period ended (**38**). P. Turin 1898+1926+1937+2094, dated to year 3 of Ramses X, may record a work-free period from IV Shemu 30 to I Akhet 2 (*KRI* VI, 698: 10–2).
[48] P. Louvre E 25416 C, verso (Posener-Kriéger and de Cenival 1968, pl. 14, A, col. 3).
[49] Luft 1992, 45.
[50] Griffith 1889, pl. 6, l. 278, pl. 7, ll. 297–8, and pl. 8, ll. 305 and 312.
[51] While IV Shemu was considered the end of the year (Grimm 1994b, fig. 2), the epagomenal days somewhat had an arbitrary character as a distinctive celebration, as evidenced in the Middle Kingdom tomb of Khnumhotep III, count of Menat-Khufu, at Beni Hasan (PM IV, 148; Newberry 1893, pl. 25, ll. 90–5), whereas the Buto Stela of Thutmose III places the first evening meal, probably on IV Shemu 30, at the beginning of the year (Bedier 1994a, 4, z. 14; Bedier 1994b, 38, l. 14 for identical article with better facsimiles and a photograph). The Banishment Stela (Louvre C 256) of the Twenty-First Dynasty records the epagomenal days as part of IV Shemu (von Beckerath 1968, 12, l. 9; Jansen-Winkeln 2007, vol. 1, 72).
[52] Leitz 1994a, 428.
[53] Leitz 1994a, 366.
[54] Neugebauer and Parker 1960, 67–8 and 72–6; von Lieven 2007, 82 and 86–91 for translation and parallel texts.

Ptolemy VI, records a series of rituals to be performed until I Akhet 4.[55] P. Brooklyn 47.218.50 (XVI, 21), dated to the fifth or fourth century BC, attests a duration until I Akhet 9.[56] The same duration may be recorded at Esna (**62**). The decree of Rosetta, dated to the time of Ptolemy V, specifies IV Shemu 30 (**1405**) and a period from I Akhet 1 to 5 as festival days (**25**).

4.2.3. Association of the New Year Festival with other celebrations: perception as a set?

The previous section proves that the duration of the New Year Festival proper was nine days from IV Shemu 30 to I Akhet 3 during the New Kingdom and that it could be supplemented by other arbitrarily occurring cycles. As these ancillary cycles indicate, it is evident that the Festivals of the New Year and Khoiak were doubles of each other. Whether either was a copy of the other, and, if so, which was the original cannot be resolved. More complex is that the characteristics of the New Year Feast may also be seen in association with the Wag and Thoth Festivals, taking place on I Akhet 18 and 19 respectively.

There are various views on the calendrical significance of the latter two celebrations but it is generally accepted that they were originally associated with the beginning of the lunar cycle. In fact, there are similarities between them and the civil New Year Feast not only in their calendrical positions in proximity but also on a ritualistic level. At the Wag and Thoth Feasts, various kinds of cloth were distributed for the mortuary cult in the Old Kingdom.[57] The same holds for the New Year. Was it a result of copying ceremonies from these lunar celebrations? None of the Abusir account papyri attests the New Year celebration, but it is not impossible that an identical ceremony was repeated for the civil and lunar New Years. However, it is hardly plausible that the distribution of linen was likewise repeated in the same month. Hence, I will attempt briefly to explore the Festivals of Thoth and Wag, as well as the *tḫy*, in the following pages with a view to suggesting that the New Year Feast had taken over the function of the Wag and Thoth Festivals by the New Kingdom.

4.2.3.1. Wag Festival

The Wag Feast was of two-day duration, from I Akhet 17 to 18, as evidenced by some sources from the Middle Kingdom onwards (**86, 88, 90, 96–7**, and **99**). A nocturnal performance took place on the first day, followed by a morning one on the second day (BD 169, 14). The feast is referred to in a parallel spell found in the Pyramid Texts (PT 408, Pyr. 716c) and also in the Coffin Texts (*CT* III, 159b [207]), where it is likened to the occasions that oxen are slaughtered in honour of the deceased.[58] It was one of the celebrations commonly listed in the *ḥtp-di-nsw.t*-formula from the Old Kingdom. Its significance, together with the Thoth Festival, is evident when one observes that these celebrations often represent other mortuary celebrations where the formula is shortened. The chapel at Saqqara of Ankhmeryre, vizier perhaps under Pepi I, gives a remarkable example of the Wag Festival standing alone. The formula is followed by an abridged reference to celebrations to be performed for the dead as: 'invocation offerings (for) him at the Wag Festival and every festival'.[59]

Etymological approaches can offer an insight into the meanings and functions of the Wag Festival.[60] As examined previously in 3.2.1, there were two Wag Festivals—one was governed by the lunar cycle and the other by the civil one. The lunar version supposedly marked the inundation of the Nile but was no longer recorded after the Middle Kingdom. According to Winter (1951, 35), the Wag Feast was characterized by the navigation to Abydos and offering the dead the *mȝḥ*-headband/plant. He added that the Wag Feast underwent changes and came to be known under a different name by the Ptolemaic Period, and offered this explanation to justify its absence from later records. However, the paucity of evidence is a factor in the New Kingdom. Unlike during the Old and Middle

[55] Goyon (1972a, 42, n. 2) reads *ir mit.t r tpy ȝḫ.t sw 4 r mḥ hrw 5* as 'du 4 au 13 du meme mois', a translation opposed by Grimm (1994, 158) who renders 'bis zum 1. Monat der *ȝḫt*-Jahreszeit, Tag 4, bis zum 5. (Fest-)Tag', followed by Corthals (2004, 11) who translates 'until the 1st month of *ȝḫt*, day 4, until the 5th day (of the festival)'. el-Sabban (2000, 155) incorrectly reads it as 'from 1st of Akhet, day 4, until the 12th of Akhet'. Grimm's reading is securely confirmed because the last sign is 5, rather than 13.

[56] Goyon 1972a, 42 and 74.

[57] Posener-Kriéger 1976; Abusir X, 429–38.

[58] In the tomb of Nenkhefetka at Saqqara (D 47), the Festivals of Thoth and Wag are referred to as occasions when forelegs of meat (*stp.w*) were offered to the deceased (PM III-2², 580 (5)). A parallel to this is attested in the tomb of Sekhemka, where the celebrations of the new moon and full moon are mentioned alongside these two festivals (PM III-2², 596; Spieß 1991, 192).

[59] PM III-2², 621; Altenmüller 1998b, 249, pl. 95.

[60] Only early scholars attempted to interpret the meaning *wȝg*: for example, Brugsch (1864c, 105–6) proposed the meanings of 'inactif, paresseux ou impuissant' by citing a verbal form of a homonym and regarded the triple and determinatives as indicating the mortuary nature of the feast. The determinative is attested from the Middle Kingdom, which Brugsch disregarded as a phonetic complement. Birch (1864, 95–6) associated another determinative , which appeared in the New Kingdom, with a ship's 'beam' or 'log', in which he was supported by Legrain (1905, 130) who read 'flanc de navire' or 'carène' and referred to the king Wegaef (*Wgȝ=f*) of the Thirteenth Dynasty as integrating the word in his name. Then, Brugsch (1867, vol. 1, 317 and vol. 5, 352) pictured a river journey in the inundation season and defined the *wȝg*-Feast as 'das Fest der Schiffsrippe'. Renouf (1896, 169) pointed out that *wgȝ* or *wȝg* was another name of the Nile. Based on the Pyramid Texts (PT 442, Pyr. 819c–820a), Erman (1934, 23) associated the first observation of Orion with 'Weinlese' (at the Wag Feast), which fell in June/July (Gregorian). The idea of the Wag Feast as a 'Weinlesefest' was followed by Hopfner (1940, vol. 1, 145) and Badawy (1964, 200–1), but opposed by Winter (1951, 10), who put emphasis on the river journey to Abydos but saw no relationship with the Nile's inundation. Supporting Erman again, Krauss (1998, 57–8) demonstrates that the movable (lunar) Wag Feast was celebrated between 5 June and 4 August (Gregorian).

Kingdoms, we know of no single accounting document regarding the distribution of linen at this celebration in the New Kingdom. Even a bare mention to the festival is completely absent from records originating from Deir el-Medina and it is hard to imagine that people celebrated it. Winter (1951, 37) related the *mꜣḥ*-headband to the tying of onions to the dead performed at the Khoiak Feast, but apparently overlooked the significance of the New Year Feast, when a similar headband called *sšd* played a key role (4.6.3). In fact, the *sšd*-headband is attested in association with the Wag Feast, as well. Thus, the text carved on the statue of Amenhotep, a royal scribe and overseer of the houses of gold and silver under Amenhotep III, lists cloths among the invocation offerings to be given to the deceased. The text reads:[61]

> *... sfḫ.w n wp.t nṯr šsp(=i) sšd.w m ḥb wꜣg m wꜣḏ.t ḥr insy(.t) ḫnd=i nšm.t m bꜣ iḳr*
>
> ... and cast-off cloths of the forehead of the god. May (I) receive the *sSd*-headbands at the Wag Festival, namely, green cloths with red cloths, so that I will go (on) the neshemet-barque as a beneficial ba.

The contemporaneous stela of Hor and Suty, perhaps twin brothers both being overseer of works, also includes the following wish by the deceased:[62]

> *di=k n=i ṯꜣw nḏm ḫft mn ṯꜣy sšd.w hrw n ḥb wꜣg*
>
> May you give me a sweet wind when fastening the *sSd*-headbands on the day of the Wag Festival.

It is clear that at the Wag Feast the deceased was supposed to receive a headband originating from a god. Such is evident in some Abusir papyri. For instance, a few fragments belonging to P. Cairo JE 97348, discovered at the mortuary temple of the king Reneferef, record the distribution of various textiles to temple attendants at the Wag and Thoth Festivals.[63] Posener-Kriéger, Verner, and Vymazalová observe that particular kinds of fabric were associated with these festivals.[64] An accounting document similar to the Abusir papyri is also attested in P. Cairo CG 58065 from Lahun, dated to year 9 of a ruler belonging to the Twelfth Dynasty.[65] This account, however, does not include linen offerings. The absence of textiles is also evident in the entry for the Wag Feast in the Medinet Habu calendar.[66] It is, therefore, apparent that by the New Kingdom this festival underwent a considerable change, and that its association with the delivery of linen remained only in liturgical or canonical literature.

4.2.3.2. Thoth Festival (ḏḥwty.t)

Parker (1950, 31) hypothesized that the Thoth Festival was originally a celebration of the lunar intercalary month, thus taking place only every two or three years.[67] It was subsequently fixed to I Akhet 19 (**102**). Spalinger (1993a, 301) asserts that day 19 was selected for this feast because it was exactly a month after the end of the last lunar year, provided that the last lunar year started on I Akhet 1. Like the Wag Festival, the Thoth Feast was presumably a lunar celebration in origin, and its original form as such did not last long. No source attests it celebrated on various dates, apart from one dated text from the Old Kingdom—one of the aforementioned Abusir papyri. The Festivals of Thoth and Wag are recorded together for an entry dated to I Akhet 26 on which cloths were distributed to temple attendants (**134**). Posener-Kriéger (1985, 38–40) postulated that on that day the two festivals took place in accordance with the lunar calendar although she did not rule out the possibility of their being fixed to the civil calendar (This is largely because the rendition of the date is not on firm ground. Note that she provisionally reads the date as I Akhet 23, 25, 26, or 29). She further posited that the Thoth Feast took place together with the Wag Feast in non-intercalary years, but was celebrated separately when the intercalary month was inserted.[68]

Also based on Parker's idea of the intercalary lunar month, Nolan (2003, 88–94) regards cattle counts as taking place at the Thoth Feast in order to explain the irregular occurrence of censuses at roughly two- or three-year intervals, known, for instance, from the Palermo Stone.[69] Nolan based his proposal on two Fifth Dynasty tombs at Saqqara that include a representation of a livestock count as part of preparations for the Thoth

[61] Statue BM 632 from Abydos (PM V, 43; *Urk.* IV, 1803: 8–9; *Hieroglyphic texts from Egyptian stelae*, vol. 5, 11, pl. 38, ll. 5–6; Petrie 1902, vol. 2, pl. 36).

[62] Stela BM 826, provenance unknown (*Urk.* IV, 1947: 15; Lichtheim 1973, vol. 2, 86–9 for translation; *Hieroglyphic texts from Egyptian stelae*, vol. 8, 25, l. 21, pl. 21).

[63] Abusir X, 220–5, pl. 11, A and B, pl. 12, A.

[64] Abusir X, 431–4.

[65] Parker 1950, 68, pl. 6, B for partial transcription of the upper part and full photograph; Winter 1951, 54 for partial transcription and translation of the lower part; Luft 1992, 135 for partial transcription and translation of the upper part.

[66] *MH* III, pls 152–3, lists 24–5. Textiles are recorded only for the Sokar Feast in this calendar (*MH* III, pl. 160, list 47, 1097–8).

[67] The idea of the lunar intercalary month was first posited by Parker (1957a, 89–90), supported by Depuydt (1997, 39–45), but opposed by Gardiner (1955b, 26) and Barta (1981, 12–3). Barta assumes that the last and the intercalary lunar months were identically called *wpy-rnp.t*.

[68] Regarding the case in question, she believed that the gap between I Akhet 19 and 23 could not be explained other than by its occurrence being based on the lunar calendar. Her thinking is, however, questioned by Depuydt (2000, 174) and Vymazalová (2008, 140).

[69] Nolan (2008) further develops his idea and proposes that the later Babylonian intercalary system already existed in Old Kingdom Egypt in order to explain the occurrence of the Sed Feast in regnal year 30, which is ultimately destined to shorten the conventionally accepted length of the Old Kingdom.

Feast.[70] His idea is, however, challenged by Verner (2008, 39–43), who considers that the scenes represent the bringing of animal offerings, rather than a census, based on the inclusion of, what he believes are, wild animals, not only domestic ones. We suffer from the paucity of evidence to define the true nature of the Thoth Feast in the Old Kingdom, but the presence of the wild animals does not necessarily preclude the feast's association with censuses. The purpose of the census was to assess the national estate, which perhaps included any kind of resource available to be registered.[71]

Although highly hypothetical, the idea of the lunar intercalary month might explain the scarcity of evidence relating to the Thoth Festival. The celebration might have seen a rapid decline during the Middle Kingdom or even earlier in the Old Kingdom. In most cases, the Thoth Festival is mentioned together with the Wag Festival in the Abusir archives and barely appears as an independent celebration. This also holds for later evidence.[72] The stela of the king Neferhotep I of the Thirteenth Dynasty records that the king and his officials visited Abydos to perform a celebration to Osiris in year 2, the date of which is not recorded.[73] Following the procession of Osiris to the house of gold in order to fashion him (*r ms nfr.w ḥm=f*), the god expressed his appreciation of the deeds of the king, as follows:

> [two or three groups missing *ib*]*=f ḥr ꜥ3b. t=k tp tr.w n pr.w nṯr nb m w3g m ḏḥwty.t ḫn.ty rnp.wt=k im*
>
> [ ] his [heart rejoices(?)] at your seasonal great offerings at the coming-out of every god at the Wag Festival, at the Thoth Festival, and (through) the period of your years therein.

Because the text is a historical account rather than an ideological narrative, the Wag and Thoth Festivals are likely to have been celebrated, at Abydos at least, before the New Kingdom. Our knowledge of these celebrations during the New Kingdom is very limited. There are only three sources that give a glimpse into the Thoth Festival under its own name. First, Hatshepsut's inscription at the Speos Artemidos records the appearance of the god Thoth at two celebrations of Nehebkau and of Thoth (4.3.2). Second, a stela of Merenptah, carved on a pylon belonging to the Thoth temple at Hermopolis, portrays the king dedicating the temple to Thoth and six other deities at the Thoth Festival. Unfortunately, the second text is not dated and it is only the three-day duration of the celebration that is mentioned.[74] It is perhaps best to disregard these two examples for the present examination because the feast in question may not be the one that fell on I Akhet 19 but could be one of several occasions celebrated at Hermopolis in honour of Thoth. Third, O. DeM 57, dating from the time of Ramses III, records that on IV Shemu 19, a man called Pentaweret took a juridical oath to do what was due 'by the Thoth Festival' (**1357**). However, this text does no more than mention the festival as his deadline.[75]

Hence, little is known of what was performed at the Thoth Feast in the New Kingdom.[76] By examining work journals from the Ramesside Period, Helck (1964, 156) concluded that the Wag and Thoth Festivals did not affect the work shifts of the workmen at Deir el-Medina.

4.2.3.3. *Festival of tḫy*

The *tḫy*-Feast is more elusive than the two festivals examined above, due to the extreme paucity of evidence. This celebration is included neither in festival lists in private tombs nor in known temple archives before the New Kingdom. The earliest evidence, but arguably in the meaning of its name as a lunar month rather than that of the festival, is found in the Ebers calendar.[77] Parker (1950, 37) assumed that the *tḫy*-Feast fell on a full moon day in the first month of the original lunar calendar. The association with the full moon cannot be confirmed by the contemporaneous sources, but this feast certainly occupied a significant position in the lunar cycle. Spalinger (1993a, 302) posits that when the feast came to be fixed to the civil calendar, I Akhet 20 was selected because it was the beginning of the first full lunar month, provided that the previous lunar year started on I Akhet 1. It remained as the name of the first

[70] The tomb chapel of Akhethotep (PM III-2², 599 (8–9); Davies 1900, vol. 2, 16–7, pls 18–21). The tomb of Usernetjer (PM III-2², 485 (4–5); Murray 1905, vol. 1, pl. 22), and the Thoth Festival is also referred to in association with animal offerings in the tombs of Nenkhefetka (PM III-2², 580 (5)), of Reshepses (PM III-2², 495 (3)), and of Niankhkhnum and Khnumhotep (PM III-2², 642 (5, b); Moussa and Altenmüller 1977, 62, Tafel 16).

[71] Bleiberg 1999, 762.

[72] *CT* I, 276a [64] and VII, 137b [936].

[73] Stela Cairo, location unknown, originating from Abydos (Pieper 1929, 30, l. 23 for full publication; Helck 1975, 26 for transcription; Simpson 2003, 343 for translation).

[74] *KRI* IV, 28: 5.

[75] O. DeM 603 (*KRI* V, 568: 8), also dated to the time of Ramses III, refers to *hrw Ḏḥwty* the 'day of Thoth' in association with a scribal duty, which Jauhiainen (2009, 87–8) associates with the Thoth Feast. Undated O. IFAO 1088 records *Ḏḥwty* between *wpy-rnp.t* and *ḥb n ỉmn*, but this may refer to the month name (van Walsem 1982, 242, O. DeM 1088).

[76] A scene related to the cult of Thoth is found in the tomb of Tjay (TT 23), dated to the time of Merenptah (PM I-1², 38 (4, II); Borchardt 1907, 59–61; Zinn 2011, 191–2). As a royal scribe, he is portrayed working and performing a ritual at *t3 s.t n3 šꜥ.wt pr-ꜥ3* 'the seat of the royal documents' at Pi-Ramses, where Thoth is worshipped in the form of a baboon. However, the association of this scene with the Thoth Festival on I Akhet 19 is not evident. P. Leiden T 32 (III, 5), dated to the Roman Period, records the Khonsu temple at Karnak as one of the settings of the Wag and Thoth Feasts (Herbin 1994, 148–9 for full publication; M. Smith 2009, 412 for translation).

[77] Depuydt 1997, 91.

civil month before the later theophoric designation *ḏḥwty* was employed.

Scholars seem to split into two groups regarding the nature of this celebration—one rendering the *tḫy* as 'weight'[78] and the other as 'drunkenness'[79]. This has led to arguments on the association of the *tḫy* with either Thoth or Hathor, characterized as the god of weights and measures and the goddess of intoxication respectively. The first group bases their theory, first, on the myth that Thoth weighs the heart, as is well-known from the Book of the Dead (BD 125), and second, that the Festival of Thoth is immediately followed by that of the *tḫy*. This naturally develops into the thesis that the *tḫy*-Feast was part of the Thoth celebrations and, by extension, those of Wag as well, making three consecutive festival days from I Akhet 18 to 20. The second group is not obviously based on the semantic interpretation of the word but focuses on its calendrical significance. It is perhaps only Spalinger (1993a, 301), who belongs to the second group, who contends that the *tḫy*-Feast was a distinct celebration independent of the Wag Feast in origin and later associated with the Hathoric cult.

Insofar as state records are concerned, very little is known of the *tḫy*-Feast. There is only one dated text attesting it before the Ptolemaic-Roman Period. P. Berlin 10282 from Lahun records the occurrence of *tp ꜥ tḫ* (lit. 'before the *tḫ*' or *tp ꜥtḫ* the 'first of brewing(?)') on I Akhet 20 (**112**). Later sources are also reticent, apart from those from the temple of Dendera, where we find four texts associating the *tḫy*-Feast with that day (**118**). The limited geographical range of the sources may or may not be the result of how little evidence survives, but the Hathoric character of this celebration is evidenced by Ramesside texts mainly from Deir el-Medina, that bridge the gap between the Middle Kingdom and the later periods.

P. Cairo 86637 (verso XXII, 8), dated to the Ramesside Period, records the Hathor Festival as taking place on I Akhet 20 (**115**). This papyrus scroll is a calendar of a magical, mythological nature, including the annotation of lucky and unlucky days, and is not necessarily to be seen as encompassing the realities of ritual performances. However, more than a few work journals bear witness to the fact that people actually celebrated it. More significantly, P. UC 34336, dated to the time of Siptah or Ramses III, documents that beer was supplied from temples in western Thebes to the workmen at Deir el-Medina on I Akhet 20, corresponding to a work-free day (*wsf*) for the entire community.[80] In addition, O. BM 5634 (recto, 2 and verso, 18), dated to year 40 of Ramses II, records *swr* a 'drinking' as taking place on I Akhet 14 (**74**), which Janssen (1980, 145) associated with a feast. The festival of Hathor was not exclusively celebrated only on I Akhet 20 but on various other days and over different seasons. As Janssen pointed out, the Deir el-Medina journals recorded the Hathor celebrations mostly as a personal feast and the rest of the community was not always involved. Hence, O. Gardiner 61, dating from the time of Ramses III, records the death of a woman on I Akhet 1, when her husband seems to have celebrated 'his Hathor festival (*pꜣy=f ḥb n Ḥw.t-ḥr*)' at the same time.[81] Hathoric traits are not at all evident for the Festivals of Wag and Thoth.

4.2.3.4. Brief summary

The examinations above demonstrate that the Festivals of Wag, Thoth, and *tḫy* were never celebrated or conceived as a set although Jauhiainen (2009, 89) suggests that this may have been the case, based on the entries of work-free days of O. Cairo 25539, dating from year 3 of Merenptah. The first two celebrations disappeared from administrative documents in the New Kingdom, during the same time the *tḫy* seems to have emerged as a popular feast. Thus, only the latter celebration reveals its real form. Over the course of the long history, the religious, fiscal functions of the first two celebrations were perhaps taken over by the civil New Year celebration. As a result, the Wag and Thoth Festivals remained only nominal but the doubling of the function between them and the New Year continued to appear in texts. Hence, the tomb of Hepdjef, count of Asyut under Senusret I, attests that candles were used on the fifth epagomenal day and on New Year's Day as well as on the eve of the Wag Feast.[82] On a statue of the overseer of the works of Thutmose III Minmes, found at Medamud, the Festivals of the New Year, Wag, and Thoth are recorded perhaps as a set.[83] This points to how Egyptians perceived the New Year. Just as 'the New Year' evokes various meanings and associated events

[78] Borchardt (1935, 33, n. 4) 'Zünglein an der Waage', an interpretation followed by Gardiner (1955b, 25) 'plummet of the balance' and Luft (1992, 188–9) 'Waagelot'.

[79] Sethe 1919, 34 'Trunkenheit', a translation followed by Schott (1950, 82 (27)) and Depuydt (1997, 50).

[80] *KRI* V, 439: 15–6. An undated 'drinking of Hathor' is recorded in O. Cairo 25705+O. IFAO 01322+O. Varille 38, dated to the Twentieth Dynasty (*KRI* VI, 161: 5–6 for transcription of the Cairo fragment; Janssen 1997, 56–9 for full translation and commentary). Also see O. DeM 570, dated to the time of Ramses IX, which records a group of men and women as drinking together at the Enclosure of the Necropolis while others worked (*KRI*, VI, 664: 1–5). Other personal Hathoric celebrations at Deir el-Medina are recorded in: O. Queen's College, Oxford, 1115, verso (*KRI* VI, 167: 7); O. Gardiner 61 (*KRI* V, 596: 16); O. Liverpool 13625, recto (*KRI* IV, 163: 2); O. Cairo 25782 recto (*KRI* IV, 221: 7–8); O. Cairo 25780 and 25782 recto (*KRI* IV, 221: 3 and 8); O. Cairo 25533 (*KRI* VI, 176: 3); O. Cairo 25521 (*KRI* IV, 402: 3–4). For a general survey on the Hathoric drinking rituals, see Gutbub (1961, 46–50) who associated it with the Valley Festival for the New Kingdom.

[81] *KRI* V, 596: 15–6.

[82] Griffith 1889, pl. 8, cols 305–6.

[83] Six festivals appear to have been performed for him: the Festivals of Mentu, the New Year, Wag, Thoth, Sokar, and the Coming-Out of Min, but those of Wag and Thoth are not separated by from  (*Urk.* IV, 1441: 7–8).

to us today, a certain degree of ambiguity regarding the marginal happenings pertaining to with it may have existed in Egypt. Such is evidenced by various designations and expressions related to the New Year and celebrations that fell in I Akhet.

It was only in the Ptolemaic Period that the three celebrations of Wag, Thoth, and the *tḫy* were apparently regarded as a set. The calendars at Edfu and Dendera attest a celebration lasting from I Akhet 18 to 22 (Table 24). P. Leiden T 32 (V, 29), dated to the Roman Period, attests that on the day of the Wag Feast, loaves were offered in the presence of Hathor, perhaps to make beer, followed by the day of *sbi tḫ.w* 'presenting beer jars ( )'.[84] The *tḫy*-Feast seems to have gained increasing importance at Roman Dendera. The day of *sbi tḫ.w* 'presenting the intoxicant plants' (with the determinative) is recorded as having taken place on II Akhet 5 in a text at the Hathor temple (**162**). Elsewhere in the same temple, it is specified as the last day of a celebration started on I Akhet 20, making a 16-day duration (**118**). This probably explains the period of time required to brew alcoholic beverages for the goddess. There is no evidence for the consecutive sequence of the various New Year celebrations from the beginning of the year to the *tḫy*-Feast, but the doubling of the mythology between them is apparent. Cauville (2002, 141) concludes that on I Akhet 1 and I Akhet 20 the king was assigned an heir in the name of Horus and undertook a ritual to appease the raging goddesses Sekhmet on the former day and Hathor on the latter one.

4.3. Ceremonies of the New Year Festival

Unlike the elaborate reliefs depicting the Opet and the Valley Festivals, the New Kingdom temples are not promising regarding the sequence of the New Year celebrations. On the other hand, sources from the Ptolemaic-Roman temples are abundant, particularly from their New Year complexes. According to Corthals (2004, 18), the complexes can be defined as a 'set of rooms constructed for the purpose of celebrating the rituals of the New Year festival which led to the enactment of the "touching the sun" (*ḫnm itn*)'.[85] Corthals goes on to suggest that the architectural evolution of this complex can be traced back to the Old Kingdom.[86]

While the Festivals of Opet and the Valley were indigenous to Thebes and exclusively associated with the cult of Amun-Re, the New Year Festival was celebrated all over Egypt and an independent celebration was performed at each temple in the name of its local god, such as Ptah at Memphis, Upwaut at Asyut, and Khnum at Elephantine.[87] It was, of course, for Amun to celebrate the New Year at Thebes.

As demonstrated in the previous sections, this festival employed many elements from earlier celebrations and had a very complex character on a mythological level. Its official functions were, however, straightforward—the renewal of the year, coupled with the economic functions which marked the beginning of the administrative, fiscal cycle. A difficulty lies in the fact that there is no single illustration attesting the sequence of this feast and more significantly that two distinctive types of event took place in different settings at the same time, namely, the temple ceremony and the royal ceremony. The king probably celebrated the feast in his residential city because there is little evidence for royal attendance at the Theban New Year celebration during the Ramesside Period. Thus, the exploration in the following sections is mostly limited to the Eighteenth Dynasty before the royal residence moved outside Thebes.

4.3.1. Renewal of the world: the rituals of fresh water, cloth, and candle

Among the earliest New Kingdom evidence for the New Year ceremonies is Thutmose III's calendar at the Akh-menu in Karnak, where one reads: [.....] *ḏbꜣ m mnḫ.t ir.t mḏ.t m pr r-ḏr=f mi ir.t m ḥb wpy-rnp.t ḥnꜥ rdi.t pr sfḫ* [....] '[.....] clothing in linen and using oil in the entire house, as is done at the New Year Festival, together with letting out removed [garments....]'.[88] Despite its very fragmentary condition, the text bears witness to a purification ritual enacted for the entire temple to be renewed at this festival.

The New Year purification is attested earlier in P. Berlin 10218 b from Lahun as being performed during the epagomenal days.[89] The earliest pictorial evidence may come from the temple of Luxor. On the west wall of Room VIII, a procession of the vases of Amun is represented.[90] Three large vases, each topped with a ram's head, are carried on poles by priests. The procession is followed by two rows of 16 priests, each holding a small vase of the same form, who are in turn followed by the king

[84] The Book of Traversing Eternity (Stricker 1953, 24 for transcription; Herbin 1994, 212–3 for full publication; M. Smith 2009, 421 for translation).
[85] The complex consists of an axial sanctuary, the wabet, the New Year court, stairways to/from the roof, and a roof kiosk(s). Such a complex is attested in nine temples from the Greek-Roman Period (Coppens 2010, 40).
[86] For other supporting arguments regarding earlier parallels to the New Year complex, see Coppens 2010, 40, n. 4. More recently, Janák, Vymazalová, and Coppens (2011, 439) relate the sun temples of the Old Kingdom to the sun court, called *šw.t-Rꜥ*, of temples at western Thebes.
[87] The festival was called *ḥb ꜥꜣ n tꜣ r-ḏr=f* the 'great festival of the entire land' at Philae (Junker 1958, 108).
[88] Gardiner 1952, 12, l. 23.
[89] Luft 1992, 107–9.
[90] PM II², 322 (128, III, 1).

Amenhotep III. The legend accompanying the large vases reads:[91]

> *ḏd in Ꞽm[n] wꜥb wꜥb wp=f rnp.t m [mw] in nsw.t Nb-mꜣꜥ.t-rꜥ di ꜥnḫ*
>
> Word spoken by Amu[n]: 'Be pure! Be pure! May he open the year with [the water][92] by the king Nebmaatre, given life.'

Traunecker (1972) relates the scene to the New Year Festival. Ryhiner (1995, 20–30 and 52) includes the neighbouring scenes in the middle register as depicting the same celebration. They depict a similar procession but carrying chests. A scene akin to this is attested at Dendera, with a legend that reads:[93]

> *kꜣwt.n=ꞽ n bꜣḳsw ẖr nbꜣ.w n.w štꜣ ꜥprw.tꞽ m wꜥb.t wꜥb.tꞽ r sẖkr nb.t nṯr.w m nfr.w=s m hrw pn nfr wpy-rnp.t*
>
> I lift to the neck with carrying poles of the box containing washed clean cloths to adorn the Golden One of the gods (Hathor) with her beautiful cloths on this beautiful day of the New Year.

A text at the Great Hypostyle Hall at Karnak, dated to the time of Seti I, also refers to purification with fresh water, as follows:[94]

> *rꜣ n inḏ-ḥr m nms.t n wpy-rnp.t Ꞽmn m n=k tp=k ꜥb n=k ir.ty=k in(=i) n=k pr.t m nnw ḥꜣ.t pr m [Ꞽtm] m rn=s pw n nms.t*
>
> Spell of saluting with the *nms.t*-vase of the New Year. (O) Amun, take for yourself your head. Purify for yourself your eyes. (I) have brought to you what comes from the first primeval water, which comes from [Atum] in this its name of *nms.t*.

The water came from the river and was equated with the primeval flow emitted by the demiurge Atum. For what purposes the water was used is not clearly stated in the New Kingdom sources.[95] This scene is followed by another, where Seti I is portrayed holding two candles accompanied by a spell, which reads:[96]

> *rꜣ n ḫfꜣ.t pr ḫfꜣ.t(ꞽ) pr pn in Ꞽmn nb ns.wt tꜣ.wy wp=f rnp.t nfr.t ḥnꜥ Rꜥ swḫꜣ=f ḥnꜥ hb tkꜣ m ḥḏ.t ḥbs.w m rḫ.t ḫfꜣ.t pr pn in Ꞽmn-rꜥ-kꜣ-mw.t=f wp=f rnp.t nfr.t in Ḥr-ꜣḫ.ty wp=f rnp.t nfr.t mit.t nn in Pt[ḥ] nb ꜥnḫ-tꜣ.wy wp=f rnp.t nfr.t mit.t nn Ḏḥwty nb ḫmnw wp=f rnp.t nfr.t Mw.t nb.t išrw ḥnw.t nṯr.w ḥry-ib ip.t-s.wt mit.t nn pꜣ ꜥḥꜥ-nfr n pꜣ pr=f wp=f rnp.t nfr.t Rnw n pr pn wp=f rnp.t nfr(.t) iw ẖ.t n nsw.t Mn-mꜣꜥt-rꜥ mḥ.ti wsr.ti m ḥw n=k rꜥ nb*
>
> Spell of the *ḫfꜣ.t*[97] of the temple: '*ḫfꜣ* this temple! It is Amun, lord of the thrones of the Two Lands, who will open the good year with Re[98] and bring the night with the ibis (with) the torch (made) of white (fat) and the clean *ḥbs*-cloths at the *ḫfꜣ.t* of this temple. It is Amun-Re-Kamutef who will open the good year. It is Horakhety who will open the good year likewise. It is Pta[h], lord of Memphis, who will open the good year likewise. Thoth, lord of Hermopolis, will open the good year. Mut, lady of Isheru,

[91] Gayet 1894, pl. 39 (the text in question is incorrectly recorded); Schott 1970, 43; Traunecker 1972, 232 for the correct text.

[92] An undulant sign of 𓈖 is surviving after 𓅃, probably as part of 𓈗.

[93] PM VI, 57 (110–4), first register on the north wall; *Dendara* IV, 128: 8–9, pl. 282; Ryhiner 1995, 59; Cauville 2001, 220–1 for transliteration and translation.

[94] PM II², 46 (155, IV, 6); Nelson 1949, 216; *idem* 1981, pl. 219. Phraseology similar to this is attested in the Coffin Texts (*CT* I, 287i–288b [67]). A text at Edfu reads: *inḏ-ḥr m nms.t ḏd mdw m n=k nms.t nty wḥm ꜥnḫ r swꜥb ḥw.t-nṯr=k n.t mw rnpi ini n=k tp=k ꜥb n=k ir.ty=k snṯr ꜣḫꜣḫ.w=k sḫm.w=k* 'Saluting with the *nms.t*-jar. Word to recite: 'Take for yourself the *nms.t*-jar that repeats life to purify your temple with the young water. Bring to you your head. Purify for you your eyes. Deify your bones and your strength' (PM VI, 167 (339–40); *Edfou* VII, 202: 11–4, X, pl. 173 (XIV); Kurth 2004, 367). For parallel phrases, see PM VI, 141 (154), *Edfou* I, 470: 11–3, pl. 35, c; PM VI, 138 (126, a–b), *Edfou* II, 142: 10, pl. 41; PM VI, 67 (183–4), *Dendara* II, 144: 10–4, 154: 10–4, pls 127 and 135. None of these later sources explicitly refers to the New Year. The formula of 'take for yourself your head' appears as part of the recitations of the Opening-of-the-Mouth ritual in association with purification with the *nms.t*-jar (Otto 1960, 37). This is the case for TT 107 (2), where the passage 'take for yourself the eye of Horus' is repeated within an offering list dedicated at the New Year, below which is represented the Opening-of-the-Mouth ritual (Helck 1956b, 14).

[95] Another text at Dendera mentions the use of milk instead, taken from the sacred cows of Hathor, to purify shrines at the New Year (PM VI, 91; Simonet 1995, 104). A text at Edfu portrays the king saying: *in=ꞽ n=k nms.t šps pr m nw rnpi wbn m siꜣty r inḏ ḥr=k m ḥry rnp.t* 'I bring to you the august *nms.t*-jar that comes from the young Nun, rising from the leg (of Osiris) in order to salute to you during the epagomenal days' (*Edfou* II, 232: 6–7; Germond 1981, 328–9; Pécoil 1993, 109, n. 53). The purification rites were usually performed with the *snb.t*-jars and the *nms.t*-jars (Traunecker 1972, 202). In particular, the latter functioned to carry the primeval water of Nun (Kurth 1983, 104–5). This type of jar was also used during the process of embalming performed by Anubis and the goddess Qebehet, a deified pure water (B. Altenmüller 1975, 329).

[96] PM II², 46 (155, IV, 7); Nelson 1949, 339–40, fig. 39; *idem* 1981, pl. 220.

[97] The meaning of the verb *ḫfꜣ* is not clear. *Wb* does not include this word but Nelson (1949, 339, n. 166) translates it as 'illuminate', an interpretation followed by Goyon (1986, 333) who proposes 'éclairer'. Because it denotes an action of the god and appears with the determinative of 𓉴, the implication is likely to be the god's return to the temple after the whole edifice had been purified.

[98] Nelson (1949, 339, n. 167) translates as 'when it (the torch) inaugurates a good year'. It can be either a designation of the festival 'His Beautiful Opening of the Year' or a verbal clause, but the latter is more likely.

> mistress of the gods, residing at Karnak, likewise. Ahanefer[99] of his temple will open the good year. Renu[100] of this temple will open the good year. The body of the king Menmaatre is filled and strengthened with food for you everyday!'

This episode presumably marked the end of the temple rejuvenation rituals, which were completed by the eve of the New Year. According to Nelson (1949, 216), the spells of Seti I are part of the daily rituals to be performed before the statue of Amun.[101] If so, the New Year may be seen as the annual culmination of the daily routines. It is also not impossible that the fresh water collected at the beginning of the year was stored and subsequently used when required on different occasions, including during daily rituals, a possibility of which will be discussed in 4.5.12. Note that water from the inundation was also used at the Khoiak Festival.[102]

Representations of Amun's large vase are also attested in two private tombs on the West Bank. First, in the tomb of Panehesy (TT 16), a priest of Amenhotep-of-the-Forecourt in the later years of Ramses II, a procession of Amun's vase is represented coming out of a pylon, perhaps of Karnak.[103] A large ram-headed vase is accompanied by eight small ones.[104] Unlike the scene at Luxor temple, the small vases here vary in form. One of the small vessels is in the shape of an *ꜥnḫ* topped with a ram's head. The *ꜥnḫ*-jar perhaps represents the life force contained in the primeval water.[105] The scene may depict a procession going to the Nile, or a sacred lake within a temple district, to collect the water for ritualistic use.[106] Because the priest censing towards the large vase has the title *wꜥb n ḥꜣ.t Ỉmn* 'wab-priest of the front of Amun',[107] the vase is considered to be a manifestation of Amun.

The second tomb belongs to Imiseba (TT 65), chief temple-scribe of the temple of Amun under Ramses IX. A procession of vases is represented in the uppermost register on the northwest wall and continues onto the north wall.[108] As in the first tomb, there are one large vase carried on poles by priests, and eight small vases, three of which are missing today (Figure 28). These vessels are followed by four smaller ones and a long row of men carrying offerings on their heads. The entire procession travels to a temple precinct, where the Theban triad and a board of priests await.

The fresh water was used for symbolically regenerating not only temples but also the statues of the dead, and by extension, the entire land in order to imbue with new life force all that had passed with the old year. Hence, P. Cairo 86637 (recto III, 3–4), dated to the Ramesside Period, records for New Year's Day as:[109]

> *ꜣḫ.t 1-nw sw 1 nfr nfr nfr msw.t Rꜥ-ḥr-ꜣḫ.ty wꜥb m-ḫt tꜣ ḏr=f m mw n ḥꜣ.t Ḥꜥp pr m Nw rnpi ḥr.(t)w r(n)=f is.t nṯr.w nṯr.wt nb.w m ḥb ꜥꜣ m hrw pn ir.t nb m mit.t*
>
> I Akhet 1, good-good-good, Birth of Re-Horakhety: Purification throughout the entire land with the water of the beginning of the Inundation that comes from the young Nun, so called is his na(me). O all gods and goddesses are at the great festival on this day, every one doing likewise.

The collection of the fresh water took place prior to New Year's Day, as evidenced in the tomb of Neferhotep, a divine father of Amun-Re from the time of Horemheb or later, (TT 50) (4.5.8). The purification ceremony was essentially a precursor for New Year's Day, when all was confirmed as renewed and then returned to its original owners.

4.3.2. Dedication of the building and statue, and awakening of the god

The purification ritual was followed by the consecration of statues and buildings. It fell before the dawn of the New Year.[110] Evidence for this is attested from the Middle Kingdom onwards. A passage from the aforementioned tomb of Hepdjef at Asyut, concerning a contract made with a temple priest, states:[111]

> *hrw n wpy-rnp.t m ḏꜣw ḫft rdi.t pr n nb=f m-ḫt rdi n=i wnwt.w ḥw.t-nṯr pꜣ t ḥḏ*
>
> The day of the New Year, at night, when the temple is given to its owner after the hour

[99] Protective snake god.
[100] Snake god, often as a brother of Apis.
[101] Corthals (2004, 10) maintains that certain rituals at the New Year Festival were no more than an extended version of the daily rituals. It is worth noting that the scene at Luxor seems to be part of a series of rituals relating to the ithyphallic Amun because the adjacent wall (PM II², 322 (127, III)) depicts a procession of this deity. In fact, the text of Seti I accompanies a scene depicting the king presenting a *nms.t*-jar to the ithyphallic Amun, named 'Amun-Re-Kamutef, great god, foremost of Karnak'.
[102] Traunecker 1992, 119.
[103] PM I-1², 28 (5, II); Baud and Drioton 1932b, fig. 16. Based on the number of flag stakes, four at each wing, the pylon is identified with the second pylon.
[104] The large vase is painted in a bright yellow colour, suggesting that it is made of gold (Schott, 1970, 44).
[105] Sugi 2007, 245. Based on the presence of the *ꜥnḫ*-vessels, she regards a depiction of the tomb of Amenhotep-Sise (TT 75: PM I-1², 147 (3); Davies 1923, pl. 12) as representing the New Year.
[106] Schott 1970, 46.
[107] *Wb* III, 21: 10.
[108] PM I-1², 130 (8–9).
[109] Leitz 1994a, 13.
[110] Bissing and Kees 1922, 13.
[111] Griffith 1889, pl. 7, col. 298; Jankuhn 1972, 8.

> priests of the temple give me the white bread.

Another short passage, concerning a contract made with those who are in charge of the necropolis, refers to a statue of Hepdjef:[112]

> *n ḫn.ty=f ḫr-ꜥ n ḥm-kꜣ=f m tpy ꜣḫ.t sw 1 hrw n wpy-rnp.t ḫft sꜣḫ=sn s*
>
> For his statue in charge of his ka-priest on I Akhet 1, the day of the New Year, when they glorify it.

Whether the glorification in question took place within a temple or within the tomb of the deceased is not specified in the text. The statue may have been placed within a temple so that it could receive regular rituals. It is also likely that the statue was brought out from the temple to the tomb of the deceased because *ḫn.ty* seems to denote a processional statue.

At the Speos Artemidos, Hatshepsut's text refers to the Festivals of *nḥb-kꜣ.w* and Thoth in association with the recovery of Hermopolis.[113] The queen speaks of the restoration of the Thoth temple, as follows:

> *[sḫ(?)]ꜥ.n=i ḥm n nṯr pn m ḥb.wy nḥb-kꜣ.w ḥb Ḏḥwty wꜣḥ.n=i n=f [m] mꜣw.t iw=w m rꜣ nn m tp-tr.w=f ḏr wꜥ sšm-ḥb ḳb.n=i n=f ḥtp-nṯr ... sb.wt m snt.t grg.n=i s sḥb.n=i s di=i pr.w n nb[=sn]*
>
> I [caused(?)] the majesty of this god [to appear(?)][114] at two festivals, Nehebkau and the Festival of Thoth, that I established anew for him. They were in the mouth, not among his annual festivals[115] because the festival-leader was alone. I multiplied the divine offering for him. ... The enclosure walls were in foundation. I provided it and made it festal while I gave the temples to [their] lords.

Whether Nehebkau refers to I Akhet 1 or I Peret 1 cannot be confirmed because the dedication of a temple could take place at the Khoiak Feast. A fragment of Amenemhat II's annals, discovered at Memphis, alludes to the dedication of a temple at least four times, seemingly each on a different occasion.[116] The incomplete condition of the block onto which they are carved does not give a clear context as to when the dedication was performed, except one instance on the 25th and 26th of an unknown month of Akhet. This is most likely to be the Khoiak Festival that took place on those days in IV Akhet. Two stelae also of Amenhotep II from Amada and Elephantine record the erection of temples at those sites, the establishment of temple services, and the dedication of the temples (*rdi n=f pr nb=f*). The stelae are dated to III Shemu 15 of year 3 (**1242**), but just when the dedication of the temples actually took place is not clear.[117]

After the temple had been rejuvenated, the god was re-installed in the sanctuary. In the tomb of Imiseba (TT 65), chief temple-scribe of the temple of Amun under Ramses IX, a spell evoking the god follows a list of 17 hypostases of Amun.[118] It accompanies a scene of offering to the Theban triad and is most probably associated with the New Year (Figure 28). It reads:

> *rsi=k m ḥtp rsi=k Ỉmn-rꜥ nb nb.w m ḥtp rsi=k (ḥtp).ti rsi=k bꜣ imnt.t Ḥr iꜣbt.t [rs] i=k ḥtp.ti rsi=k Ỉmn-rꜥ-kꜣ-mw.t=f m ḥtp rsi=k ḥtp.ti rsi=k m ḥtp rsi=k itn=k ḏd.w sḫm(.w) ḫpr(.w m) Nw ḫw=k sꜣ=k mr=k nb tꜣ.wy Nfr-kꜣ-rꜥ-stp-n-rꜥ sꜣ rꜥ Rꜥ-ms-sw-ḫꜥ-(m)-wꜣs.t-mrr-imn m ꜥnḫ ḏd wꜣs nb di=k (n)=f nḥḥ (m) nsw.t tꜣ.wy ḏ.t m ḥḳꜣ ꜣw.t ib tꜣ.w nb.w ḫꜣ.w nb.w dmd ḫr ṯb.ty=k n ḫsf=tw ꜥ=k nmt.n=k tꜣ nb m k(s) n rn=k*
>
> May you awake in peace. May you awake, Amun-Re, lord of the lords, in peace. May you awake. Be (in peace)! May you awake, the soul of the west and Horus of the east. May you [awa]ke. Be in peace! May you awake, Amun-Re-Kamutef, in peace. May you awake. Be in peace! May you awake in peace. May you awake, your sun-disk being sturdy and strong, and appearing (from) Nun. May you protect your beloved son, lord of the Two Lands Neferkare-setepenre, son of Re, Ramses-kha(em) waset-meryamen (Ramses IX) in all life, stability, and dominion. May you give him

112 Griffith 1889, pl. 8, col. 315.

113 *Urk.* IV, 388: 14–389: 14; Gardiner 1946, 47 for transcription and translation; Goedicke 2004, 63 for translation; Allen 2002a for translation and more accurate transcription.

114 Allen (2002a, 4) restores *sꜥꜣ* 'magnify'.

115 Or 'not on his calendar', thus speaking of abandoned festivals remembered only in the oral tradition.

116 Altenmüller and Moussa 1991, 5–6 and 20–1.

117 Also refer to Hannig 2003, II-1, 894 for examples from the Middle Kingdom to the Second Intermediate Period; *Wb, Belegstellen* I, 513, 8 for those from the New Kingdom; Parker 1979, 55, n. 7 and Wilson 1997, 350 for those from the Ptolemaic Period. Undated dedication texts from New Kingdom Thebes are temple inscriptions: of Thutmose III at Medinet Habu (PM II², 468 (42, 2)); of Amenhotep III at Luxor (PM II², 316–7 (90, a and b); Schwaller de Lubicz 1957, vol. 2, pl. 29, B, vol. 3, 120, fig. 220; *Façade*, 28, pl. 176); of Ramses II at Luxor (PM II², 306 (16, III-2); Schwaller de Lubicz 1957, vol. 2, pl. 29, A, vol. 3, 119, fig. 219) and at Karnak (PM II², 46 (157, III, 5); Nelson 1981, pl. 26); of Seti I at Karnak (PM II², 49 (162, b, II); Nelson 1981, pl. 187); of Pinedjem I at Karnak (PM II², 229 (12, e and f, IV); *Khonsu* II, pls 120 A and 125 A).

118 PM I-1², 130 (9); *LD* III, pl. 236 for the scene and text; *KRI* VI, 549–50; Bács 2004 for translation and commentary.

> eternity (as) the king of the Two Lands and everlastingness in rulership (with) the dilated heart, all lands and islands being united under your soles. No one opposes you when you have gone. Every land bows (down) to your name.

Later sources explicitly state that the renewal of temples and gods was performed at the New Year.[119] The calendar of Kom Ombo records *gb mnḫ.t ir mḏ.t ir n.t-ꜥ nb m ḥb tpy* 'presenting the cloth, using oil, and performing every ritual at the first festival' as occurring on IV Shemu 30 (**1404**). Likewise, *ḥb mnḫ.t* is recorded for I Akhet 1 in the calendar of Dendera (**29**). The Ptolemaic calendar at the Mut precinct at Karnak records *sꜥḥꜥ sḫm m 4 n pr=s* 'erecting the effigy at four corners of her house' for IV Shemu 29 (**1391**). These were probably followed by a final ritual in the morning to evoke the divine statues by exposing them to the sunlight.[120]

4.3.3. *Renewal of the reign: Hatshepsut's obelisks at Karnak and the Sed Festival*

In addition to the customary rituals, special events were co-celebrated at the New Year. This is recorded on the base of the standing obelisk of Hatshepsut between the fourth and fifth pylons at Karnak, a space once called the *wꜣḏ.t*-hall. The queen completed the 'two great obelisks' on IV Shemu 30 in year 16 (**1394**). The enterprise began on II Peret 1 in year 15 and it took about seven months to quarry the stone and bring it to Thebes. The north side of the obelisk itself has a text referring to the first Sed Festival, for which the monument was created.[121] Whether the reference to the jubilee is a commonly used formula for obelisks, because it is also to be seen on the standing obelisk of Senusret I at Heliopolis,[122] or an account of a historical fact is not confirmed.[123] Hatshepsut's temple at Deir el-Bahari attests to the Sed Feast and New Year's Day together as a day of the royal appearance.[124] Based on various references to the Sed Festivals at Deir el-Bahari, Uphill (1961, 250, n. 17) contended that Thutmose III and Hatshepsut celebrated a joint jubilee in year 16. Along similar lines, Redford (1967, 14) posited that Hatshepsut may have celebrated her coronation at the New Year. Białostocka (2010, 19–20) maintains that the queen celebrated the Sed Feast on the same day as the New Year on account of their parallel characteristics, but also notes that such might only be the ideal and would not reflect any historical fact.[125]

The erection of the obelisks in question is depicted elsewhere on the Red Chapel, but the context is not entirely clear.[126] However, the dedication of two unspecified obelisks in relation to the New Year Festival is attested in a scene belonging to the tomb of an unknown person (TT 73), who was contemporary with Hatshepsut and bore the titles 'overseer of works on the two great obelisks in the temple of Amu[n] at Kar[nak]' (*imy-r kꜣ.t ḥr nꜣ tḫn.wy wr m pr Ỉm[n] m ip[.t-s.wt]*) and 'chief steward of the king'.[127] On the north wall of the tomb are depicted various objects including two large obelisks (Figure 34). The beginning of the broken text behind them reads:[128]

> [two groups lost] *n Ỉmn (iḫ.t) nb.t nfr.t m wpy-[rnp.t m(?)] nḥb-kꜣ.w*
>
> [Bringing(?)] to Amun every good (thing) at the New [Year and at(?)] Nehebkau.

This scene continues onto the adjacent wall, where the tomb owner is portrayed offering collars to the queen seated in a kiosk. According to Habachi (1957, 98), these obelisks are identical with those completed in year 16 of Hatshepsut. A similar scene is found in the tomb of Puymre (TT 39), second-priest of Amun, who is depicted inspecting (*mꜣꜣ*) 'two great obelisks' dedicated by Thutmose III to Amun alongside various other items represented in three registers.[129] The context of this scene is not obvious but likely to be related to the New Year Feast, based on the presence of other precious goods and its location on the northwest wall of the

[119] Fairman (1954/1955, 173) assumed that the temple of Edfu was consecrated on New Year's Day. The link between the New Year and the dedication of buildings appears to be manifest in archaeological evidence from the time of Aspelta of the Napatan Kingdom. Many inscribed faience objects, found in a pit located at Building 294 at Meroe, bear a standard formula, beginning with 'May such and such god open the good year for the king' (PM VII, 240). Al-Rayah (1981, 125–32, pls 4–6 and 10–4) holds that the building was used for certain New Year ceremonies.

[120] Corthals (1994, 16) maintains that such a solar cult is attested in P. Louvre E 25416 c+P. Cairo 602, frame X verso, originating from Abusir (Posener-Kriéger and de Cenival 1968, 6, pl. 13; Posener-Kriéger 1976, vol. 1, 61 for translation). It records the Sokar Festival, during which were used two religious symbols (*wḫ*), each called *iꜥ n rꜥ* 'one which ascends to the sun' and *twt n rꜥ* 'one which unites with the sun'. Arnold (1997, 57) relates the ritual involving these emblems to the mock burial of a ka-statue of the king, followed by his rebirth.

[121] *Urk.* IV, 359: 1.

[122] *LD* II, pl. 118, h.

[123] For other references to the queen's Sed Festival, see Hornung and Staelin 2006, 23. The authors (1974, 56 and 64–5) do not regard them as historical accounts.

[124] PM II², 348 (20); *Urk.* IV, 262: 7–8; Naville 1895, vol. 3, pl. 63; Białostocka 2010, 19 for partial translation. Gardiner (1945, 26) suggested that her inscription was borrowed from a Middle Kingdom text. In fact, a text parallel to this is attested in a fragmentary inscription belonging to Senusret III (Berlin 15801–4: Roeder 1913, vol. 1, 138 and 268; Barta 1985, 7, n. 44). For more arguments regarding this famous text, see Spalinger 1990, 293, n. 9.

[125] Alliot (1949, vol. 1, 207) and Corthals (2004, 303) proposed that the New Year was called the 'Sed Festival of Re' in the calendar of Edfu, but the passage is fragmentary and thus their rendition cannot be confirmed. The erection of an obelisk during Akhenaten's Sed Festival at Thebes was proposed by Bell (1985, 292).

[126] Block 302 on the south exterior wall (*Urk.* IV, 374–5; Burgos and Larché 2006, vol. 1, 77).

[127] *Urk.* IV, 461: 12.

[128] PM I-1², 143 (2); *Urk.* IV, 459: 13; Säve-Söderbergh 1957, 7, pl. 6.

[129] PM I-1², 72 (12); Davies 1922, pls 37–8.

antechamber, where the royal appearance is often represented (4.5.12).

An obelisk to be consecrated at the New Year is first attested in the tomb of Intefiker (TT 60), vizier in the reign of Senusret I. A man is portrayed carrying a small, decorated obelisk (Figure 36).[130] Obelisks are depicted in private tombs in two contexts. First, they appear as part of the Opening-of-the-Mouth ritual. According to Porter and Moss, there are 12 scenes depicting the setting-up of obelisks.[131] Of them eight are located in the inner-room, all dated to the Eighteenth Dynasty. Those obelisks stand in front of the tombs and are associated with the funerary cult. The second type is found among other New Year gifts.[132] At Karnak, Ramses II is portrayed erecting two obelisks before Re on an unspecified occasion.[133]

If Re played a key role as a recipient of obelisks, then their erection would best suit New Year's Day, which was known as the 'birth of Re-Horakhety' or 'birth of Re' (**15–6**, **18**, and **27**).[134] In fact, that the *bnbn*-stone and the Heliopolitan gods are associated with the New Year is evidenced by a scene on the eastern wall of the Great Hypostyle Hall at Karnak.[135] Seti I is portrayed kneeling and extending his arms over offerings to be dedicated to Amun-Re. The New Year formula, which will be examined in 4.5.2, follows the legend that begins as:

> *r3 n srwd ḥtp-nṯr inḏ ḥr=k 'Itm inḏ ḥr=k Ḫpri rn=k m k3w wbn=k m bnbn m ḥw.t-b3 m iwn išš=k m Šw Tfn.t di=k ʿ[.wy=k] ḥ3 nsw.t Mn-m3ʿ.t-rʿ di ʿnḫ ḏ.t*
>
> Spell of securing the divine offering. 'Hail to you, Atum. Hail to you, Khepri. Your name is raised. You rise as a *bnbn*-stone in the House of the Ba at Heliopolis. Your saliva is Shu and Tefnut. May you extend [your ar]ms around the king Menmaatre, given life forever.'

As signified by the designation of *nḥb-k3.w* (4.2.1.2), the myth entailing Horus as an heir to Osiris encompassed the New Year celebrations and the image of the young successor was realised by borrowing the figure of the rising sun. In the hymn to the sun god, Re and Osiris represented tomorrow/son and yesterday/father respectively when the day changed.[136] The narrative was echoed in the renewal of all objects on earth with the power of Re. Hence, New Year's Day was not only the beginning of the calendrical cycle but also of the world order. This conforms to the reference to the New Year as 'the beginning of the eternity' (4.2.1.4). For the same reason, the renewal of the kingship was performed at the New Year, as described by P. Brooklyn Museum 47.218.50, dated to the fourth century BC.[137] A significant difference from the Khoiak Feast is that the cult of Re took precedence over that of Osiris at the New Year celebrations.

4.3.4 Consecration of the New Year gift: examination of Thutmose III's reliefs at Karnak

As noted in 4.3, the New Year complex of the Ptolemaic-Roman temples was probably the result of architectural evolution from the Old Kingdom. A small open-air court containing an altar located in the north Akh-menu is one early New Kingdom example.[138] Its location at the northeast of the temple of Karnak parallels the Middle Kingdom edifice erected by Senusret I (Figure 19).[139] It lies half way to the roof, being reached by a stairway from the pillared hall (Figures 20, a–b). There is another stairway leading from the west, presumably connecting a corridor and the roof directly (Figures 21, a–b).[140] Some reliefs carved in the surrounding rooms parallel one another and display a link to the New Year. One spreads over the north wall of Corridor XL leading to the second stairway.[141] The scene has only partially been published.[142] I have, therefore, reproduced it in Figures 22, a–b. It comprises four episodes:

[130] PM I-1², 122 (11); Davies and Gardiner 1920, pl. 13.
[131] PM I-1², 472, h.
[132] Other celebrations can be associated with obelisks. For instance, small obelisks (or bread or incense in the shape of them) appear among offerings to the Theban triad in the reliefs of the Opet Festival at the temple of Luxor (*Opet*, 3, n. h, pls 43 and 55).
[133] The girdle wall located to the north of the sacred lake (PM II², 128 (469, 32); *LD* III, 148, A left).
[134] See Baines (1970) for the mythological and linguistic meanings of obelisks; Habachi (1978, 3–14) and Curran, Grafton, Long, and Weiss (2009, 13–33) for general introduction; Gregory (2012, 13–6) for their symbolism and historical development.
[135] PM II², 45 (155, I, 1); Nelson 1981, pl. 202.
[136] Assmann 1983b, 62.
[137] Goyon 1972a. Barguet (1962, 291) noted that the king's unification with the sun was aimed at the New Year. Daumas (1980, 264) assumed that the king was united with the sun in the solar court of the Akh-menu by performing the ritual of *ḫnm itn*. Based on Old Kingdom sources, Kessler (1987, 80) posited the king's transformation to the cosmic parentage of Re and Hathor, which was realised in his re-enthronement.
[138] For recent studies on the Akh-menu, see Haeny 1997, 96–8, and Blyth 2006, 68–77. For the open-air court and the related solar cult from the New Kingdom onwards, see Kees 1949 and Caminos 1958, 134, n. rr. It was probably called *ḫʿw.t Rʿ tp-ḥw.t pr 'Imn* 'the Altar of Re on the Roof of the Temple of Amun', which is first attested in a text on the Bubastite Gate at Karnak, dated to the Twenty-Second Dynasty (*RIK* III, pl. 22, col. 11). The 'place of the First Festival' *s.t ḥb-tpy* is attested in Ptolemaic texts and described as being located on the roof above the Chamber of Mesen in the temple of Edfu (Wilson 1997, 634).
[139] Gabolde 1998, 141–2, pl. 2. While Carlotti (2000) presents a reconstruction similar to Gabolde, Larché (2009, 149, figs 14–7) proposes a different configuration of the original architecture as comprising two parts, facing each other, as if they are a contra temple. For the altar located at the northeast of this building, see Hirsch 2004, 229, pl. 3, a.
[140] For these stairways, see Christophe 1954, 257–8. Blyth (2006, 75–6) proposes that this was the original stairway to the solar platform and the one leading from the south was added by later kings.
[141] PM II², 123 (432, II).
[142] Schott 1937, pl. III (c); Myśliwiec 1985, pls 13 (2), 16, and 24 (1).

1. Thutmose III offering incense to a statue of the ithyphallic Amun without his plume crown;
2. Thutmose III purifying a statue of the ithyphallic Amun-Re without his plume crown;
3. two rows of singers and priests carrying various vases, torches, and a royal statue;
4. Thutmose III censing and making libations over offerings, accompanied by a torch-bearer, two candle chests, and two figures of Hapi, to the seated Amun-Re with his plume crown.

The whole scene may be related to the Opening-of-the-Mouth ritual because Amun appears to undergo different phases of a ritual, being purified and finally adorned with two tall plumes (Figures 22, c and e–f).[143] One of the vases in Episode 3 is topped with a ram's head (Figure 22, d). The representations of two figures of Hapi and two candle-chests in Episode 4 have parallels in Hatshepsut's temple at Deir el-Bahari and in Thutmose III's dedication relief at Karnak.[144] Other iconographic features parallel New Year scenes at the temples of Edfu and Dendera.[145]

In fact, the New Year is mentioned in Room XXXVII, lying to the west of the first stairway (Figure 23).[146] The scene comprises three episodes:

1. Thutmose III censing and making a libation to the seated Mut;
2. two rows of singers and priests carrying various objects, mostly royal statues;[147]
3. Thutmose III (censing? and) making a libation to a seated god.

The second episode closely parallels Episode 3 of Corridor XL, and a broken legend in the final episode says: [... *ỉhhy*] *n ḥꜣ.t-rnp.t* '[laudation] of the front of the year'.[148] The unusual designation of *ḥꜣ.t rnp.t* is attested elsewhere in a few texts belonging to the early Eighteenth Dynasty (4.2.1.3).[149] For example, the so-called coronation text of Hatshepsut at Deir el-Bahari records that Thutmose I decided to appoint his daughter Hatshepsut the next ruler, whose accession was described as *ḫꜥ.w n wpy-rnp.t m ḥꜣ.t rnp.wt ḥtp.wt n.t ỉr=s ḥḥ.w m ḥb sd ꜥšꜣ wr.t* the 'appearances of the New Year in the front of the peaceful years that she performs millions of the Sed Festival very many times'.[150]

The two reliefs at the Akh-menu display a close association with the New Year on architectural, textural, and iconographic grounds. They probably represent the dedication of annual offerings to the Theban triad after their statues had been rejuvenated through the Opening-of-the-Mouth ritual. The pile of offerings represented in Episode 4 of Corridor XL is a temple version of the New Year gift scenes attested in private tombs (4.5.12). Corthals (2004, 118–9) suggests that the sight of a large pile of offerings is the most remarkable element of the New Year courts at Edfu, Dendera, and Philae.[151] The obelisks dedicated by Hatshepsut at the New Year can be seen as part of the New Year gifts to Amun-Re.

Relating to this subject, there is one more significant representation at Karnak, which has hitherto been unexplored in the New Year context. It is carved on the north wall surrounding the sanctuary.[152] Thutmose III offers a substantial number of offerings to Amun-Re. As in Corridor XL, two figures of Hapi and two candle-chests are included in the third and sixth registers.[153] Moreover, two enormous obelisks dominate a space in front of the king. No captions indicate the date and context of this scene but the annals inscribed at the bottom might suggest a dating. According to this retrospective account, Thutmose III began his first war campaign before IV Peret 25 in year 22 and continued it for at least 27 days until I Shemu 21 in year 23, when his army reached Megiddo (Table 25).[154] It is known elsewhere in the annals that the king was back at Thebes to celebrate the 'first victory festival' ([*tpy n ḥb n pꜣ ḥb nḫt*]), corresponding to the 'first Amun festival'

143 Representations parallel to this are carved inside the Red Chapel, where an episode of *ỉṯỉ r rꜣ ỉṯỉ r ꜥ* 'bringing to the mouth and bringing to the arm' is followed by the Opening-of-the-Mouth ritual performed by Hatshepsut to the ithyphallic Amun (Lacau and Chevrier 1977, vol. 1, 341–2, vol. 2, pl. 19 (Blocks 217 and 181); Burgos and Larché 2006, vol. 1, 221). This formula is also attested for the Opening-of-the-Mouth ritual (Otto 1960, vol. 1, 9 (4a), 12 (5b), etc.).

144 Hatshepsut's reliefs (four figures of Hapi in each: PM II^2, 358 (83, II-1), 365 (132), and 366 (133); Schott 1937, pls I (b) and IV (a)); Thutmose III's relief (PM II^2, 97 (282); *Urk.* IV, 634; Schott 1937, pl. III (b); Baines 2001, 52, fig. 29). Schott (1937, 20 and 22) related these motifs to the Feasts of the New Year and the Valley.

145 Corthals 2004, 22.

146 PM II^2, 123 (426–7); Pécoil 2000, pls 115–7.

147 These royal statues, renewed or newly created, were brought to temples and then sanctified. A royal statue to be used at festivals (*sšm ḥb ḥr ỉr.t snṯr* 'festival statue performing fumigation') is depicted among gifts to Amun-Re at the temple of Medinet Habu (PM II^2, 508 (135 g); *MH* V, pl. 331).

148 Barguet (1962a, 291–4) first noted the relevance of this text to the New Year but put more emphasis on the Khoiak Feast to explain a scene associated with Buto in Corridor XLA (PM II^2, 124 (439)). For the association of *ḥꜣ.t-rnp.t* with *ỉhhy*, see 4.2.1.3.

149 A stone fragment of Amenhotep I's building at Karnak, dated to I Akhet 13 (Spalinger 1992, 22, pl. IV); the tomb of Puymre (TT 39), dated to the time of Thutmose III (PM I-1^2, 73 (14); Davies 1922, pl. 64).

150 *Urk.* IV, 261: 9; Naville 1895, vol. 3, pl. 62; Naville 1896b, 100, l. 33 for translation. Her coronation (*hrw ḥb* [two groups lost] *smꜣ tꜣ.wy*) scene is also represented on the Red Chapel, where it is called *sp tpy ḫꜥ.t* the 'first occasion of the appearance' and the queen's *ꜣtf*-crown is described as *ḫꜥ.w Rꜥ n sp tpy* the 'diadems of Re of the first occasion' (Blocks 95, 172, and 261: Burgos and Larché 2006, vol. 1, 78–9 and 83; Goebs 2011, 84–8 for translation).

151 Edfu (PM VI, 144 (192–4); *Edfou* I, pl. 34 c–d); Dendera (PM VI, 59 (124–5); *Dendara* IV, pls 301–2); Philae (PM VI, 240 (309); *Philae* I, pl. 6).

152 PM II^2, 97 (282); Wreszinski 1923, vol. 2, pl. 33; Sherrat and Sherrat 1991, 386, fig. 2 (from Baines's rendition).

153 The two figures of Hapi here are captioned as *ḥw* 'nourishment' and *ḏfꜣ* 'food'. There are two reliefs in the Khonsu precinct at Karnak, where *ḥw* and *ḏfꜣ* are represented as a papyrus and a lotus to be offered to the god by Herihor (Dittmar 1986, 88).

154 *Urk.* IV, 647: 12 and 657: 2; Redford 2003, 8 and 29.

(*ḥb tpy n ỉmn*), before the Opet Feast to start on II Akhet 14 in that year.[155] If the annals and the scene above were executed at the same time and relate one another, the ceremonial dedication of gifts, including the booty from the campaign, must have taken place between those dates.[156] This could be the Valley Feast, the New Year Feast, or the Opet Feast, but the presence of the obelisks among the gifts indicates the New Year.

Elsewhere on Stela Cairo 34013, found in the Ptah temple at Karnak, Thutmose III is recorded as having dedicated offerings to Amun, Ptah, and Mut-Hathor after the 'first occasion of victory'.[157] The king commissioned the erection of the Ptah temple as a station of Amun-Re, who went to the Treasury of the Head of the South, located to the north of the precinct of Amun-Re, 'for all his annual festivals'.[158] The stela is dated to I Akhet 26, the significance of which is not defined.[159] Amun's procession to the Treasury of the Head of the South is also recorded on the barque chapel of Amenhotep II at the Mentu precinct of Karnak.[160]

A link between Thutmose III's first campaign and the New Year celebrations is also suggested by an inscription carved on the seventh pylon, recording that Amun's Userhat barge was constructed along with four great obelisks shortly after the first campaign.[161] Significantly, this event is represented in Room XV to the north of the sixth pylon (Figure 24).[162] The south wall preserves only the lowest part, where the Userhat is depicted being towed by a royal barge and then consecrated by the king through the Opening-of-the-Mouth ritual, captioned as *wp r3 n ỉmn*. Ptah is depicted behind the king.[163] On the north wall is represented a pylon being approached by the king, who erects masts in front of a temple pylon, accompanied by high officials, including the viziers of Upper and Lower Egypt.[164] The east wall represents a large pile of offerings dedicated to Amun by the king.

Given the Opening-of-the-Mouth ritual, Traunecker (1989, 106) identified the rooms in this area with *ḥw.t nb* the 'house of gold', where temple offerings were sanctified, a hypothesis followed by Blyth (2006, 89–91).[165] The association of the New Year with temple storerooms is attested in a text at the Maat temple, located in the Mentu precinct of Karnak, dated to the time of Ramses III, as follows:[166]

> *ḥ3.t-sp [22(?)] 3bd 4-nw šmw sw 12 ḫr ḥm [n nsw.]t-bi.ty Wsr-m3ʿ.t-rʿ-mry-imn wḏ ḥm=f rdi.t m ḥr n imy-r niw.t ṯ3ty T3 m3ʿ ḫrw s[ʿ3(?)] [...] [m(?)] m3w r rdi.t n=s s.t ḥb tpy pr.wy ḥḏ šps pr mn[w?] [..........*
>
> Year [22(?)], IV Shemu 12 under the person of the king of [Upper] and Lower Egypt, Usermaatre-meryamen. His person commissioned the mayor, vizier Ta, true of voice, to en[large(?)] anew in order to dedicate to her (Maat) the place of the First Festival, august double-treasury of the house of [..........

[155] Sixth pylon of Karnak (PM II², 90 (245); *Urk.* IV, 740: 14–6; Redford 2003, 137–8).

[156] With regard to the date of the erection of the north wall in the ambulatory by defacing Hatshepsut's northern rooms, Laskowski (2006, 201) postulates year 42 or later. Redford (2003, 3) suggests that the annals were carved after year 40.

[157] *Urk.* IV, 767: 4.

[158] *Urk.* IV, 765: 11.

[159] Jacquet-Gordon (2009, 123) relates the date to the cult of Amenhotep I and Ahmes-Nefertari, for whom a celebration took place on I Akhet 29 and 30 (**139** and **142**).

[160] van Siclen 1986, 359–7, fig. 3, pl. 55. The tomb of Neferhotep (TT 50) may attest the same celebration. A reward ceremony is recorded to have taken place in year 3 of Horemheb, who appeared from the palace *m-ḫt ir.t ʿḳ.w n it=f ỉmn m p3 pr.t ir.n=f m ḥw.t nb* 'when making food offerings to his father Amun at the Coming-Forth that he performed in the house of gold' (PM I-1², 95 (2); Hari 1985, 18–9, pl. 6).

[161] The text on the doorway of the seventh pylon of Karnak (PM II², 169 (498, c); *Urk.* IV, 186: 13). Thutmose III replaced the barge of Amun constructed in later years of Hatshepsut (Traunecker 1989, 103, n. 75; Redford 2003, 209 and 211; Laskowski 2006, 201).

[162] PM II², 104 (310). Fully published by Traunecker (1989, 96–7). Murnane (1979, 19, pl. 7) and Le Saout (1989, pls 11–3) also published part of it. This scene is again retrospective because the northern suites of rooms were erected after the Akh-menu had been built. Laskowski (2006, 198) postulates that the rooms were completed after year 33. Barguet (1962a, 336) and Haikal (1970, vol. 2, 13) related this scene to the Valley Feast, which is unlikely. Amun's barge is also represented in Room XLI (PM II², 124 (442)).

[163] The key role of Ptah in this area is evident. In a relief of the next room XVA, dated to the time of Ptolemy X, Ptah-Foremost-of-the-Gold-House is captioned as giving an *imy.t-pr* document to the king (PM II², 104 (312)). The reception of this document by a child god became a festival celebrated on I Akhet 2 at Ptolemaic-Roman Dendera (**34**). This was probably more characteristic of the Khoiak Feast in the Middle and early New Kingdoms, when official titles were transferred to heirs (**455**, **542**, and **547**). Ptah evoking Osiris in the house of gold is mentioned in 'the First Letter for Breathing' (M. Smith 2009, 507). Golden vases of Ptah are referred to in a text of the tomb of Neferhotep (TT 50) in association with the New Year (4.5.8). The Middle Kingdom tomb of Intefiqer (TT 60) also specifies Ptah as the origin of the New Year gifts (Davies and Gardiner 1920, 16, pl. 10). Ptah was certainly associated with the gold house in one of his forms (Leitz 2002a, vol. 3, 174). It was Osiris-of-Koptos-in-the-House-of-Gold who was worshipped at one of the chapels located to the northeast of Karnak (Haikal 1970, vol. 2, n. 152; Coulon, Leclère, and Marchand 1995, 222, pl. 12). Loeben (1987, 238) proposes that Amenhotep I played a key role in the house of gold as a patron deity of the artisans of western Thebes and, by extension, as a god to whom paraphernalia were dedicated at Karnak, a role taken by Sokar at Memphis.

[164] *Urk.* IV, 584–5. Pillet (1939, 247), following Legrain (1917, 28), identified the portal with the entrance to Thutmose III's barque chapel erected between the seventh and eighth pylons, while identification with the seventh pylon is proposed by Traunecker (1989, 104).

[165] Other northern rooms include references to the Sed Festival, the *ḥdn*-Plant Feast of Hathor (**374** and **381**), and foundation ceremonies.

[166] PM II², 13 (39); *KRI* V, 231: 1–4; Bouriant 1890, 173. Awad (2002, 185) reads the date as IV Shemu 4. For examples of *ḥb tpy* from the Ptolemaic texts, see Wilson 1997, 634. Vesting the deceased is mentioned in connection with the 'first festival' and the epagomenal days in mortuary papyri from the Ptolemaic-Roman Period (M. Smith 2009, 409, 418, and 436). This Maat temple was erected first by Amenhotep III in line with the Akh-menu on the same axis (O'Connor 1998, 157).

The king ordered the vizier to enlarge the double-treasury of Maat, located to the north of Karnak, in order to accommodate a 'place of the First Festival'.[167] The significance of the treasury for the New Year is also suggested by the location of the *pr ḥḏ* at the entrance to the New Year court at Dendera. References to the New Year and 36 figures representing the decans are attested in this room.[168]

A wider spectrum may be required here to understand how the consecration of offerings was performed in a chronological order within the year. At the same time, emphasis is to be placed on the fiscal aspects of the New Year Festival. Elsewhere, Thutmose III is known to have issued a decree on I Shemu 27 in year 15 (**1038**). It concerns new offerings to be established for Amun 'from the annual allowance on behalf of the life, prosperity, and health of my person' (*m ẖr.t-rnp.t ḥr-tp ꜥnḫ wḏꜣ snb ḥm=i*). The offerings include various precious objects to be used at annual festivals and their provision is described as being done 'as on the first occasion' (*mi sp tpy*). It may be that the first occasion is analogous to the New Year as well as the mythical primeval time. The decree was probably issued in a ceremonial setting on a new moon day about three months before New Year's Day to allow sufficient time to prepare the new offerings.

There may be a few more New Kingdom examples that bear witness to New Year offerings.[169] For example, a large pile of offerings is also attested in two scenes on Hatshepsut's Red Chapel.[170] Each scene is followed by the dedication of two obelisks. A representation more elaborate and comparable to Thutmose III's grandiose dedication scene is seen at the unpublished peristyle hall of Thutmose IV.[171] It consisted of two wings and once stood in front of the fourth pylon at Karnak but was dismantled by Amenhotep III in order to erect the third pylon. Many of its stone blocks have been re-assembled into nearly a complete building, which is displayed at the Open-Air Museum today. Two large dedication scenes are represented on the rear wall of each wing. The king offers to the seated Amun-Re various goods, which occupy a large space between them. While the scene on the right wing depicts provisions ranging from bread to bulls, that on the left focuses on paraphernalia, such as statues and vases as well as Amun's barge (Figures 25, a–d).[172] The legends include a reference to the Sed Festival and do not indicate a link to the New Year, but the iconographical features closely parallel other examples examined so far. The court in front of the fourth pylon was initially constructed by Thutmose II and called *wsḫ.t ḥby.t* the 'festival hall'. According to the Northampton Stela of the tomb of Djehuty (TT 11), overseer of the double-treasury under Hatshepsut and Thutmose III, the young king Thutmose III ordered the construction of a double-treasury within the festival hall in order to 'measure grain for Amun before the land in its entirety' on behalf of the queen Hatshepsut.[173] Gabolde (1993, 58–9) identifies this hall with that of Thutmose II and relates it to the New Year.

The dedications, which are divided between animated offerings and craft objects, is also seen in tomb scenes related to the New Year, which will be presented in 4.5.12. If Thutmose III's dedication scene had the other half for animal offerings, then it would have existed on the other side over the sanctuary (i.e. to the south).

4.3.5. Locations of the New Year celebrations

4.3.5.1. Temple ceremony on the East Bank (Figure 18)

The function of the treasuries differed from time to time and from location to location. The English word 'treasury' is used to translate a number of different Egyptian words. Three institutions can be grouped under this category, namely, *pr-ḥḏ*, *pr-nb*, and *ḫtm*.[174] Moreover, the orthography for the first two can appear as *pr.wy* 'double-', sometimes with *ḥḏ* and *nb* being combined.[175] The significance of treasuries in administrative, economic activities is evident but their distinctive functions, if any, and interrelationship with other governmental institutions are not easy to surmise.

There were two kinds of temple treasury in the opinion of Haring (1997, 128), Hovestreydt (1997, 202), and Awad (2002, 20 and 40)—one for ritualistic use in the core temple area and the other for administrative use in the marginal temple precincts. The latter was used as a setting to host religious celebrations, as evidenced by the aforementioned visit of Amun to the remote treasury in the time of Thutmose III. Some archaeological evidence supports this idea. Thutmose I's treasury, located in the north vicinity of Karnak, to which Thutmose III added outer enclosure walls and workshops, had a barque station of Amun.[176] The same

[167] For official titles associated with the Maat temple and a relation between this temple and the treasury of Amun, see Awad 2002, 185–6.

[168] The decans are represented in a narrow overhead band surrounding Room XI (PM VI, 58–9; *Dendara* IV, 176: 4–178: 5, pls 292–7; Cauville 2001, 284–7 for transliteration and translation). See *Dendara* IV, 150: 1 and 175: 6 for references to the New Year in this room.

[169] Room XVIII at central Karnak (PM II^{2}, 105 (319); Myśliwiec 1985, pl. 11 (2)); Room XIII at the Akh-menu (PM II^{2}, 115 (363)). Hovestreydt (1997, 200) points out the architectural and decorative similarities of Hatshepsut's ambulatory rooms, including Room XVIII, to other temple treasuries.

[170] Blocks 53 and 196 (Burgos and Larché 2006, vol. 1, 76, 128).

[171] PM II^{2}, 72. It bears the name of a portal or the building itself: *sbꜣ ꜥꜣ m ḏꜥm Mn-ḫpr.w-rꜥ di ꜥnḫ sḥb ꜣImn ip.t* the 'great gate in electrum of Menkheperure, given life, Amun-Makes-Opet-Festive' (Gabolde 1993, 32).

[172] See Grimal and Larché 1995, xxx for a part of the bull scene.

[173] PM I-1^{2}, 22 (5); *Urk.* IV, 429: 9–10.

[174] Desplancques 2006, 9–10.

[175] Bryan 1991, 247–9; Desplancques 1999.

[176] Jacquet-Gordon 1988, fig. 23. Gundlach (2010, 93–5) proposed that

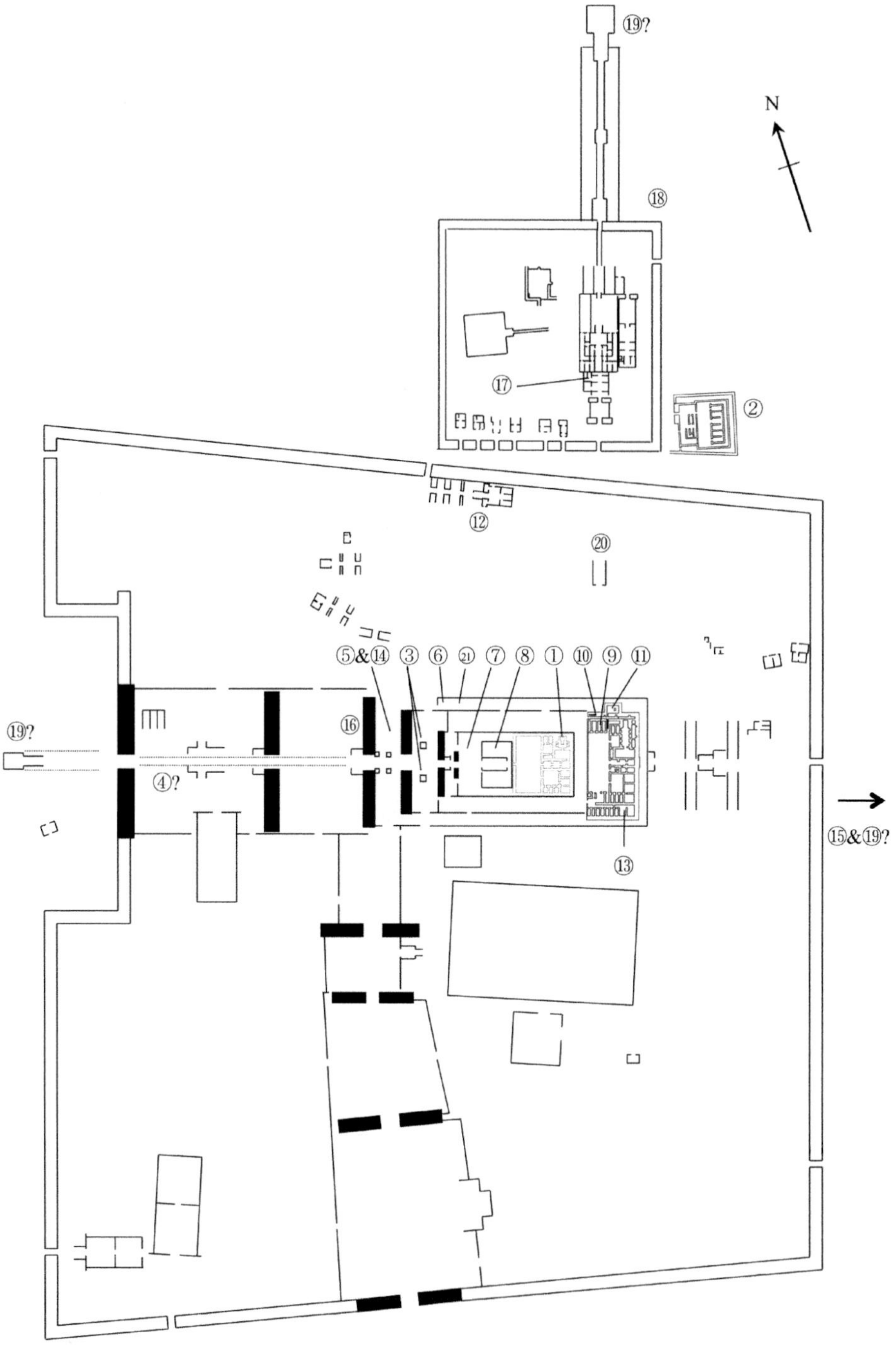

1. Solar court (Senusret I)
2. Treasury of Thutmose I (until the time of Seti I)
3. Hatshepsut's obelisks
4. *wꜣ.t wḏḥw* the 'way of the libation offerings' (Hatshepsut)
5. Double-treasury at *wsḫ.t ḥby.t* the 'broad hall' (Thutmose II)
6. Userhat and the Opening-of-the-Mouth ritual (Thutmose III)
7. *pr ḥḏ n ꜥntyw* 'treasury of the frankincense' (Thutmose III)
8. Dedication scene (Thutmose III)
9. Reference to the New Year (*ḥꜣ.t rnp.t*) (Thutmose III)
10. Dedication and the Opening-of-the-Mouth ritual (Thutmose III)
11. Solar court (Thutmose III)
12. Ptah temple as a way station for the procession to the treasury (Thutmose III)
13. Storerooms (Thutmose III)
14. Dedication scenes of the peristyle hall (Thutmose IV)
15. Treasury of the Aten temple (Amenhotep IV)
16. New Year scenes and text (Seti I)
17. Reference to the New Year Feast (*ḥb tpy*) and the double-treasury of Maat (Ramses III)
18. Double-treasury of the Mentu temple (Ramses IX)
19. *ḏꜣḏꜣ* (Menkheperre)
20. Treasury of Shabaka
21. Ptah giving an *imy.t-pr* document to the king (Ptolemy X)

Figure 18. Locations of the New Year texts and scenes, and of treasuries.

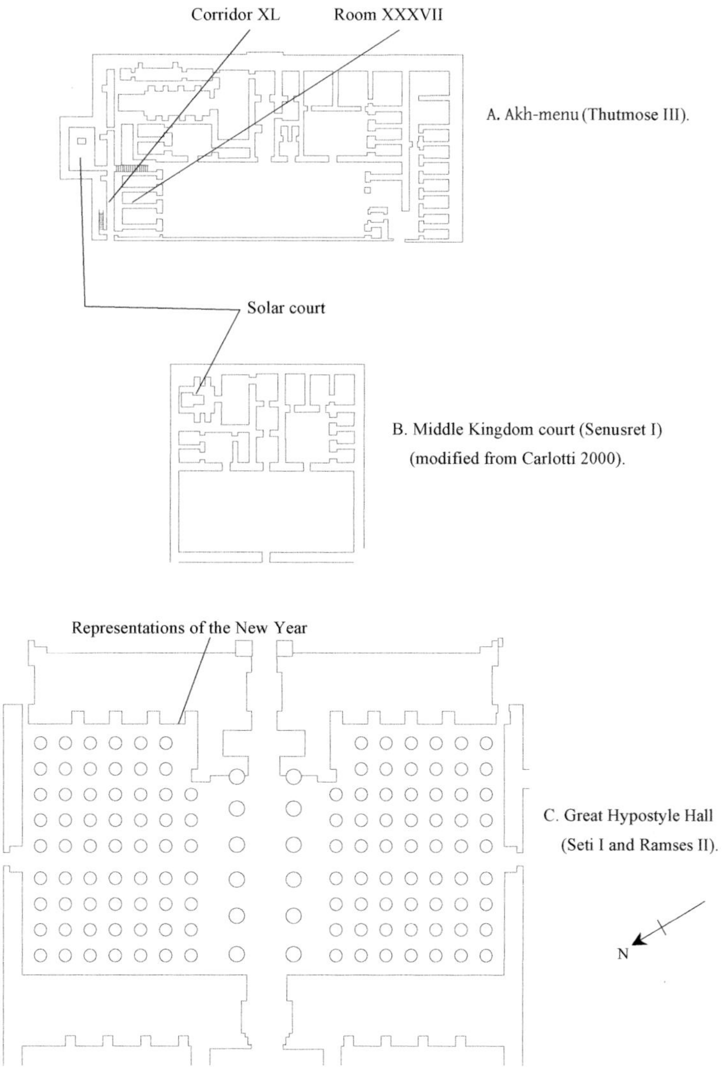

Figure 19. New Year quarters at the Karnak temple.

holds for some temple granaries. In the tomb of Pahemnetjer (TT 284), a scribe of the offerings for all the gods in the time of Ramses II or earlier, the processions of the Theban triad are represented proceeding to an unspecified granary at a harvest celebration.[177] The northwest storeroom area of the Ramesseum included a ceremonial raised platform reached by steps, on which a statue may have been placed. By identifying this quarter with a treasury and the house of gold, Goyon (1976, 209) argues that the king himself stayed at this site to receive the New Year gifts.

It is hardly surprising that a structure similar to this may have existed in every storage facility attached to major temples and palaces. There were four New-Kingdom temples that contained a treasury called *pr ḥḏ* within its core quarter: Hatshepsut/Thutmose III's rooms at Karnak,[178] Seti I's temple at Abydos,[179] Ramses II's temple at Abu Simbel,[180] and Ramses III's temple at Medinet Habu.[181] In the last three temples, reliefs covering their blocked entrance suggest that there

the treasury of Thutmose I, together with the Ptah temple at northern Karnak, can be traced back to the time of Senusret I, based on the name of the latter king carved on a stone block discovered in the treasury (Jacquet-Gordon 1988, vol. 1, 214, vol. 2, pl. 55 for the stone block). For a general reference, see Cabrol 2001, 492–3.

[177] PM I-1², 366 (6–7); Norman Davies and Nina Davies 1939. Kozloff and Bryan (1992, 274) propose that the harvest celebration took place at a granary located in northern Karnak during the reign of Amenhotep III.

[178] *pr ḥḏ n ꜥntyw* the 'treasury of the frankincense' (PM II², 93; *Urk.* IV, 853: 9).

[179] PM VI, 27 (250–2).

[180] PM VII, 106–9 (Rooms I–III and VI–VIII).

[181] PM II², 507 (Rooms 9–13).

was a hidden access. The king is portrayed dedicating offerings and foreign captives to gods at Abu Simbel and Medinet Habu. As Hovestreydt (1997, 194–5) rightly demonstrates, the subject was modelled on the scenes of foreign gifts to the king depicted in private tombs belonging to the Eighteenth Dynasty. A difference between them is that the foreigners are portrayed coming to Egypt of their own will in the private tomb decorations, some of which clearly indicate a context of the New Year (4.5.12). It may be that the inner temple treasuries contained only selected items due to their smaller capacity. On the basis of the wall reliefs in the magazines belonging to Thutmose I's treasury, Awad (2002, 19) assumes that that treasury was designed to store commodity items, rather than precious materials, such as gold and silver. There is another structure that Awad believes was a treasury, which may be associated with the beginning of the year. It consists of three rooms located at the southeast corner of the Akh-menu.[182] A relief in Room XIII portrays the king, accompanied by Thoth, dedicating treasures to Amun and Amenet. The legend says that Thutmose III erected monuments for his father Amun-Re to dedicate divine offerings at many great festivals, and then the following line reads:[183]

> *rdi.t mꜣʿ wḏḥ.w wḥ.wt ʿšꜣ wr.t wsḫ.w wḏꜣ [mni.wt] m ḏʿm mꜣʿ iny n ḥm=f m ḫꜣs.wt rsy.(w)t m bꜣk.wt=sn n.t ḫr.t-rnp.t*
>
> Presenting very many *wḏḥ.w*-offerings and cauldrons, as well as broad collars, the *wḏꜣ*-necklace, and [menits] made of fine electrum that was brought to his person from the southern countries as their levies of the annual revenue.

Whether those valuable objects were crafted in Egypt or in the places where the raw materials were produced, they were destined initially for the hand of the king and then passed on to the temple treasuries for the god. The flow of the material resources on an annual basis is evoked by *ḫr.t-rnp.t* (lit. 'that which is under the year'), a category defining what is collected for the needs of a given body to be consumed over one year, which sometimes appears in texts in association with the New Year (4.6.1).

The treasury and the Maat temple at Karnak were undoubtedly central to the beginning of the year. Whether the treasury of Thutmose I continued to function in the Ramesside Period is not clear, but one treasury seems to have remained, at least until the time of the high-priest of Amun, Menkheperre, of the Twenty-First Dynasty, as evidenced by Stela Cairo 3.12.24.2, found at the east part of Karnak.[184] This stela records the northern enclosure wall of Karnak as extending from the southern *ḏꜣḏꜣ* to the northern treasury. The Banishment Stela tells us that Menkheperre performed the New Year Feast when Amun appeared 'before the *ḏꜣḏꜣ*' on the fourth epagomenal day.[185] Cabrol (2001, 590–3) proposes three possibilities regarding the location of the *ḏꜣḏꜣ*—the quay at west Karnak, the quay of the Mentu precinct, or the quay at east Karnak.[186]

A key function of the treasury is also attested in a scene of the tomb of Imiseba (TT 65), chief temple-scribe of the domain of Amun under Ramses IX.[187] By examining the procession of Amun's vases in this scene, Schott (1970, 46–8) related it to the New Year, an interpretation followed by Bács (2001, fig. 2) who further suggested that the three festivals of Opet, of the Valley, and of the New Year are represented in the same chamber. The New Year scene has only partially been published, so its overall layout is reproduced in Figure 28. The procession of Amun's vases is represented in the top register, which extends over two walls. On the north wall is depicted a group of men carrying offering trays aloft (mainly the *bit*- and *psn*-bread) towards a temple treasury.[188] Small rolled objects, perhaps linen[189], are counted within the enclosure of the treasury. On the other side of the treasury, four rows of priests proceed towards the treasury where they appear to receive the cloths and liquid containers from Pairy, chief guardian of the treasury of the temple of Amun (*ḥry sꜣwty pr ḥḏ*

[182] PM II², 15 (Room XIII, XIV, and XV).

[183] PM II², 115 (363, a); *Urk.* IV, 871: 8–11; Awad 2002, 22–3 for transcription and translation.

[184] PM II², 210; Cabrol 2001, 592; Ritner 2009, 136–7 for transliteration and translation.

[185] von Beckerath 1968, 12, l. 9.

[186] Also see Spencer (1984, 133), who considers the *ḏꜣḏꜣ* a way station or peripteral chapel beside a canal or lake used for temple processions.

[187] PM I-1², 130 (8–9). Originally the tomb of Nebamen, overseer of the granary in the early Eighteenth Dynasty. Wasmuth (2003, 94) proposes that the tomb was usurped on two occasions.

[188] By examining scenes parallel to this, though not including our scene, Haring (1997, 102–5) concludes that they are associated with festivals, rather than with the daily rituals. An example from Ramses II's temple at Abydos specifies this particular performance as *wn-ḥr* the 'Opening of the Face (with the determinative)' (*MH* III, pl. 169, B). This idiom is attested in the Pyramid Texts (PT 268, Pyr. 373a and 341, Pyr. 555a), where the dawn is referred to, while the king is likened to Horus emerging from the eastern horizon, and may first appear in Middle Kingdom texts as 'every good festival of *wn-ḥr*' (Barta 1968, 41). This suggests that the *wn-ḥr* was an essential part of any celebration, including the daily rituals (Lohwasser 1991, 28–31). Spell 113 of the Book of the Dead speaks of it in association with the second and fifteenth lunar days. It also appears in administrative documents, such as P. Harris I (VI, 2; XXVII, 2; XLVII, 10; LVII, 10; and LVIII, 4), where *šnʿ.w n wn-ḥr* the 'workshops of ' are referred to in association with the daily cult. Later evidence from Edfu (*Edfou* I, 554: 4) and Esna (**1154**) shows a link to the New Year. Also see Wilson (1997, 230) for other late attestations.

[189] We are not aware of an object parallel to this from any surviving source. Its flexibility is obvious because it is rolled. Similar, but not exactly the same, objects made of flax are attested in the mastaba of Werirenptah, dating from the Fifth Dynasty (*Hieroglyphic texts from Egyptian stelae*, vol. 4, pls 10–11). More revealing evidence is attested on the coffin of Mentuhotep, dating from the Middle Kingdom, which depicts two round objects, each painted in a light and a dark colour and bound with a red strip (Steindorff 1896, vol. 2, 27, pl. 5, top). The accompanying text identifies these objects as the *ḥbs*-linen.

Figure 20a. Stairway leading from the pillared hall to the solar courtat the Akh-menu, viewed from south (photograph taken by the author).

Figure 20b. Stairway to the solar court and Corridor XL at the Akh-menu, viewed from west. The corridor continues to another group through a door behind the palm tree (photograph taken by the author).

Figure 21 a. Corridor XL and the opening to another stairway at the Akh-menu, viewed from south (photograph taken by the author).

Figure 21b. Stairway leading from Corridor XL perhaps directly to the roof of the Akh-menu, viewed from west (photograph taken by the author).

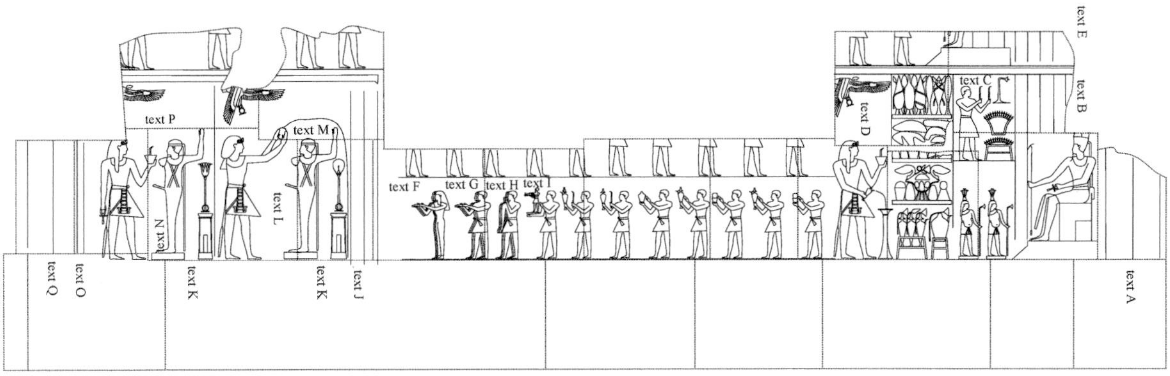

Figure 22a. Elevation of the north wall of Corridor XL at the Akh-menu (PM II[2], 123 (432)), drawn by the author.

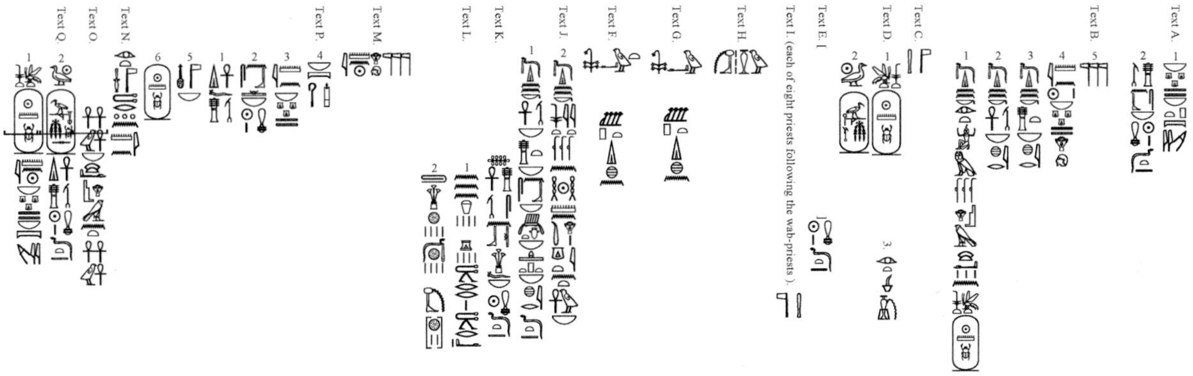

Figure 22b. Text on the north wall of Corridor XL at the Akh-menu.

Figure 22c. Thutmose III performing rituals to the ithyphallic Amun-Re. The god is not yet in full investiture (Episodes 1 and 2, Corridor XL at the Akh-menu). Photograph taken by the author.

Figure 22d. Priests carrying a vase and a candle taper (part of Episode 3, Corridor XL at the Akh-menu). Photograph taken by the author.

Figure 22e. Thutmose III dedicating offerings to Amun-Re. Between them are represented a priest holding two tapers in front of two candle chests and two figures of Hapi below (Episode 4, Corridor XL at the Akh-menu). Photograph taken by the author.

Figure 22f. Priest holding two tapers in front of two candle chests towards Amun-Re, who wears the double-plume headdress (part of Episode 4, Corridor XL at the Akh-menu). Photograph taken by the author.

Figure 23. Scene of *ḥ3.t-rnp.t* depicted on the west wall of Room XXXVII at the Akh-menu (after Pécoil 2000, pls 115–7). To the right, a seated god receives offerings from Thutmose III, behind whom is a broken text including '[jubilation] for the front of the year'.

Figure 24. Present state of Room XV at Karnak, viewed from west (photograph taken by the author).

n pr ꞽImn).[190] From above the first and second rows of priests represent the schools of Mut and Khonsu.[191] The last two rows below belong to that of Amun, headed by three priests—the second-, third-, and fourth-priests of Amun, who also appear in the procession of Amun's vases above. Finally, the Theban triad sits in a kiosk and receives a libation from Imiseba, accompanied by musicians and the portable images of Ahmes-Nefertari and Amenhotep I. The accompanying text enumerates 17 hypostases of Amun worshipped at different temples, followed by a formula to evoke the deity (4.3.2).

Imiseba seems to have acted as top administrative officer in his capacity as chief temple-scribe of the domain of Amun. His official service included not only attending religious ceremonies but also maintaining regular supplies to the temples. He is recorded at Karnak as the chief distributor of 80 loaves of the white bread (*t ḥḏ*)[192] destined for the temple audience hall (*wbꜣ*) every day.[193] The depiction of his tomb is astonishing with respect to his role of presenting offerings to the Theban triad, which was usually performed by the vizier on behalf of the king only when royal attendance was not possible. In fact, P. Turin 2004+2007+2057+2106, also dated to the time of Ramses IX, records that the vizier Khaemwaset

[190] The same title was also given to an Amenmesu under Ramses IX (Awad 2002, 172, n. 124). Whether they were the same individual is not clear.

[191] Some remarks on the legends are necessary here because Kitchen's documentation has errors. The person leading the first row of priests is the high-priest of Mut *Rꜥ-ms-sw-nḫt*, rather than the high-priest of Amun as recorded in *KRI* VI, 551: 4. The leader of the second group of priests below is the high-priest of Khonsu [ ]-*tꜣ* (*KRI* VI, 551: 6).

[192] The conical white bread (*dḳw t ḥḏ*) took precedence over other offerings, indicating its significance and rarity. In the tomb of Imiseba (TT 65), the man carrying the white bread is the second of the offering bringers. See Stroot-Kiraly 1989 for its implication and association with the solar cult and Haring 1997, 110 for its association with the production of beer. H. Wilson (1989, 99) regards the funerary cones as representing the white bread. Deliveries of this bread to the workmen are recorded in O. Cairo 25763 and 25765, dated to the Twenty-First Dynasty. II Peret 21 and III Peret 1 (O. Berlin 14258 dating from the Twentieth Dynasty) and II Shemu 10 (O. Berlin 14254 dating from the Nineteenth Dynasty) are known to have been the days on which it was delivered.

[193] PM II[2], 83 (213); *KRI* VI, 543–4; Sethe 1907b, 39–41 for translation; Frood 2010a, 117–9, figs 4–5 for transliteration, translation, and photograph.

rewarded officials and selected workmen with the *ḥbs*-linen at the temple of Maat on IV Akhet 19 in year 16 (**485**).[194] This event was preceded by the payment of salaries 'from the hand (*m-ḏr.t*)' of the vizier to the workmen 'on the West Bank' the previous day. For what reason the vizier stayed at eastern Thebes is, however, not given in the text although the ceremonial nature of the visit is evident.[195] To date, there is no festival known to have taken place on IV Akhet 19. It may have been related to the Khoiak Feast, the auxiliary rituals of which began from IV Akhet 20, according to the Medinet Habu calendar (**487**).

The treasury depicted in Imiseba's tomb was presumably that of Karnak. The fact that the priests of the Theban triad gathered there suggests that there was no ideal place to accommodate them other than Karnak.[196] Indeed, the temple of Luxor had hardly any function as an economic centre at celebrations. Apart from the central treasuries of Hatshepsut/Thutmose III and one founded by Thutmose I, both at Karnak, two other treasuries are known to have existed on the East Bank of Thebes during the New Kingdom—one belonging to the Mentu precinct[197], the other to the Aten temple[198], located to the north and east of Karnak respectively. The latter was, of course, maintained only during the reign of Amenhotep IV. The treasury of Thutmose I was functioning throughout the Eighteenth Dynasty but abandoned after the time of Seti I.[199] Hence, only the domain of Mentu, which included the temple of Maat, remained active during the rest of the Ramesside Period. It is known that the 'granary' of the Maat temple and the treasury of Mentu temple were still in operation as distributors of copper under Ramses IX.[200]

In addition, a ceremonial route used for water rituals existed near the royal palace in the time of Hatshepsut. Her Red Chapel refers to the palace as being located 'on the way of the *wḏḥw*-offering' (*ꜥḥ nsw.t ḥr m wꜣ.t wḏḥw*).[201] The word *wḏḥw* appears in a text carved on the western quay of Karnak, dating from the time of Taharqa, in association with a ritual, when the Nile's water was collected for ceremonial use.[202] It was a general term denoting water offerings carried in various vessels, such as the *nms.t*-, *ḥs.t*-, and *ꜥnḫ*-jars.[203] Large ornamental versions of those vessels for the New Year were perhaps taken from Amun's precinct of Karnak to its western vicinity, where the processional route met the Nile.[204] This seems to have been performed at all the temples because it is also represented at the temple of Luxor (4.3.1). There is no evidence attesting the reversionary supply of the sacred water from Karnak to different temples, nor vice versa.

It is significant to observe the pictorial, textual, and architectural evidence relating to the New Year celebrations in the north half of Karnak temple. Barguet (1962a, 157–217) proposed dividing the Akh-menu into three parts: 'la salle des fêtes' to the west, 'les salles sokariennes' to the southeast, and 'les salles solaires' to the northeast. Janák, Vymazalová, and Coppens (2011, 440) suggest that the location of the solar complexes in the Theban temples on their north side displays a bearing on Heliopolis when seen from southern Egypt.

4.3.5.2. Royal ceremony on the West Bank

While the temenos of Karnak was undoubtedly a key setting on the East Bank, various sources reveal that the king stayed at a palace on the West Bank at some point during the New Year celebrations. For example, two accounts of the new vizier Useramen testify that Thutmose III was there for the installation ceremony on I Akhet 1 in year 8. First, P. Turin 1878 reads (**4**):

> *ḥꜣ.t-sp 5 ꜣbd 1-nw ꜣḫ.t sw 1 ḫr ḥm nsw.t-bỉ.*
> *ty Mn-ḫpr-rꜥ ꜥ.w.s. sꜣ-rꜥ Ḏḥwty-ms ꜥ.[w.s]*
> *hrw pn sṯꜣ sš ḫtmw nṯr Wsr-ỉmn n pr ỉmn*
> *m-bꜣḥ ḥm=f ꜥ.w.[s.* a few groups lost] *hꜣnꜣ*
> *Wsr-ỉmn r ꜥꜣ.t my ṯꜣy wr n rnp.[wt pw ḏr*
> *fḫ.t=f] 30 n rnp.t tꜣy pr-ꜥꜣ ꜥ.w.s. pꜣy(=ỉ) nb*
> *nfr ḳnw nꜣ [n rnp.wt] ỉrr=ỉ tꜣ ỉꜣ.t n pꜣy=k*[sic] *ỉt*
> *gr ỉr ṯꜣty sš* [one or two groups lost]

194 Copper was also another item with which the workmen were rewarded, given as a royal favour rather than as their prescribed work tools (Janssen 1994, 94).

195 There is another text attesting the vizier as a provider of linen. O. Cairo 25504 records that the vizier Panehesy supervised the lowering of a sarcophagus into the tomb of Merenptah and subsequently rewarded (*mk*) the workmen at the Enclosure of the Necropolis on IV Shemu 19 in year 7 (**1342**). He left Thebes to the north on IV Shemu 20. The reward included six oxen and 80 fine cloths (*šmꜥ nfr ḥbs.w*), probably one for each workman. A similar quantity of linen (78 in number) is attested in P. Turin 1881, III, 2–4 as distributed to the workmen in I Peret, year 7 of Ramses IX, but the provider is not specified (**693**; *KRI* VI, 612: 5–6).

196 P. Berlin 3047, dated to year 46 of Ramses II, records that Theban priests gathered for a tribunal at a place called Heriheramen (*ḥr=ỉ-ḥr-ỉmn* 'My-Face-is-towards-Amun'), which Sauneron (1954, 121) and Traunecker (1982, 310) proposed to locate at eastern Karnak. Traunecker does not rule out that any building located on a temple axis could be called by this name.

197 P. Leopold II+P. Amherst VII, 1, 7, dated to III Akhet 23 of year 16 of Ramses IX (**391**; *KRI* VI, 482: 7–8; Capart and Gardiner 1939, pl. 1, l. 7).

198 A text originating from the temple *gm-pꜣ-ỉtn* (*Urk.* IV, 1995: 5; Awad 2002, 181).

199 Jacquet-Gordon (2009, 123) argues that brick sanctuaries were erected by the following Ramesside rulers to replace the treasury for the cult of Amenhotep I and Ahmes-Nefertari.

200 See P. Turin 1881, recto, II, 5 and 12 (*KRI* VI, 611: 7 and 15–6) for the granary of the Maat temple; P. Leopold II+P. Amherst VII, 1, 7 (Awad 2002, 126) for the treasury of Mentu temple.

201 Lacau and Chevrier 1977, vol. 1, 98, vol. 2, pl. 6 (Block 222); Burgos and Larché 2006, vol. 1, 31; Cabrol 2001, 66–70; Assmann 1984, 225–6 for translation. See Gundlach (2006, 20, Abb. 7) for its presumed location to the west of Karnak.

202 Traunecker 1972, 203, fig. 2.

203 Sugi 2007, 242–5.

204 Hatshepsut is also known to have erected *ỉḫm.t sdni* a 'paved bank' anew at *ḫft-ḥr-nb=s* (Stela Vatican 266: Cabrol 2001, 636–9).

> Year 5, I Akhet 1 under the person of the king of Upper and Lower Egypt Menkheperre l.p.h., son of Re Thutmose l.[p.h]. This day of bringing the scribe of the divine seal Useramen to the temple of Amun before his person, l.p.[h. His person said: 'I] assent [to] Useramen very much. How many year[s] has the man passed [since his departure]?' 'It is 30 years. King l.p.h., (my) good lord. Many are the [years]. I take the office of my father as for the vizier and the scribe [ ].'

This account is complemented by another source from Useramen's own tomb (TT 131), which adds some more detail.[205] It represents soldiers and officials leading Thutmose III, who is carried in a palanquin to the gate of an unspecified edifice. Useramen is clad in the costume of the vizier and accompanies the king. This episode leads to another portrayal of Useramen, with his father Aametju, being ushered to the king, who is seated in a kiosk. The accompanying text specifies where the ceremony took place as:

> *ḫpr sw.t ḥms.t nsw.t m* [*ḏꜣdw n*] *ꞽmy wr.t nsw.t-bi.ty Mn-ḫpr-rꜥ di ꜥnḫ sṯꜣ sr.*[*w smr.w n stp-sꜣ*] *sꜥḥ.w s.t wꜥꜥw ꞽmy.w ḫnt wr.*[*w n tꜣ ḏr*] *šny.t Ḥr m ꜥḥ=f r ꞽnḏ-ḫrt nsw.*[*t ꜥ.w.s. ꜥḳ*] *ṯꜣty r ꞽnḏ-rꜣ ḥr ḫr.t tꜣ.wy r šsr.t m* [*w* two or three groups lost] *n sḫr.w Ḏḥwty* [*ṯꜣty*(*?*)] *ẖr-ꜥ=f ḥr* [two or three groups lost]

> Now it occurred: the seating of the king in the [*ḏꜣdw*-hall of] the West of the king of Upper and Lower Egypt, Menkheperre, given of life. The magistrate[s, friends of the palace], dignitaries of the private place, chamberlains, chief[s of the entire land], and entourages of Horus in his palace came to salute the kin[g l.p.h]. The vizier [entered] to advice on matters on the Two Lands and to express at [ ] the plans of Thoth, under whom [the vizier(?)] is in control of [ ].

Some early rulers of the Eighteenth Dynasty are known to have used the *ḏꜣdw*-building on ceremonial occasions. Thutmose III is elsewhere known to have issued a royal decree when a 'royal sitting took place in the *ḏꜣd*[*w*]-hall [o]f the West at [his p]alace [...], resting at the gate which was at the [northern] lake of the temple, purifying [...]' (*ḫpr ḥms.t nsw.t m ḏꜣd*[*w ꞽ*]*my wr.t m* [*ꜥ*]*ḥ=*[*f*...long lacuna] *ḥtp m rwy.t n.t m š* [*mḥy*] *n ḥw.t-nṯr ḥr twr* [...long lacuna]) on I Shemu 2 in 'year after 23', which Gardiner (1952, 9) read as year 24 (**967**). Phraseology parallel to this appears in Stela Cairo 34002, which records the king Ahmes' decision to establish the cult of his grandmother Tetisheri at Abydos,[206] and in the so-called coronation text of Hatshepsut at Deir el-Bahari, which tells us that Thutmose I proclaimed that the kingship be given to his daughter Hatshepsut at the New Year.[207] Stadelmann (1996, 226) proposes that the *ḏꜣdw* was located in el-Tarif to the northeast of the later temple of Seti I until Amenhotep III had erected a large residential complex at Malkata.

The king's sojourn in western Thebes is also evidenced in the tomb of Menkheperreseneb, high-priest of Amun (TT 86), where Thutmose III is portrayed receiving gifts from northern countries.[208] The legend, which Manniche (1986, 58) associates not with the Valley Feast but with the New Year celebration, says:

> *ꞽ.t m ḥtp r bw ẖr nsw.t ẖr ꜥnḫ* [*Ꞽmn-rꜥ*] *m* [*ꞽ*]*p.t-s.*[*wt*] *m-ḫt ꞽr.t ḥss.t Ꞽmn-rꜥ m ḥb=f n ḏsr-ꜣḫ.t m ḫꜥ.w=f* [2 groups lost] *m ẖn.t=f n.t tpy-rnp.t*

> Coming in peace to the place before the king with a bouquet [of Amun-Re] from [Kar]nak after giving the praises of Amun-Re at his festival of Djeser-akhet in his diadems [ ] at his navigation of the beginning of the year.

Phraseology parallel to this is attested in the tomb of Nakht (TT 161), a bearer of the floral offerings of Amun under Amenhotep III, where the deceased and his wife are portrayed returning to the tomb.[209] The accompanying text reads: [two groups lost] *ḥtp m ḥw.t=f ḫft ꞽꞽ.t* [one group lost] *ḥr šms Ꞽmn m* [one group lost] *ḥb=f nfr m ḫꜥ.w=f* [one group lost] *wꞽꜣ ꜥꜣ m ẖn.t=f n tpy-rnp.t* 'resting in his house when coming [ ] at following Amun from [ ] at his beautiful festival in his diadems [ ] great barge at his navigation of the beginning of the year'. It is known that the accession of Thutmose I was called *ḥb n ḫꜥ.w* the 'festival of the diadems', where *ḫꜥ.w* has the determinative of .[210] This recalls Hatshepsut's coronation text, where her appearance (*ḫꜥ nsw.t*) is called *ḥb* (*s*)*šd* the 'festival

[205] PM I-1², 246 (8–9); *Urk.* IV, 1380–3; Murnane 1977, 36; Dorman 1988, 33–4; Dziobek 1994, pl. 72 for facsimile; Dziobek 1998, 3–15 for transliteration and translation. Stela Grenoble Museum 10, perhaps originating from the same tomb, also records an account of his career (PM I-1², 247; *Urk.* IV, 1029–33; Kruchten 1989, 188–9 and Frandsen 1998, 980 for partial transcription, transliteration, and translation).

[206] Discovered in the tomb of the grandmother of Ahmes, Tetisheri, at Abydos (PM V, 92; *Urk.* IV, 26: 12).

[207] PM II², 348 (19); *Urk.* IV, 257: 1 and 261: 8–9; Naville 1895, vol. 3, pl. 60, l. 11; *idem* 1896b, 98, l. 11 for translation.

[208] PM I-1², 177 (8); *Urk.* IV, 928–9; Davies 1933b, 3, pl. 3.

[209] PM I-1², 274 (4). Manniche (1986, 56, fig. 8, left) relates this scene to the New Year.

[210] *Urk.* IV, 81: 4.

of the (*s*)*šd*-headband', taking place at the New Year (4.6.3). Coppens and Vymazalová (2010, 95) points out the possibility that the elevated wabet-hall of Greek-Roman temples had functions parallel to the throne placed on a platform, and that the renewal of the kingship was performed at the New Year, as was done at the Sed Feast.

As a historical fact, Hatshepsut did celebrate the New Year by receiving gifts, as depicted in the tomb of Amenhotep (TT 73), overseer of works on the great obelisks in the temple of Amun.[211] The queen appeared at a palace (*ʿḥ*), which may have been located on the West Bank. Likewise, a scene in the tomb of Qenamen, chief royal steward (TT 93), portrays Amenhotep II receiving the New Year delegation at a palace. The accompanying text reads:[212]

> *sp tpy ir.t bw nfr m ʿḥ wr ms ind-ḥr n wpy-rnp.t*
>
> The first occasion of performing the good occasion at the great palace, bringing salutation for the New Year.

Similarly, Thutmose III is depicted receiving foreign tributes on his *ḫʿ.t nsw.t m s.t wr.t m ʿḥ n iwn šmʿy* 'royal appearance on the throne in the palace of Southern On' in the tomb of Iamnedjeh, first royal herald (TT 84), although this particular occasion is not specified.[213] The large queue of representatives lined up waiting to see the king suggests that it could be a time-consuming ceremony. It may have been performed only on special occasions, when officials, priests, and foreign delegations assembled.

Soldiers also appear in the scenes of inspection and presentation of the New Year gifts. In some cases, the tomb owner is portrayed registering them in a book roll, in his capacity as an army scribe. They are probably young soldiers recruited from various parts of the country and outside. In the tomb of Nebamen (TT 90), captain of troops of the police on the west of Thebes from the time of Thutmose IV to Amenhotep III, a multitude of short-wigged men are represented gathering in one place on an unknown occasion, perhaps at the beginning of the year. Some are seated on chairs and receive greetings from a different group. Above their figures a royal chariot draws up by the royal barge, ready to convey the king elsewhere. This scene is likely to continue onto the next wall, where rows of soldiers are portrayed marching with standards and weapons towards Nebamen. As the result of a royal decree issued in year 6 of Thutmose IV, Nebamen is here given the emblem of a new title by the royal scribe Iuny for his long service as the standard bearer of the royal barge, called 'Beloved-of-Amun'. Then he proceeds to the king, who is seated in a kiosk. The legend accompanying the royal barge refers to geographical directions, as follows:[214]

> *imy wr.t imy r imnt.t ini pꜣ mw nḏm ḫn[t]y pr [Imn] r ir.t ḥss.[t n Imn]*
>
> Starboard: 'Come to the West. The sweet water brings him who sails south[ward]s (to) the temple of [Amun] to perform [what Amun] praises.

Given the presence of the soldiers, Davies (1923, 37) argued that this scene represents a return journey from an Asian campaign in the northwest. However, there is no official evidence attesting a campaign by Thutmose IV in Asia.[215] Moreover, the 'West' here does not imply the relative location of Egypt seen from Asia but the Theban West. The scene was intentionally painted on the south wall, in accordance with the orientation of the scene. This scene parallels those depicted in the contemporaneous tombs of Qenamen, chief royal steward (TT 93),[216] and Amenhotep-Sise, second-priest of Amun (TT 75).[217] In Qenamen's tomb, the royal barge is represented towing a boat which conveys statues of the deceased to the Theban West. The boat is likened to the *nšm.t*-barque of Osiris. The processions of the statues depicted in the upper registers give a delightful impression with dancers moving towards shrines. In Amenhotep-Sise's tomb, again a barge is depicted, below which are portrayed priests carrying vases and candles towards two empty booths. This scene gives way to one where the deceased couple receives an offering list and cloths from a man clothed in a panther skin. In the tomb of Ptahemhat, child of the nursery (TT 77), Thutmose IV is portrayed receiving gifts that were produced under the direction of Ptahemhat. He is described as: *mꜣꜣ [iḫ].wt nb(.wt) [nfr.wt wʿb.wt m] pꜣ mr ʿꜣ ḥw.t Mn-ḫpr.w-rʿ m [pr Imn]* 'Inspecting all [good and pure thin]gs [at] the great canal of the temple Menkheperure in the [domain of Amun]'.[218] This scene is not explicitly associated with the New Year but argues for at least the location of such reception ceremonies.

Now one may wonder whether a divine presence was required for ceremonies held at the palace. The aforementioned texts of the tomb of Menkheperreseneb (TT 86) and tomb of Nakht (TT 161) include references to Amun and the valley temple of Thutmose III. Do

211 PM I-1², 143 (3); Säve-Söderbergh 1957, 2, pl. 2.
212 PM I-1², 191 (9); Davies 1930, 24, pls 11 and 13.
213 PM I-1², 168 (9); *Urk.* IV, 951: 4.
214 PM I-1², 183 (3); Davies 1923, pls 24–5; *Urk.* IV, 1620: 16–8; Radwan 1969, 102, pl. 16 (1).
215 Bryan 1991, 336.
216 PM I-1², 190 (3, IV); Davies 1930, vol. 1, 41, pl. 42.
217 PM I-1², 149 (8); Davies 1923, 17, pl. 17.
218 PM I-1², 151 (4); *Urk.* IV, 1599: 13; Radwan 1969, pl. 15.

they bear witness to Amun's journey to the West Bank? Surviving evidence does not substantiate it. We perhaps should see, in these controversial texts, amalgamated elements brought together from different subjects. Theoretically, the gods were supposed to stay in their temples and be the subject of purification rituals in preparation for the New Year. Thus, an offering scene in the tomb of Amenemhat, a counter of the grain of Amun under Thutmose III (TT 82), which probably depicts this celebration, includes a harper's song, as follows:[219]

> *nfr.w[y] n tꜣ ḥw.t n.t'Imn-rꜥ tꜣ wrš.t mm ḫ[b]*
> *ḫr nsw.t nṯr.w im=s*
>
> Ho[w] beautiful the house of Amun-Re is!
> She who spends the day at the festi[val]
> with the king of the gods in it.

The gods moved about within their own temples but did not have a good reason to go out in public. The static state of the god is corroborated by the fact that there is no single representation depicting a barque procession of Amun at the New Year celebrations. On the contrary, the king might have visited Karnak to dedicate to Amun gifts that he received on the West Bank although the Ramesside rulers hardly visited Thebes for this occasion.

4.4. Other official ceremonies

4.4.1. Visits to Thebes of officials at the New Year

Unlike for the Opet Festival, there is no source attesting the visit of a Ramesside king to Thebes for the New Year. The Ramesside rulers remained in the north. Stela BM 1189, for example, records that Seti I was in Memphis on II Shemu 30 to perform a ceremony for Horakhety, Ptah, and Atum, after which he issued a decree concerning a new endowment to Min-Amun at Buhen. Some evidence witnesses that the vizier was sent to Thebes on behalf of the king. According to P. Turin 1999+2009, an unnamed vizier stayed at Thebes on the first and second epagomenal days in year 13 of Ramses IX (**1414**). The vizier seems to have appointed the second-priest of Amun on the second epagomenal day. As was shown in Table 7, the New Year was one of two occasions, when high officials were dispatched to Thebes, the other being the Opet Festival. Another unnamed vizier is also known to have visited the West Bank to accompany the workmen to the riverbank on I Akhet 5 in year 28, perhaps of Ramses III, for an unknown ceremony (**47**).

4.4.2. Oracle and the appointment of the high-priest of Amun

The vizier and the high-priest of Amun probably celebrated the New Year at Thebes jointly in the Ramesside Period. However, the political situation for the Twenty-First Dynasty onwards may not always have allowed this to take place. Only the high-priest was chiefly documented in association with the New Year. Before Pinedjem I self-appointed himself as a king, he was the high-priest of Amun. According to Graffito 1001 located in the Theban West, Pinedjem I visited the West Bank on I Akhet 3 in year 10, perhaps of Smendes I (**41**). This corresponds to nine years after he assumed the office of the high-priest and had six years to go until he called himself a king. Thus, he was probably sent on a mission parallel to those assigned to the vizier.

The Banishment Stela records that one generation later, Menkheperre became the high-priest of Amun at Thebes, probably for an oracular session, during which Amun-Re appeared (**45**). The event took place on I Akhet 4 or 5 in year 25, either of the reign of his father Pinedjem I or of Smendes I. This account is followed by a retrospective one concerning another oracular session that took place at the 'Festival of Amun at the New Year' on the fourth epagomenal day (**1429**).

It is also not impossible that Menkheperre's son Pinedjem II was appointed (*stꜣ r*) the high-priest at the New Year. In a badly preserved text carved on the tenth pylon of Karnak, the account of his appointment is followed by the date of I Akhet 1 in year 5, perhaps of the king Amenemopet (**19**). Because this passage is now completely destroyed and its original location within the whole text cannot be identified, it is difficult to be entirely certain whether or not the date refers to Pinedjem's appointment. The main subject of the text is a proprietary claim concerning the noblewoman Henuttauy, a daughter of a woman named Asetemkheb. She was probably one of the wives of a high-priest of Amun in that period because she or her mother bore the title the 'first chief of the harem of Amun'.[220]

4.5. Representations in the private tomb at the Theban West

As described in the previous chapter (3.5.1), the New Year celebrations were one of the more frequent subjects depicted in private tombs. The scenes are characterized

[219] PM I-1², 165 (12, II); Davies and Gardiner 1915, 63, pl. 15; Engelmann-von Carnap 1999, pl. 4. The song in this scene has drawn attention from some scholars. Opposing Davies, Lichtheim (1945, 184–7) stressed on the funerary nature of the song. In the same line, Fox (1982, 275 and 296) regards it as a funeral banquet, a continuation from wall 10. Darnell (1995, 60) relates the scene to a Hathoric drinking ceremony but does not rule out an association with the New Year. More significantly, another harper's song similar to this one is attested in the same tomb (wall 5, II) and it praises Amun's temple at *wpy-rnp.t* (4.5.12). In fact, this scene contains a legend parallel to the one in the contemporaneous tomb of the vizier User representing the New Year Festival (TT 61 (7); Dziobek 1994, 29–30).

[220] Gardiner 1962, 63.

by several elements (Table 19), which can be broadly divided into two categories: official representations and private ones. The former is most distinctively exemplified by New Year gifts either to be presented to the king or inspected by the tomb owner. The styles and subjects of depictions varied depending on the office that the tomb owner bore. The latter is represented by an evening banquet held by the family of the deceased. Individual characteristics are still visible but the styles of the cultic performance are by and large uniform, as evidenced by standardized formulae and components, such as candles, cloths, and mortuary priests. In these scenes, the tomb owner is normally depicted being a dedicatee of such rituals, displaying the posthumous nature of the monument.

4.5.1. Evening meal

The *msy.t* was a general term that denotes the evening meal, as opposed to *iꜥw* the 'morning meal'. Its nocturnal character is obvious in the orthography that includes the  -sign. The *msy.t*-Festival is occasionally attested in festival lists from the First Intermediate Period.[221] A statue of Hepseneb, high-priest of Amun under Thutmose II, records *msy.t tp* the 'Festival of the First Evening Meal' before the Birth of Osiris on the first epagomenal day, suggesting the date of IV Shemu 30.[222] In a similar fashion, the Buto Stela of Thutmose III places the *msy.t* before I Akhet 1.[223] It came to be explicitly associated with IV Shemu 30 from the New Kingdom onwards.[224] No surviving records attest it in connection with the Valley Festival, at which a similar banquet was performed (Table 19, no. 46). In the tomb of Neferhotep, divine father of Amun-Re from the time of Horemheb and later (TT 50), the *msy.t tp* is described as taking place on IV Shemu 30, when 'rituals were performed on the day of Osiris' (**1395**). There are three other Ramesside tombs which attest the *msy.t* on that day, and they all include a banqueting scene.[225] In these scenes, the deceased couple receives offerings from their family. O. DeM 32, dated to year 25 of Ramses III, also records an evening meal on the same day as in these tombs (**1399**).

[221] The earliest attestation is the tomb of Khety at Asyut (Brunner 1937, 62, l. 82).

[222] Statue Bologna 1822 (*Urk.* IV, 483: 3–4). The tomb of Amenemhat (TT 48) also attests the *msy.t* before the Birth of Osiris (PM I-1², 89; Säve-Söderbergh 1957, pl. 40).

[223] Stela provisionally numbered 209 (Bedier 1994a, 4, z. 14; *idem* 1994b, 38, l. 14 for identical article with better facsimiles and a photograph; Klug 2002, 100 for transliteration and translation).

[224] Jauhiainen 2009, 194–5.

[225] TT 2 (10, III), TT 4 (5, II), and TT 9 (6, II) (Černý 1949, 16, 45, and 71).

4.5.2. Candle and the New Year formula

Lighting for the dead was probably a convention that was practised on various occasions.[226] However, in any attempt to differentiate the representations of the New Year from those of the Valley Feast, candles can be used as a primary criterion for identification because there are no examples attested for the latter celebration (Table 19, no. 29).

A formula associated with the lighting performance is documented in four private tombs at Thebes (Text 1). The most complete version is carved with a painted scene in the tomb of Tjay (TT 23), also known as Ta who was royal secretary of the lord of the Two Lands under Merenptah.[227] Long after the publication of the first translation and a partial drawing by Davies (1924, 13, pl. 7 (14)), a revised translation plus a photograph and a facsimile were published by Haikal (1985). Her facsimile does not include the scene with a lit candle, but Davies had a complete drawing of it which has hitherto been unpublished. Hence, it is presented in Figure 29. The New Year formula occupies a major part of the scene. It contains a litany repeating the phrase *mi rwd* 'as flourish' followed by names of different gods, mostly those associated with Heliopolis (see Text 1 for transliteration):

> (1) [Evening me]al of the New Year, performing (2) [O]siris, [royal] secretary of the lord of the Two Lands, (3) [Ta, true of voice]. On this day of smearing (4) the [*m*] *ḏ.t*-oil, performing the torch-lighting, and presenting offerings to (5) Osiris, royal scribe, Ta, true of voice. Hail to you, this beautiful torch to Osiris, (royal) secretary, Ta, true of voice. Hail to you, the eye of Horus, who guides the gods (6) at night and guides Osiris, royal scribe, Ta, true of voice, from any seat of his [to] any place wherein that he desires to be. This (7) beautiful [to]rch is set for Osiris, (royal) secretary Ta, true of voice, with fresh fat [and clean linen] from [what is given to you] by your [father] Geb, your mother Nut, (8) Osiris, Isis, Seth, and Nephtys. May they wash your face. May they wipe away [your tea]rs. May they open [your mouth with th]ese bright fingers, (9) with which the mouth of the gods is opened. There is give[n to you the sky]. There is given to you the land. There is given to you the field of (10) Iaru at night on this beautiful day of the New [Year] to e[stablish the months. There] is given to you fresh

[226] In the tomb of Hepdjef, dated to the Middle Kingdom, three occasions (the fifth epagomenal day, New Year's Day, and Wag Feast) are specified as when a candle is to be offered to the god (Griffith 1889, pl. 7, cols 296–9 and pl. 8, cols 305–6).

[227] PM I-1², 39 (8, II).

water of the god. There (11) is given to you divine fresh water in accordance with [all the stars of] unweary ones in purification(?) (12) and imperishable ones. This beautiful torch to Osiris, royal scribe, Ta, true of voice, shall be forever. May this beautiful torch to Osiris, (royal) secretary, (13) Ta, true of voice, endure, as endures Atum, lord of [the Two Lands] and of the Heliopolitan pillar(?) at Heliopolis. May this beautiful torch to Osiris, royal scribe, Ta, true of voice, endure, (14) as endures the name of Shu of Upper Menset at Heliopolis. May this beautiful torch to Osiris, (royal) secretary, Ta, true of voice, endure, as endures (15) the name of Tefnut of Lower Menset at Heliopolis. May this beautiful torch to Osiris, royal scribe, Ta, true of voice, endure, as endures the name of Geb, (16) [manly] soul [at] Heliopolis. May [th]is beautiful torch to Osiris, (royal) secretary, Ta, true of voice, endure, as endures the name of Nut in the house of the ba at Heliopolis. (17) May this beautiful torch to Osiris, royal scribe, Ta, true of voice, endu[re], as endures the name of Isis at the Iseum. May this beautiful torch to Osiris, (royal) secretary, (18) Ta, true of voice, endure, as endures the name of Nephtys at Heliopolis. May this beautiful torch to Osiris, royal scribe, Ta, true of voice, endure, as endures the name of Horus at Pe. (19) May this be[auti] ful torch to Osiris, (royal) secretary, Ta, true of voice, [endure], as endures the name of Uadjet at Buto. May this beautiful torch to Osiris, royal scribe, Ta, (20) [true] of voice, endure, as endures [the name of the Ba] at Mendes. May this be[auti]ful torch to Osiris, (royal) secretary, Ta, true of voice, endure, as endures the name (21) of Thoth at Hermopolis. This beautiful torch to [Osiris], [royal] secretary of the lord of the Two Lands, Tjay, true of voice, (22) shall be (on) the night barque and the morning barque. It will never perish. It will never be destroyed. Forever, forever, pure, pure! Osiris, royal secretary of the lord of the Two Lands, (23) Ta, true of voice. The sky is open to you. The land is open to you. The wa[y] in the necropolis is open to you. May you come out and enter w[i]th Re, being free of your foot like the lords of eternity, as Hapi gives you water as sustenance. May he give you bread, as Hathor gives you beer, and as Hesat gives you milk. Be pure, be pure! Osiris, royal scribe Tjay!

Tjay and his wife Raya are portrayed to the extreme left seated in front of an offering table. A candle-stand and a tall container, perhaps of the *md̠.t*-oil,[228] are represented below the table. To the extreme right a man in a panther skin is portrayed censing and making a libation over offerings piled on a table in front of him. A large conical candle stands beyond the offering table. The candle is supported by a shrine-like stand, in which five tapers of candle are inserted, probably symbolizing the five epagomenal days.

Archaeological evidence reveals that such a stand was actually used at the New Year in the Middle Kingdom.[229] In fact, the formula in question survived from the Old Kingdom, as evidenced by the Pyramid Texts.[230] Other texts may belong to this genre, such as a part of the Book of the Dead[231] and P. Louvre N 3083, dated to the Ptolemaic Period,[232] both carrying the title *r3 n rdi.t hpr bs hr d3d3 3h* 'Spell for igniting a flame beneath the head of a transfigured one.'[233] The Second Letter for Breathing, which had been composed by the first century AD, is also classified in the same category.[234]

Later, during the New Kingdom, the New Year formula came to be employed in temple decorations. Three reliefs in the Great Hypostyle Hall of Karnak attest a temple version of it intertwined with the cult of Amun (Figure 27). A text accompanying one of them, where Seti I offers a taper to Amun-Re, reads (see Text 1, K1):

> Spell of the torch of the New Year. [Hail to] you, this beautiful torch to Amun-Re, lord of the thrones of the Two Lands. Hail to you, the eye of Horus, who guide[s on the way of] darkness and guides Amun, lord of the thrones of the Two Lands, in every place that your ka desires therein, living forever. [ ] torch of Amun, lord of the thrones of the Two Lands, (made) of fresh fat and clean linen from what is given to you by

[228] For a vessel characteristic of the *md̠.t*-oil, see Nelson 1981, pls 205, left and 208, right.

[229] A limestone candle-stand discovered in the valley temple belonging to the pyramid complex of Sneferu at Dahshur (PM III-2², 880; Fakhry 1959, vol. 2 (2), 63–9, pls 68–9). It belongs to the chief sculptor Seshenu. A large square cavity is seen on the top surface, probably for a large candle. It is surrounded by nine small holes for tapers. A link to the New Year is evident from the formula carved on the top, which echoes the one in the tomb of Tjay.

[230] PT 601, Pyr. 1660a–1671d.

[231] BD 162, heading.

[232] Herbin 1999, 155–7 and 188–9; M. Smith 2009, 490–3.

[233] Other parallels from the Roman Period are: P. BM 10819, verso, 6–18 and 89–96 (unpublished); P. BM 9977, 10110+10111, 10116, 10124, 10125, 10264, 10275, 10282, 10286, 10304, 10331, and 71513A (Herbin 2008).

[234] For example, P. Cairo 58018 (Golénischeff 1927, 74–80, pls 17–8; M. Smith 2009, 514–25 for translation).

your father Geb, your mother Nut, Osiris, Isis, [Seth], and Nephtys. May [th]ey wash your face. May they wipe away your tears. May they open your mouth with these [th]eir bright fingers. There is given to you the sky. There is given to you the land, as the field of Iaru belongs to you at this night of [ ] establisher of every month, provider of the day, and provider of fresh water for the gods [ ] fresh water (in) accordance with the stars [ ] imperishable ones. This torch for Amun, lord of the thrones of the Two Lands, is from what the king Menmaatre gives.

The equation of the recipient of the spell with Osiris is deliberately eliminated here but the original mortuary characteristics remain in the references to 'tears' and the 'field of Iaru'. The surviving corpora of the formula attest that torches were ignited at the same time as oil and linen were presented to a recipient at the creation of months and days, i.e. at the start of the new yearly cycle.[235]

Contracted versions of the formula are attested in three scenes in the tombs of the scribe Amenemhat (TT 82),[236] Menkheperreseneb, high-priest of Amun (TT 112),[237] and Senemiah, a royal scribe (TT 127), all dated to the time of Hatshepsut and Thutmose III. These scenes are associated with the epagomenal days. In the hitherto unpublished scene of the last tomb, a man offers a libation and incense to the deceased couple.[238] The legend says:

hrw.w 5 ḥr.w rnp.t msw.t nṯr.w ir.t [ḳbḥ] snṯr n ꜥḫ st.t tkꜣ šsp ꜣḫ.w m wꜣ.t kkw ir.t Ḥr rs.ti m sꜣ[=k]

The Festival[239] of the five epagomenal days, births of the gods. Performing [a libation] and censing to a brazier bowl, and lighting a torch. Receive the illumination on the way of the night. The eye of Horus is awake in [your] protection.

Large conical candles were the most distinctive of the offerings dedicated to the deceased. They often appear as torches or tapers carried by offering bringers, and were used to clear the darkness of the night and evoke the dead. Often considered to be the eye of Horus, as any offering could be, candles were burnt to guide the gods and the deceased. O. Berlin 12631, dated to year 1 of Ramses IV, records a substantial number of timber pieces to be used for IV Shemu 30 and the epagomenal period, the purpose of which is, however, not clearly stated (**1296**).

It is remarkable to see in the New Year formula a reference to the Opening-of-the-Mouth, which was enacted on 'this day of smearing the *mḏ.t*-oil, performing the torch-lighting, and presenting offerings' to the dead. These performances were major components of the Opening-of-the-Mouth ritual. The following sections will, therefore, focus on each component that is particularly associated with the New Year.

4.5.3. Opening-of-the-Mouth ritual

Although various occasions seem to have involved the Opening-of-the-Mouth ritual, it is exclusively associated with the New Year when compared with the Valley Feast (Table 19, no. 56). A New Year performance and the Opening-of-the-Mouth ritual are well represented together in the tomb of Amenhotep (TT 415), overseer of the carpenters of Amun under Amenhotep III.[240] The scene has only partially been published to date, and hence schematized in Figure 30. The deceased couple receives an offering list from Amenhotep's brother clad in a panther skin, the costume of the sem-priest. The legend says: *smꜣ iḫ.t nb.t nfr.t wꜥb.t ḳmꜣ.t p.t srd.t tꜣ inn[.t] ḥꜥpy sn=f wꜥb n Ḫnsw Nfr-ḥtp* 'Partaking every good and pure thing[241], what the sky creates, what the land makes to grow, and wha[t] the inundation brings, (by) his brother, wab-priest of Khonsu, Neferhotep.' Two sub-registers follow the brother, each representing the rituals of the Opening-of-the-Mouth and of the New Year. The first is captioned as: *šsp nw Ꞽnpw m sp tpy wp rꜣ n Wsir* 'taking the *nw*-adze of Anubis for the first time and opening of the mouth for Osiris'; the latter as: *sḏy.t(?) tkꜣ.w n wpy-rnp.t rdi.t wꜥb* [unknown number of groups lost] 'Kindling(?) the candles of the New Year and presenting the pure linen [ ]'.

It seems that the elements of the Opening-of-the-Mouth ritual represented in private tombs were selected from a limited number of components. Their sequence is essentially the same as those deployed during the daily temple cult and the royal accession ceremony.[242] What they consisted of can be surmised and will be examined in the following sections, based on the sequence presented by Otto (1960):

[235] *smn ꜣbd.w* is also attested in association with the night of *wpy-rnp.t* in TT 50 (Hari 1985, 42, pl. 28, col. 13).
[236] PM I-1², 166 (17, III).
[237] PM I-1², 230 (6, III).
[238] PM I-1², 242 (5, II); Davies 1915, 98 for text.
[239] The *rnp.t*-sign is followed by that of *ḥb*.

[240] PM I-1², 456 (1, II); Loret 1889, 29–31.
[241] *smꜣ iḫ.t* is also attested as a temple ritual at Luxor (PM II², 327 (153, I, 2); Gayet 1894, pl. 70, fig. 209). Nelson (1949, 331) related this rite to temple scenes depicting *fꜣy iḫ.t* the 'elevation of the offering'. Our term, conventionally translated as 'partaking of the food', literally means 'uniting with the thing'. The earliest attestation is the Pyramid Texts (PT 406, Pyr. 708c), where Re is evoked for food and the king desires to share it with him. Phraseology parallel to this is found in the Coffin Texts (*CT* III, 21c [167]).
[242] Goebs 2011, 62–5 and 84–94.

no. (Otto)	ritual	section
nos. 6–7)	burning *snṯr*	4.5.4;
nos. 48–53)	clothing statues with various pure linen	4.5.5;
no. 55)	anointing statues with the *mḏ.t*-oil	4.5.6;
no. 56)	adorning statues with the *msḏm.t* eye-paint	4.5.7;
nos. 62–3)	*inḏ-ḥr* with the *nms.t*/*ḥs*/ *kbḥ*-jars	4.5.8;
no. 70)	offerings (*ḥtp-di-nsw.t* ritual)	4.5.9;
no. 71)	hymn to Re-Horakhety	4.5.10.

An abridged version is represented in the tomb of Amenmes, a servant in the Necropolis in the time of Ramses III or later (TT 9).[243] The scene contains four episodes that occurred on IV Shemu 30, each portraying the deceased couple receiving a ritual performed by their children. First, a daughter presents the *mḏ.t*-oil for anointing (*wrḥ*). Second, a son pours from a *ḳbḥ*-jar and burns the *snṯr*-incense. Third, a son performs a ritual (destroyed). Fourth, a daughter offers food (*sn.w*).

4.5.4. Burning the *snṯr*-incense

A New Year scene in the tomb of Menkheperreseneb, high-priest of Amun under Thutmose III (TT 112), includes five men carrying small cups of incense (Figure 32).[244] They are captioned with a spell which reads:

> *r3 n snṯr swʿb m snṯr wʿb Ḥr snṯr r=f sw m ir.t=f n ḏ.t=f wʿb r3=k Wsir ḥm nṯr tpy n ʾImn Mn-[ḫpr-rʿ]-sn[b] m3ʿ ḫrw p[r]=k tw m ir.t Ḥr pḏ.t n ḥtm tw im=s m rn=k pwy n pḏ(.t) ḏd mdw sp 3 snṯr.n=k tw im=s m rn=s pwy n snṯr k3p ḥr=k im=s*
>
> Spell of fumigation and purification with the incense. Horus is pure, fumigating himself with his eye of his body. May your mouth be pure, Osiris, high-priest of Amun, Men[kheper]resene[b], true of voice. May you sh[ow] yourself with the eye of Horus, the pellet of incense for equipping you with it in this your name of the pellet of incense. Word to be recited three times: 'You have fumigated yourself with it in this its name of the incense. May your face be censed with it.'

A spell parallel to this is attested in the Book of the Opening-of-the-Mouth written on the coffin of Butehamen, a secretary of the king's draughtsmen during the Twenty-First Dynasty,[245] and in the funerary papyrus of a woman named Sais, dated to the Ptolemaic-Roman Period.[246]

4.5.5. Adorning with cloth and amulet, and archaeological evidence

As was the case for the Valley Festival (3.6.3), changing the cloths of tomb statues was also performed at the New Year. Insofar as the Theban tombs are concerned, a priest bringing cloths to the deceased is portrayed as early as the time of Senusret I. Hence, although not explicitly associated with the New Year, the tomb of the vizier Intefiqer (TT 60) attests a priest in a panther skin together with a large offering list, which parallels the New Kingdom examples.[247] By examining Thutmose III's inscription (4.3.1) and a text in the tomb of Paheri, count of Nekheb and Inyt from the time of Thutmose I to Thutmose III, Schott (1970, 47) hypothesized that cloths brought to the private tombs originated from divine statues.[248]

---

243 PM I-1², 19 (6, II); Černý 1949, 71.

244 PM I-1², 161 (6, II); Davies 1933b, 23, pl. 29.

245 Turin 2237, IX, 15–8.

246 Louvre 3155, XII, 2–8. Scene 58 (Otto 1960, vol. 1, 148–9). Also see the tomb of the queen Tausret (KV 14 (17): Lefébure 1889, pl. 66) and the Saite tomb of Padiamenopet (TT 33 (34)) for a comparable passage, which is associated with Scene 6 of the Book of the Opening-of-the-Mouth (Otto 1960, vol. 1, 18). In addition, three later sources prove that the spell was recited as part of the daily ritual within temples: an inscription of the Amun temple in Umm Ebeida at the Siwa Oasis (Fakhry 1944, 102, pl. 22; Otto 1960, vol. 1, 19–20) and two papyri discovered in the archive belonging to the Sobek temple at Tebtynis, dated to the first or second century AD: P. Florence PSI inv. I 79 A+P. Berlin P 14473 a A (III, 5–7) and P. Florence PSI inv. I 70 A (II, 11–3) (Osing and Rosati 1998, vol. 1, 109, vol. 2, pls 15, A2 and 16, A1–4).

247 His tomb at el-Kab (PM I-1², 122 (15); Davies 1920, pls 31–2).

248 The tomb of Paheri records that *ʿrḳ.tw n=k wʿb.w m p3ḳ.t iry.w m sfḫ.w ḥʿ nṯr s3s3.tw n=k mḏ.t wʿb.t* 'May be bound for you pure cloths from the *p3ḳ.t*-cloth, which belong to the removed cloths of the god's body. May the pure *mḏ.t*-oil be smeared for you' (PM V, 180 (10–11); *Urk.* IV, 112: 13–5; Tylor 1895, pl. 16; Assmann 2005, 227). A text carved on a statue of the royal scribe Amenhotep, dated to the time of Amenhotep III, describes cast-off cloths as coming from the forehead (*wp.t*) of the god (Petrie 1902, vol. 2, 45, pl. 36). A cast-off cloth of Hathor is referred to in the Coffin Texts (*CT* I, 258f [61]) as: 'You are dressed in the pure garment of Ptah and in the cast-off garment of Hathor' (Hall 1985, 239). This passage has a parallel in the tomb of Rekhmire, vizier from the time of Thutmose III to Amenhotep II (TT 100 (16); Assmann 2005, 193). Spell 397 (*CT* V, 93f–94a) refers to a cloth (*w3b*, not *wʿb*) which 'Horus and Seth kissed at the New Year (*tpy-rnp.t*)'. Elsewhere in the aforementioned tomb of Amenhotep (TT 415), the deceased expresses his desire to obtain cloths made by the weaver-goddess Tayt and the *ḫnd.t*-goddesses of Neith (PM I-1², 456 (4); Loret 1889, 26). The association of a goddess with cloths is evidenced by P. Turin 2004+2007+2057+2106 (*KRI* VI, 650–1), which records that the vizier Khaemwaset supplied linen from the temple of Maat to the workmen on IV Akhet 19 in year 16 of Ramses IX. O. Cairo 25562, dated to II Shemu 1 in year 2 of Ramses IV or V, records that the *ḥbs*-linen originating from the god was delivered under the direction of the vizier (**1070**). It was delivered by a deputy of the treasury to the chief workman, who finally cut it into eight pieces, a number suggesting further allocation to the 80 members of the workmen. Later sources often name the goddess Renenutet as an origin of cloths, such as P. Louvre N 3166, dated to the Ptolemaic Period (Herbin 1999, 197 (II, 11); M. Smith 2009, 497 for translation), and the New Year texts at Dendera (Coppens 2010, 43–4). The latter texts record a cast-off garment of Osiris as adorning the head of the deceased. The red *sšd*-linen (*sšd m insy*), which originated from a cast-

It was also at the New Year that statues were adorned with cosmetics and ornaments, such as collars and jewellery, including amuletic objects. In fact, the aforementioned Amenhotep (TT 415) has two amulets hanging from his neck.[249] One may also draw attention to a passage in the Opening-of-the-Mouth, which includes references to *s3 ꜥnḫ* the 'protection of life'.[250] The *s3 ꜥnḫ* is also referred to in P. Edwin Smith (XIX, 9–14), perhaps dated to the Second Intermediate Period, in a prescription against possible dangers in the year:[251]

> *ḏd mdw ḥr Sḫm.t B3s.tt Wsir Nḥb-k3.w sš m ꜥntyw ḥr sšd n p3ḳ.t rdi n s r ḫḫ=f tm rdi ꜥḳ ꜥ3.w Nfri bsbs r=i w3ḏ-ḥ3.t iw s3.w ꜥnḫ N.t ḥ3=i ḫnt.t wh st grḥ B3st.t r pr s ḏd s m ꜥnḫ.w rnp.t*
>
> Words to be recited over (images of) Sekhmet, Bastet, Osiris, and Nehebkau, written in frankincense on a *sšd*-headband of the *p3ḳ.t*-linen, attached to a man to his neck in order not to let donkeys enter. O Nefer, the *bsbs*-goose is against me and the green-breasted goose. The protection of the life of Neith is around me, she who is in front of the failed sower. Bastet is repelled from the house of the man, so that the man shall say among the living of the year.

Given the prophylactic nature of this document, the amulet is likely to have been issued for the living. The Book of the Epagomenal Days (P. Leiden I 346, II, 3), dated to the Ramesside Period, describes a similar linen band in slightly more detail:[252]

> *ḏd mdw ḥr stp n p3ḳ.t sš nn nṯr.w ḥr=f ir m ṯs.t 12 wdn=sn t ḥnḳ.t snṯr ḥr ḫ.t di=w n s r ḫḫ=f nḥm s [m] i3d.t rnp.t n sḫm n ḫfty im=f*
>
> Words to be recited on a band of the *p3ḳ.t*-linen, written with these gods on it and made with 12 knots, their offerings being bread, beer, and incense on fire, while they are given to a man to his neck, so that the man shall be saved [from] the plague of the year and the force of the enemy shall not be in him.

The 12 knots seem to represent the 12 deities that appear at the end of this papyrus scroll.[253] It is also not impossible that the numeral 12 represented the month because this performance was undoubtedly intended as a year-round prescription.[254]

In addition, *s3 rnp.t* the 'protection of the year' may belong to the same group as the *s3 ꜥnḫ*. Ramses III's great north stela at Karnak records in its introduction a variety of Amun-Re's attributions, one of which is *s3.w rnp.t* 'for one who seeks your (Amun-Re) great name', witnessing to its divine origin.[255] The gods could also be recipients. P. Harris I (XXVI, 5–6) recounts that Ramses III made amulets to be consecrated to divine statues within the temple at Heliopolis:[256]

> *iry=i n=k wḏ3.wt špsy n nb nfr m mḥ m ḫsbd m3ꜥ mfk m3ꜥ di=i ḫnm=w šnb.t=k m ḥw.t sr ḥw=k špsy=k m s.t=k ḏsr.t iw=w (m) mki ḥꜥ.w=i špsy m s3.w rnp.t n ḫpri=k ꜥ3 wr mry.ty*
>
> I made for you the august udjat-amulets, (made) of quality gold and inlayed with true lapis lazuli and true malachite. I gave them to be attached to your limbs in the house of the magistrates that you protect your augustness in your holy place. They protect my[257] august limbs as the amulets of the year for your grand form, great of love.

If the first-person suffix pronoun in the last passage is correct, it may argue for a reciprocal transfer of amulets between the god and the king.

Another phraseology characteristic of the annual prescription is the one beginning with the name of Horus repeated twice. This formula is attested in Ptolemaic-Roman temples in scenes of the New Year celebration, known as the 'Ceremony of the Great Seat'.

off garment of Osiris and was provided at the Khoiak Feast, is referred to together with the rite of onion-tying in the tomb of Tjay (TT 23; Assmann 2005, 486–7) and the tomb of Kheruef (TT 192; *Kheruef*, pl. 64, B; Assmann 2005, 374–5). The Medinet Habu calendar records that fine linen originating from the *sfḫ*-cloth was destined 'for a candle for every day of the *idg*-cloth (*r tk3 n hrw nb idg*)' and that two pieces of such fine linen were used every month (*MH* III, pl. 146, section II, 291).

249 PM I-1², 456 (1, II); Loret 1889, pl. 3.

250 Otto vol. 1, 67, f, vol. 2, 84, Scene 27.

251 Breasted 1930, 481–2.

252 Stricker 1948, 63–4; Bommas 1999, 14.

253 Raven (1997) publishes five strips of linen now kept in the Leiden Museum (Leiden I 134), on two of which 12 deities comparable to our papyrus are portrayed, while three other strips each show one different deity. Raven (1997, 285) does not rule out the possibility that the five strips were discovered together with our papyrus. These linen strips were once twisted to form a cord, with no trace of knots visible today. The 12 hostile deities apparently represent the 12 months of the year, as specified by an oracular amuletic papyrus (P. BM 10308: Edwards 1960, vol. 1, 24, vol. 2, pl. 7).

254 An elaborate version of such amuletic linen was applied to the king. P. Brooklyn 47.218.50, dated to the fourth century BC, records that a red *sšd*-linen formed *p3 wḏ3 n s.t wr.t r ḫḫ n nsw.t* 'the amulet of the Great Seat (bound) to the neck of the king', in which 30 white crowns and 30 red crowns were painted with a figure of Ptah between them, and was finally tied to the king's neck with 60 knots. Goyon (1972a, 85–6, n. 24) related the numbers 30 and 60 to the Sed Feast, which theoretically occurred at the thirtieth anniversary of the royal accession.

255 PM II², 131 (483); *KRI* V, 239: 7.

256 Erichsen 1933, 30: 11–4; Grandet 1994, vol. 1, 259.

257 Erichsen marked 'sic', suggesting =*k* here, an interpretation opposed by Grandet who remains with the original reading.

According to Goyon (1974, 77), this formula dates to no later than the New Kingdom because P. Edwin Smith records it for different prescriptions.[258] One example includes a spell against malign air, for which the Horus formula is required:[259]

> *ḥm.t r3 n.t rnp.t tn m nf3.t n ṯ3w nb ḏw Ḥr Ḥr w3ḏ n Sḫm.t ḥ3 iwf=i tm n ꜥnḫ*
>
> Spell of this year against the breath of every evil wind: 'Horus, Horus! The *w3ḏ*-amulet of Sekhmet is around my flesh, complete of life.'

After examining a liturgical text at the temple of Edfu, Jankuhn (1972) classified it as the Book of 'Protection of House' (*s3 pr*). He demonstrated that this liturgy can originate from the Pyramid Texts and be associated with the New Year. In fact, the aforementioned P. Leiden I 346 (III, 4–6) includes a reference to a house to be safeguarded:[260]

> *md3.t n.t hrw.w 5 ḥr.w rnp.t ist ḥr rnp.t m3w.t iw k3=i m ḥtp swḏ3 tw=i swḏ3 pr=i h3=i r sḏm md.wt nṯr.w nḥm=tn wi ḫw=tn wi ṯs pḫr m ꜥw3y.w n ḥr.w rnp.t ḥr nt.t ir rḫ rn=sn n ḫr.n=f n imy.w-ḫt Sḫm.t n šmm.wt n.t ꜥ w.t rnp.t iw iw=f (r) ḥtp*
>
> Book of the Five Epagomenal Days. O (it is) at the New Year! My ka is in peace. Keep me safe. Keep my house safe. I wish to hear the words of the gods. May you save me and protect me, may you protect me and save me, from the robbers of the epagomenal days. With regard to the one who knows their names, he does not fall to the followers of Sekhmet and the fevers of plague(?) of the year, but he shall be in peace.

In a manner similar to this, P. Cairo 58027 (IV, 6–7), perhaps dated to the first century AD, includes the Horus formula regarding the protection of the palace.[261]

Other genres of prophylactic literature may fill in the temporal gap between the New Kingdom and the Ptolemaic Period. What Edwards (1960) named the oracular amuletic decrees are attested from the Twenty-Second to the Twenty-Third Dynasty.[262] During the Twenty-Sixth Dynasty, New Year bottles were widely used.[263] A large proportion of the bottles carry a standard text wishing a good year for the owners.[264] Although the archaeological contexts and applications of the bottles are largely unknown, D. Darnell (2000, 118, nn. 4–5) proposes that these bottles are attested from the New Kingdom onwards. The New Year bottles were probably produced exclusively for the New Year together with other items, such as rings, scarabs, and various forms of amulets.[265] Indeed, amulets of other forms could bear the same formula as the New Year bottles, such as those combining the three signs of *ꜥnḫ*, *w3s*, and *ḏd* (sometimes added by that of *ḥḥ*). This type of object is commonly attested in the Twenty-Fifth Dynasty and later, but Berlandini-Grenier (1994, 12) suggests that the triple amulets can be dated back to the Eighteenth Dynasty. The use of amuletic objects in the royal residence is evidenced by scarabs commemorating selected celebrations, mostly the Sed Feast under Amenhotep III (at Malkata) and Ramses II. Although the number is not high, some are associated with the New Year[266] and it may be that they were given by the king to his subordinates in return for the New Year gifts brought to the palace.[267]

4.5.6. Ointment jar

Various kinds of oil are recorded in several Eighteenth Dynasty tombs. In a scene from the tomb of Qenamen, chief royal steward under Amenhotep II (TT 93), his wife is portrayed offering two containers of ointment to her husband. The texts above each of the couple read:[268]

> *ms ind-ḥr n nḥb-k3.w m ꜥntyw b.t ti-šps n sn.t=f nb.t pr T3-dd.t=s*
>
> Bringing a greeting of the Nehebkau Festival, consisting of frankincense and

[258] Breasted 1930, 477, 480, and 486.

[259] Breasted 1930, 475.

[260] Stricker 1948, 65; Jankuhn 1972, 7; Bommas 1999, 18.

[261] Golénischeff 1927, 130; Jankuhn 1972, 6–7.

[262] They were issued from various gods and written on a papyrus sheet for the protection of petitioners, mainly young individuals. However, our knowledge of their provenance and archaeological contexts is very limited and association with the New Year is not evident.

[263] They were usually made of green faience. One specimen was discovered in the residential area of priests within the temple of Karnak (Masson 2007, 614, pl. 27). The formula written on this bottle refers to the Theban triad and Mentu.

[264] Yamani 2002.

[265] Blanquet 1991, 52.

[266] Budge 1896, 218–9, nos. 483–8; Hornung, Staehelin, and Brack 1976, 331 and 401–2. Two scarabs (UCL 18.6.18 and 18.14.1) name Thutmose III and Horemheb as *mn tḫn.wy m pr Imn* the 'furnisher of the two obelisks in the temple of Amun', which may be associated with a particular celebration (Petrie 1917, pls 26 and 38). One specimen from Medinet Habu, roughly dating from the Twentieth to Twenty-Fifth Dynasty, may be associated with the New Year (Teeter 2003, 59).

[267] A statuette of Neith, dated to the Twenty-Sixth Dynasty, is of some interest. Being 12 centimeters in height, made of green faience, and inscribed with the New Year formula, it was, according to Yoyotte (1983), presented by a high official to the then prince Necho (future king Necho II). This example may prove that the New Year talismans were also circulating within the court in that time.

[268] PM I-1², 193 (G, d); *Urk.* IV, 1399: 10–11; Davies 1930, 55, pl. 59, B.

a cruse of the *ti-šps*-oil,[269] by his wife, mistress, Tededetes.

sḫmḫ-ib m wrḥ.[t] ꜥntyw tpy.t m nwd n is pr ꜣ[mn two or three groups lost]

Recreation[270] with the quality ointment[t] of frankincense and with the unguent of the *is*-plant of the temple of A[mun   ].

In the tombs of Ramose, a royal scribe perhaps in the post-Amarna period (TT 46), of Useramen, vizier under Thutmose III (TT 61), and of Sennefer, overseer of the seal under Thutmose III (TT 99), *sṯy ḥknw nwd* the 'fragrance of the *ḥknw*-oil' is recorded.[271] As one of the significant components of the Opening-of-the-Mouth ritual, ointment jars are more frequently referred to in association with the New Year than the Valley Festival. In the Ramesside tombs, it was the *mḏ.t*-oil that was primarily documented. The tomb of Qen, a chiseller of Amun in the Necropolis under Ramses II (TT 4), records *ir.t mḏ.wt wrḥ.w tpy.w hrw pn n ir.t m[s]y* 'Presenting the *mḏ.t*-jars and the quality *wrḥ*-jars on this day of performing the evening m[ea]l'.[272] The *mḏ.t*-oil is represented with candles in the tomb of Tjay, royal secretary of the lord of the Two Lands under Merenptah (TT 23 (8, II)) and the tomb of Amenemhat, a scribe in the time of Hatshepsut and Thutmose III (TT 82 (17, III)), the former of which has been examined in 4.5.2.

4.5.7. *Eye-paint msdm.t*

Usually understood as the black eye-paint, *msdm.t* was applied to cult statues and perhaps to the living as well. In the tomb of Menkheperreseneb, high-priest of Amun under Thutmose III (TT 112), it is referred to in a scene depicting priests carrying oil jars and torches (Figure 32):[273]

hrw.w 5 ḥr.w rnp.t wrḥ sdm stk3 tk3 šsp 3ḫ.w m w3.t [k]kw ir.t Ḥr rs.ti m [s3=k] Wsir

The Festival of the five epagomenal days. Anoint, apply the eye-paint, kindle the candle, and receive illumination on the way of the [n]ight. The eye of Horus is awake as [your protection] Osiris!

A more elaborate version of what can be called the 'Spell of the Eye-Paint' is found in the Ramesside calendrical script P. Cairo 86637, verso XII, 1–6:[274]

ry.(t) km ms m tpy.t k3p m snṯr ḥr sḏ.t wꜥb. ti sfḫ.ti ḫ3ꜥ.ti r mw n it=f Nw n mw.t Nw.t ḥr-s3 hrw ms Rꜥ ḥnꜥ ntk ir ist ir n=k ꜥ3b.wt ꜥ3.(w)t m t.w ḥnḳ.wt k3.w 3pd.w snṯr ti-špsy ḥnḳy.wt rn(p)y.wt nb wꜥb sp-sn m-b3ḥ Rꜥ-ḥr-3ḫ.ty wbn=f m 3ḫ.t i3bt.t n.t p.t ḥtp=f m 3ḫ.t imnt.t ist wꜥb=k m mw rnpy n ḥ3.t ḥꜥpy sdm n=k ir.ty=ky m w3ḏ ms[dm.t] ṯḫ.ti m irp.w ms.t[i long lacuna]

Black paint to be applied with the quality oil and fumigation with the incense on fire. Purify, remove, and throw into the water[275] of his father Nun and the mother Nut after the day of the Birth of Re, and you perform: O make for yourself the great *ꜥ3b.t*-offerings consisting of bread, beer, oxen, birds, incense, the *ti-šps* oil, the *ḥnḳ.t*-offerings, and all fresh plants. Be pure, be pure before Re-Horakhety when he rises from the eastern horizon of the sky and sets in the western horizon. O purify yourself in the fresh water of the beginning of the flood. Adorn your eyes for yourself with the green and bla[ck] eye-paint. Be drunk with the wine and smear [oil(?)   ]!

As one of several cultic cosmetics, the black eye-paint was, according to Janot and Vezie (1999, 224), used not for the embalming ritual but for the Opening-of-the-Mouth performed for mummies to secure well-being in the afterlife.

4.5.8. *Fresh water mw rnpi*

As described in 4.3.1, the performance of the 'fresh water' played a key role in temple rituals at the New Year. P. Cairo 86637, presented in the previous section, includes a reference to the 'fresh water of the beginning of the flood' to be dedicated to the deceased in the morning of the New Year. A description in the tomb of Neferhotep, a divine father of Amun-Re in the time of Horemheb or later (TT 50), likewise specifies when fresh water was brought into his tomb, as follows:[276]

---

[269] Janssen (1975a, 366) proposed to identify the *ti-šps* with cinnamon, whose oil could be a perfume when used with *snṯr*.
[270] For the interpretation of *sḫmḫ-ib* (lit. 'diverting the heart'), see Fox (1982, 269) who defines the songs of this genre as the 'entertainment songs'. The idiomatic expression *sḫmḫ-ib* is attested in association with the New Year in the tomb of Paheri at el-Kab (4.6.1).
[271] TT 46 (PM I-1², 86 (1); Kawai 2010, 215, fig. 5 for photograph); TT 61 (PM I-1², 125 (7); Dziobek 1994, 29, pl. 53); TT 99 (PM I-1², 205 (pillar A, a); Dziobek 1994, 30).
[272] PM I-1², 11 (5, II); Černý 1949, 45. Phraseology akin to this is attested in TT 2 (10, III) and TT 9 (6, II).
[273] PM I-1², 230 (6, III); Davies 1933b, 24, pl. 29.

[274] Bács 1990, 45; Leitz 1994a, 446.
[275] It is not clear what was thrown in the water. In the Gebel el-Silsila inscriptions, dated to the reigns of Ramses II, Merenptah, and Ramses III, *ḫ3 mḏ3.t ḥꜥpi* 'throwing the Book of Hapi' is recorded to have taken place on I Akhet 15 (**78**) and III Shemu 15 (**1243**). P. Harris I (XXXVIIb, 1; LIVa, 2; and LXVII, 2) documents this book as a list of offerings.
[276] PM I-1², (9–10); Hari 1985, 55, pl. 40, cols 227–40; Assmann 2005, 429.

> *ꜣbd 4-nw šmw ꜥrḳy hrw pn n ir.t msy tpy ir ir.wt m hrw n Wsir it-nṯr n ꞽImn Nfr-ḥtp mꜣꜥ ḫrw r rdi.t wdḥ.w ꜥšꜣ.w itrw r in.t mw rnpy iw wnw.t 8 (m) pḫr m hrw pn šꜣꜥ* [two groups lost] *nfry.t r msw Stḫ ḏd mdw mw rnpy* [three or four groups lost] *ḥs.w nb n Ptḥ* [long lacuna]
>
> IV Shemu 30: this day of performing the first evening meal, performing rituals on the day for Osiris, god's father of Amun, Neferhotep, true of voice, to give many *wdḥ.w*-jars of the river in order to bring fresh water when the eighth hour is (in) the course on this day until good [ ] to the Birth of Seth. Words to be spoken: 'Fresh water [ ] the gold *ḥs*-jars of Ptah [ ].'

In a fashion similar to this, the flood and mortuary offerings are referred to together in the tomb of another Neferhotep, chief scribe of Amun, who lived roughly in the same time as the previous Neferhotep (TT 49):[277]

> *ir.tw n=i tkꜣ ḥr pgꜣ r-gs nb.w imḥ.t* [*šs*]*p=i sn.w m ḥꜣ.t ḥꜥpy dwꜣw.t wpy-rnp.t sb.tw n=i* [two groups lost] *m iḫ.wt hrw n ṯꜣ.t ḥ.wt(?) šsp iḫ.wt grḥ msy iry=i ḫpr.w nb mry=i* [*in*]*k wḏ(ꜣ) tp tꜣ*
>
> May one perform for me lighting at the entrance beside the lords of the underworld. May I [rece]ive provisions from the beginning of the flood (in) the morning of the New Year. May one travel for me [ ] with things on the day of taking offerings(?) and receiving things (at) the night of the evening meal, when I accomplish all forms that I desire, and I am healthy on earth.

4.5.9. *Offering list and the ḥtp-di-nsw.t formula*

Scenes with an offering list typically illustrate the seated deceased with his wife and a man, usually clad in a panther skin, standing in front of them. The list appears above an offering table set between the dead couple and the ritual conductor. According to PM I-1² (473, 35 (e)), there are 45 instances of offering list represented in private tombs. Some of the lists are linked to the New Year, such as in the tomb of Amenhotep, overseer of the carpenters of Amun under Amenhotep III (TT 415 (1, II)), which is not included in the list of PM (Figure 30). In the tomb of Amenemhat, a scribe under Hatshepsut and Thutmose III (TT 82), a list is presented to the deceased couple by a son clad in a panther skin, who recites the *ḥtp-di-nsw.t* formula (Figure 33, a).[278] Because the New Year is referred to below in the third register, the entire wall seems to represent a scene from that feast. Elsewhere in the same tomb, another son, also clad in a panther skin, is portrayed reciting the *ḥtp-di-nsw.t* formula for the New Year, but without an offering list.[279] The *ḥtp-di-nsw.t* formula in the latter case refers to Geb as the benefactor of offerings, which is reminiscent of the New Year formula where that god is addressed in the first instance as a leading member of the Heliopolitan pantheon (4.5.2). In a fashion similar to this, a scene of Menkheperreseneb, high-priest of Amun under Thutmose III (TT 112), attests an offering list and a reference to the New Year in different registers on the same wall (Figure 32).[280] On a wall of the partially published tomb of Nefersekheru, a royal scribe under Amenhotep III (TT 107), a New Year banquet (*msy.t tpy-rnp.t*) is represented with an offering list in the upper register and the Opening-of-the-Mouth ritual in the lower one.[281] The latter scene is captioned as follows:[282]

> *ir.t wp rꜣ m* [*mꜥ*]*ḥꜥ.t n twt sp tpy di.w ḥr šꜥy m mꜥḥꜥ.t ḥr=f r rsy ḥꜣ.w m tꜣ hrw mnḫ.t ḥꜣ=f*
>
> Performing the Opening-of-the-Mouth in the [to]mb for the statues for the first time, being placed on the sand in the tomb, its face being towards the south and naked on the ground on the day of clothing, which is around it.

It is significant to see references to the 'first time' (4.2.1.5), and to the 'day of clothing', which was performed from IV Shemu 30 to I Akhet 1 as a festival at later temples (**29**, **1404**, **1417–8**, and **1433**).[283] This performance in the tomb of Nefersekheru is followed by an offering rite labelled *rꜣ n wꜣḥ iḫ.wt* the 'spell of presenting the offerings', which contains the *ḥtp-di-nsw.t*-formula addressed to Re-Horakhety, Atum, and Hathor.[284]

Another example worth considering may be the tomb of Menna, a scribe of the fields of the lord of the Two Lands of Upper and Lower Egypt from the time of Thutmose IV to Amenhotep III (TT 69), where a wall

[277] PM I-1², 91 (1); Davies 1933a, vol. 1, 49, pl. 34, ll. 19–20; Assmann 2005, 195 for partial translation.

[278] PM I-1², 166 (17, I); Davies and Gardiner 1915, pls 21–3; Engelmann-von Carnap 1999, pl. 5.

[279] PM I-1², 164 (5); Davies and Gardiner 1915, pls 4–6, A; Engelmann-von Carnap 1999, pl. 3.

[280] PM I-1², 230 (6); Davies 1933b, pls 28–9.

[281] PM I-1², 225 (2).

[282] Helck 1956b, 16.

[283] Hermann (1940, 99) suggested that the ceremony of erecting mummies towards the sun was performed in the antechamber at funerals. A rite parallel to this probably took place at the New Year.

[284] Helck 1956b, 17.

scene is divided in two registers.[285] The second register, which contains a list, probably depicts the New Year Festival on account of men bringing ointment jars and candles.

Apart from one instance in the tomb of Tjanefer, third-priest of Amun from the time of Ramses III to Ramses IV (TT 158), which is associated with the Sokar Feast,[286] the offering list was almost exclusively presented at the New Year (Table 19, no. 37). This conforms to the occurrence of a ritual performer, clad in a panther skin, whose performances were similarly confined to the New Year (Table 19, no. 58).

4.5.10. Hymn to Re-Horakhety

See 3.7.1.

4.5.11. Bouquet of Amun-Re and Re-Horakhety

Similarly to what took place at the Valley Festival (3.6.5), bouquets of Amun were delivered at the New Year.[287] They were not an essential component of the Opening-of-the-Mouth ritual but played a distinctive, ideological role in expressing the divine power from the New Kingdom onwards.[288] In the tomb of Amenemheb, lieutenant-commander of soldiers from the time of Thutmose III to Amenhotep II (TT 85), the deceased offers *[ꜥnḫ n Ỉmn]-rꜥ m ḥb=f n wpy-rnp.t* a '[bouquet of Amun]-Re at His Festival of the New Year' to his wife, who suckles a young prince.[289] Elsewhere in the same tomb his wife offers a bouquet of 'Amun' to the king at the Valley Feast (3.5.2.3). The difference between 'Amun-Re' and 'Amun' here is probably not accidental.

It is documented elsewhere that bouquets were distributed within the royal court as well. In the tombs of Re, high-priest of Amun Henqet-ankh (memorial temple of Thutmose III) (TT 72), and Pehsukher, lieutenant of the king (TT 88), both dating from the time of Thutmose III to Amenhotep II, bouquets of Amun-Re are presented by the deceased to Amenhotep II seated in a kiosk.[290] These two scenes are not explicitly related to the New Year, but the royal appearance is often associated with that celebration with regard to the New Year gifts (4.5.12). In fact, bouquets exchanged between Amun and the king were mostly associated with the powerful rulership in the guise of Re.[291]

There may be other instances relevant to the New Year although they are again not explicit. The vizier Ramose (TT 55), for instance, is portrayed offering a bouquet of the Theban triad to Amenhotep IV.[292] The bouquet of 'your (king's) father Amun' is rephrased as the 'bouquet of your father Re-Horakhety'. An alternation between the two hypostases is also attested in the tomb of Benia, overseer of works under Thutmose III (TT 343), where the deceased is represented receiving an offering list.[293] Two legends accompany the scene—one says: *prr.t nb.t [ḥr] ḫ3w.t n.t [Ỉmn]-rꜥ nsw.t nṯr.w ḫft ḥtp=f m ḥnḳ.t-ꜥnḫ* 'all that came [on] the altar of [Amun]-Re, king of the gods, when he rested at Henqet-ankh', and the other: *sm3 r iḫ.t nb.t nfr.t wꜥb.t ḥr ḫ3w.t n.t Rꜥ-ḥr-3ḫ.ty m ḫr.t hrw n.t rꜥ nb* 'Partaking of every good and pure thing on the altar of Re-Horakhety every day.' In the tomb of Minnakht, overseer of the granaries of Upper and Lower Egypt under Thutmose III (TT 87), the deceased receives a bouquet of Re-Horakhety from a 'scribe of divine offerings of Amun in Henqet-ankh of Menkheper[re]'.[294] In the tomb of Amenhotep, overseer of carpenters of Amun under Amenhotep III (TT 415), six deities—Werethekau, Re-Atum of Heliopolis, Ptah of the *s.t wr.t*, and three other whose names are lost—are referred to as the providers of a bouquet to be presented to the deceased.[295]

It is not impossible that although offerings were delivered from Amun's temples, including royal memorial temples on the West Bank, they were associated with the solar aspect of that god at the New Year, resulting in the reference to Re-Horakhety in the *ḥtp-di-nsw.t*-formula and the delivery of bouquets.

4.5.12. Royal appearance (*ḫꜥ.t-nsw.t*) and the New Year gift

Not a few private tombs contain a portrayal of the king, who is often accompanied by a goddess.[296] Such scenes are usually located beside the entrance to the inner-room.[297] Being labelled the *ḫꜥ.t-nsw.t* in some cases, the

[285] PM I-1², 137 (7).
[286] PM I-1², 269 (3, III, 2).
[287] Dittmar 1986, 121.
[288] Bouquets of Osiris are referred to in association with the first epagomenal day in P. Leiden T 32 (IV, 9), dated to the Roman Period (Stricker 1953, 21; M. Smith 2009, 416 for translation).
[289] *Urk.* IV, 925: 13–4. The tomb of Paheri at el-Kab, dated to the time of Thutmose III, contains a scene depicting the deceased tutoring the short-lived prince of Thutmose I Uadjmes who is on Paheri's lap. Paheri receives offerings from his children 'in the morning of the New Year' (PM V, 179 (7–8); *Urk.* IV, 109: 17; Tylor 1895, pl. 4; Roehrig 1990, 289, pl. 16; Figure 27). To depict the deceased suckling or fostering a young prince was neither uncommon nor exclusively associated with the New Year. Such a representation is attested in association with the Valley Feast in the tomb of Heqaerneheh (TT 64: PM I-1², 128 (3, I)).
[290] TT 72 (PM I-1², 142 (5); *Urk.* IV, 1457: 9) and TT 88 (PM I-1², 180 (4); *Urk.* IV, 1460: 13).
[291] Dittmar 1986, 87.
[292] PM I-1², 109 (7); Davies 1941, pl. 30.
[293] PM I-1², 412 (11); Guksch 1978, pl. 22.
[294] PM I-1², 179 (8); Guksch 1995, 64, pl. 12.
[295] PM I-1², 456 (3); *Urk.* IV, 1936: 7–10.
[296] Brock and Shaw (1997, 176, n. 89) propose that the goddess depicted behind the king can be seen as an image of the queen.
[297] Aldred 1969, 73; Engelmann-von Carnap 1999, 246; el-Menshawy 2000, 86. According to Engelmann-von Carnap (1995, Abb. 14), the scene of the royal appearance is mostly attested in large tombs belonging to high-ranking individuals in the first half of the Eighteenth Dynasty. See Hartwig 2004, 54–73 for this particular genre of scene.

scenes are associated with various occasions, such as reward ceremonies and installations of officials (Table 21). The occasion, when specified, was either the Sed Feast or the New Year celebration.[298] The latter typically represented a ceremony when gifts were presented to the king seated in a kiosk. The gifts often originated from foreigners, but were invariably presented by the tomb owner to the sovereign.

In the tomb of Sennefer, mayor of the Southern City (TT 96), for example, the deceased is portrayed offering New Year gifts to Amenhotep II. The beginning of the legend reads: *ms inḏ-ḥr n wpy-rnp.t ḫꜣ.t n nḥḥ pḥ ḏ.t* 'Bringing the salutation of the New Year, the beginning of eternity and the end of everlastingness'.[299] The New Year gifts vary in form and character. They include several statuettes of Amenhotep II, of the queen Meryre, and of Amenhotep I, jars, fans, offering tables, and boxes, all in different styles, as well as one plain stela.

The tomb of Amenhotep, overseer of the works on the two great obelisks in the temple of Amun under Hatshepsut (TT 73), represents a wider variety of goods than those depicted in the aforementioned tomb of Sennefer (TT 96; Figure 34).[300] The items of prime importance are collars (perhaps made of gold) and two obelisks being presented to the queen Hatshepsut (4.3.3). Other objects include: a few chariots and a bow, all made of gold; a ram-headed jar; a bed; large shrines; several royal and divine statues; and fat bulls with a flower decoration around their necks to be dedicated at the Opet Feast (2.5.4). On the adjacent wall are two episodes: Amenhotep fishing and fowling, and receiving a bouquet from a man. That these scenes are consecutive is confirmed by the fact that each scene continues onto the next wall. The whole sequence seems to start from the last-mentioned episode of the bouquet, which is labelled: *[n kꜣ=k] šꜣ nḏm-sty pr [m-bꜣḥ] nb nṯr.w Ꞽmn nb ns.wt tꜣ.wy* '[For your ka], a flower, sweet of scent, that comes [before] the lord of the gods, Amun, lord of the thrones of the Two Lands'.[301] A sequence of episodes parallel to this is also attested in the tomb of Puymre, second-priest of Amun under Hatshepsut and Thutmose III (TT 39).[302] These scenes are reminiscent of the widely attested scenes where a tomb owner is portrayed inspecting products in relation to the harvest. It is significant that our scenes depict fishing and fowling, which have been associated with various subjects by scholars.[303] It may be misleading to explore them only in an ideological context—the tomb owner's wish for repeating entertaining activities in the hereafter—because the scenes bear witness, to some extent, to a series of economic activities.[304] In fact, as Kessler (1987, 84) rightly pointed out, a link to the New Year can also be seen in this particular genre of representation. From the scenes of the aforementioned tomb of Amenhotep (TT 73), we are able to reconstruct a sequence illustrating the state income to be collected, inspected, and finally presented to the king during the harvest season. Hence, a song recorded in the tomb of Amenemhat, a scribe under Hatshepsut and Thutmose III (TT 82), praises the gathering of supplies at the New Year (Figure 33):[305]

> *nfr.w(y) n tꜣ ḥw.t-nṯr n.t [Ꞽmn] wpy-rnp.t m smꜣ.wy [n Ꞽmn nb ns.wt tꜣ.wy] nb r-ḏr=s ti sw šsp=f nfr.w=s sft.tw iwꜣ.w=s m št.w ḥkꜣ.wt=s ḫꜣs.wt m ḫꜣ.w n [Ꞽmn m imn]y.t=f m ḥb[y.t n.t tp-tr.w]*
>
> How good for the temple of [Amun] the New Year is in renewing[306] [for Amun, lord of the thrones of the Two Lands] and lord in its entirety, when he receives its good things—its oxen are slaughtered by hundreds and its foreign *heqa*-beasts by thousands for [Amun as] his [offer] ings, (consisting) of [seasonal] festival [offerings].

This text is remarkable because it says that when renewal was completed at the New Year, sacrificial animals, probably together with other supplies, were brought together and registered for the year to come. The contracted formula 'hundreds and thousands of offerings' is far more attested when it appears beside an offering table in offering and inspection scenes,

298 In the tombs of Meryre (II) (*Urk.* IV, 2003: 5; Davies 1903, vol. 2, pls 37–8) and of Huya (*Urk.* IV, 2006: 11; *LD* III, pl. 100, b; Davies 1903, vol. 3, pl. 13) at Amarna, Akhenaten and his queen are portrayed appearing (*ḫꜥ*) on the throne of 'his father Aten' and receiving foreign tributes. The scenes are dated to II Peret 8 in year 12 (**711**). It might be that Amarna Letter EA 27 records a celebration relating to this event, dated to I Peret 5 (or 6 or 9) in year 2 or 12 (**608**).

299 PM I-1², 198 (6); *Urk.* IV, 1417: 5; Davies 1928b, fig. 6.

300 PM I-1², 143–4 (1–3); Säve-Söderbergh 1957, pls 1–9.

301 *Urk.* IV, 462: 9.

302 PM I-1², 72 (7–9); Davies 1922, pls 8–19.

303 Balcz (1939, 37) thought that the scene depicted a cultic performance in association with the goddess Hathor. Westendorf (1967, 142) sees an implication of sexual union between the tomb owner and his wife. For references to the symbolism evoked by spearing two fish representing Upper and Lower Egypt, see Kanawati and Woods 2010, 63, n. 43. Feucht (1992, 159) seems to reject the cultic interpretations of the scene and stresses its sporting/entertainment aspects. For a more recent study on the Hathoric association in a sexual context, see Darnell 2010, 127.

304 Fishing and fowling tend to be represented in the antechamber of private tombs belonging to the first half of the Eighteenth Dynasty (Engelmann-von Carnap 1999, 232). An agricultural scene normally appears in the left half of the antechamber, which seems to be juxtaposed with the waterfront scene in the right half (Engelmann-von Carnap 1999, 283). Some scenes of fishing and fowling, such as in TT 125 (2) and 127 (11), are labelled as *sḫmḫ-ib mꜣꜣ bw nfr ir sm m kꜣ.t sḫ.t* 'recreation, the inspection of the good thing, and performing a job in the field work', which is usually attested in inspection scenes.

305 PM I-1², 164 (5); *Urk.* IV, 1056: 8–14; Davies and Gardiner 1915, 40–1, pl. 5; Lichtheim 1945, 184.

306 The expression *m smꜣ.wy* is characteristic of the New Year (*Wb* IV, 126 (14)).

occasions which ideologically evoke the acceptable number of offerings to be presented to the deceased on any occasion for eternity.[307] The sum of deliveries presented to a given recipient for each year was called *ḫr.t-rnp.t* (lit. 'what is under the year'), a designation comparable to *ḫr.t-hrw* and *ḫr.t-3bd*, denoting the daily and monthly requirement respectively.[308] In all likelihood, the New Year was simply considered the epitome of many occasions throughout the year when tax was collected. Such a view is reinforced by the candles represented in the above-mentioned tomb of Amenemhat (TT 82).[309] They are eight in number, five of which are used on the epagomenal days and two on New Year's Day. The last candle is used for the rest of the year, as the legend says: *t[k3] n [ḫr.t hrw] n.t rʿ nb sḥḏ ḥr.t n.t bw kkw n NN* 'Ca[nd]le for [every] day, illuminating the way of the nocturnal place for NN.'[310]

Because the gifts presented to the king ranged from military equipment to ritual paraphernalia, the king's private department does not seem to have been the final destination for every object. The divine statues at least were certainly destined as endowments for temples.

4.6. Economic functions of the New Year Festival

4.6.1. Sequence of the annual revenue collection

The seasonal sequence between the harvest and the New Year is remarkably represented in two New Kingdom tombs. First, it is depicted on a single wall of the unpublished tomb of Mentuiyuy (TT 172), a royal butler from the time of Thutmose III to Amenhotep II.[311] There are four episodes: 1) the deceased hunting in a desert; 2) wine production offered to the goddess Renenutet and the deceased; 3) a man presenting handiworks as New Year gifts to the deceased, labelled: *ms in n wpy-rnp.t ir n nsw.t* 'Presenting the output of the New Year made for the king'; 4) the deceased and his mother receiving offerings (Figure 35). The fact that a sub-scene of agriculture runs through all the episodes above supports the interpretation that this represents a temporal succession. Hunting, which is the first episode, may appear here in place of fishing and fowling. It may be that hunting, coupled with wine production, and the craftsmen represent respectively an income stream from natural resources and from workshops. The representation of the deceased after each episode appears to receive reports on these products. The third figure, of the deceased with his mother, receives annual offerings at the New Year. The *ḥtp-di-nsw.t* recited by a man clad in a panther skin suggests that this episode represents a mortuary cult performed at this tomb on that occasion.

Second, the aforementioned tomb of Paheri, count of Nekheb and Inyt, at el-Kab, dated to the time of Thutmose III, attests that the presentation of offerings to the tomb owner was performed in the morning of the New Year (Figure 37b).[312] The offerings were brought in as the result of his supervision of production, including fishing, cattle counting, production of gold and wine, and harvesting of grain and flax. The agricultural scenes are represented in the top register, presiding over other productions because they represent an essential component of the tax income. The New Year as an occasion to receive the 'first (yield) of the harvest' (*tpy n šmw*) is evidenced in the Middle-Kingdom tomb of Hepdjef, count of Asyut under Senusret I.[313] It is not hard to imagine that the collection of tax was the main duty of these local governors.

It was hardly possible that each tomb owner represented in the scene of the New Year gifts could have afforded to furnish all these items on his own. He was not boasting about the wealth in his possession but did boast about the extent of his official service, that encompassed a wide range of annual productions. Ideologically, it was the 'breath' that was given to him in return from the king.[314] In reality, some of the collected products seem to have been apportioned to officials as a reward. According to Delvaux (2010, 75), even a statue of the deceased king could be given to officials as a royal favour. Such was described as: *ḫft ḥs.wt n.t ḫr nsw.t* 'according to the favours of the king'. This reciprocal relation was, however, not limited to the royal court and officials but extended to the god and the deceased. Hence, in the tomb of Sennefer, overseer of the seal under Thutmose III (TT 99), he is portrayed receiving New Year gifts from his wife, who is described as:[315]

---

307 This formula is already attested in the Pyramid Texts (663, Pyr. 1882 and 667, Pyr. 1957a–c).

308 The *ḫr.t-rnp.t* can denote festivals celebrated throughout the year, as evidenced by the Pyramid Texts (726, Pyr. 2253). In administrative documents, *dmḏ ḫr.t-rnp.t* appears in relation to the share of goods required for each year (Abusir X, 423, n. 106). A sum of divine offerings to Mut was recorded at the end of the year as the *ḫr.t-rnp.t* on an unnumbered stone fragment of Amenhotep I from Karnak (Spalinger 1992, pl. IV; Grimm 1994b, fig. 2 for better facsimile). Such usage of the phrase is attested in P. Berlin 10056, dated to the Middle Kingdom (Luft 1992, 74), whereas the *ḥtri-rnp.t* (P. Harris I, 51, b, 6) or *ḥtri-n-ṯnw-rnp.t* (*Urk.* IV, 503, 8) is widely used in the New Kingdom.

309 PM I-1², 166 (17); Davies 1915, pl. 23.

310 Such candles were also reserved for upcoming temple rituals. A candle intended for a Hathor feast to be celebrated on III Shemu 30 or the next day is recorded among other offerings on a stela from the Ptah temple at Karnak (**1295**).

311 PM I-1², 280 (8–10).

312 PM V, 179 (7–8); *Urk.* IV, 10: 17; Tylor 1895, pl. 4.

313 Griffith 1889, pl. 6, col. 279; Leibovitch 1953, 110.

314 Texts carved on columns of Amenhotep II at Karnak (PM II², 80; *Urk.* IV, 1326: 4–6; Bleiberg 1984, 157, no. 6). Also see TT 86 (8) where foreign chiefs are depicted bringing New Year gifts with a reference to *ṯ3w n ʿnḫ* (PM I-1², 177 (8); Davies 1933b, pl. 4). A rare example of *ṯ3w* given from a son to a father in the form of a raised sailing mast, not in a New Year context though, is represented in the tomb of Sennedjem, dated to the Nineteenth Dynasty (TT 1: PM I-1², 3 (6)).

315 PM I-1², 205 (A, a); *Urk.* IV, 539: 3–6; Dziobek 1994, 30. Significantly, phraseology similar to this is attested in a temple relief at Karnak,

ḏd=s n kꜣ=k sṯy-ḥb ḥnḳ.wt nwd.w n is.wy m ḫꜣw pn n rnp.t wḏ.n n=k nb=k [Ỉ]mn[-rꜥ] iw=k m pr=k n ꜥnḫ.w nḏm ib=k im[=s]

She says: 'For your ka. Festival oil, beer, and unguents of the double-chamber in this bowl of the year that your lord [A] mun[-Re] ordered for you while you are in your house of lives with your sweet heart [there]in.'

This text may argue for a further re-distribution channel that connects the temple and tomb through the living family, at least, on an ideological level.

The flow of annual products between the harvest and the New Year is also visible in a fragmentary relief of Thutmose III at the Akh-menu (**967**). The king appears on the throne at the *ḏꜣḏ*[w]-hall on I Shemu 2 in 'year after 23', perhaps corresponding to year 24. This is followed by long vertical columns of inscription recording a decree concerning a new endowment for festivals. At the end of this a list of feasts begins with the New Year celebration.[316] The heading of the list reads: *ir.t mi mꜣꜥ.t n ḥb.w tp tr.w wꜣḥ n=sn nb ꜥnḫ wḏꜣ snb ꜥꜣb.t m mꜣꜥw.t m ḫr.t-rnp.t ḥr-tp ꜥnḫ wḏꜣ snb nsw.t-bity* 'Performance, according to Maat, for the seasonal festivals, for which the lord, l.p.h., established the *ꜥꜣb.t*-offerings anew as yearly revenue on behalf of the l.p.h. of the king of Upper and Lower Egypt'. From this we can imagine a possible scenario where the king issued the decree at the time of the harvest celebrations, when he then received a report on the prolific agricultural production. By this time, in anticipation of regular incomes to be collected, the yearly budget for the next year had already been calculated and approved by an administration office.[317]

That foreign delegations visited the king to present exotic New Year gifts may hint at a regular income stream brought from the other lands to Egypt to be delivered at ceremonies because their handing over most probably required a formal setting.[318] Foreign tributes were called the *in.w* and received by the king in the first instance and some were certainly passed on to temples.[319] Hence, in an inspection scene in the tomb of Ineni, overseer of the granary of Amun from the time of Amenhotep I to Thutmose III (TT 81), they are described as:[320]

in.w n ḫꜣs.wt nb r di.n ḥm=f r ḥw.t-nṯr n.t Ỉmn m ḥtr r tnw rnp.t ḥr-tp ꜥnḫ wḏꜣ snb nsw.t-bi.ty ꜥꜣ-ḫpr-kꜣ-rꜥ

Tributes of all foreign lands that his person gave to the temple of Amun as an annual levy on behalf of the l.p.h. of the king of Upper and Lower Egypt, Aakheperkare (Thutmose I).

The *bꜣk.wt* (lit. 'labour') also appear elsewhere as part of *ḥtr rnp.t* the 'yearly levy' or *bꜣk.wt n.t ḫr.t-rnp.t* the 'annual *bꜣk.wt*'.[321]

Temples were not economically and administratively independent but rather counted on the state's institutions in large and were part of its re-distribution systems.[322] They received revenue both from their own estates and from governmental institutions. In addition, from time to time kings established new endowments for temples. By examining New Kingdom records, Haring (1997, 395–6) explains that temples functioned as 'important landholders and producers' but their economy was limited when compared with 'the efforts required for the maintenance of their own organization and cults'. The collection of yearly levies was a major responsibility of the king and sometimes took place during an official ceremony.[323] The New Year was one of those occasions, when the king presented a portion of the newly collected tax to temples.

It is, however, evident that once royal donations were made to temples, they were seen to belong to the gods and ritualistically given back to the king as divine offerings.[324] This constituted an essential part

where Ramses II offers the *mḏt*-oil to Amun-Re in the form of a hawk god who resides in the temple of the akh of the king (PM II², 46 (156, IV, 2); Nelson 1981, pl. 32). The legend says: 'Offering the *mḏ.t*-oil, purification of the double-chamber (*is.wy*) of the father Amun-Re.'

316 *Urk.* IV, 1272: 4–5.

317 The end of the fiscal year may be recorded in P. Northumberland II (*KRI* I, 241: 11–4). The amount of provision supplied to the army was summed up a year later on II Shemu 29 in year 3 of Seti I.

318 For foreign delegations visiting the Egyptian king, see Gnirs (2009, 29–37) who emphasizes ceremonial settings at festivals in the court and their impact on international politics.

319 Bleiberg (1988, 165) distinguishes the *bꜣk.wt*, which went to the king as an intermediary in the first place and were passed on to temples afterwards, from the *in.w* forming the private royal income. But such a clear distinction cannot be easily drawn (Warburton 1997, 236; Katary 2011, 13). Haring (1997, 205) asserts that the *in.w* donated by the king to temples did not occupy a high proportion of temple income and were considered only royal tokens.

320 PM I-1², 161 (5); *Urk.* IV, 70: 4–7.

321 See Katary (2011, 4) for the annual taxation.

322 Haring 2007, 165; Janssen 1975b, 183–4. On the other hand, Kemp (1989, 232–60) questions the application of Polanyi's theory to Egypt without consideration of differing economic systems at different times. He argues, for example, for the existence of a merchant class (*šwty*) and local economy independent of central government during the First Intermediate and Amarna Periods.

323 Bleiberg 1988, 165. Although the existence of central tax administration is only conjectural (Katary 2011, 7), it is evident that the royal institution played a key role in collecting products.

324 Even if the temple economy formed only a small part of the entire state produce, its function as an ideological origin or storehouse of resources cannot be underestimated. The reversion of divine offerings (*wḏb.w*) was exercised from the Old Kingdom onwards. By examining Abusir papyri of the Fifth Dynasty, Papazian (2010, 143) concludes that at Memphis the Ptah temple and solar temples played only 'a ritualistic role of receiving the donations' and 'reverting them' to funerary temples or personnel attached to them. According

of the re-distribution system with many complex and peripheral ramifications before they reached people.[325] In the following sections, an attempt will be made to demonstrate that such was actually the case for animal offerings and cloths collected at the New Year.

4.6.2. Cattle

The Buto Stela of Thutmose III records the largest number of offerings for the New Year Feast including four bulls, which is more than for any other of the celebrations recorded in that stela (**8**). An account of O. Cairo 25504, dated to year 7 of Merenptah, may also be understood in association with the New Year. It records that six oxen and 80 fine cloths were awarded by the vizier Panehesy to the Deir el-Medina workmen on IV Shemu 19 as a reward (**1356**). The number of the cloths perhaps signifies that each workman received one piece of linen.[326]

As described in 4.5.12, it is evident that oxen destined for the Opet Feast were collected at the New Year. Hence, the New Year was not only the occasion for meat consumption but also for apportioning supplies for the following festivals within the same year. This may be deduced in the Middle-Kingdom tomb of Sarenput (I), count and overseer of the priests of the goddess Satis at Elephantine under Senusret I. The tomb owner is portrayed:[327]

> *m33 k3.w iw3.w wnḏ.w ir=f r šms ḥb.w n nṯr.w nb 3bw*
>
> Inspecting oxen, the *iw3*-bulls, and the *wnḏ*-cattle that he made to follow the festivals of all the gods of Elephantine.

Those yearly supplies could amount to 365 items, corresponding to the total number of civil days.[328] This was manifest only after the New Kingdom but could have been a tradition from earlier times.[329]

4.6.3. Cloth

Cloths were essential to the New Year. Two documents from the Neferirkare archive at Abu Sir record that cloths were distributed in IV Shemu, probably in preparation for the New Year.[330]

According to Vogelsang-Eastwood (1992, 5), flax sowing took place in mid-November, corresponding to I Peret, and the seed required roughly three months to mature. In the tomb of the vizier Rekhmire, from the time of Thutmose III to Amenhotep II (TT 100), men are portrayed carrying bunches of various cloths to the memorial temple of Thutmose III under the supervision of the vizier after the 'victory in the lands of the south and the north'. The legend further says:[331]

> *r ir.t sšr.w nsw.t ḥḏ.t p3k.t* [*sẖr*]*.w mty ḫrp.w mnḫ.t iry n* [*Imn*] *m ḥ*[*b.w*]*=f nb.w* [*n*]*ḫt* [one group lost] *m* [*pr*] *ḥḥ.w n rnp.t n ity* [*Mn-ḫpr-rꜥ* unknown groups lost ...
>
> in order to make royal linen, consisting of the white-, *p3k.t*-, and [*sẖr*]-cloths precisely when he supervises the linen belonging to [Amun] at all his festi[vals] of [v]ictory [ ] in [the house] of millions of years for the sovereign [Menkheperre ...

to Stela Cairo 34013, dated to the time of Thutmose III, offerings for Amun were passed on to the hour-priests (*wnw.t*) of the temple of Karnak as well as to a royal statue that *šms r ḥw.t-nṯr tn* 'participated in this temple' (*Urk.* IV, 768: 11–769: 5; Klug 2002, 140). The Buto Stela of the same king more explicitly refers to reversionary offerings from the god to a royal statue (Bedier 1994a, 6, z. 1–4, Abb. 4; Klug 2002, 103, Abb. 10). The Medinet Habu calendar records that *swr n wnw. tyw ḥw.t-nṯr iꜥb.n=i m-b3ḥ p3 twt n ḫꜥ-nsw.t* an occasion of 'drinking for the hour-priests of the temple that I brought together before the statue of the appearance of the king' took place during the accession anniversary of Ramses III (*MH* III, pl. 152, list 22). This reveals that the divine offerings were consumed for the royal statue and the temple personnel in the same location at the same time. Later sources, such as P. Rylands 9 (XVII, 17–8), prove that a similar pattern of re-distribution from the god to a royal statue and priests was maintained in the Third Intermediate Period (Muhs 2005, 2–3). Offerings presented to the god and king could also be redirected to the statues of individuals set up within temple precincts, as recorded on a statue of chief steward Amenhotep-Huy, dated to the time of Amenhotep III (Statue Ashmolean 1913.163: PM III-2², 836; *Urk.* IV, 1797: 12–3; Morkot 1990, 331 for translation).

[325] Insofar as grains was concerned, the monthly and yearly festivals recorded in the Medinet Habu calendar could not have had a large impact on the delivery of re-distributed temple offerings (Table 26). According to Janssen (1979, 513, n. 23), the total number of grain sacks consumed at these festivals was very small, about 2200 against the 40,150 required for the daily ritual throughout the year. However, Janssen also maintained that some major celebrations played a key role in the delivery of a larger number of offerings and that additional supplies were made from more than one temple. In fact, the making of the daily offerings was not skipped during the annual festivals, as evidenced by the indication of their daily total multiplied by 365 days (Haring 1997, 77).

[326] Janssen 1975a, 492.

[327] PM V, 238 (6–7); *Urk.* VII, 7: 8; Gardiner 1908, 136.

[328] Redford 1972, 153.

[329] 365 oxen are documented in the chronicle of Osorkon (Caminos 1958, 142) and Stela Cairo 39410 from Herakleopolis, dated to the time of Sheshonq I (PM IV, 121; Tresson 1961, 821; Redford 1972, 153 for translation). The Book of Opening-of-the-Mouth for Breath (P. Berlin 8351) refers to water brought at ten-day intervals from Elephantine (col. II, l. 5) and associated with 365 tables (col. IV, l. 9) (M. Smith 1993, 31 and 34). At Philae 365 offerings (*ḥtp.w*) were made in association with the decade ceremony (PM VI, 254 (5); Junker 1913, 18). 360 bowls to be filled with milk every day is recorded by Diodorus Siculus (LXXI and LXXXVII).

[330] Posener-Kriéger 1976, vol. 2, 356 and 358. Private sources also record the distribution of cloths in the Old Kingdom. For example, in the mastaba of Mereruka, vizier under the king Teti, he is portrayed receiving cloths supplied from the 'Residence' (*ẖn*) as royal gifts (PM III-2², 530 (49); *Mereruka* I, pl. 96). Although the context of this scene is not clear, it is noteworthy that other scenes in the same room attest *iḫhy*, an expression characteristic of the beginning of the year and reign (4.2.1.3).

[331] PM I-1², 210 (13, IV–V); *Urk.* IV, 1147–8; Davies 1943, vol. 1, 47, vol. 2, pl. 57; Davies 1928b, 38–40, figs 1–2.

Figure 25a. Distant view of Thutmose IV's peristyle hall, east wing, now at the Open-Air Museum, Karnak (photograph taken by the author).

Figure 25b. Beasts dedicated to Amun-Re, east wing of Thutmose IV's peristyle hall (photograph taken by the author).

Figure 25c. King dedicating paraphernalia and royal statues to Amun-Re, west wing of Thutmose IV's peristyle hall. The stern of Amun's barge is visible below left (photograph taken by the author).

This scene continues into the register above, where foreign female captives with their children are portrayed receiving the cloths. The legend reads:

> *ir.t mꜣ m* [*mr.wt n.wt ḥw.t*]*-nṯr* [*n Ỉmn*] *m-ꜥb šnꜥ.w n ḥtp.w nṯr in n nsw.t m sꜥ*[*ḳ*]*.w ꜥnḫ ḥtr ms.w=sn m bꜣk.w r rdi.t n=sn sšr.w mrḥ.wt ḥbs.w mi n.t-ꜥ=sn n ẖr.t-rnp.t n* [unknown groups lost ...
>
> Supervision of [the personnel of the te]mple [of Amun] together with the magazines of the divine offerings that have been brought to the king as living capti[ve]s, levying on their children as servants, in order to give them linen, ointment, and the *ḥbs*-cloths as their yearly supply of [...

Foreigners could form part of the temple workforce.[332] This scene may illustrate newly installed labour or a regular review. It is not impossible to link our scene to the New Year because foreign tributes including children are represented among New Year gifts elsewhere in the contemporaneous tomb of Menkheperreseneb, high-priest of Amun (TT 86).[333] The stress to be placed here is that foreign captives formed part of the output but could also receive a part of it as their annual supply. The re-distribution of cloths from temples may also be illustrated in the tomb of the scribe Amenemhat (TT 82), also contemporary with Rekhmire and Menkheperreseneb, where the deceased is portrayed rewarding his draughtsmen. The legend reads:[334]

> *dwꜣ nṯr n* [*ḥm.*]*w snm.t=st m ḥtp-nṯr t ḥnḳ.t kꜣ.w ꜣpd.w fḳꜣ=st m sšr.w nb nf*[*r* one group lost] *n sḏd.w sšd.w r tp.w=sn*
>
> Praise of the god for the [craftsm]en. Feeding them with divine offerings, (consisting of) bread, bear, oxen, and

[332] Haring 1997, 198–9.

[333] PM I-1^2, 177 (8, II); Davies 1933b, pl. 5.

[334] PM I-1^2, 164 (4, I); *Urk.* IV, 1055: 10–4; Davies and Gardiner 1915, pl. 8; el-Kordy 1984, 126 for translation.

Figure 25d. Vessels dedicated to Amun-Re, west wing of Thutmose IV's peristyle hall, continued from Figure 25c (photograph taken by the author).

> birds, and rewarding them with all fin[e] linen [ ] giving(?) the *sšd*-headbands to their heads.

In agreement with this caption, the craftsmen are each depicted with a band tied to their head with a fillet hanging down behind. Amenemhat was probably commissioned to reward them in his capacity of a steward of the vizier. Because this scene is located next to a New Year representation, a link cannot be ruled out.

There are two other examples perhaps associated with the New Year on account of the representations of candles. First, in the tomb of Qenamen (TT 93), chief royal steward under Amenhotep II, a lector-priest carrying two tapers to the deceased announces: *ḏd in ḥry-ḥb in.n(=i) n=k ꜥrf n wꜣḏ ꜥrf n msdm.t sfḫy snṯr ḥr st wꜥb wꜥb n kꜣ=k ḥbs.w m ꜥ.wy tꜣ ii.t m ḥm n stp-sꜣ* 'Word spoken by the lector-priest: "(I) have brought to you a bag of the green paint, a bag of the black paint, the removed linen, and the incense on fire. Be pure! Be pure! For your ka, the *ḥbs*-linen in the arms and that which comes from the person of the palace".'[335] Second, in the tomb of Hori (TT 259), a wab-priest during the Ramesside Period, his son gives a large cone-candle to Hori, whose head is bound with a fillet painted in yellow and red.[336]

Evidently, linen was included among the New Year gifts as a reward from the king, as attested in the Middle-Kingdom tomb of Intefiqer, vizier under Senusret I (TT 60), where *mnḫ.t ḥss.n tw ns*[*w.t*] the 'cloth that the king rewarded you' is recorded (Figure 36).[337] As a valuable material, cloths were probably distributed only a few times (or less) a year. By extension, they represented annual supplies. While linen met the need of every person for personal, domestic use, it was also given as a token of royal honour to workers and officials, and presented to the dead on a symbolic level.

On the other hand, there were cloths that undoubtedly originated from temples. Numerous bunches of cloths

335 PM I-1², 193 (C, b, I); Davies 1930, 52, pl. 61 (C and D).
336 PM I-1², 343 (2, I); Feucht 2006, Faltplan 4 and Farbtafel 20.
337 PM I-1², 122 (11); Davies and Gardiner 1920, 16, pl. 10.

are depicted in the tomb of Imiseba (TT 65), chief temple-scribe of the temple of Amun under Ramses IX, being sorted into individual units within a temple warehouse (Figure 28). They were perhaps to be allocated to the group of priests portrayed next to the building. Unlike the ideological functions of oracle-givings at the Opet Feast and of bouquets at the Valley Feast as a means of conveying Amun's divine power to people, cloths at the New Year seem to differ in nature. The recipients of the New Year cloths were not limited to common folk.

The coronation text of Hatshepsut at her Deir el-Bahari temple records that the royal appearance and *ḥb (s)šd* the 'festival of the *(s)šd*-headband' took place at the New Year (Figure 26).[338] Unfortunately, the figure of the queen accompanying the text has been thoroughly hacked out so that it is impossible to confirm whether she was wearing a headdress of that kind. Significantly, a formula parallel to Hatshepsut's is attested in the entry of the Fourth-Dynasty king Shepseskaf carved on the Palermo Stone.[339] It records the royal appearance (*ḫꜥ nsw.t-bi.ty*) and the festival of *sšd* taking place together on the same day. In a fashion similar to this, P. Berlin 3029 (known as the Leather Roll) records that Senusret I 'appeared in the Double-crown when a sitting took place at the *ḏꜣdw*-hall' (*ḫꜥ.t nsw.t m sḫm.ty ḫpr ḥms.t m ḏꜣdw*) on III Akhet 8 in year 3 (**329**). This account is followed by the stretching-the-cord ritual when the 'king appeared in the *sšd*-headband and double-feather' (*ḫꜥ.t nsw.t m sšd šw.ty*). This date corresponded to one day after his father Amenemhat I had died three years earlier (**324**), thus marking Senusret I's accession anniversary day. The combination of a double-feather and a linen headband may have been an aspect of some deities, such as Amun and Min. Representations of these gods show a long narrow object fastened to the head and running behind the back down to the lower legs. This was presumably a cloth used to secure the tall headdress placed on it. Ramses II also wore the same headdress when he performed rituals in the Ptah temple at Memphis on I Peret 4 in year 3, perhaps on the occasion of the *kꜣ-ḥr-kꜣ*.[340]

As a royal emblem the *sšd* was often combined with other ornaments, such as the double-feather and Double-crown.[341] Its association with the New Year is manifest in earlier and later texts, and very likely during the New Kingdom as well.[342] This headband had a close link to the resurrection of the dead person as the sun.[343] By associating it with the homonymous word *sšd* 'window', Pécoil and Maher-Taha (1983, 74) regard this headband as a symbol of the solar rays but also point out that because the appearance of the sun inevitably evokes the resurrection of the dead, the band was also used for the mortuary cult, including during the Sed Feast when the king underwent ritualistic death and rebirth.[344]

From the New Kingdom onwards, the magical aspect of the *sšd* as an amulet came to be pronounced. The Book of the Dead, for example, instructs that the *sšd* be made of the royal linen (*sšr nsw.t*) and tied to the neck of the deceased on the day of burial (BD 101, 9).[345] The same holds for a prescription of P. Edwin Smith (verso XIX, 11), perhaps dated to the Second Intermediate Period (4.5.5).

Attention could be drawn to the fact that the 'chamber of cloth' (*ḥw.t sšr*) is located to the other side of the inner vestibule from the New Year complex at the temple of Dendera.[346] The chamber of cloth also exists at Philae directly to the north of the New Year complex.[347] Corthals (2004, 90) proposes that at Edfu the offering of linen is closely related to the legitimation of the kingship. The king received divine linen in return for offering cloths to the god. According to Coppens (2010, 48), a part of the temple of el-Qal'a had a function parallel to the linen chamber.[348] By examining the Greek-Roman temples, he rightly draws attention to a set of various cloths, unguents, and amulets as the essentials of the New Year celebrations. They were

[338] PM II², 348 (20–1); *Urk.* IV, 262: 7–8 and 265: 5; Naville 1895, vol. 3, pls 63–4; el-Kordy 1984, 126 for partial translation. Naville (1897, 212) related the 'festival of the *(s)šd*-headband' to the Sed Feast.

[339] *Urk.* I, 239: 12; Wilkinson 2000, 149, fig. 3.

[340] *KRI* II, 355: 2.

[341] See S. Collier (1996, 64–7) for the *sšd* as a symbol of regeneration in the next world, and el-Kordy (1984) for other evidence of the *sšd* from the New Kingdom onwards and its association with Isis and Hathor. Barta (1984, 7–8) also presents other evidence for the New Kingdom and earlier.

[342] Spell 669 of the Pyramid Texts (Pyr. 1964) records that the deceased king sets forth for his rebirth in the eastern sky as a ferryman adorned by a goddess with the *sšd* during the five epagomenal days (Goebs 2008, 150). Spell 466 (Pyr. 883d) likens the year to a presenter of the *sšd* to the king. Sethe (1936, vol. 4, 151) explained that the *sšd*-headband is associated with the new birth, and 'the year' in question is to be seen as the rising of Sothis. This headband is also attested together with other various cloths in two texts at Edfu temple as being given to adorn the god's statue at the New Year (Coppens 2010, 42, texts 1–2).

[343] It is referred to as a means to withstand the rays of the sun in the Book of the Dead (BD 78, 33), written on P. BM 10477 (the papyrus of Nu: Allen 1974, 78, 9 for translation; Carrier 2010, 238, 33, pl. 110 for transcription, transliteration, and translation).

[344] The *sšd* was also associated with the Wag Feast in a New Kingdom text, which reads: *sšp(=i) sšd.w m ḥb wꜣg m wꜣḏ ḥr ins* 'May (I) receive the *sšd*-headbands at the Wag Festival as green cloths upon red cloths' (statue of the royal scribe Amenhotep found at Abydos: PM V, 43; Petrie 1902, vol. 2, 45, pl. 36). For other texts associating this feast with headdresses, see Assmann 2005, 303–4. In the Book of the Dead (BD 136, 1–2), it is related to the sixth lunar festival (P. BM 10477 (the papyrus of Nu): Allen 1974, 111, 2 for translation; Carrier 2010, 275, 3, pl. 127 for transcription, transliteration, and translation).

[345] P. BM 10477 (the papyrus of Nu): Allen 1974, 83, T1 for translation; Carrier 2010, 452–3, pls 224–5 for transcription, transliteration, and translation.

[346] References to cloths in association with the New Year are also attested in texts carved on the north wall and on the entrance thickness of Room X (PM VI, 57 (109, d, 111–2); *Dendara* IV, 104: 10, 112: 3, 124: 15, and 128: 9).

[347] *Philae* 55–6, pl. 21.

[348] *el-Qal'a* II, 117–9.

Figure 26. Hatshepsut's 'coronation text' at her Deir el-Bahari temple
(after Naville 1895, vol. 3, pl. 63).

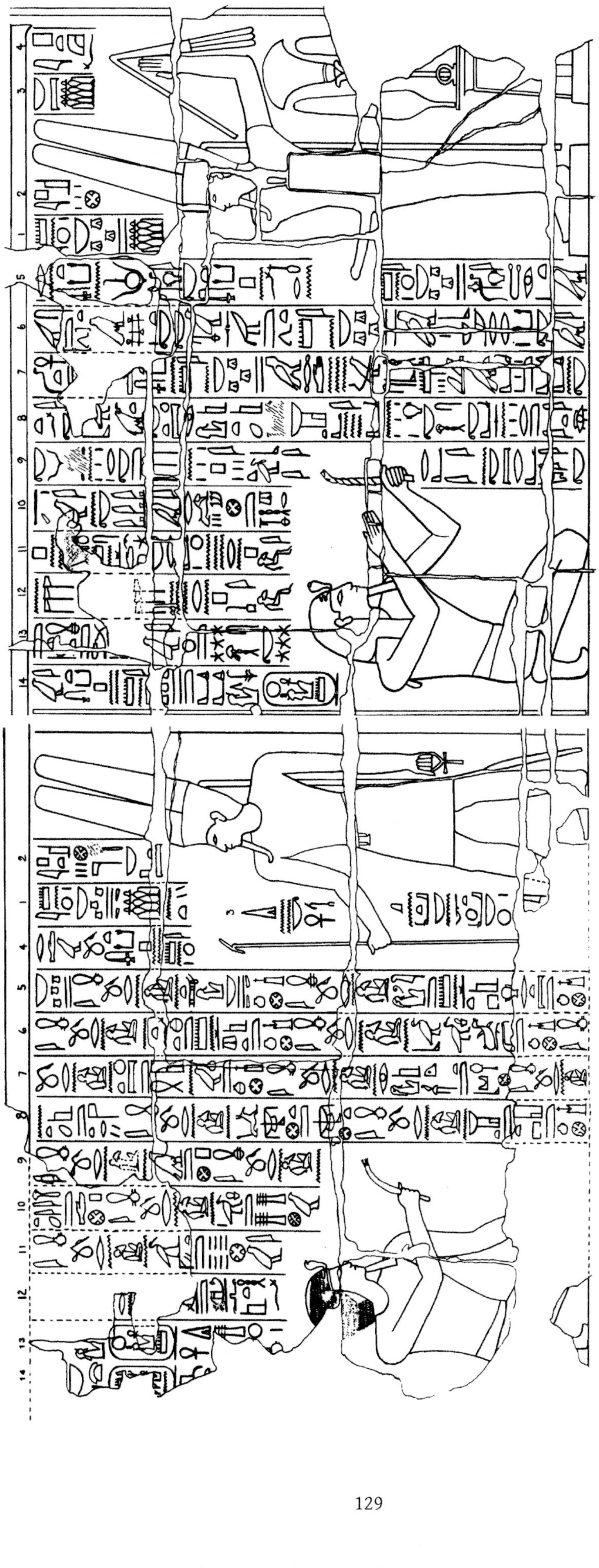

Figure 27. New Year formula carved on the west wall of the Great Hypostyle Hall at Karnak, by courtesy of the Oriental Institute, University of Chicago. (PM II[2], 45 (155, III, 2–3); after Nelson 1981, pls 211–2).

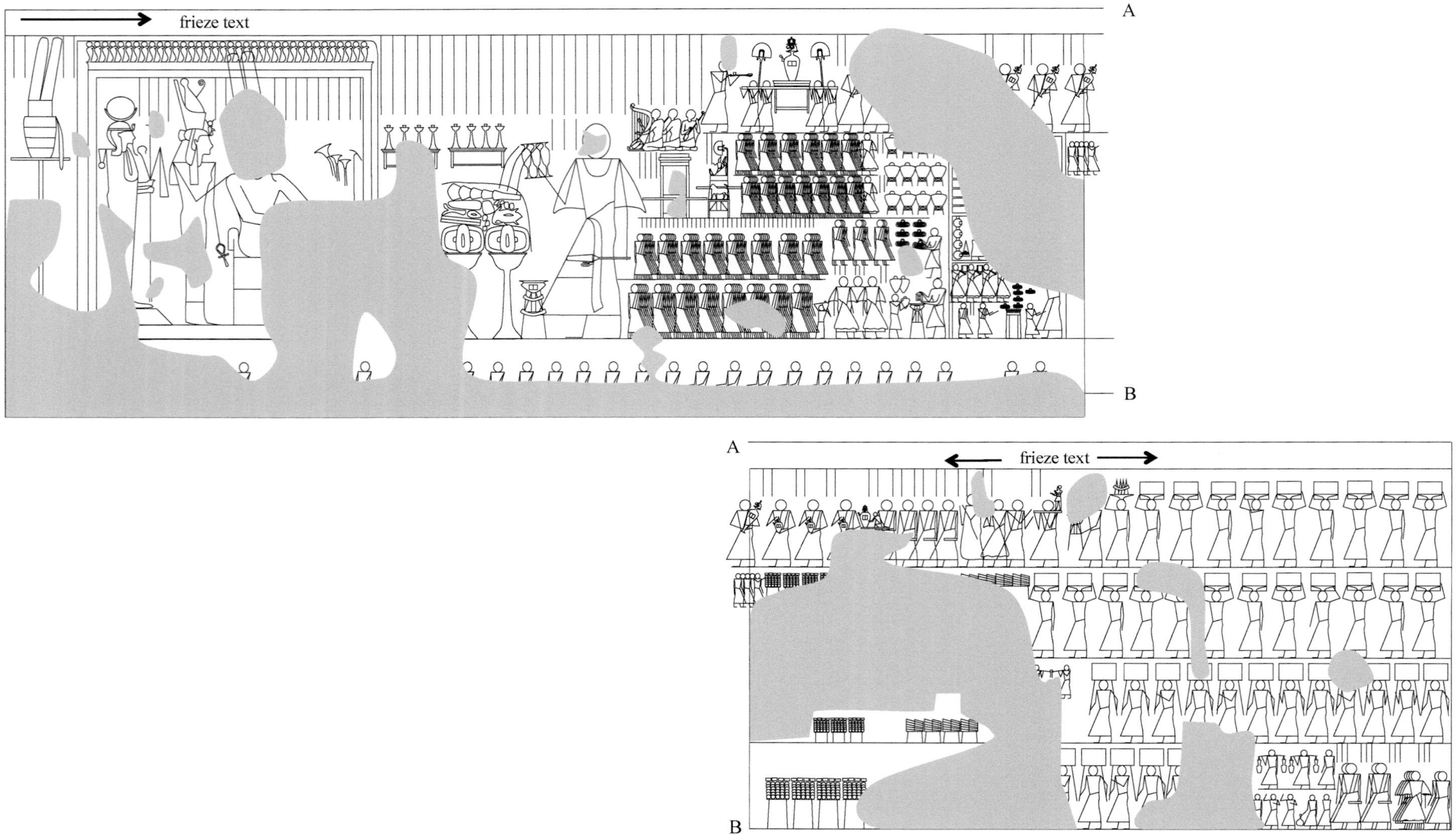

Figure 28. Northwest and north walls of the tomb of Imiseba (TT 65 (8–9)).
Imiseba offers before the Theban triad. Behind him are elaborate representations of individuals, who carry Amun's sacred vase in the uppermost register, which continues onto the north wall depicting offering bringers. Below the vase, priests, who belong to the Theban triad, are portrayed moving towards a treasury, where they seemingly receive divine offerings. Musicians and the portable images of Ahmes-Nefertari and Amenhotep I are represented behind Imiseba (drawing made by the author).

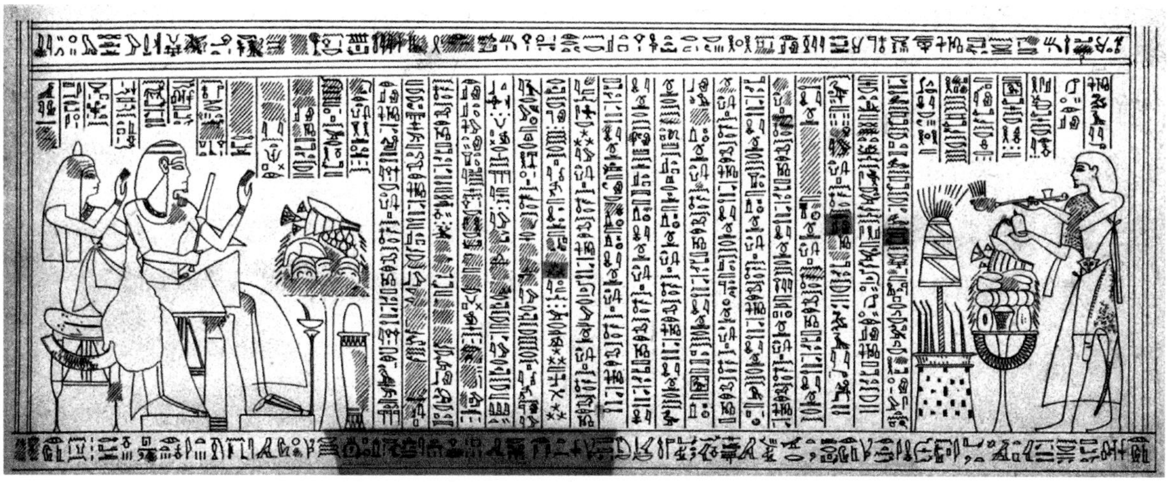

Figure 29. Kindling candles, accompanied by the New Year formula, in the tomb of Tjay (TT 23 (8, II)).
Davies MSS. 10.10.9 by courtesy of the Griffith Institute, University of Oxford.

Figure 30. New Year scene in the tomb of Amenhotep (TT 415 (1, II), according to Loret's (1889, 30–1) description.

Figure 31. North wall of the tomb of Qen (TT 4 (5)), by courtesy of the Griffith Institute, University of Oxford.
The upper register portrays Qen's family adoring Ptah and Maat, a representation parallel to that of TT 2 (10, II) which depicts the Festival of the Two Goddesses on I Peret 22. To the left of the lower register, Qen and his wife Nefertere receive ointment from their daughter, with a caption mentioning the 'meal on IV Shemu 30'. The right half, largely hacked out, portrays Qen and his another spouse Henutmehyt receiving a mortuary performance from their three sons.

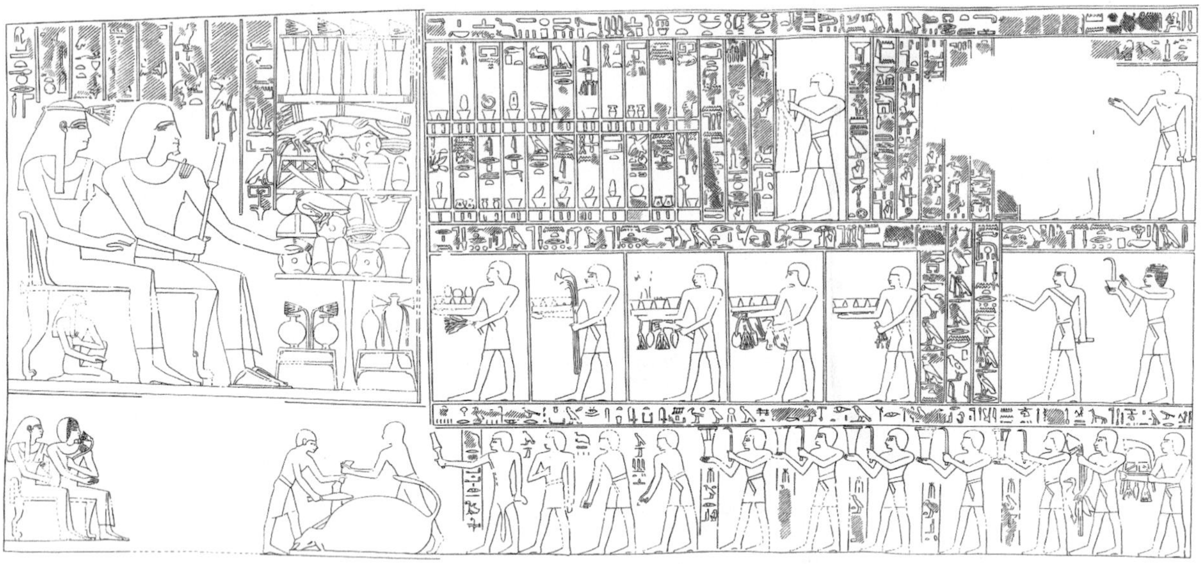

Figure 32. Tomb of Menkheperreseneb (TT 112 (6)), after Davies 1933b, pls 28–9.
The lowest horizontal text begins with a mention of the five epagomenal days.
The five men carrying an eye-paint vessel and a torch represent those days.

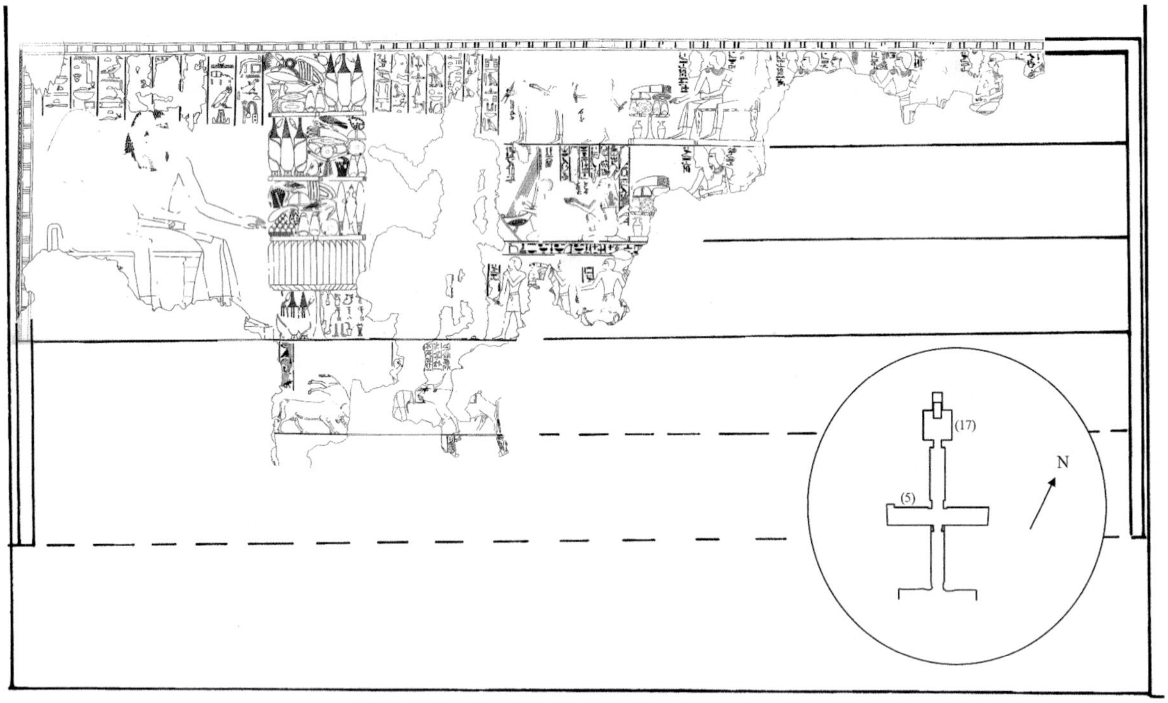

Figure 33a. Tomb of Amenemhat (TT 82 (5)), after Davies and Gardiner 1915, pls 4–6, and Engelmann-von Carnap 1999, pl. 3, by courtesy of the Deutsches Archäologisches Institut Kairo.
In front of the female singers in the second register, a passage includes the 'New Year Festival'.

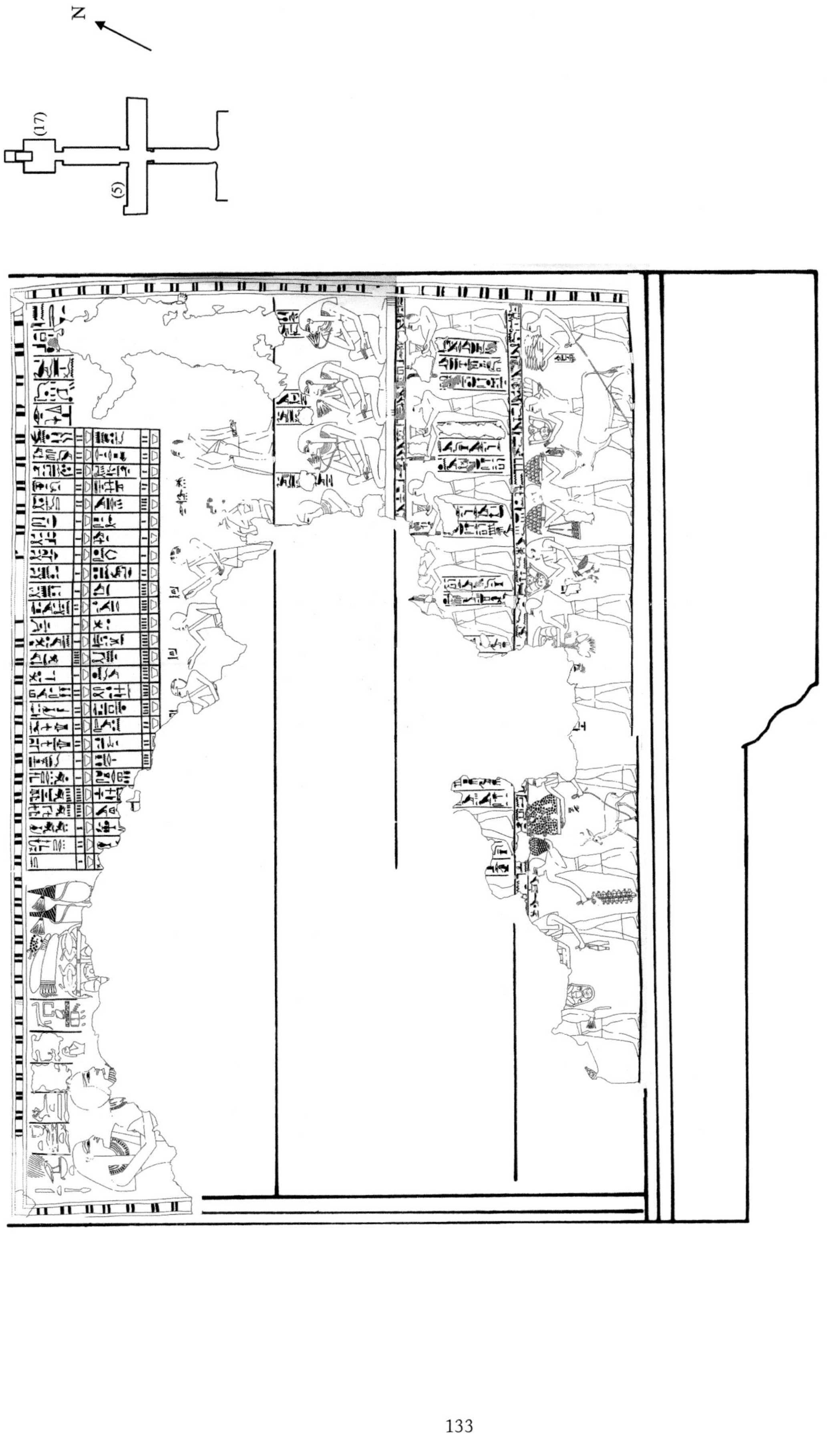

Figure 33b. Tomb of Amenemhat (TT 82 (17)), after Davies and Gardiner 1915, pls 21–3, and Engelmann-von Carnap 1999, pl. 5, by courtesy of the Deutsches Archäologisches Institut Kairo. In the third register, men carrying a torch and an ointment vessel represent the epagomenal days, New Year, Nehebkau, and every day respectively.

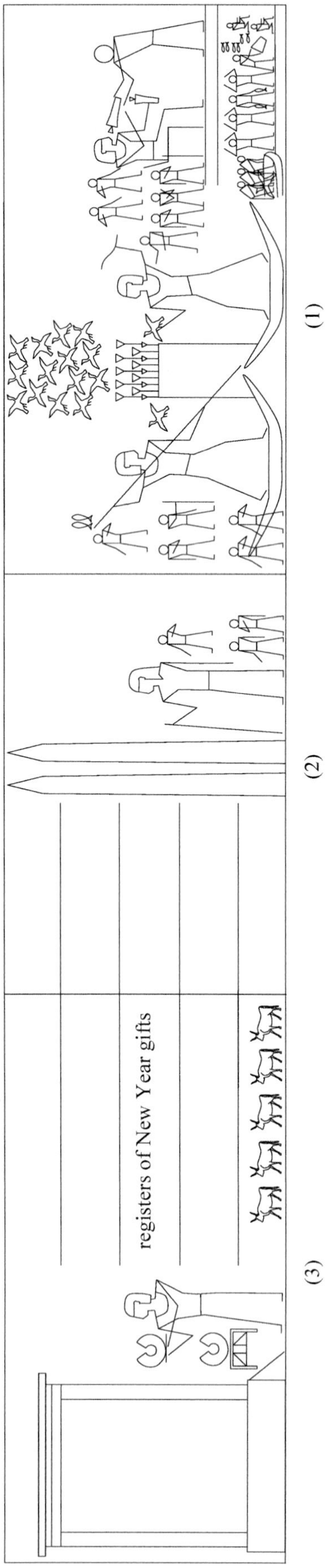

Figure 34. Sequence of the New Year scenes in the tomb of Amenhotep (TT 73 (1–3)).

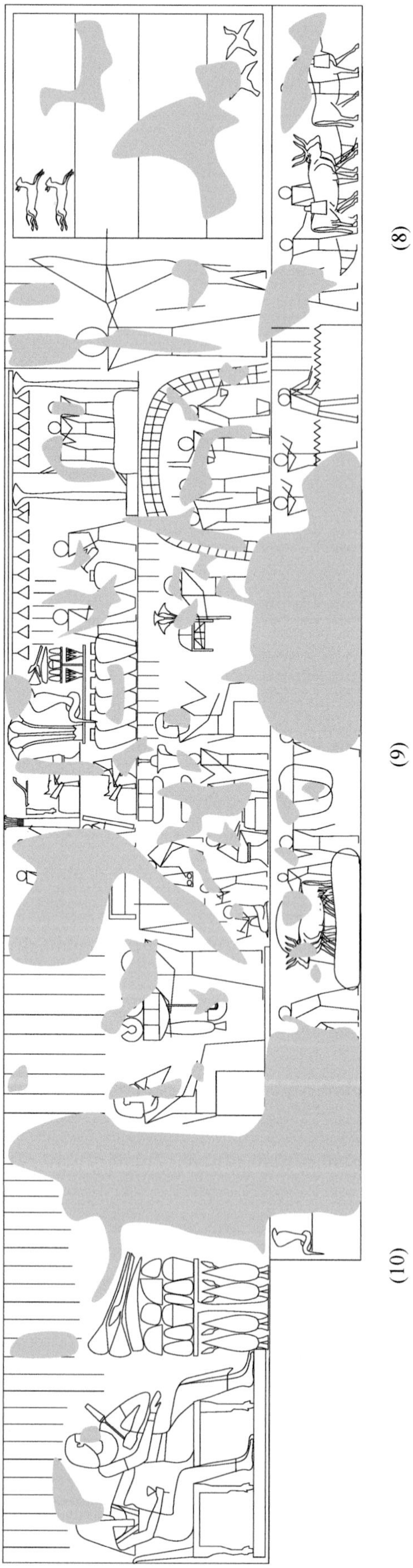

Figure 35. Scenes of annual taxation and the New Year in the tomb of Mentuiyuy (TT 172 (8–10)).

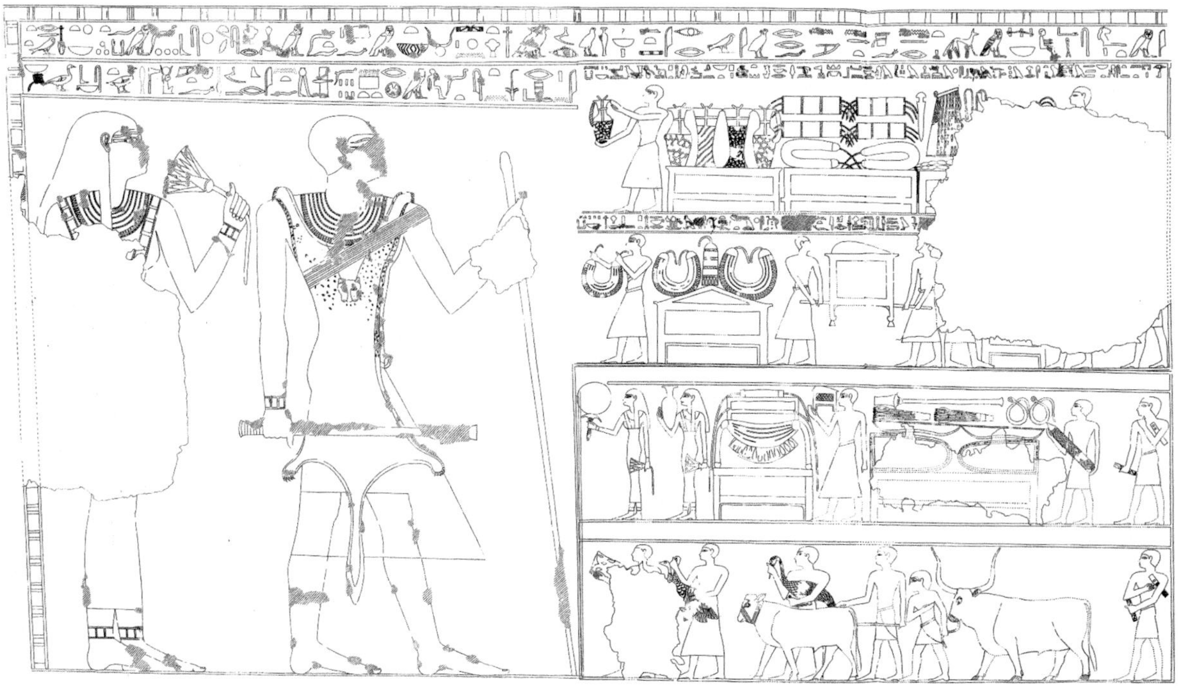

Figure 36. Tomb of Intefiqer (TT 60 (11)), after Davies and Gardiner 1920, pls 10 and 13–4.
The uppermost text describes Intefiqer as receiving the 'salutation on the day of the New (Year) Festival'.

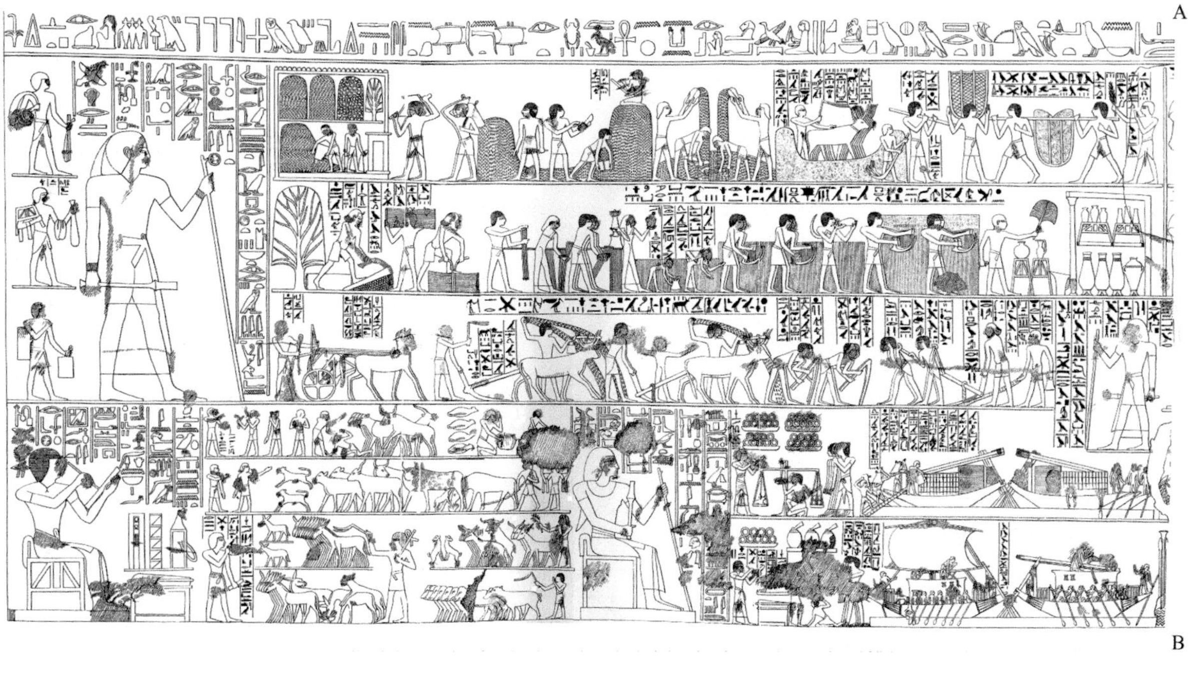

Figure 37a. West wall of the tomb of Paheri at el-Kab, left half (after Tylor and Griffith 1894, pls 3–5).

A

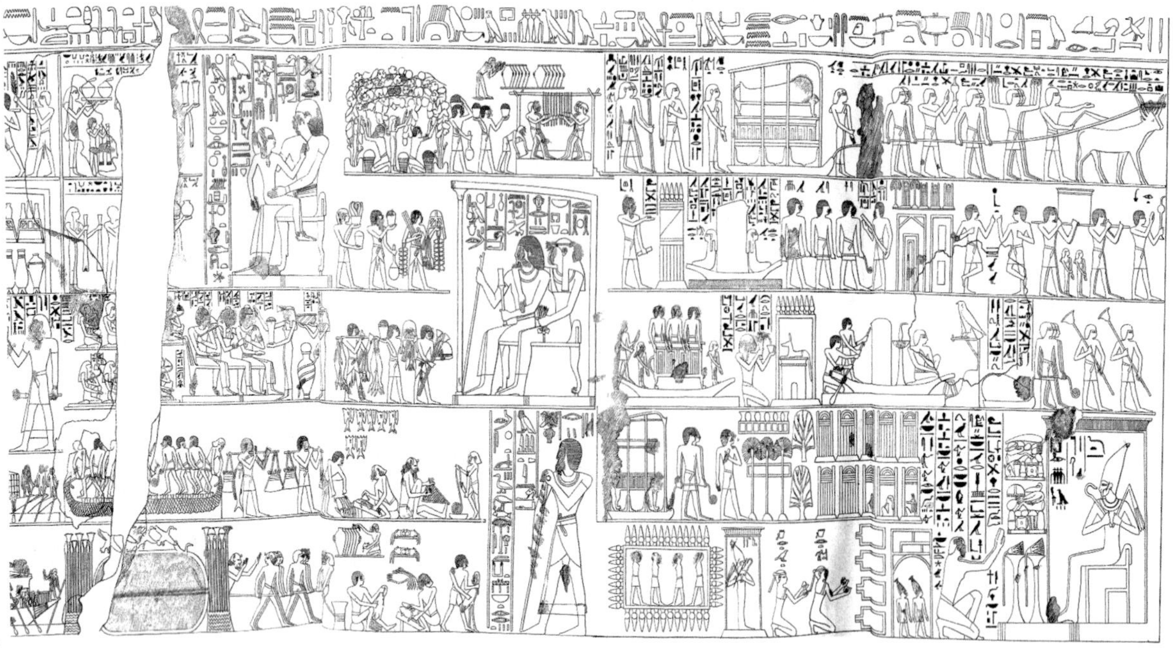

B

Figure 37b. West wall of the tomb of Paheri at el-Kab, right half (after Tylor and Griffith 1894, pls 3–5). On the upper left corner, Paheri is portrayed seated and holding Wadjmes, a son of Thutmose I, on his lap. The morning of 'Nehebkau', 'Ka-(her)-ka', and the 'New Year' is respectively referred to in the captions in front of him and above each of the two registers representing offering bringers.

dedicated to adorn a divine statue when it underwent ritual renewal, transforming from the dead to life through a process similar to embalming. Hence, the Book of Embalmment (P. Boulaq III, 3, 21–4, 2), dated to the Roman Period, records that the *ḥbs*-linen was to be distributed to the deceased when he returns to this world at the Opet Feast, the Decade Ritual, and possibly the Valley Feast.[349] Then comes the following passage:

> *ir=k mr=k m ẖnw n wꜣs.t di.tw=w n=k mnḫ.wt n nṯr.w nṯr.wt imy.w ip.t-s.wt šsp=k ḥbs nfr m ꜥ n ꞽImn-rꜥ ḫnty ip.t=f ḥnꜥ imy=f*
>
> You (the deceased) will do as you wish within Thebes. May one give you the cloths of the gods and goddesses who are at Karnak. May you receive the fine *ḥbs*-linen from the hand of Amun-Re, foremost of his Opet, together with what accompanies it.

Linen connected Amun of Karnak and the deceased through an agency, probably of a living family, a scenario parallel to the distribution of bouquets and sistra at the Valley Feast (3.6.5). Cloths were used to secure not only the renewal of the kingship but also that of the divine power on a mythological level. They were destined to adorn the main god of each temple and then delivered to the king and people, dead or alive.

[349] Sauneron 1952, 9–10 for transcription; Goyon 1972b, 52–3 for translation. Note that the Valley Feast may not be included here because the text only refers to Amenhotep, undoubtedly son of Hapu, and Imhotep, a sage of the New Kingdom and the Old Kingdom respectively, worshipped at the *in.t* (Deir el-Bahari).

Chapter 5

Conclusions

Each of the Festivals of Opet, the Valley, and the New Year had distinctive functions in many respects. First, on a seasonal level they marked Nile's inundation, recession, and the heliacal rising of Sothis respectively. Since the civil calendar was dislocated from the natural cycle by one day every four years, the association of these festivals with the seasonal markers was not always visible throughout the pharaonic time over three thousand years. The harmony of the calendar with the seasons had been maintained only in canonical traditions. However, at the beginning of the Nineteenth Dynasty, the civil calendar once again accorded with the natural cycle. Hence, the calendar could have been used within the minimal disharmony of about two months during the New Kingdom. The religious calendar was no loner notional but adequately reflected the movement of the sun and the Nile, which underpinned the mythological background of each celebration.

Second, each festival represented a specific geographical domain. The Theban festivals were, of course, celebrated in honour of the city god Amun in the first instance. This was particularly true for the Festivals of Opet and the Valley, which were exclusively Theban in nature. The loci of these celebrations were the temples of Luxor and Deir el-Bahari respectively. The temple of Luxor was considered the primordial site, origin of the life-giving power, which was embodied in its location at the south end of the residential area on the East Bank. This, of course, reflected the flow

	Opet Festival (section)	**Valley Festival** (section)	**New Year Festival** (section)
date	II Akhet 19 (2.2.2)	II Shemu (3.2.3)	I Akhet 1 (4.2.2)
duration	27 (at longest) (2.2.2)	2 (3.2.3)	9 (4.2.2)
season	Nile's inundation (2.2.2)	Nile's recession (3.2.3)	heliacal rise of Sothis (4.2.2)
locus	Luxor temple (2.4.8)	Deir el-Bahari (3.4.4)	north Karnak (4.3.5)
bearing	south (1.3.2)	west (1.3.2)	north (1.3.2)
mythology	Theban (2.3)	Osiride (3.3)	Heliopolitan (4.3.3)
deity	Amun-Re and Nun (2.4.6)	Osiris (3.4.4)	Re-Horakhety (4.5.11)
ideology	creation in primeval water (2.4.6)	resurrection from the dead (3.4.4)	renewal of the world (4.3.1)
function (royal)	renewal of the kingship (2.4.9)	ancestral cult (3.4.3)	dedication of supplies (4.5.12)
function (non-royal)	oracular session (2.5.1)	ancestral cult (3.6)	reception of supplies (4.6)
attendance	king in his first year (2.4.3)	————	high officials (4.4.1)
offering	special kind (such as meat) distributed to (limited?) people (2.5.4)	bouquet delivered to the dead (3.6.5)	yearly supply delivered to all (4.6)

of the Nile from the south. On the other hand, at the Valley Feast Amun travelled to the West Bank, where the necropolis stretched out at the foot of the barren mountains.The New Year celebration differed from the other two. Surviving evidence does not securely attest the god's journey outside of the temenos of Karnak but rather suggests that rituals took place mainly within the northern precinct of that temple. This may explain the location of an open-air solar court or stairway to the north of the sanctuary at many well-preserved Theban temples. It is not impossible that this specific orientation symbolized the relative location of Thebes against Heliopolis, which was the Egyptian centre of the solar cult. The Heliopolitan traits are manifest in reference to the Heliopolitan deities in textual evidence of the New Year celebrations. The beginning of the civil year was coupled with the renewal of the world through the first rising of Re-Horakhety and Sothis. This was desired to take place every year. By extension, the New Year was referred to as the 'beginning of the eternity'. The repetition of everlastingness naturally entailed the renewal of divine statues and temples. Such was theoretically possible only if the god remained in his original place. This may explain the reason why Amun appears not to have come out of Karnak at the New Year. On the same ground, the kingship was renewed at the same time. It had been an age-old tradition that rulers before the New Kingdom counted their regnal year from I Akhet 1, rather than after the predecessor died. Such notional ascension to the throne remained in the New Kingdom and was shared by the Khoiak Festival, when Horus's assumption of the crown from his father Osiris was performed. Mythical narratives underpinned the ritual performances. This is the third point to be stressed for my conclusions. For the Opet Festival the myth centred on Amun-Re, who retired from the temple of Karnak to gain the divine force generated by the primeval water Nun and Amenopet at the temple of Luxor. Amun's barge was likened to the *mskt.t*, night-barque of Re. On the contrary, his barge was referred to as the *mꜥnḏ.t*, day-barque of Re, at the Valley Feast. This was not accidental because sources elsewhere argue for Amun to be an embodiment of the solar power from the beginning of the latter celebration. He conveyed, rather than received, the divine force to the western gods and dead spirits, who were all ideologically identified with Osiris.

Finally, the divine force was displayed in different ways at these celebrations. This was most visible when it was delivered to people. The significance of the Opet Feast is evidenced by the fact that some Ramesside rulers visited Thebes in II Akhet and III Akhet in their first regnal year. It was through oracular sessions that divine messages were sent to people. Insofar as dated records are concerned, this divine performance took place only after Amun renewed himself at Luxor temple and hence his oracles could have been issued with full effect. The more petitions he had to handle, the more time he required. This probably explains the very long duration of this celebration, being 27 days in the time of Ramses III. It is not surprising that no oracular session is known to have taken place during the Valley Festival, which lasted two days only. The divine force was disseminated by means of physical objects instead at this mortuary celebration. This feast stands out in that the popular ancestral cult was geared to the royal counterpart. These two settings were connected by the delivery of Amun's offerings, which most commonly carried his force in the form of *ꜥnḫ* a 'bouquet', a word homonymous with 'life'. It is, however, difficult to define how extensive the delivery of divine offerings to the private tombs was. All the deceased were theoretically promised to witness Amun, who visited the West Bank. Whether royal, private, dead or alive, all beings converged on the ancestral cult and this functioned for Amun as a vehicle to distribute his power at once. The divine offerings were largely symbolic and appeared not to have met people's needs for maintaining their households. Such an economic function was certainly the case for the New Year celebration, when the annual revenue was collected and approved. The king's role on this occasion was twofold. He was administratively responsible for collecting taxes and then dedicating part of them to temples for the sake of gods. Ideologically, gods were regarded as the ones who promised wealth for Egypt as well as the kingship. Hence, the dedication of supplies to the temples by the king was followed and preceded by gods' promise. On the other hand, towards the end of the New Year celebration, the king probably played a receiver of the divine offerings. This comes as no surprise because the god was also a recipient of offerings as well as a distributer. This proves to be true on the part of people. They received specific kinds of valuable supply, such as linen and meat, which could not have been available to them on a frequent basis. The New Year was most likely to have been one of rare occasions when such materials were delivered. The extent of this fiscal function is again impossible to conclude. However, it is noteworthy that the New Year followed the actual harvesting during the New Kingdom. Be that as it may, the precious offerings of the New Year ideologically originated from the god and regarded as an epitome of all that would be supplied within the year. This was particularly evident in later periods, when amuletic objects began to be made in association with the beginning of the year, such as the New Year bottles, which was widely attested in the Twenty-Sixth Dynasty. Such was probably one of practices that could have been dated back to earlier times.

Appendices

Appendix 1

List of dated religious events

The following list of dated texts is arranged in calendrical order. The events included here are mainly associated with New Kingdom religious ceremonies. Some important events from other periods are also indicated for the various purposes of future studies on extended subjects. For example, the calendar of Esna temple (Sauneron 1963, vol. 1, 122–9) and the geographical list of Edfu temple (Chassinat 1897, vol. 1, 329–44) are fully covered because the former seems to be partially archaic in content and the latter gives a good insight into local religious celebrations in each nome, including the Theban area, a focus of this study. Also included are a series of the Middle Kingdom papyri found in Lahun, which may allow us to seek the possible origins of some feasts (Luft 1992).

As one of the primal New Kingdom sources, the calendar of the temple of Medinet Habu (hereafter MHC), published by the Epigraphic Survey in 1934 (*MH* III), is the backbone of this list. It records for each festival celebrated at this temple the total number of consumed offerings (*ḥtp-nṯr*), which is given in parentheses to give the sense of the relative scale of each celebration and listed below on this page for readers' convenience (also see Haring 1997, 399–404 for a table of offerings measured by grain sack).

Month names are given as the earlier Egyptian/later Egyptian (theophoric names)/Coptic, and decade names are given at the beginning of each ten days (based on Neugebauer and Parker 1960, pls. 26–9). King's name, regnal year, and the provenance of source are indicated in square brackets, if available (king's name in *italic* when securely attested). Events are written in capital letters when translated from the original texts. The names of private individuals appear in transliteration to avoid possible confusion, except well-known historcial figures, whose names are usually referred to in conventional forms. The original location of evidence, particularly temple reliefs and private tombs, is referred to based on PM.

Civil-based festivals recorded in the Medinet Habu calendar

1. I Akhet 1: Coming-Forth of Sothis (112)
2. I Akhet 17: Eve of the Wag Festival (285)
3. I Akhet 18: Wag Festival (295)
4. I Akhet 19: Thoth Festival (160)
5. I Akhet 22: Great Going-Forth of Osiris (292)
6. I Akhet 28: Festival of the Victory over the Meshwesh (1616)
7. II Akhet 18: Eve of the Opet Festival (295)
8. II Akhet 19–III Akhet 12: Opet Festival (11,341)
9. III Akhet 17: Amun Festival after the Opet Festival (296)
10. IV Akhet 1: Hathor Festival (640)
11. IV Akhet 20–30: Sokar Festival (7003)
12. I Peret 1: *Nḥb-k3.w* Festival (4531+)
13. I Peret 6: Amun Festival of Writing the King's Name on the *išd*-Tree in the temple of Ptah (640)
14. I Peret 22: Festival of the Two Goddesses (1034)
15. II Peret 1: Festival of the procession of Anubis (140+)
16. II Peret 29–III Peret 1: Festival of Lifting-Up the Sky (1150)
17. III Peret 29–IV Peret 1: Festival of Entering the Sky (unknown)
18. IV Peret 1: Sokar(?) Festival (122)
19. IV Peret 4: Festival of Chewing Onions for Bastet (320)
20. I Shemu 1: Renenutet Festival (293)
21. I Shemu 10: Festival of Clothing Anubis (122)
22. I Shemu 11: Going-Forth of Min to the Stairs (299)
23. I Shemu 26: Accession of Ramses III (4860+)
24. II Shemu: Valley Festival (1150)
25. III Shemu 16: Victory Festival (1056)

1st MONTH of *3ḫ.t* (*ṯḫy*/*ḏḥwty*/Thoth); 1st decade (*ṯm3t ḥrt*) I Akhet

No.) Day: Event

1) 1: Festival Offering of the New Year [MK, 2, Lahun][1]
2) 1: New Year Festival and *ihhy* [Amenemhat III, 35, Lahun][2]
3) 1: Hatshepsut's coronation(?) and the Festival of the (*s*)*šd*-headband at the New Year [*Hatshepsut*, DB][3]
4) 1: Installation of the vizier *Wsr-imn* [*T III*, 8, TT 131 (8)][4]
5) 1: New Year Festival, Beginning of Eternity [*T III*, year after 23, Akh-menu][5]
6) 1–3: Amun Festival at Thebes [*T III*, Elephantine][6]
7) 1–3: Khnum Festival at Elephantine [*T III*, Elephantine][7]
8) 1: New Year Festival [*T III*, Buto][8]
9) 1: King renewed the 'Great Stairs' for Amun-Re and Sokar [*Horemheb*, 6, memorial temple of A III][9]
10) (1): Coming-Forth of Sothis [*Seti I*, Abydos][10]
11) 1: Oath taken by the workman *P3-nb* [*R II*, 66][11]
12) 1: Coming-Forth of Sothis (112) [*R III*, MHC][12]
13) 1–4: Workmen at DeM were off duty [R III, QV][13]
14) 1: Unknown royal [butler] visited Deir el-Medina [R IV, 1, DeM][14]
15) 1: Birth of Re-Horakhety [R IX, 13][15]
16) [1]: Birth of Re-Horakhety, when a delivery from the vizier to the workmen took place [R IX, 16][16]
17) 1: Second New Year [Ramesside][17]
18) 1: Birth of Re-Horakhety [Ramesside][18]
19) 1: Oracle of Amun-Re concerning the lady *Ḥnw.t-t3.wy* and the appointment? (*sṯ3 r*) of Pinedjem II as HPA [Amenemopet, 5, Karnak][19]
20) 1: Devotion of a temple to Amun-of-Kawa and a royal decree [*Taharqa*, 10, Kawa][20]
21) 1: Piankhi celebrated the New Year to cause Amun to appear at Napata [*Piankhi*, 21?, Gebel Barkal][21]
22) 1?: Amun Festival at Kawa [Aryamani: 3rd cent. BC, 23?, Kawa][22]
23) (1): First Festival of Atum [*Ptolemy II*, 16, Pithom][23]
24) 1: Festival in the 7th Lower Egyptian nome [*Ptolemy IV*, Edfu][24]

---

1 P. Berlin 10007, recto (Luft 1992, 45).
2 P. UC 32191 (Luft 1992, 138–40; Collier and Quirke 2006, 92–5).
3 North side of the middle colonnade at DB (PM II^2, 348 (19–20); *Urk.* IV, 261: 8–9, 262: 7–8; Naville 1895, vol. 3, pls. 62–3).
4 *hrw pn sṯ3 sš ḫtm nṯr Wsr-imn n pr 'Imn m-b3h ḥm=f ꜥ.w.s.* 'this day of bringing the scribe of the god's seal Useramen to the temple of Amun before his person l.p.h.' (P. Turin 1878: Dziobek 1998, 98). This papyrus is a Ramesside (or later) copy of an original text. Useramen was probably appointed the co-vizier with his father *ꜥ3-mṯw*. The year in question appears to be 8 in the original document (Pleyte and Rossi 1869, vol. 1, pl. 1) but altered to year 5 in *Urk.* IV, 1384: 3.
5 *wpy*[*-rnp.t*] *ḥ3.t nḥḥ* (PM II^2, 126 (462); Gardiner 1952, 21).
6 Stone block (*Urk.* IV, 824: 9; Bommas 2000, 468).
7 Stone block (*Urk.* IV, 823: 13; Bommas 2000, 493).
8 Buto Stela 209 (Bedier 1994a, 4, z. 15; Bedier 1994b for better facsimiles and a photograph; Klug 2002, 96–105, Abb. 10 for transliteration, translation, and a photograph of the side face). The largest offerings were dedicated on this day.
9 *rd.w ꜥ3* the 'Great Stairs' (stela location unknown: Haeny 1981). In the base inscription of Hatshepsut's obelisk, Karnak is likened to *ḳ3y šps n sp spy* the 'august hill of the first time' in a New Year context (*Urk.* IV, 364: 3).
10 Ceiling of the cenotaph, west side (PM VI, 30; Frankfort 1933, vol. 1, 72, vol. 2, pl. 81).
11 O. Cairo 25237, verso (*KRI* III, 530: 5).
12 *pr spd.t* (*MH* III, pl. 152, list 23).
13 O. Turin 57032 (*KRI* V, 620 : 7).
14 O. DeM 40+O. Strasbourg H 42 (*KRI* VII, 330: 1–2).
15 P. Turin 1999+2009, verso (Gardiner 1906a, 139; *KRI* VI, 564: 8). *p3 šm Ḥr* 'the Proceeding of Horus' associated with the New Year is attested in O. BM 29560 (Černý and Gardiner 1957, pl. 85 for transcription and facsimile; Erman 1901, 128 for examination) and P. DeM 2 (*KRI* VI, 260: 8). A bed was delivered to the vizier on this day, which Jauhiainen (2009, 79) relates to a New Year gift. Belmonte Avilés (2009, 108) asserts that in the time of Mentuhotep II, who had just unifieid Egypt, the winter solstice took place on I Akhet 1 (2004 BC) and that this explains the association of the east-west axis of Karnak with the winter solstice.
16 P. Turin 1884+2067+2071+2105, recto (*KRI* VI, 644: 14–5).
17 *wpy-rnp.t 2-nw* (P. Cairo 86637, recto, I, 2: Leitz 1994a, 428). In a similar fashion, the second Sokar Festival is attested in the tomb of Khnumhotep III at Beni Hassan (PM IV, 147 (13); Newberrry 1893, pl. 33).
18 P. Cairo 86637, recto, III, 3 (Bakir 1966, 11; Leitz 1994a, 13). *wꜥb m-ḫt t3 ḏr=f m mw n ḥ3.t ḥꜥp* 'purification of the entire land with the water of the beginning of inundation'.
19 North face of 10th pylon (PM II^2, 187 (580); Gardiner 1962, 58; Winand 2003, 641; Jansen-Winkeln 2007, vol. 1, 177). Cf. III Shemu 19 for Amun's another oracle concerning this lady.
20 Stela (Eide, Hägg, and Pierce 1994, vol. 1, 177). The decree concerns cedar trees from Lebanon to erect flag-staves at this temple.
21 Stela Cairo 48862 (*Urk.* III, 14: 11; Grimal 1981a, 15*; Jansen-Winkeln 2007, vol. 2, 341). Piankhi requested Amun's decree to send him to celebrate the Opet Feast on the way to his war campaign in the north.
22 Fragments of Stela BM 1777 (Eide, Hägg, and Pierce 1994, vol. 2, 530).
23 *ḥb tpy n it=f Itm* (Stela Cairo 22183: *Urk.* II, 95: 2 and 104: 6; Müller 2006, 195 and 199 for translation). The king and queen went on a tour in the country (*pḫr t3-mri*) and arrived in the Eastern Harpoon nome, where they offered annual offeings (*ḥtr n tp rnp.t*).
24 Geographical list on the exterior of the sanctuary (PM VI, 146 (219–20)).

I Akhet

25) 1–5: Festival when a garland was placed on their (Egyptian temples' or gods'?) heads [*Ptolemy V*, Rosetta][25]
26) 1–4: Opening of the Year and offerings to Re [*Ptolemy VI*, Kom Ombo][26]
27) 1: Festival of Horsematauy and His Beautiful Festival of the Birth of Re [*Ptolemy* X, Edfu][27]
28) 1: Festival of Re at the Opening of the Year and the Festival of All Gods at the 8th hour [Ptolemy XII, Dendera][28]
29) 1: Festival of the Cloth [Ptolemy XIII, Dendera][29]
30) 1: New Year Festival and *Nḥb-kꜣ.w* Festival of Khnum with his Ennead [Roman, Esna][30]
31) 1: Heliacal rising of Sothis [Antoninus Pius: AD 139][31]
32) 2: Dated docket of a copy recording thieves in the Necropolis [*R XI*, 19 (w1), Thebes?][32]
33) 2: Ennead comes to Re to see his young figure and defeats Apophis [Ramesside][33]
34) 2: Ihy Festival and His Beautiful Festival of Receiving the *imy.t-pr*-Document [Dendera][34]
35) 2: Day of Drinking (*swr*) and the Appearance (*ḫꜥ*) of Djeme [Ptolemy IX, 8?, MH][35]
36) 3: Dated letter concerning an unknown subject [Pepi II, temple of Neferirkare at Abusir][36]
37) 3: Oath-taking when the qenbet is urged to act according to the Laws of Truth [*R II*, 38][37]
38) 3: Last day of a holiday period(?) of the workmen of DeM, making 11 days [R IV, KV][38]
39) 3: Officials visited western Thebes [*R V*, 2, QV][39]
40) 3: Personal festival? [NK, Qurnet Murai][40]
41) 3: Royal scribe *Bw-th-imn* & HPA Pinedjem I visited western Thebes [Smendes I, 10, western Thebes][41]
42) 3: King and queen went on a tour in the country and arrived in the Eastern Harpoon nome [*Ptolemy II*, 12, Pithom][42]
43) 4: Thoth Festival [Roman, Esna][43]
44) 4+: Festival in the 18th Upper Egyptian nome [*Ptolemy IV*, Edfu][44]
45) 4 or 5: Appearance of Amun-Re & the promotion of *Mn-ḫpr-rꜥ* to HPA at Thebes [Pinedjem I/Smendes I, 25, Karnak][45]
46) 5: A woman appealed over a female servant before witnesses [*A III*, 33, Lahun][46]
47) 5: Unnamed vizier visited the Enclosure to take men to the riverbank [R III, 28, DeM][47]
48) 5: Ritual of Ptah-Sokar? [Bocchoris, 6, Serapeum][48]
49) 6: Visit(?) of an unnamed vizier [DeM][49]
50) 7: Taking the River [Ramesside, DeM][50]
51) 7: Initiation (*sḫn*) of a Buchis bull at Armant [*Ptolemy V*, 24, Armant][51]

[25] Decree of Memphis recorded on the Rosetta Stone (*Urk.* II, 195: 8; Spiegelberg 1922, 62; Quirke and Andrews 1988, 22 for transliteration and translation).
[26] *wdn iḫ.wt nb nfr r wdn n pꜣ Rꜥ m-bꜣḫ=f* (Grimm 1994a, 20–1 and 157–8). *šsp iḫ.wt* is referred to in TT 49 (1) as taking place during the 'night of the evening meal' (PM I-1², 91 (1); Davies 1933a, vol. 1, 49, l. 20).
[27] *ḥb Ḥr-smꜣ-tꜣ.wy nb kꜣdy ḥb=f nfr n msy.t Rꜥ* (Grimm 1994a, 20–1, 182–3).
[28] *hrw ḥb Rꜥ m wpy-rnp.t ḥb nṯr.w nb nṯr.wt nb* (inner hypostyle hall: Grimm 1994a, 20–1 and 225).
[29] *ḥb mnḫ.t* (western crypt: *Dendara* VI, 158: 2; Alliot 1949, 239; Grimm 1994a, 22–3 and 236).
[30] *ḥb wpy-rnp.t nfr nfr ḥb nḥb-kꜣ.w ḫnm ḥnꜥ psdt=f* (Sauneron 1963, vol. 1, 123; Grimm 1994a, 22–3 and 239–40).
[31] Censorinus 21: 10 (Meyer 1904, 23).
[32] P. Abbott (BM 10221): *KRI* VI, 764: 3; Peet 1930b, 131. II Akhet 24 is also recorded. The text concerns a tomb robbery dating from year 16 of Ramses IX (*KRI* VI, 468–81).
[33] O. Cairo 86637 (Leitz 1994a, 14).
[34] *ḥb=f nfr n šsp imy.t-pr* (*Dendara* V, 153: 5 and VI, 92: 1; Waitkus 1997: 151; Cauville 2002, 19–21). The *imy.t-pr* document was not only a secular legal document but also related to divine decrees. For general discussion on this document, see van den Boorn 1988, 180–1 and Logan 2000.
[35] P. Berlin 3115 (de Cenival 1972, 104; Pestman 1993, 199 for translation).
[36] P. Berlin 15729, recto (Posener-Kriéger and de Cenival 1968, 52, pl. 103, B for facsimile and transcription; Posener-Kriéger 1976, vol. 2, 428 for translation).
[37] *imy ir.tw tꜣ ḳnb.t m pꜣ ḫr* 'Let the qenbet be held in the Necropolis' (O. Michaelides 47: *KRI* III, 514: 14; Goedicke and Wente 1962, pl. 50; Allam 1973, 212).
[38] O. Cairo 25533 (*KRI* VI, 177: 4–5).
[39] Graffito 1252 (*KRI* VI, 246: 11; Černý 1956: 14, pl. 35). See O. Cairo 25788 (*KRI* IV, 159: 3) for high officials(?) who visited western Thebes in this month.
[40] O. DeM 739 (Grandet 2000a, 34–5, 141; Jauhiainen 2009, 242).
[41] Graffito 1001 (Spiegelberg 1921, 83, no. 1001; Jansen-Winkeln 2007, vol. 1, 37).
[42] *pḥr tꜣ-mri* (Stela Cairo 22183: *Urk.* II, 94: 5; Müller 2006, 195 for translation).
[43] Sauneron 1963, vol. 1, 124; Grimm 1994a, 24–5, 240.
[44] Geographical list on the exterior of the sanctuary (PM VI, 147 (223–4)).
[45] Banishment Stela (=Louvre C 256: von Beckerath 1968, 9; Jansen-Winkeln 2007, vol. 1, 72).
[46] P. Gurob II, 1 (Gardiner 1906b, 36).
[47] O. DeM 427 (*KRI* V, 523: 9).
[48] Stela Louvre SN 22 (Jansen-Winkeln 2007, vol. 2, 378–9).
[49] O. DeM 1190 (Posener 1938, vol. 2, 23, pl. 37). The vizier also bears the titles of 'fan-bearer on the right hand of the king' and 'royal [scribe]'.
[50] P. Cairo 86637 (Leitz 1994a, 18).
[51] Bucheum stela no. 7 (Mond and Myers 1934, vol. 2, 4–5, vol. 3, pl. 40; Goldbrunner 2004, pl. 4).

52) 8: Oath-taking before witnesses [*A III*, 33, Lahun][52]
53) 8: The workmen of DeM received royal favours (*ḥs.w*) [*R IX*, 7][53]
54) 8: Festival in the 10th Lower Egyptian nome [*Ptolemy IV*, Edfu][54]
55) 9: Offering of Anubis [MK, 10, Lahun][55]
56) 9: *iḥhy*(?) [MK , 24, Lahun][56]
57) 9: A festival [*T III*, Akh-menu at Karnak][57]
58) 9: Scribe *Ḥri* arrived at the Enclosure of the Necropolis [*R IV*, 6, KV][58]
59) 9–10: Vizier *Nfr-rnp.t* (with royal butler *Stẖ-ḥr-wnmj=f*) arrived at Thebes (*niw.t*) on day 9 and visited the Enclosure of the Necropolis on day 10 [*R IV*, 6, W. Thebes][59]
60) 9: Reference to Re [Ramesside, DeM][60]
61) 9: A festival(?) performed by Osorkon (III) [*Takelot II*, 12, Karnak][61]
62) 9: Festivals of Amun-Re and of Re as the New Year Festival [Roman, Esna][62]
63) 9: Festival in the 17th Lower Egyptian nome [*Ptolemy IV*, Edfu][63]
64) 10: Investigation concerning a man's death/burial [R VI or VII, 4, DeM or MH?][64]
65) 10: Counting of properties by *ꜥꜣ-nḫt* and the scribe of the treasury *Pꜣ-bꜣ-sꜣ*, concerning a coffin and copper [R VI or VII, 7, DeM or MH?][65]
66) 10: Hereditary claim by a priest and his wife [*R XI*, 18, near Herakleopolis Magna][66]
67) 10: Tefnut Festival [Roman, Esna][67]

1st MONTH of *ꜣḫ.t* (*tḫy*/*ḏḥwty*/Thoth); 2nd decade (*tmꜣt ḫrt*)

No.) Day: Event
68) 12: Vizier *Nfr-rnp.t* visited western Thebes with the royal butler *Stẖ-ḥr-wnmj=f* [*R IV*, 6, KV][68]
69) 13: Unknown seasonal festival [*T III*, Akh-menu at Karnak][69]
70) 13: *Ỉhhy* of the Front of the Year [Amenhotep I, Karnak][70]
71) 13–6: Visit of officials for a festival on the 15th day [*R V*, 2, W. Thebes][71]
72) 13: The wab-priest *Mniw-nfr* visited KV 38 to open it for reburial [Ramesside, near KV 38][72]
73) 13: *Ỉhhy* of the Front of the Year [Ptolemaic-Roman, Edfu][73]
74) 14–5: Personal festival? [*R II*, 40][74]
75) 14–7: Offerings to the gods at the small temple of Medinet Habu on the first day [Ptolemy XII, 5, MH][75]
76) 15: Report of *Ỉ-m-iꜥt-ib* concerning well-maintained administration [MK, Lahun][76]

---

[52] P. Gurob II 1 (Murnane and Meltzer 1995, 45).
[53] P. Turin 1881+2080+2092 (*KRI* VI, 613: 3; Janssen 1994, 94, n. 22). The favours comprised copper, the *ḥbs*-linen, the *nḥḥ*-oil, etc.
[54] Geographical list on the exterior of the sanctuary (PM VI, 146 (219–20)).
[55] P. Cairo 58066, recto (Luft 1992, 136).
[56] P. Berlin 10052, verso. Luft (1992, 67) and Grimm (1994, 73) regard the missing event as *iḥhy*, a restoration rejected by Krauss (1994, 89–90).
[57] South wall of the Akh-menu (PM II², 126 (462); *Urk.* IV, 1272: 8; Gardiner 1952, pl. 8).
[58] O. Cairo 25273 (*KRI* VI, 145: 8).
[59] Graffito 790 (*KRI* VI, 145: 3–6). He seems to have stayed there, at least, until I Akhet 12.
[60] P. Cairo 86637 (Leitz 1994a, 20). Goyon (1972a, 42–3) posits that the New Year celebrations continued up to this day on account of this text, which however cannot be well corroborated.
[61] Bubastite Gate (*RIK* III, pl. 21, l. 1; Caminos 1958, 76; Jansen-Winkeln 2007, vol. 2, 187). Cf. Spalinger 2011, 734.
[62] *ḥb Ỉmn-rꜥ ḥb Rꜥ m wpy-rnp.t* (Sauneron 1963, vol. 1, 124; Grimm 1994a, 25–6, 241). Spalinger (1992, 51–6) rejects a link to the heliacal rising of Sothis, an assumption proposed by Parker (1950 , 49), but relates to, what he believes, a historical fact that the introduction of the civil calendar took place on the 9th day of the lunar year in 2768 BC (Spalinger 2011, 727). Depuydt (2003, 60–1) dates this calendar to the reign of Marcus Aurelius, more specifically to AD 170s, as Parker (1950, 49) said, and associates with the heliacal rising of Sothis.
[63] Geographical list on the exterior of the sanctuary (PM VI, 146 (219–20)).
[64] *smtr n=f* (P. Turin 1907+1908: *KRI* VI, 405: 2).
[65] *ir.t* [*ḫ*]*sb.w n iḫ.wt* (P. Turin 1907+1908: *KRI* VI, 408: 12; Peet 1925a, 74; Janssen 1966, pl. 19).
[66] P. Ashmolean 1945.96 (Gardiner 1940, 24; *KRI* VI, 736: 9). See III Shemu 20 for the same case.
[67] Sauneron 1963, vol. 1, 124; Grimm 1994a, 26–7, 241–2.
[68] O. Cairo 25274 (*KRI* VI, 145: 12). For other dates recorded for this particular visit, see I Akhet 9–10 and I Peret 19.
[69] South wall of the Akh-menu (PM II², 126 (462); *Urk.* IV, 1272: 9; Gardiner 1952, pl. 8).
[70] *iḥhy n ḥꜣ.t-rnp.t* (unnumbered stone fragment: Spalinger 1992, 22, pl. IV; Grimm 1994b, fig. 2 for better facsimile). Grimm proposes that this event came to be fixed to the civil calendar since the time of Amenhotep I because the same date is attested from Edfu, and that this date modeled on a Middle Kingdom tradition.
[71] Graffito 1696 (*KRI* VI, 246: 13).
[72] Graffito 2061 (Peden 2001, 242).
[73] *hrw tpy n* [*ḥb*] *ihy ḥr ḥꜣ.t-rnp.t* (*Edfou* V, 349: 1; Alliot 1949, vol. 2, 220; Grimm 1994a, 28–9, 180).
[74] O. BM 5634, verso, 10 (*KRI* III, 522: 7–8). The workmen *Ḥnsw* was absent for his festival (*ḥb=f*). Also on recto, 2 (*KRI* III, 517: 1–2) and verso, 18 (*KRI* III, 525, 3–4), a drinking (*swr*) is recorded for I Akhet 14.
[75] Graffito MH no. 44 located at the small temple of Medinet Habu (Thissen 1989, 18–29). This was followed by supplying food to priests.
[76] P. UC 32198, verso (Collier and Quirke 2002, 95).

I Akhet

77) 15: Nubian campaign(?) involving Akuyata [*A III*, Amada][77]
78) 15: Offerings to Amun-Re and Hapi
[*R II*, 1, Gebel el-Silsila], [*Merenptah*, 1, Gebel el-Silsila], [*R III*, 6, Gebel el-Silsila][78]
79) 15: Unnamed royal butler mustered the workmen at the Enclosure of the Necropolis [R IV, 6][79]
80) 15: Buchis bull entered Armant [Ptolemy II, 26, MH][80]
81) 15: Initiation (*sẖn*) of a Buchis bull at Armant [*Ptolemy III*, 25, Armant][81]
82) 15: Festival of Tithoes (*Twtw*), son of Neith [Roman, Esna][82]
83) 16: King received a report on a rebellion in Nubia [*A IV*, Amada][83]
84) 16: Oath taken by a water carrier [R IV, 4 DeM][84]
85) 16: Visit of an unnamed royal butler [6, KV][85]
86) 17: Night of the Wag Festival [Senusret I, Asyut][86]
87) 17 or 18: A festival [*T III*, Akh-menu at Karnak][87]
88) 17: Wag Festival [*Horemheb*, TT 50][88]
89) 17 or 18: Ritual during the night on the jouney to Abydos [*Horemheb*, TT 50][89]
90) 17: Laudation of the Wag Festival (285) [*R III*, MHC][90]
91) 17: Foundation of the tomb of a royal child [R III, 28, DB][91]
92) 17: Sailing to Abydos [R III–IV, TT 359][92]
93) 17: The *nbḥ*-plant appears from Osiris, being given by Thoth [Ptolemaic][93]
94) 18: Dated administrative papyrus [OK, Temple of Reneferef at Abusir][94]
95) 18: Dated account papyrus [Djedkare-Isesi, year after the 14th census, Reneferef's temple at Abusir][95]
96) 18: Wag Festival [Senusret I, Asyut][96]
97) [1]8: Wag Festival with *i͗hhy* [MK, Lahun][97]
98) 18: Moistening Barley [*Horemheb*, TT 50][98]
99) 18: Wag Festival (295) [*R III*, MHC][99]
100) [18]: Filling of the Udjat-eye and the sixth day lunar festival [*Ptolemy* X, Edfu][100]
101) 19: Assessor of the cattle of Amun-Re's domain *Sꜣ-mw.t* donated his properties to Mut [*R II*, TT 409][101]
102) 19: Thoth Festival (160) [*R III*, MHC][102]
103) 19: Coming-Out-of-Thoth in the Necropolis [Ramesside][103]

---

77 Stela Cairo 41806 (*Urk.* IV, 1963: 4).
78 Rock inscriptions (*LD* III, pls. 175, a: 9, 200, d: 9, and 218, d: 15; *KRI* I, 90: 14–6). Is this a celebration for the high rising of the Nile? This was called the day of *ẖꜣ mḏꜣ.t ḥꜥpi* the 'Throwing the Book of Hapi' (*KRI* I, 91: 4–6), which is described in P. Harris I (XXXVIIb, 1; LIVa, 2; and LXVII, 2) as a list of numerous offerings dedicated at Kheraha (272 in number) and at Memphis (Breasted 1906, vol. 4, 156, n. e). See III Shemu 15 for rituals parallel to these.
79 O. Berlin 9906 (unpublished). The royal butler was probably *Stẖ-ḥr-wnmj=f.*
80 Graffito MH no. 220 (PM II^2, 506 (127); Thissen 1989, 129 (no. 220); Edgerton 1937b, pl. 54). *pꜣ hrw šm i͗.i͗r bẖ r i͗wnw-Mnṯ* 'day on which a Buchis bull went to Armant'.
81 Bucheum stela no. 6 (Mond and Myers 1934, vol. 2, 4, vol. 3, pl. 39; Goldbrunner 2004, pl. 3).
82 Sauneron 1963, vol. 1, 124; Grimm 1994a, 28–9 and 242.
83 Stela JE 41806 (*Urk.* IV, 1963: 4; Murnane and Meltzer 1995, 102).
84 *ꜥnẖ n nb* (O. DeM 412; *KRI* VI, 136: 12–3).
85 O. Cairo 49557 (unpublished).
86 Tomb of *Ḥp-ḏf* (Griffith 1889, pl. 8, cols. 306, 307, and 320).
87 South wall of the Akh-menu (PM II^2, 126 (462); *Urk.* IV, 1272: 10; Gardiner 1952, pl. 8).
88 'Striking the ships of Osiris' took place (PM I-1^2, 96 (9–10, I); Hari 1985, 43, pl. 29, l. 36).
89 *nhsi i͗n ẖry-ḥb m gs n grḥ rdi.t nꜣ n ꜥḥꜥ.w r šmꜥ=f mw.t fꜣi ḥtpy.t=sn* 'Evocation by the lector-priest at the night. Placing the boats to its south of the mother. Elevating their *ḥtpy.t*-linen' (PM I-1^2, 96 (9–10); Hari 1985, 44, pl. 31, col. 69). The original text states day 9, perhaps an error.
90 *hrw ꜣꜥꜥ n wꜣg* (*MH* III, pl. 152, list 24). Leeuwenburg (1940, 334) provisionally translates *ꜣꜥꜥ* as 'vooravodfeest'.
91 O. Berlin 10663 (*KRI* V, 558: 16).
92 *rꜣ n md.t n ẖd r ꜣbḏw hrw sb.t ḳrf.t m tpy ꜣḫ.t sw 17* 'invocation of going downstream to Abydos, the day of sailing on I Akhet 17' (PM I-1^2, 422 (6–7); Saleh 1984, 93).
93 P. Salt 825, XV, 5–8 (Derchain 1965, 143). The 9th hour of the day is documented. The same entry is recorded for II Akhet 24.
94 Abusir X, 241, pl. 26.
95 Abusir X, 290, pl. 66.
96 Tomb of *Ḥp-ḏf* (Griffith 1889, pl. 7, ll. 283 and 290).
97 *[i͗]hhy [wꜣ]gi͗* (P. Berlin 10282, recto, 3: Luft 1986, 77, n. 31; Luft 1992, 116; Spalinger 1992, 25). Luft (1986) demonstrates that this festival was celebrated after the civil New Year's Day in relation to the heliacal rising of Sothis.
98 *i͗wḥ bšꜣ* (Bénédite 1893, 519, fig. M; Hari 1985, 46, pl. 33).
99 *ḥb n wꜣg* (*MH* III, pl. 154, list 25). This festival was fixed to this day from MK onwards (Krauss 1985, 86–94), and as a lunar-based event it was, according to Luft (1994, 41), also held on the 18th day of the second lunar month after the heliacal rising of Sothis during the Middle Kingdom.
100 Grimm 1994a, 28–9, 181.
101 PM I-1^2, 462 (4–6); Wilson 1970, 192; Vernus 1978, 133; Frood 2007, 89 for translation.
102 *ḥb Ḏḥwty* (*MH* III, pl. 154, list 26). Parker (1950, 36) suggested that it took place in the lunar intercalary month every 2 or 3 years.
103 *pr i͗[n Ḏḥwty m] ẖr.t-nṯr* (P. Cairo 86637, recto, V, 12: Leitz 1994a, 32).

104) 19: Thoth Festival [*Ptolemy VI* , Kom Ombo][104]
105) 19: Festival in the 15th Upper Egyptian nome [*Ptolemy IV*, Edfu][105]
106) 19: Day of Drinking (*swr*) [Ptolemy IX, 8?, MH][106]
107) 19?: Consecration of Dendera temple [*Augustus*, 1, Dendera][107]
108) 19: Dated graffito [Ptolemy II, 20, MH][108]
109) 19: Thoth Festival in the entire land [Roman, Esna][109]
110) 19: Festival of Hedjhotep [AD 1st to 2nd century, Tebtynis][110]
111) 20: Burial of the treasurer of the king of Lower Egypt *Ni-kꜣ.w-issi* [Teti, 11, Saqqara][111]
112) 20: 'Before-Intoxication' [MK, Lahun][112]
113) 20: Report (complaint) made by the workman *Ỉmn-m-ip.t* before witnesses [R III][113]
114) 20: Beer supplied from temples in western Thebes to the workmen on holiday [R III or Siptah, 5][114]
115) 20: Hathor Festival [Ramesside][115]
116) 20: Graffito on the roof of the Khonsu temple [Sheshonq IV, 6, Karnak][116]
117) 20: [Appearance of] the goddess (Hathor) and Anubis Festival at Dendera [*Ptolemy X*, Edfu][117]
118) 20: Purifying of Re at the Intoxication Festival of Hathor until II Akhet 5 [Ptolemaic-Roman, Dendera][118]
119) 20: Receiving-of-the-Letters [Ptolemaic][119]

1st MONTH of *ꜣḫ.t* (*tḫy*/*ḏḥwty*/Thoth); 3rd decade (*wšt bkꜣt*/*wšꜣti*)

No.) Day: Event
120) [21]: A Hermopolitan festival? [*Ptolemy* X, Edfu][120]
121) 21: Performance of *mꜣꜥ ḫrw* of Thoth in front of Re [Roman, Esna][121]
122) 22: Great Going-Forth [MK, Lahun][122]
123) 22: Festival of the Great Going-Forth of Osiris (292) [*R III*, MHC][123]
124) 22: Festival in the 21st Upper Egyptian nome [*Ptolemy IV*, Edfu][124]
125) 22: Induction of Apis bull to the temple of Ptah at Memphis [*Ptolemy V*, 21, Serapeum at Memphis][125]
126) 22+: Thutmose III's decree to renew Thutmose II's statue at Thebes [*T III*, 42, Karnak][126]

---

104 *ḥb Ḏḥwty* (Grimm 1994a, 28–9, 173).
105 Geographical list on the exterior of the sanctuary (PM VI, 147 (223–4)).
106 P. Berlin 3115 (de Cenival 1972, 104; Pestman 1993, 199 for translation).
107 The temple construction began in year 27 of Ptolemy XII and ended 34 years later in year 9 of Augustus. In the mean time, the temple was dedicated to Hathor 'in year 1, on the 19th day' (30 BC), generally regarded as I Akhet 19 (Amer and Morardet 1983, 258). Skeat (1994, 311) opts for IV Shemu 26, based on that Augustus began his rule in Egypt on conquering Alexandria on IV Shemu 8 and counted his year from this day for the first four years.
108 Graffito MH no. 224 located at the slaughter house of Medinet Habu (Thissen 1989, 132).
109 *ḥb Ḏḥwty ꜥꜣ wr m tꜣ ḏr=f* (Sauneron 1963, vol. 1, 124; Grimm 1994a, 30–1, 243).
110 P. Firenze PSI inv. I 72, x+5, 7 (Osing and Rosati 1998, 171, pl. 20, A and B).
111 Graffito inscribed on a wall of the tomb of *Ni-kꜣ.w-issi* (Kanawati 2000, 28; Baud 2006, 146).
112 *tp ꜥ tḫy* (P. Berlin 10282, recto: Luft 1992, 116). Luft (1992, 188–9) translates 'vor dem Waagelot'. This feast may be related to Hathor because Niuserre's solar temple attests [*šms tp*] *wiꜣ n* [*Ḥw.t-ḥr*] 'following the bark of Hathor' for this day (Helck 1977, 57), a restoration questioned by Spalinger (1993, 297) who reads [*tḫy*] instead.
113 O. Berlin 10655 (*KRI* V, 573: 16). Complaints against two water-carriers concerning non-payment, and a subsequent oath taken by one of the latter. This case continued from III Shemu 9.
114 P. UC 34336 (*KRI* V, 439: 15). Colllier (2011, 119) dates this papyrus to the time of Siptah.
115 P. Cairo 86637, verso, XXII (Leitz 1994a, 440).
116 Graffito 100 (Jacquet-Gordon 2004, 40–1, pl. 36; Jansen-Winkeln 2007, vol. 2, 220).
117 Calendar for Hathor (Alliot 1949, vol. 1, 216; Grimm 1994a, 30–1, 182).
118 *wꜥb n Rꜥ ḥb tḫy*. Four references to the feast of *tḫy* on this day are found at Dendera: the smaller calendar in the west crypt, which reads *ḥb wḥm.t tḫy* the 'Festival of the Repetition of *tḫy*' (Alliot 1949, vol. 1, 239; Grimm 1994a, 30–1 and 46–7); the larger calendar attesting the five days duration (Alliot 1949, vol. 1, 241; Grimm 1994a, 30–1, 227–8); the east crypt (*Dendara* V, 75: 16–76: 1, pl. 381); and an outer hypostyle hall inscription, dated to the time of Nero, recording 16 days duration until II Akhet 5 (PM VI, 47 (20); Cauville 2002, 76–7, pls. 6 and VIII). Spalinger (1993b, 166, l. 16) relates a part of the inscription carved on the Ptolemaic gate of the Mut precinct at Karnak to this feast. Darnell (1995, 47) adds a text from the Medamud temple (Bisson de la Roque and Drioton 1927, vol. 2, 13 and 27–8).
119 *hrw šsp mḏꜣ.wt wḏ.wt* (P. Salt 825, V, 9: Derchain 1965, 139). The living and dead come out (*pr*) on this day.
120 Grimm 1994a, 30–31, 181–2.
121 *ir mꜣꜥ ḫrw ny Ḏḥwty m-bꜣḥ Rꜥ* (Grimm 1994a, 30–31, 243).
122 *pr.t ꜥꜣ.t* (P. Berlin 10282, recto: Spalinger 1992, 25; Luft 1992, 116).
123 *pr.t ꜥꜣ.t n Wsir* (*MH* III, pl. 154, list 27). At Edfu and Dendera, days from 18 to 22 seem to be grouped as one category. For the detailed episodes of this festival, see Iikherneferet's stela (Stela Berlin 1204: *LD* II, pl. 135, h; Schäfer 1904). See a lengthy entry for this day on P. Cairo 86637 (Leitz 1994a, 38–9).
124 Geographical list on the exterior of the sanctuary (PM VI, 147 (223–4)).
125 Unnumbered stela (Brugsch 1884, 125; Goldbrunner 2004, 89).
126 A statue of Thutmose II in fornt of the 8th pylon of Karnak (PM II^2, 176, O; *LD* III, pl. 16, b; *Urk.* IV, 606: 6; Mariette 1975, 38, c 2, e 2). Laskowski (2006, 207) relates this date to the proscription of Hatshespsut.

I Akhet

127) 23: Filling(?) of the granary [OK, Gebelein][127]
128) 23: Dated Greek graffito [Ptolemaic-Roman, 20, DB][128]
129) 24+: *Ỉḥhy* [MK, Lahun][129]
130) 24: Burial of Ramses III [*R IV*, 1, DeM][130]
131) 24: Festival in the 9th Lower Egyptian nome [*Ptolemy IV*, Edfu][131]
132) 24: The *nbḥ*-plant appears from Osiris, being given by Thoth [Ptolemaic][132]
133) 24: Dated Greek graffito [Ptolemaic-Roman, 20, DB][133]
134) 26: Payprus document concerning the Festivals of Wag and Thoth written by the scribe of the treasury *Ṯnni* [Djedkare-Isesi, Reneferef's temple at Abusir][134]
135) 26: Amun Goes to the Treasury [*T III*, Temple of Ptah at Karnak][135]
136) 26: Offering to Amun-Re at Kawa and his oracle-giving [*Irike-Amannote* (2nd half of 5th century BC), 2, Kawa][136]
137) 28: Festival of Victory over the Meshwesh (1933+) [RIII, 11, MHC][137]
138) 29: Royal decree to commission the royal scribe *Ỉti* to carry out inspection [*Merenptah*, 2, MH][138]
139) 29: Appearance of AmenhotepI[R IV, 6, KV][139]
140) 29: Festival in the 14th Lower Egyptian nome [*Ptolemy IV*, Edfu][140]
141) 30: Royal decree [*Hatshepsut*, 17, Karnak][141]
142) 30: Appearance of AmenhotepI[R IV, 6, KV][142]
143) 30: Osiride ritual [Ptolemaic][143]

1st MONTH of *ꜣḫ.t* (*tḫy*/*ḏḥwty*/Thoth); unknown decade

144) ?: *ꜣbd sꜣḏ* [*Niuserre*, Abu Gurob][144]
145) ?: Foundation ritual [*Niuserre*, Abu Gurob][145]
146) ?: Cloths dedicated to a royal statue [*R III*, 24, Memphis][146]
147) New moon?: *iḥhy* [MK, Lahun][147]

[127] P. Gebelein II, verso, B (Posener-Kriéger 2004, pl. 15).
[128] Graffito no. 77 located at Hatshepsut's temple at Deir-el-Bahari (Bataille 1951, 51–3).
[129] P. Berlin 10412 d, recto (Luft 1986, 77, n. 31; Luft 1992, 132). Krauss (1994, 109–11) dates to I Akhet 27 or 28.
[130] O. DeM 40+O. Strasbourg H 42 (*KRI* VI, 107: 1–2; Janssen 1992, 108; McDowell 1999, 225). Prior to this date, burial equipment was transported to the Valley of the Kings on I Akhet 4.
[131] Geographical list on the exterior of the sanctuary (PM VI, 146 (219–20)).
[132] P. Salt 825, XV, 5–8 (Derchain 1965, 143). The 9th hour of the day is documented. The same entry is recorded for II Akhet 17.
[133] Graffito no. 78 located at Hatshepsut's temple at Deir-el-Bahari (Bataille 1951, 53–4).
[134] A document concerning various kinds of linen to be distributed (Abusir X, 222, pl. 12). Posener-Kriéger (1985, 42), who incorrectly dated this papyrus to I Akhet 23, regarding this day as the 18th lunar day.
[135] *wḏꜣ=f r pr-ḥḏ* (Stela Cairo 34013: *Urk.* IV, 770: 3; Legrain 1902, 107–11; Lacau 1909, 27–30, pl. 9; Klug 2002, 137–46 for transliteration and translation). This ceremony is also attested in the chapel of Amenhotep II at the Mentu precinct, north Karnak (van Siclen 1986, 356). Spalinger (1992, 14) points out that the date in question is located in the part restored by Seti I. Jacquet-Gordon (2009, 123) associates this feast with the cult of Amenhotep I and Ahmes-Nefertari, for whom festivals were celebrated on the 29th and 30th of the same month. An offering list is attached. See a detailed entry for this day in P. Cairo 86637 (Leitz 1994a, 54–6).
[136] Graffito on the E. wall, S. side of the Hypostyle Hall of temple T (Eide, Hägg, and Pierce 1994, vol. 2, 408).
[137] *pꜣ smꜣ pꜣ mšwš ir.n nsw.t-bi.ty N* (*MH* III, pl. 163, lists 53–5).
[138] Two texts at the small temple of Medinet Habu (*KRI* IV, 26: 4–5 and 8–9; Spalinger 1991, 26). The inspection continued at least until III Akhet, year 3 (*KRI* IV, 26: 13–4). Demarée (1985, 176, n. 4) regards I Akhet 29 as the last day of the regnal year, thus I Akhet 30 as the accession day of Merenptah.
[139] *ẖꜥ in Ỉmn-ḥtp* (O. Cairo 25275: Černý 1927, 182; Daressy 1901, 70).
[140] Geographical list on the exterior of the sanctuary (PM VI, 146 (219–20)).
[141] Inscription at Chapel 5 (PM II^{2}, 93; *Urk.* IV, 376: 13).
[142] *ẖꜥ n Ỉmn-ḥtp* (O. Cairo 25276: Černý 1927, 182; Daressy 1901, 70–1).
[143] Ritual to be performed on the last day of this month is known from P. MMA 35.9.21 (M. Smith 2009, 152–66).
[144] The solar temple of Niuserre (Helck, 1977, 57, pl. 2, l. 2).
[145] *pḏ šs sẖ.t ḏb bꜣ ḏbꜣ snṯ m šꜥ ir.t kꜣ* 'stretching the cord, making the brick, hacking the earth, filling foundation with sand, and working' (Helck 1977, 58, pl. 2, l. 2). Also held in III Akhet and IV Peret?
[146] Stela Cairo, number unknown (*KRI* V, 250: 10; Schulman 1963, 178 for translation and photograph).
[147] P. Berlin 10001 B, verso (Luft 1992, 27).

2nd MONTH of *ꜣḫ.t* (*mnḫ.t*/*pꜣ-n-ip.t*/Phaophi); 4th decade (*ipḏs*/*sšpt*) II Akhet

No.) Day: Event

148) 1–2: Funeral and burial of Ramses V [*R VI*, 2, KV][148]

149) 1: Offering to Amun-Re at Pnubs (*pr-nbs*) and his oracle-giving [*Irike-Amannote* (2nd half of 5th century BC), 2, Kawa][149]

150) 2: Graffito of the scribe *Ḳn-ḥr-ḫpš=f* [*Merenptah*, 1, W Thebes][150]

151) 2: Graffito on the roof of the Khonsu temple [*Osorkon II*, 1?, Karnak][151]

152) 2–III Akhet 1: His Beautiful Festival of Entering His Town for 30 days [*Ptolemy VI*, Kom Ombo][152]

153) 2+: Festival in the 3rd Lower Egyptian nome [*Ptolemy IV*, Edfu][153]

154) 3: A wonder of the god Min happened during an expedition [*Mentuhotep IV*, 2, Wadi Hammamat][154]

155) 3: Inundation of the Nile [*Merenptah*, 2, W. Thebes][155]

156) 3: Festival in the 2nd Lower Egyptian nome [*Ptolemy IV*, Edfu][156]

157) 4: Inundation of the Nile [19 Dyn., W. Thebes][157]

158) 4: Festival of Finding Her Souls [Roman, Esna][158]

159) 5: Decree to establish offerings to Amun-Re and Hapi [*Merenptah*, 1, Gebel el-Silsila][159]

160) 5: Inundation of the Nile [R II, 22, W. Thebes][160]

161) 5: A woman named *Tꜣ-mry* gave a man food including a portion of meat (*iwf*) [R VI/VII, 6, DeM/MH?][161]

162) 5: Day of Bringing the Intoxicant Plant [Roman, Dendera][162]

163) 6: Pouring the Sand [MK, Lahun][163]

164) 6: Pouring the Sand [MK, Lahun][164]

165) 6: Offering to Hathor [Amenmes or Merenptah, 1, DeM][165]

166) 6: Menehet Festival [Roman, Esna][166]

167) 7: Qenbet session concerning the herdsman *Msi* [*A IV*, 4, Lahun][167]

168) 7: Inundation of the Nile [Merenptah, 10, W. Thebes][168]

169) 7: The royal butler *Stẖ-ḥr-wnmj=f* visited western Thebes [*R IV*, 6, W. Thebes][169]

170) 7: Herihor decreed to rebury Seti I [*R XI*, 6, coffin of Seti I][170]

171) 8: Appearance (*ḫꜥ.t*) of Thutmose II [*T II*, 1, Aswan][171]

---

148 O. Cairo 25254 (K*RI* VI 343: 13–5; McDowell 1999, 225–6). The body of the king arrived at KV on day 1 and was interred (*ḳrs*) next day.

149 Graffito on the E. wall, S. side of the Hypostyle Hall of temple T (Eide, Hägg, and Pierce 1994, vol. 2, 409).

150 Graffiti 854b and 855 (K*RI* IV, 180: 11; Spiegelberg 1921, 70, nos. 854b and 855; Peden 1994b, 69).

151 Graffito 8 left by the god's father of Khonsu *Pꜣ-di-mꜣꜥ.t-stp-n=s* (Jacquet-Gordon 2004, 14, pl. 3; Jansen-Winkeln 2007, vol. 2, 151–2).

152 *ꜣbd 2-nw ꜣḫ.t sw 2 ir m pr Ḥr nb nb.t sḫꜥ nṯr pn m ḥb=f nfr n ꜥḳ dmi=f m-ḫt wnn=f m pꜣ tꜣ mḥy.t ir n.t-ꜥ=f ḥtp m tꜣy=f ip.t mḥ sw 2 ḫꜥ nṯr pn ir n.t-ꜥ=f ir mit.t r ꜣbd 3-nw ꜣḫ.t sw 1 r mḥ sw 30 ḥtp ḥr s.t=f* 'II Akhet 2: celebrated in the house of Horus, lord of Ombos, is the appearance of this god at His Beautiful Festival of Entering His Town when he is in the north land, performing his rituals, resting in his Opet. The second day: the appearance of this god, performing his rituals, doing likewise until III Akhet 1 to complete 30 days, (when) resting in his place' (PM VI, 190 (94); Grimm 1994a, 32–3; el-Sabban 2000, 155, pl. 33). Klotz (2008, 574–5 and 2012, 386) relates this to the Opet Festival.

153 Geographical list on the exterior of the sanctuary (PM VI, 146 (221–2)).

154 Rock inscription carved by the vizier *Ỉmn-m-ḥꜣt* (probably future Amenemhat I). The miracle occurred when two gazelles appeared on a rock befitting the lid of a royal sarcophagus (*LD* II, pl. 149, c). The king decreed later on II Akhet 15 to carve rock inscriptions at Wadi Hammamat. Cf. II Akhet 15 and 23 for subsequent events.

155 Unnumbered graffito (Spiegelberg 1898, no. XIX; K*RI* IV, 151: 3).

156 Geographical list on the exterior of the sanctuary (PM VI, 146 (221–2)).

157 Graffito 1064 (Černý 1956, no. 1064).

158 *ḥb gmy bꜣ.w=s* (Sauneron 1963, vol. 1, 125; Grimm 1994a, 34–5).

159 Rock inscription (*LD* III, pl. 200, d; K*RI* I, 84: 15). Also see parallel decrees issued by R II on III Shemu 10 and by R III on III Peret 14. These are all decrees to hold celebrations on II Akhet 15 and III Shemu 15. Janssen (1987, 136) regards these dates as recording the days of setting-up the stelae, rather than the beginning of the inundation of the Nile.

160 Graffito 881d (Spiegelberg 1921, 72, no. 881d).

161 P. Turin 1907+1908 (K*RI* VI, 407: 4–7).

162 *hrw sb tḫ.w* (eastern inner jamb of the entrance to the outer hypostyle hall; Cauville 2002, 98-9, pls. 7 and XI). This feast began on I Akhet 20 (Cauville 2002, 76–7, pls. 6 and VIII). Preys (2007) associates this celebration with the cult of divine ancestors. A ritual was also performed at the roof kiosk *m hrw tp n tḫ ḏr di n=s s.t=s m ḥb mꜣꜣ nḥḥ nṯr m ḥḥ.w n rnpw.t r-ꜥ nḥḥ* 'on the day of the first of the drunkenness when her seat was given to her at the festival of seeing the eternity of the god in millions of years to the extent of eternity' (*Dendara* VIII, 9: 12).

163 *ḫnp-šꜥ* (P. Berlin 10079, recto: Luft 1992, 60). Cf. P. Berlin 10344 b, recto (Luft 1992, 120); P. UC 32191 where the *ḫnp-šꜥ* and the *mnḫ.t* always occur together (Collier and Quirke 2006, 94). P. Berlin 10001 B, verso indicates that this was a lunar celebration (Luft 1992, 27). A rite called *wšꜣ-šꜥ* 'dispersing the sand' is attested from NK (Gabolde 1989, 161). Are these part of the foundation ceremony (Weinstein 1973, 421–3)?

164 *ḫnp-šꜥ* (P. Berlin 10018, recto: Luft 1992, 86; Luft 2006, 36). It was followed by the *mnḫ.t*.

165 *wdn n Ḥw.t-ḥr* (O. Cairo 25779: Černý 1935b, 98*: 13–4, pl. 101; K*RI* IV, 212: 15–6).

166 Sauneron 1963, vol. 1, 125; Grimm 1994a, 36–7.

167 P. Berlin 9785 (Gardiner 1906b, 40; Murnane and Meltzer 1995, 46).

168 Unnumbered graffito (Spiegelberg 1898, no. XVIII; K*RI* IV, 160: 3).

169 Graffito 2056 (K*RI* VI, 146: 3; B. Davies 1997b, 51 for translation).

170 *wḏ.t ir n ṯꜣty imy-r mšꜥ ḥm-nṯr tpy Ỉmn-rꜥ nsw.t nṯr.w Ḥry-ḥr* (Coffin Cairo 61019: Gauthier 1907, vol. 3, 232). Cf. III Peret 15 for the reburial of R II in the same year.

171 Rock inscription (*LD* III, pl. 16, a; *Urk.* IV, 137: 9; Sethe 1896, 38 and 81; Klug 2002, 83–7). Redford (1966, 117) regarded this day as the accession of T II.

172) 8: Session concerning a payment to *Pꜣ-di-ḫnsw* before witnesses [21 or 22 Dyn., 14, Thebes?][172]
173) 8: Payment for a male servant and an oath-taking before witnesses by the choachyte *Ỉt-šri* [*Piankhi*, 21, Thebes][173]
174) 9: Offering to Amun of Kawa [Aryamani: 3rd cent. BC, Kawa][174]
175) 10: Appeal over a donkey made by the builder *Ḥrw-nfr* [R III, 20, DeM][175]
176) 10: Qenbet session [R III, 27, DeM][176]
177) 10: Dispute(?) over lamp oil [*R III*, 30][177]
178) 10–13: Seti II visited Thebes, including the West Bank on day 13 [*Seti II*, 1, DeM][178]
179) 10: Petition(?) to a deity at Deir el-Bahari [Ramesside, 2, DB][179]
180) 10: Induction (*sḫn*) of a Buchis bull to Thebes by the king himself [*Augustus*, 28, Armant][180]
181) 10: Coptic beginning of the sowing season [Coptic][181]

2nd MONTH of *ꜣḫ.t* (*mnḫ.t/pꜣ-n-ip.t*/Phaophi); 5th decade (*sbššn/tpy-ꜥ ḫntt*)

No.) Day: Event

182) 11: Distribution of 60 cloths to temple personnel [Djedkare-Isesi, year of the 11th census, Neferirkare's temple at Abusir][182]
183) 12: *Wꜣḥ-mw* performed by the workman *Ḳn* [Amenmes, 1, KV][183]
184) 12: Vizier *Ḥri* commissioned the workmen [Seti II–Siptah, 1, KV][184]
185) 12: Vizier *Ḥri* registered work for the construction of a royal tomb [Siptah, 1, KV][185]
186) 12: Vizier *Ḥri* came to the West Bank of Thebes to register work (*šsp bꜣk*) [Siptah, 1, KV][186]
187) 12+: Workmen of DeM sat at the gate of the royal palace [R IX, 16][187]
188) 12: Restoration of Horemheb's burial by a vizier [R XI, 6, KV 57 (Horemheb)][188]
189) 12: Inundation of the Nile [R II, DeM][189]
190) 12: Inundation of the Nile [early 18 Dyn., 5, Karnak][190]
191) 13: Chief archivist *Pn-pꜣ-tꜣ* was commissioned to investigate Upper Egyptian temples [*R III*, 15, Tod][191]
192) 13: Unnamed vizier came to the village [R III, QV][192]
193) 13: Inundation of the Nile [Merenptah, 10, W. Thebes][193]
194) 13: HPA Pinedjem I 'came' while the royal scribe *Bw-th-imn* was on the west bank [Smendes I, 11, W. Thebes][194]

---

172 P. BM 10800 (Edwards 1971).
173 P. Leiden F 1942/5.15 (Jansen-Winkeln 2007, vol. 2, 361; Vleeming 1980, 13).
174 Fragments of Stela BM 1777 (Eide, Hägg, and Pierce 1994, vol. 2, 531).
175 *ḏd* 'appeal'. O DeM 73 (*KRI* V, 472: 16; Allam 1993, 88–9).
176 O. Gardiner 81 (*KRI* V, 515: 15).
177 P. Turin 1880 (Strike Papyrus).
178 O. Cairo 25560 (*KRI* IV, 302: 2–3; Černý 1935b, 45*, pl. 29). His future tomb was already under construction by III Akhet 12 (O. MMA 14.6.217: KRI IV, 298: 9–10; Altenmüller 1994, 28). A date (the second month of an unknown month in year 1) perhaps close to this is recorded on a fragmentary stela discovered at Buhen (Smith 1976, 130, pl. 30).
179 Graffito DB 65 (Marciniak 1974, 116: 7). These graffiti, found from the memorial temple of Thutmose III at DB, probably record pilgrimages to this place and not convey juridical contexts.
180 Bucheum stela no. 15 (Mond and Myers 1934, vol. 2, 14–5, vol. 3, pl. 44; Goldbrunner 2004, 67, pl. 8). The bull was carried on Amun's barge.
181 Wissa-Wassef 1991b, 444. This season continued until I Peret 10, corresponding to 20 October to 18 January (Gregorian).
182 P. BM 10735, frame 1 (Posener-Kriéger and de Cenival 1968, 21, pl. 53 A for facsimile and transcription; Posener-Kriéger 1976, vol. 2, 359–60 for translation).
183 O. Cairo 25779, recto (*KRI* IV, 213: 10). For the dating to Amenmes, see Gutgesell 2002, 37–8. Cf. III Akhet 17 for the same ritual performed by the same man.
184 O. Cairo 25517 (*KRI* IV, 387: 13; McDowell 1999, 35).
185 O. Cairo 25536 (*KRI* IV, 402: 11; McDowell 1999, 216–7).
186 O. Cairo 25537 (Černý 1935b, vol.1, 16, 34*, vol. 2, pl. 22; *KRI* IV, 396: 3). He came to execute his plan from II Akhet 12 to III Akhet 2. He was the (northern?) vizier under some Ramesside rulers (Černý 1958a, 24, n. 9, 25, n. 1; Wolterman 1996, 162–4).
187 P. Turin 1884+2067+2071+2105 (*KRI* VI, 648: 9).
188 Graffito in KV 57 (Reeves 1990, 234; Peden 2001, 207–8; Jansen-Winkeln 2007, vol. 1, 35–6). For another occurrence of reburial in the same tomb, see IV Akhet 22.
189 O. DeM 436 (Černý 1935a, vol. 5, 26, pl. 25). Janssen (1987, 136) dated to the time of Ramses II, whereas Černý opted for the 20 Dyn.
190 New Kingdom graffito on a block belonging to a chapel of Senusret I (Cotelle-Michel 2003, 348, fig. 8, pl. 5 b). *r ḥꜣ.t-sp 5 ꜣbd 2-nw ꜣḫ.t sw 12 r n ḥꜥpy wr ii n sḏꜣwty imy-r mšꜥ.w Ỉꜥḥ-ms* 'In year 5, II Akhet 12: beginning of the great inundation. The chancellor, overseer of the army, Ahmes has come.'
191 Temple of Tod (Barguet 1952b, 99; *KRI* V, 233: 3). He, also as a royal treasurer, was commissioned (*di m ḥr n*) to investigate (*sip*) temples from Memphis to Elephantine. A record referring to the same decree is known at Edfu (PM VI, 168; *KRI* V, 233: 7) and Elephantine (*KRI* V, 233–4; Awad 2002, 153–4 for translation). At Karnak there is a record of a royal decree, dated to II Shemu in year 16, which was eight months later, perhaps relating to this revision (Spalinger 1991, 24; Haring 1997, 95).
192 O. Turin 57032 (*KRI* V, 621: 1).
193 Unnumbered graffito (*KRI* IV, 160: 6; Spiegelberg 1898, no. XVII).
194 Graffito 1021 (Spiegelberg 1921, 86, no. 1021; Kitchen 1973a, 418; Jansen-Winkeln 2007, vol. 1, 38). The year is misread as 21 by Spiegelberg.

II Akhet

195) 13: Festival in the 18th Lower Egyptian nome [*Ptolemy IV*, Edfu][195]
196) 13: Opet Festival? [Christian era][196]
197) 14: Mentu Festival and Pouring the Sand on the 2nd lunar day [MK, Lahun][197]
198) 14: Overseer of the treasury *Mry-ptḥ* visited W. Thebes with a king's letter [*Merenptah*, 8, KV][198]
199) 14: Opet Festival of Thutmose III in year 23 [*T III*, 23, Karnak][199]
200) 14: Day of the Hall of the Pharaoh in Thebes at Heriheramen and a qenbet session [*R II*, 46][200]
201) 14: Visit of the vizier *Tꜣ* with the scribe *Ỉmn-nḫt* [*R III*, 18][201]
202) 14: Quarrel happened at Deir el-Medina [R IV, 6, DeM][202]
203) 14+: Crossing of the river of Amun-Re [R IX, 15][203]
204) 14: Petition(?) to a deity at Deir el-Bahari [R III, 23, DB][204]
205) 14: Great Festival when Horus was crowned [Ramesside][205]
206) 14: Nitocris was appointed the priestess of Amun at Thebes [*Psametik I*, 9, Karnak][206]
207) 14: Piankhi went to the north to celebrate the Opet Festival? [*Piankhi*, 4, Gebel Barkal][207]
208) 14: Appearance of Khnum [Roman, Esna][208]
209) 15: Address by the member of *pꜥt*, *Ỉmn-m-ḥꜣ.t*, to tomb visitors [*Senusret I*, 43, Beni Hasan][209]
210) 15: Clothing of the king Senusret II [*Amenemhat III*, 28, Lahun][210]
211) 15: Royal decree to erect a stela for the god Min at Wadi Hammamat
[*Mentuhotep IV*, 2, Wadi Hammamat][211]
212) 15: Second anniversary of the accession of Thutmose I [*T I*, 2, Tombos][212]
213) 15–25: Opet Festival of Thutmose III in unspecified year [T III, Elephantine][213]
214) 15: Vizier's visit to the Valley of the Kings [R III, 6][214]
215) 15: Buchis bull entered Thebes [*Ptolemy VI*, 2, Armant][215]
216) 15: Dated Greek graffito [*Domitian*, 2, DB][216]
217) 16: Clothing of the king Senusret II [MK, Lahun][217]
218) 16: Pouring of the Sand [A I, Karnak][218]
219) 16: Ritual of *iwṯt* [18 Dyn., Karnak][219]
220) 16: Delivery of the *šꜥ.t-bi.t*-bread to DeM [R II or III, 26][220]
221) 16: Vizier *Pn-sḫm.t* visited western Thebes [*Merenptah*, 8, KV][221]

195 Geographical list on the exterior of the sanctuary (PM VI, 146 (219–20)).
196 Liturgical text of Triadon (Nagel 1983, 45, 311). The date is recorded in the original text as corresponding to 9 October.
197 *ꜣbd ḥb Mntw ḫnp-šꜥ* (P. Berlin 10282, recto: Luft 1992, 116; Krauss 2006b, 423). Part of the foundation ceremonies (Weinstein 1973, 421–3)?
198 O. Cairo 25504 (*KRI* IV, 157: 10–5; McDowell 1999, 224). Cf. II Akhet 16 and 20 for subsequent events.
199 6th pylon at Karnak (PM II², 90 (245); *Urk.* IV, 742: 1; Redford 2003, 138). Horemheb celebrated his coronation in year 1 during the Opet Festival (Gardiner 1953).
200 *hrw pn ꜥrꜥy.t n.t pr-ꜥꜣ ꜥ.w.s. m niw.t šmꜥy.t* (P. Berlin 3047: Helck 1963). The HPA *Bꜣk-n-ḫnsw* and other priests attended this session regarding a land property of the royal scribe of offerings *Nfr-ꜥꜣb.t*.
201 Graffiti 524+525+2538 (*KRI* V, 379: 14; Černý and Sadek 1969, IV (1)). 'He (vizier?) came from the capital city (*pꜣ pr-ꜥꜣ*)'.
202 O. Cairo 25286 (*KRI* VII, 337: 15).
203 *ḏꜣi n Ỉmn-rꜥ nsw.t nṯr.w* (P. Turin 1960+2071: *KRI* VI, 643: 8). This took place in a security crisis at Thebes caused by the Libyans and the Meshwesh tribe.
204 Graffito DB 119 (Marciniak 1974, 146: 3; *KRI* V, 431–2). Peden (2001, 122, n. 393) dates to the time of Ramses III.
205 *ḥb ꜥꜣ* (P. Cairo 86637 and P. Sallier IV: Budge 1922, 36; Leitz 1994a, 82).
206 Stela Cairo 36327 (PM II², 27; Caminos 1964, 74; Jansen-Winkeln 2014, vol. 1, 17: 3).
207 Fragments of a stela? Berlin 1068 and Cairo 47085 (PM VII, 218; *Urk.* III, 78–9 for the Berlin fragment; Jansen-Winkeln 2007, vol. 2, 351–2).
208 *mk m hrw pn sḫꜥ n Ḫnm-rꜥ* (Sauneron 1963, vol. 1, 125; Grimm 1994a, 38–9).
209 Tomb of Amenemhat (PM IV, 141 (5); Newberry 1893, 24, pl. 8).
210 P. Berlin 10039, verso (Luft 1992, 62). Cf. P. Berlin 10282, recto bearing the date of II Akhet 16.
211 Two rock inscriptions executed during an expedition led by the vizier *Ỉmn-m-ḥꜣt*, founder of the 12 Dyn. (*LD* II, pl. 149, d and e). Cf. II Akhet 3 and 23 for relating records of the expedition.
212 Tombos Stela *in situ* (*Urk.* IV, 82: 9; Kruchten 1989, 168; Klug 2002, 71). His actual accession day was III Peret 21.
213 Stone block from a festival list (present location unknown: *Urk.* IV, 824: 10; Bommas 2000, 468–9). Lepsius (*LD* III, pl. 43, c) published a different reproduction of the date in question. Spalinger (1993, 294, n. 16) suggests to add four vertical signs to the gap indicated by Lepsius, thus rendering the date I Akhet 19. Sayed Mohamed (2004, 72–5) associates the food supply recorded in P. Boulaq XI (Cairo 58070) and P. Cairo 58081 with the Opet Feast in the same reign.
214 O. Ashmolean 115 (=O. Gardiner 115): *KRI* VII, 283: 6; Helck 2002, 226.
215 Bucheum stela no. 8 (Mond and Myers 1934, vol. 2, 5–6, vol. 3, pl. 40; Goldbrunner 2004, 56, pl. 4).
216 Graffito no. 107 located at Hatshepsut's temple at Deir-el-Bahari (Bataille 1951, 74).
217 P. Berlin 10282, recto (Luft 1992, 116).
218 Unnumbered stone block. *ḫnp-šꜥ* (Spalinger 1992, 5, pl. I).
219 Unnumbered stone block (Spalinger 1992, 22 and 28, pl. IV).
220 O. Gardiner AG 69 (Haring 1997, 259). It was delivered from the memorial temple of T IV. Haring relates this delivery to a preparation for the Opet Feast.
221 O. Cairo 25504 (*KRI* IV, 157: 10–5; McDowell 1999, 224). Cf. II Akhet 14 and 20 for relating events.

II Akhet

222) 16: Ptah Festival [*R IV*, 2, DeM][222]
223) 16: Osiris Festival at Abydos [Ramesside][223]
224) 16: Festivals of Neith and of the eye of Horus [Roman, Esna][224]
225) 17: Delivery of the *šʿ.t-bi.t*-bread to DeM [*R II*, 34, DeM][225]
226) 17: Inundation of the Nile [R III, W. Thebes][226]
227) 17: Vizier *Nfr-rnp.t* and two royal butlers *Ḥri* and *ỉmn-ḫʿw* visited Thebes [*R IV*, 2, DeM][227]
228) 17: Royal Appearance (*ḫʿ-nsw.t*) [*Ptolemy V*, Rosetta][228]
229) 18: Pouring the Sand of Anubis at the temple of Senusret II [MK, 14, Lahun][229]
230) 18: Vizier *Nfr-rnp.t* and royal butlers *Ḥri* and *ỉmn-ḫʿw* visited W. Thebes to seek a place for the future tomb of Ramses IV [*R IV*, 2, DeM][230]
231) 18: Festival of Khnum and Anuket at Elephantine [*T III*, Elephantine][231]
232) 18: Two workmen were absent for brewing [Amenmes, 1, KV][232]
233) 18: Eve of Opet Festival of Ramses III (295) [*R III*, MHC][233]
234) 18: Appearance and oracle of an unidentified god; Inscribing the king's name in the granary of the Enclosure; Unknown HPA, prob. Ramsesnakht, with the royal butler *Ḳd-r-n* and the overseer of the treasury *Mnṯw-m-tꜣ.wy*, visited Thebes [*R VI*, 3][234]
235) 19: Clothing [MK, Lahun][235]
236) 19–III Akhet 12 (24 days): First day of Opet Festival under Ramses III (190–407) [*R III*, MHC][236]
237) 19–III Akhet 15 (27 days): First day of Opet Festival under Ramses III (recorded in P. Harris I, XVIIa, 5) [*R III*, 1–31, DeM][237]
238) 19: Royal butler *Stẖ-ḥr-wnmj=f* ordered two wooden chests to be brought out [*R IV*, 6, KV][238]
239) 19: A letter of a woman concerning some oxen for Amun [late 20 Dyn., Thebes?][239]
240) 19: Appearance of the Goddess (Hathor) and her Ennead for 15 days until III Akhet 3 [*Ptolemy X*, Edfu][240]
241) 19: Opet Festival [Augustus/Nero, Thebes][241]
242) 19: Festival of Amun in His Opet [Roman, Esna][242]
243) 19: Opet Festival [Roman][243]
244) 20: *Mry*'s commission to build a mortuary complex for the king [*Senusret I*, 9, Abydos][244]
245) 20: Clothing of Anubis at the temple of Senusret II [MK, 14, Lahun][245]

---

222 O. DeM 45+O. Berlin P 12651+O. Vienna H 4 (*KRI* VI, 120: 9–10). This was lunar day 3 or 4, given that year 2 of Ramses IV was 1157 BC.
223 P. Cairo 86637 and P. Sallier IV (Leitz 1994a, 83).
224 *ḥb N.t ḥb ir.t Ḥr* (Sauneron 1963, vol. 1, 125; Grimm 1994a, 38–9).
225 O. DeM 447 (*KRI* III, 512: 8; Haring 1997, 259). It was delivered from the memorial temple of Thutmose I. Haring relates this delivery to a preparation for the Opet Feast.
226 Unnumbered graffito (Spiegelberg 1898, no. XX; *KRI* V, 484: 13).
227 O. DeM 45+O. Berlin P 12651+O. Vienna H 4 (*KRI* VI, 120: 10–3; McDowell 1999, 207).
228 Decree of Memphis recorded in the Rosetta Stone (*Urk.* II, 194: 3; Spiegelberg 1922, 61; Quirke and Andrews 1988, 21 for transliteration and translation). The Demotic version records the different date of II Peret 17.
229 P. Berlin 10248, recto (Luft 1992, 112). This was the 2nd lunar day, followed by the *mnḫ.t* of Anubis on the 4th lunar day. Krauss (2006b, 424) dates this document to the time of Senusret III. Is this Part of the foundation ceremony (Weinstein 1973, 421–3)?
230 O. DeM 45+O. Berlin P 12651+O. Vienna H 4 (*KRI* VI, 120: 10–3; McDowell 1999, 207).
231 Stone block from a festival list (*LD* III, pl. 43, f; *Urk.* IV, 823: 14).
232 O. Cairo 25779, recto (*KRI* IV, 214: 7–9). Jauhiainen (2009, 99) relates this to the Opet Feast.
233 *hrw n iḫ.t ḫꜣw.t* 'day of evening offering' (*MH* III, pl. 154, list 28).
234 P. Bibliothèque Nationale 237, Carton 1 (*KRI* VI, 339: 13), dated to the time of Ramses VI by Helck (2002, 447–8).'I Akhet' in the original text is to be amended to II Akhet because the account starts with the date II Akhet 14. The god in question (deified Amenhotep I?) *ḫꜣʿ pḥty r nꜣ sr.w r dr r mit.t n nꜣ ḏd.w tꜣ rḫ.t* 'turned the back to all the officials in accordance with what the wise woman said.' A similar expression *pnʿ=f r rmṯ* 'he turned to/against people' is attested in an oracular text at the Khonsu precinct, Karnak (*Khonsu* II, 17, l. 11). Our scroll is docketed as *ʿ.t 2 mḏꜣ.t imy-pr ir n nsw.t* 'two pieces of an *imy-pr*-document made by the king', which may parallel the oracular text of Djehutymes (Kruchten 1986, 80–3) and the adoption stela of Nitocris (Caminos 1964, 75, ll. 16 and 86). For 'the wise woman', see Borghouts 1982, 25–6.
235 *mnḫ.t* (P. Berlin 10166, verso: Luft 1992, 104).
236 *ḥb ỉmn m ḥb=f nfr n ip.t* (*MH* III, pl. pls. 154–6, lists 29–38). The total number of bread consumed during the festival is 11,341.
237 Erichsen 1933, 21: 2–3; Grandet 1994, vol. 1, 246. Ramses III could not celebrate the Opet Festival in his last regnal year 32 because he died on III Shemu 14 before the festival.
238 *hrw pn hꜣb in* [*wdpw*] *nsw.t Stẖ-ḥr-wnmj=f* (O. Cairo 25277: *KRI* VII, 337: 12–3).
239 ....] *tw=i tꜣ md.t nꜣ kꜣ.w m-bꜣḥ ỉm*[*n* half of the line lost] *r tꜣj rj.t m ꜣbd 2-nw ꜣḫ.t sw 19* 'I (speak of) the matter of the oxen before Amu[n] to this side on II Akhet 19' (P. Bournemouth 17/1931: Černý 1939, 65; Wente 1967, 78). O. Gardiner 362 also concerns oxen for the Opet Feast (*KRI* III, 637–9; Wente 1990, 119–20 for translation).
240 PM VI, 127 (52), 161 (310); Alliot 1949, 216; Grimm 1994a, 40–1.
241 Book of Traversing Eternity (P. Leiden T 32, III, 7–9: Stricker 1953, 18; Herbin 1994, 151; Klotz 2008, 576; M. Smith 2009, 413).
242 *ḥb ỉmn m ip.t=f* (PM VI, 113 (15); Sauneron 1963, vol. 1, 125; Grimm 1994a, 40–1).
243 P. Boulaq III, 3, 22 (Sauneron 1952, 10; Klotz 2008, 575–6; Klotz 2012, 387).
244 Stela Louvre C 3 (Vernus 1973).
245 P. Berlin 10248, recto (Luft 1992, 112). This was the 4th lunar day (*pr.t sm*). Krauss (2006b, 424) dated this to Senusret III. Cf. II Akhet 18 for the

246) 20: The workmen was rewarded (*mk*) for the work on the tomb of Merenptah [*Merenptah*, 8, KV][246]
247) 20: Report and oath(?) [20 Dyn., DeM][247]
248) 20: Rebellion of Seth began and Osiris was killed [Ramesside][248]

2nd MONTH of *ꜣḫ.t* (*mnḫ.t/pꜣ-n-ip.t*/Phaophi); 6th decade (*ḫntt ḥrt*)

No.) Day: Event
249) 22: Pouring the Sand and the Mentu Festival [MK, Lahun][249]
250) 23: The god (Min) revealed himself during an expedition [*Mentuhotep IV*, 2, Wadi Hammamat][250]
251) 23: Vizier *Tꜣ* was appointed the vizier of Upper and Lower Egypt [*R III*, 29, Thebes][251]
252) 23?: Hearing of thieves [R XI, 9][252]
253) 23: Appearance of Amun-Re at Kawa and his oracle-giving [*Irike-Amannote* (2nd half of 5th century BC), 2, Kawa][253]
254) 24: Clothing of the king [MK, Lahun][254]
255) 24: First Nubian campaign [A III, 5, Island of Sai][255]
256) 24: Royal scribe *Ḥri* came to reward (*mk*) the workmen [R IV, 1, DeM][256]
257) 24: Hearing of the wab-priest *Pn-wn-ḥb* over a theft from a temple [R XI, 18][257]
258) 24: Recording of the thieves of the Necropolis [*R XI*, 19 (w1), Thebes?][258]
259) 25: Decree during the Half-Monthly Festival [8 Dyn. or later, Koptos][259]
260) 25: Dated inscription [*R II*, 1, Abu Simbel][260]
261) 25 (or 24): Oracle of Ahmes in Abydos [*R II*, 14, Abydos][261]
262) 25: Qenbet and an oath over a donkey [R IV, 7][262]
263) 25: Burial of an Apis bull at the Serapeum [*Psametik I*, 20, Serapeum][263]
264) 25: Festival of Ptah, lord of Memphis, and the Festival of *ḥkꜣ* [Roman, Esna][264]
265) 26: Thutmose III's endowment to festivals [*T III*, 7(?), Akh-menu][265]
266) 26: Transaction of a property before a witness [*R II*, 32][266]
267) 26: Workmen of DeM were rewarded (*mk*) with meat [Amenmes][267]
268) 26–28: Mentu Festival [13 Dyn., Dra Abu el-Naga][268]

'pouring the sand' 2 days earlier.

246 O. Cairo 25504, verso (*KRI* IV, 157: 15; McDowell 1999, 224 for translation). The northern vizier *Pn-sḫm.t* was probably present for this occasion. The reward included ten oxen to be slaughtered.

247 O. IFAO 290 (Janssen 2005, 26–7).

248 P. Cairo 86637 and P. Sallier IV (Leitz 1994a, 90). Leitz proposes 70 days duration of embalmment until IV Akhet 30.

249 P. Berlin 10130 B c, recto (Luft 1992, 99). Part of the foundation ceremony (Weinstein 1973, 421–3)? Cf. II Akhet 6 for other attestations of the Pouring the Sand.

250 *wḥm biꜣ.t* 'a wonder repeated': a rainfall happened and a well was discovered (rock inscription: *LD* II, pl. 149, f; Shirun-Grumach 1989, 380–1). Cf. II Akhet 3 and 15 for relating records of the expedition. The expedition was completed when the lid of the king's sarcophagus was descended from the mountains on day 28.

251 O. Berlin P 10633 (*KRI* V, 530: 1–2). *iw.tw ḥr di.t ṯꜣty Tꜣ r ṯꜣty n šmꜥw mḥw* 'The vizier Ta was promoted to the vizier of the south and north.' According to Wolterman (1996, 164), he had previously been the northern vizier, at latest, from year 16, an idea opposed by Peden (2000, 14) who is inclined to the idea of the southern vizier.

252 P. BM 10053, verso (Peet 1930b, 116).

253 Graffito on the E. wall, S. side of the Hypostyle Hall of temple T (Eide, Hägg, and Pierce 1994, vol. 2, 410). Cf. I Akhet 26 and II Akhet 1 and 30 for relating events.

254 P. Berlin 10130, recto (Luft 1992, 99).

255 Stone fragment (*Urk.* IV, 1959: 11). Cf. III Akhet 2 for the kimg's appearance subsequently performed.

256 O. DeM 41 (*KRI* VI, 108: 15–6).

257 P. BM 10054, recto (Peet 1930b, 62). *šsp-r* 'hearing' or 'deposition'.

258 P. Abbott (Peet 1930b, 132). Cf. I Akhet 2 for a relating event.

259 One of the Koptos decrees from the First Intermediate Period (Strudwick 2005, 125).

260 PM VII, 108; *LD* III, pl. 189, a; Redford 1971, 110.

261 *smi [n] Nb-pḥty-rꜥ* (Stela Cairo 43649: *KRI* III, 464–5; Frood 2007, 102).

262 *hrw tꜣ ḳnb.t* (O. Gardiner 181: Allam 1973, 186; *KRI* VI, 148: 12).

263 Stela Louvre IM 3733 (Malinine, Posener, and Vecoutter 1968, 146, no. 192). The bull died on IV Shemu 21.

264 *ḥb Ptḥ nb ꜥnḫ-tꜣ.wy ḥb ḥkꜣ* (Sauneron 1963, vol. 1, 125; Grimm 1994a, 42–3).

265 Texts on the south exterior wall of the Akh-menu (PM II², 126 (462); *Urk.* IV, 1256: 8). Gardiner (1952, 12) read the date I Akhet 16 while Redford (2003, 135) reads the year as 24.

266 O. Varille 20 (*KRI* VII, 175: 12). Cf. IV Shemu 29 for the same subject.

267 O. DeM 353 (*KRI* IV, 236: 15–6).

268 P. Boulaq 18 (=JE 58069: Scharff 1922, 63; Griffith 1891, 115–6; Bisson de la Roque and Drioton 1927, vol. 2, 12). Ryholt (1997, 244) proposes to date this papyrus to the time of Imyremeshaw or Intef V. See Spalinger 1985, 233 for partial translation. The location for each day is:1st day) Ritual of Mentu at Medamud; 2nd day) Mentu visits the palace (at Karnak?); 3rd day) Mentu returns to Medamud (*mnmn r mꜣdw*). The scenes of this festival are depicted in TT 31 (4–6), but the date is unknown and the topography is different. The episodes can be summarized as follows (Davies and Gardiner 1948, 12–9, pls. 11–3): 1) Outward river procession to Tod (*ḏrty*); 2) Offering at Tod; 3) Return river procession from Tod to

II Akhet

269) 26: Day of the Clothing [*R III*, MHC][269]
270) 27: Clothing [MK, 5, Lahun][270]
271) 27–III Akhet 2: Chantress of Amun-Re *Ḥnw.t-tꜣ.wy* supplied divine offerings [R XI, w2][271]
272) 27?: Appearance of Theban triad at Luxor at the Opet Festival [*Pinedjem II*, 5, Karnak][272]
273) 27: Death of a Hesat cow [*Ptolemy I*, 12?, Atfih][273]
274) 28: Festival of Satet and Anuket at Elephantine [*T III*, Elephantine][274]
275) 28: Burial of an Apis bull [*Sheshonq V*, 11, Serapeum][275]
276) 28: Offering to Amun of Kawa [Aryamani: 3rd cent. BC, 23?, Kawa][276]
277) 28: Festival of Menehet-Nebetu [Roman, Esna][277]
278) 30: Nun Festival [Ramesside][278]
279) 30: Amun-Re's appearance and procession in the town at night [*Irike-Amannote* (2nd half of 5th century BC), 2, Kawa][279]
280) 30: Amenopet's procession with a Buchis bull to be installed at Thebes [*Ptolemy VI*, 24, Armant][280]

2nd MONTH of *ꜣḫ.t* (*mnḫ.t*/*pꜣ-n-ip.t*/Phaophi); unknown decade

No.) Day: Event
281) 2nd lunar day: Pouring the Sand [MK, Lahun][281]
282) ?: Pouring the Sand [MK, Lahun][282]
283) ?: Royal appearance (*ḫꜥ*) and decree to promote *Nb-nfr* to an office before witnesses [*A III*, 20, Thebes][283]
284) ?: An unidentified person visited the Step Pyramid [R II, 48, Saqqara][284]
285) ?: Sailing southwards to the Opet [Ramesside?][285]
286) ?: The goddess Nehemetaway 'entered (*ꜥḳ*)' her temple at Hermopolis and the king dedicated offering according to a royal decree [*Nectanebo I*, 8, Hermopolis][286]

Armant (*iwn*); 4) Landing and returning to the temple of Thutmose III; 5) Offering to Thutmose III's barque in a shrine.

[269] *hrw pn n mnḫ.t* (MH III, pl. 156, list 34).

[270] *mnḫ.t* (P. Berlin 10092 b, recto; Luft 1992, 89). Niuserre's solar temple records *mnḫ.t Inpw* 'clothing of Anubis' (Helck 1977, 58). In a Lahun papyrus (UC 32191) is recorded 'Clothing of Senusret II (*mnḫ.t Ḫꜥ-ḫpr-rꜥ*)', of which the date is unknown, except for the month (Collier and Quirke 2006, 94). Cf. P Berlin 10056 A, recto (Luft 1992, 71).

[271] P. Geneva D 191 (Wente 1990, 174–5). Sweeney (1994, 212, n. 41) regards this as a result of a demand for extra deliveries during the Opet Festival.

[272] The eastern exterior wall of Court IV at Karnak (PM II^2, 183 (553); Kruchten 1986, 254). This day is recorded as the 9th day of the festival, which means that the festival began on II Akhet 19.

[273] Stela Cairo 22180 (*Urk.* II, 160: 5; Roeder 1960, 353 for translation).

[274] Stone block from a festival list (*Urk.* IV, 823: 15).

[275] Stela Louvre IM 3049 (Jansen-Winkeln 2007, vol. 2, 281).

[276] Fragments of Stela BM 1777 (Eide, Hägg, and Pierce 1994, vol. 2, 530).

[277] *ḥb Mnḫ.t-nb.t-ww sḫꜥ n nṯr.t tn r swꜣḏ sḫ.t* (Sauneron 1963, vol. 1, 125; Grimm 1994a, 42–3).

[278] P. Sallier IV (Leitz 1994a, 107).

[279] Graffito on the E. wall, S. side of the Hypostyle Hall of temple T (Eide, Hägg, and Pierce 1994, vol. 2, 412). Török (1997, 227) relates this ritual to the Opet Festival. Kormyscheva (1998, 85) associates the coronation of this king with the Opet Festival. The king's accession day must have fallen between II Shemu 20 and I Akhet 9. The related rituals following are: III Akhet 1 (appearance of Amun-Re and procession in the town at dawn); III Akhet 7 (Irike-Amannote stands alone with Amun-Re); III Akhet [?] (offering to Amun-Re; Irike-Amannote comes out of the temple and holds celebration); III Akhet 16 (offering to Amun-Re and his oracle-giving); III Akhet 23 (invocation to Amun-Re). Cf. I Akhet 26 and II Akhet 1 for seemingly associated ceremonies performed earlier.

[280] Bucheum stela no. 9 (=Cairo JE 53147: Mond and Myers 1934, vol. 2, 6–9, vol. 3, pl. 41; Goldbrunner 2004, 56, pl. 5; Klotz 2008, 77). The bull travelled from Esna to the temple of Luxor in company with the king and remained there until I Shemu.

[281] *ḫnp-šꜥ* (P. Berlin 10001 B, verso: Luft 1992, 27).

[282] *ḫnp-[šꜥ]* (P. Berlin 10399 b, recto: Luft 1992, 124).

[283] Statuette Brussels E 1103 (PM II^2, 444; *Urk.* IV, 1884–6; Capart and Spiegelberg 1902; O'Connor and Cline 1998, 15, n. 72). The king's appearance 'on the throne of Horus'.

[284] Graffito at the south chapel of the Step Pyramid (Firth and Quibell 1935, vol. 1, 83).

[285] *ḥb.wt nb.w m ḫnty r ip.t* (O. DeM 1265: van Walsem 1982, 220, 25; Jauhiainen 2009, 93).

[286] Stela Cairo 72130 (Roeder 1954, 407).

3rd MONTH of *3ḫ.t* (*ḥw.t-ḥr*/Hathyr); 7th decade (*ḫntt ḫrt*) III Akhet

No.) Day: Event

287) 1: Horemheb's decree to restore the burial of Thutmose IV [*Horemheb*, 8, KV 43][287]
288) 1: Decree to construct a lake at Djarukha for the queen Tye [*A III*, 11][288]
289) 1: Passing of Khepri [R II or III, 29][289]
290) 1: Installation of funerary equipment at KV [*Merenptah*, 7, near KV][290]
291) 1: Appeal to Amun-of-Pakhenty and oracle-giving during the Opet Festival [R IV, 2][291]
292) 1: Hathor Festival [Ramesside][292]
293) 1: Festival in the 6th Upper Egyptian nome [*Ptolemy IV*, Edfu][293]
294) 1–I Peret: Navigation of Hathor [Ptolemy XIII, Dendera][294]
295) 1–30: Appearance of Horus [*Ptolemy VI*, Kom Ombo][295]
296) 1–30: Hathor Festival at Dendera [*Ptolemy* X, Edfu][296]
297) 1: Sekhmet Festival [Roman, Esna][297]
298) 2: Appearance (*ḫʿ*) of A III during the 1st Nubian campaign [*A III*, 5, Aswan][298]
299) 2: Oath over a donkey [R III, 25][299]
300) 2: Return journey of Amun at the Opet Festival [*Piankhi*, 21?, Gebel Barkal][300]
301) 2: Day of Drinking (*swr*) [Ptolemy IX, 8?, MH][301]
302) 3: Festival of Uadjet [*T III*, Buto][302]
303) 3: Inundation of the Nile [*Merenptah*, 1, W. Thebes][303]
304) 3: Vizier *T3* visited western Thebes with the scribe *Imn-nḫt* [*R III*, 18][304]
305) 3: 6th expedition to the Eastern Desert by the scribe of the double-treasury *Ḫnsw-ms* [R VII, 1][305]
306) 3: Decree to restore the house of the divine adoratice of Amun [*Psametik I*, 26][306]
307) 4: Oath-taking [*R II*, 66][307]
308) 4: Devotion of silver to Ptah by the lector priest *ʿnḫ=f-n-ḫnsw* [*Siamen*, 16, Memphis (Fustat)][308]
309) 4: His (king) Festival of Life, Prosperity, and Health in the morning [*Ptolemy II*, 6, Pithom][309]
310) 5: Inundation of the Nile [Merenptah, 7, W. Thebes][310]
311) 5: Vizier *Ḥri* visited western Thebes to register work [*Siptah*, 2][311]
312) 5: Inundation of the Nile [R III, 18, W. Thebes][312]
313) 5: Burial of a person called *Wn-t3-w3.t* at Kom Ombo [21 Dyn., 49, Kom Ombo][313]

---

287 Graffito on the S. wall of Chamber 1 in KV 43 (*Urk.* IV, 2170: 15; Hari 1964, pl. 60; Peden 2001, 142). The decree was given to the fan-bearer on the right hand of the king *Mʿy3*, who was also a royal scribe, overseer of the treasury, overseer of the work in the Place of Eternity, and festival leader of Amun at Karnak.

288 Scarab MMA 35.2.1 (*Urk.* IV, 1737: 8; Murnane and Meltzer 1995, 20). Baines (1976, 15–6) associates the event with the agricultural year. The lake, measuring 3700 x 600 cubits, was completed 15 days later on III Akhet 16.

289 *sš Ḫpri* (O. Berlin 14689, unpublished).

290 *st3 n n3 mn.w nḥḥ n B3-n-rʿ-mry-[imn]* (Graffito 87: *KRI* IV, 154: 12; Peden 2001, 150).

291 P. BM 10335 (*KRI* VII, 416: 7; Blackman 1925, 250). Jauhiainen (2009, 96, n. 3) posits that Amun-of-Pakhenty (Leitz 2002a, vol. 1, 316) was worshipped at western Thebes. Haring (2004, 219–20) points out that Pakhenty is a shortened toponym of Pakhentykheru.

292 *ḥb nb.t p.t Ḥw.t-ḥr m p.t Rʿ* (P. Cairo 86637 and P. Sallier IV: Leitz 1994a, 108). The Hathor Feast took place on IV Akhet 1 as well. The one on III Akhet 1 may only be theoretical, reflecting the name of that month '(the month of) Hathor'.

293 Geographical list on the exterior of the sanctuary (PM VI, 147 (223–4)).

294 *ḫn.t n nṯr.t tn* (Alliot 1949, vol. 1, 239). Grimm (1994a, 46–7) regards this feast as occurring on I Peret 1 only.

295 Grimm 1994a, 44–5.

296 Grimm 1994a, 46–7.

297 Sauneron 1963, vol. 1, 125; Grimm 1994a, 46–7.

298 Rock stela (*Urk.* IV, 1665: 15; Berman 1998, 10–11; Klug 2002, 423). Is this a coronation or an accession ceremony (van Siclen 1973)? Cf. II Akhet 24 for another dated of this Nubian campaign.

299 O. Gardiner 196 (Allam 1973, 188; *KRI* V, 502: 3).

300 *ḫrw sʿḳ nṯr* (Stela Cairo 48862: *Urk.* III, 15: 3; Grimal 1981a, 15*; Jansen-Winkeln 2007, vol. 2, 341). This is the latest surviving attestation of the Opet Feast, apart from liturgical texts from the Roman Period.

301 P. Berlin 3115 (de Cenival 1972, 104; Pestman 1993, 199 for translation).

302 Buto Stela 209 (Bedier 1994a, 5, z. 16; Klug 2002, 96–105). This feast took place on I Peret 2, II Peret 26, and III Peret 9, with intervals possibly of lunar nature. Bedier (1994a, 40) proposes to date the stela to year 47 while Redford (2003, 164) suggests year 49–50.

303 Graffito 862 (Spiegelberg 1921, 71, no. 862; *KRI* IV, 150: 14).

304 Graffito 508 (Spiegelberg 1921, 44, no. 508; *KRI* V, 380: 2). See Graffito 1149 for his visit in the same year (*KRI* V, 379: 11) and Graffiti 1154 (*KRI* V, 468: 11) and 1158 (*KRI* V, 468: 8) with the date of III Akhet in year 18.

305 P. IFAO (Koenig 1979, 192, pl. 30).

306 Statue Cairo 36158 (Graefe 1994, 87, l. 11).

307 O. Cairo 25237, recto (*KRI* III, 529: 8). For the same ostracon, see I Akhet 1.

308 Stela Cairo 70218 (Jansen-Winkeln 2007, vol. 1, 151).

309 *ḥb=f n.t ʿnḫ wḏ3 snb* (Stela Cairo 22183: *Urk.* II, 88: 11; K. Müller 2006, 194 for translation). This was celebrated for the completion of the Atum temple at Tjeku.

310 Graffito 856 (Spiegelberg 1921, 70, no. 856; *KRI* IV, 154: 15).

311 O. Ashmolean 118 (O. Gardiner 118); *KRI* VII, 253: 2.

312 Graffito 1158 (Černý 1956, no. 862; *KRI* V, 468: 8). Helck (2002, 237) dates to the time of Ramses III.

313 A tomb 1.5 km to the east of the temple of Kom Ombo (Jansen-Winkeln 2004, 74; Jansen-Winkeln 2007, vol. 1, 94). This is the only example of

III Akhet

314) 6: Royal decree concerning the protection of the pyramid city of Menkaure [*Pepi II*, 50, valley temple of Menkaure's pyramid][314]
315) 6: Offerings for a new moon day and the 2nd lunar day on day 7 [*Amenemhat III*, 32, Lahun][315]
316) 6: Qenbet session [R III, 11, DeM][316]
317) 6: Vilification (*sḫwr*) against a wab-priest arose [R III, KV][317]
318) 6: A royal burial [R VI or X?, 8, western Thebes][318]
319) 6: A Royal butler visited western Thebes [8, western Thebes][319]
320) 6: Reburial of R II [Pinedjem I, 15, mummy shroud][320]
321) 6?: Oracular session of Amun-Re in the morning at the Silver Floor of Karnak [*Pinedjem II*, 2?, Karnak][321]
322) 6: Vizier *Ḥri* entered a temple [*Takelot II*, 14][322]
323) 6: Day of Drinking (*swr*) [Ptolemy IX, 8?, MH][323]
324) 7: Death of Amenemhat I [*Amenemhat I*, 30, Story of Sinuhe][324]
325) 7: Document was drawn up concerning Asiatic female servants [29, Lahun][325]
326) 7: Visit of the scribe *ỉmn-m-ḥ3.t* to the temple of Sahure [A II or T IV, 2, Abusir][326]
327) 7: Burial of the queen Tiye or Satamen [T IV–A IV, 3, WV 22][327]
328) 7: Vizier *T3* commanded *Mry-rʿ* to work at the Necropolis, and an oath taken by *Ḫnsw* [*R III*, 16, DeM][328]
329) 8: Royal decree to construct Atum's temple at Heliopolis [*Senusret I*, 3, Thebes][329]
330) 8 (or 7): Royal decree to dedicate offerings to a personal statue at the Hathor temple [*R II*, 9, DeM][330]
331) 8: Appearance and oracular session of Amun in the morning at the Opet Festival [*R VI*, 7, stela of Merimaat from Karnak][331]
332) 9: Going-Forth of Amun [T III, Elephantine][332]
333) 9: Appeal to Amenhotep I over a shed [R III, 11, DeM][333]
334) 9: Inundation of the Nile [R III, 24, W. Thebes][334]
335) 9: Dispute over a donkey hired by *Pn-t3-wr.t* [R III, 28][335]
336) 9: A letter from the vizier *Ḏḥwty-ms* and the overseer of the treasury *ỉmn-ḥtp* [R IX, 4][336]

dated tomb usurpation outside Thebes.

314 Stela Boston 47.1654 (*Urk.* I, 277: 9; Reisner 1931, 280–1, pl. A, 1 for translation and facsimile). Due to the badly weathered condition of the stela, the date has been interpreted differently to be: IV Akhet 6, year 31 by Goedicke (1967, 148, Abb. 12) and III Akhet 3, year 31 by Baud (2006, 153).

315 P. Berlin 10006, recto (Parker 1950, 63; Luft 1992, 40).

316 The matter was discussed again during an Amenhotep I's session held on day 9 this month (O. Geneva 12550, recto: 8: Allam 1973, 193–5; McDowell 1990, 128 and 256–9). The qenbet session was held when a scribe of the vizier came to Deir el-Medina to allocate regular rations.

317 O. BM 50734+O. Gardiner 99+O. Cairo 25673 (*KRI* V, 564: 1–2; Wente 1990, 51).

318 Graffito 1860 a (*KRI* VI, 681: 7; Peden 2001, 199–201). *hrw pn ḫni p3 ḫr* 'day of closing the tomb', which was performed by the HPA *Rʿ-ms-sw-nḫt*, the royal butler *P3-rʿ-ḥr-wnmj=f*, and the chief workmen *ỉmn-nḫt*.

319 Graffito 1860 (Černý and Sadek 1969, IV (1)).

320 Jansen-Winkeln 2007, vol. 1, 22–3.

321 The eastern exterior wall of Court IV at Karnak (PM II², 183 (553)). First published by Naville (1883) and re-examined by Kruchten (1985 and 1986, 57–61). Also see Valbelle and Husson 1998, 1061.

322 *hrw ʿḳ r pr n ḥm-nṯr n ỉmn-rʿ nsw.t nṯr.w imy-r niw.t ṯ3ty Ḥri* (P. Berlin 3048, verso: Jansen-Winkeln 2007, vol. 2, 170, ll. 4–5).

323 P. Berlin 3115 (de Cenival 1972, 105; Pestman 1993, 199 for translation).

324 Lichtheim 1973, vol. 1, 223.

325 P. UC 32167 (Collier and Quirke 2004, 118–9). It was created at the office of the vizier Khety.

326 Graffito (Peden 2001, 60; Navrátilová 2007, 51–3).

327 Graffito on the passage into the antechamber of WV 22 (Kondo 1995, 25–33; Peden 2001, 141–2). Hornung (2006, 204) attributes the date to Amenhotep III.

328 O. DeM 10045 (=O. IFAO 10002: Grandet 2006a, 97). Elsewhere the vizier's visit with the scribe *ỉmn-nḫt* in III Akhet in year 16 is recorded in Graffiti 1111, 1140 A–1143 (Černý 1956). Their cooperation in unknown years is also attested to from Graffiti nos. 82, 84, 94, and 96 (Spiegelberg 1921, 11–2).

329 Berlin Leather Roll (P. Berlin 3029: de Buck 1938; Lichtheim 1973, vol. 1, 115–8; Osing 1992, 111). The king appeared at the *ḏ3dw*-hall at the Unification of the Two Lands (*sm3-t3.wy*) and subsequently performed the stretching-the-cord in the *sšd-šw.ty* headdress. Gundlach (2011, 113–4) regards this as the 'coronation' of Senusret I, corresponding to the beginning of his sole reign and the ritual in question as having taken place on a day after it.

330 Statue of *Rʿ-ms* (Cairo 72000: KRI II, 363: 2; Bruyère, *Deir el-Médineh (1935–40)*, fascicule II, 56–7, pls. 12 and 35, n. 115; Černý 1961, 151). The day is called [*ḥ3.t n*]*ḥḥ* the 'front of eternity'. The divine offerings were delivered from the Ramesseum to the Hathor temple at the Necropolis.

331 *sḫʿ ḥm nṯr šps ỉmn-rʿ nsw.t nṯr.w m ḥb=f nfr n ip.t* (Stela Cairo 91927: PM II², 13; Vernus 1975, 107).

332 *ḥb pr.t ỉmn* (Stone block from a festival list: LD III, pl. 43, c; *Urk.* IV, 824: 11–2).

333 *ʿš n ỉmn-ḥtp* (O. Geneva 12550, recto: 8; Allam 1973, 193–5; McDowell 1990, 128 and 256–9).

334 Graffito 1159 B (Černý 1956, no. 1159 B; *KRI* V, 492: 13). Helck (2002, 257) dates to the time of Ramses III.

335 *ḏd* 'appeal' or 'dispute' (O. Berlin 1121: *KRI* V, 524: 13; McDowell 1999, 89). The identical lawsuit is recorded in O. Petrie 9 and O. Ashmolean 1933.

336 O. Louvre E 11178 a (*KRI* VII, 377: 9). It concerns wages to the workmen.

337) 10: Thutmose III set up a stela concerning his war campaigns [*T III*, 47, Gebel Barkal][337]
338) 10: Graffito of the wab-priest *Pꜣ-wꜣḥ* [*Neferneferuaten*, 3, TT 139][338]
339) 10: A *Rꜥ-ms-s* was appointed as a scribe of the Necropolis [*R II*, 5, KV][339]
340) 10: Oath over a property of *Niw.t-nḫti* at Deir el-Medina [*R V*, 3, DeM][340]
341) 10: Oath taken by *Ḳn-ḫpš=f* over a payment [R V or VI, 3][341]
342) 10: Donation of daily offerings to Seth by the official *Ḥr-tꜣ-bi* [*Piankhi*, 24, Dakhla Oasis][342]
343) 10: Festival of Neith and her son Tithoes (*Twtw*) [Roman, Esna][343]
344) 10?–17?: Accession of Ramses V [*R V*, 4, DeM][344]

3rd MONTH of *ꜣḫ.t* (*ḥw.t-ḥr*/Hathyr); 8th decade (*ṯms n ḫntt*)

No.) Day: Event

345) 11: HPA *Mꜣy* was commissioned to bring a bekhen-stone for a divine statue [*A IV*, 4, Wadi Hammamat][345]
346) 11: Overseer of the double-treasury *Ṯꜣy* visited W. Thebes to reward the workmen [*Merenptah*, 7, KV][346]
347) 11: Report (*ḏd*) by the scribe *ꜥḫ-p.t* followed by an oath-taking [R III, 16][347]
348) 11: Vizier *Tꜣ* visited western Thebes [*R III*][348]
349) 11: The workmen were rewarded (*mk*) with 11 oxen (at the Opet Festival?) [R IV, 2, DeM][349]
350) 12: Building future tomb of Seti II began after his visit to West Thebes [*Seti II*, 1, DeM][350]
351) 12: Last Day of the Opet Festival under Ramses III [*R III*, MHC][351]
352) 12: Appearance (induction) of a Buchis bull at Djeme and the Maru temple at Thebes [*Hadrian*, 12 to 13, Armant][352]
353) 13: Rituals(?) for two manifestations of Amun (inundation of the Nile?) [R III, 18, QV][353]
354) 13: Oath over a payment [R III, 25, DeM][354]
355) 14: 12 workmen were given a cloth each [R III, 15, DeM][355]
356) 14: Examination of thieves, esp. the quarryman *ỉmn-pꜣ-nfr*, by the vizier *Ḫꜥ-m-wꜣs.t* [*R IX*, 16][356]
357) 15: A letter concerning a royal decree on gains from an expedition [*Pepi II*, 2, Aswan][357]
358) 15: Dated graffito at Wadi Hilâl [6 Dyn., year of the 2nd occasion, Wadi Hilâl near el-Kab][358]
359) 15: Last day of the Opet Festival under Ramses III (recorded in P. Harris I, XVIIa, 5) [*R III*, 1–31, DeM][359]
360) 16: The king celebrated the Feast of Opening the Lake to perform rowing at Djarukha [*A III*, 11][360]
361) 17–8: Mentu Festival [13 Dyn., 3, Dra Abu el-Naga][361]

337 Stela Boston 23.733 (*Urk.* IV, 1228: 6; Reisner and Reisner 1933, 26; Klug 2002, 193–208).
338 Hymn to Amun (PM I-1², 253 (5); *Urk.* IV, 2024: 14; Gardiner 1928, 10–11).
339 O. Cairo 25671 (*KRI* III, 636: 10).
340 P. Ashmolean 1945.97 (Pestman 1982, 176–8; McDowell 1999, 38–40). Cf. III Akhet 17 and IV Akhet 5 for the same juridical case.
341 P. Ashmolean 1945.95 (*KRI* VI, 242: 16).
342 Stela Ashmolean 1894.107b (Janssen 1968; Jansen-Winkeln 2007, vol. 2, 364).
343 Sauneron 1963, vol. 1, 125; Grimm 1994a, 48–9.
344 P. Ashmolean 1945.97 (Pestman 1982).
345 Graffito (Murnane and Meltzer 1995, 68).
346 O. Cairo 25504, recto (*KRI* IV, 155: 7; Awad 2002, 98 for translation). The 'reward' (*mk*) took place at the Enclosure of the Necropolis. He is also recorded as visiting somewhere on day 22.
347 O. Louvre E 27677 (Grandet 2002, 205, no. 156). Cf. IV Shemu 22 for the same case.
348 O. Ashmolean 192 (unpublished).
349 O. DeM 46 (*KRI* VI, 122: 12–3). *n pꜣ n ip.t* 'for the (month) of Opet'. They also received another portion of meat later on the 18th and 28th of the same month, which Janssen (1979, 514–5) explained as deliveries from more than one temple.
350 O. MMA 14.6.217 (*KRI* IV, 298: 9–10; Altenmüller 1994, 28). The king sojourned in Thebes at least from II Akhet 10 to 13.
351 *sꜥḳ n ỉmn* (*MH* III, pl. 156, list 35). This celebration lasted 24 days. See Leitz (1994a, 118) for the entry 'letting the gods rest in their places' for this day.
352 Stela Pushkin 5863 (Hodjash and Berlev 1982, 217–20, no. 147; Goldbrunner 2004, 74, 104, pl. 19 left).
353 Graffito 1154 (*KRI* V, 468: 11; Černý 1956, 7, pl. 15). Helck (2002, 237) dates to the time of Ramses III. 1) *ỉmn-n-niw.t-pꜣ-ḥꜥpy-n-pꜣ-sr-ꜥꜣ-n-ḫnty-nfr* 'Amun of the Town, Hapi of the Great Nobleman of Khenty-Nefer', whom Leitz (2002a, vol. 1, 318) associates the name of a place to the south of Memphis and 2) *ỉmn-n-tꜣ-wdn.t* 'Amun of the Offerings' (Leitz 2002a, vol. 1, 315). This was probably a ritual relating to the high rise of the Nile, which had taken place 8 days earlier on III Akhet 5 that year. For similar dated graffiti recording inundation, see Graffiti 1064, 1158–60 (Černý 1956); 850b, 856, 862, 881c–d (Spiegelberg 1921), all of which fall in II Akhet and III Akhet but without any indication of a ritualistic performance.
354 O. DeM 56 (*KRI* V, 502: 12; McDowell 1999, 170).
355 O. DeM 406 (*KRI* V, 459: 1–5). The cloths are called a 'remainder' (*spy.t*).
356 The Great Tomb Robbery (P. BM 10054, verso: *KRI* VI, 490: 2; Peet 1930b, 60). Also present as investigators were the royal butlers *Ns-imn* and *Nfr-rꜥ-m-pr-imn*, and the mayor *Pꜣ-sr*. Other judicial sessions followed on days 19 and 21.
357 Tomb of Harkhuf (Wente 1990, 20–1).
358 LD II, pl. 117, q; Vandekerckhove and Müller-Wollermann 2001, vol. 1, 183–6, O 74. Carved by the overseer of the priests *Ni-ꜥnḫ-Ḥr*.
359 This celebration lasted 27 days (Erichsen 1933, 21: 2–3; Grandet 1994, vol. 1, 246).
360 *ḥb wbꜣ* (Scarab Metropolitan 35.2.1: *Urk.* IV, 1737: 15; Berman 1998, 13–4). The construction of the lake began on III Akhet 1.
361 P. Boulaq 18 (L) (=Cairo 58069: Bisson de la Roque and Drioton 1927, vol. 2, 12). Ryholt (1997, 244) dismisses the dating of this document to the

III Akhet

362) 17: *W3ḥ-mw* performed by the workman *Ḳn* [Amenmes, 1, KV][362]
363) 17: Amun Festival after the Opet Festival (296) [*R III*, MHC][363]
364) 17: Qenbet session on the properties of a woman called *Niw.t-nḫti* at Deir el-Medina [*R V*, 4, DeM][364]
365) 17: Installation of an official [*Sheshonq I*, 2, Karnak][365]
366) 18: Report(?) made by the guardian *Ỉmn-m-ip.t*, and a reference to an unidentified vizier [19 Dyn., 6][366]
367) 18–30: Visit of the vizier *T3* to take the workmen to KV [*R III*, DeM][367]
368) 18: Festival in the 11th Lower Egyptian nome [*Ptolemy IV*, Edfu][368]
369) 19: Horemakhet appeared in a dream to Thutmose IV [*T IV*, 1, Giza][369]
370) 19: Visit of the overseer of the treasury *Ḫʿ-m-ti* and the high-priest *Wsr-m3ʿ.t-rʿ-nḫt* [*R III*, DeM][370]
371) 19: HPA *Ỉmn-ḥtp* received a reward from the king in the great court of Amun [*R IX*, 10, Karnak][371]
372) 19: Inspection of tombs at QV by the vizier *Ḫʿ-m-w3s.t* and the royal butler *Ns-imn*, and a subsequent juridical session at the temple of Ptah [*R IX*, 16, Thebes?][372]
373) 19: Prescription not to sail to either north or south [Ramesside][373]
374) 20: The *hdn*-Plant of Hathor [MK, Lahun][374]
375) 20: The king's appearance (*ḫʿ*) and commission to the viceroy of Kush [*A IV*, 12?, Buhen][375]
376) 20: Appeal to Amenhotep I [R III, 30, DeM][376]
377) 20: Scribe of the Necropolis *Ḥri* visited HPA in the Great Hall of Karnak with regard to copper [R VI, 6][377]
378) 20: Inundation of the Nile [Ramesside, 4, KV][378]
379) 20: Offering to Hathor at Deir el-Bahari [Ramesside, 10, DB][379]
380) 20: Festival in the 6th Lower Egyptian nome [*Ptolemy IV*, Edfu][380]
381) 20: Hathor, Lady [of the *hdn*-Plant] [AD 1st century, Tanis][381]

3rd MONTH of *3ḫ.t* (*ḥw.t-ḥr*/Hathyr); 9th decade (*ḳdty/spty*)

No.) Day: Event

382) 21: Visit of the vizier *T3* to investigate the workmen [*R III*, DeM][382]
383) 21: Visit of the royal butler *Stḫ-ḥr-wnmj=f* to reward (*ḥs.t*) the workmen [*R IV*, 5, KV][383]
384) 21: Great qenbet was held before the vizier *Ḫʿ-m-w3s.t* [*R IX*, 16, Thebes?][384]
385) 21: Shu Festival [Ramesside][385]
386) 22: The royal scribe *Bw-th-imn* visited the tomb of Horemheb to work on it [Smendes I, 4, KV 57][386]

---

time of Sobekhotep II. Krauss (2006b, 422–4) dates to the time of one of the predecessors of Khendjer and relates this feast to the 2nd lunar day.

362 O. Cairo 25779, verso (*KRI* IV, 216: 9). Cf. II Akhet 12 for the same ritual performed by the same man.

363 *ḥb Ỉmn ḫpr s3 ḥb ip.t* (*MH* III, pl. 158, list 39). Osiris died this day (Graindorge-Héreil 1994, 212).

364 P. Ashmolean 1945.97 (Pestman 1982, 174–5; *KRI* VI, 239: 10). Cf. III Akhet 10 and IV Akhet 5 for the same case.

365 Legrain 1900, 54; Kruchten 1989, 49; Jansen-Winkeln 2007, vol. 2, 36.

366 O. Berlin 14843 (unpublished).

367 O. DeM 148 (*KRI* V, 505: 12 and 506: 12). Cf. III Akhet 19, 21, and 30 for events recorded in the same text.

368 Geographical list on the exterior of the sanctuary (PM VI, 146 (219–20)).

369 Great Sphinx Stela at Giza *in situ* (*Urk.* IV, 1540: 2; Zivie 1976, 127; Klug 2002, 297).

370 O. DeM 148 (*KRI* V, 505–6). Cf. III Akhet 18, 21, and 30 for events recorded in the same text.

371 Eastern exterior wall of Court II (PM II², 172 (505); *KRI* VI, 455: 14; Warburton 1997, 186; Frood 2007, 68–72 for translation).

372 Great Tomb Robbery (P. Abbott (=P. BM 10221) and P. Amherst VII (=P. Pierpont Morgan Library Eg. 7): *KRI* VI, 473: 16, 475: 15, and 487: 10; Peet 1930b, 39–40, 49; McDowell 1999, 194–8). Cf. III Akhet 14 and 21 for associating events.

373 O. Cairo 86637 and P. Sallier IV (Leitz 1994a, 14). Leitz regards this day as the autumnal equinox.

374 P. Berlin 10282, recto and 10344 c, recto (Luft 1992, 116 and 121; Spalinger 1998b, 57–8). For an undated 'Festival of *hdn* of Hathor of Thebes', see Le Saout (1989). On 'the lord of *hdn*' as an epithet of Thoth, see Caminos 1958, 44, n. m.

375 Fragments of a stela (Smith 1976, 125, pl. 29; Helck 1980; Murnane and Meltzer 1995, 101).

376 *ʿš n nsw.t Ỉmn[-ḥtp]* (O. DeM 448, recto: Černý 1935a, vol. 5, 29, pl. 28; *KRI* V, 541: 1–5).

377 P. Turin 1879+1899+1969, verso, col. 2, 7 (*KRI* VI, 338: 3; Janssen 1994, 92). The copper was sent from the Necropolis to Karnak on IV Akhet 1 and officially received by HPA *Rʿ-ms-sw-nḫt* on IV Akhet 7. Janssen (1994, 95) related these events to the security unrest in that time, which required metal resources to produce weapons.

378 O. Cairo 25801 (*KRI* IV, 405: 2). Černý (1973, 206) dates to the time of Ramses III, while Gutgesell (1983, vol. 2, 284–5) opts for Seti II or Siptah.

379 Graffito DB 79 (Marciniak 1974, 126: 3). Cf. the *prt b3st* recorded for this day (Leitz 1994a, 134).

380 Geographical list on the exterior of the sanctuary (PM VI, 146 (219–20)).

381 P. BM ESA 10673 (Griffith and Petrie 1889, pl. 12; Spalinger 1993b, 165 (14)).

382 O. DeM 148 (*KRI* V, 505–6). Cf. III Akhet 18, 19, and 30 for events recorded in the same text.

383 O. Cairo 25565 (*KRI* VI, 142: 15). TT 50 (2) also attests *ḥs.t* in a reward scene.

384 Great Tomb Robbery (P. Abbott (=P. BM 10221): *KRI* VI, 479: 14; Peet 1930b, 42; McDowell 1999, 194–8). Held at a place to the north of the great court of Amun with other notable judges, the royal butler *Ns-imn*, the HPA *Ỉmn-ḥtp*, and the mayor *P3-sr*. Cf. III Akhet 14 and 19 for associating events.

385 P. Cairo 86637 and P. Sallier IV (Leitz 1994a, 136).

386 Graffito at the entrance of KV 57 (Kitchen 1973a, 418; Peden 2001, 208).

III Akhet

387) 22?: Dated graffito [Ptolemaic-Roman, 8, MH][387]
388) 22: Beginning of the Herka Festival [Roman, Esna][388]
389) 23: Ramses II left Thebes to the north after celebrating the Opet Festival [*R II*, 1, Seti I's temple at Abydos][389]
390) 23: Vizier *Pꜣ-nḥsy* supervised dragging divine statues to Merenptah's tomb [*Merenptah*, 7, KV][390]
391) 23: The tomb robbery was reported at the double-treasury of the Mentu precinct at Karnak [R IX, 16][391]
392) 23: Inundation of the Nile [20 Dyn., W. Thebes][392]
393) 23: Khonsu Festival [*Ptolemy VI*, Kom Ombo][393]
394) 23: Day of Drinking (*swr*) [Ptolemy IX, 8?, MH][394]
395) 23: Festival of the Field [*Ptolemy* X, Edfu][395]
396) 24: Vizier *Pꜣ-rʿ-m-ḥb* visited western Thebes to give rations [Seti II, DeM][396]
397) 25: Taking the River [MK, Lahun][397]
398) 25: Asiatic war campaign [*A II*, 9, Memphis][398]
399) 25: Vizier *Tꜣ* came to the Necropolis to inspect a work [*R III*, 22, QV][399]
400) 25: Festival of Shu and Khnum, lord of the field [Roman, Esna][400]
401) 27: Unspecified HPA and the scribe of the double-treasury *Ḫnsw-ms* received gold as the result of a mining expedition [R VII][401]
402) 27: Burial of an Apis bull [*Sheshonq V*, 37, Serapeum][402]
403) 28: Wag Festival [Djedkare-Isesi, Reneferef's temple at Abusir][403]
404) 28: Vizier *Nfr-rnp.t* ordered to increase workforce for the construction of a royal tomb [*R IV*, 2][404]
405) 28: Five oxen were given to four workmen [R IV, 2, DeM][405]
406) 28: Appeal to AmenhotepI[R IV, 5, DeM][406]
407) 28–IV Akhet 5: Appearance of Hathor, lady of Kom Ombo [*Ptolemy VI*, Kom Ombo][407]
408) 28: Ritual performed for the gods of the mound Djeme [Cleopatra VII, 3, MH][408]
409) 28: Dated graffito [Ptolemaic-Roman, 19, MH][409]
410) 28: Dated graffito [Ptolemaic-Roman, 6, MH][410]
411) 29: Workmen received rations from the royal butler *Ns-imn* [*R IX*, 8][411]
412) 29: Festival of the goddess Nebetu [Roman, Esna][412]
413) 29–IV Akhet 1: Appearance of Hathor, lady of Dendera [*Ptolemy* X, Edfu][413]
414) 29–IV Akhet 1: [Appearance of Horus, lord of Edfu] [*Ptolemy* X, Edfu][414]

---

[387] Graffito MH no. 146 located on the roof of the second court of the temple of Medinet Habu (Thissen 1989, 107).
[388] *ḥꜣ.t n wp Ḥr-kꜣ* (Sauneron 1963, vol. 1, 126; Grimm 1994a, 50–1). For a study on this feast, see Sauneron 1962, 29–46.
[389] This jounery was called *wḏy.t=f tpy.t r wꜣs.t* 'his first travel to Thebes' (PM VI, 3 (34–7); *KRI* II, 325: 5–6; Gauthier 1910, 55; Spalinger 2009, 22).
[390] O. Cairo 25504 (*KRI* IV, 155: 12–3; McDowell 1999, 224). Cf. IV Shemu 13–20 for the sarcophagus subsequently brought into this this tomb.
[391] Great Tomb Robbery (P. Leopold II (=P. Brussels E 6857)+P. Amherst VII (=P. Pierpont Morgan Library Eg 7), 1, 1: Capart and Gardiner 1939, pl. 1, l. 1 for photograph and transcription; *KRI* VI, 481: 13).
[392] Graffito 1160 (Černý 1956, no. 1160).
[393] *ḥb Ḫnsw* (Grimm 1994a, 50–1).
[394] P. Berlin 3115 (de Cenival 1972, 105; Pestman 1993, 199 for translation).
[395] *ḥb sḫ.t* (Grimm 1994a, 50–1).
[396] O. DeM 595 (*KRI* IV, 328: 11).
[397] P. Berlin 10079, recto and 10166, verso (Luft 1992, 86 and 104).
[398] Stela Cairo 86763 (*Urk.* IV, 1305: 13; Badawy 1943, 17; Edel 1953, 121; Klug 2002, 248).
[399] O. Turin 57047 (*KRI* V, 483: 2).
[400] *ḥb Š*[*w sꜣ Rʿ* one group lost] *H̱nm nb sḫ.t* (Sauneron 1963, vol. 1, 126; Grimm 1994a, 50–1).
[401] P. IFAO (Koenig 1979, 194, pl. 34).
[402] Stelae Louvre IM 2846 and 3085 (Jansen-Winkeln 2007, vol. 2, 271 and 286). The bull was induced as a Ptah's sacred animal on IV Peret 4 in year 12 of the same king. Cf. Stela Louvre IM 3721 (Jansen-Winkeln 2007, vol. 2, 285).
[403] Papyrus fragment from the archive of Reneferef (Abusir X, pl. 11, 220–2). The name of the season is missing, but Luft (1994, 42) proposes Akhet while Depuydt (2000, 173) gives Peret. For more on the month in question, see Vymazalová, 2008, 140–2.
[404] This was done according to a royal decree (P. Turin 1891: *KRI* VI, 76: 13). He was accompanied by the royal butler *Stẖ-ḥr-wnmy=f* and the overseer of the treasury *Mntw-m-tꜣ.wy*.
[405] O. DeM 46 (*KRI* VI, 124: 1). One ox was also given to three officials.
[406] *ʿš n nsw.t Ỉmn-ḥtp* (O. Gardiner 4: Černý 1927, 178–9; *KRI* VI, 142: 4–5; Gardiner 1917, 43).
[407] Grimm 1994a, 52–3.
[408] Graffito MH no. 45 located at the small temple of Medinet Habu (Thissen 1989, 30–6).
[409] Graffito MH no. 95 located on the roof of the second court of the temple of Medinet Habu (Thissen 1989, 81).
[410] Graffito MH no. 126 located on the roof of the second court of the temple of Medinet Habu (Thissen 1989, 96).
[411] P. Turin 1881+2080+2092 (*KRI* VI, 613: 13). *Ns-ỉmn* was in Thebes at least until IV Akhet 5 (*KRI* VI, 614: 11).
[412] This festival was established 'according to a stela of Thutmose III', which had previously been discovered in this temple (Grimm 1994a, 52–3).
[413] Grimm 1994a, 52–5.
[414] Grimm 1994a, 52–5.

III Akhet

415) 30: Anuket Festival in Elephantine [*T III*, Elephantine][415]
416) 30: Visit of the vizier *Tȝ* to investigate the workmen [*R III*, DeM][416]
417) 30: King received his provisions from Isis and Nephtys [*Ptolemy II*, 16, Pithom][417]
418) 30: Day of Drinking (*swr*) [Ptolemy IX, 8?, MH][418]
419) 30: Appearance of Herka [Roman, Esna][419]

3rd MONTH of *ȝḫ.t* (*ḥw.t-ḥr*/Hathyr); unknown decade

No.) Day: Event
420) ?: Taking the River [*Niuserre*, Abu Gurob][420]
421) ?: Evening Offering of the Taking the River, and the Taking the River [*Amenemhat III*, 35, Lahun][421]
422) ?: Clothing [MK, Lahun][422]
423) ?: Ramses II left Thebes to the north after celebrating the Opet Festival and *Nb-wnn=f* was appointed HPA [*R II*, 1, TT 157 (8)][423]
424) ?: Vizier *Tȝ* visited western Thebes to appoint *Ỉmn-nḫt*, son of Ipuy, a Necropolis scribe (*sš n pȝ ḫr*) [*R III*, 16, Theban West][424]
425) ?: Ceremonies in the precinct of Mut at Karnak and on the river [Ptolemaic, Mut precinct at Karnak][425]
426) ?: Royal decree to commission the royal scribe and festival leader *Mʿyȝ* to renew the burial of T IV [*Horemheb*, 8, KV 43][426]

---

415 Stone fragment from a festival list (*LD* III, pl. 43, f; *Urk.* IV, 823: 16).
416 O. DeM 148 (*KRI* V, 505–6). Cf. III Akhet 18, 19 and 21 for events recorded in the same text.
417 Stela Cairo 22183 (*Urk.* II, 104: 9; K. Müller 2006, 199 for translation).
418 P. Berlin 3115 (de Cenival 1972, 105; Pestman 1993, 199 for translation).
419 Sauneron 1963, vol. 1, 126; Grimm 1994a, 54–5.
420 *šsp-itrw* (the solar temple of Niuserre: Helck 1977, 73, pl. 2, l. 3 and pl. 3, l. 3). Helck's restoration of the text is very dubious.
421 *iḫ.t ḫȝwy n.t šsp-itrw* followed by *šsp-itrw* (P. UC 32191: Collier and Quirke 2006, 94; Luft 1992, 140). For discussion on this event, see Willems 1996, 218–21.
422 P. Berlin 10206 a, recto (Luft 1992, 105).
423 Tomb of *Nb-wnn=f* (PM I-1^2, 267 (8); *KRI* III, 283: 2; Sethe 1907a, 30–1; Frood 2007, 36).
424 Graffiti 1111, 1140A–43 (Černý 1956, 4 and 7; *KRI* V, 379: 2 and 8). Amennakht, son of Ipuy, left a number of records at Deir el-Medina. He is attested from the end of the Nineteenth Dynasty to year 7 of Ramses VI or VII (P. Turin 1885: von Beckerath 2000).
425 Inscription on the Ptolemaic gate (PM II^2, 255 (1, e); Sauneron 1983, pl. 8, l. 17; Spalinger 1993b, 167).
426 Graffito on the south wall of chamber I in the tomb of T IV (*Urk.* IV, 2170: 15; Peden 2001, 143; Awad 2002, 115).

4th MONTH of *3ḫ.t* (*nḥb-k3.w/k3-ḥr-k3*/Khoiak); 10th decade (*ḫnwy*) IV Akhet

No.) Day: Event

427) [1]: Procession of Hathor [MK, Lahun][427]
428) 1: Festival of the accession of Amenhotep II, followed by a royal decree [*A II*, 23, Semna][428]
429) 1: Date of a stela [*Ay*, 4][429]
430) 1: Seti I's decree to make an expedition during a night celebration at Thebes [*Seti I*, 6, Silsila][430]
431) 1?: Completion of a building at Luxor [*R II*, 3, Luxor][431]
432) 1: Second(?) Sed Festival of Ramses II [*R II*, 32, DB][432]
433) 1: Hathor Festival (640) [*R III*, MHC][433]
434) 1: Offering to Hathor [R III or IV][434]
435) 1: Petition to Hathor at Deir el-Bahari [Ramesside, DB][435]
436) 1: A man paid a visit to Hathor at Deir el-Bahari [Ramesside, DB][436]
437) 1: *P3y-m3ʿ.t- m-niw.t* praised Hathor at the Festival of the West [Ramesside, DB][437]
438) 1: Date of the bandage of a mummy [Amenemopet, 1, mummy no. 105][438]
439) 1: Day of Drinking (*swr*) [Ptolemy IX, 8?, MH][439]
440) 1: *k3-ḥr-k3* Festival and Appearance of Khnum-Re [Roman, Esna][440]
441) 1: Hathor Festival [AD 1st century, Tanis][441]
442) 1–6: Gods gathered from cities in the regions to attend the Khnum Festival on day 2 [Roman, Esna][442]
443) 2: A festival [Ramesside][443]
444) 3: Royal decree concerning the temple of Osiris at Abydos [*Teti*, Abydos][444]
445) [3]: Taking the River [MK, Lahun][445]
446) 4: Offering to Hathor when she appeared at Deir el-Bahari [R II or III, 20, DB][446]
447) 4: Festival in the 15th Lower Egyptian nome [*Ptolemy IV*, Edfu][447]
448) 5: A man called *Ptḥ-ḥtp*(?) visited the Step Pyramid when T III was in Thebes [*T III*, 1, Saqqara][448]
449) 5: Qenbet session on the properties of a women called *Niw.t-nḫti* at Deir el-Medina [*R V*, 3, DeM][449]
450) 5: Appearance of This August God [*Ptolemy X*, Edfu][450]
451) 5: Procession of Ptah [AD 1st century, Tanis][451]
452) 5: A contract made by the servant *P3=f-tw-ʿw-ḫnsw* [*Amasis*, 8, El-Hiba][452]

---

427 *ḫn.t Ḥw.t-ḥr* (P. Berlin 10282, recto; Luft 1992, 116 and 177). The *šsp-itrw* took place next day. For an undated Hathor's procession see P. UC 32191 (Collier and Quirke 2006, 94). For 'procession' in this month see P. Berlin 10079, recto.

428 *ḥb ḫʿ-nsw.t*. The decree issued to the Nubian viceroy *Wsr-s.tt* (Stela BMFA 25.632: Helck 1955b, 23; *Urk.* IV, 1343: 10; Wente 1990, 27–8). Redford (1965, 121–2), opposed by Bierbrier (1980, 108), took this day as the beginning of his co-regency with his father T III (Cf. IV Peret 1 for the beginning of his sole reign).

429 Stela Louvre C 55 & Stela Berlin 2074 (*Urk.* IV, 2110: 13; *LD* III, pl. 114, i). This is the highest known date of the king Ay.

430 Rock stela (*LD* III, pl. 141, e; *KRI* I, 60: 4).

431 Inscription on the S. face of the E. wing of the 1st pylon of the temple of Luxor (PM II^2, 306, (17, III-2); Redford 1971, 114). Abd el-Razik (1967, 69) read the date as IV Akhet 3.

432 Graffito DB 17 (*KRI* III, 374: 3; Marciniak 1974, 76: 1; Sadek 1984a, 83–4 for translation). The scribe of the double-treasury *Imn-m-ḥb* and his mother visited Deir el-Bahari to present offerings to Amun-Re, lord of *ḏsr.t*, and Hathor of the West.

433 *ḥb Ḥw.t-ḥr* (*MH* III, pl. 158, list 40). This festival began on the 29th of the previous month at Dendera. Cf. Leitz (1994a, 147–8) for a lengthy entry for this day.

434 O. Michaelides 33 (*KRI* V, 613: 10; Jauhiainen 2009, 108–9).

435 Graffito DB 63 (Marciniak 1974, 114: 11).

436 Graffito DB 114 (Marciniak 1974, 144).

437 Graffito DB 58 (Marciniak 1974, 110). *ir nfr ir nfr Ḥw.t-ḥr ir nfr n ḥr ḥb n imnt.t* 'Make good! Make good!. May Hathor make good at the Festival of the West.' Dolińska (2007, 73, n. 39) relates Graffito DB 7, dated to IV Akhet, to this celebration.

438 Kitchen 1973a, 421.

439 P. Berlin 3115 (de Cenival 1972, 105; Pestman 1993, 199 for translation).

440 *ḥb k3-ḥr-k3 sḫ3 n Ḫnm-rʿ* (Sauneron 1963, vol. 1, 126; Grimm 1994a, 54–5). The appearance of the goddess Nebetu is also recorded.

441 *ḥb Ḥw.t-ḥr* (P. BM ESA 10673: Griffith and Petrie 1889, pl. 12).

442 Sauneron 1963, vol. 1, 126–7; Grimm 1994a, 56–9. It is recorded that those gods appeared in the 'house of Khnum of the field' and that this celebration corresponded to one on III Shemu 20.

443 P. Cairo 86637 and P. Sallier IV (Leitz 1994a, 149).

444 Stela BM 626 (*Urk.* I, 208: 8; Goedicke 1967, 37, Abb. 3).

445 P. Berlin 10282, recto (Luft 1992, 116). On the previous day is held *ḫ3w n.t šsp-itrw* 'night of Taking the River'. Cf. IV Akhet 1 for the Rowing of Hathor the previous day.

446 *wdnw n Ḥw.t-ḥr* [ ] *m ḫʿw=s nfr* (Graffito DB 1: Marciniak 1974, 56: 33–4; Sadek 1984a, 71). The scribe *Ns-imn* visited Deir el-Bahari to make offerings to Hathor. Kitchen (*KRI* V, 433–4) and Peden (2001, 121, n. 390) date the graffito to the time of Ramses III.

447 Geographical list on the exterior of the sanctuary (PM VI, 146 (219–20)).

448 Graffito at the south chapel of the Step Pyramid (Firth and Quibell 1935, 80).

449 P. Ashmolean 1945.97 (Černý 1945, 31; Pestman 1982, 174; *KRI* VI, 237: 2). Cf. III Akhet 10 and 17 for the same juridical case.

450 *sḫʿ nṯr pn šps* (Grimm 1994a, 58–9).

451 *ḫn n Ptḥ* (P. BM ESA 10673: Griffith and Petrie 1889, pl. 12). Clagett (1995, 90) concludes that these papyrus fragments were used as a shadow clock.

452 P. Rylands 7 (Menu 1985, 85).

IV Akhet

453) 6: Royal decree to protect the personnel for the cult of Amenhotep, son of Hapu [*A III*, 31, Thebes][453]
454) 7: Offering of the Rowing [MK, 7, Lahun][454]
455) 7: Decision that the queen Ahmes-Nefertari be appointed the 2nd-priest of Amun and the divine wife [*Ahmes*, Karnak][455]
456) 7: Visit of the vizier *Nfr-rnp.t* to lay out the plan of the king's tomb [*R IV*, 5, KV][456]
457) 8: Day of osirifying the princess Ahmes-Satkames [Psusennes I, 7, shroud of mummy][457]
458) 9: Oath over a donkey [20 Dyn., DeM][458]
459) 9–26: Ritual in the Shetyt chamber [Edfu][459]
460) 10: Dated graffito at Wadi Hilâl [6 Dyn., Wadi Hilâl near el-Kab][460]
461) 10+: Dedication text attesting the completetion a work of Ramses II [*R II*, 3, Luxor][461]
462) 10: The workmen received rations in the presence of the vizier *Nfr-rnp.t*, etc. [*R IV*, 3][462]
463) 10: Vizier *Nfr-rnp.t* and the high-priest *Rꜥ-ms-nḫt* visited western Thebes [*R IV*, 4, KV][463]
464) 10: Dispute and oath over a payment [6][464]

4th MONTH of *Ꜣḫ.t* (*nḫb-kꜢ.w/kꜢ-ḥr-kꜢ*/Khoiak); 11th decade (*ḥry-ib wiꜢ*)

No.) Day: Event
465) 11: Taking of the River? [MK, Lahun][465]
466) 11: Festival of Osiris in the Neshmet-barque at Abydos [Ramesside][466]
467) 12: Dated account of grain (*pḫ*) [OK, year of 21st occasion, Abusir][467]
468) 12–21: Rituals of Osiris [Dendera][468]
469) 12–24: Grain germing from 12th to 24th day [Harsiesis: 22 Dyn.][469]
470) 12–30: Osiris Festival [Dendera][470]
471) 14: Taking of the River [MK, Lahun][471]
472) 15: Royal decree to the viceroy of Kush *PꜢ-nḥsy* [*R XI*, 17][472]
473) 16: Royal decree to establish monuments [*Senusret III*, 14, Wadi Hammamat][473]
474) 16: A festival [A I?, Karnak][474]
475) 16: Festival of Sekhmet and Bastet at Isheru [Ramesside][475]
476) 16: Burial of an Apis bull at the Serapeum [*Necho II*, 16, Serapeum][476]
477) 17: Burial of the God [*R II*, 40][477]

453 Stela BM EA 138, one of the earliest known hieratic stela (Varille 1968, 68; Jansen-Winkeln 2007, vol. 1, 167). A later replication (21 Dyn.?) of an original text erected within the mortuary temple of Amenhotep, son of Hapu? He was still active in year 34 (Hayes 1951, 100).
454 P. Berlin 10232 b, recto (Luft 1992, 110).
455 Unnumbered stela (PM II², 73; Harari 1959; Logan 2000, 63–4). This was secure with an *imy.t-pr* document according to the order of her husband Ahmes. She was subsequently given the office in the presence of Amun and the king at the Khoiak Feast.
456 O. Cairo 25565 (*KRI* VI, 142: 16). Cf. III Akhet 21 for another associating event.
457 Gauthier 1907, vol. 3, 268; Kitchen 1973a, 420; Jansen-Winkeln 2007, vol. 1, 21.
458 O. DeM 309 (Černý 1935a, vol. 4, 18, pls. 20 and 20A).
459 Graindorge-Héreil 1994, 178.
460 *LD* text IV, 40; Vandekerckhove and Müller-Wollermann 2001, vol. 1, 210–1, O 144. Carved by the sole companion *Mr-ppy*, who was appointed *dꜢs.ti* in the 'year after the 1st occasion'.
461 PM II², 306 (17, III-2); Abd el-Razik 1974, 145, col. 11 for facsimile; Abd el-Razik 1975, 126 for translation.
462 P. DeM 24 (*KRI* VI, 134: 4; Eyre 1987a; Awad 2002, 101 for translation). The vizier was accompanied by the overseer of the treasury *Mnṯw-tꜢ.wy*, the royal scribe *Ḫꜥ*-[ ], the HPA *Rꜥ-ms-nḫt*, and an unnamed mayor of Thebes (*ḥꜢty-ꜥ niw.t*).
463 O. Cairo 25271 (*KRI* VI, 151: 2). An unnamed overseer of the treasury also accompanied them.
464 P. Turin (unnumbered and unpublished).
465 P. Berlin 10130 B c, recto (Luft 1992, 99).
466 P. Cairo 86637 and P. Sallier IV (Bakir 1966, 27–8; Graindorge-Héreil 1994, 178; Leitz 1994a, 160). For IV Akhet 18 enters the 'making the ointment for Osiris in front of the hall of embalmment'. Van Walsem (1982, 233, n. 22) dates this to R III's time.
467 P. BM 10735, frame 7, verso (Posener-Kriéger and Cenival 1968, 16, pl. 41).
468 Chassinat 1966, 69–73.
469 Cairo 37516 (von Känel 1984, 303).
470 Cauville 2002, 25.
471 P. Berlin 10344 b, recto (Luft 1992, 120).
472 P. Turin 1896 (*KRI* VI, 735: 7).
473 Rock inscription (Couyat and Montet 1912, 49).
474 Unnumbered stone block (Spalinger 1992, 5, pl. I).
475 P. Cairo 86637 and P. Sallier IV (Leitz 1994a, 167).
476 Stela Louvre 193 (Piehl 1886, vol. 1, 21 A).
477 *krs.t pꜢ nṯr* (O. BM 5634: *KRI* III, 518: 9–10 and 520: 15–6; Janssen 1980, 149). According to Plutarch (*Iside et Osiride*, XXXIX), this day corresponds to the first day of the lamentation of Isis, suggesting the death of Osiris whose body was discovered three days later on day 19.

478) 18: Vizier *Ḫꜥ-m-wꜣs.t* paid royal wages (*ḥtri n pr-ꜥꜣ*) to the workmen, and appointed (*swḏ*) two chief workmen and a scribe [R IX, 16][478]
479) 18–25: Moistening Barley for Osiris [*Horemheb*, TT 50][479]
480) 18–26: Khoiak Festival [Alexander II][480]
481) 19: Scribe *Ꞽꜥḥ-ms* visited the Step Pyramid [*A I*, 20, Saqqara][481]
482) 19: Appearance of the king and the restoration of monuments [*Tutankhamen*, 1, Karnak][482]
483) 19: Fan-bearer on the right hand of the king, city-governor *Ḥri* visited KV prior to a royal(?) burial on IV Akhet 22 [Siptah–Tausret, KV][483]
484) 19: Amenhotep I's oracle? [R IV, 2, DeM][484]
485) 19: Vizier *Ḫꜥ-m-wꜣs.t* supplied linen (*ḥbs*) to officials and selected workmen at the Maat temple [R IX, 16][485]
486) 20: Appeal to Amenhotep I by the workman *Ḫꜥ-m-wꜣs.t* and his oracle-giving [R III, 29, DeM][486]
487) 20: Purifying the Ennead (145) [*R III*, MHC][487]
488) 20: Festival of He who Spreads and Extends [*Ptolemy X*, Edfu][488]

4th MONTH of *ꜣḫ.t* (*nḥb-kꜣ.w/kꜣ-ḥr-kꜣ*/Khoiak); 12th decade ('crew'/*sšmw*)

No.) Day: Event
489) 21: Opening the Window in the Shetyt-Chamber (145) [*R III*, MHC][489]
490) 21: Royal butler *Sṯḫ-ḥr-wnmj=f* departed Thebes after resigning some officials [*R IV*, 6, KV][490]
491) 21: Qenbet session concerning a payment [*R XI*, 14][491]
492) 21: Mentu-Re-Horakhety rests at the mound Djeme [Ptolemy II, 18, MH][492]
493) 22: Dated record of a counting of grain [Djedkare-Isesi, year of the 21st census, Neferirkare's temple at Abusir][493]
494) 22: Digging the Earth [*T III*, Akh-menu at Karnak][494]
495) 22: Festival of Ptah, South of His Wall, Lord of Ankhtawy, at Thebes [*Horemheb*, 1, Ptah precinct in Karnak][495]
496) 22: Burial of the king Siptah by the vizier *Ḥri* [Siptah–Tausret, KV][496]
497) 22: Digging the Earth (310) [*R III*, MHC][497]
498) 22: Burial restoration by the royal scribe *Bw-th-imn* at KV 57 [R XI, 4, KV 57 (Horemheb)][498]
499) 22: Night of the Sokar Festival [AD 1st century][499]
500) 22–6: Festival of the Two Kites [*Alexander IV* (305 BC), 12, Thebes?][500]
501) 23: Dragging(?) [*T III*, Karnak][501]
502) 23: Proceeding in the Shetyt-Chamber (298) [*R III*, MHC][502]

---

478 P. Turin 2004+2007+2057+2106 (*KRI* VI, 650: 14). The chief workmen *Wsr-ḫpš* and *Ḥri-ms-sw*, and the scribe *Ḥri-šri*. Cf. IV Akhet 19 for an event the next day.
479 *hrw n iwḥ bšꜣ* (PM I-1^2, 96 (9–10, I); Hari 1985, pl. 33, col. 104).
480 P. Louvre N 3176 (Barguet 1962b; Gaballa and Kitchen 1969, 32).
481 Graffito at the south chapel of the Step Pyramid (Firth and Quibell 1935, 79; Navrátilová 2007, 81–2).
482 Restoration Stela (Cairo 34183: PM II^2, 10 and 52–3; *Urk.* IV, 2025: 18; Cumming and Davies 1982, vol. 6, 1995).
483 O. Cairo 25792 (*KRI* IV, 415: 1).
484 *iw pꜣ nṯr ḏd* 'the god said' (O. DeM 342: Černý 1935a, vol. 5, 2, pl. 1; *KRI* VI, 128: 7–8).
485 P. Turin 2004+2007+2057+2106 (*KRI* VI, 651: 2). Cf. IV Akhet 18 for an event the previous day.
486 *smi n nsw.t Ꞽmn-ḥtp* (O. Cairo 25242, recto: Černý 1927, 179; *KRI* V, 532: 1). Hornung (2006, 205) dates this ostracon to the time of Amenhotep III.
487 *wꜥb psḏ.t* (*MH* III, pl. 158, list 41).
488 *ḥb [d]wn pd ḥry-ib dmꜣ.t* the 'festival of he who spreads and extends, who dwells in the wing' (Grimm 1994a, 60–1).
489 *wn wsy m šty.t* (*MH* III, pl. 158, list 42).
490 O. Cairo 25283 (*KRI* VII, 453: 4). He visited Thebes from at least I Akhet 9 (Graffito 790; *KRI* VI, 145: 3).
491 P. Berlin P 10460 (*KRI* VI, 863: 9; Allam 1973, 275–6).
492 Graffito MH no. 234 located at the slaughter house of the temple of Medinet Habu (Thissen 1989, 140–2; Klotz 2012, 394).
493 Posener-Kriéger (1976, 329) does not see any association of this date with a particular event, but it is probably related to the harvest.
494 South wall of the Akh-menu (PM II^2, 126 (462); *Urk.* IV, 1273: 7; Gardiner 1952, pl. 8).
495 Wall stela (PM II^2, 200 (18); Hari 1964, pl. 60; *Urk.* IV, 2132: 4). This stela records: 'the offerings of the ancestors were founded'. Offerings to Ptah are referred to elsewhere in connection with Sokar (Graindorge-Héreil 1994, 40).
496 O. Cairo 25792 (*KRI* IV, 415: 5).
497 *ḫbs tꜣ* (*MH* III, pl. 158, list 43; Traunecker, Le Saout, and Masson 1981, 124–5).
498 Graffito in KV 57 (Niwiński 1984, 152; Reeves 1990, 234; Peden 2001, 207–8; Jansen-Winkeln 2007, vol. 1, 35). For another occurrence of reburial at the same tomb, see II Akhet 12.
499 Liturgy of the Opening-of-the-Mouth for Breathing (P. Berlin 8351, col. IV, l. 5: M. Smith 1993, 32; M. Smith 2009, 363).
500 P. BM EA 10188=P. Bremner-Rhind (Faulkner 1936 and 1937; M. Smith 2009, 104).
501 *sṯ* (South wall of the Akh-menu (PM II^2, 126 (462); *Urk.* IV, 1273: 8; Gardiner 1952, pl. 8).
502 *ir.t wꜣ.t m šty.t* (*MH* III, pl. 158, list 44). Also see P. BM 10188 (Faulkner 1937, 12–6). At the Akh-menu of Thutmose III, the Day of Purification is

IV Akhet

503) 23: Wab-priest of Ptah *Ḫ*ʿ*-m-w*ȝ*s.t* and a chantress visited DB to petition [R III, 18, DB][503]
504) 23+: Festival in the 5th Upper Egyptian nome [*Ptolemy IV*, Edfu][504]
505) 24: Offering to the deceased Senusret II at the Sokar Festival [MK, 4 and 14, Lahun][505]
506) 24: Placing Sokar in Their Midst (258) [*R III*, MHC][506]
507) 24: Workmen received leather material from the royal butler *Ns-imn* [*R IX*, 7][507]
508) 2[4]: Princess *Ḫb* assumed a priestly title at the temple of Amun-Re-Bull-of-Bowland [*Aspelta*, 3, Gebel Barkal][508]
509) 24: Festival of He who is in Edfu [*Ptolemy X*, Edfu][509]
510) 24: Appearance of Osiris at the Night [Ptolemy XII, Dendera][510]
511) 24–5: Commemoration of the Two Sisters and Great Rite of the Opening-of-the-Mouth at Karnak [Alexander II][511]
512) 25: Sokar Festival [Djedkare-Isesi, year of the 3rd census, Neferirkare's temple at Abusir][512]
513) 25: Day of the Full Moon when a contract was made [8th Dyn., (1), Koptos][513]
514) 25: Sokar Festival [MK, 8, Lahun][514]
515) 25: *Nṯry.t* Ritual (1237) [*R III*, MHC][515]
516) 25: Taharqa renewed the enclosure wall of Karnak during a festival [*Taharqa*, Mut precinct][516]
517) 25 Appearance of Osiris at the 12th hour of the day [Ptolemy XII, Dendera][517]
518) 25: Osiride ritual [Ptolemaic, Thebes][518]
519) 25: Opening the Doors of the Temple and Evening Offering [Roman, Esna][519]
520) 26: Sokar Festival [MK, Lahun][520]
521) 26: Ritual of Sokar (3694) [*R III*, MHC][521]
522) 26: Sokar-Osiris Festival [R III or Siptah, 6][522]
523) 26: Tying Onions [Ramesside, TT 219][523]
524) 26: Offering to Amun of Kawa [Aryamani: 3rd cent. BC, Kawa][524]

---

attested for this day (Gardiner 1952, pl. 8).

503 Graffiti DB 23 and 24 (*KRI* V, 423–4; Marciniak 1974, 81–3; Sadek 1984a, 86–7; Peden 2001, 121, n. 389). In Graffito DB 24 *Ḫ*ʿ*-m-w*ȝ*s.t* appealed to Hathor, saying 'Let my heart be gladdened, when I am in your house today. Indeed, there is no one with me except you'. This statement may allude to an incubation ritual over the night. On 10 June 2008 at a seminar in Oxford, Hans-Werner Fischer-Elfert presented an unpublished ostracon (O. DeM 1059), which records that an ill man *Mri-sḫm.t* performed the same kind of ritual on the 7th(?) day of the Festival of *k*ȝ*-ḥr-k*ȝ (*rn n nṯr.t hrw 7 n k*ȝ*-ḥr-k*ȝ 'name of the goddess of the day 7 of Khoiak'). For incubation rituals see Szpakowska 2003, 142–51.

504 Geographical list on the exterior of the sanctuary (PM VI, 147 (223–4)).

505 P. Berlin 10042, recto and 10053, recto (Luft 1992, 64 and 68).

506 *rdi Skr n ḥry-ib=sn* (*MH* III, pl. 158, list 45). The 'Coming-Out of Isis and Nephtys' is elsewhere known for this day (Leitz 1994a, 181). Ritualistic Osiris drama performed during this festival is recorded at Dendera (Parker 1950, 59–60). In Edfu the 28th day is described as the fifth lunar day, which means the 24th day is the first lunar day (Parker 1950, 60). Note that a pig (*iph*) is listed among the offerings.

507 P. Turin 1881+2080+2092 (*KRI* VI, 611: 10).

508 Stela Louvre C 257 (Eide, Hägg, and Pierce 1994, vol. 1, 260). She succeeded her mother *Mdknn*.

509 *ḥb bḥd.ty nḥm.n=f šs n it=f m-*ʿ *pf* 'Festival of he who is in Edfu. He took away the cloth of his father from the hand of this (Seth)' (Grimm 1994a, 62–3).

510 *ḫ*ʿ *in Wsir m d*ȝ*w ḥtp m-ḥr pš.t* 'resting in fornt of the sea' (Grimm 1994a, 62–3).

511 The *sḫ*ȝ *sn.ty* taking place from the evening of day 24 to the morning of day 25 at the House of Gold in Karnak (P. Louvre N 3176: Barguet 1962b, 16, ll. 7–10).

512 P. Louvre E 25416 c+P. Cairo 602, frame X, verso (Posener-Kriéger and de Cenival 1968, 6, pl. 13; Posener-Kriéger 1976, vol. 1, 61 for translation).

513 Stela Cairo 43290 (Goedicke 1994, 72, pl. 9). The contract, concerning temple offerings, was made between the god Min and a member of the *pat Ḥtp-k*ȝ*-mnw*.

514 P. Berlin 10056, recto (Luft 1992, 71).

515 *nṯry.t* (*MH* III, pl. 158, list 46). In TT 2 (9), *ṯsi.tw ḥḏ.t grḥ nṯry.t ḥḏ t*ȝ *m tri n dw*ȝ*.t* 'onion is tied (to neck?) (from) the night of *nṯry.t* (to) the sunrise in the time of the morning' is recorded (Černý 1949, 14). Also see a similar record in TT 50 (9–10, I): *hrw nṯry.t rn ṯsi ḥḏ n Wsir* 'day of the *nṯry.t* ritual, that is, tying onion to Osiris' (Dümichen 1866, pl. 36: 42–3). TT 9 (6, I) represents this feast (Černý 1949, 71 for text). Also see Frood 2007, 135. The 25th and 26th days are always referred to as 'the day of the Sokar Festival' in the Old Kingdom (Strudwick 2005, 88, 166), and the days following until the 30th seem to be grouped as a single festival at Esna and Dendera. The extended duration of the festival was perhaps first created by Ramses II because Amenhotep III began the festival on the 26th (Aldred 1969, 76). The eve of this festival celebrated for Osiris at Abydos and for Sokar was called the *h*ȝ*kr*-Feast and *nṯry.t*-Feast respectively (Assmann 2001, 355). For the former festival, followed by the processions of Upwaut and Osiris, see Iskander 2011.

516 *iw sm*ȝ *n sbty n ḥw.t-nṯr n.t 'Imn m ip.t-s.wt* (PM II^2, 258 (12); Mariette 1875, pl. 42: 23).

517 Grimm 1994a, 62–3.

518 P. Berlin 3008, I, 1 (M. Smith 2009, 129).

519 *wn* ʿȝ*.wy m r*ȝ*-pr.w iḫ.t ḫ*ȝ*w.t* (Sauneron 1963, vol. 1, 127; Grimm 1994a, 62–3).

520 P. Berlin 10001B, verso (Luft 1992, 27).

521 *ḥb Skr* (*MH* III, pl. 160, list 47). Some pieces of papyri from Lahun also record this festival on the 26th day (P. Berlin 10001 B, verso, and 10104, recto: Luft 1992, 27 and 93).

522 P. UC 34336 (*KRI* V, 445: 6). Colllier (2011, 119) dates this papyrus to the time of Siptah.

523 *hrw pn n tpy n ṯs ḥḏ.w* 'this day of the first of tying onions' (PM I-1^2, 321 (5); Schott 1950, 91 (75) for translation).

524 Fragments of Stela BM 1777 (Eide, Hägg, and Pierce 1994, vol. 2, 528).

IV Akhet

525) 26: Osiris Festival [Ptolemy III, Hibeh (but related to Sais)][525]
526) 26: Day of Drinking (*swr*) [Ptolemy IX, 8?, MH][526]
527) 26: Sokar Festival in the morning [*Ptolemy X*, Edfu][527]
528) 26: Appearance of Sokar at the 1st hour of the day [Ptolemy XII, Dendera][528]
529) 26: Mentu of Armant visited Medinet Habu to present offerings to fathers and mothers [Greek-Roman, MH][529]
530) 26: Dated graffito [Ptolemaic-Roman, 10, MH][530]
531) 26: Moistening (at) the Appearance of Mentu [Ptolemaic-Roman, 1, MH][531]
532) 26: Sokar Festival [Roman, Esna][532]
533) 26–30: Resting at Begau [*Ptolemy VI*, Kom Ombo][533]
534) 27: Ritual of Anointing the Ennead (304) [*R III*, MHC][534]
535) 27: Royal decree concerning an inspector of wab-priests and land tenants [Djedkare-Isesi, year of the 15th census, Reneferef's temple at Abusir][535]
536) 27: Great qenbet at Thebes [R IX, 14][536]
537) 27?: Dated graffito [Ptolemy XII, 18, MH][537]
538) 27: Neith Festival, Opening of the Doors at the Seats, and Anointing the Gods [Roman, Esna][538]
539) 28: Day of Dragging the Benben (50) [*R III*, MHC][539]
540) 28: Graffito of the royal scribe *Bw-th-imn* to perpetuate his father's name [Smendes I, 10, West Thebes][540]
541) 28: Festival of the Offerings on the Altar [*Ptolemy X*, Edfu][541]
542) 29 (or 19): Controller of the phyle (*mty n sꜣ*) *Mry* gave his title to his son *Ꞽn-it=f* [MK, 37, Lahun][542]
543) 29: Procession of Re [*Niuserre*, Abu Gurob][543]
544) 29: Unspecified festival (385) [*R III*, MHC][544]
545) 29: Appearance of Hathor, lady of Dendera, at the *nḥb-kꜣ.w* Festival [*Ptolemy X*, Edfu][545]
546) 29: Ritual performed for the gods of the mound Djeme [Cleopatra VII, 3, MH][546]
547) 30: Mayor of el-Kab *Kbsi* sold his office to his relative *Sbk-nḫt* [*Nebiryaut* of 17 Dyn., 1, Karnak][547]
548) 30: Khnum Festival in Elephantine [*T III*, Elephantine][548]
549) 30: Erecting the Djed-Pillar (177) [*R III*, MHC][549]
550) 30: Appeal to AmenhotepIby the workman *Ḳn-nꜣ* and an oath-taking [R V, 4, DeM][550]
551) 30: Qenbet session, followed by an oath taken by a man called *Wsr-ḥꜣ.t* [*R III*, 29][551]

---

525 P. Hibeh 27, l. 60 (Grenfell and Hunt 1906, 144).
526 P. Berlin 3115 (de Cenival 1972, 105; Pestman 1993, 199 for translation).
527 *ḥb Skr m tri n dwꜣ.t* (Grimm 1994a, 62–3).
528 *ḫꜥ in Skr* (Grimm 1994a, 64–5).
529 Graffiti on the Ptolemaic pylon and the doorway of the Roman court at Medinet Habu (Egberts 1995, 348–9, pl. 150, a and b; Klotz 2012, 393). The first text says that he visited the mound of Djeme to present offerings (*wꜣḥ iḫ.t*) to fathers and mothers.
530 Graffito MH no. 128 located on the roof of the second court of Medinet Habu temple (Thissen 1989, 97–8).
531 Graffito MH no. 129 located on the roof of the second court of Medinet Habu temple (Thissen 1989, 98–9; Klotz 2012, 394). *tḫb pꜣ ḫꜥ Mnṯ.*
532 *ḥb Skr* (Sauneron 1963, vol. 1, 128; Grimm 1994a, 64–5).
533 *ḥtp m bg[ꜣw]* (Grimm 1994a, 62–3).
534 *ḥb n wrḥ psḏ.t* (*MH* III, pl. 160, list 48). Also see *wrḥ nṯr.w* 'anointing of the gods' recorded in a Middle Kingdom papyrus (Collier and Quirke 2006, 95).
535 Abusir X, 236–7, pl. 20. The decree was sealed in the presence of the king and dispatched(?) next day.
536 P. Turin 2071+1960 (*KRI* VI, 641:16; Allam 1973, 329).
537 Graffito MH no. 77 located at the slaughter house of Medinet Habu temple (Thissen 1989, 72–3).
538 *ḥb N.t wn ꜥꜣ.wy m s.wt wrḥ nṯr.w* (Sauneron 1963, vol. 1, 128; Grimm 1994a, 64–5).
539 *hrw n stꜣ bnbn* (*MH* III, pl. 160, list 49).
540 Graffito 1286 (Černý 1956; Kitchen 1973a, 418).
541 *ḥb iḫ.wt ḥr ḫꜣw.t* (Grimm 1994a, 64–5).
542 An *imy.t-pr* document regarding a title transfer from a father to his son (P. UC 32037: Collier and Quirke 2004, 100–1).
543 *ḫn.t rꜥ.* The festival took place on the 29th of every month at Niuserre's solar temple (Helck 1977, 59, etc.).
544 Damaged inscription (*MH* III, pl. 160, list 50). P. Berlin 10104, recto records an unknown ritual *stp nṯr* (Luft 1992, 93).
545 *ḫꜥ in Ḥw.t-ḥr* (Grimm 1994a, 64–5). She appeared with her Ennead to the *ḏꜣḏꜣ*-hall.
546 Graffito MH no. 45 located at the small temple of Medinet Habu (Thissen 1989, 30–6).
547 Juridical Stela (Cairo 52453: PM II², 52; Helck 1975, 65–9; Logan 2000, 60–3). The transfer of the office was insured by an *imy.t-pr* document. All the witnesses swore next day on I Peret 1.
548 Stone fragment from a festival list (*LD* III, pl. 43, f; *Urk.* IV, 823: 17).
549 *sꜥḥꜥ ḏd.* (*MH* III, pl. 160, list 51).
550 *smi n Ꞽmn-ḥtp pꜣ nb ꜥ.w.s. pꜣ dmi* (O. BM 5625: *KRI* VI, 252: 3–4; Blackman 1926, 181, pl. 35; McDowell 1990, 112). A divine verdict was given on the spot of the real estate over which a dispute arose.
551 P. Turin 1880 (Strike Papyrus): Gardiner 1948, 47; McDowell 1999, 36. The man took an oath not to be separated from his daughters perhaps after his wife's death.

552) 30: Report (or complaint) over an unspecified matter [20 Dyn., DeM][552]
553) 30: Second day of the Hathor Festival and the Festival of Erecting the Djed-Pillar [*Ptolemy* X, Edfu][553]
554) 30: Mentu-Re-Horakhety rests at the mound Djeme [Cleopatra VII, 9, MH][554]
555) 30: Festival of Erecting the Djed-Pillar of Osiris [Roman, Esna][555]
556) 30–I Peret 4 (or 5): Appearance of Haroeris and Hathor [*Ptolemy VI*, Kom Ombo][556]

4th MONTH of *ꜣḫ.t* (*nḥb-kꜣ.w/kꜣ-ḥr-kꜣ*/Khoiak); unknown decade

No.) Day: Event
557) ?: Taking of the River [MK, Lahun][557]
558) ?: Scribe *Bꜣki*, a native of Thebes, visited the Step Pyramid [18 Dyn., 36?, Step Pyramid][558]
559) ?: Reward (*ḥs.w*) given by the king to a person [R III or IV, 1, Thebes][559]
560) ?: Following Khonsu at Deir el-Bahari [Ramesside, 20, DB][560]
561) ?: Sed Festival of Osorkon II [*Osorkon II*, 22, Bubastis][561]

[552] O. IFAO 294 (unpublished).
[553] *ḥb sꜥḥꜥ [n] ḏd* (Grimm 1994a, 66–7).
[554] Graffito MH no. 53 located at the small temple of Medinet Habu (Thissen 1989, 58–60).
[555] *ḥb sꜥḥꜥ ḏd n Wsir* (Sauneron 1963, vol. 1, 128; Grimm 1994a, 66–7).
[556] *sḫꜥ n Ḥr-wr Ḥw.t-ḥr* (Grimm 1994a, 66–7).
[557] P. Berlin 10282, recto (Luft 1992, 116).
[558] Graffito at the south chapel of the Step Pyramid (Firth and Quibell 1935, vol. 1, 81).
[559] O. Ashmolean 264+O. Cochrane (older text of a palimpsest document which has been unpublished, but referred to by Janssen (1994, 94, n. 22). The reward included copper.
[560] Graffito DB 7 (Marciniak 1974, 66; Sadek 1984a, 79). Dolińska (2007, 73, n. 39) dates this to IV Akhet 1.
[561] Inscription on the gate of the festival hall at Bubastis (Naville 1892, pl. 6). Accession ceremonies were also held (van Siclen 1973, 294) and tax exemption for Thebes was declared (Spalinger 1991, 29–30; Galán 2000).

1st MONTH of *pr.t* (*šf-bd.t*/*t3-ꜥ3b.t*/Tybi)*; 13th decade (*knm*/*tp-ꜥ smd*) I Peret

No.) Day: Event

562) 1?: Scribe *Ḫꜥw-m-mn-nfr* visited the Step Pyramid [*AII*, 4, south chapel of the Step Pyramid at Saqqara][562]
563) 1: *Nḥb-k3.w* [Amenemhat III, 35, Lahun][563]
564) 1: *Nḥb-k3.w* [*T III*, 15, Karnak][564]
565) 1?: Morning of the *nḥb-k3.w* [*Horemheb*, TT 50][565]
566) 1: Decree while the king performed ceremonies to various gods in Memphis [*Seti I*, 4, Nauri][566]
567) 1: Decrees to prepare for the Sed Festival [*R II*, 42 and 44, Gebel el-Silsila] [*R II*, 54, Armant][567]
568) 1: *Nḥb-k3.w* and Appearance of the King (4531+) [*R III*, MHC][568]
569) 1?: Royal decree to donate a land to statues of Amun-Re & Ramses III [*R III*, 2, Medamud][569]
570) 1: Festival? (*wp*) [R IV][570]
571) [1 or later]: *K3-ḥr-k3* Festival when the *šꜥ.t-bi.t* bread was delivered [20 Dyn.][571]
572) 1: Amun-Re's procession and oracle at the *Nḥb-k3.w* Feast, and HPA Osorkon (III) issued two decrees [*Takelot II*, 2, Karnak][572]
573) 1: Donation of a land plot to Hathor [*Sheshonq III*, 32, Kom el-Hisn?][573]
574) 1: Donation to Sekhmet and Heka [Sheshonq V, 30, Kom Firin?][574]
575) 1: Festival in the 20th Upper and the 1st Lower Egyptian nomes [*Ptolemy IV*, Edfu][575]
576) 1: New Year Festival of Horus of Edfu, son of Osiris and Re, and Appearance of the King [*Ptolemy X*, Edfu][576]
577) 1: Ritual performed for the gods of the mound Djeme [Ptolemy XII, 26, MH][577]
578) 1: Ritual performed for the gods of the mound Djeme [Cleopatra VII, 11, MH][578]
579) 1: Mut proceeds to Thebes [Ptolemaic, Mut temple at Karnak][579]
580) 1: Dated private inscription [Augustus, 42 (18 Dec AD 12), near Malgata village to the north of Karnak][580]
581) 1: Dated Greek graffito [*Domitian*, 6, DB][581]
582) 1–2: Slaughtering a donkey for the god [*Constantine the Great*, AD 324, DB][582]
583) 1: Tefnut Festival [Roman, Esna][583]
584) 1: Dated graffito [Ptolemaic-Roman, 39, MH][584]
585) 1: Horus began his battle against his enemies at Edfu and then Tod [*Ptolemy XI*, year 363 of Re's divine era, Edfu][585]
586) 2: Unknown event [A III, 20, Mortuary temple of Amenhotep, son of Hapu][586]
587) 2: Offering to Re-Horakhety [*Seti I*, 8, Serabit el-Khadim][587]
588) 2: Viceroy of Kush *St3w* installed a stela at the Wadi el-Sebua temple [*R II*, 44, Wadi el-Sebua][588]

*For the popular name of this month in the late New Kingdom *p3 ḫnw Mw.t*, see Depuydt 1997, 58–9.

562 Graffito (Navrátilová 2007, 92–4).

563 P. UC 32191 (Luft 1992, 140; Collier and Quirke 2006, 94 for better transcription and facsimile).

564 PM II², 106 (329); *Urk*. IV, 177; el-Sabban 2000, 19.

565 *dw3y.t n.t nḥb-k3.w* (PM I-1², 96 (9–10, I); Dümichen 1866, pl. 37: 10). The bark of Sokar is depicted enshrined in the next scene.

566 Rock stela (*KRI* I, 46: 2; Griffith 1927, 196; Černý 1961, 150; Spalinger 1991, 31–8; B. Davies 1997a, 277–308). The year is called the 'front of eternity' (*ḥ3.t nḥḥ*).

567 Records from Armant and Gebel el-Silsila include the proclamation of the 5th Sed Festival in year 42, the 6th in year 44 (or 45), and the 9th in year 54 (Mond and Myers 1940, pl. 93; *KRI* II, 394: 5 and 15, and 396: 10).

568 *nḥb-k3(.w) n ḫꜥ-nsw.t* (*MH* III, pl. 163, list 52). The *nḥb-k3.w*-serpent was considered a manifestation of the young Horus (Gardiner 1917, 40; Parker 1950, 62).

569 Stela IFAO 5413 (Kitchen 1973b, 195; *KRI* V, 227: 7).

570 O. Ashmolean 70 (Černý and Gardiner 1957, 20, pl. 48, 1, recto; Jauhiainen 2009, 245).

571 O. Berlin 12406, verso (not yet fully published).

572 *ḥb=f nfr m nḥb-k3.w* 'his beautiful festival at Nehebkau' (Bubastite Gate: Caminos 1958, 34–5, 54, and 57–8; Jansen-Winkeln 2007, vol. 2, 161–8). The oracle was given to appoint Osorkon (III) the HPA, and the two decrees concerned endowment to Karnak.

573 Stela Cairo TN 21.3.25.15 (Meeks 1979, 669 (22.8.32); Jansen-Winkeln 2007, vol. 2, 201).

574 Stela IFAO 14456 (Meeks 1979, 666 (22.0.30); Jansen-Winkeln 2007, vol. 2, 276).

575 Geographical list on the exterior of the sanctuary (PM VI, 146 (221–2) and 147 (223–4)).

576 *ḥb wpy-rnp.t n Ḥr* (Grimm 1994a, 66–7).

577 Graffito MH no. 43 located at the small temple of Medinet Habu (Thissen 1989, 15–8).

578 Graffito MH no. 51 located at the small temple of Medinet Habu (Thissen 1989, 51–5).

579 Ptolemaic gate (PM II², 255 (1, f); Sauneron 1983, pl. 9, l. 24; Spalinger 1993b, 171). The date is double-dated as being the 6th (lunar?) day.

580 A Greek stone fragment dedicated by an individual named Epaphroditos in honour of his friend Isidoros (Wagner 1971, 37, pl. 8).

581 Graffito no. 121 located at Hatshepsut's temple at Deir-el-Bahari (Bataille 1951, 82).

582 Greek graffito, left by the iron-workers of Armant at Hatshepsut's temple at Deir el-Bahari (PM II², 364, niche D; Łajtar 1991, 55–6; Klotz 2012, 397).

583 *ḥb Tfnw.t* (Sauneron 1963, vol. 1, 128; Grimm 1994a, 66–7).

584 Graffito MH no. 140 located on the roof of the second court of Medinet Habu temple (Thissen 1989, 104).

585 Horus myth (Egberts1997, 49).

586 Inscription on a stone fragment (Varille 1968, 96–7).

587 Stela *in situ* (Gardiner, Peet, and Černý 1952, vol. 1, pl. 68, vol. 2, 175).

588 He was the chief officer of the military campaign (Stela Cairo 41395: *KRI* III, 92: 5; Frood 2007, 207 for translation).

I Peret

589) 2: *Nḥb-k3.w* Festival [*R II*, TT 341][589]
590) 2: *K3-ḥr-k3* Festival [20 Dyn., DeM][590]
591) 2: Uadjet Festival [*T III*, Buto][591]
592) 2: Oath taken by the door-keeper *Ḫꜥ-m-w3s.t* concerning an assignment of workmen [*R III*, 29][592]
593) 2: 7th expedition to the Eastern Desert by the scribe of the double-treasury *Ḫnsw-ms* [R VII, 1][593]
594) 2: Inundation of the Nile [*Osorkon III*, 3, Luxor][594]
595) [2?]: Festival of *tḫy* of the Eye of Re [*Ptolemy X*, Edfu][595]
596) 2+: Mut Festival [AD 1st century, Tanis][596]
597) 2: Battle between Horus and his enemies at Dendera [*Ptolemy XI*, year 363 of Re's divine era, Edfu][597]
598) 3: Unknown festival [Karnak][598]
599) 3: Vizier *T3* and the scribe *Ỉmn-nḫt* were present at West Thebes [*R III*, 21][599]
600) 3: Appearance of Haroeris on the Great Seat [*Ptolemy VI*, Kom Ombo][600]
601) 4: *K3-ḥr-k3* Festival as the first day of *Nḥb-k3.w* Festival(?) [18/20 Dyn.][601]
602) 4: Decree to dig a well in Akuyata (*i-k3-y-t*) [*R II*, 3, Kubban][602]
603) 4: Oath concerning a mistreated woman [R III, 23][603]
604) 4: Dated Greek graffito [Ptolemaic-Roman, DB][604]
605) 4: Coming-Around of Sekhenu-Nefer [Roman, Esna][605]
606) 5: *K3-ḥr-k3* Festival of Meretseger [R V, West Thebes][606]
607) 5: Amun's oracle to make a decision on a military campaign [*Harsiyotef*: 4th cent. BC, 35][607]
608) 5, 6, or 9: King is in the 'Mansion of Rejoice in the Horizon (*bḫn n ḥꜥ m 3ḫ.t*)' at Thebes [A IV, 2 or 12, Amarna][608]
609) 6: Dated letter from a qenbet court to the king [Amenemhat III, 17, Lahun][609]
610) 6: Amun's Festival of Writing the King's Name on the *išd*-Tree in the Temple of Ptah (640) [*R III*, MHC][610]
611) 6: Appearance of the goddesses Tasenetneferet and Hathor, and of the god Panebtauy [*Ptolemy VI*, Kom Ombo][611]
612) 6: Battle between Horus and his enemies at a town called *ḥbnw* [*Ptolemy XI*, year 363 of Re's divine era, Edfu][612]

[589] The deceased is portrayed receiving offerings (PM II^2, 409 (8–9); *KRI* III, 363: 15; Davies 1948, 39, pl. 28). TT 46 (1), TT 93 (G, a), and TT 345 (3 and 5) also depict an offering scene that took place at the Nehebkau Feast.

[590] O. Berlin P 12635, recto, ll. 9–10 (Gardiner 1955b, 30–1). 'My Uplifting of Horus (*p3=i f3i Ḥr*)', 'the navigation of the god (*t3 d3y n p3 nṯr*)', 'the Coming of the Gods from the East (*p3 ii n3 nṯr.w m i3bt.t*)', 'My Feast of Taweret (*p3y=i ḥb n T3-wr.t*)', and a 'night supper (*msy*)' are recorded perhaps as preceding I Peret 1. The Feast of Taweret is elsewhere recorded in O. DeM 230.

[591] Buto Stela 209 (Bedier 1994a, 5, z. 18; Klug 2002, 96–105).

[592] P. Turin 1880 (Strike Papyrus): Černý 1973, 188. Cf. III Peret 28 for a possibly relating event.

[593] P. IFAO (Koenig 1979, 192, pl. 31).

[594] Graffito at Luxor (Bell 1975, 244; Jansen-Winkeln 2007, vol. 2, 298).

[595] *ḥb tḫy* [*n*] *ir.t Rꜥ* (Grimm 1994a, 68–9).

[596] P. BM ESA 10673 (Griffith and Petrie 1889, pl. 12).

[597] Horus myth (Egberts1997, 49).

[598] Unnumbered stone block (Spalinger 1992, 15, pl. II).

[599] Graffiti nos. 245+247 (*KRI* V, 380: 12; Spiegelberg 1921, 23, nos. 245 and 247). Also see nos. Graffiti 99+100, dated to this year, recording *T3* and *Ỉmn-nḫt* (*KRI* V, 380: 7–10).

[600] *ḥꜥ n Ḥr-wr ḥr s.t wr.t* (Grimm 1994a, 68–9).

[601] *m tpy pr.t sw 4 n ir.t k3-ḥr-k3 m tpy nḥb* (or *n ḥb*) [ ] (Book of the Dead belonging to Neferrenpet, now in Bruxelles (E 5043), corresponding to Chapter 42: Speleers 1917, pls. 26 and 29; Gardiner 1955b, 15).

[602] Kubban Stela now in Grenoble (*KRI* II, 353: 14, 354: 14). The decree was issued when the king performed ceremonies for his fathers and all the gods of south and north at Memphis. Akuyata is thought to be the area of Wadi Allaqi in Lower Nubia (Frood 2007, 252, n. 10). The text portrays the king appearing (*ḥꜥ*) with the *sšd*-headdress but the vignette of the stela does not show it.

[603] O. Bodleian Library 253 (Allam 1973, 40; *KRI* V, 485: 4; McDowell 1999, 33).

[604] Graffito no. 64 located at Hatshepsut's temple at Deir-el-Bahari (Bataille 1951, 41).

[605] *pr r ḥ3 in Sḫnw-nfr* (Grimm 1994a, 68–9).

[606] Graffito 2087 (*KRI* VI, 271: 9; Černý and Sadek 1969, vol. 4, 38).

[607] Stela Cairo 48864 (Eide, Hägg, and Pierce 1994, vol. 2, 453).

[608] Amarna Letter EA 27 (Knudtzon, Ebeling, and Weber 1915, 240–1; *Urk.* IV, 1995: 16; Fritz 1991, 213). See II Peret 8 of year 12, recorded in the tombs of *Mry-rꜥ* and *Ḥwy3* at Amarna, for an event perhaps relating to this. Murnane (1976, 165–6) argued the event in discussion was not one held at Amarna but one to be celebrated in Mitanni, based on his emended reading of the text and date.

[609] P. Berlin 10045 (Luft 2006, 87).

[610] *ḥb Ỉmn w3ḥ.n nsw.t-bi.ty N m-ḥ.t gb.t išd ḥt.ti ḥr rn n nsw.t-bi.ty N m pr Ptḥ* (*MH* III, pl. 163, list 56; Haring 1997, 96 for translation). See II Shemu 23 and IV Shemu 12 for the same ceremony.

[611] *ḥꜥ n T3-sn.t-nfr.t Ḥw.t-ḥr P3-nb-t3.wy* (Grimm 1994a, 68–9).

[612] Horus myth (Egberts1997, 49).

613) 6: Coptic feast of circumcision[613]
614) 7: Festival in the 5th Upper Egyptian nome [*Ptolemy IV*, Edfu][614]
615) 7: Renenutet Festival [*Ptolemy* X, Edfu][615]
616) 7: Battle between Horus and his enemies at the Oxyrhynchites, moving to the Herakleopolites [*Ptolemy XI*, year 363 of Re's divine era, Edfu][616]
617) 8: Oath taken regarding a list of the household of the soldier *Snfr* [*Amenemhat* V, 5, Lahun][617]
618) 8: Nubian mission [*Senusret I*, 18, Buhen][618]
619) 8: Renewal of a decree concerning boundary stelae [*A IV*, 8, Amarna][619]
620) 8: Construction of Tausret's tomb began [Siptah or Seti II, 2, KV][620]
621) 8: Hearing of thieves by a vizier at the Maat temple in Thebes [*R IX*, 17][621]
622) 8: Festival of Horus, Lord of the Mountains [AD 1st century, Tanis][622]
623) 9: Festival of the Lady of Dendera [*Ptolemy* X, Edfu][623]
624) 9–10: Three A I's oracular sessions to order the policeman *Ỉmn-ḫ*ʿ to pay for a donkey [20 Dyn., 4, DeM][624]
625) 10: Scribe *Ḫ*ʿ*-m-mn.w-nfr* visited the Step Pyramid [*A II*, 4, Step Pyramid][625]
626) 10: Execution of Amun (or Amenhotep?)'s decree to appoint *Ḥwr-n=f* a vizier [*R III*, 15][626]
627) 10: Oath taken by the water carrier *Ḫ*ʿ*-m-tr* concerning a donkey [R III, 28, DeM][627]
628) 10: Oath taken by the water carrier *Pꜣ-*ʿ*-m-tꜣ-in.t* [*R III*, 31][628]
629) 10: Qenbet session [R IX, 17, DeM][629]
630) 10: Donation to the god Thoth of Amheida [Takelot III, 13, Dakhla Oasis][630]
631) 10: Payment for a male servant and oath-taking by Amun's singer *Di-ꜣs.t-ḥb=s* [*Taharqa*, 10][631]
632) 10: Dated graffito [Ptolemaic-Roman, 8, MH][632]

1st MONTH of *pr.t* (*šf-bd.t*/*tꜣ-*ʿ*ꜣb.t*/Tybi); 14th decade (*smd srt*)

No.) Day: Event
633) 11: Coptic beginning of the harvest season [Coptic][633]
634) 13: Stela concerning the blessing of Ptah for Ramses II [*R II*, 35, Abu Simbel][634]
635) 13: Festival in the 19th Lower Egyptian nome [*Ptolemy IV*, Edfu][635]
636) 13: Initiation of a Buchis bull at Armant [*Nechtharmais*, 3, Armant][636]

613 Gregorios 1991, 1106. See Bailey 1996 for general discussion on circumcision.
614 Geographical list on the exterior of the sanctuary (PM VI, 147 (223–4)).
615 *ḥb Rnnw.t* (Grimm 1994a, 68–9).
616 Horus myth carved in the time of Ptolemy XI (PM VI, 160 (308–11, 2nd register); *Edfou* VI, 121, 7; Fairman 1935, 33–4; Egberts1997, 49). This was called *ḥb ḫn* the 'Festival of Navigation'. Plutarch (*De Iside et Osiride*, 50) remarked the significance of this day as 'the arrival of Isis from Phoenicia'. The battle took place in year 363 of the god Re and continued until I Peret 14.
617 P. UC 32163 (Griffith 1898, IX, 9–10; Wilson 1948, 142; Collier and Quirke 2004, 110–1). The list was drawn up on IV Akhet 25 and an oath concerning it was taken on I Peret 8 at a vizier's office.
618 Stela Florence 2540 (Smith 1976, 40, pl. 69).
619 Boundary stelae (Davies 1903, vol. 5, 19–34, pls. 25–8; *Urk.* IV, 1986: 12; Lichtheim 1973, vol. 2, 51). Redford and Murnane (1976) suggested that this event was related to the king's accession anniversary.
620 O. Cairo 72452 (*KRI* IV 404: 4). Altenmüller (1984, 45) dates the ostracon to the time of Siptah, while Roehrig (2012, 50) opts for Seti II.
621 P. BM 10053, recto (Peet 1930b, 104). The examination was done by the vizier *Ḫ*ʿ*-m-wꜣs.t* and the HPA *Ỉmn-ḥtp*. Cf. II Peret 21 for the outcome of the hearing.
622 P. BM ESA 10673 (Griffith and Petrie 1889, pl. 12).
623 *ḥb nb(.t) iwn.t* (Grimm 1994a, 70–1).
624 O. DeM 133, recto (*KRI* VI, 425–6; Allam 1973, 100–1; McDowell 1999, 174–5). Prior to I Peret 8 Amenhotep I ordered *Ỉmn-ḫ*ʿ to pay for a donkey, and the issue was put again before oracles on these consecutive days for the 2nd and 3rd sessions, followed by *Ỉmn-ḫ*ʿ's oath-taking before witnesses.
625 Graffito at the south chapel of the Step Pyramid (Firth and Quibell 1935, vol. 1, 80).
626 O. Florence 2619 (Wolterman 1996, 151). Wolterman suggests that he succeeded the northern vizier *Ḥri*.
627 O. DeM 782 (Grandet 2000a, vol. 8, 58 and 184).
628 O. Gardiner 104 (*KRI* V, 155: 11).
629 P. Turin 2029+2078+2083, etc. (*KRI* VI, 593: 13; Botti and Peet 1928, pl. 43).
630 Hieratic block SCA 2816 (Kaper and Demarée 2005; Jansen-Winkeln 2007, vol. 2, 329).
631 P. Louvre E 3228 d (Menu 1985, 77).
632 Graffito MH no. 122 located on the roof of the second court of Medinet Habu temple (Thissen 1989, 94–5).
633 Wissa-Wassef 1991b, 444. This season continued until II Shemu 11, corresponding to 19 January to 18 June (Gregorian). The coldest period of the year ends on this day (from IV Akhet 1 for 40 days) and another agricultural cycle of 40 days began for preparing for grinding the first crops until II Peret 20.
634 Stela in the main hall in the great Abu Simbel temple (PM VII, 106; *LD* III, pl. 194).
635 Geographical list on the exterior of the sanctuary (PM VI, 146 (219–20)).
636 Bucheum stela no. 1 (Mond and Myers 1934, vol. 2, 2, vol. 3, pl. 37; Goldbrunner 2004, pl. 1).

I Peret

637) 13: Horus chased his enemies from the Herakleopolites (20th Upper Egyptian nome) to Nubia [*Ptolemy XI*, year 363 of Re's divine era, Edfu][637]
638) 14–15: Offering to a god [*R II*, 40][638]
639) 14: Qenbet session concerning donkeys [*R IX*, 7][639]
640) 14: Horus finally defeated his enemies near a town called *š3s-ḥrt* in Nubia [*Ptolemy XI*, year 363 of Re's divine era, Edfu][640]
641) 15: A man and a woman were arrested and released 10 days later [R III, 25, QV][641]
642) 16: Offering to Sekhmet-of-Sahure [*R II*, 50, Abusir][642]
643) 17: Decrees of Ramses II to prepare for the Sed Festival [*R II*, 57 and 60, Armant][643]
644) 17: Rewards (*sndm-ib*) to workmen for fashioning statues at the Hathor temple [R II/Merenptah, 3, KV][644]
645) 17: Rowing of Menehet [Roman, Esna][645]
646) 17–20: Death and a festival of the princess Berenice, a daughter of Ptolemy III [*Ptolemy III*, 9][646]
647) 18: Brewing beer [*R II*, 40][647]
648) 18: Neith Festival, Great Festival of Heka, and Grand Festival of the Child in Sais [Roman, Esna][648]
649) 18: Dated graffito [Ptolemaic-Roman, 18, MH][649]
650) 19: Death of Seti II [*Siptah*, 1, KV][650]
651) 19: Vizier *Nfr-rnp.t* sent his message to western Thebes [*R IV*, 6, KV][651]
652) 19–21: Festival of Hathor of Dendera who returns from Nubia [*Ptolemy X*, Edfu][652]
653) 19–II Peret 4: Festival of Hathor, including a ritual at the temple lake [Ptolemaic-Roman, Dendera][653]
654) 20: A festival [A I, Karnak][654]
655) 20: Festival of the Procession of Uadjet [T III, Mut precinct at Karnak][655]
656) 20: Procession of Uadjet [*T III*, Buto][656]
657) 20: Offering beer to Meretseger and Renenutet [R II, DeM][657]
658) 20: Oath [R III, 16][658]
659) 20: Oath concerning the delivery of an ox by the policeman *P3-sd* [*R V*, 2][659]
660) 20: Festival of Phitorois [Ptolemy III, Hibeh (but related to Sais)][660]
661) 20: Festival in the 1st Upper Egyptian nome [*Ptolemy IV*, Edfu][661]
662) 20: Pouring the Water for One-who-is-in-Khadi by the King (or by Horus) [Ptolemy XII, Dendera][662]

---

637 Horus myth (Egberts1997, 50).
638 O. BM 5634 (Sadek 1987, 184; *KRI* III, 516: 5–6, 518: 11–2, 519: 7–8, 520: 3–4, and 522: 15–6; Janssen 1980, 148).
639 *hrw pn ir.t ḳnb.t* (P. Turin 1881, recto: Allam 1973, 313–4; *KRI* VI, 614: 13).
640 Horus myth (Egberts1997, 50). The gods retired to Edfu.
641 O. Turin 57556 and 57031 (*KRI* VII, 293: 13 and V, 502: 16; McDowell 1999, 193).
642 *wdn n Sḫm.t n S3ḥ-rꜥ* (Graffito by the scribe *Ptḥ-m-wi3*: *KRI* III, 437: 3; Peden 2001, 95–6; Navrátilová 2007, 58–61). For the popular cult of Sekhmet at Abusir, see Sadek 1988, 29–36.
643 The proclamation of the 10th Sed Festival in year 57 and the 11th in year 60 (Mond and Myers 1940, pl. 93, 1). A stone fragment discovered from the same temple may also record (the proclamation of?) the 8th Sed Festival in year 51, the 12th in year 63, and the 13th in year 66 (Mond and Myers 1940, pl. 93, 3).
644 O. Cairo 25552 (*KRI* IV, 154: 2–4; Helck 2002, 51).
645 *ḫn pw n Mnḫ.t* (Sauneron 1963, vol. 1, 128; Grimm 1994a, 70–1).
646 Decree of Canopus (*Urk.* II, 146: 8–10; Budge 1904, vol. 3, 31, ll. 27–9). Her death perhaps occurred on an earlier day. I Peret 17 is equated to 7 March 238 BC by Depuydt (2003, 58). For the association of this feast with the wandering goddess, see Richter 2010, 169.
647 O. BM 5634 (*KRI* III, 525: 3; Janssen 1980, 146).
648 *ḥb N.t ḥb wr ḥk3 ḥb ꜥ3 ḫrd m s3w* (Sauneron 1963, vol. 1, 128; Grimm 1994a, 70–1).
649 Graffito MH no. 100 located at the treasury of Medinet Habu temple (Thissen 1989, 82–3).
650 O. Cairo 25515, verso, col. II, ll. 25–8 (McDowell 1999, 205–6; *KRI* IV, 327).
651 O. Cairo 25287 (*KRI* VII, 453: 15).
652 PM VI, 130 (310); *Edfou* V, 351: 6; Alliot 1949, vol. 1, 227 for translation. This celebrated 'her (Hathor's) coming from Nubia for [the Nile?] to Egypt' (*iw=s n t3 Bw-gm rr* [ ] *n kmt*), and the same was performed from I Peret 28 to II Peret [4?].
653 Four texts related to the wandering goddess (Richter 2010, 168; Cauville 2002, 28–9).
654 Unnumbered stone block (Spalinger 1992, 15, pl. II).
655 *ḥb ḫn.t W3dy.t.* A granite stela (Champollion 1844, text, vol. 2, 264; Schott 1950, 94; Spalinger 1992, 17). Some personal festivals, performed by the DeM workmen and related to their family members, are also known (Sadek 1987, 184). P. BM 10763, 1, 4 (Altenmüller 1979, 7–12; Gardiner 1955c, pl. 43), P. BM 10769, 8, 3 (Altenmüller 1979, 7–12; Gardiner 1955c, pl. 51), and Statuette Cairo 69771 (Altenmüller 1979, 7–12), all originating from the Ramesseum and dating from the Second Intermediate Period, attest the 'festivals of Uadjet'.
656 *ḫn.t W3dy.t* (Buto Stela 209: Bedier 1994a, 5, z. 19; Klug 2002, 96–105).
657 Stela of the sculpture *Ḳn* in the collection of the Musée des Beaux-Arts in Bordeau (Clère 1975, 76).
658 P. DeM 26 (*KRI* V, 465: 8; Allam 1973, 297–301). Cf. I Shemu 7–8 and 20 for other dates recorded in the same text.
659 *ꜥnḫ n nb ꜥ.w.s.* 'oath to the lord, l.p.h.' O. IFAO Inv. 388 (*KRI* VI, 250: 1; Allam 1973, 195). Cf. III Shemu 13 for a relating event.
660 P. Hibeh 27, l. 62 (Grenfell and Hunt 1906, 144).
661 Geographical list on the exterior of the sanctuary (PM VI, 147 (225–6)).
662 *sty mw n nty m ḫ3di in nsw.t*(?) (Grimm 1994a, 72–3).

I Peret

1st MONTH of *pr.t* (*šf-bd.t*/*tꜣ-ꜥꜣb.t*/Tybi); 15th decade (*srt*)

No.) Day: Event

663) 21: Personal festival [Siptah, 2, KV][663]
664) 21: Processions of Uadjet and Renenutet at the Granary of Amun's Temple [AD 1st century, Tanis][664]
665) 22: Festival of the Two Goddesses [*Horemheb*, TT 50][665]
666) 22: Festival of the Two Goddesses [2nd half of R II, TT 2][666]
667) 22: Festival of the Two Goddesses (1034) [*R III*, MHC][667]
668) 23: Royal decree concerning the pyramid town of Snefer [*Pepi I*, 21, Dahshur][668]
669) 24: Going-Forth of [?] [AD 1st century, Tanis][669]
670) 24–5: A libation (*wꜣḥ-mw*) performed by three different families [*R II*, 40][670]
671) 25: Festival of Hathor, lady of Dendera [*Ptolemy X*, Edfu][671]
672) 25–7: Festivals of Offerings to the Gods of Edfu [*Ptolemy X*, Edfu][672]
673) 27: Great Festival of the Snake [Ramesside][673]
674) 27: Day of Drinking (*swr*) [Ptolemy IX, 8?, MH][674]
675) 27: Re-Horakhety was seated on the throne [*Ptolemy XI*, year 363 of Re's divine era, Edfu][675]
676) 28: Brewing for a personal festival [Siptah, 2, KV][676]
677) 28: Oath taken by the water-carrier *Pꜣ-ꜥn* over a donkey before witnesses [R III][677]
678) 28: Rowing for four days [Roman, Esna][678]
679) 29: Festival of the Rowing of Bastet [T III, Mut precinct at Karnak][679]
680) 29: Festival of Erecting the *Ṯr.t*-Tree (122) [*R III*, MHC][680]
681) 29: Festival of Entering His Town and Appearance of Khnum-Re [Roman, Esna][681]
682) 30: Festival of the Procession of Sekhmet [T III, Mut precinct at Karnak][682]
683) 30: Day of Filling the Sacred Eye in Heliopolis [18 Dyn., Memphis][683]
684) 30: Rowing of Mut, Mistress of Isheru [R IX?, 7][684]
685) 30: Crossing before Nun [Ramesside][685]
686) 30: Festival in the 11th Upper Egyptian nome [*Ptolemy IV*, Edfu][686]
687) 30: Rowing of [?] [AD 1st century, Tanis][687]
688) 30: Hathor Festival [Roman, Esna][688]

---

663 O. Cairo 25521 (*KRI* IV, 398: 10).
664 *ẖn.t Wꜣḏy.t* [ ] *Rnw.t* [ ] *iḫ.t m šnꜥ pr ꞽImn* (P. BM ESA 10673: Griffith and Petrie 1889, pl. 12).
665 Tomb of Neferhotep (PM I-1^2, 96 (9–10, I); Hari 1985, 50, pl. 37).
666 Tomb of Khabekhenet (PM I-1^2, 7 (10, II); Černý 1949, 17). TT 4 (PM I-1^2, 11 (5, I); Černý 1949, 45) is also likely to depict this festival.
667 *ḥb hr.ty* (*MH* III, pl. 163, list 57).
668 Stone Berlin 17500 (*Urk*. I, 209: 11; Goedicke 1967, 55, Abb. 5).
669 *pr.t* [ ]. P. BM ESA 10673 (Griffith and Petrie 1889, pl. 12).
670 *wꜣḥ mw* (O. BM 5634: *KRI* III, 516: 5–6, 519: 3–4, and 523: 1–2; Janssen 1980, 149).
671 *ḥb Ḥw.t-ḥr nb(.t) iwn.t* (Grimm 1994a, 74–5).
672 *ḥb.w n [wꜣ]ḥ iḫ.wt n nṯr.w n bḥd.t* (Grimm 1994a, 74–5).
673 P. Cairo 86637 and P. Sallier IV (Leitz 1994a, 223).
674 P. Berlin 3115 (de Cenival 1972, 105; Pestman 1993, 199 for translation).
675 Horus myth (PM VI, 160 (308–11); *Edfou* VI, 134: 2; Egberts1997, 50). This feast was called 'the great offering to Pre' (*pꜣ wdn ꜥꜣ n pꜣ Rꜥ*).
676 O. Cairo 25521 (*KRI* IV, 402: 3–4). Date uncertain but Janssen (1980, 147) speculated this day.
677 O. Varille 41 (*KRI* VII, 308: 1).
678 *ẖn(.t) pw nfr.t* (Sauneron 1963, vol. 1, 128; Grimm 1994a, 74–5).
679 *ḥb ẖn.t Bꜣst.t*. A granite stela (Champollion 1844, text, vol. 2, 264; Schott 1950, 95; Spalinger 1992, 17).
680 *sꜥḥꜥ ṯr.t* 'erecting the willow tree' (*MH* III, pls. 163–5, list 58). For rites parallel to this see Spalinger 1993b, 167. A branch of willow tree is depicted in TT 50 (9–10) for the Bastet Feast celebrated on IV Peret 4 (Hari 1985, pl. 38).
681 *ḥb ꜥḳ r niw.t=f sḫꜥ n Ḫnm-rꜥ* (Sauneron 1963, vol. 1, 128; Grimm 1994a, 74–5).
682 *ḥb ẖn.t Sḫm.tt*. A granite stela (Champollion 1844, text, vol. 2, 264; Schott 1950, 95; Spalinger 1992, 17).
683 *hrw mḥ wḏꜣ.t m iwn* (stela of Djehutymes (BM 155): Edwards 1939, 48, l. 9), pl. 39 for transcription and photograph; Assmann 2005, 313 for translation). Also see the Book of the Dead, spell 125. An event parallel to this was celebrated in I Shemu at Edfu and Dendera, and in III Shemu at the Mut temple at Karnak (Spalinger 1993b, 176; 1995, 36–7). 'Filling of the udjat-eye' is associated with the sixth-day festival (Barta 1969, 75–6).
684 *hrw n ẖn.t Mw.t wr.t nb.t išrw* (P. Turin 68: Peet 1930a, 487). Gardiner (1906, 140) regarded the feast as continuing until II Peret 1. For the association of *išrw* with other goddesses, see Yoyotte 1962, 101–11.
685 P. Cairo 86637 and P. Sallier IV (Leitz 1994a, 226).
686 Geographical list on the exterior of the sanctuary (PM VI, 147 (223–4)).
687 *ẖn.t* [ ] (P. BM ESA 10673: Griffith and Petrie 1889, pl. 12).
688 *ḥb Ḥw.t-ḥr* (Sauneron 1963, vol. 1, 128; Grimm 1994a, 76–7).

1st MONTH of *pr.t* (*šf-bd.t*/*tꜣ-ꜥꜣb.t*/Tybi); unknown decace

No.) Day: Event

689) ?: Rowing of Hathor, Lady of Hutnennesut [*Amenemhat III*, 35, Lahun][689]
690) ?: Raising the Field(?) [*Amenemhat III*, 35, Lahun][690]
691) ?: Appearance of Sothis [A I, Karnak][691]
692) ?: Temple revision [*R III*, 5, Tod][692]
693) ?: Delivery of precious materials to the Necropolis [R IX, 7][693]

[689] *ẖn.t n.t Ḥw.t-ḥr nb.t Ḥw.t-nn-nsw.t* (P. UC 32191: Collier and Quirke 2006, 95). The date is not recorded, but this event was possibly held in this month. Cf. P. BM ESA 10673 for the *fꜣi* [ ] *m nn-nsw.t* taking place on I Peret 1.
[690] *fꜣ.t ꜣḥ.t* (P. UC 32191: Collier and Quirke 2006, 94).
[691] Unnumbered stone block (Spalinger 1992, 15–8, pl. II). This is probably a copy of an ealier document (Krauss 2006c, 445, n. 26).
[692] Temple of Tod (Barguet 1952b, 100–1; Spalinger 1991, 22–6). Haring (1997, 95) relates this to new endowment made for Karnak in year 6.
[693] P. Turin 1881, III, 2–4 (*KRI* VI, 612: 1).

2nd MONTH of *pr.t* (*rkḫ-wr*/*pꜣ-n-mḫr*/Mecheir); 16th decade (*sꜣwy srt*) II Peret

No.) Day: Event

694) 1: Execution of the two Karnak obelisks began [*Hatshepsut*, 15, Karnak][694]
695) 1: Festival of the Procession of Anubis (140+) [*R III*, MHC][695]
696) 1: Festival of Lifting-Up the Sky [Ramesside][696]
697) 1: Burial of the chief of Ma *Pꜣ-di-ꜣs.t* [*Pami*, 2, Serapeum][697]
698) 1: Serapeum stela [*Pami*, 2, Serapeum][698]
699) 1: Festival and rowing of the gods and goddesses [Roman, Esna][699]
700) 1: Festival in the 1st Lower Egyptian nome [*Ptolemy IV*, Edfu][700]
701) 1: Seizure of the Foreleg in Front of Him [*Ptolemy VI*, Kom Ombo][701]
702) 2: Day of a stone work to begin at *Ḏsr-mn.w* [T III, 43, western Thebes][702]
703) 2?: A scribe visited the Step Pyramid [*A IV*, 14, Step Pyramid][703]
704) 4: Oath cencerning a property before witnesses [R III, 17][704]
705) 4: Very Very Grand Festival with animal offerings until the 8th hour of the day [*Ptolemy* X, Edfu][705]
706) 4: Last day of a festival at the 3rd hour of the day at the temple lake [Ptolemy XII, Dendera][706]
707) 5: Qenbet session concerning a donkey [R III, 22, DeM][707]
708) 6: Festivals of Shu and of the Eye of Horus [Roman, Esna][708]
709) 7+: Slaughtering a bull for a personal festival(?) [Siptah/Tausret][709]
710) 7: Herihor's decree to renew the burial of Seti I [*R XI*, w6, coffin of Seti I][710]
711) 8: Arrival of tributes from foreign lands [*A IV*, 12, Amarna][711]
712) 8: Ramses III's victorious war campaign against the Meshwesh [*R III*, 11, MH][712]
713) 8: Festival of Great Fire [Roman, Esna][713]
714) 8: Neith Festival [Roman, Esna][714]
715) 9?: Fire Festival [*Niuserre*, Abu Gurob][715]
716) 9: Decree to procure turquoise in Sinai for the 3rd Sed Festival [*A III*, 36, Sinai][716]
717) 9: Festival of the Great Fire [*Ptolemy* X, Edfu][717]
718) 9–13: Festival of the *ṯr.t*-Tree and Eating the Calf [*Ptolemy VI*, Kom Ombo][718]
719) 10: Thutmose III erected a victory stela in Armant [*T III*, 22, Mentu temple at Armant][719]

694 Inscription on the base of the standing obelisk at Karnak (PM II², 81–2; *LD* III, pl. 24, n; *Urk*. IV, 367: 3–5; Lichtheim 1973, vol. 2, 28; Bell 2002, 19–22, n. 13). The work was completed on IV Shemu 30 in year 16.

695 *ḥn.t Inpw* (*MH* III, pl. 165, list 59). Also recorded in P. BM ESA 10673 (Griffith and Petrie 1889, pl. 12).

696 P. Cairo 86637 and P. Sallier IV (Leitz 1994a, 228).

697 Stela Louvre IM 3697 (Jansen-Winkeln 2007, vol. 2, 261; Malinine, Posener, and Vercoutter 1968, 21–2).

698 Stela Louvre IM 3441 (Jansen-Winkeln 2007, vol. 2, 266; Malinine, Posener, and Vercoutter 1968, 24–5).

699 Sauneron 1963, vol. 1, 129; Grimm 1994a, 76–7.

700 Geographical list on the exterior of the sanctuary (PM VI, 146 (221–2)).

701 *Ṯꜣy p(ꜣ) ḫpš m-bꜣḥ=f* (Grimm 1994a, 76–7). The same ritual took place on days 19 and 21 of the same month.

702 O. Berlin P 10615 (*Urk*. IV, 1374: 8; Hayes 1960, 51–2; Lipińska 1967, 31). *hrw pn ir.t bḥ ḥr imnt.t m dsr-mnw*. There is no evidence of building by Thutmose III at Deir el-Bahari before this date. Cf. O. Gardiner 5 for the date II Peret 1–2 in year 43, on which a stone work took place (Hayes 1942, 40–1).

703 Graffito at the south chapel of the Step Pyramid (Firth and Quibell 1935, vol. 1, 81; Malek 1995, 106).

704 O. Florence 2610 (*KRI* V, 467: 7).

705 *ḥb ꜥꜣ wr wr* (Grimm 1994a, 76–7).

706 Grimm 1994a, 78–9.

707 O. Gardiner 53 (*KRI* V, 484: 2; Allam 1973, 158). The litigant had appealed the same matter earlier, at least, four times.

708 *ḥb Šw ḥb ir.t Ḥr* (Sauneron 1963, vol. 1, 129; Grimm 1994a, 78–9).

709 O. Ashmolean 37 (*KRI* IV, 447: 6–8).

710 Gauthier 1907, vol. 3, 232; Kitchen 1973a, 417.

711 Tombs of *Mry-rꜥ* and *Ḥwyꜣ* (*LD* III, pl. 100, b; *Urk*. IV, 2003: 5 and 2006: 11). The king with his queen appeared (*ḫꜥ*) on the seat of his father Aten. See I Peret 5, 6, or 9 in year 2 or 12 for an event perhaps relating to this.

712 Inscriptions on the north wing of the 1st pylon of the temple of Medinet Habu (de Rougé 1877, pl. 121). Cf. I Akhet 28 and IV Shemu 10+ for festivals celebrated for the victory of the war in the same year.

713 This festival is attested only from the Old Kingdom and the Ptolemaic Period (Altenmüller 1977, 177).

714 Sauneron 1963, vol. 1, 129; Grimm 1994a, 78–9.

715 The part of the text referring to this, however, is completely destroyed (Helck 1977, 60).

716 Rock inscription of the scribe *Imn-ms* (*Urk*. IV, 1891: 4; Murnane 1998, 191). The royal scribe, overseer of the treasury *Sbk-ḥtp*, called *Pꜣ-nḥsy*, was dispatched.

717 *ḥb rkḫ wr* (Grimm 1994a, 78–9).

718 *ḥb=f nfr n ḥb ṯr.t pꜣ wnm ib* (Grimm 1994a, 78–9 and 394, fig. 11).

719 Stela Cairo 67377 (*Urk*. IV, 1244: 14; Mond and Myers 1940, pl. 103; Klug 2002, 153). Hornung (2006, 201) proposes that Thutmose III's sole reign began from this day on, because Josephus gives Hatshepsut a reign of 21 years and nine months.

II Peret

2nd MONTH of *pr.t* (*rkḥ-wr/p3-n-mḫr*/Mecheir); 17th decade (*ḫry ḫpd srt*)

No.) Day: Event

720) 11: Neith Festival in Sais [Ramesside][720]

721) 11: Festival of Imhotep [Ptolemaic Period, Memphis?][721]

722) 12?: Dated graffito [Ptolemaic-Roman, 6, MH][722]

723) 14: Oath taken by the chief policeman *Mnṯw-ms* over a payment [*R IV*, 4][723]

724) 14?: The scribe *Imn-ḥtp* and his son *Imn-nḫt* visited KV 9 [*R IX*, 9, KV 9][724]

725) 14: Property divided among brothers [20 Dyn., 6, DeM][725]

726) 15: Oath concerning a property before witnesses [R III, 31][726]

727) 15: Divine adoratice of Amun sent a man to Lower Egypt [21 Dyn.][727]

728) 15: Amun selected Aspelta as the king [*Aspelta*, 1, Geber Barkal][728]

729) 16: Reburial of Seti I [Menkheperre, 7, mummy shroud][729]

730) 16: Assembly at Sais in honour of Neith [Ptolemy III, Hibeh (but related to Sais)][730]

731) 17: Burial of Meresankh III at Giza [Khafre, year after the 1st census, Giza][731]

732) 17: The overseer of the treasury *Ḫꜥ-m-try* visited western Thebes to lower an alabaster stone to the tomb of Ramses V, and to give wages to the workmen [*R V*, 4][732]

733) 17: Festival of Neith, lady of Lower Egypt [Roman, Esna][733]

734) 18: Festival of Horus, Lord of the Mountains [AD 1st century, Tanis][734]

735) 19: Report to Amenhotep I by the workman *Mn-n3* [R III, 8][735]

736) 19: Seizure of the Foreleg in Front of Him [*Ptolemy VI*, Kom Ombo][736]

737) 19: [Appearing? of] Horus as the Ruler [AD 1st century, Tanis][737]

738) 20: Royal decree concerning a land property at Koptos [*Neferkauhor*, Koptos][738]

739) 20: A man called *Idi* was appointed the overseer of Upper Egypt [*Neferkauhor*, Koptos][739]

740) 20: Royal decree concerning a brother of the overseer of Upper Egypt *Idi* [*Neferkauhor*, Koptos][740]

741) 20: Royal decree concerning the mortuary cult of the vizier *Šm3y* and his wife *Nb.t* [*Neferkauhor*, Koptos][741]

742) 20: Ceremonies of Amun-Re and Ptah in Memphis, and a royal decree [*R I*, 2, Wadi-Halfa][742]

743) 20: Provisions to a man (*ꜥ3-nḫt?*) for the offering of Ptah [R VII, 4, DeM or MH?][743]

744) 20: Appearance of Amenhotep I [R IX, 8, DeM][744]

745) 20: Udjat/goddess comes to the low sky [Ramesside][745]

---

720 P. Cairo 86637 and P. Sallier IV (Leitz 1994a, 237).

721 Stone statue base (Gauthier 1918, 37).

722 Graffito MH no. 88 located at the slaughter house of Medinet Habu temple (Thissen 1989, 77–8).

723 O. OIC 12073 (*KRI* VI, 139: 10). Cf. II Shemu 5 for the same case litigated in the previous year.

724 Graffito (*KRI* VI, 658: 12; Peden 2001, 205).

725 *sḏm r3* (O. DeM 434).

726 *iry=f ꜥnḫ n nb.* O. Gardiner 68 (*KRI* V, 555: 16; Černý and Gardiner 1957, pl. 67, 3; Allam 1973, 166–7; McDowell 1990, 150).

727 P. Straßburg 25 (Wente 1990, 207–8; Jansen-Winkeln 2007, vol. 1, 202).

728 Stela Cairo 48866 (Eide, Hägg, and Pierce 1994, vol. 1, 234; Grimal 1981b, 23).

729 Gauthier 1907, vol. 3, 264; Kitchen 1973a, 420; Jansen-Winkeln 2007, vol. 1, 79.

730 P. Hibeh 27, l. 76 (Grenfell and Hunt 1906, 144).

731 Meresankh III, a queen of the 4th Dynasty, was buried at Giza after 273 or 274 days of embalming after her death on I Shemu 21 (*Urk*. I, 156–7; Simpson 1974, vol. 1, 15, pl. 7, a, fig. 7). Gardiner (1945, 14) reads the year as regnal year 3, an interpretation supported by Spalinger (1994c, 286), while Simpson regards it as year 2. Her burial was perhaps performed in association with the Ptah Festival.

732 O. Edgerton 14 (*KRI* VI, 253: 8).

733 *ḥb N.t nb(.t) t3 mḥy ir mit.t nty r ḥb Mnw nb s3w* 'do likewise according to the Min Festival in Sais' (Sauneron 1963, vol. 1, 129; Grimm 1994a, 80–1).

734 P. BM ESA 10673 (Griffith and Petrie 1889, pl. 12).

735 *smi n nsw.t Imn-ḥtp* (O. DeM 672: Černý 1935a, vol. 8, 11; *KRI* V, 449: 5).

736 *ṯ3y p(3) ḫpš m-b3ḥ=f* (Grimm 1994a, 80–1). The same ritual took place on days 1 and 21 of the same month.

737 *s*[ ] *Ḥr m ḥk3* (P. BM ESA 10673: Griffith and Petrie 1889, pl. 12).

738 Cairo 41895 (*Urk*. I, 296: 17; Goedicke 1967, 166, Abb. 17).

739 Stela MMA 14.7.11 (*Urk*. I, 299: 4; Hayes 1946, 16, pl. 4; Goedicke 1967, 178, Abb. 19).

740 Stela MMA 14.7.12 (*Urk*. I, 300: 10 and 302: 4; Hayes 1946, 18–9 for translation; Goedicke 1967, 190, 193, Abb. 21–2). The father of *Idi* was perhaps promoted to a vizier at this time (Stela MMA 14.7.13: *Urk*. I, 297–9; Hayes 1946, 14; Goedicke 1967, 197–202, Abb. 24).

741 Stone stela (*Urk*. I, 300: 10 and 303: 12; Goedicke 1967, 206, Abb. 27).

742 Stela Louvre C 59 (*KRI* I, 2: 9). Decree to establish new offerings and temple personnel for the cult of Min-Amun at Buhen. This is the only surviving complete date of Ramses I.

743 P. Turin 1907+1908, recto, col. II, 1. 16 (*KRI* VI, 405: 16; Janssen 1966, 83). This continued from I Akhet 10.

744 *ḫꜥ n Imn-ḥtp* (P. Turin 1906+1939+2047: *KRI* VI, 629: 14).

745 O. Cairo 86637 and P. Sallier IV (Leitz 1994a, 258). Leitz regards this entry as indicating the winter solstice.

II Peret

746) 20: Birth of a priest of Amun [Late period][746]

2nd MONTH of *pr.t* (*rkḥ-wr/p3-n-mḫr*/Mecheir); 18th decade (*tpy-ˁ 3ḫwy*)

No.) Day: Event

747) 21: Recovery of the gold and silver stolen at the Maat temple in Thebes [*R IX*, 17][747]
748) 21: Delivery of the white bread (*t-ḥḏ*) [20 Dyn., DeM][748]
749) 21: Festival in the 17th Upper Egyptian nome [*Ptolemy IV*, Edfu][749]
750) 21+: Festival in the 4th Lower Egyptian nome [*Ptolemy IV*, Edfu][750]
751) 21: Seizure of the Foreleg in Front of Him [*Ptolemy VI*, Kom Ombo][751]
752) 21: Day of Drinking (*swr*) [Ptolemy IX, 8?, MH][752]
753) 21: Festival of the Victory in the Entire Land [*Ptolemy* X, Edfu][753]
754) 21–30: Plants of Leaves of the Gods [*Ptolemy* X, Edfu][754]
755) 21: Appearance of Hathor at the roof kiosk at the 10th hour of the day [Ptolemy XII, Dendera][755]
756) 21: Ritual performed for the gods of the mound Djeme [Cleopatra VII, 15, MH][756]
757) 21: Victory Festival and Appearance of Hekha-the-Child [Roman, Esna][757]
758) 21: Victory rites (drama?) of Horus of Behedet as the winged sun-disc against his enemies [Ptolemy XI, Edfu][758]
759) 22: Qenbet session concerning a dead donkey [R III, 27][759]
760) 22: Qenbet and oath [*R III*, 28][760]
761) 22: Vizier *Nfr-rnp.t* visited the Enclosure of the Necropolis to announce R VI's accession [*R VI*, 1, KV][761]
762) 24: Lawsuit (qenbet?) [R IV, DeM][762]
763) 24–III Peret 1: Ptah Festival [*Ptolemy X*, Edfu][763]
764) 25: Festival of Seeing her (Uadjet) Souls [*T III*, Buto][764]
765) 25: Visit of scribes to the Step Pyramid [*R II*, 47, Saqqara][765]
766) 25: Day of Drinking (*swr*) [Ptolemy IX, 8?, MH][766]
767) 26: Uadjet Festival [*T III*, Buto][767]
768) 26: Going-Forth of Min in Koptos [Ramesside][768]
769) 27: New moon day at Piramses [*R II*, 52][769]

---

746 *hrw n ms ḥm-nṯr Ỉmn* (Statue Cairo 39146: Daressy 1905, vol. 1, 285).
This may be the appointment of a priest. The following four days are documented as following:
21st: Day of Great Annual Purification (*hrw swˁb wr n tp-rnp.t*);
22nd: Appearance from *ṯbsty* (*ḫpr m ṯbsty*);
23rd: Placing the Oil (*w3ḥ mrḥ.t*);
24th: Offering to Sekhmet (*wdn n Sḫm.t*).

747 P. BM 10068, recto (Peet 1930b, 90). The recovery was made by the vizier *Ḫˁ-m-w3s.t* and the HPA *Ỉmn-ḥtp*. Cf. I Peret 8 for an appeal made earlier.

748 O. Berlin 14258, recto (unpublished).

749 Geographical list on the exterior of the sanctuary (PM VI, 147 (223–4)).

750 Geographical list on the exterior of the sanctuary (PM VI, 146 (221–2)).

751 *Ṯ3y p(3) ḫpš m-b3ḥ=f* (Grimm 1994a, 80–1). The same ritual took place on days 1 and 19 of the same month.

752 P. Berlin 3115 (de Cenival 1972, 105; Pestman 1993, 199 for translation).

753 *ḥb ḳn m t3 ḏr=f* (Grimm 1994a, 80–1). This was performed 'like I Akhet 19'.

754 *srd.w sm.w nṯr.w* (Grimm 1994a, 80–1).

755 *ḫˁ in Ḥw.t-ḥr* (Grimm 1994a, 80–1).

756 Graffito MH no. 47 located at the small temple of Medinet Habu (Thissen 1989, 41–4).

757 *ḥb ḳn sḫˁ n Ḥk3-p3-ẖrd* (Sauneron 1963, vol. 1, 129; Grimm 1994a, 82–3).

758 PM VI, 160 (308–11, 2nd register); Fairman 1935, 34; Blackman and Fairman 1944, 14. Horus hurled ten harpoons to a hippopotamus, a manifestation of Seth. The triumph of Horus over Seth may be likened to the rising of Sothis (Säve-Söderbergh 1953, 26–7). The text instructs that the same rites be performed on I Akhet 2 and IV Akhet 24.

759 *spr r ḳnb.t* (O. Gardiner 1: Allam 1973, 191; *KRI* V, 518: 2).

760 O. Gardiner 150 (*KRI* V, 527: 3).

761 O. KV 18/6.924+O. Cairo 25726+O. BM 50722 (*KRI* VI, 364: 4; McDowell 1999, 206; Demarée 2002, 33, pl. 115 for O. BM 50722). Ramses VI's accession date is supposed to be between II Peret 8 and 11 (Dorn 2011, 164).

762 O. DeM 645 (*KRI* VI, 160: 6).

763 *ḥb Ptḥ* (Grimm 1994a, 82–3).

764 *ḥb gm b3.w=s* (Buto Stela 209: Bedier 1994a, 5, z. 20; Klug 2002, 96–105).

765 Graffito at the Step Pyramid (*KRI* III, 148: 4; Firth and Quibell 1935, vol. 1, 82–3; Peden 2001, 99; Navrátilová 2007, 108–11). The visit was made by the scribes *Ḥd-nḫt* and *P3-nḫt*.

766 P. Berlin 3115 (de Cenival 1972, 105; Pestman 1993, 199 for translation).

767 Buto Stela 209 (Bedier 1994a, 5, z. 21; Klug 2002, 96–105).

768 P. Cairo 86637 and P. Sallier IV (Bakir 1966, 35; Leitz 1994a, 262). *šsp ˁbw* 'taking lettuce'.

769 P. Leiden 350, verso 3: 6 (*KRI* II, 809: 12; Janssen 1961, 12; Casperson 1988, 181; Krauss 2006b, 395–43).

II Peret

770) 27: Festival of Sokar in Ra-setau before Wennefer in Abydos [Ramesside][770]
771) 27: Festival of Prometheus-Iphthimis [Ptolemy III, Hibeh (but related to Sais)][771]
772) 28: Festival of Khnum in Elephantine [Osorkon II, Elephantine][772]
773) 28–9: Festivals of Laying-Down the Dead on the Island of the Fire (Osiris), and of Ptah [*Ptolemy X*, Edfu][773]
774) 29: Ritual at Luxor temple during the Festival of Amun [*Hatshepsut*, 2, Karnak][774]
775) 29: First Day of Amun's Festival of Lifting-Up the Sky (1150) [*R III*, MHC][775]
776) 29: Report on a payment [R III, 17][776]
777) 29: Festival of Amun, procession, and oracle-giving [*Anlamani*: 7th cent. BC, Kawa][777]
778) 29: Offering to Amun of Kawa [Aryamani: 3rd cent. BC, Kawa][778]
779) 30: Dated papyrus concerning cloth allocations [OK, Temple of Reneferef at Abusir][779]
780) 30: Foundation ceremony of the Akh-menu at Amun's Festival on a new moon day [*T III*, 24, Karnak][780]
781) 30: Second Day of Amun's Festival of Lifting-Up the Sky (offerings not recorded) [*R III*, MHC][781]
782) 30: Osiride ritual of injuring the *wḏꜣ.t*-eye [*Nectanebo I*, 17, Thebes][782]

2nd MONTH of *pr.t* (*rkḥ-wr*/*pꜣ-n-mḫr*/Mecheir); unknown decade

No.) Day: Event

783) ?: Establishment of divine offerings [*R III*, 4, MHC][783]
784) ?: Sokar Festival, Dragging of Sokar for two days [*Amenemhat III*, 35, Lahun][784]

---

[770] P. Cairo 86637 and P. Sallier IV (Bakir 1966, 35; Leitz 1994a, 263).
[771] P. Hibeh 27, l. 85 (Grenfell and Hunt 1906, 144).
[772] Stela reused as a roof stone of a temple (Jansen-Winkeln 2007, vol. 2, 120).
[773] *ḥb dr ḫp m iw nsrsr ḥb Ptḥ* (Grimm 1994a, 82–3).
[774] *m sr n=i tꜣ.wy m wsḫ.t n.t ip.t-rsy* 'promising the Two Lands for me in the Broad Hall of Southern Opet' (Lacau and Chevrier, 1977, vol. 1, 133, block no. 287; Shirun-Grumach 1993, 138; Burgos and Larché 2006, vol. 1, 40). This festival is referred to as the 3rd Amun's Festival, corresponding to the 2nd day of offering to Sekhmet (*wdn Sḫm.t hrw 2-nw*). For the lunar dating, see Meyer 1904, 49.
[775] *tpy n ḥb ꞽImn m ḥb=f n ꜥḫy.t p.t.* (*MH* III, pl. 165, list 60). The date seems to have been misspelled as 9. The Festival of Lifting-Up the Sky is also attested from Lahun, but was celebrated in III Akhet. Belmonte Avilés (2009, 108) associates this celebration with either the winter solstice or the summer solstice, depdending on from which period one looks.
[776] *ḏd* 'report' (O. Leipzig 2/inv. 1892: K*RI* V, 467: 14).
[777] Stela Copenhagen 1709 (PM VII, 187; Macadam 1949, 46; Eide, Hägg, and Pierce 1994, vol. 1, 220; Török 1997, 224). The king assigned a third-priest and four royal sisters for the cult of Amun.
[778] Fragments of Stela BM 1777 (Eide, Hägg, and Pierce 1994, vol. 2, 529).
[779] Abusir X, 232, pl. 17.
[780] *ḥb mḥ 10 n ꞽImn m ip.t-s.wt* 'the 10th day of (or 10th) Festival of Amun' (Stela Cairo 34012: *Urk.* IV, 836: 2; Wente 1975; Klug 2002, 123). Based on the date of the new moon on I Shemu 21 of the previous year, this day also falls on a new moon day. A royal decree to coordinate the ritual was issued before the new moon day, as the text tells 'my person ordered that the extension of the cord be prepared [ ] the day of a new moon festival' (Read 1996, 104). The link between the foundation ceremony and a new moon day is also evident from the ritual of 'loosening of the cord (*wḥꜥ wꜣwꜣ.t*)' of Ramses II at Luxor (Redford 1971, 114). For the astronomical aspect of the stretching of the cord, see Park 1998.
[781] *ḥb=f n ꜥḫy.t p.t* (*MH* III, pl. 165, list 60). This day is also referred to in the Book of the Dead (Spell 125) as the day on which the Sacred Eye in Heliopolis was filled.
[782] P. BM 10252 (*Urk.* VI, 139: 23).
[783] *MH* III, pl. 140, section 2, col. 60; K*RI* V, 119: 12; Haring 1997, 63.
[784] *ḥb Skr stꜣ Skr* (P. UC 32191: Collier and Quirke 2006, 94). Cf. P. Berlin 10332 a recto for the dragging of Sokar performed on [III Peret] 28 (Luft 1992, 118).

3rd MONTH of *pr.t* (*rkḥ-nḏs*/*p3-n-imn-ḥtpw*/Phamenoth); 19th decade (*3ḫwy*) III Peret

No.) Day: Event

785) 1: Festival of the Great Fire [Senusret III, 7, Lahun][785]
786) 1: Great Fire [MK, 3, Lahun][786]
787) 1: Festival of Lifting-Up the Sky [*T III*, Buto][787]
788) 1: Entering of Amun on Festival of Lifting-Up the Sky (offerings not recorded) [*R III*, MHC][788]
789) 1: Ptah Festival [*R X*, 3][789]
790) 1: Delivery of the white bread (*t-ḥḏ*) and beer [20 Dyn., DeM][790]
791) 1: Festival of Entering the Sky [Ramesside][791]
792) 1: Festival in the 5th Lower Egyptian nome [*Ptolemy IV*, Edfu][792]
793) 1: Opening of the Face in the House of Gold [*Ptolemy VI*, Kom Ombo][793]
794) 1: Day of Drinking (*swr*) [Ptolemy IX, 8?, MH][794]
795) 1: Festival of Lifting-Up the Sky by Ptah (began from II Peret 24) [*Ptolemy* X, Edfu][795]
796) 1: Festival of Ptah, lord of Lifting-Up the Sky, Festival of Khnum, lord of Esna [Roman, Esna][796]
797) 2: A scribe visited the Step Pyramid [*Hatshepsut & T III*, 20, Step Pyramid][797]
798) 2: King consulted Amun on a Nubian campaign during a celebration at Karnak in the morning [*T IV*, 8, Konosso][798]
799) 3: Graffito of a man called *Sbk-nḫt* at the pyramid of Reneferef [OK, Temple of Reneferef at Abusir][799]
800) 3: A letter concerning a royal decree on a juridical case [13 Dyn., 6][800]
801) 3: 'When asked, you (Ptah?) answer in Ra-Setau' [18 Dyn., Memphis][801]
802) 3: Festival in the 12th Upper Egyptian nome [*Ptolemy IV*, Edfu][802]
803) 3?: Festival of Alexander IV [*Alexander IV*, 12, MH][803]
804) 4: Day of Offerings to Ptah at the Great Field (KV) by the workmen [R IV, 2, DeM][804]
805) 5: Nebetu Festival [Roman, Esna][805]
806) 6: Unknown event [T IV, Elephantine][806]
807) 6: Day of bringing Ramses II out his burial place by Pinedjem I [Smendes I, 15, mummy shroud][807]
808) 7: Oath taken by the washerman *B3k-n-wr-n-r* [R III, 9, DeM][808]
809) 7: Pinedjem I renewed the burial of Thutmose II [Smendes I, 6, mummy shroud of T II][809]
810) 8?: Royal decree to build a divine barque (*p3 sšm n* [*ḫwy*]) [*T III*, 27, Sai][810]
811) 8: Dated stela [*T IV*, 7, Konosso][811]

---

785 P. Berlin 10069, verso (Borchardt 1935, 56; Altenmüller 1977, 177).
786 P. Berlin 10069, recto (James 1955, 123; Luft 1992, 81).
787 *ḥb ˁḫy.t p.t* (Buto Stela 209: Bedier 1994a, 5, z. 22; Klug 2002, 96–105).
788 *ˁḳ n ỉmn m ḥb=f n ˁḫy.t p.t* (*MH* III, pl. 165, list 60).
789 P. Turin 1898+1926+1937+2094 (Botti and Peet 1928, 47, pl. 50; K*RI* VI, 687: 12). Altenmüller notes that this is the last day of the Ptah Festival.
790 O. Berlin 14258, recto and verso (unpublished).
791 *ḥb ˁḳ m p.t* (P. Cairo 86637 and P. Sallier IV: Leitz 1994a, 267).
792 Geographical list on the exterior of the sanctuary (PM VI, 146 (219–20)).
793 *wn ḥr n pr nb* (Grimm 1994a, 84–5). The same rite was performed on III Peret 9, IV Peret 1, 11, 17, 20, 24, 25, and 27.
794 P. Berlin 3115 (de Cenival 1972, 105; Pestman 1993, 199 for translation).
795 *ḥb* [ ] *ḥb ˁḫy p.t in Ptḥ* (Grimm 1994a, 84–5).
796 *ḥb Ptḥ nb ˁnḫy p.t ḥb Ḫnm nb t3-sn.t* (LD IV, pl. 78, b: 10; Sauneron 1963, vol. 1, 167; Grimm 1994a, 84–5). The unification with the sun was performed at this feast (Sauneron 1962, 121).
797 Graffito at the south chapel of the Step Pyramid (Firth and Quibell 1935, vol. 1, 80; Navrátilová 2007, 90–2).
798 Rock stela (*Urk.* IV, 1545: 6; Bryan 1991, 333; Shirun-Grumach 1993, 80–1; Johnson 1998, 64–6; Klug 2002, 346).
799 Abusir IX, 194, no. 28.
800 P. Brooklyn 35.1446 (Wente 1990, 25). Cf. III Peret 20+ for another date recorded in the same text.
801 *nis.tw=k wšb=k m r3-st3.w* (stela of Djehutymes (BM 155): Schott 1950, 98; Edwards 1939, 48, l. 10, pl. 39 for transcription and photograph; Assmann 2005, 313 for translation).
802 Geographical list on the exterior of the sanctuary (PM VI, 147 (223–4)).
803 Graffito MH no. 235 located at the slaughter house of Medinet Habu temple (PM II², 507, Room 6; Thissen 1989, 142–5; Edgerton 1937b, pl. 59). *p3 ḥb p3 nb wn p3 nṯr ˁ3 n pr-ˁ3 3r-str-s* 'the feast of the lord of light, of the great god, and of the king Alexander'. Also see no. 86 (PM II², 506 (124); Thissen 1989, 145).
804 *hrw n wdn n Ptḥ m sḫ.t ˁ3 in t3 is.wt r gs p3 rˁ-b3k iw=sn ir ḥb ˁ3 m-b3ḥ p3 rˁ-b3k* 'the day of offering to Ptah at the Valley of the Kings by the workmen, putting aside the work. They held a great festival in front of the work place' (O. DeM 401: Černý 1935a, vol. 5, 17, pl. 16; K*RI* VI, 125: 8–9). Note that the workmen celebrated on the spot of their work, which was temporarily halted.
805 *ḥb Nb.t-ww* (Sauneron 1963, vol. 1, 167; Grimm 1994a, 86–7). The 'Coming-forth of Neith in Sais' is elsewhere attested for this day (P. Cairo 86637 and P. Sallier IV: Leitz 1994a, 273).
806 Stela in the Elephantine Museum (Klug 2002, 343).
807 Gauthier 1907, 245; Young 1963, 102, n. 15; Jansen-Winkeln 2007, vol. 1, 22–3. Kitchen (1973, 419) included an error to read Ramses III, instead of Ramses II.
808 O. DeM 564 (K*RI* V, 451: 11; McDowell 1999, 170–1).
809 Kitchen 1973a, 418; Jansen-Winkeln 2007, vol. 1, 21.
810 Stela, present location unknown (Klug 2002, 191).
811 Stela *in situ* (*Urk.* IV, 1556: 2; Klug 2002, 354).

III Peret

812) 8: Royal scribe *Sꜣ-n-r* was commissioned to donate a land [*R III*, 6, Memphis][812]
813) 9: Uadjet Festival [*T III*, Buto][813]
814) 9: Installation of a priest? [Psusennes II or III, 13, Karnak][814]
815) 9: Installation of a priest? [*Sheshonq I*, 13, Karnak][815]
816) 9: Festival of Hacking the Earth [AD 1st century, Tanis][816]
817) 9: Festival of Edu? [Ptolemy III, Hibeh (but related to Sais)][817]
818) 10?: An unknown scribe petitioned to Amun (or Theban triad) at Deir el-Bahari [Ramesside, 8, DB][818]
819) 10–11: Appearance of Khnum at night on the first day until the morning on the second day [Roman, Esna][819]

3rd MONTH of *pr.t* (*rkḥ-nḏs*/*pꜣ-n-imn-ḥtpw*/Phamenoth); 20th decade (*imy-ḫt ꜣḫwy*)

No.) Day: Event
820) 11: Rowing [MK, Lahun][820]
821) 11: Burial of Seti II [*Siptah*, 1, KV][821]
822) 11: Festival of Hera (Mut?) [Ptolemy III, Hibeh (but related to Sais)][822]
823) 11: Festival (birthday) of Amenhotep, son of Hapu [*Ptolemy VIII*, DB][823]
824) 11: Opening of the Face in the House of Gold [*Ptolemy VI*, Kom Ombo][824]
825) 12: Oath taken by the policeman *ỉmn-ḫꜥ* [R V, 3][825]
826) 12: Amun-of-Opet appeared at Luxor when the Nile flooded [*Osorkon III*, 3, Luxor temple][826]
827) 13: The royal army arrived in Nubia [*Seti I*, 4, Amara West and Sai][827]
828) 13: Visit of a chief to Deir el-Bahari [R IV, 2, DB][828]
829) 14: Decree to establish offerings for Amun-Re and Hapi [*R III*, 6, Gebel el-Silsila][829]
830) 14–18: Appearance of Khnum [Roman, Esna][830]
831) 15: Festival(?) of Amenhotep I [R III][831]
832) 15: Herihor's decree to renew the burial of Ramses II [*R XI*, w6, coffin of R II][832]
833) 17: Procession from a royal temple [MK, 9, Lahun][833]
834) 17: Festival in the 16th Lower Egyptian nome [*Ptolemy IV*, Edfu][834]
835) 18: Visit of the vizier *Ḫꜥ-m-wꜣs.t* to KV [*R X*, 3, western Thebes][835]

---

812 Stela Cairo 66612 (*KRI* V, 229: 11; Gaballa 1973, 111; Fitzenreiter 2007, 237).
813 Buto Stela 209 (Bedier 1994a, 5, z. 23; Klug 2002, 96–105).
814 Inscription at the Akh-menu (Legrain 1900, 54; Jansen-Winkeln 2007, vol. 1, 162).
815 Inscription at the Akh-menu (Legrain 1900, 54; Kruchten 1989, 50; Jansen-Winkeln 2007, vol. 2, 36).
816 *bꜣ tꜣ* (P. BM ESA 10673: Griffith and Petrie 1889, pl. 12). Part of the foundation ceremony (Weinstein 1973, 12)? Cf. III Peret 20 for the same ritual recorded in the same text.
817 P. Hibeh 27, l. 92 (Grenfell and Hunt 1906, 144).
818 Graffito DB 67 (Marciniak 1974, 118: 2). Petition to protect his family and to obtain commodities.
819 *sḫꜥ n Ḫnm pꜣ ḫw nfr ḫnm itn* 'uniting with the sun' (Sauneron 1963, vol. 1, 167; Grimm 1994a, 86–7).
820 P. Cairo 71583, recto (Luft 1992, 137; Luft 2006, 120).
821 Rock Graffito (no. 551) between the tombs of Tausret (KV 14) and Bay (KV13): *hrw n smꜣ tꜣ n Wsr-ḫpr-rꜥ[-mry-imn]* (Reeves 1992, 148, fig. 19; Altenmüller 1994, 21–2). Prior to this date, the king's death was reported to the gang on I Peret 19 (O. Cairo 25515, verso, col. IV, 1–3 and col. II, 21–8).
822 P. Hibeh 27, l. 112 (Grenfell and Hunt 1906, 144).
823 *nṯr mnḫ ḫꜥ=f wiꜣ=s m hrw pn nfr ꜣbd 3-nw pr.t sw 11 m rn=s ḥꜥ.t* 'beneficial god appears (in) her (Hathor) ship on this beautiful day of III Peret 11 in her name "joy".' Sanctuary of Hatshepsut's Deir el-Bahari temple (PM II², 368 (147); Laskowska-Kusztal 1984, 38).
824 *wn ḥr n pr nb* (Grimm 1994a, 88–9).
825 O. Gardiner 137 (*KRI* VI, 251: 2).
826 Hieratic graffito left by the priest of Amun-Re *Nḫt* (PM II², 317 (98); Daressy 1896, 184; Bell 1975, 244; Jansen-Winkeln 2007, vol. 2, 298). Daressy read the date as I Peret 12.
827 Stelae at Amara West (Brooklyn 39.424; PM VII, 159) and at Sai (*KRI* VII, 10: 7–8). The king seized his enemy seven days later on III Peret 20 (Darnell 2011, 136).
828 Graffito DB 96 (Marciniak 1974, 134–5). Kitchen (*KRI* VI, 97) and Peden (2001, 122, n. 395) date this record to the time of Ramses III.
829 Rock inscription (*KRI* I, 84: 16). Cf. II Akhet 5 and III Shemu 10 for decrees parallel to this.
830 Sauneron 1963, vol. 1, 167; Grimm 1994a, 88–9.
831 P. Turin 1961+2006 (Pleyte and Rossi 1869, 134–5, pls. 93–9).
832 Coffin Cairo 61020 (Gauthier 1907, vol. 3, 232; *KRI* VI, 838: 9; Kitchen 1973a, 417). The decree was issued by Herihor in his capacity of the king, not of a vizier, as attested in a docket of Seti I's coffin, dated to II Akhet 7, year 6 (*wḏ.t i.ir nsw.t imy-r mšꜥ* [ ] *srw n tꜣ* [*r*] *ḏr* [ ] *ḥm-nṯr tpy ỉmn-rꜥ nsw.t nṯr.w* [ ] *Ḥry-ḥr*). The date is wrongly transcribed as III Akhet 15 by Daressy (1909, 32).
833 P. Berlin 10003 B, recto (Luft 1992, 35). *ḫn.t n.t tꜣ* 'navigation of the land'.
834 Geographical list on the exterior of the sanctuary (PM VI, 146 (219–20)).
835 Graffito 1756 (Černý and Sadek 1969, vol. 4; *KRI* VI, 681, 1). Cf. Graffito no. 109 for the presence of *Ḫꜥ-m-wꜣs.t* the same day (Spiegelberg 1921, 14). According to P. Turin 2056+2075+2096, the workmen were off duty 'because of the desert dwellers (*r-ḥꜣ.t nꜣ ḫꜣsty.w*)' on this particular day (*KRI* VI, 688: 7).

836) 18: Festival of Nun or Nut [Ramesside][836]
837) 18: Festival in the 15th Lower Egyptian nome [*Ptolemy IV*, Edfu][837]
838) 19: Letter sent by the estate servant (*b3k n pr-ḏt*) *ỉpy* [*A IV*, 5, Gurob near Fayum][838]
839) 19: Induction of a Buchis bull to Thebes by the king and queen themselves
[Ptolemy XIII and Cleopatra VII, 1, Armant][839]
840) 20: Day of re-founding the Nubian border [*Seti I*, 4, Sinn el-Kaddab near Kurkur Oasis][840]
841) 20: Festival of Hacking the Earth [AD 1st century, Tanis][841]
842) 20+: Letter concerning a royal decree on a juridical case [13 Dyn., 5][842]

3rd MONTH of *pr.t* (*rkḥ-nḏs*/*p3-n-imn-ḥtpw*/Phamenoth); 21st decade (*b3wy/ḫmtw*)

No.) Day: Event
843) 21: Festival of the accession of ThutmoseIand his decree [*T I*, 1, Wadi-Halfa and Kubban][843]
844) 21: Lifting-Up of AmenhotepIto the Valley (KV) [R V or IV, 1, KV][844]
845) 21: Vizier *Ḫ*ʿ*-m-w3s.t* visited QV and found the violated tomb of the princess *3st* [*R IX*, 17][845]
846) 21: Oath taken by a man called *Nb-imn* concerning a payment [unknown][846]
847) 22: Royal decree to tax the entire land of Egypt [*Tutankhamen*, 8, Thebes or Aswan?][847]
848) 22: Qenbet session [R III, 28, DeM][848]
849) 22: Oath concerning a payment by the oversser of the district *Pn-rnnwt* [R IV or VI, 5][849]
850) 23: Vizier *Ḫ*ʿ*-m-w3s.t* and the HPA, royal butler *Ns-sw-imn* visited KV to hear complaints [*R IX*, 17][850]
851) 23: Horus Festival in Athribis [Ramesside][851]
852) 24: Offerings of a full moon festival [MK, 9, Lahun][852]
853) 25: Amenhotep I [20 Dyn.][853]
854) 25: A letter concerning a decree of Nebkheperre-Intef to punish an official at the Min temple in Koptos
[*Nebkheperre-Intef*: 17 Dyn., 3, Koptos][854]
855) 25: Property document concerning the family of the tutor of the prince *W3ḏ-ms*, *Sni-ms*
[*T III*, 21, temple of *W3ḏ-ms* at W. Thebes][855]
856) 25: Hearing of a matter over dividing properties among brothers [R III, 8, Assasif][856]
857) 25: Oath taken by a man called *Knr* concerning a donkey [R III, 21][857]

[836] P. Cairo 86637 and P. Sallier IV (Leitz 1994a, 287).
[837] Geographical list on the exterior of the sanctuary (PM VI, 146 (219–20)).
[838] P. UC 32782 (Sandman 1938, 148: 7; Wente 1980; Murnane and Meltzer 1995, 51). The letter is a report concerning the soundness of estates. This is the last known record of 'Amenhotep', who later became Akhenaten.
[839] Bucheum stela no. 13 (Mond, Myers, and Fairman 1934, vol. 2, 32, vol. 3, pl. 43; Goldbrunner 2004, 67, pl. 7, no. 13). The bull was carried on Amun's barge.
[840] Sandstone stela, catalogue number unknown (Darnell 2011, 132). The royal army had reached Nubia seven days earlier on III Peret 13.
[841] *b3 t3* (P. BM ESA 10673: Griffith and Petrie 1889, pl.12). Part of the foundation ceremony (Weinstein 1973, 12)? Cf. III Peret 9 for the same ritual recorded in the same text.
[842] P. Brooklyn 35.1446 (Wente 1990, 24–5). Cf. III Peret 3 for another date recorded in the same text.
[843] Stela Cairo 34006+Buhen ST 9 (*Urk.* IV, 81: 4; Wente 1990, 27; Klug 2001, 68). *hrw n ḥb n ḫ*ʿ*.w* 'day of the festival of the diadems. A royal decree to declare the king's full titulary was issued.
[844] *ṯsi in ỉmn-ḥtp* ʿ*.w.s. iw=f pḥ t3 in.t* (O. Cairo 25559: Černý 1962, 41–8; Černý 1927, 185–6; *KRI* VI, 104: 5–9). Several festivals of different dates in honour of this king are known, but many of them fall at the end of this month. The mortuary nature of this festival is clear, because Thutmose I succeeded his father Amenhotep I on this day (Sadek 1979, 52). The processions of some goddesses of funerary nature are likely to have been performed at the sane time (O. Gardiner 31).
[845] P. Turin 2029 (*KRI* VI, 579: 4; McDowell 1999, 198). The vizier, accompanied by a royal butler, also visited KV to supervise work two days later. Cf. III Akhet 19 for the same vizier inspecting QV in the previous year.
[846] O. Petrie 60 (=O. UC 39655): Allam 1973, 241–2; Černý and Gardiner 1957, pls. 18 and 18A.
[847] Stela Univ. of Liverpool E. 583 (Amer 1985a, 18; Awad 2002, 118). The decree was given to the overseer of the treasury and the fan-bearer on the right hand of the king *M*ʿ*y3* to tax the entire land (*ḥtri t3 r ḏr=f*) from Aswan to *Sm3-nb-bḥd.t* (Mediterranean coast) in order to establish divine offerings (*w3ḥ ḥtp-nṯr*) for all the gods of Egypt.
[848] O. Gardiner 150 (Vleeming 1982; *KRI* V, 527: 3; Allam 1973, 181).
[849] O. Petrie 67 (=O. UC 32054): *KRI* VI, 143: 3.
[850] P. Turin 2029 (*KRI* VI, 580: 3; McDowell 1999, 198).
[851] P. Cairo 86637 and P. Sallier IV (Leitz 1994a, 296).
[852] P. Berlin 10003 B, recto (Luft 1992, 37). For other full moon celebrations, see P. Berlin 10011, recto.
[853] P. Turin (Pleyte and Rossi 1969, 134, pl. 98: 5; Černý 1927, 183).
[854] Stela Cairo 30770 (PM V, 125; Petrie 1896, 10, pl. 8; Goebs 2003; Wente 1990, 25–6).
[855] Stela Cairo 34016 (PM II^2 444–5; Daressy 1900, 101–3; *Urk.* IV, 1066: 10). This is an *imy.t-pr* document, perhaps issued as a royal favour.
[856] *sḏm r3 n N* 'listening of the word of N'. P. Boulaq X (=P. Cairo 58092): *KRI* V, 450: 10; Janssen and Pestman 1968: 137–70; Allam 1973, 289–93. Prior to this day, there was a qenbet session in the presence of Amenhotep I.
[857] O. DeM 364 (*KRI* V, 475: 2).

III Peret

858) 26: Dated record concerning a sale of house with an oath [Menkaure, year after the 3rd census, Gebelein][858]
859) 26: Offering to Khentykhety, lord of Kemuy, and to other gods at Sinai [Amenemes IV, 9, Serabit el-Khadim][859]
860) 27: Renenutet Festival [A III, TT 48][860]
861) 27: Oath by a workman *Ḥr-m-wiꜣ* [R II or III, 14, DeM][861]
862) 28: Priest of priests *Dd-sbk* visited Thebes to make offerings to Mentuhotep [*Amenemhat III*, 30, Wadi el-Hôl][862]
863) 28: *Wꜣḥ-mw* performed by a workman [Amenmes, KV][863]
864) 28: Vizier *Tꜣ* left Thebes after collecting the statues of the southern gods for the Sed Feast [*R III*, 29][864]
865) 28: Osiris Festival in Abydos [Ramesside][865]
866) 28: Day of inspecting the queen Merytamen [Smendes I, 19, coffin of the queen][866]
867) 29: Dated scene of burial preparation with a legal formula [Djedkare-Isesi, year of the *smꜣ-tꜣ.wy*, mastaba of *Wp-m-nfr.t*, Giza][867]
868) 29: First Day of Amun's Festival of Entering the Sky (offerings not recorded) [*R III*, MHC][868]
869) 29: Great Festival of 'Amenhotep I, Lord of the Village' [R VI, 7, KV 9][869]
870) 29: Pinedjem I's decree to osirify Ahmes I and the prince Siamen [*Pinedjem I*, 8, mummy shroud][870]
871) 30: Distribution of offerings of special nature(?) [Teti, temple of Neferirkare at Abusir][871]
872) 30: Appearance of Khnum [T III, Aswan][872]
873) 30: Death of Thutmose III and accession of Amenhotep II next day [*T III*, 54, TT 85][873]
874) 30: Second Day of Amun's Festival of Entering the Sky (offerings not recorded) [*R III*, MHC][874]
875) 30: Festival in Busiris [Ramesside][875]

3rd MONTH of *pr.t* (*rkḥ-nḏs*/*pꜣ-n-imn-ḥtpw*/Phamenoth); unknown decade

No.) Day: Event
876) ?: Procession of the Land [*Amenemhat III*, 35, Lahun][876]
877) ?: Royal decree (on an expedition to Sinai?) [Ramesside, 3, Serabit el-Khadim][877]
878) ?: Dated mortuary formula [Ramesside, 8, DB][878]
879) ?: Nectanebo I erected the temple of Thoth at Hermopolis [*Nectanebo I*, 8, Hermopolis][879]
880) ?: Day of Ptah [*Harsiyotef*, 4th cent. BC, 35, Gebel Barkal][880]
881) ?: Ritual of the Emmer [Ptolemaic, Mut precinct at Karnak][881]

858 P. Gebelein I, verso, B, 1–2 (Posener-Kriéger 2004, pl. 5; Strudwick 2005, 185). For the dating to Menkaure, see Verner 2006b, 135.
859 Rock stela (Gardiner, Peet, and Černý 1952, vol. 1, pl. 45, vol. 2, 125).
860 *hrw pn ḫꜣw sk* 'this day of measuring the corn' (PM I-1², 88 (3); *Urk.* IV, 1907: 9). Säve-Söderbergh (1957, 42, n. 2) regards III Peret as an error for IV Peret because the latter date is attested from TT 38 (3).
861 O. Turin N 57173 (*KRI* V, 457: 14; McDowell 1999, 88).
862 Rock graffito in the western desert near Luxor (Darnell 2002, 96–8).
863 O. Cairo 25786 (*KRI* IV, 235: 9–10). For the dating, see Gutgesell 2002, 123.
864 P. Turin 1880 (=Strike Papyrus: Gardiner 1948, 45–8; Allam 1973, 310–2). Elsewhere in the tomb of Setau at el-Kab (Gardiner 1910; Kruchten and Delvaux 2010, 114–5, pls. 27 and 59), Ta is recorded to have visited that city to collect the divine barge of Nekhbet for the Sed Festival to be celebrated in the north, perhaps at Memphis (P. Harris I, XLIX, 10). Ramses II commissioned his prince Khaemwaset to celebrate the 1st, 2nd, 3rd, 4th, and 5th Sed Festival, and the vizier Khay was also assigned to the same task for, at least, the 5th and 6th jubilations (*ARE* III, 552–60).
865 P. Cairo 86637 and P. Sallier IV (Leitz 1994a, 299).
866 Winlock 1932, 51, pl. 41, B: 8; Kitchen 1973a, 419; Jansen-Winkeln 2007, vol. 1, 28.
867 The legend concerns the burial place of *Wp-m-nfr.t*'s son *Ỉby* and its legal testimony (PM III-1², 282 (6); *Giza* II, 190).
868 *tpy n ḥb Ỉmn m ḥb=f n ꜥḳ n p.t* (*MH* III, pl. 165, list 61). The Festival of Entering the Sky was celebrated from MK but in the Akhet season.
869 *ḥb ꜥꜣ n nsw.t Ỉmn-ḥtp-pꜣ-nb-pꜣ-dmi.t* (O. Cairo 25234: Černý 1927, 182–4; *KRI* VI, 370: 10). This festival lasted four days and was celebrated by 120 people from outside and inside the Village. Helck (1964, 158) postulated that III Peret 29 here might be a scribal error for III Peret 19.
870 Gauthier 1907, vol. 3, 248–9; Kitchen 1973a, 420; Jansen-Winkeln 2007, vol. 1, 22.
871 P. Berlin 10474 A and B (Posener-Kriéger and de Cenival 1968, 45, pl. 94 A).
872 Rock inscription of the overseer of works of Amun *Ḥw-mn* (Habachi 1950, 14–5).
873 PM I-1², 172 (17); *Urk.* IV, 895:16.
874 *MH* III, pl. 165, list 61.
875 P. Cairo 86637 and P. Sallier IV (Leitz 1994a, 301).
876 *ẖn.t n.t tꜣ* (P. UC 32191: Collier and Quirke 2006, 94–5, Luft 1992, 140).
877 Stela *in situ* (Gardiner, Peet, and Černý 1952, vol. 1, pl. 77, vol. 2, 94).
878 Graffito DB 67 (Marciniak 1974, 117–8; Sadek 1984b, 73 for translation). Curse for those who obliterate the text.
879 Stela Cairo 72130 (Roeder 1954, 410).
880 Stela Cairo 48864 (PM VII, 218; Eide, Hägg, and Pierce 1994, vol. 2, 454). The stela itself was set up on II Peret 13 in year 35, so that the 'day of Ptah' would have been fallen before that date.
881 Inscription of the Ptolemaic gate (PM II², 255 (1, f); Sauneron 1983, pl. 9, l. 28; Spalinger 1993b, 173).

4th MONTH of *pr.t* (*p3-n-rnnw.tt*/Pharmouthi); 22nd decade (*kd*) IV Peret

No.) Day: Event

882) 1: Dated account concerning distribution of linen [OK, year of the 15th census, Abusir][882]
883) 1: Festival of the Small Fire [*Senusret III*, 7, Lahun][883]
884) 1: Day of Entering the Sky [*T III*, Buto][884]
885) 1: Accession of Amenhotep II [*A II*, 1, TT 85][885]
886) 1: Amenhotep III was in the House of Rejoicing [*A III*, 36, Amarna][886]
887) 1: Entering of Amun at the Festival of Entering the Sky (offerings not recorded) [*R III*, MHC][887]
888) 1: Sokar(?) Festival on a new-moon day (122) [*R III*, MHC][888]
889) 1: Great Festival [Ramesside][889]
890) 1: Festival in the 5th Lower Egyptian nome [*Ptolemy IV*, Edfu][890]
891) 1: Opening of the Face in the House of Gold [*Ptolemy VI*, Kom Ombo][891]
892) 1: Induction of a Buchis bull to Thebes by the king himself [*Ptolemy IX*, 35, Armant][892]
893) 1: Festival of Holding the Sky [Roman, Esna][893]
894) 4: Bastet Festival [*Horemheb*, TT 50][894]
895) 4: Bastet Festival [2nd half of R II, TT 2][895]
896) 4: Bastet Festival [R II, TT 341][896]
897) 4: Festival of Chewing the Onions for Bastet (320) [*R III*, MHC][897]
898) 5: Bastet appeared in her barque [26 Dyn.][898]
899) 7: Festival of the Gods (particularly Min?) [Ramesside][899]
900) 7: Pinedjem I's decree to renew the burial of Amenhotep I [Smendes I, 6, coffin of A I][900]
901) 9: Oath concerning a donkey? [R IX, 10][901]
902) 10: A festival established anew at Thebes after an Asiatic campaign [*Seti I*, 1?][902]
903) 10: King ordered to send a copy of his royal decree to all Egyptian temples [*Ptolemy II*, 6, Pithom][903]
904) 10: Dated papyrus concerning the founfation of regulations regarding choachytes [Ptolemy IX, 8?, MH][904]

4th MONTH of *pr.t* (*p3-n-rnnw.tt*/Pharmouthi); 23rd decade (*ḫ3w*)

No.) Day: Event

905) 11: Masaharta's decree to renew the burial of Amenhotep I [Smendes I, 16, coffin of AI][905]
906) 11: Burial of the princess *Nbt-i3* [Menkheperre, 27, mummy docket][906]
907) 11: Morning of the Opening of the Face in the Birth House [*Ptolemy VI*, Kom Ombo][907]
908) 11: Opening of the Face in the House of Gold [*Ptolemy VI*, Kom Ombo][908]

---

882 P. Cairo 58063, frame 1, recto (Posener-Kriéger and de Cenival 1968, 19, pl. 47).
883 P. Berlin 10069, verso (Borchardt 1935, 56; Altenmüller 1977, 177).
884 *hrw ʿḳ n p.t* (Buto Stela 209: Bedier 1994a, 5, z. 24; Klug 2002, 96–105).
885 PM I-1², 172 (17); *Urk.* IV, 895:16. A different day of his accession is known (IV Akhet 1).
886 Amarna Letter from the Mitanni king Tushratta, concerning the travel of the goddess Ishtar from Nineveh to Egypt (BM 29793: Moran 1992, 62, n. 6).
887 The last day of the Festival of Entering the Sky beginning from the end of the previous month (*MH* III, pl. 165, list 61).
888 The inscription is damaged, but the festival is regarded as a new-moon festival (*MH* III, pl. 165, list 63; Spalinger 1995b, 27).
889 P. Cairo 86637 and P. Sallier IV (Leitz 1994a, 302).
890 Geographical list on the exterior of the sanctuary (PM VI, 146 (219–20)).
891 *wn ḥr n pr nb* (Grimm 1994a, 92–3).
892 Bucheum stela no. 12 (Mond and Myers 1934, vol. 2, 11, vol. 3, 42; Goldbrunner 2004, 62, pl. 6). The bull was carried on Amun's barge from Armant.
893 *hrw ḥb k3w.t n(.t) p.t* (Sauneron 1963, vol. 1, 167; Grimm 1994a, 92–3).
894 Tomb of Neferhotep (PM I-1², 96 (9–10, III); Hari 1985, 51, pl. 38, col. 185).
895 Tomb of Khabekhenet (PM I-1², 7 (9, II); Černý 1949, 14).
896 Tomb of Nakhtamen (PM I-1², 409 (8–9, II); *KRI* III, 364: 3; Assmann 2005, 426).
897 *wšʿ ḥd.w n B3s.t* (*MH* III, pl. 165, list 62). Her festival is recorded on a MK stela as *ḥb=s n ḫw niw.t=f* 'her festival of protecting his town', but the date is not known (Vernus 1987). P. Carlsberg 69 (unpublished) attests rites relating to this feast.
898 *iw sḫʿ n=i B3s.t r wi3=s m ḥb=s nfr* (Statue Louvre A 88: Vercoutter 1950, 90).
899 P. Cairo 86637 and P. Sallier IV (Leitz 1994a, 307).
900 Gauthier 1907, vol. 3, 244; Kitchen 1973a, 418; Jansen-Winkeln 2007, vol. 1, 21.
901 P. Turin CGT 54021 (*KRI* VI, 634: 9; Janssen 2005, 59–60).
902 [*wḏ ḥm*]*=f ir n.t-ʿ ḥb m3w.t nty ḫpr=f 3bd 4-nw pr.t sw 10 ḥr w3s.t* (Stela BM 1665: *KRI* I, 231: 11; Shorter 1933). The date was not the day on which the royal decree was issued, but the festival took place.
903 Stela Cairo 22183 (*Urk.* II, 92: 12; K. Müller 2006, 195 for translation).
904 P. Berlin 3115, Text A, I, 1 (de Cenival 1972, 15, pl. 8; Pestman 1993, 197–201 for translation).
905 Gauthier 1907, vol. III, 249; Kitchen 1973a, 419; Jansen-Winkeln 2007, vol. 1, 28.
906 Discovered from a tomb near TT 131 (Jansen-Winkeln 2007, vol. 1, 92; Dodson and Janssen 1989, 128).
907 *ḥd t3 wn ḥr n pr ms.t* (Grimm 1994a, 94–5).
908 *wn ḥr n pr nb* (Grimm 1994a, 94–5).

IV Peret

909) (11): Festival of the God's Birth [Ptolemy XIII, Dendera][909]
910) 11?: Dated graffito [Ptolemaic-Roman, 12, MH][910]
911) 11: Appearance of Neith and Herka-the-Child in the Morning, and Unification with the Sun [Roman, Esna][911]
912) 13: Royal oath to found the city Akhetaten [*A IV*, 5, Amarna][912]
913) 13: Royal decree concerning the layout of Akhetaten [*A IV*, 6, Amarna][913]
914) 13: Qenbet session [Siptah, 5, DeM][914]
915) 13: Festival in the 2nd and 3rd Upper Egyptian nomes [*Ptolemy IV*, Edfu][915]
916) 13: Opening of the Face in the House of Gold [*Ptolemy VI*, Kom Ombo][916]
917) 14?: Going-Forth to the Sky (death of a king) [MK, Lahun][917]
918) 15: Offering of the Rejuvenation of the Prince [MK, 14, Lahun][918]
919) 15: Inscription referring to royal enterprises all over Egypt [*Darius*, 30, Wadi Hammamat][919]
920) 16: Rising of Sothis [*Senusret III*, 7, Lahun][920]
921) 16: Petition to Hathor at Deir el-Bahari [Ramesside, 6, DB][921]
922) 17: Taking the coffins of R I, Seti I, and R II out from the tomb of Seti I for reburial [*Siamen*, 10, coffin dockets A][922]
923) 17: Opening of the Face in the House of Gold [*Ptolemy VI*, Kom Ombo][923]
924) 20: Bringing the coffins of Seti I and R II into the tomb of A II [Siamen, 10, coffin dockets B][924]
925) 20: Burial of Pinedjem II [Siamen, 10, cache at DB 320][925]
926) 20: Opening of the Face in the House of Gold [*Ptolemy VI*, Kom Ombo][926]

4th MONTH of *pr.t* (*p3-n-rnnw.tt*/Pharmouthi); 24th decade (*ʿryt*)

No.) Day: Event

927) 21: Festival of the Defense against Bedouin in honor of Senusret III [*T III*, 2, Semna][927]
928) 21: Scribes *Rʿ*-[ ], *ỉmn-m-ỉp.t*, and *Ḥy* visited the Step Pyramid [Ramesside, 14, Saqqara][928]
929) 22: Dated wooden chest [Djedkare-Isesi, year of the 6th census, Saqqara][929]
930) 23?: Accession of Djer(?) [Djer, 1, Palermo Stone][930]
931) 23: Burial of an Apis bull at Memphis [*Taharqa*, 24, Serapeum][931]
932) 24: Senusret I decided to renew the temple of Karnak [*Senusret I*, 10, Karnak][932]

---

909 *ḥb ms nṯr* (Grimm 1994a, 94–5).
910 Graffito MH no. 69 located at the small temple of Medinet Habu (Thissen 1989, 65–7).
911 *sḫʿ N.t Ḥr-k3-p3-ẖrd m tr n dw3w ẖnm ỉtn* (Sauneron 1963, vol. 1, 167; Grimm 1994a, 94–5).
912 Boundary stelae K, M, and X. Davies (1903, vol. 5, 28) translated as IV Peret 4 of year 4, emended by Murnane and van Siclen (1993, 35) as IV Peret 13 of year 5. Wells (1987, 331) demonstrates that the sun came out from the wadi Abu Hasah el-Bahri on the city's east-west axis on this day, corresponding to 20 February (Gregorian). Krauss (2006b, 419) further proposes that this celebration was followed by a foundation ceremony next day, on which the new moon fell.
913 Boundary stelae A, B, F, J, N, P, Q, R, S, U, and V (Murnane and van Siclen 1993, 99).
914 O. Berlin 11241 (*KRI* IV, 406: 5; Allam 1973, 34).
915 Geographical list on the exterior of the sanctuary (PM VI, 147 (225–6)).
916 *wn ḥr n pr nb* (Grimm 1994a, 94–5).
917 P. Berlin 10332 a, recto (Luft 1992, 118).
918 P. Berlin 10077, recto (Luft 1992, 84). *ỉn.w ḥby.t n.t rnp.wt n.t s3 nsw.t.*
919 Rock inscription (Couyat and Montet 1912, 97). Also see inscription dated to years 26 (I? Shemu 4), 27 (IV Peret 13), 29 (I Shemu 11), and 36 (Couyat and Montet 1912, 39, 67, 87, and 90).
920 P. Berlin 10012 A, recto, and B, recto (Borchardt 1899, 99; Parker 1950, 34; Luft 1992, 55–8; von Beckerath 1997, 227). Krauss (2006c, 441–2) regards this day as when the heliacal rising of Sothis was announced 22 days earlier. Based on this text, Depuydt (1995, 50, n. 34) interprets the astronomical ceiling of Seti I's cenotaph at Abydos as displaying the same date for the heliacal rising of Sothis and being a copy of a Middle Kingdom original.
921 Graffito DB 39 (Marciniak 1974, 96: 4).
922 Černý 1946, 28; Kitchen 1973a, 423; Jansen-Winkeln 2007, vol. 1, 114–5.
923 *wn ḥr n pr nb* (Grimm 1994a, 94–5).
924 Jansen-Winkeln 2007, vol. 1, 116.
925 Graffito at the entrance to DB 320 (Černý 1946, 26; Kitchen 1973a, 423; Jansen-Winkeln 2007, vol. 1, 141).
926 *wn ḥr n pr nb* (Grimm 1994a, 94–5).
927 *ḥb ḫsf ỉwnt.y*. Inscription on the eastern exterior wall of the Semna temple (*Urk.* IV, 195: 12–3; *LD* III, pl. 55, a). Cf. II Shemu 8 for a relating event.
928 Graffito at the north chapel of the Step Pyramid (Firth and Quibell 1935, 79; Navrátilová 2007, 124–5).
929 A wooden linen chest discovered in the tomb of Nefer and Kahay, attesting its deposing in the tomb (PM III-2^2, 641; Moussa and Altenmüller 1971, 18).
930 Wilkinson 2000, 92, fig. 1.
931 Stela Louvre IM 2640 (Malinine, Posener, and Vercoutter 1968, 99–100, no. 125; Kitchen 1973a, 489).
932 The Middle Kingdom court of Karnak (Gabolde 1998, 40, 123, pl. 5). Gabolde (1998, 123–4) suggests that this date was seven days after the

933) 25: Beginning of the 1st war campaign of T III at the city *Ṯ3-r* [*T III*, 22, Karnak][933]
934) 25: Delivery of the *šꜥ.t-bi.t*-bread to DeM [*R* X, 3][934]
935) 25: Oracle of Seth in the Dakhla Oasis [Sheshonq I, 5, Dakhla][935]
936) 25: Opening of the Face in the House of Gold [*Ptolemy VI*, Kom Ombo][936]
937) 26: First day of the first Sed Festival of Amenhotep III [*A III*, 30, Soleb][937]
938) 26: Visit of an unnamed vizier to reward (*mk*) the workmen on a holiday [R III, 26, DeM][938]
939) 26: Vizier *Nfr-rnp.t* came to perform the libation *w3ḥ mw* (at western Thebes?) [*R IV*, 5][939]
940) 26: 9th expedition to the Eastern Desert by the scribe of the double-treasury *Ḫnsw-ms* [R VII, 2][940]
941) 27: Day of Measuring the Corn, and harvest offerings to Amun and Renenutet [T IV, TT 38][941]
942) 27: Brewing for Hathor [Amenmes, 3, DeM][942]
943) 27: Opening of the Face in the House of Gold [*Ptolemy VI*, Kom Ombo][943]
944) 28: Offering to Hathor [Amenmes, 3, DeM][944]
945) 28: Festival of Horus of Sepa, son of Sekhmet [*Ptolemy* X, Edfu][945]
946) 28: Birth of Horus [*Ptolemy* X, Edfu][946]
947) 28: Harsies Festival [Roman, Esna][947]
948) 29: Offering to Amun of Kawa [Aryamani: 3rd cent. BC, Kawa][948]
949) 30: Graffito of two scribes [TIP, Ptah precinct at Karnak][949]
950) 30: Awakening in the Birth House [*Ptolemy VI*, Kom Ombo][950]
951) 30–I Shemu (1): Renenutet Festival [Ptolemaic, Mut precinct at Karnak][951]
952) 30: Appearance of Nebetu of Esna, Resting in the Birth House [Roman, Esna][952]

4th MONTH of *pr.t* (*p3-n-rnnw.tt*/Pharmouthi); unknown decade

No.) Day: Event
953) ?: Foundation ritual [*Niuserre*, solar temple of Niuserre at Abu Gurob][953]
954) ?: Offering of the Appearance of Sothis [MK, 1, Lahun][954]
955) ?: Dragging of Sokar [MK, 8, Lahun][955]
956) ?: Heliacal rising of Sothis [A I, Karnak][956]
957) ?: Tax collection [*Ptolemy II*, 21, Pithom][957]

---

heliacal rising of Sothis.

933 Enclosure wall around the granite sanctuary at Karnak (PM II², 98 (282, II); *Urk.* IV, 647: 12).

934 P. Turin 1898+1926+1937+2094 (*KRI* VI, 690: 7; Botti and Peet 1928, pl. 52). It was delivered from the memorial temple of R III. Haring (1997, 260) relates this delivery to an unknown feast.

935 *ḥb=f nfr n wrš* (Stela Ashmolean 1894.107a). Krauss sees this festival as a new moon celebration as *wrš* is a word associated with temple personnel based on the lunar calendar (Gardiner 1933, 22; Krauss 1985, 165–6; Jansen-Winkeln 2007, vol. 2, 24).

936 *wn ḥr n pr nb* (Grimm 1994a, 96–7).

937 Inscription at the Soleb temple (*Urk.* IV, 1961: 16). The rite of 'illuminating the throne (*tk3 ḫf tnṯ3.t*)' continued from this day to I Shemu. The ritual of 'raising the djed pillar' is attested in TT 192. Van Siclen (1973, 291) asserts that the festival continued until III Shemu 2 for 67 days. Cf. II Shemu 27 and III Shemu 2 for relating events during the festival.

938 *iw.n ṯ3ty r t3 s.t p3 mk*. O. Turin 57153, recto (López 1978, 26, pl. 68).

939 *hrw pn ii in imy-r niw.t ṯ3ty Nfr-rnp.t r w3ḥ mw* (O. BM 50744: Krauss 1985, 149; *KRI* VII, 336: 13). On the *w3ḥ-mw*, see Donker van Heel 1992.

940 P. IFAO (Koenig 1979, 193, pl. 32).

941 *ḫ3t sk* 'measuring the corn' (TT 38 (3); *Urk.* IV, 1640: 6). Scenes parallel to this are found in TTs 57 (8), 96 (A), 120 (1), and 253 (2). Cf. III Peret 27 for a different date for this ritual attested in TT 48.

942 *ꜥtḫ n Ḥw.t-ḥr* 'brewing for Hathor' (O. Cairo 25782, recto: *KRI* IV, 221: 7–8.; Černý 1935b, 87, pl. 103*, 4).

943 *wn ḥr n pr nb* (Grimm 1994a, 96–7).

944 *wdn n Ḥw.t-ḥr* (O. Cairo 25780 and 25782, recto: *KRI* IV, 221: 3, 9; Černý 1935b, 86–7, pls. 102–3*).

945 *ḥb Ḥr sp3 w3ḏ Sḫm.t* (Sauneron 1963, vol. 1, 217; Grimm 1994a, 96–7).

946 *msw.t=f* (Alliot 1949, 218; Sauneron 1963, vol. 1, 218; Grimm 1994a, 96–7). Isis conceived Horus on III Shemu 4.

947 Sauneron 1963, vol. 1, 168; Grimm 1994a, 98–9. The birth (of Horus) is documented for this month at Edfu and Dendera (el-Sabban 2000, 171, 181, and 183). This day was regarded as the 2nd lunar day (Parker 1950, 59).

948 Fragments of Stela BM 1777 (Eide, Hägg, and Pierce 1994, vol. 2, 529).

949 Western half of the southern exterior wall of the Ptah precinct at Karnak (PM II², 201 (36); Ragazzoli and Frood 2013, 33 for photograph).

950 *rs n pr ms* (Grimm 1994a, 98–9).

951 *ḥb Rnn.t* (Ptolemaic gate of the Mut precinct: Sauneron 1983, pl. 9, col. 31; Spalinger 1993b, 174; Klotz 2012, 391).

952 *sḫꜥ n Nb.t-ww m iwny.t ḥtp m pr ms* (Sauneron 1963, vol. 1, 168; Grimm 1994a, 98–9). It continued until the morning.

953 *pḏ-šs sḫ.t-ḏb b3 ḏb3-snṯ-m-šꜥ ir.t-k3* 'stretching the cord, making the brick, hacking the earth, filling foundation with sand, and working' (Helck 1977, pl. 2, l. 5).

954 *ḥby.t n.t pr.t spd.t* (P. Berlin 10007, recto: Luft 1992, 45; Spalinger 1992, 22).

955 *sṯt Skr* (P. Berlin 10056 A, recto: Luft 1992, 71).

956 *pr.t spd.t r hrw=s* (unnumbered stone block: Spalinger 1992, 19–21, pl. III). The date is not recorded but Grimm (1994b, 74) suggests IV Peret and postulates that this record was a copy of a Middle Kingdom document.

957 Stela Cairo 22183 (*Urk.* II, 104: 10; K. Müller 2006, 199 for translation).

1st MONTH of *šmw* (*pꜣ-n-ḫnsw*/Pachons)*; 25th decade (*ẖry ꜥryt*) — I Shemu

No.) Day: Event

958) 1: Scribe of the house of life *ỉn-(tf)* spent a day at Wadi el-Hôl [MK, 2, Wadi el-Hôl][958]
959) 1: Iahhotep's decree to give gifts to her steward *Kꜣ-rs* [*A I*, 10, Dra Abu el-Naga][959]
960) [1]: Dated stela recording an endowment [*A III*, 35, Silsila][960]
961) 1: Offering to the goddess Renenutet and birthday of (her son) Nepri [A III, TT 57][961]
962) 1: Renenutet Festival (293) [*R III*, MHC][962]
963) 1: Horus Festival [Ramesside][963]
964) 1: Appearance of Haroeris in the Birth House [*Ptolemy VI*, Kom Ombo][964]
965) 1–II Shemu 1: Festival of the God's Hand of Hathor-Iusas [*Ptolemy X*, Edfu][965]
966) 1: Festival of Khnum, Nebetu, and Her-Ka, Appearance of Min-Amun, and Renenutet Festival [Roman, Esna][966]
967) 2: Royal decree to offer a thanks-giving to Amun [*T III*, year after 23, Akh-menu at Karnak][967]
968) 3: Thutmose III listed booty and tributes from his war campaign [*T III*, 31, Karnak][968]
969) 3: Rituals with different headdresses [Roman, Esna][969]
970) 4: The lector (*ꜥšꜣ*) *Ḫꜥ-kꜣ.w-rꜥ-snfr* swore regarding his household document [*Sekhemre-Khutauy*, 3, Lahun][970]
971) 4?: Birth of the goddess Meretseger [20 Dyn., KV][971]
972) 4: Accession of Thutmose III [*T III*, 1, Karnak][972]
973) 4: Accession of Thutmose III [*T III*, 15, Karnak][973]
974) 4: Festival of appearance of Thutmose III in Gaza during his Asian campaign [*T III*, 23, Karnak][974]
975) 4: Accession day of Thutmose III [*T III*, Buto][975]
976) 4: Anuket Festival in Armant [*A II*, 4, Armant][976]
977) 4: Installation of tomb equipment (cloth?) in the tomb of R IV [R V, KV 2][977]
978) 5: Festival of the Soul-of-the-Lord-of-Busiris [Ramesside][978]
979) 5: Appearance of Amun-Re and oracle-giving on the Silver Floor [*Psametik I*, 14, Thebes][979]
980) 6–7: Dispute over a tomb at Deir el-Medina [R III, 21, DeM][980]
981) 6: Installation of a priest? [*Sheshonq III*, 18?, Karnak][981]
982) 7–8: Qenbet session on the 1st day and the appearance of AmenhotepIon the 2nd day [R III, 16][982]

---

* A festival solely celebrated for Khonsu is rarely attested, apart from the statue of Horsaaset, which lists *ḥb=f nfr n Ḫnsw* before the Valley Feast (Cairo 42210: PM II^2, 150; Jansen-Winkeln 1985, vol. 1, 63–82, vol. 2, 462–69; Jansen-Winkeln 2007, vol. 2, 234; Spalinger 1996, 74).

958 Rock graffito at Wadi el-Hôl, Western Desert, recording a holiday (*hrw nfr*). Darnell 2002, 136–7.

959 Kares Stela (Cairo 34003; *Urk.* IV, 45: 9). Based on the lunar date recorded in P. Ebers, dated to year 9 of Amenhotep I, I Shemu 1 in year 10 corresponds to a new moon day.

960 Two rock stelae (*Urk.* IV, 1678: 8 and 1920: 3; *LD* III, pl. 81, c; Klug 2002, 415).

961 *wdn ḫ.t nb.t nfr.t wꜥb.t n Rnw.tt nb.t šnꜥ.t m ꜣbd 1-nw šmw sw 1 hrw pn ms.t Npri* (TT 57 (8); *Urk.* IV, 1844: 10–1; Davies 1929, 41–9). The festival is also recorded in TT 50 (9–10, I) (Dümichen 1866, pl. 38). This event was associated with the birth of the god Khonsu, thus the designation of this month (P. Leiden T 23: M. Smith 2009, 414).

962 *ḥb Rnnw.tt* (*MH* III, pl. 165, list 64).

963 P. Cairo 86637 and P. Sallier IV (Leitz 1994a, 329).

964 *ḫꜥ n Ḥr-wr* (Grimm 1994a, 98–9).

965 *hrw ḥb ḏr.t nṯr Ḥw.t-ḥr-ỉwsꜥs.t* (Grimm 1994a, 98–9).

966 *ḥb Ḫnm Nb.t-ww Ḥr-kꜣ* (Sauneron 1963, vol. 1, 168; Grimm 1994a, 100–1). The unification with the sun was performed in the 2nd hour of the day.

967 *ḫpr ḥms.t nsw.t m ḏꜣd[w ỉ]my wr.t m [ꜥ]ḥ=[f]* 'royal seating took place in the *ḏꜣd*[*w*]-hall [o]n the West at [his p]alace' (PM II^2, 126 (462); *Urk.* IV, 1252: 11; Gardiner 1952, 9; Redford 2003, 127). Parallel ceremonies of Hatshepsut (*Urk.* IV, 257: 1) and of Ahmes (*Urk.* IV, 26: 12) are attested (Stadelmann 1996, 226, n. 9). Gardiner (1945, 16) read 'year after 23' as year 24.

968 Annals near the sanctuary (PM II^2, 89 (240–4); Mariette 1875, pl. 13, ll. 9–16; *Urk.* IV, 690: 14).

969 Sauneron 1963, vol. 1, 168; Grimm 1994a, 104–5. A series of rituals with royal crowns were held on the 3rd, 7th, 14th, 15th, 16th, 18th, 20th, and 22nd in this month.

970 P. UC 32166 (Collier and Quirke 2004, 116–7). Another date (I Shemu 9, year 26) is recorded for a previous(?) oath.

971 O. Cairo 25535 (Černý 1935b, vol. 1, 32*).

972 *ḫpr ḫꜥ.t-nsw.t* (Doorway of the 7th pylon at Karnak: PM II^2, 170 (498, c); *Urk.* IV, 180: 15). The accession was approved by Amun-Re-Horakhety.

973 *ḥb ḫꜥ.w nsw.t n nsw.t-bi.ty Mn-ḫpr-rꜥ* 'Festival of the Royal Diadems of Menkheperre' (PM II^2, 106 (329); *Urk.* IV, 177; el-Sabban 2000, 19).

974 *hrw n ḥb ḫꜥ-nsw.t.* Annals near the sanctuary (PM II^2, 98 (282, II); *Urk.* IV, 648: 9).

975 *ḫꜥ-nsw.t n nsw.t-bi.ty Mn-ḫpr-rꜥ* (Buto Stela 209: Bedier 1994a, 5, z. 25; Klug 2002, 96–105).

976 Stela Cairo 34019 (Lacau 1909, 40). Also see O. Turin 57062, which records a ritual performed for Anuket in this month: *ink in mw n ꜥnḳ.t* 'I brought water to Anuket', dated to year 47 of Ramses II (K*RI* III, 524: 2 and 525: 15).

977 Graffito found in KV 2 of R IV (Warburton 1990, 133; Peden 2001, 203–4). See II Shemu 7 for another occasion of installation in the same tomb.

978 P. Cairo 86637 and P. Sallier IV (Leitz 1994a, 331).

979 P. Brooklyn 47.2183. Parker (1962, 7–8) asserted that this day was the 1st lunar day.

980 O. BM 5624 and P. Berlin 10496 (K*RI* V, 475: 5–14; Blackman 1926, 176–8; Allam 1973, 43–5). See II Shemu 1 for another date recorded in the same text.

981 Inscription at the Akh-menu (Kruchten 1989, 144).

982 P. DeM 26 (K*RI* V, 462: 11, 463: 2 and 11; Allam 1973, 297–300). The people involved in this juridical case made an oath the previous day. Cf. I Peret 20 andIShemu 20 for other dates recorded in the same text.

983) 9: Burial(?) of Horemheb [*Horemheb*, 27, MH][983]
984) 10: Royal decree to devote a land to the Mentu temple [*T IV*, 5, Medamud][984]
985) 10: Festival of Clothing Anubis (122) [*R III*, MHC][985]
986) 10 or 12: Day of the Rest of Amun (at Karnak?) and Appearance of the Theban triad, and an oracular session [*Pinedjem II*, 3, Karnak][986]

1st MONTH of *šmw* (*p3-n-ḫnsw*/Pachons); 26th decade (*rmn ḥry s3ḥ/ṯs ꜥrḳ*)

No.) Day: Event
987) 11: Going-Forth of Min to the Stairway When the New Moon is in the Morning (299) [*R III*, MHC][987]
988) 11: Visit of the prince Osorkon (III) and a hereditary claim by the wab-priest *Ḥri* at the Festival of I Shemu [*Takelot II*, 11, Karnak][988]
989) 11: Payment of a man called *P3-di-ḫnsw* and an oath to a priest of Amun [*Takelot II*, 23][989]
990) 11: Appeal on a contract before many priests [*Takelot II*, 24][990]
991) 11–21: Birth of Iusas-Hathor, lady of Dendera [*Ptolemy X*, Edfu][991]
992) 11: Appearance of Hathor [Ptolemy XII, Dendera][992]
993) 12: Oracle of Amun [Siamen, 3, Karnak][993]
994) 13: Oath-taking [*R II*, 40][994]
995) 13: Strike at Thebes [*R III*, 29][995]
996) 13: Festival in the 18th Lower Egyptian nome [*Ptolemy IV*, Edfu][996]
997) 14: God appeared at a festival [R IV or VIII, DeM][997]
998) 15: Scribe *Sn-wsr.t* spent a day at Wadi el-Hôl [MK, 2, Wadi el-Hôl][998]
999) [15]: Visit of HPA *Rꜥ-ms-sw-nḫt* to the Enclosure of the Necropolis [R IV, 1, DeM][999]
1000) 15: Burial of an Apis bull at Memphis [*Amasis*, 23, Serapeum][1000]
1001) 15: Appearance of Min-Amun in (or from) the Birth-House [Roman, Esna][1001]
1002) 16: 9th lunar day [*Amenemhat III*, 29, Lahun][1002]
1003) 16: Royal decree concerning the temple of Amun and the overseer of Amun's temple *Sn-mw.t* [*T III*, 4, Karnak][1003]
1004) 16: Accusation against some men [*R III*, 29][1004]
1005) 17: Scribe *ʾIn-ḥr.t-nḫt* spend a holiday (*hrw nfr*) with his people at Wadi el-Hôl [MK, 17, Wadi el-Hôl][1005]

---

983 *ꜥḳ ir.n Ḥr-m-ḥb* (Graffito on a statue of the king: Anthes 1939, 107; Peden 2001, 74). Year 27 is contentious because the highest known regnal year of Horemheb is 13. This perhaps includes the reigns of all the proscribed kings of the Amarna Period (Hornung 2006, 209).
984 Stela then in sale (Bigler and Geier 1994, 15).
985 *ḥb ḏb3 ʾInpw m3ꜥ n ʾImn-rꜥ ḥnꜥ psḏ.t=f m ḥb pn m imny.t n hrw 1 ḥb* 'Feast of Clothing Anubis, offering to Amun-Re with his Ennead at this festival for the duration of one festive day' (*MH* III, pl. 167, list 65).
986 *sḫꜥ n nṯr pn šps nb nṯr.w ʾImn-rꜥ*. Amun appeared while 'Mut and Khonsu stayed in the sanctuary' (text of Djehutymes at Karnak (PM II^2, 183 (553); Kruchten 1986, 231–47).
987 *pr.t Mnw r ḫ.t* (*MH* III, pl. 167, list 66). The same date is attested from Niuserre's solar temple (Helck 1977, pl. 2, l. 10), but a different date (III Peret 19) is known from the reign of Ptolemy VIII, year 29 (Parker 1950, 47). Spalinger (1995, 27) notes that the festival coincidentally fell on day 11 in both civil and lunar calendars in a given year of Ramses III. Dolińska (2007, 71) attributed this record to Ramses II. The duration of five or six days in association with the new moon is attested from a text dating from the Thirtieth Dynasty to Ptolemaic Period (Guermeur 2004, 250).
988 Block Louvre C 258 (Daressy 1913, 130; Krauss 1985, 166–7; Kruchten 1989, 257; Jansen-Winkeln 2007, vol. 2, 168–9). He made a hereditary claim before the overseer of Upper Egypt. Osorkon (III), son of Takelot II, was the HPA and general.
989 P. Berlin 3048, verso (Jansen-Winkeln 2007, vol. 2, 169).
990 P. Berlin 3048, verso (Jansen-Winkeln 2007, vol. 2, 169).
991 *ms.t n ʾIwsꜥs Ḥw.t-ḥr nb(.t) iwn.t* (Grimm 1994a, 106–7).
992 *ḫꜥ in Ḥw.t-ḥr* (Grimm 1994a, 106–7).
993 East end of the 10th pylon at Karnak (PM II^2, 183 (553); Kitchen 1973a, 422; Jansen-Winkeln 2007, vol. 1, 175).
994 O. Ashmolean 215 (*KRI* VII, 184: 3).
995 P. Turin 1880 (Strike Papyrus): McDowell 1999, 235–6.
996 Geographical list on the exterior of the sanctuary (PM VI, 146 (219–20)).
997 O. DeM 115 (*KRI* VI, 448: 13–4; Wente 1990, 163).
998 Rock graffito at Wadi el-Hôl, Western Desert (Darnell 2002, 135–6). Cf. I Shemu 1 for a graffito possibly recorded on the same occasion.
999 O. Berlin 12640+O. DeM 161+O. Strasbourg H 82 (*KRI* VI, 114: 12).
1000 Stela Louvre 190 (Chassinat 1900, 22). This bull died on III Peret 6. Cf. IV Peret 23.
1001 Sauneron 1963, 169; Grimm 1994a, 108–9.
1002 P. BM 10062 A (Parker 1950, 63).
1003 Donation stela of *Sn-mw.t in situ*? (PM II^2, 17; Christophe 1951, 87, pl. 15). Dorman (1988, 29 and 2006, 44) leaves the year dating open to question because it was re-carved in the Ramesside Period.
1004 P. Turin 1880 (Strike Papyrus): McDowell 1999, 192–3.
1005 Rock graffito at Wadi el-Hôl, Western Desert, referring to *hrw nfr* a 'holiday' (Darnell 2002, 129–35). Cf. I Shemu 1 for a graffito similar to this in context.

I Shemu

1006) 17: Visit of HPA *Rꜥ-ms-sw-nḫt* to DeM [R IV, 1, DeM][1006]
1007) 18: Unspecified festival [R II, KV][1007]
1008) 18: Arrival of a scribe and two chief policemen to punish a water carrier and two washermen [R III/V, QV][1008]
1009) 19: Appeal to Amenhotep I [*R III*, 14][1009]
1010) 19: Unnamed vizier went downstream (*ḫd*) [R III, 24, QV][1010]
1011) 19: Report to Amenhotep I [R III, 27, DeM][1011]
1012) 19: Great Festival [Ramesside][1012]
1013) 19: Installation (*bsi*) of the priest of Amun-Re and vizier *Pꜣ-nty-iw=f-ꜥnḫ* before Amun at Karnak [*Padibast I*, 8, Karnak][1013]
1014) 19: Appearance of Khonsu of Behedet [*Ptolemy X*, Edfu][1014]
1015) 20: Dated rock stela [*Amenemhat III*, 2, Wadi el-Hôl][1015]
1016) 20: Graffito of the fan-bearer on the right of the king *Sṯḫy* [*Siptah*, 3, Sehel][1016]
1017) 20?: Appeal to Amenhotep I(?) [R III, 16, DeM][1017]
1018) 20: Installation (*bsi*) of the divine father of Amun-Re *Ns-pꜣ-nfr-ḥr* in the presence of all priests in a procession [*Osorkon the Elder*, 2, Karnak][1018]
1019) 20: Festivals of I Shemu and of Mentu at Armant [*Ptolemy XII*, 28, Armant][1019]
1020) 20: Dated graffito [Ptolemaic-Roman, 10, MH][1020]

1st MONTH of *šmw* (*pꜣ-n-ḫnsw*/Pachons); 27th decade (*rmn ḫry sꜣḥ*)

No.) Day: Event

1021) 21: New-moon festival corresponding to a coronation event(?) at Megiddo [*T III*, 23, Karnak][1021]
1022) 22: Thutmose I's decree to clean up a canal after his Nubian campaign [*T I*, 3, Sehel][1022]
1023) 22: Thutmose III's decree to clean up a canal [*T III*, 50, Sehel][1023]
1024) 22: Induction of a Buchis bull to Thebes by the king himself [*Ptolemy VIII*, 51, Armant][1024]
1025) 23: Dated lid of the sarcophagus of the overseer of the priests of the mother of the king Khentkaues *Ꞽdw* [Djedkare-Isesi, year after the 17th census, Abusir][1025]
1026) 24: The king entered the temple of Ptah in Memphis [*R III*, 20+, Memphis][1026]
1027) 25: Dated stela recording an Asiatic war campaign [*A II*, 7, Memphis][1027]

1006 O. Berlin 12640+O. DeM 161+O. Strasbourg H 82 (*KRI* VI, 114: 14).
1007 O. Cario 25815, a (*KRI* III, 567: 7).
1008 O. Turin 57058 (López 1978, 35, pls. 35–35a).
1009 *ꜥš n Ꞽmn-ḥtp* (O. Cairo 25555, recto: 5; *KRI* V, 456: 11; McDowell 1999, 179). This appeal was the second session on a property dispute previously raised by *Knr* on III Shemu 24.
1010 O. Turin 57055 (*KRI* V, 495: 11).
1011 *smi n nsw.t Ꞽmn-ḥtp* (O. Petrie 21: Allam 1973, 237–8; *KRI* V, 518: 9).
1012 O. Cairo 86637 (Leitz 1994a, 343). Leitz regards this day as the vernal equinox.
1013 Stone block Cairo 36494 found in the Middle Kingdom court (Legrain 1900, 52; Kruchten 1989, 36; Jansen-Winkeln 2007, vol. 2, 213). The ceremonial appointment was performed before the statue of Amun at the sanctuary of Karnak in the presence of the high-priest of Amun: *r tꜣ gꜣy.t ꜥꜣ.t šps.t n Ꞽmn in ḥm-nṯr tpy n Ꞽmn imy-r šmꜥy Ḥr-sꜣ-ꜣs.t* [ ] *m=f mꜣ=f Ꞽmn m sšm=f pw ḏsr*.
1014 *sḫꜥ nṯr pn Ḫnsw n bḥd.t* (Grimm 1994a, 110–1).
1015 Rock stela at Wadi el-Hôl, Western Desert (Darnell 2002, 138). The context is not clear.
1016 Graffito (*LD* III, pl. 202, b; *KRI* IV, 363: 12).
1017 *my n=i pꜣy=i nb nfr* 'come to me my beautiful lord!' (P. DeM 26: *KRI* V, 464: 5–6; Allam 1973, 297–300). Also see I Peret 20 and I Shemu 7–8 for other dates recorded in the same text.
1018 Inscription at the Akh-menu (Legrain 1900, 53; Young 1963, 100; Kruchten 1989, 45). Kruchten (1989, 18–20, 45) argues that the initiation rituals of priests could have involved divine processions.
1019 Bucheum stela no. 13 (Mond and Myers 1934, vol. 2, 11–3, vol. 3, pl. 43; Goldbrunner 2004, 67, pl. 7). A Buchis bull entered Armant on this day to be raised.
1020 Graffito MH no. 61 located at the small temple of Medinet Habu (Thissen 1989, 61–3).
1021 Annals on the enclosure walls around the sanctuary (PM II^2, 97 (280); *Urk.* IV, 657: 2). The king co-celebrated his coronation in the morning at Megiddo during his war campaign (*hrw n ḥb n psḏntyw r mty ḫꜥ.t-nsw.t tp dwꜣ.t* 'exact day of the new-moon festival, the king's appearance in the morning'). Faulkner (1942, 11, n. hh), later supported by Parker (1957c, 40), proposed that the date be emended to I Shemu 20. See Lello (1978) and Casperson (1986) for subsequent arguments on this issue offered by some scholars. Whether this refers to a coronation event or the king's waking up in the morning remains uncertain. Cf. Redford 1967, 3–27; Redford 2003, 29; Read 1996, 104.
1022 *šꜣd mr pn*. Rock inscription (*Urk.* IV, 89: 16).
1023 *šꜣd mr pn*. Rock inscription (*Urk.* IV, 814: 10; Gardiner 1927, 3rd ed., 335; Klug 2002, 165).
1024 Bucheum stela no. 11 (Mond and Myers 1934, vol. 2, 10–1, vol. 3, pl. 42; Goldbrunner 2004, pl. 6). The bull was carried on Amun's barge.
1025 Sarcophagus *in situ* (Verner 1980, 259, pl. 16; Strudwick 2005, 382–3 for translation; Verner 2006a, 328, n. 54 for the corrected dating).
1026 Door-jamb fragment Cairo 45570 (*KRI* V, 230: 12; Gaballa 1973, 111). There is a reference to 200 persea trees planted at the temple.
1027 Stela Cairo 86763 (*Urk.* IV, 1301: 3; Badawy 1943, 4; Edel 1953, 113; Klug 2002, 243).

I Shemu

1028) 25–6: Amenhotep II's victory at the Orontes in his Asiatic campaign [*A II*, 7, Karnak][1028]
1029) 25: Installation (*bsi*) of a divine father [*Takelot II*, 11, Karnak][1029]
1030) 25: Appearance of the Great Gods [Roman, Esna][1030]
1031) 25: Installation of priests and singers at the great *wbꜣ*-hall of the Ptah temple [*R III*, 24, Memphis][1031]
1032) 26: Accession of Ramses III, who decreed to establish new offerings for Amun-Re (4860+) [*R III*, MHC][1032]
1033) 26–II Shemu 15: Accession anniversary of Ramses III for 20 days [*R III*, 22–32, DeM][1033]
1034) 26: Appearance of the king [R III, 31, DeM][1034]
1035) 26: Dated rock inscription of the HPA *Rꜥ-ms-sw-nḫt* [*R IV*, 3, Wadi Hammamat][1035]
1036) 26: Appearance of Ramses III [*R X*, 3][1036]
1037) 26: Amun Festival and the installation (*bsi*) of the vizier *Ḥr-sꜣ-ꜣs.t* [*Sheshonq III*, 39, Karnak][1037]
1038) 27: Thutmose III's decree to establish new offerings for Amun [*T III*, 15, Karnak][1038]
1039) 27: Rainfall [*Merenptah*, 4, western Thebes][1039]
1040) 27: Amenhotep I's Festival [*R X*, 3][1040]
1041) 28: Appearance of Min-Amun to His Stairway during a festival [*Taharqa*, Karnak][1041]
1042) 30: Festival of two Meret Deities of the South and the North [*T III*, Buto][1042]
1043) 30: Graffito at the Step Pyramid [*Seti I*, 4, Saqqara][1043]
1044) 30: Qenbet and oath concerning the ownership of a tomb [*R III*, 24][1044]
1045) 30: Report and oath concerning an ox [R IV, 2, DeM][1045]
1046) 30: A festival [Ramesside][1046]

1st MONTH of *šmw* (*pꜣ-n-ḫnsw*/Pachons); unknown decade

No.) Day: Event
1047) ?: Day of the Rowing to Mentuhotep II's Valley [Amenemhat I, West Thebes][1047]
1048) ?: Festival of I Shemu [A I, Karnak][1048]
1049) ?: Rising of Sothis [*T III*, Buto][1049]

1028 Stela located by the 8th pylon (*Urk.* IV, 1310: 18; Edel 1953, 115; Klug 2002, 260–70). The king subsequently celebrated his war victory for Amun on the second day.
1029 Inscription at the Akh-menu (Legrain 1900, 60; Kruchten 1989, 121; Jansen-Winkeln 2007, vol. 2, 168).
1030 *mḥ hrw* 6 'for six days(?)' (Sauneron 1963, vol. 1, 169; Grimm 1994a, 112–3).
1031 Stela Cairo, number unknown (Schulman 1963, 178; *KRI* V, 250: 1). Helck (1966b) proposed a restoration of the beginning of the text. They served a cult statue of the king, which was to be given offerings originating from the treasuries of Ptah and the king in I Akhet.
1032 *hrw ḫꜥ-nsw.t ḥr s.t Ḥr šsp.n=f ḥkr.w n it=f Rꜥ* (*MH* III, pls. 140 and 152, lists 1 and 19–22). The accession day is also alluded to on O. Turin 57033 (*KRI* V, 496: 10). Parker (1950, 61) noted that Ramses III may have celebrated this event during the Sed Festival, which Spalinger (1991, 26) regards as having taken place in year 22.
1033 P. Harris I (XVIIa: 3–4): Erichsen 1933, 21: 1; Grandet 1994, vol. 1, 246.
1034 O. DeM 55 (*KRI* V, 557: 7).
1035 Rock inscription (*KRI* VI, 12: 5; Couyat and Montet 1912, 108, pl. 40).
1036 P. Turin 1898+1926+1937+2094 (Gardiner 1906a, 138; *KRI* VI, 692: 8; Helck 1990). *ḫꜥ Wsr-mꜣꜥ.t-rꜥ-stp-n-(imn)*. The workmen at DeM were off duty on this day.
1037 Inscription at the Akh-menu (Legrain 1900, 55; Krauss 1985, 166; Kruchten 1989, 59). The 'first month (*tpy*)' is omitted in Legrain's copy. The initiation ritual was again held in the sanctuary of Amun at Karnak.
1038 The south wall of a group of rooms to the south of the granite sanctuary (PM II², 106 (328); *Urk.* IV, 172: 15; el-Sabban 2000, 18). Based on the new moon day on I Shemu 21, eight years ago, this day also falls on a new moon day.
1039 Graffito 3012 (Černý and Sadek 1969, IV/3, 154, no. 3012; Peden 2001, 178).
1040 *ḥb* [*n*] *nsw.t ꞽImn-ḥtp* (P. Turin 1898+1926+1937+2094: Černý 1927, 183; *KRI* VI, 692: 9–10). Cf. III Shemu 11 for the same festival celebrated on a different day, recorded in the same text.
1041 *iw ḫꜥ n Mnw-imn r ḫ.t=f m pr wꜣs m ḥb=f nfr* [ ] (Mariette 1875, pl. 42: 5; Gauthier 1931, 28). The copy of Mariette shows the date as II Shemu 28, but it may better be understood as I Shemu 28.
1042 *ḥb Mr.wt rsy.t mḥy.t* (Buto Stela 209: Bedier 1994a, 6, z. 27; Klug 2002, 96–105).
1043 Graffito at the south chapel of the Step Pyramid (Firth and Quibell 1935, vol. 1, 82).
1044 P. Berlin 10496, verso (*KRI* V, 478: 1; Blackman 1926, 177–81; Allam 1973, 278).
1045 *smi* 'report' (O. DeM 433: *KRI* VI, 130: 13).
1046 P. Cairo 86637 and P. Sallier IV (Leitz 1994a, 351).
1047 Graffiti no. 968 and 981 (Spiegelberg 1921, 81, no. 968 and 82, no. 981; Winlock 1947, 84, pl. 40 (1); Egberts 1995, vol. 1, 407 for translation; Ullmann 2007, 8 for transliteration and translation).
1048 Unnumbered stone block (Spalinger 1992, 19, pl. III; Grimm 1994b, fig. 1). *ḥb=f n tpy* [*šmw*] preceded by *ḫꜣw.t n.t ḥb=f* [ ] the 'altar of his festival of [ ]'.
1049 Buto Stela 209 (Bedier 1994a, 5–6, z. 26; Klug 2002, 96–105). If one seeks an alternative interpretation other than just an error, the date might indicate the accession day of Thutmose III, which was I Shemu 4. In the Ptolemaic-Roman Period, the birthday of rulers was referred to as *wpy-rnp.t* in the calendar of Esna and the Decree of Canopus, and as the 'Festival of Isis' in Stela Louvre 335 (Depuydt 2003). The Decree of Memphis (Rosetta Stone) records the birthday of Ptolemy V for IV Shemu 30 as a festival day.

I Shemu

1050) ?: Festival of Anuket of Nubia of I Shemu [*A II*, 4, Elephantine, later moved to Armant][1050]
1051) ?: Installation of the divine father *Ḫri* at Karnak [*Siamen*, 17, Karnak][1051]
1052) ?: Amun's procession during the Festival of I Shemu [*Osorkon II*, Karnak][1052]
1053) ?: Installation of the divine father of Amun *Pꜣ-di-imn* at the sanctuary of Mut and Khonsu [*Padibast I*, 7, Karnak][1053]
1054) ?: Installation of a priest? [*Padibast*, 14 and 23, Karnak][1054]
1055) ?: Installation of the divine father of Khonsu *ꜥnḫ-n=f-ḫnsw* [*Takelot III*, 7, Khonsu precinct at Karnak][1055]
1056) ?: Festival of I Shemu for Amun [*Psametik I*, 26, Thebes][1056]
1057) ?: Day of the Drinking (*swr*) and *ḫnmy* of the Djeme mound [Ptolemy IX, 8?, MH][1057]
1058) New moon: Amun-Re's Festival of I Shemu for five days (256) [*R III*, MHC][1058]
1059) New moon: Festival of Bringing It, lasting eight days [*Ptolemy VI*, Kom Ombo][1059]
1060) New moon: Appearance of Min [*Ptolemy VI*, Kom Ombo][1060]
1061) New moon: His Beautiful Festival of Going to Khadi, lasting five days [*Ptolemy X*, Edfu][1061]
1062) New noon: Going to Khadi [Ptolemy XII, Dendera][1062]
1063) Full moon: Great Festival in the Entire Land, lasting 23 days [*Ptolemy X*, Edfu][1063]
1064) Full moon: Greta Festival in the Entire Land [Ptolemy XII, Dendera][1064]

[1050] Stela at Elephantine (Vienna 141+Cairo 34019). The duration was expanded from three days to four days, according to a royal decree of A II (PM V, 229; Kuentz 1925, 23). Cf. I Shemu 4 for another date referring to Anukis Festival in the same reign.
[1051] Inscription at the Akh-menu (Legrain 1900, 53–4; Young 1963, 100; Kruchten 1989, 47).
[1052] *mꜣ=i nṯr wḏꜣ=f ḫft-ḥr=i m ḥb=f n tpy šmw* (Statuette Cairo 42228: Legrain 1906, vol. 3, 69).
[1053] Cairo JE 36494 (Krauss 1985, 166–7; Kruchten 1989, 25; Jansen-Winkeln 2007, vol. 2, 212).
[1054] Inscription at the Akh-menu (Kruchten 1989, 52–3; Jansen-Winkeln 2007, vol. 2, 213).
[1055] Block on the roof of the Khonsu temple (Jansen-Winkeln 2007, vol. 2, 326–8).
[1056] Statue Cairo JE 36158 (Graefe 1994, 88, col. 25).
[1057] P. Berlin 3115 (de Cenival 1972, 105; Pestman 1993, 199 for translation).
[1058] *ḥb=f tpy n šmw hrw pr nṯr pn* (*MH* III, pl. 167, list 67). This celebration lasted five days (*ḥr hrw.w 4 n psḏntyw*). The Bentresh Stela (Louvre C 824: *KRI* II, 285: 14) records this festival taking place at Thebesin year 26 of Ramses II.
[1059] *in.tw=s* (Grimm 1994a, 100–3).
[1060] *sḫꜥ Mnw* (Grimm 1994a, 102–3).
[1061] *ḥb=f nfr n šm r ḫꜣdi* (Grimm 1994a, 102–3).
[1062] *pꜣ šm r ḫꜣdi* (Grimm 1994a, 104–5).
[1063] *ḥb ꜥꜣ m tꜣ ḏr=f* (Grimm 1994a, 104–5).
[1064] *ḥb ꜥꜣ m tꜣ ḏr=f* (Grimm 1994a, 108–9).

2nd MONTH of *šmw* (*ḫn.t-ḫty*/p3-n-in.t*/Payni); 28th decade (*ʿbwt*) II Shemu

No.) Day: Event

1065) 1: King dedicated monuments to Amun-Re [*Senusret IV*, 1, Karnak][1065]
1066) 1: Wag Festival [MK, Lahun][1066]
1067) 1: Dated graffito concerning the discovery of water in a desert [*T III*, 13, Bir Dunqash][1067]
1068) 1: Accession day of Amenhotep III celebrated during the Sed Festival [*A III*, 30, Soleb][1068]
1069) 1: Amenhotep I's oracle [R III, 21, DeM][1069]
1070) 1: Linen was delivered by the treasury deputy *Ti-m-nsw.t-bi.ty* and the scribe of the vizier *P3-(s)r* [R IV/V, 2, KV][1070]
1071) 1: Oath taken by a workman [R IX, 1, KV 6][1071]
1072) 1: Dated royal stela, perhaps concerning endowment [*Osorkon III*, 15, Hermopolis][1072]
1073) 1: Heliacal rising of Sothis, and the Festivals of the New Year and of Bastet [*Ptolemy III*, 9][1073]
1074) 1–30: Festival of Hathor, lady of Dendera [*Ptolemy X*, Edfu][1074]
1075) 1: Appearance of Khnum, Neith, and Nebetu, and the Unification with the Sun [Roman, Esna][1075]
1076) 2: Graffito on the roof of the Khonsu temple [Iuput I, 9, Karnak][1076]
1077) 2: Graffito on the roof of the Khonsu temple [Osorkon III, 1, Karnak][1077]
1078) 4: Festival of Imhotep [Ptolemaic Period, Memphis?][1078]
1079) 5: Oath taken by the chief policeman *Mntw-ms* concerning a payment before witnesses [*R IV*, 3, DeM][1079]
1080) 5: Division of the property of the scribe *Imn-nḫt* between his wife and children [R VI or VII, 7][1080]
1081) 5: Dated graffito [Ptolemaic-Roman, 10?, MH][1081]
1082) 6 or 7: Thutmose IV's decree to establish new offerings for Amun [*T IV*, 1, Luxor temple][1082]
1083) 6: Dispute over payment for a male servant [*Taharqa*, 6][1083]
1084) 6: Appearance of Tasenetneferet and Panebtauy [*Ptolemy VI*, Kom Ombo][1084]
1085) 7: Installation of shrines in the tomb of Ramses IV under the supervision of the vizier *Nfr-rnp.t*, the HPA *Rʿ-ms-nḫt*, the royal butler *Stḫ-ḥr-wnmy=f*, etc. [*R V*, 1][1085]
1086) 8: Decree to renew offerings established by Senusret III at Semna temple [*T III*, 2, Semna][1086]
1087) 8: Presenting a Libation (*w3ḥ n=f mw*) [*R II*, 40][1087]
1088) 8: Presenting a Libation (*w3ḥ-mw*) [R III, 22, QV][1088]
1089) 8: Oracle of Khonsu-in-Thebes concerning a payment [Amenemope, 4, Thebes][1089]

* *ḫn.t-ḥ.ty-pr.ty* with a divine determinative after *pr.ty* (James1962, 33, pl. 6 A, col. 32).

1065 Stela, location unknown (PM II², 293; Legrain 1908, 15–6; Helck 1975, 41; Ryholt 1997, 391).

1066 P. Berlin 10007, recto (Luft 1992, 45; Spalinger 1992, 22).

1067 Graffito located at Bir Dunqash to the east of Kom Ombo (Rothe, Miller, and Rapp 2008, 297–8, DN 14).

1068 A relief at the temple of Soleb (PM VII, 170 (7); *LD* III, pl. 86, b). The king's 'appearance' and the Sed Festival seem to have been co-celebrated (van Siclen 1973, 294 and fig. 1; Galán 2000, 255–6 for translation). The ceremonies were followed by the issue of a royal decree concerning an exemptin of some Theban population from tax collection. Helck (1956a, 67) instead regarded A III's accession as taking place on III Shemu 3.

1069 O. BM 5624, recto (*KRI* V, 476: 5; Blackman 1926, 177; Allam 1973, 43–5). Cf. I Shemu 6–7 for another date recorded in the same text.

1070 O. Cairo 25562 (*KRI* VI, 131: 6). The *ḥbs*-linen was delivered from(?) 'the god' (Amun?) to KV and cut into eight pieces by the chief workman *Nḫt-mw.t*.

1071 O. Cairo 25253 (*KRI* VII, 458: 15).

1072 Spencer 1989, 59, pl. 100. This very fragmentary stela included references to the epagomenal days, I Akhet [3+], I Peret [12+], and a new moon feast.

1073 Decree of Canopus (*Urk.* II, 138: 3–4 and 9–10; Budge 1904, vol. 3, 25–6, ll. 18–20; Spiegelberg 1922, 19 for original texts; Clagett 1995, 327 for translation; Simpson 1996, 2–3; Depuydt 2003, 59; Corthals 2004, 5 for renewed translation). This celebration lasted five days. Van Oosterhout (1992, 92) suggests that the heliacal risings of Sothis recorded in this decree and by Censorinus were observed at Heliopolis.

1074 *ḥb Ḥw.t-ḥr nb(.t) iwn.t* (Grimm 1994a, 112–3).

1075 *sḫʿ Ḥnm N.t Nb.t-ww ḫnm itn* (Sauneron 1963, vol. 1, 169; Grimm 1994a, 112–3). Four fish were offered to four doors.

1076 Graffito 245 A (Jacquet-Gordon 2004, 85, pl. 93; Jansen-Winkeln 2007, vol. 2, 173).

1077 Graffito 101 left by the god's father [glyph] *d-sw-ḫnsw* (Jacquet-Gordon 2004, 41, pl. 13; Jansen-Winkeln 2007, vol. 2, 311).

1078 Stone statue base (Gauthier 1918, 37).

1079 O. OIC 12073 (Allam 1973, 73–6; *KRI* VI, 139: 4; Manning, Greig, and Uchida 1989, 119). Possibly a qenbet session, this being the 4th session on this matter. Cf. II Peret 14 for the same case appealed the next year.

1080 P. Turin 1885 (*KRI* VI, 371: 3). His wife is *T3-wrt-m-ḥb*.

1081 Graffito MH no. 130 located on the roof of the second court of Medinet Habu temple (Thissen 1989, 99–100).

1082 Stela located in front of the pylon (Higazy and Bryan 1986, 98). Klug (2002, 327) dates to I Shemu 8.

1083 P. Louvre E 3228 c (Malinine 1951, 159; Menu 1985, 78). Dispute between the soldier *P3-di-ḫnm* and the coachyte *P3-di-b3s.t*.

1084 *ḫʿ n T3-sn.t-nfr.t P3-nb-t3.wy* (Grimm 1994a, 114–5).

1085 P. Turin 2002 (*KRI* VI, 244: 12; McDowell 1999, 222–3). These officials also include three royal butlers *P3-rʿ-nḫt*, *Itm-nḫt*, and *Sbk-ḥtp* as well as the overseer of the treasury *Mnt-t3.wy*. Cf. I Shemu 4 for another installation in the same tomb.

1086 Inscription on the eastern exterior wall of Semna temple (*LD* III, 55, a; *Urk.* IV, 193: 13). Based on the new moon day on I Shemu 21 in year 23, this day also falls on a new moon day. Cf. IV Peret 21 for a relating event.

1087 O. BM 5634 (*KRI* III, 520: 15; Černy and Gardiner 1957, pls. 83–4; Janssen 1980, 139, and 149; Donker van Heel 1992, 27).

1088 *wsf w3ḥ-mw* 'work-free day, offering of the water' (O. Turin 57034: Krauss 1985, 149). Cf. II Shemu 12 for a river procession recorded in the same text.

1089 P. Brooklyn 16.205 (Parker 1962, 50; Jansen-Winkeln 2007, vol. 1, 102).

1090) 8: Festival in the 2nd Lower Egyptian nome [*Ptolemy IV*, Edfu][1090]
1091) 9: Dated accounting document [Mentuhotep III, 5, Deir el-Bahari][1091]
1092) 9: Vizier *Ḥri* visited western Thebes [Siptah-Tausret, 4, KV][1092]
1093) 9: Festival of the Uniting with Osiris and the Valley Festival on the 6th lunar day [*Ptolemy VIII*, 30, Edfu][1093]
1094) 10: Report to the king that Egypt is in peace [*Sethnakht*, 2, Elephantine][1094]
1095) 10: Delivery of the white bread (*t-ḥḏ*) [19Dyn., DeM][1095]
1096) 10: Graffito at Deir el-Bahari [Ramesside, 8, DB][1096]
1097) 10: Resting of Herka-the-Child and the Unification with the Sun [Roman, Esna][1097]

2nd MONTH of *šmw* (*ḫn.t-ẖty/p3-n-in.t*/Payni); 29th decade (*ẖrt wꜥrt*)

No.) Day: Event

1098) 11–12: Coptic 'Night of the Droplet' [Coptic][1098]
1099) 12: River procession [R III, 22, QV][1099]
1100) 12–13: Vizier *Nfr-rnp.t* visited western Thebes(?) [R IV onwards, 4, KV][1100]
1101) 12+: Oath taken by a man called *Wsr-ḥ3.t*, son of *ꜥ3-nḫtw* [20 Dyn., 6][1101]
1102) 12–17: Festival in the 20th Lower Egyptian nome [*Ptolemy IV*, Edfu][1102]
1103) 12: Visit of a private family to the god Amenophis at Deir el-Bahari [*Hadrian*, 3 (6 June AD 119), DB][1103]
1104) 13: Uadjet Festival in Buto [Ramesside][1104]
1105) 13: Full moon day in I Shemu, when an oath was taken before the god Khonsu [Amasis, 12][1105]
1106) 14: Dated stela [*T III*, 51, Ellesia][1106]
1107) 14: Navigation of the queen Nefertari [*R X*, 3][1107]
1108) 14: Donation of a land plot to Uadjet of Buto [Sheshonq V, 36][1108]
1109) 14: Hathor Festival [Roman, Esna][1109]
1110) 15: Last day of the accession anniversary of Ramses III [*R III*, 22–32, DeM][1110]
1111) 15: Navigation of the queen Nefertari [R V or VI?, 2][1111]
1112) 15: Resting at Esna [Roman, Esna][1112]
1113) 15–28: Festival of the Appearance of Amun-who-Dwells-in-Ombos, [*Ptolemy VI*, Kom Ombo][1113]
1114) 16: Dated letters concerning an unknown subject [*Djedkare-Isesi*, Neferirkare's temple at Abusir][1114]

1090 Geographical list on the exterior of the sanctuary (PM VI, 146 (221–2)).
1091 Letter V of the Heqanakht papyri (P. MMA 22.3.520, recto: T. James 1962, 52, pl. 10; A. James 2002, 18, pl. 40).
1092 O. Cairo 25794 (*KRI* IV, 361: 12). His titles include the fan-bearer on the right hand of the king.
1093 *ḥb ḫnm Wsir i3b.t n.t Rꜥ snw.t pw n.t ḥb int.t* 'Festival of Uniting with Osiris, left eye of Re, this 6th Day Festival of the Valley Festival' (*Edfou* III, 86: 15–87: 1 and VII, 8: 8; de Wit 1961b, 292; Depuydt 1997, 124; Belmonte Avilés 2003, 14).
1094 Stela (*KRI* V, 672: 10; Bidoli 1972). Altenmüller (1982) regards the stela as referring to the end of the civil war against the queen Tausret. It has been suggested that the accession of Sethnakht fell on this day (van Dijk 2000, 304).
1095 O. Berlin 14254, recto (unpublished).
1096 Graffito DB 105 (Marciniak 1974, 140).
1097 *ḥtp n Ḥr-k3-p3-ẖrd ḫnm itn* (Sauneron 1963, vol. 1, 170; Grimm 1994a, 114–5).
1098 Wissa-Wassef 1991b, 443. The beginning of the Nile's flooding, which continued until II Akhet 9, corresponding to 18 June to 19 October (Gregorian). Also see another date of II Shemu 25.
1099 *p3 ḏ3y* (O. Turin 57034, recto: López 1978, 27, pl. 23; Krauss 1985, 145). Cf. II Shemu 8 for the *w3ḥ-mw* ritual recorded in the same text.
1100 O. Cairo 25272 (Daressy 1901, 70, pl. 56; Černý 1973, 235 n. 2; Janssen 1997, 165).
1101 P. Turin 1966, verso (unpublished).
1102 Geographical list on the exterior of the sanctuary (PM VI, 146 (219–20)).
1103 Dated Greek graffito no. 123 (PM II^2, 360 (100); Łajtar 2006, 205–6). Łajtar (2006, 49 and 65) excludes a probability that the Valley Feast continued to be celebrated in that time, opposed by Klotz (2012, 390–1).
1104 P. Cairo 86637 and P. Sallier IV (Leitz 1994a, 359).
1105 P. Louvre 7848 (=P. Louvre Eisenlohr IV): Parker 1957b, 210–1; Donker van Heel 1996; Belmonte Avilés 2003, 14.
1106 Stela Turin (*LD* III, pl. 45, e; *Urk.* IV, 811: 10; Klug 2002, 169–71).
1107 *ḫn.t Nfr-ii* (P. Turin 1898+1926+1937+2094: Gardiner 1906a, 138; *KRI* VI, 693: 1). The workmen at DeM were off duty this day. This event was probably fixed to the civil calendar. On the reading of the name of the queen, see van Walsem 1982, 225. Cf. II Shemu 15 for the same event.
1108 Stela of unknown provenance (Meeks 1979, 670 (22.10.36); Jansen-Winkeln 2007, vol. 2, 272–3).
1109 Sauneron 1963, vol. 1, 170; Grimm 1994a, 116–7.
1110 P. Harris I, XVIIa, 3 (Erichsen 1933, 21: 1; Grandet 1994, vol. 1, 246). The original text reads II Shemu 14. This celebration began on I Shemu 26 to last 20 days.
1111 *p3 r ḫnw Nfr-tri* 'the [day] of rowing Nefertari' (O. Gardiner 11=O. Ashmolean 11, recto: *KRI* VI, 248: 13). Cf. II Shemu 14 for the same event.
1112 *ḥtp n t3-sn.t* (Sauneron 1963, vol. 1, 170; Grimm 1994a, 116–7).
1113 *ḥb ḫꜥ n'Imn ḥry-ib nb.t* (PM VI, 191 (107); Grimm 1994a, 116–7, 155, and 171). Two different durations are attested from the same temple. Klotz (2012, 389) associates this celebration with the Valley Feast.
1114 P. BM 10735, frame 4 (Posener-Kriéger and de Cenival 1968, 37–8, pl. 80 B, C).

1115) 16: Graffito made by a visitor to TT 161 [*Horemheb*, 12, TT 161][1115]
1116) 16: Vizier *P3-rꜥ-m-ḥb* came to the Field (KV) to instruct the workmen [*Seti II*, 6, KV][1116]
1117) 16: Vizier *P3-rꜥ-m-ḥb* came to the Field (KV) [*Seti II*, 6, KV][1117]
1118) 16: Petition and offering to Hathor at Deir el-Bahari by the scribe *P3-k3-t3-n3* [R VI, 7, DB][1118]
1119) 16: Bastet Festival [Ptolemy III, Hibeh (but related to Sais)][1119]
1120) 16: Festival of Menhyt, Festival of Bastet, Satisfying Sekhmet [Roman, Esna][1120]
1121) 17: Wag Festival [MK, 18, Lahun][1121]
1122) 18: Rituals were performed for royal statues [OK, temple of Neferirkare at Abusir][1122]
1123) 18: Royal decree concerning a temple at Abydos [*Neferirkare*, Abydos][1123]
1124) 18: Petition to a deity at Deir el-Bahari [Ramesside, 3, DB][1124]
1125) 18: Festival (of Bastet) in the 18th Lower Egyptian nome [*Ptolemy IV*, Edfu][1125]
1126) 18: Day of the Drinking (*swr*) [Ptolemy IX, 8?, MH][1126]
1127) 18: Dated graffito [Ptolemaic-Roman, 8, MH][1127]
1128) 19: Petition to Hathor at Deir el-Bahari [Ramesside, 4, DB][1128]
1129) 19: Dated Greek graffito [*Trajan*, 9?, DB][1129]
1130) 20: Heliacal rising of Sothis [17 Dyn., 11, Gebel Tjauti][1130]
1131) 20: Qenbet and oath concerning a donkey by the scribe *Nfr-ḥtp* [R III, 10][1131]
1132) 20: A wab-priest of Mentu visited Deir el-Bahari to petition a deity [Ramesside, 1, DB][1132]
1133) 20: Amun stayed in the memorial temple of Ramses II [Ramesside, 3, DB][1133]
1134) 20: Contract made by the female servant *Ḏd-t3-wr.t-ꜥnḫ* [Psametik II, 4, Thebes][1134]
1135) 20: Festival in the 1st Upper Egyptian nome [*Ptolemy IV*, Edfu][1135]

2nd MONTH of *šmw* (*ḫn.t-ḫty/p3-n-in.t*/Payni); 30th decade (*tpy-ꜥ spd*)

No.) Day: Event
1136) 21 or 22: Qenbet session [*R III*, 25, QV][1136]
1137) 21: Goddess Nut conceived(?) her children [Ramesside][1137]
1138) 21: Offering to Amun of Kawa [Aryamani: 3rd cent. BC, Kawa][1138]
1139) 22: Day of Wag [MK, Lahun][1139]

1115 PM I-1², 274 (5, IV); Quirke 1986, 85. Quirke relates the text to the Valley Festival.
1116 O. Cairo 25515, recto (*KRI* IV, 322: 3; Černý 1935b, 11*, col. I: 1–5; McDowell 1999, 205–6). The verso (*KRI* IV, 382–4) records Seti II's death on I Peret 19 (nine months later), the accession of Siptah, and the beginning of the construction of the new king's tomb.
1117 O. Cairo 25538 (*KRI* IV, 315: 3). The vizier set off to the north on II Shemu 25.
1118 Graffito DB 29 (Marciniak 1974, 86: 7; Sadek 1984a, 88; Sadek 1987, 57 and 186). Kitchen (*KRI* VI, 363: 9) and Peden (2001, 122, n. 397) date to the time of Ramses VI.
1119 P. Hibeh 27, l. 146 (Grenfell and Hunt 1906, 144).
1120 Sauneron 1963, vol. 1, 170; Grimm 1994a, 116–7 and 261.
1121 P. Berlin 10016, recto (Parker 1950, 36; Luft 1992, 59; Luft 2006, 30). The date is followed by the 'second of the full moon', which is difficult to interpret. Krauss (1994, 88) reads 'II Shemu 17, which was two days after the full moon', corresponding to lunar day 17. He (2006b, 424) dates this papyrus to Senusret III.
1122 P. BM 10735, frame 7, recto (Posener-Kriéger and de Cenival 1968, 2, pl. 4). Another Abusir papyrus (P. Louvre E 25279, recto) records that such rituals took place on a new moon day as *hrw n ḥb* a 'day of festival' (Posener-Kriéger and de Cenival 1968, 2–3, pl. 5).
1123 Stela Boston 03.1896 (*Urk.* I, 172: 11; Goedicke 1967, 24, Abb. 2; Muhs 2016, 25–6 for translation).
1124 Graffito DB 70 (Marciniak 1974, 120: 2).
1125 Geographical list on the exterior of the sanctuary (PM VI, 146 (219–20)). For the association of two Bastet Feasts in II Shemu with the *wpy-rnp.t*, recorded in the Canopus Decree, see Spalinger 1992, 57–9.
1126 P. Berlin 3115 (de Cenival 1972, 105; Pestman 1993, 199 for translation).
1127 Graffito MH no. 231 located at the small temple of Medinet Habu (Thissen 1989, 139–40).
1128 Graffito DB 28 (Marciniak 1974, 85: 1; Sadek 1984, 88).
1129 Graffito no. 138 located at Hatshepsut's temple at Deir-el-Bahari (Bataille 1951, 96–7).
1130 Rock graffito at Gebel Tjauti, Western Desert (Darnell 2002, 49–52). *m3 pr.t spd.t.*
1131 O. Michaelides 1 (*KRI* V, 451: 16).
1132 Graffito DB 60 (Marciniak 1974, 112: 1).
1133 Graffito DB 32 (Marciniak 1974, 89: 4). Sadek (1984a, 90) does not date this to the time of Ramses II, whose temple was not yet completed by this year. Dolińska (2007, 70) dates to the time of Merenptah, while Krauss (1985, 139) had opted for Ramses II and later changed to Ramses VI (2006b, 416).
1134 Vessel Louvre E 706 with Demotic texts written on both the sides (Menu 1985, 82).
1135 Geographical list on the exterior of the sanctuary (PM VI, 147 (225–6)).
1136 O. Turin 57033 (*KRI* V, 496: 2; Allam 1973, 247–9).
1137 *hrw pwy n wꜥr.ty ꜥnḫ ms.w Nw.t* 'that day of the thighs when the children of Nut lived' (P. Cairo 86637: Leitz 1994a, 366). Sothis ideologically began to disappear from this day to the end of the year for 70 days.
1138 Fragments of Stela BM 1777 (Eide, Hägg, and Pierce 1994, vol. 2, 529).
1139 P. Berlin 10165, recto (Luft 1992, 101; Luft 1994, 39). A link to the full moon is suggested by a full moon date on day 19 of an unknown month in the same year recorded in the same text.

II Shemu

1140) 22: Opet Festival [*R II*, 23, Karnak][1140]
1141) 22: Valley Festival [R II/III/XI, 22, DB][1141]
1142) 22: Dated graffito [Ptolemaic-Roman, 8, MH][1142]
1143) 23: Festival at Karnak celebrated with a dedication list of offerings to Amun-Re [*R IV*, 1, Karnak][1143]
1144) 23: Royal butler *Rꜥ-ms-sw-nfr* visited western Thebes on the 6th or 9th lunar day [R IV or IX, 4, KV][1144]
1145) 23: Offering to Hathor at Deir el-Medina [Ramesside, 2, DB][1145]
1146) 23?: Graffito at the Step Pyramid [Ramesside, Saqqara][1146]
1147) 23: Festival in the 8th Lower Egyptian nome [*Ptolemy IV*, Edfu][1147]
1148) 24: Divine statues were brought in joy to the entrance of the Queen's Valley [20 Dyn., 1, DeM][1148]
1149) 25: Amun's Rowing to the Town (*niw.t*) and the vizier *Pꜣ-rꜥ-m-ḥb* went downstream [*Seti II*, 6, KV][1149]
1150) 25: Amun's river procession [R V or VI, 2][1150]
1151) 25 or 26: Coptic beginnings of the Nile's inundation and of the tax year[1151]
1152) 26 or 28: Royal decree concerning the Min temple [*Pepi II*, year after the 11th census, Koptos][1152]
1153) 26: Graffito on the roof of the Khonsu temple [Sheshonq III, 4, Karnak][1153]
1154) 26: New Year Festival and Opening of the Face in the Neith temple [Roman, Esna][1154]
1155) 27: Sed Festival; reward ceremony; rowing on a lake [*A III*, 30, tomb of Kheruef (TT 192)][1155]
1156) 27: Appearance of Ramses IV and establishing a stela [*R IV*, 3, Wadi Hammamat][1156]
1157) 27: HPA Pinedjem I's decree to dispatch officials to rebury Ramses III [Smendes I, 13, mummy shroud of R III][1157]
1158) 27: Unknown festival [Ptolemy III, Hibeh (but related to Sais)][1158]
1159) 27: Appearance of Hathor [Ptolemy XII, Dendera][1159]
1160) 28: Amun stayed in Tausret's memorial temple on the West Bank of Thebes [Tausret, 7, DB][1160]
1161) 28: Night of the River Procession [R III, 26, QV][1161]

[1140] Bentresh Stela (=Louvre C 824: *KRI* II, 285: 5–6; Wilson 1969, 29, n. 7). Created in the Persian or Greek time, this stela retrospectively records a tale in the time of Ramses II in a pseudo-archaic style. Wilson interpreted the date in the context of the Valley Festival, whereas Murnane (1982, 577, n. 9) took it as the date of text composition.

[1141] *smꜣꜥ n nb.t Ḥw.t-ḥr nb.t ḏsr.t m ḥb nfr in.t n ꞽImn-rꜥ nsw.t nṯr.w Mw.t Ḫnsw* 'offering to the lady Hathor, lady of Deir el-Bahari, at the Beautiful Festival of the Valley of Amun-Re, king of the gods, Mut, and Khonsu' (Graffito DB 31: Marciniak 1971, 54–6; Marciniak 1974, 88: 1; Sadek 1984a, 89; Krauss 1985, 138). Marciniak translated day 23, but the original text reads day 22. Krauss (1985, 138) had first dated this document to the time of Ramses II but later suggested Ramses XI (Krauss 2006b, 417) while Dolińska remains with Ramses II (2007, 79). Kitchen (*KRI* V, 417–8) and Peden (2001, 122, n. 392) date to the time of Ramses III.

[1142] Graffito MH no. 263 located at the treasury of the temple of Medinet Habu (Thissen 1989, 158).

[1143] Wall stela at Karnak (PM II^2, 131 (485); *KRI* VI, 8: 36; Peden 1994a, 144–5 and el-Sabban 2000, 152 for translation). This was perhaps his 3rd accession anniversary after Heliopolis and Memphis, when the ceremony of the *išd*-tree was performed in all these places. See I Peret 6 and IV Shemu 12 for the same ceremony and note that a curious delivery of 260 feathers of falcon from the treasury [of the king] is recorded in col. 3. Le Saout (1982, 244) corresponds this day to the Valley Feast.

[1144] O. Cairo 25247 (*KRI* VII, 334: 6; Helck 2002, 475–6).

[1145] *wdnw n Ḥw.t-ḥr nb(.t) ḏsr.t / iw* [*ꞽImn*] *m* [*imnt.t wꜣs.t ḥr šsp ḥtp*] (Graffito DB 4: Marciniak 1974, 61: 1; Sadek 1984a, 77). A woman and her daughter visited Hathor with other people of the village (*dmi*). The name of season is illegible, but restored here as Shemu.

[1146] Graffito at the south chapel of the Step Pyramid (Firth and Quibell 1935, vol. 1, 84).

[1147] Geographical list on the exterior of the sanctuary (PM VI, 146 (219–20)).

[1148] O. Turin 57366 (Janssen 1992, 110; McDowell 1999, 221–2).

[1149] *ḏꜣy n ꞽImn r niw.t.* This may well refer to the Valley Festival (O. Cairo 25538: Černý 1935b, 16, 34*; *KRI* IV, 315: 4). The vizier *Pꜣ-rꜥ-m-ḥb* came to the Field (*sḫty*) prior to this day (II Shemu 16).

[1150] *wsf iw.tw m pꜣ ḏꜣj* [ ] *iw tm ꞽImn ḏꜣj* 'work-free day, one participates in a river procession [ ] Amun has not crossed the river' (O. Gardiner 11=O. Ashmolean 11: *KRI* VI, 249: 2–3). Krauss (1985, 145–8) dates the ostracon to the time of Ramses V.

[1151] Popper 1951, 66. The summer solstice is traditionally regarded as taking place on Coptic II Shemu 26, corresponding to 20 June (Julian).

[1152] Stela Cairo 41893 (PM V, 126; *Urk.* I, 280: 14; Goedicke 1967, 87, Abb. 8).

[1153] Graffito 145 left by the god's father of Khonsu *Ḏd-iꜥḥ* (Jacquet-Gordon 2004, 55, pl. 55).

[1154] *wpy-rnp.t wn ḥr m ḥw.t N.t* (Sauneron 1963, vol. 1, 170; Grimm 1994a, 120–1 and 261). The clothing (*mnḫ.t*) of the gods was performed as was 'done on II Peret 8'.

[1155] TT 192 (6) (*Urk.* IV, 1867: 2; *Kheruef*, 43, pl. 28; van Siclen 1973, 292). *ḫꜥ.t-nsw.t r r.wt wr.ty m ꜥḥ=*[*f n*] *ḥꜥ* 'royal appearance to the great double gates at his palace House of Rejoicing (i.e. the palace of el-Malqata)'. The ceremony of rowing seems to have continued until III Shemu (*Urk.* IV, 1869: 2). See a parallel text and depiction in TT 57 (15) dated to year 30. Cf. IV Peret 26 and III Shemu 2 for relating events during the festival.

[1156] Rock stela (*KRI* VI, 12:15; Couyat and Montet 1912, 36). *sḫꜥ.n=f sw ḥr wṯs r nb tꜣ.wy* 'he caused himself to appear on a palanquin (the throne?) to the lord of the Two Lands'. However, Ramses IV's accession day is elsewhere known to be III Shemu 15.

[1157] PM I-2^2, 661; Kitchen 1973a, 419; Jansen-Winkeln 2007, vol. 1, 22. The scribe of the Necropolis *Bw-th-imn* was dispatched.

[1158] P. Hibeh 27, l. 154 (Grenfell and Hunt 1906, 144).

[1159] *ḫꜥ in Ḥw.t-ḥr* (Grimm 1994a, 120–1).

[1160] Graffito DB 3 (*KRI* IV, 377: 4; Marciniak 1974, 60: 9; Sadek 1984a, 75–6; Krauss 1985, 138). Hornung (2006, 214), Krauss (2006, 415), and Dolińska (2007, 70) date to the time of Tausret. Ullmann (2002, 436) posits that a temporal architecture was used during the festival because the temple would not have been completed in year 7.

[1161] *wsf ḫꜣ pꜣ ḏꜣj* 'work-free day, night of the river procession' (O. Turin 57044: *KRI* V, 510: 12; Krauss 1985, 145).

1162) 28: Arrival of officials to have the gang to take an oath of loyalty? [R IV, 1, KV][1162]
1163) 28: Offering to Amun of Kawa [Aryamani: 3rd cent. BC, Kawa][1163]
1164) 29?: Accession of Neferirkare [*Neferirkare*, 1, Palermo Stone][1164]
1165) 29: Offering to the king Senusret II on the Day of Wag [MK, 9, Lahun][1165]
1166) 30: Waiting of the men of the sanctuary [18 or 19 Dyn.][1166]
1167) 30: Hereditary claim by a woman at Deir el-Medina [R IV, 1, DeM][1167]
1168) 30: Inunadtion [Ptolemy III, 2, MH][1168]
1169) 30: Inunadtion [Ptolemy III, 5, MH][1169]
1170) 30: Satisfying Sekhmet [Roman, Esna][1170]

2nd MONTH of *šmw* (*ḫn.t-ḫty/p3-n-in.t*/Payni); unknown decade

No.) Day: Event
1171) X: Valley Festival (575) [*R III*, MHC][1171]
1172) X+1: Second Day of the Valley Festival (575) [*R III*, MHC][1172]
1173) ?: Month of the Sadj [*Niuserre*, Abu Gurob][1173]
1174) ?: Festival of the Ruler [*Amenemhat III*, 35, Lahun][1174]
1175) ?: Royal decree to build the temple of Buhen and its divine statue [*T III*, 35, Buhen][1175]
1176) ?: Decree to establish divine offerings for Amun-Re [*R III*, 16, Karnak][1176]
1177) ?: Decree to build the memorial temple of R IV [*R IV*, 5, Serabit el-Khadim, Sinai][1177]
1178) ?: Date of a stela portraying the king offering to a god [*R IV*, 5, Serabit el-Khadim, Sinai][1178]
1179) ?: Visit of the wab-priest of Amun-Re and chief workman *Ḥr-m-ḳni-3s.t* to do work at KV (*t3 in.t ʿ3.t*) [Pinedjem I, 20, West Thebes][1179]
1180) ?: Decree to erect monuments for Amun-Re at Karnak [*Sheshonq I*, 21, Silsila][1180]

[1162] O. Cairo 25255 (Allam 1973, pl. 29; Daressy 1901, 66; Helck 2002, 366).
[1163] Fragments of Stela BM 1777 (Eide, Hägg, and Pierce 1994, vol. 2, 530).
[1164] Wilkinson 2000, 172, fig. 3.
[1165] P. Cairo CG 58065 recto (Luft 1992, 135; Luft 1994, 39). Krauss (2006b, 424) dates to the time of Amenemhat III.
[1166] *n3 n isḳ n t3 n rmt pr ḥn* (P. Berlin 11253, unpublished).
[1167] O. DeM 235 (*KRI* VI, 105: 10). A woman claimed (*smi*) that she should own her husband property.
[1168] Graffito MH 311 (PM II^2, 506 (125); Edgerton 1937, pl. 86; Thissen 1989, 171–2, no. 311). Thissen dates those graffiti recorded in the Slaughter's Room to 245–242 BC under Ptolemy III. If his assumption is correct, the dates referred to are about 18 days earlier than the expected the Nile's maximum in that time. Hence, they may record the plenitude (a certain required level of water), rather than the maxim, a practice excercised in medieval Cairo (Popper 1951, 191).
[1169] Graffito MH 312 (PM II^2, 506, pillar in Room 5 (h); Edgerton 1937, pl. 86; Thissen 1989, 172–3, no. 312).
[1170] *sḥtp Sḫm.t* (Sauneron 1963, vol. 1, 170; Grimm 1994a, 122–3).
[1171] *ḥb=f n in.t* (*MH* III, pl. 142, lists 3–4; Haring 1997, 68). Unfortunately the date is not illegible, but the duration is clearly two days.
[1172] *mḥ hrw 2* (*MH* III, pl. 142, list 4; Haring 1997, 68–9).
[1173] *3bd s3ḏ* (Solar temple of Niuserre: Helck 1977, 63, pl. 2, l. 12).
[1174] *ḥb ḥk3* (P. UC 32191: Collier and Quirke 2006, 94).
[1175] Stela BM EA 1021+Cairo 34014 (*Urk.* IV, 820–1 for the Cairo fragment; Klug 2002, 187, Abb. 16).
[1176] Temple of Ramses III at Karnak, E. exterior wall (PM II^2, 33 (118); *KRI* V, 235: 11; *RIK* II, pl. 108; Nelson 1936, 237; Haring 1997, 89–90). For similar decrees of R III in years 6 and 7, see *KRI* V, 237: 1 and 6.
[1177] Stela Chadwick Museum 58.05.4 (Gardiner, Peet, and Černý 1952, vol. 1, pl. 71, vol. 2, 188).
[1178] Stela *in situ* (Gardiner, Peet, and Černý 1952, vol. 1, pl. 74, vol. 2, 187).
[1179] Graffito 2138 (Jansen-Winkeln 2007, vol. 1, 40).
[1180] Stela at Silsila (Caminos 1952, 50).

3rd MONTH of *šmw* (*ỉp.t-ḥm.t*/*ỉpỉp*/Epeiph); 31st decade (*spd/tpy-ꜥ knmt/štwy*) III Shemu

No.) Day: Event

1181) 1: Dated papyrus concerning the transmission of an office from a father to his son [OK, temple of Reneferef at Abusir][1181]

1182) 1?: Jar label recording the 3rd Sed Festival of A III [*A III*, 38, Malkata][1182]

1183) 1: Ay's decree in Memphis to reward an official with lands [*Ay*, 3, Giza][1183]

1184) 1: Festival of Amenopet [R II, 11][1184]

1185) 1: Qenbet session and oath-taking concerning domestic violence [R III, 20][1185]

1186) 1: Petition to Hathor at Deir el-Bahari [R III, 21, DB][1186]

1187) 1: Great Festival in the Southern Sky, relating to the goddess Ipet-Hemet [Ramesside, DeM][1187]

1188) 1: Inspection of the major Theban temples & installation of a priest by the HPA Menkheperre [Menkheperre, 40, Karnak][1188]

1189) 1: Appearance of the August Image of Haroeris [*Ptolemy VI*, Kom Ombo][1189]

1190) 1: Festival of Khnum-Re, lord of the Field [Roman, Esna][1190]

1191) 1–14: Defeat of Seth [*Ptolemy X*, Edfu][1191]

1192) 1: Festival of This Goddess [Ptolemy XIII, Dendera][1192]

1193) 2: Last day(?) of A III's Sed Festival [*A III*, 30, temple of Amenhotep, son of Hapu][1193]

1194) 2: Qenbet session [Seti II, 5, DeM][1194]

1195) 2: Oath concerning a transaction [19 Dyn., DeM][1195]

1196) 2: A festival [*R III*, 25, QV][1196]

1197) 2: Workman's graffito [R VI, 1, western Thebes][1197]

1198) 2: Qenbet session [R VII,7, DeM][1198]

1199) 2: Dated graffito [Ptolemy II, 26, MH][1199]

1200) 3: Distribution of meat offerings to temple personnel [Teti, year after the 1st census, temple of Neferirkare at Abusir][1200]

1201) 3?: Dated graffito [A III, 10, south chapel of the Step Pyramid at Saqqara][1201]

1202) 3: Commemoration of a victory over the Libyans [*Merenptah*, 5, memorial temple of Merenptah][1202]

1203) 3: Visit of the vizier *Tꜣ* with the scribe *Ỉmn-nḫt* [*R III*, 32, western Thebes][1203]

1204) 3: An unnamed man received some items from an unidentified vizier [R VI or VII, 5, DeM or MH?][1204]

1205) 3: Offering to Hathor at Deir el-Bahari [Ramesside, 2, DB][1205]

1206) 4: Isis's conception of Horus [*Ptolemy* X, Edfu][1206]

1207) 4: Khnum-Re Festival [Roman, Esna][1207]

1181 [*ꜣbd 3*]*-nw* [*š*]*mw sw wp* (Abusir X, 240, pl. 25).

1182 Hayes 1951, fig. 11, no. 142. Cf. *Urk.* IV, 1954: 12 for a parallel jar label of year 37 recording the 3rd Sed Festival.

1183 Stela Cairo 34187 (*Urk.* IV, 2109: 8; Lacau 1909, 233–4).

1184 *pꜣ ḥb n Ỉmn-n-ỉp.t* (O. DeM 354: K*RI* III, 508: 15).

1185 O. Nash 5 (K*RI* V, 471: 12; Allam 1973, 221–2; McDowell 1999, 34). Cf. III Shemu 13 for another session recorded in the same text.

1186 Graffito DB 36 (Marciniak 1974, 92: 7). Kitchen (K*RI* V, 442), Peden (2001, 122, n. 391), and Dolińska (2007, 70) dated to the time of Ramses III.

1187 *ḥb ꜥꜣ m p.t rsy.t* (P. Cairo 86637: Leitz 1994a, 375).

1188 Stela Cairo TN 3.12.24.2 (PM II^{2}, 210; Legrain 1900, 53; Jansen-Winkeln 2007, vol. 1, 75). Installation of the 4th-prophet of Amun-Re *Ṯꜣ-nfr.*

1189 *ḫꜥ n pꜣ mtr šps n Ḥr-wr* (Grimm 1994a, 122–3).

1190 *ḥb H̱nm-rꜥ nb sẖ.t* (Sauneron 1963, vol. 1, 170; Grimm 1994a, 124–5).

1191 *šꜥw.t Stẖ m hrw pn rdỉ.t mtꜣt=f ỉnsw=f ḥr rmn.t* 'cutting of Seth on this day, his phallus and testicles were placed on the shoulder' (Alliot 1949, 217, 233; Grimm 1994a, 200–1).

1192 *ḥb n nṯr.t tn* (Grimm 1994a, 122–3).

1193 Painted stone block (PM II^{2}, 455; *Urk.* IV, 1837: 9; Robichon and Varille 1936, vol. 1, pl. 35; Parker 1950, 61). *dhn sš nsw.t mꜣꜥ mry=f* [*sš nfr.w*] *Ỉmn-ḥtp ꜥd-mr ẖft ꜥrḳ ḥb sd tpy n ḥm=f šsp.n=f ẖkr.w m nb.w ꜥꜣ.t nb.t šps.*[*t*] 'the true royal scribe, beloved of him, [scribe of recruits], Amenhotep was appointed an administrator when the first Sed Festival of his person ended. He received the adornments of gold and every precio[us], noble stone.' This festival began on IV Peret 26 (*Urk.* IV, 1961: 16).

1194 O. Cairo 25556 (K*RI* IV, 302: 10; Allam 1973, 61–3; Collier 2004, 41–2 for dating).

1195 O. DeM 61 (K*RI* III, 546: 8; Allam 1973, 85).

1196 *nꜣ nwḥ m ḥb* 'the ropes at a festival' (O. Turin 57033: Allam 1973, 248; Sadek 1987, 187; K*RI* V, 497: 4).

1197 Graffito 1269 (K*RI* VI, 364: 12; Černý 1956).

1198 O. Ashmolean 36 (=O. Gardiner 36: K*RI* VI, 430: 6; Allam 1973, 155–7).

1199 Graffito MH no. 257 located at the slaughter house of Medinet Habu temple (Thissen 1989, 154–5).

1200 P. Berlin 10474 A and B, verso (Posener-Kriéger and de Cenival 1968, 45, pl. 94 A for facsimile and transcription; Posener-Kriéger 1976, vol. 1, 322–3 for translation).

1201 Navrátilová 2007, 95–6.

1202 The Israel Stela (=Cairo 34025, verso: PM II^{2}, 448; K*RI* IV, 13: 7; Petrie 1897, 26, pl. 14, l. 1; Lacau 1909, 54).

1203 Graffito Carter 1450 (Peden 2000).

1204 P. Turin 1907+1908 (K*RI* VI, 406: 6).

1205 Graffito DB 71 (Marciniak 1974, 121: 4).

1206 *ỉwrt n Ḥr* (Alliot 1949, 218; Grimm 1994a, 124–5). Horus was born on IV Peret 28 after 299 days of pregnancy.

1207 Sauneron 1963, vol. 1, 170; Grimm 1994a, 124–5.

III Shemu

1208) 5: Offering of deceased Senusret II and drinking at the Sobek Festival [MK, Lahun][1208]
1209) 5: Date of a rock inscription left by the overseer of HPs [*R II*, 1, Wadi Hammamat][1209]
1210) 6: Preparation for the 6th lunar and new-moon festivals [A II, 19][1210]
1211) 6: Date of the heading of P. Harris I [*R III*, 32, DeM][1211]
1212) 6: Delivery of the *šˁ.t-bi.t*-bread to DeM [R II or III, 24, DeM][1212]
1213) 7: Consecrating of an ox to Ptah [*R III*, 25, QV][1213]
1214) 9: Heliacal rising of Sothis and new moon day [*A I*, 9, Thebes][1214]
1215) 9: Report by the workman *Imn-m-ip.t* and oath concerning a debt [R III][1215]
1216) 9+: Qenbet session [R VI, 2, DeM][1216]
1217) 9: Amun-Re stayed at the memorial temple of Ramses IV? [Siptah/R IV?, 6, DB][1217]
1218) 9: Amun-Re stayed at the memorial temple of Ramses III? [R III, 7, DB][1218]
1219) 9: Installation of an Apis bull [*Psametik II*, 1, Serapeum at Memphis][1219]
1220) 9: Appearance of These Gods [*Ptolemy VI*, Kom Ombo][1220]
1221) 9: Inunadtion [Ptolemy III, 1, MH][1221]
1222) 9 or 10: Dated graffito [Ptolemaic-Roman, MH][1222]
1223) 10: Decree of Ramses II to establish offerings for Amun-Re and Hapi [*R II*, 1, Gebel el-Silsila][1223]
1224) 10: First day of the work of masons at a quarry [R II, 36, Saqqara][1224]
1225) 10: Qenbet session concerning a female thief [Seti II, 6][1225]
1226) 10: The workmen were rewarded (*mk*) by the vizier *Ḥri* at the Enclosure of the Necropolis [Sitptah, 4][1226]
1227) 10: Graffito on the roof of the Khonsu temple [*Iny*, 5, Karnak][1227]

3rd MONTH of *šmw* (*ip.t-ḥm.t*/*ipip*/Epeiph); 32nd decade (*knmt*)

No.) Day: Event
1228) 11: Appearance of Amenhotep I [*R X*, 3][1228]
1229) 11: Inspection by the royal scribe *Bw-th-imn* [Pinedjem, 6, West Thebes][1229]
1230) 11 or 2: Graffito on the roof of the Khonsu temple [2, Karnak][1230]

1208 P. Berlin 10127 B, recto (Luft 1992, 97).

1209 Couyat and Montet 1912, 64. Subsequent dates recorded are: IV Akhet 4, 6, and 20, all of year 38.

1210 P. Leningrad 1116A (Golénischeff 1913, pl. 22: 192–5; Helck 1961, vol. 4, 629; Parker 1969, 76–9). This day was recorded to be the 6th lunar day or close to it, thus the next new moon fell on about III Shemu 30.

1211 P. Harris I (=BM 9999, I, 1: Erichsen 1933, 1; Haring 1997, 157). Grandet (1994, vol. 1, 120) regards this day as the beginning of the *de facto* rulership of Ramses IV. Goedicke (1963, 82–3) assumed that Ramses III was already dead by this day as the result of the harem conspiracy during/after the ceremony of the Valley Festival celebrated at Thebes.

1212 O. DeM 101 (*KRI* V, 491: 3). It was delivered from the memorial temple of T IV. Haring (1997, 260) does rule out a link to the Valley Feast. Also see O Berlin 8380 recording the deliveries of the *šˁ.t*-bread from I Shemu to III Shemu.

1213 *rḫs kꜣ n Ptḥ* (O. Turin 57033: *KRI* V, 497: 4; Allam 1973, 248). This was probably a lunar day, based on O. Turin 57044 recording a river procession on II Shemu 28 in year 26, perhaps of Ramses III.

1214 Ebers Calendar (Gardiner 1906a, 141; Clagett 1995, 193–216). Edgerton (1937, 194) proposed that the observation was done at Heliopolis. Spalinger (2011, 732, n. g) regards this calendar as only representing a schematic table of the lunar cycle and as reflecting a historical fact that when the civil year was first introduced, the heliacal rising of Sothis was placed on the 9th day of the lunar calendar.

1215 *smi* (O. Berlin 10655: *KRI* V, 573: 11; Allam 1973, 30). This case continued until I Akhet 20.

1216 O. Berlin 12654 (*KRI* VI, 344: 15–6; Allam 1973, 35–8).

1217 Graffito DB 9 (Marciniak 1974, 68: 7; Sadek 1984a, 80; Ullmann 2002, 531). Various datings have been proposed: Ramses IV (*KRI* VI, 102; Peden 2001, 122, n. 395), Ramses VII (Krauss 1985, 138; Dolińska 2007, 70), Siptah (Krauss 2006b, 415). The date in the original text is as clear as Graffito DB 10 below. Is this the Decade Festival?

1218 Graffito DB 10 (Marciniak 1974, 69: 1; Sadek 1984a, 81; Krauss 1985, 138; Ullmann 2002, 503–4). Kitchen (*KRI* V, 337), Peden (2001, 121, n. 338), Ullmann (2002, 521), Krauss (2006b, 415), and Dolińska (2007, 70) date the graffito to the time of Ramses III. Marciniak (1971, 63–4) related this event to the Valley Feast.

1219 Stela Louvre IM 132 (Jurman 2010, 248–9, fig. 10). This bull was dead on IV Peret 12 and buried on II Shemu 21 in year 12 of Apries, taking 70 days for embalmment.

1220 *ḫˁ n nṯr.w ipn* (Grimm 1994a, 128–9).

1221 Graffito MH no. 308 (PM II^2, 506 (125); Edgerton 1937, pl. 85; Thissen 1989, 169–71, no. 308).

1222 Graffito MH no. 83, located at the slaughter house of Medinet Habu temple (Thissen 1989, 75, no. 83).

1223 Rock inscription (*KRI* I, 84: 14). Cf. II Akhet 5 for a decree of Merenptah parallel to this.

1224 Graffito at the south chapel of the Step Pyramid (Firth and Quibell 1935, vol. 1, 85).

1225 O. Nash 1 (=O. BM 65930: *KRI* IV, 315: 8; Allam 1973, 214; Collier 2004, 43 for dating). A vizier was involved in this session.

1226 O. DeM 10051, recto (Grandet 2006a, 55–6 and 241).

1227 Graffito 146 left by the wab-priest of Khonsu *Ḏd-iˁḥ* (Jacquet-Gordon 2004, 55, pl. 54; Jansen-Winkeln 2007, vol. 2, 383).

1228 P. Turin 1898+1926+1937+2094 (*KRI* VI, 695: 14; Černý 1927, 183). Cf. I Shemu 27 for the same feast celebrated on a different day, recorded in the same text.

1229 Graffito 1358 (Jansen-Winkeln 2007, vol. 1, 21).

1230 Graffito 44 left by the wab-priest of Khonsu *Pꜣ-di-ḫnsw* (Jacquet-Gordon 2004, 26, pl. 16; Jansen-Winkeln 2007, vol. 2, 446).

III Shemu

1231) 12: Appearance of Amenhotep I [Siptah, 4][1231]
1232) 12: Payment for labor and an oath-taking before witnesses [*Piankhi*, 22][1232]
1233) 12: Isis visited the Bigeh Island from Philae on a new moon day(?) [Roman, Philae][1233]
1234) 13: Graffito at the Step Pyramid [*A III*, 10, Step Pyramid][1234]
1235) 13: Qenbet session and oath-taking [R III, 20?][1235]
1236) 13: Appearance of Amenhotep I, when an appeal concerning a theft was made [R III, DeM][1236]
1237) 13: Report and oath concerning a bull [*R V*, 2][1237]
1238) 13?: Assembly at Sais in honour of Neith [Ptolemy III, Hibeh (but related to Sais)][1238]
1239) 13: Neith Festival [Roman, Esna][1239]
1240) 15: Offering [MK, 3, Lahun][1240]
1241) 15: Unknown king came to Thebes [MK, 11, Gebel Tjauti][1241]
1242) 15: King erected stelae recording his accession anniversary [*A II*, 3, Amada and Elephantine][1242]
1243) 15: Offering to Amun-Re and Hapi
[*R II*, 1, Gebel el-Silsila], [*Merenptah*, 1, Gebel el-Silsila], [*R III*, 6, Gebel el-Silsila][1243]
1244) 15: Accession (*ḫʿ-nsw.t*) of Ramses IV [*R IV*, 2, DeM][1244]
1245) 16: Tutankhamen's decree to endow an official with a land [*Tutankhamen*, 1, Memphis][1245]
1246) 16: Festival of victory (1056) [*R III*, MHC][1246]
1247) 16: Death of Ramses III was reported to the workmen [*R III*, 32, DeM][1247]
1248) 16: Criminal *ʿ3-nḫt* was sent to masonry as a punishment, and the *w3ḥ-mw* for the kings [R IV, 6][1248]
1249) 16: Vizier *Nfr-rnp.t* visited to inspect work and performed the *w3ḥ-mw* for a goddess [*R IV*, 6, KV][1249]
1250) 16: Vizier *Nfr-rnp.t* visited to inspect work and the guardian *Ḫʿy* visited DB [*R IV*, 6, KV][1250]
1251) 16: Birthday of Imhotep [*Ptolemy VIII*, DB][1251]
1252) 16: Festival of Imhotep [Ptolemaic-Roman, Memphis][1252]
1253) 18: Oath concerning cattle [*R IX*, 2][1253]
1254) 19: Oath concerning a property by a man called *Ti-r-niw.t=f* [19 Dyn., DeM][1254]

1231 O. DeM 10051, verso (Grandet 2006a, 55–6 and 241). The workmen were off their duty.
1232 P. Vatican 10574 (Menu 1985, 75; Jansen-Winkeln 2007, vol. 2, 362).
1233 PM VI, 255, frieze text (Junker 1913, 28).
1234 Graffito at the south chapel of the Step Pyramid (Firth and Quibell 1935, vol. 1, 81).
1235 O. Nash 5 (*KRI* V, 472: 5; Allam 1973, 221–2). Cf. III Shemu 1 for another session recorded in the same text.
1236 O. BM 5637 (*KRI* V, 577: 11; Černý 1927, 183; Blackman 1926, 183–4; Allam 1973, 50).
1237 *ʿnḫ n nb* 'oath to the lord' (O. IFAO Inv. 388: *KRI* VI, 249: 13; Allam 1973, 195). Also seeIPeret 20 for a relating event.
1238 P. Hibeh 27, l. 165 (Grenfell and Hunt 1906, 144).
1239 *ḥb N.t* (Sauneron 1963, vol. 1, 170–1; Grimm 1994a, 128–9). For a study on this feast, see Sauneron 1962, 245–308.
1240 P. Berlin 10090, recto (Luft 1992, 87).
1241 Rock graffito written in red ink at Gebel Tjauti, Western Desert (Darnell 2002, 53–5).
1242 *Urk.* IV, 1289: 1; Kuentz 1925, 5; Klug 2002, 279 and 287. One stela engraved on the wall of the sanctuary at the temple of Amada (PM VII, 70 (49); *LD* III, pl. 65, a), and the other from Elephantine divided in two fragments (Stela Cairo JE 28585 and Vienna ÄS 5909: PM V, 229). The extension and dedication (*rdi n=f pr n nb=f*) of the temples of Amada and Elephantine are also recorded (*Urk.* IV, 1294: 3–4). Hornung (2006, 203) proposes that this event marked the beginning of Amenhotep II's sole reign.
1243 Rock inscriptions (*KRI* I, 90: 14–6; *LD* III, pls. 175, a: 9, 200, d: 9, and 218, d: 15). Cf.IAkhet 15 for rituals parallel to these. They were called the day of *ḫ3 md3.t ḥʿpi* the 'Throwing the Book of Hapi' (*KRI* I, 91: 4–6), which is described in P. Harris I (XXXVIIb, 1; LIVa, 2; and LXVII, 2) as a list of offerings dedicated at Kheraha (272 in number) and at Memphis (Breasted 1906, vol. 4, 156, n. e). See Popper (1951, 68) for Coptic traditions parallel to this.
1244 O. DeM 44 (*KRI* VI, 116: 3; Helck 1964, 153). Also see O. Cairo 25255 for II Shemu 28 in year 1, on which the workmen took an oath of loyalty (Allam 1973, pl. 29; Daressy 1901, 66).
1245 Stela Cairo 34186 (Lacau 1909, 232–3). The decree was issued when the king was performing a ceremony for Ptah (*ḥm=f ḥr ir.t ḥss.t it Ptḥ*).
1246 *MH* III, pl. 142, list 5. This was celebrated for *p3 ḫpš tn[r n] pr-ʿ3 ʿ.w.s. m nty.w ḫr.w n ḫpr m ḥ3.t-sp* [ ] 'the strong-armed one, king, l.p.h., among those enemies, which occurred in year [ ].' Haring (1997, 69–70) dates the year to 6 or earlier. Grain was supplied from Karnak, rather than from MH as at other feasts.
1247 O. DeM 39 (*KRI* V, 553: 5) and P. Turin 1946+1949 (*KRI* V, 557: 15) for a report on R III's death to the workmen at DeM. Donker van Heel (1992, 20) assumes that the king died on III Shemu 14 or 15.
1248 *w3ḥ mw n n3 nsw.t-bi.ty.w m hrw pn* (P. Geneva MAH 15274+P. Turin 54063: *KRI* VI, 144: 1; Krauss 1985, 149; McDowell 1999, 186). Donker van Heel (1992, 20) associates *w3ḥ mw* with a mortuary rite for R III, who, he believes, had died on III Shemu 14 or 15. Peden (2001, 209, n. 477) does not regard this text as referring to a punishment. For the dating to the time of Ramses IV, see Černý (1973, 165) and Gutgesell (1983, vol. 1, 235–6).
1249 O. Cairo 25290 (*KRI* VI, 143: 8; Daressy 1901, 37, pl. 58; Helck 2002, 398). A libation (*w3ḥ-mw*) and offering of the garland (*p3 m3ḥw*) are recorded for this day (Donker van Heel 1992, 20).
1250 O. Cairo 25291 (*KRI* VI, 143: 12; Daressy 1901, 74, pl. 57; Helck 2002, 398). The vizier went downstream (*ḫd*) to the capital city (*r p3 nty twtw im*) on the same day. Cf. O. Cairo 25303 (*KRI* VII, 455) for the same vizier attested in a different month.
1251 He was born in *ḥ3.t-mḥy.t* (Mendes). Sanctuary of Hatshepsut's DB temple (PM II^2, 367, (146); Laskowska-Kusztal 1984, 47).
1252 Statue base of the overseer of granaries *P3-di-b3s.t* (BM 512: Gauthier 1918, 37; Łajtar 2006, 64, n. 242).
1253 O. Gardiner 143 (*KRI* VII, 376: 8).
1254 O. DeM 58 (*KRI* III, 546: 4; Allam 1973, 84).

III Shemu

1255) 19: Amun-Re's oracle concerning the lady *Ḥnw.t-t3.wy* [Siamen, 6, Karnak][1255]
1256) 19: Contract concerning three servants and an oath-taking [Taharqa, 5][1256]
1257) 19–23: Festival of the Stamping on the Fish [*Ptolemy VI*, Kom Ombo][1257]
1258) 19–21: Appearance of Khnum [Roman, Esna][1258]
1259) 20: Festival of the Souls of Nekhen [*T III*, Buto][1259]
1260) 20: Herdsman *Nb-mḥy* appealed over a female servant before witnesses [*A III*, 27, Lahun][1260]
1261) 20: Seti I's decree to dig a well in the Eastern Desert [*Seti I*, 9, Kanayis][1261]
1262) 20: A woman put a hereditary claim at Amun's appearance [R XI, 1, near Herakleopolis Magna][1262]
1263) 20: Transfer of a donkey to a water-carrier by the workman *Wsr-ḥ3.t* [1, DeM][1263]
1264) 20: Graffito on the roof of the Khonsu temple [1?, Karnak][1264]

3rd MONTH of *šmw* (*ip.t-ḥm.t*/*ipip*/Epeiph); 33rd decade (*s3wy knmt*)

No.) Day: Event
1265) 21: *w3ḥ-mw* performed by some workmen [Amenmes, 4, KV][1265]
1266) 21: Appearance of Khnum-Re, Lord of the Field, the Unification with the Sun [Roman, Esna][1266]
1267) 23: The royal scribe *Bw-th-imn* visited East Thebes when work began at KV 42 [R XI, w10?, KV 42][1267]
1268) 23: Anubis Festival [Ptolemy III, Hibeh (but related to Sais)][1268]
1269) 24: A note of a man having divorced his wife [*Sethnakht*, 2, Ramesseum][1269]
1270) 24: A property claim by *Knr* [*R III*, 13][1270]
1271) 24: Oath-taking in front of witnesses by the watercarrier *P3-šd* [*R III*, 27][1271]
1272) 24: Navigation of Seti [R V or VI?, 2][1272]
1273) 25: Day of [?] of Amun-Re [Siptah-Tausret or R III, 4, KV][1273]
1274) 25: Qenbet? [R III, 8][1274]s
1275) 25: Brewing for Hathor [R IV, KV][1275]
1276) 25: Return of a loaned donkey and a payment by a workman [R IX, 6][1276]
1277) 27: Rock inscription concerning the 1st Sed Festival [*Pepi I*, after the 18th census, Wadi Hammamat][1277]
1278) 27?: Navigation of Ramses II [Siptah or Tausret, KV][1278]
1279) 27: Siptah killed the chancellor *B3y* [Siptah, 5, DeM][1279]

1255 The north face of the 10th pylon at Karnak (PM II², 187 (580); Gardiner 1962, 58; Kitchen 1973a, 422; Winand 2003, 641; Jansen-Winkeln 2007, vol. 1, 177). Note that this date is annotated to be 'good, good, good', probably expressing a festive day. Cf. I Akhet 1 for Amun's another oracle concerning this lady.
1256 P. Louvre E 3228 f (Menu 1985, 78). The oath was taken by the coachyte *P3-di-b3s.t*.
1257 *ḥb tktk rm.w* (Grimm 1994a, 128–31).
1258 *r snfr ib=f ḥr ir ḳbḥw sntr n nṯr.w n nty.w i3m* 'in order to satisfy his heart, performing a libation and fumigation of the gods and those who were before' (Sauneron 1963, vol. 1, 171; Grimm 1994a, 130–3 and 263). Also see Sauneron 1962, 309–78.
1259 *ḥb b3.w nḫn* (Buto Stela 209: Bedier 1994a, 6, z. 28; Klug 2002, 96–105).
1260 P. Berlin 9784 (Gardiner 1906b, 31; Murnane and Meltzer 1995, 43).
1261 Text at the rock temple at el-Kanayis, east of Redesiya (*LD* III, pl. 140, b; *KRI* I, 65: 14; Lichtheim 1973, vol. 2, 52–7). The decree also concerns establishing Amun's temple at a divine command.
1262 P. Ashmolean 1945.96 (*KRI* VI, 735: 10; Gardiner 1940, 23). Cf. I Akhet 10 for another recorded in the same text.
1263 O. DeM 781 (Grandet 2000a, vol. 8, 57 and 184).
1264 Graffito 43 of a wab-priest of Khonsu (Jacquet-Gordon 2004, 25, pl. 15; Jansen-Winkeln 2007, vol. 2, 445).
1265 O. Cairo 25784 (*KRI* IV, 227: 9). For the dating, see Gutgesell 2002, 9–10.
1266 *sḫʿ Ḥnm-rʿnb sḫ.t ḥnʿ psḏ.t=f ḫnm itn* (Sauneron 1963, vol. 1, 171; Altenmüller 1977, 179; Grimm 1994a, 132–3).
1267 Graffito 714 at the entrance of KV 42 (*KRI* VI, 849: 9; Jansen-Winkeln 1995; Eaton-Krauss 1999, 122). He was awaiting the arrival of the general Piankhi from the south. Cf. letters sent to/from *Bw-th-imn* with the date of I Shemu 25 in year 10 (P. BM 10326: Wente 1967, 37–42) and P. BM 10375 dated to I Shemu 29 (Wente 1990, 194–5).
1268 P. Hibeh 27, l. 170 (Grenfell and Hunt 1906, 144).
1269 O. UC 19614 (*KRI* V, 1: 15; McDowell 1999, 43–4).
1270 O. Cairo 25555+O. DeM 999 (*KRI* V, 456: 6; Allam 1973, 59–61; McDowell 1999, 179). This case was again discussed before Amenhotep I later onIShemu 19 in the same regnal year.
1271 O. Ashmolean 106 (*KRI* V, 515: 10).
1272 *p3 ḫnw Sthy* (O. Gardiner 11=O. Ashmolean 11: *KRI* VI, 249: 7). This day was a lunar day as the Valley Festival was recorded for II Shemu 25 on the same ostracon. Helck (1966a and 1990, 208) regarded this date as the accession day of Seti I, a hypothesis opposed by Murnane (1975/1976).
1273 *hrw pn n* [ ] *ir n Imn-rʿ* [ ] (O. Cairo 25794: Černý 1935b, 90, pl. 112*; *KRI* IV, 361: 15). Helck (1964, 159) regarded the date as II Shemu 25 to associate it with the Valley Festival, an interpretation followed by Černý (Notebook), Krauss (1985, 146), and McDowell (1999, 96–7).
1274 P. Boulaq X, verso (=P. Cairo 58092): Spiegelberg 1892, 16–28; Janssen and Pestman 1968, 147.
1275 *ʿtḫ n Ḥw.t-ḥr* (O. Cairo 25533: Černý 1935b, 15; *KRI* VI, 176: 3).
1276 P. Turin 1976 (*KRI* VI, 599: 10; Wente 1990, 137–8; McDowell 1999, 171–2).
1277 Written by the overseer of all royal works *Mry-ptḥ* (*LD* II, pl. 115, g; Couyat and Montet 1912, 74).
1278 O. Cairo 25503 (*KRI* IV, 425: 10–1). *p3 ḫn.t* [*Wsr-m3ʿ.t*]*-rʿ-*[*stp-n-rʿ*]. The workmen at DeM were off duty.
1279 O. IFAO 1864 (Grandet 2000b, 341). The other side of the ostracon records deliveries including pigs.

1280) 27: Appearance(?) of Ramses II [R IV, KV][1280]
1281) 27: Appearance of Ramses II in the time of Ramses X [*R X*, 3][1281]
1282) 27–IV Shemu 12: Appearance of Hathor, Lady of Dendera [*Ptolemy X*, Edfu][1282]
1283) 27: Festival of Hacking the Earth [AD 1st century, Tanis][1283]
1284) 28: Heliacal rising of Sothis, celebrated with festival offerings [*T III*, Elephantine][1284]
1285) 28: A personal festival [19 Dyn., 2][1285]
1286) 28: Oracular appointment of an official by Amun-Re in the morning at the Ipet-Hemetes Festival [*R XI*, w7, Karnak][1286]
1287) 28?: Qenbet session gave a man a sentence of 50 blows [Merenptah, DeM][1287]
1288) 29: Workmen off duty until I Akhet 3 for the New Year Festival [Amenmes, 2][1288]
1289) 29: Overseer of the treasury *Ḫ*ʿ*-m-tir* visited DeM to hear the workmen [*R IV*, 2, DeM][1289]
1290) 29: Festival of Mut of Isheru [Ramesside, DeM][1290]
1291) 29: Amun-Re's Festival [Pinedjem I or Smendes I, 25, Karnak][1291]
1292) 29: Ankhnesneferibre was adapted by Nitocris before Amun at Karnak [*Psametik II*, 1, Karnak][1292]
1293) 29: Festival of the Gods at Her (Nebtu) Majesty's Festival for three days(?) [Roman, Esna][1293]
1294) 30: Dated papyrus concerning a shift change of temple personnel [Djedkare-Isesi, year of the 18th census, Reneferef's temple at Abusir][1294]
1295) 30: Day of the Evening of the Festival (of Hathor?) [*T III*, Ptah precinct in Karnak][1295]
1296) 30: Delivery of timber to be used for IV Shemu 20, 30, and the epagomenal days [R IV, 1, DeM][1296]

3rd MONTH of *šmw* (*ip.t-ḥm.t*/*ipip*/Epeiph); unknown decade

No.) Day: Event
1297) ?: First of Wine was offered [MK, 1, Lahun][1297]
1298) ?: Festival of Uniting [...] [MK, 41, Lahun][1298]
1299) ?: Wag Festival [MK, 38, Lahun][1299]
1300) ?: Dated rock stela recording a monumental construction for Thoth of Hermopolis [*A III*, 1, Wadi el-Nakhla][1300]
1301) ?: Dated stela [*R II*, 40, Heliopolis][1301]

1280 O. Cairo 25533 (*KRI* VI, 176: 5; Jauhiainen 2009, 183). The workmen at DeM were off duty. Helck (1959, 119), Krauss (1977, 147), and Kitchen (1982, 43) agree to regard this day as Ramses II's accession, a hypothesis opposed only by Murnane (1975/1976, 25). The accession year of Ramses II is proposed to have been 1304 BC by Černý (1961, 151); 1290 by Parker (1957c, 43), Hornung (1964), Redford (1966, 124), and Baines and Malek (1980, 37); 1279 by Hornung (2006, 493). Based on *wḥm msw.t* recorded on the north exterior wall of the Hypostyle Hall at Karnak (PM II², 57 (170); LD III, pl. 129, a), Sethe (1930), later opposed by Černý (1961, 151), proposed that the date in question is more accurately 1318 BC, corresponding to the accession of Seti I.

1281 P. Turin 1898+1926+1937+2094 (*KRI* VI, 697: 1–2).

1282 *ḫ*ʿ *in Ḥw.t-ḥr nb(.t) iwn.t* (Grimm 1994a, 132–3).

1283 *b3 t3* (P. BM ESA 10673: Griffith and Petrie 1889, pl. 13). Foundation ceremony (Weinstein 1973, 12)?

1284 *hrw n pr.t spd.t* (Stone Louvre D 68: *Urk.* IV, 827: 8; Ziegler 1982, 264–5 for photograph; el-Sabban 2000, 34). Krauss (2006c, 445, n. 29) dates this to the last years of Thutmose III, based on the epigraphy.

1285 O. DeM 209 (*KRI* IV, 218: 12).

1286 *sḫ*ʿ *ḥm nṯr pn šps ʾImn-r*ʿ *m tri n dw3.t m ḥb=f nfr n ʾIp.t-ḥm.t=s* (chapel of Amenhotep II: PM II², 186 (576); *KRI* VI, 702: 11–3; Nims 1948, 159; Spalinger 1993a, 292, n. 11). *Ns-imn* was appointed a scribe of the storehouse of Amun's temple, a position of his fathers'.

1287 O. IFAO 1357 (*KRI* IV, 162: 3; Allam 1973, 197–8). This man appears to be blamed for *swr m p3 dmi* 'drinking in the town' from III Shemu 29 to IV Shemu 2 while other workmen were at work. It is not entirely clear whether his behaviour was simply the result of his lazy personality or associated with a personal celebration.

1288 O. DeM 209 (*KRI* IV, 219: 5–6; Černý 1935a, vol. 3, pl. 8: 20).

1289 O. DeM 44 (*KRI* VI, 117: 7). The case concerns the delay of provision supplies for III and IV Shemu.

1290 P. Cairo 86637 (Bakir 1966, 47; Leitz 1994a, 395).

1291 *ḥb ʾImn-r*ʿ. The Banishment Stela (=Louvre C 256: von Beckerath 1968, 9; Kitchen 1973a, 419; Jansen-Winkeln 2007, vol. 1, 72).

1292 Stela Cairo 36907 (PM II², 166; Leahy 1996). Ankhnesneferibre was a daughter of Psametik II.

1293 *ḥb nṯr.w m ḥb ḥm=s* (Sauneron 1963, vol. 1, 171; Grimm 1994a, 134–5).

1294 Abusir X, 262, pl. 45.

1295 Stela Cairo 34013 (*hrw n ḫ3w.t ḥb n.t ḥb sḫpr m 3bd 3-nw šmw* ʿ*rḳy*). *Urk.* IV, 771: 7; Legrain 1902, 107–14; Lacau 1909, 27–30, pl. 9; Kees 1955, 335; Klug 2002, 142). An offering list is attached.

1296 O. Berlin 12631 (unpublished). 110 pieces of timber for IV Shemu 20 and 200 pieces for IV Shemu 30.

1297 P. Berlin 10007, recto (Luft 1992, 45).

1298 *hrw n ḥb sm3y* [ ] (P. UC 32137 J: Collier and Quirke 2006, 241).

1299 P. Berlin 10419 a, recto (Luft 1992, 134).

1300 *Urk.* IV, 1677: 11; Klug 2002, 367.

1301 Stela from Heliopolis, present location unknown (*KRI* II, 398: 15). *ḥ3.t nḥḥ šsp ḏ.t ir.t ḥḥ.w n ḥb.w-sd* 'front of the eternity, receiving the everlastingness, and performing millions of the Sed Festivals' is documented .

III Shemu

1302) ?: Royal decree issued for the royal butler *Sbk-ḥtp* to procure turquoise on the 4th expedition [R V, 3, Serabit el-Khadim, Sinai][1302]
1303) ?: Graffito on the roof of the Khonsu temple [*Iuput I*, 9, Karnak][1303]
1304) ?: Graffito on the roof of the Khonsu temple [TIP, 10, Karnak][1304]
1305) ?: Graffito at the treasury of the temple of Medinet Habu [Ptolemaic-Roman, 16, MH][1305]
1306) New moon: Festival of *sḫn* (Reunion) [*Ptolemy* X, Edfu][1306]
1307) New moon: Beautiful Festival of *sḫn* [Ptolemy XII, Dendera][1307]

[1302] Stela Yale University Art Gallery 28.53 (Gardiner, Peet, and Černý 1952, vol. 1, pl. 75, vol. 2, 194; Schulman 1988, 137–8).
[1303] Graffito 244 left by the divine father *Ḫnsw-ḥ3.t-nṯr-*[*nb*] (Jacquet-Gordon 2004, 84–5, pl. 93).
[1304] Graffito 135 left by a man called *Ḏd-ḫnsw-*[ ] (Jacquet-Gordon 2004, 52, pl. 51). For another graffito carved probably in this month, see Graffito 147 (Jacquet-Gordon 2004, 56, pl. 56; Jansen-Winkeln 2007, vol. 2, 173).
[1305] Graffito MH no. 24 B, located at the treasury of Medinet Habu temple (Thissen 1989, 11).
[1306] *ḥb sḫn* (Grimm 1994a, 124–7; Altenmüller 1998). Its longest known duration at Edfu is 13 or 14 days.
[1307] *ḥb nfr sḫn* (Grimm 1994a, 126–7). The procession of Hathor took place at the 10th hour of the day and lasted four days.

4th MONTH of *šmw* (*wpy-rnp.t*/*msw.t-rꜥ*/Mesore); 34th decade (*ẖry ḫpd n knmt*) IV Shemu

No.) Day: Event

1308) 1: Royal decree regarding the cult of the two queens *Mry-rꜥ-ꜥnḫ-n=s* and *N.t*
[Pepi II or later, year of *smꜣ-tꜣ.wy*, Saqqara][1308]
1309) 1: Divine offering of the first wine [MK, Lahun][1309]
1310) 1: Delivery of the fat of pigs of the barn of the Residence [Seti I, DeM][1310]
1311) 1: Amun-Re crossed to the western Thebes to perform a libation (*wꜣḥ mw*) to kings [R IV?, 5, KV][1311]
1312) 1: Appearance of the August Image of Haroeris [*Ptolemy VI*, Kom Ombo][1312]
1313) 1: Festival of Her Majesty [*Ptolemy* X, Edfu][1313]
1314) 1: Appearance of Hathor at the 3rd hour of the day [Ptolemy XII, Dendera][1314]
1315) 1: Khnum-Re Festival [Roman, Esna][1315]
1316) 1–2: Workmen in Deir el-Medina off duty for a festival [Amenmes, 2, DeM][1316]
1317) 2: Scribe *Ṯꜣy* visited the Step Pyramid to worship Osiris [*Tutankhamen*, 4, Saqqara][1317]
1318) 2: Ipet Festival and the workmen of Deir el-Medina were off duty [*R* X, 3][1318]
1319) 2: Amun-Re's amuletic decree concerning ushabtis for *Ns-ḫnsw*, a wife of Pinedjem II [Siamen, 5][1319]
1320) 2: Festival of Apollo (Horus) [Ptolemy III, Hibeh (but related to Sais)][1320]
1321) 3: Oath (or petition?) by the scribe *Ỉmn-nḫt* to Amenhotep I [R III, 16][1321]
1322) 4: Offering to a god [*R II*, 40][1322]
1323) 4: Erection of a stela by Ramses II to honour his father Seti I [*R II*, Tanis][1323]
1324) 4: Rainfall [Ramses V, 2, western Thebes][1324]
1325) 5: Expedition to Sinai [*Pepi I*, year after the 18th census, Magharah in Sinai][1325]
1326) 5 or 6: Decree of Merenptah [*Merenptah*, 2, Gebel el-Silsila][1326]
1327) 5–10: Investigation of the thieves of royal tombs by the vizier *Nb-mꜣꜥ.t-rꜥ-nḫt* [*R XI*, w1][1327]
1328) 5: Oath taken by the workman *Mry-sḫm.t* concerning a love affair in front of witnesses [20 Dyn.][1328]
1329) 5: Min Festival at Akhmin [Ramesside, DeM][1329]
1330) 5: Installation of a priest? [*Siamen*, 14, Karnak][1330]
1331) 8: Scribe *Ỉmn-m-ḥb* visited western Memphis with the scribe *Pꜣy-m-sꜣ-imn*
[NK, 10, tomb chapel of the king Horemheb at Saqqara][1331]
1332) 8: Royal decree concerning the cult of Pepi II [Pepi II, Abydos][1332]
1333) 8: Decree for *Ns-ḫnsw*, a wife of Pinedjem II [Siamen, 5][1333]
1334) 9: Festival of Imhotep [Ptolemaic Period, Memphis?][1334]

1308 Stela Cairo 56370 (PM III-2^2, 431; *Urk*. I, 307: 9; Goedicke 1967, 158, Abb. 15).
1309 *ḥtp-nṯr ḥꜣ.t irp* (P. Berlin 10007: Luft 1992, 45).
1310 *mrḥ.t* [*n*] *šꜣy.w n nꜣ n mḏ.wt ẖnw* (O. Berlin 14213, unpublished).
1311 O. Cairo 25265. *ḏꜣj r imnt.t niw.t in Ỉmn-rꜥ nsw.t* [*nṯr.w*] *r wꜣḥ mw n nsw.t-bi.tyw*. The date is IV Shemu 1 in the original text, which is maintained by Donker van Heel (1992, 20), but emended by Černý (1927, 186, n. 1) to III Shemu, and then by Černý (Notebook, 101.23), Krauss (1985, 146), McDowell (1999, 96–7), and Jauhiainen (2009, 151) to II Shemu, in order to relate it to the Valley Festival. Following this day, the 10th of the same month is recorded. Gutgesell (1983, vol. 2, 423–4) dates the ostracon to the time of Ramses IV.
1312 *ḫꜥ n pꜣ mtr šps n Ḥr-wr* (Grimm 1994a, 134–5).
1313 *ḥb ḥm=s* (Grimm 1994a, 136–7).
1314 *ḫꜥ in Ḥw.t-ḥr* (Grimm 1994a, 136–7).
1315 *ḥb Ḫnm-rꜥ* (Sauneron 1963, vol. 1, 171; Grimm 1994a, 136–7).
1316 O. DeM 209 (*KRI* IV, 218: 14–5; Černý, 1935a, vol. 3, 5, pl. 8).
1317 Graffito at the north chapel of the Step Pyramid (Firth and Quibell 1935, 78; Navrátilová 2007, 77–9).
1318 P. Turin 1898+1926+1937+2094 (*KRI* VI, 697: 8; Gardiner 1906a, 137–8 for commentary).
1319 McCullum Tablet (=BM 16672): Černý 1942b; Jansen-Winkeln 2007, vol. 1, 120: 12–4. The decree was issued by Amun-[Lord-of]-the-Thrones-of-the-Two-Lands-of-the-Khonsu-Temple (*Ỉmn* [*nb*] *ns.wt tꜣ.wy n ḥw.t bnn.t*). See Maspero (1880, 15) for a text parallel to this. Cf. IV Shemu 8 and 21 for other documents recording the same woman.
1320 P. Hibeh 27, l. 186 (Grenfell and Hunt 1906, 144).
1321 O. Varille 40 (*KRI* VII, 286: 3).
1322 O. BM 5634 (Sadek 1987, 187; *KRI* III, 518: 11–2).
1323 The Year 400 Stela (=Cairo 60539: Stadelmann 1965, 50; Goedicke 1981).
1324 Graffito 2868 (Černý and Sadek 1969, IV-2, 128, no. 2868; *KRI* VI, 250: 6).
1325 Rock inscription (Gardiner, Peet, and Černý 1952, vol. 1, pl. 8, vol. 2, 63; *Urk*. I, 91: 17).
1326 Rock stela (PM V, 212 (39); Champollion 1844, vol. 2, pl. 114; *KRI* IV, 74: 2).
1327 P. BM 10052 (Peet 1930b, 142, 147, 149, 156, and 157). Conducted by the vizier *Nb-mꜣꜥ.t-rꜥ-nḫt*, the overseer of the treasury *Mn-mꜣꜥ.t-rꜥ-nḫt*, and royal butlers *Y-n-sꜣ* and *Pꜣ-mry-imn*. One of the thieves was re-examined 5 days later on IV Shemu 10 (Peet 1930b, 147).
1328 P. DeM 27 (*KRI* V, 579: 2; McDowell 1999, 47–9).
1329 P. Cairo 86637 (Bakir 1966, 47; Leitz 1994a, 399).
1330 Inscription at the Akh-menu (Legrain 1900, 61).
1331 Graffito (Navrátilová 2007, 65).
1332 Broken architrave inscription (*Urk*. I, 279–80; Petrie 1902, vol. 2, 42–3, pl. 19; Goedicke 1967, 81, Abb. 7).
1333 Rogers Tablet (=Louvre E 6858: Maspero 1880, 17; Černý 1942b). Cf. IV Shemu 2 and 21 for other documents recording the same woman.
1334 Stone statue base (Gauthier 1918, 37).

1335) 10+: Ramses III's victory over the Meshwesh [*R III*, 11, MH][1335]
1336) 10: Appeal and oath by the water-carrier *Ṯ3-ʿ3* concerning a donkey [R III, 28][1336]
1337) 10: God crossed to the Town (i.e. eastern Thebes) [R IV?, 5, KV][1337]

4th MONTH of *šmw* (*wpy-rnp.t*/*msw.t-rʿ*/Mesore); 35th decade (*ḥ3t ẖ3w*/*ḥ3t ḏ3t*)

No.) Day: Event
1338) 11: Appeal by the workman *Ỉmn-p3-ḥʿpy* and oath by his wife [R IV or VII, 7][1338]
1339) 12: Writing the royal name (at Sed Festival?) [*T III*, 33, el-Bersheh][1339]
1340) 12: Royal decree to the vizier to enlarge the treasury of Maat for the New Year Feast [*R III*, 22?, Karnak][1340]
1341) 13?: Seti I established monuments for Amun-Re [*Seti I*, 11, Gebel Barkal][1341]
1342) 13–20: Vizier *P3-nḥsy* supervised lowing a sarcophagus to the tomb of Merenptah [*Merenptah*, 7, KV][1342]
1343) 13: Royal decree to dedicate offerings to the temple of Neith after his accession at Sais [*Nectanebo I*, 1, Naucratis][1343]
1344) 14: The presence of the vizier *T3* with the scribe *Ỉmn-nḫt* [*R III*, West Thebes][1344]
1345) 15: 1st examination of the tomb robbers of Seti I and R II, attended by the vizier *Nb-m3ʿ.t-rʿ-nḫt* [*R XI*, w1][1345]
1346) 15: Nun rests in his grotto [Ramesside][1346]
1347) 16: Rowing of the Water [MK, Lahun][1347]
1348) 16: Graffito of the scribe of a prince *Ỉmn-ḥtp* [*T III*, 18, Shelfak, Nubia][1348]
1349) 16: Hearing of a theft taking place at a temple [*R XI*, w2][1349]
1350) 16: Ankhnesneferibre was appointed the divine wife and divine adoratice of Amun at Karnak [*Apries*, 4, Karnak][1350]
1351) 17: Dated stela commemorating a new monument (*ḏ3ḏ3*-hall) for Mentu [*Ahmes*, Armant][1351]
1352) 17: 2nd examination of the thieves of the tombs of Seti I and R II [*R XI*, w1][1352]
1353) 17: Festival of Imhotep [Ptolemaic Period, Memphis?][1353]
1354) 18: 23rd lunar day of III Shemu [*Ptolemy VIII*, 28, Edfu][1354]
1355) 18: Dated graffito [Ptolemaic-Roman, 7?, MH][1355]
1356) 19: The workmen were rewarded (*mk*) by the vizier *P3-nḥsy* at the Enclosure of the Necropolis [*Merenptah*, 7, KV][1356]

[1335] *ḥ3.t nḫt n t3-mry mn nsw.t* 'beginning of victories of Egypt which the king achieved' (West wall of the north half of the first pylon at Medinet Habu; de Rougé 1877, pl. 116). Cf. I Akhet 28 and II Peret 8 for other occasions celebrated for the victory over the Meshwesh in this particular year.

[1336] O. Petrie 14 (=O. UC 39615): *KRI* V, 524: 3; Allam 1973, 230; McDowell 1999, 75–6. Vleeming (1982) regards this session as a qenbet, whereas McDowell (1990, 147) does not.

[1337] *ḏ3j r niw.t in p3 nṯr* (O. Cairo 25265).

[1338] O. Petrie 18 (=O. UC 39619): Allam 1973, 234–5; *KRI* VI, 430: 8. He indicted his wife for neglecting him.

[1339] Rock stela of the HP of Thoth *Sn-nfr* (PM IV, 185; *Urk.* IV, 597: 12). *ḥ3.t ḥḥ m ḥb.w ʿš3 wr.t* [*spḫr*].*n Ḏḥwty ḏs=f m sš=f ḥr išd šps* 'beginning of millions at many great festivals that Thoth himself [wrote] in his writing on the august *išd*-tree.' Helck (1957, 128) read the date as III Shemu 12. An inscription parallel to this in Krakow is dated IV Shemu 4 (Hornung 2006, 202).

[1340] The earliest attestation of *ḥb tpy*, which was widely used after the Ptolemaic Period (PM II^2, 13 (39); *KRI* V, 231: 3; Bouriant 1890, 173). Awad (2002, 185) reads the date as IV Shemu 4. The year is poorly preserved and some read as 12, which is unlikely insofar as surviving evidence is concerned because Ta is securely attested from year 16 (Dresbach 2012, 83).

[1341] Stela Khartoum Museum 1856 (*KRI* I, 75: 8).

[1342] O. Cairo 25504 (*KRI* IV, 155–6; McDowell 1999, 224; Schulman 1976, 120). The vizier was accompanied by the butler *Rʿ-ms-m-pr-rʿ*, and they sailed downstream (*ḫd*) on IV Shemu 20. Cf. III Akhet 23 for divine statues brought into this tomb earlier.

[1343] Stela Cairo 34002 (Brunner 1965, pls. 23–4 for photograph; Wente 1973, vol. 3, 87 for translation).

[1344] Graffito 1928 (*KRI* V, 380: 4).

[1345] P. Mayer A, recto (=Liverpool M 11162: *KRI* VII, 803: 12; Peet 1920, 10). Other judges include the overseer of the treasury *Mn-m3ʿt-rʿ-nḫt* and the royal butlers *Ỉni* and *P3-mry-imn*. Cf. IV Shemu 17 for the second examination.

[1346] O. Cairo 86637 (Leitz 1994a, 405). Leitz regards this as the ideological moment of the Nile's recession.

[1347] P. Berlin 10218 b, recto (Luft 1992, 108).

[1348] Hintze and Reineke 1989, vol. 1, 90.

[1349] P. BM 10403 (Peet 1930b, 171).

[1350] *n.t-ʿ.w nb n bsi dw3 nṯr n Ỉmn*. Stela Cairo 36907 (PM II^2, 166). This was performed 12 days after the death of Nitocris on IV Shemu 4 (Caminos 1964).

[1351] Stela UC 14402 (Klug 2002, 47–8, Abb. 2).

[1352] P. Mayer A, recto (=Liverpool M. 11162: *KRI* VII, 808: 15; Peet 1920, 11). Cf. IV Shemu 15 for the 1st examination.

[1353] Stone statue base (Gauthier 1918, 37).

[1354] *Edfou* IV, 2: 10; de Wit 1961a, 59; Depuydt 1997, 124; Belmonte Avilés 2003, 14.

[1355] Graffito MH no. 237 located at the small temple of Medinet Habu (Thissen 1989, 148–50).

[1356] O. Cairo 25504, recto (*KRI* IV, 156: 8). The reward included six oxen and 80 fine thin cloths (*šmʿ nfr ḥbs.w*), probably one for each workman (Janssen 1975a, 492). A similar quantity of linen (78 in number) is attested in P. Turin 1881, III, 2–4 as distributed to the workmen in I Peret, year

IV Shemu

1357) 19: Oath taken by a man called *Pn-tꜣ-wr.t* to do what is promised by the Thoth Festival [R III, 31][1357]
1358) 19: Visit(?) of a vizier, a royal scribe, and a high-priest [R IV, 3, KV][1358]
1359) 19: Departure of an unnamed vizier [20 Dyn.][1359]
1360) 19: Eye of Horus is fulfilled [Ramesside][1360]
1361) 19–21: Festival of Edfu [*Ptolemy X*, Edfu][1361]
1362) 20: Menehy Festival and the Offering on the Altar [Roman, Esna][1362]

4th MONTH of *šmw* (*wpy-rnp.t*/*msw.t-rꜥ*/Mesore); 36th decade (*pḥwy ḫꜣw*/*pḥwy ḏꜣt*)

No.) Day: Event

1363) 21: *Wdn.t-iḥhy* [Djedkare-Isesi, year after the 10th census, Neferirkare's temple at Abusir][1363]
1364) 21: Burial text of *Ns-ḫnsw*, a wife of Pinedjem II [Siamen, 5, DB 320][1364]
1365) 22: Transfer of grain by the water-carrier *Pn-tꜣ-wr.t* before witnesses [R III, 17][1365]
1366) 22: Festival of Anubis [Ramesside, DeM][1366]
1367) 22: Graffito on the roof of the Khonsu temple [Osorkon III, 14, Karnak][1367]
1368) 23: Rainfall [R IV, V, or VI, 2, near QV][1368]
1369) 24: Rainfall [R IV, V, or VI, 2, KV][1369]
1370) 23–30: Making the Offerings and Moistening the Barley for Osiris [*Horemheb*, TT 50][1370]
1371) 23: Festival of Imhotep [Ptolemaic Period, Memphis?][1371]
1372) 23: A Buchis bull entered southern Thebes [*Ptolemy I*, 14, Armant][1372]
1373) 24: Ptah Festival and his appearance in the evening [*R II*, 34, Pyramid of Khendjer at Saqqara][1373]
1374) 25: Payment made by the woman *Nssy* for a servant [*A IV*, 5][1374]
1375) 25: Unknown personal festival? [R IV, KV][1375]
1376) 25: Coppersmiths were commissioned by the Necropolis administrators and the treasury scribe *Ḥri* [*R VII*, 8][1376]
1377) 25: Investigation of a theft at the temple of Medinet Habu by the vizier *Nb-mꜣꜥ.t-rꜥ-nḫt* [R XI, w2][1377]
1378) 25: Unknown festival [AD 1st century, Tanis][1378]
1379) 26–I Akhet 3: Workmen at DeM were off duty for 13 days for an unspecified reason [*Seti II*, 6, DeM][1379]
1380) 26: A festival [AD 1st century, Tanis][1380]

7 of Ramses IX (*KRI* VI, 612: 5–6).

[1357] O. DeM 57 (*KRI* V, 554: 14; Allam 1973, 83).

[1358] O. Cairo 25267 (*KRI* VI, 133: 4).

[1359] *wḏ n ṯꜣty* (O. DeM 320: Černý 1935a, vol. 4, 24, pl. 21).

[1360] O. Cairo 86637 (Leitz 1994a, 14). Leitz regards this day as the summer solstice.

[1361] *ḥb pn n bḥd.t* (Grimm 1994a, 138–9).

[1362] *ḥb Mnḥy ḫ.t ḫꜣwy* (Sauneron 1963, vol. 1, 171; Grimm 1994a, 140–1).

[1363] P. Louvre E 25416 c+P. Cairo 602, frame X, verso (Posener-Kriéger and de Cenival 1968, 6, pl. 14 for facsimile and transcription; Posener-Kriéger 1976, vol. 1, 76–80 for translation; Spalinger 1992, 28). Five pieces of paraphernalia were inspected for their condition.

[1364] Graffito at the entrance of DB 320 (Černý 1946, 26; Kitchen 1973a, 422; Jansen-Winkeln 2007, vol. 1, 118). Cf. IV Shemu 2 and 8 for other documents recording the same woman for the same case.

[1365] O. Louvre E 27677 (Grandet 2002, 205, no. 156). Cf. III Akhet 11.

[1366] P. Cairo 86637 (Leitz 1994a, 410).

[1367] Graffito 190 left by the wab-priest *Ḫnsw-ms* (Jacquet-Gordon 2004, 68–9, pl. 71; Jansen-Winkeln 2007, vol. 2, 311).

[1368] Graffito 3013 (Černý and Sadek 1969, IV-3, 154, no. 3013; Peden 2001, 225).

[1369] Two unnumbered graffiti (Peden 2001, 225–6).

[1370] *wꜣḥ ḫ.t iwḥ bšꜣ n Wsir* (PM I-1², 96 (9–10, I); Helck 1964, 140; Hari 1985, 54, pl. 39; Assmann 2005, 428–9). See rituals parallel to this, which lasted eight days from IV Akhet 18 to 25.

[1371] Stone statue base (Gauthier 1918, 37).

[1372] Bucheum stela no. 3 (Mond and Myers 1934, vol. 2, 3–4, vol. 3, pl. 38; Goldbrunner 2004, 51, pl. 2). *sḫn(.tw?)=f m ns.t wꜣs.t rsy.t ḥꜣ.t-sp 14 ꜣbd 4-nw šmw sw 23 mn ḥr s.t=f n ḏ.t ḥḥ* 'He was inducted on the throne of southern Thebes in year 14, IV Shemu 23, being placed on his seat of eternity and everlastingness'.

[1373] *ḥr tri n rwhꜣ* (Jéquier 1933, 13–4; *KRI* III, 436: 12; Peden 2001, 99). Graffito by the scribe *Nꜣ-šwy*. While Brochardt (1934, 97–8) and Berlandini (1995, 30) related this day to the full moon, Krauss (2006b, 418) associates with the 4th lunar day called *pr.t-sm*, which recalls the high-priest of Ptah as a sem-priest. *pr.t-sm* is attested only for II Akhet during the Middle Kingdom (Luft 1992, 157).

[1374] Wooden tablet owned by Mr. W. Moir Bryce in Edinburgh (Griffith 1908).

[1375] O. Cairo 25533 (*KRI* VI, 177: 2).

[1376] P. Turin 1883+2095 (*KRI* VI, 431: 13).

[1377] P. BM 10383 (Peet 1930b, 124; Awad 2002, 127). The scribe of the army *Kꜣ-šw.ty* was investigated (*smtr*) by the vizier *Nb-mꜣꜥ.t-rꜥ-nḫt*, the overseer of the treasury *Mn-mꜣꜥ.t-rꜥ-nḫt*, and the royal butler *Y-n-sꜣ*.

[1378] P. BM ESA 10673 (Griffith and Petrie 1889, pl.12).

[1379] O. Cairo 25515, recto (Černý 1935b, vol. 1, pl. 11*, col. IV: 5; *KRI* IV, 324: 8).

[1380] P. BM ESA 10673 (Griffith and Petrie 1889, pl.12).

IV Shemu

1381) 27: Festival in the 9th Lower Egyptian nome [*Ptolemy IV*, Edfu][1381]
1382) 27: Appearance of Hathor [Ptolemy XII, Dendera][1382]
1383) 28: Royal decree concerning the temple of Min at Koptos [*Pepi II*, year after the 22nd census, Koptos][1383]
1384) 28: A letter concerning a royal decree to reward the chief justice and vizier *Snḏm-ib* [*Djedkare-Isesi*, year of the 16th(?) census, Giza][1384]
1385) 28: Carrying the Torch [R III, 28?, DeM][1385]
1386) 28: Festival of Min [Ramesside, DeM][1386]
1387) 28: Donation to a temple? [*Sheshonq III*, 30, Mendes][1387]
1388) 29: Holiday in the temple of Sokar in the estate of Ptah [Ramesside, DeM][1388]
1389) 29: Workmen at DeM were off duty until I Akhet 3 for the New Year [Amenmes, 2, DeM][1389]
1390) 29: Transaction of a property [*R II*, 32][1390]
1391) 29: A festival of Mut and renewal of her temple [Ptolemaic, Mut precinct at Karnak][1391]
1392) 30: Dated papyrus concerning allotments to temple personnel [Djedkare-Isesi, year of the 18th census, Reneferef's temple at Abusir][1392]
1393) 30: Offering of This Day [MK, 1, Lahun][1393]
1394) 30: Completion of the two obelisks at Karnak [*Hatshepsut*, 16, Karnak][1394]
1395) 30: Festival-of-Hearing-What-is-Said and the First Evening Meal [*Horemheb*, TT 50][1395]
1396) 30: Ceremonies of Horakhet, Ptah, and Atum in Memphis, and king's decree to establish offerings and temple personnel for Min-Amun at Buhen [*Seti I*, 1, Wadi-Halfa][1396]
1397) 30: Day of Evening Meal [1st half of R II, TT 4][1397]
1398) 30: Day of Evening Meal [2nd half of R II, TT 2][1398]
1399) 30: Evening meal [R III, 25][1399]
1400) 30: Day of Evening Meal [20 Dyn., TT 9][1400]
1401) 30: All Going Forth at the temple of Ptah [Ramesside, DeM][1401]
1402) 30: Payment for a male servant and an oath-taking [*Shabaka*, 10][1402]
1403) 30: Festival in the 12th Lower Egyptian nome [*Ptolemy IV*, Edfu][1403]
1404) 30: First Festival and the Opening of the Face until I Akhet 4 [*Ptolemy VI*, Kom Ombo][1404]
1405) 30: Festival celebrated for the birthday of Ptolemy V [*Ptolemy V*, Rosetta][1405]

[1381] Geographical list on the exterior of the sanctuary (PM VI, 146 (219–20)).
[1382] *ḥꜥ in Ḥw.t-ḥr* (Grimm 1994a, 140–1).
[1383] Stela Cairo 41893 (PM V, 126; *Urk*. I, 288: 1; Goedicke 1967, 119, Abb. 9).
[1384] From the mastaba of the chief justice and vizier *Snḏm-ib* (PM III-1^2, 85 (1, d); *Urk*. I, 63: 9 (last line not recorded); Wente 1990, 18–9 for translation). He was praised by the king for constructing a large lake(?), measuring 1000 cubits long and 440+ cubits wide.
[1385] O. DeM 427 (K*RI* V, 523: 1).
[1386] P. Cairo 86637 (Leitz 1994a, 413).
[1387] Stela Strasburg 1379 (Jansen-Winkeln 2007, vol. 2, 199).
[1388] P. Cairo 86637 (Bakir 1966, 105; Leitz 1994a, 414).
[1389] O. DeM 209 (Černý 1935a, vol. 3, pl. 8: 20; K*RI* IV, 219: 5–6).
[1390] O. Varille 20 (K*RI* VII, 175: 11). Cf. II Akhet 26 for the same case.
[1391] *sꜥḥꜥ sẖm m 4 n pr=s* 'Erecting the effigy at four corners of her house' (inscription on the Ptolemaic gate: PM II^2, 255–6 (1, f); Sauneron 1983, pl. 9, l. 40; Spalinger 1993b, 178; Goyon 2006, 28–9).
[1392] Abusir X, 284, pl. 63.
[1393] *ḥby.t n.t hrw pn* (P. Berlin 10007, recto: Luft 1992, 45). Cf. P. Berlin 10332 d, recto for *iḫ.t ḫꜣw*(?) the 'evening offering' for this day (Luft 1992, 119).
[1394] Inscription on the base of the standing obelisk at Karnak (PM II^2, 81–2; *LD* III, pl. 24, n; *Urk*. IV, 367: 3–5; Lichtheim 1973, vol. 2, 28; Bell 2002, 19–22, n. 13). The work began on II Peret 1 in year 15.
[1395] *ḥb sḏm.t ḏd.wt* and *msy.t tp* (PM I-1^2, 96 (9–10, IV); Hari 1985, pls. 39–40; Assmann 2005, 428–9). III Shemu 30 in the original text. The '[good] day of hearing the words (*hrw pn [nfr] n sḏm md.wt*)' is attested in TT 106 (PM I-1^2, 222 (10, II, 5, col. 13)) in association with the pilgrimage to Abydos (Assmann 2005, 463).
[1396] Stela BM 1189 (K*RI* I, 38: 2 and 100: 7). The king's decree to establish offerings for Amun of Buhen.
[1397] *hrw pn n ir.t msy* (PM I-1^2, 11 (5, II); K*RI* III, 676: 12–3; Černý 1949, 45).
[1398] *hrw pn n ir.t msy* (PM I-1^2, 7 (10, III); K*RI* III, 805: 2; Černý 1949, 16).
[1399] *msy* (O. DeM 32: K*RI* V, 499: 4).
[1400] *hrw pn n ir.t msy* (PM I-1^2, 19 (6, II); K*RI* VII, 41: 7–8 ; Černý 1949, 71).
[1401] P. Cairo 86637 (Leitz 1994a, 415).
[1402] P. Louvre E 3228 e (Menu 1985, 76). Performed by the choachyte *Pꜣ-di-bꜣs.t*.
[1403] Geographical list on the sanctuary exterior (PM VI, 146 (219–20)). Brugsch (1864a, 54) rendered day 10 instead of 30.
[1404] *ḥb tp wn ḥr n nṯr pn ... gb mnḫ.t ir mḏ.t ir n.t-ꜥ nb m ḥb tpy ...ir ꜥꜣb.t ꜥꜣ.(t) m-bꜣḥ=f* '... presenting the cloth, using oil, and performing every ritual at the first festival ... making the great *ꜣb.t*-offerings in front of him' (Grimm 1994a, 140–1, 150 and 164–5).
[1405] Decree of Memphis recorded in the Rosetta Stone (*Urk*. II, 194: 1; Spiegelberg 1922, 60–1; Quirke and Andrews 1988, 21 for transliteration and translation).

1406) 30: Offering on the Altar for Osiris at His Seat at the Beginning [*Ptolemy* X, Edfu][1406]
1407) 30: Khnum Festival [Roman, Esna][1407]

4th MONTH of *šmw* (*wpy-rnp.t*/*msw.t-rꜥ*/Mesore); unknown decade

No.) Day: Event
1408) ?: Bringing of the First Wine from the Residence [A I, Karnak][1408]

1406 *ẖ.t ẖꜣw.t n Wsỉr m s.t=f m šꜣꜥ* (Grimm 1994a, 140–1). The great *ꜣb.t*-offerings are also recorded.
1407 Sauneron 1963, vol. 1, 171; Grimm 1994a, 142–3. The god appeared at the 12th hour of the night.
1408 *ỉn.t ḥꜣ.t ỉrp m ẖnw* (Unnumbered stone fragment: Spalinger 1992, pl. IV; Grimm 1994b, fig. 2 for better facsimile).

Five Epagomenal Days (*hrw.w 5 ḥr.w rnp.t*) Epagomenal Period

No.) Day: Event

1409) Epagomenal days: Reciting a spell over the figures of Osiris, Horus, Seth, Isis, and Nephtys [Ramesside, DeM][1409]
1410) Epagomenal days: Nut (Rhea) gives a birth to her children [Plutarch][1410]
1411) 1: Birth of Osiris[1411]
1412) 1: Proceeding of Upwaut [Senusret I, tomb of *Ḥp-ḏf* at Asyut][1412]
1413) 1–5: Ritual of kindling the fire [Senusret I, tomb of *Ḥp-ḏf* at Asyut][1413]
1414) 1–2: Vizier's visit to Thebes and the appointment of 2PA on the second day [R IX, 13][1414]
1415) 1: Festival of Osiris and his procession [*Nectanebo I*, 17, Thebes][1415]
1416) 1: His (Osiris) Beuatiful Festival on the Entire Land [*Ptolemy VIII*, Opet precinct at Karnak][1416]
1417) 1: Bringing the Cloth to Osiris of Dendera and to the Grand-Pillar-of-Behedet [*Ptolemy X*, Edfu][1417]
1418) 1: Festival of Bringing the Cloth to Khnum-Re [Roman, Esna][1418]
1419) 2: Birth of Horus[1419]
1420) 2: Installation of two priests at Luxor temple [*Tanutamen*, 3, Luxor][1420]
1421) 2: Appearance of Haroeris [*Ptolemy VI*, Kom Ombo][1421]
1422) 2: Festival of Herka-the-Child at the 8th hour [Roman, Esna][1422]
1423) 3: Birth of Seth[1423]
1424) 3–4: Beginning of execution of the laws of the Great Ennead [NK][1424]
1425) 3: Ritual of the Fresh Water for Hathor and the Performance of Very Many Candles [*Ptolemy X*, Edfu][1425]
1426) 3: Offering on the Altar [Roman, Esna][1426]
1427) 4: Birth of Isis[1427]
1428) 4: A person called *ꜣ.t* appealed concerning a female servant before witnesses [*A IV*, 3, Lahun][1428]
1429) 4: Amun's Festival at the New Year and oracle-givings in front of the *ḏꜣḏꜣ*-hall [Pinedjem I or Smendes I, 25, Karnak][1429]
1430) 4: Birth of Isis [Ptolemy III, Hibeh (but related to Sais)][1430]
1431) 4: First Festival of Horus, the Festival of Opening of the Face of Hathor, and the Clothing Festival [*Ptolemy X*, Edfu][1431]
1432) 4: Night of the Child in in His Nest [Ptolemy XII, Dendera][1432]
1433) 4: Festival of the Sky and Land, and the Performance of Clothing Khnum [Roman, Esna][1433]

1409 P. Cairo 86637, verso, XVI (Leitz 1994a, 417). *sš.w ḥr stp n pꜣḳ.wt rdi n s r ḫḫ=f* 'choice scrolls of the *pꜣḳ.t*-linen that is tied to a man in his neck' are also recorded for this period.

1410 Plutarch, *De Iside et Osiride*, 12.

1411 This day was associated with the *bfn*-feast (M. Smith 2009, 416, n. 114).

1412 *wḏꜣ Wpwꜣ.wt* (Griffith 1889, pl. 6, col. 274).

1413 *grḥ n wpt-rnp.t* 'New Year's night' (Griffith 1889, pls. 7–8: cols. 297, 305, and 312).

1414 P. Turin 1999+2009, verso (*KRI* VI, 563: 12–6; Helck 2002, 504). The vizier brought (*in*) the 2PA on day 2. The workmen at DeM were off duty from IV Shemu 30 to I Akhet 4, which Jauhiainen (2009, 81) relates either to a strike or to the New Year celebration.

1415 P. BM 10252 (*Urk.* VI, 141: 6). The ritual on this day is called *ʿḥꜣ n pꜣy=f swn.t* the 'nileperch in his pond.' See P. Louvre 3129 (*Urk.* VI, 141: 13) for the ritual of 'defeating the Nehebkau snake in Heliopolis (*sḫr.tw nḥb-kꜣ.w m iwn*)'. The sequence of rituals after this day is:
2: *wḥm ir bꜣg* 'Repeating weariness';
3: *grḥ wʿb m sḫm-psg* the 'night of prurification at the Powerful of Spittle(?)' (P. Louvre 3129: *Urk.* VI, 143:7. See M. Smith 2009, 416 for the day of the 'pure bull');
4: *spd=k stp* 'Slaughtering (of the bull?)'.

1416 *ḥb=f nfr m tꜣ ḏr=f hrw pn iri p.t* 'this day that the sky was created' (PM II², 247 (21, III); de Wit 1958, vol. 1, 90, vol. 2, pl. 2, e, vol. 3, 45).

1417 *ir mnḫ.t n Wsir* (Grimm 1994a, 142–3).

1418 *ḥb ir mnḫ.t n Ḫnm-rʿ* (Grimm 1994a, 142–3). The *ḫ.t ḫꜣw.t* was also performed.

1419 P. Turin 2070 (*KRI* VI, 427: 2).

1420 *hrw pn bsi r Ỉmn-ip.t* 'on this day of induction to Amenopet'. Built-in blocks in the south exterior wall, now known as Berlin 2096 and 2097 (PM II², 335–6 (223); Vittmann 2001; Jansen-Winkeln 2009, 245–7). *Pꜣ-di-ḫnsw* and *Pꜣ-di-imn-ip.t* had the title 'stolist of Kamutef'.

1421 *ḫʿ n Ḥr-wr* (Grimm 1994a, 142–3).

1422 *ḥb Ḥr-kꜣ-pꜣ-ẖrd* (Grimm 1994a, 144–5).

1423 P. Turin 2070 (*KRI* VI, 427: 3).

1424 *šꜣʿ ir.t hp.w psḏ.t ʿꜣ.t* (P. Leiden I 346, col. II, 12 and 14: Stricker 1948, 64).

1425 [ ] *n mw rnpi* (Grimm 1994a, 144–5). The candles were brought in by the 9th hour of the night.

1426 *ḫ.t ḫꜣw.t* (Grimm 1994a, 144–5).

1427 This day was also called the 'Day of the Night of the Child in His Nest' (*hrw grḥ nḫn m sš=f*) from the Ptolemaic Period (Leitz 1993; Kurth and Waitkus 1994).

1428 P. Berlin 9784 (Gardiner 1906b, 31; Murnane and Meltzer 1995, 44).

1429 *ꜣbd 4-nw šmw sw 5 ḥr ms ꜣs.t ḫft ḥb Ỉmn m wpy rnp.t sḫʿ n ḥm nṯr pn šps nb nṯr.w Ỉmn-rʿ nsw.t nṯr.w*. Banishment Stela (Louvre C 256) (von Beckerath 1968, 12; Jansen-Winkeln 2007, vol. 1, 72). The oracle concerns people escaped to the southern oasis.

1430 P. Hibeh 27, l. 205 (Grenfell and Hunt 1906, 144).

1431 Grimm 1994a, 144–5. The great *ꜣb.t*-offerings are also recorded.

1432 *hrw pn nfr grḥ nḫn m sš=f* (Grimm 1994a, 144–5).

1433 *ḥb pn nfr n p.t tꜣ ir mnḫ.t n Ḫnm* (Grimm 1994a, 146–7).

Epagomenal Period

1434) 5: Birth of Nephthys[1434]
1435) 5: Festival of Isis' Sojourn at Per-Netjer [Roman, Esna][1435]
1436) ?: Inundation of the Nile (and a decree to restore the temple?) [*Sobekhotep VIII*: 16 Dyn., 4, Karnak][1436]
1437) ?: Bringing of the great vase of Nun for the New Year [Edfu][1437]

[1434] P. Turin 2070 (*KRI* VI, 427: 4).
[1435] *ḥb wn ꜣs.t m pr-nṯr* (Grimm 1994a, 146–7).
[1436] Unnumbered stela (PM II^2, 73; Habachi 1974, 210; Ryholt 1997, 388; Baines 1976, 11). *mꜣ ḥꜥpy wr ii.n ḥm=f (r) wsḫ.t n.t r pn mḥ.t im mw* 'witnessing great inundation, his majesty came (to) the broad hall of this temple, which was filled with water'. Baines (1974, 44) speculates that prior to the dated event the peak of floodings had already passed, and that the ritual took place subsequently on a deliberately selected day with regard to the New Year to begin.
[1437] Inscription of Edfu temple (Traunecker 1972, 233–4).

Appendix 2

Tables and text

Table 1. Festivals involving evening and morning rituals.

feast	evening	morning	section	Appendix 1
New Year	IV Shemu 30	I Akhet 1		**1397–400**
Wag	I Akhet 17	I Akhet18		**86** and **90**
Opet	II Akhet 18	II Akhet 19		**233**
Two Sisters[1]	IV Akhet 24	IV Akhet 25		**511**
Khoiak[2]	IV Akhet 25	IV Akhet 26		**515**
I Shemu				**1048**
Valley	first day	second day		**1171–2**
Ipet	III Shemu 30			**1295**
šsp-itrw	first day	second day	2.2.1	
6th lunar feast		○	1.2.3	
7th lunar feast	○		1.2.3	

1 P. Louvre N 3176 (Barguet 1962, 16, ll. 7–10).

2 The eve of this festival celebrated for Osiris at Abydos and for Sokar was called the *hꜣkr*-Feast and *nṯry.t*-Feast respectively (Assmann 2001, 355).

Table 2. Dates of the inundation of the Nile at Thebes.

source	date	year	reign (conjectural)	remark	App. 1
stela (unnumbered)	epagomenal	4	Sobekhotep VIII		**1436**
graffito (unnumbered)	II Akhet 3	2	Merenptah	earlier inundation?	**155**
Graffito 1064	II Akhet 4		(19 Dyn.)		**157**
Graffito 881 d	II Akhet 5	22	(Ramses II)		**160**
graffito (unnumbered)	II Akhet 7	10	(Merenptah)		**168**
Graffito from Karnak	II Akhet 12	5	(18 Dyn.?)		**189**
O. DeM 436	II Akhet 12		(Ramses II)		**190**
graffito (unnumbered)	II Akhet 13	10	(Merenptah)		**193**
graffito (unnumbered)	II Akhet 17		(Ramses III)		**226**
Graffito 862	III Akhet 3	1	Merenptah		**303**
Graffito 856	III Akhet 5	7	(Merenptah)		**310**
Graffito 1158	III Akhet 5	18	(Ramses III)		**312**
Graffito 1159 B	III Akhet 9	24	(Ramses III)		**334**
Graffito 1154	III Akhet 13	18	(Ramses III)	ritual for two different forms of Amun	**353**
O. Cairo 25801	III Akhet 20	4	(Ramesside)		**378**
Graffito 1160	III Akhet 23		(20 Dyn.)		**392**
Graffito Luxor	I Peret 2	3	Osorkon III		**594**
Graffito MH 311	II Shemu 30	2	Ptolemaic	*pꜣ nw* 'inundation'	**1168**
Graffito MH 312	II Shemu 30	5	Ptolemaic	Thissen (1989) dates to 245–242 BC in the reign of Ptolemy III.	**1169**
Graffito MH 308	III Shemu 9	1	Ptolemaic		**1221**

Table 3. Estimated seasonal cycle at Thebes in 1300–1299 BC (corresponding to –1299–1298 astronomical).

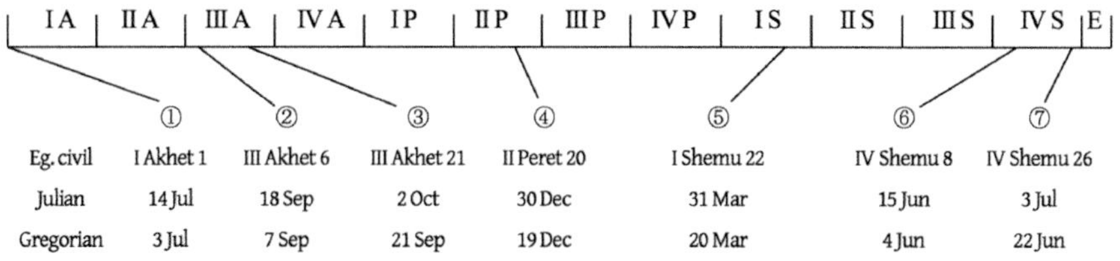

① heliacal rising of Sothis; ② maximum level of the Nile; ③ autumnal equinox; ④ winter solstice;
⑤ vernal equinox (harvest in March); ⑥ minimum level of the Nile; ⑦ summer solstice.

Table 4. Presence of the vizier Neferrenpet and the royal butler Sethherwenemyef at Thebes in year 6 of Ramses IV (E=East Bank, W=West Bank).

	I A 9	I A 10	I A 12	II A 7	II A 19	III A 15	IV A 21	I P 19
Appendix 1	**59**	**59**	**68**	**169**	**238**	**359**	**490**	**651**
Neferrenpet	E	W	W					message
Sethherwenemyef	E		W	W	message from E?		departure from E?	
Opet Feast (R III)					start	end		

Table 5. Visits to Thebes of the royal butler Sethherwenemyef.

source	reign	year	date	remark	Appendix 1
P. Turin 1891	R IV	2	III Akhet 28		**404**
O. Cairo 25565	R IV	5	III Akhet 21	reward to the workmen at DeM	**383**
Graffito 790	R IV	6	I Akhet 9	arrival at Thebes with the vizier Neferrenpet	**59**
O. Cairo 25274	R IV	6	I Akhet 12	visit to W. Thebes with the vizier Neferrenpet	**68**
O. Berlin 9906	R IV	6	I Akhet 15	mustering the workmen	**79**
Graffito 2056	R IV	6	II Akhet 7	visit to W. Thebes	**169**
O. Cairo 25277	R IV	6	II Akhet 19	message from him to have two wooden chests brought out	**238**
O. Cairo 25283	R IV	6	IV Akhet 21	return to the north	**490**
P. Turin 2002	R V	1	II Shemu 7	preparation for R IV's burial	**1085**

Table 6. Visits to Thebes of the vizier Ta in the reign of Ramses III (unnamed vizier in brackets).

source	year	date	remark	Appendix 1
O. DeM 10045	16	III Akhet 7	appointment of a workman	**328**
Graffiti 1111, 1140A–43	16	III Akhet	accompanied by the scribe Amennakht	**424**
Graffiti 524+525+2538	18	II Akhet 14		**201**
Graffito 508	18	III Akhet 3		**304**
Graffiti 245+247	21	I Peret 3		**599**
O. Turin 57047	22	III Akhet 25		**399**
(O. Turin 57055)	(24)	(I Shemu 19)		**1010**
(O. Turin 57153 recto)	(26)	(IV Peret 26)		**938**
(O. DeM 427)	(28)	(I Akhet 5)		**47**
P. Turin 1880	29	III Peret 28		**864**
Graffito Carter 1450	32	III Shemu 3		**1203**
(O. Turin 57032)	(unknown)	(II Akhet 13)		**192**
O. Ashmolean 192	unknown	III Akhet 11		**348**
O. DeM 148	unknown	III Akhet 18–30		**367**
Graffito 1928	unknown	IV Shemu 14		**1344**

Table 7. Visits to Thebes of viziers (v), the overseers of the treasury (t), and royal butlers (b).*

	I A	II A	III A	IV A	I P	II P	III P	IV P	I S	II S	III S	IV S	E
1	4[v] 14[b] 15[v] 16[v]												1414[v]
2													1414[v]
3			304[v]		599[v]						1203[v] 1204[v]		
4													
5	47[v]		311[v]									1327[v]	
6	49[v]		319[b] 322[v]									1327[v]	
7		169[b]	328[v]	456[v]						1085[v]		1327[v]	
8					621[v]							1327[v]	
9	59[v]									1092[v]		1327[v]	
10	59[v]			462[v] 463[v]	626[v]						1226[v]	1327[v]	
11			346[t] 348[v]										
12	68[v]	184–6[v] 188[v]								1100[v]			
13		192[v]								1100[v]		1342[v]	
14		198[t] 201[v]	356[v]									1342[v] 1344[v]	
15	79[b]	214[v]										1342[v] 1345[v]	
16	85[b]	221[v]								1116–7[v]	1249–50[v]	1342[v]	
17		227[v]				732[t]				1117[v]		1342[v]	
18		230[v] 234[b]	367[v]	478[v]			835[v]			1117[v]		1342[v]	
19		238[b]	367[v] 370[t] 372[v]	485[v]					1010[v] 1013[v]	1117[v]		1342[v] 1358[v] 1359[v]	
20		246[v]	367[v]							1117[v]		1342[v]	
21			367[v] 382[v] 383[b] 384[v]	490[b]		747[v]	845[v]			1117[v]			
22			367[v]	496[v]		761[v]				1117[v]			
23		251[v]	367[v] 390[v]				850[v]			1117[v] 1144[b]			
24			367[v] 396[v]	507[b]						1117[v]			
25			367[v] 399[v]							1149[v]		1377[v]	
26			367[v]					938[v] 939[v]	1037[v]				
27			367[v]										
28			367[v] 404[v]				864[v]						
29			367[v] 411[b]								1289[t]		
30			367[v] 416[v]										

*When a vizier is accompanied by an overseer of the treasury or royal butlers, only the vizier's presence is counted in this table.

Table 8. Dates of the *šsp-itrw*, Mentu Feast, and *ḫnp-šꜥ*.

a. *šsp-itrw*.

source	date	year	reign	provenance	Appendix 1
P. Cairo 86637	I Akhet 7	–	R II/III	–	**50**
Solar temple of Niuserre	[III Akhet]	–	Niuserre	Abu Sir	**420**
P. UC 32191 recto	III Akhet	35	Amenemhat III	Lahun	**421**
P. Berlin 10079 recto	III Akhet 25	–	MK	Lahun	**397**
P. Berlin 10166 verso	III Akhet 25	–	MK	Lahun	**397**
P. Berlin 10282 recto	IV Akhet [3]	–	MK	Lahun	**445**
P. Berlin 10282 recto	IV [Akhet]	–	MK	Lahun	**557**
P. Berlin 10130 B c recto	IV Akhet 11	–	MK	Lahun	**465**
P. Berlin 10344 b recto	[IV] Akhet 14	–	MK	Lahun	**471**
P. Berlin 10001 B verso[1]	before Sokar F.	–	MK	Lahun	–
P. Berlin 10064 AB recto[2]	before *stp-nṯr* & Sokar F.	–	MK	Lahun	–

b. Mentu Festival.

source	date	year	reign	provenance	remark	App. 1
P. Berlin 10282 recto	II Akhet 14	–	MK	Lahun	*ḫnp-šꜥ* (2nd lunar day)	**197**
P. Berlin 10130 B c recto	II Akhet 22	–	MK	Lahun	*ḫnp-šꜥ*	**249**
P. Boulaq 18 (S)	II Akhet 26–8	3	13 Dyn.	Thebes		**268**
P. Boulaq 18 (L)	III Akhet 17–8	3	13 Dyn.	Thebes		**361**

c. *ḫnp-šꜥ*.

source	date	year	reign	provenance	remark	App. 1
P. Berlin 10079 recto	II Akhet 6	–	MK	Lahun		**163**
P. Berlin 10018 recto	II Akhet 6	–	MK	Lahun	followed by the *mnḫ.t*	**164**
P. Berlin 10282 recto	II Akhet 14	–	MK	Lahun	Mentu Feast (2nd lunar day)	**197**
unnumbered stone fragment	II Akhet 16	–	A I	Karnak		**218**
P. Berlin 10248 recto	II Akhet 18	14	MK	Lahun	2nd lunar day, followed by the *mnḫ.t* two days later	**229**
P. Berlin 10130 B c recto	II Akhet 22	–	MK	Lahun	Mentu Feast	**249**
P. Berlin 10399 b recto	II Akhet	–	MK	Lahun		**282**
P. UC 32191[3]	–	–	MK	Lahun	followed by the *mnḫ.t*	–
P. Berlin 10001 B verso[4]	[II Akhet]	–	MK	Lahun	2nd lunar day	**281**

[1] Luft 1992, 26–30.
[2] Luft 1992, 78–81.
[3] Collier and Quirke 2006, 94.
[4] Luft 1992, 27.

Table 9. Dates of the Opet Festival during the New Kingdom and later.

reign	Dyn.	year	beginning	in progress	ending	duration	remark	Appendix 1
T III	18	23	II Akhet 14				new moon day	**199**
T III	18		II Akhet 15		II Akhet 25	11	Elephantine calendar	**213**
R II	19	1			before III Akhet 23		king's return to the north after the Opet Feast	**389**
R II	19	23		II Shemu 22			scribal error for the Valley Feast?	**1140**
Seti II	19	1	after II Akhet 10				king's visit to Thebes	**178**
R III	20	early	II Akhet 19		III Akhet 12	24	Medinet Habu calendar (eve on II Akhet 18)	**236**
R III	20	late	II Akhet 19		III Akhet 15	27	P. Harris I	**237**
R III	20	29		II Akhet 23			appointment of the vizier Ta	**251**
R IV	20	2		III Akhet 1			oracular session	**291**
R IV	20	2		III Akhet 11			workmen at DeM received offerings of the Opet Feast	**349**
R VI	20	3	II Akhet 18				oracular session (I Akhet 18 in the original text)	**234**
R VI	20	7		III Akhet 8			oracular session	**331**
R IX	20	15	after II Akhet 14				river-procession of Amun-Re	**203**
Ramesside	19/20		II Akhet 14				P. Sallier IV ('feast when Horus was enthroned')	**205**
unknown	late 20		II Akhet 19				dedication/preparation of oxen for Amun	**239**
Pinedjem I	21	11	after II Akhet 13				Pinedjem I's visit to West Thebes	**194**
Pinedjem II	21	2?	II Akhet 23?	III Akhet 6?			oracular session at Karnak	**321**
Pinedjem II	21	5		II Akhet 27?			appearance of the Theban Triad at Luxor	**272**
Takelot II	23	14		III Akhet 6			vizier Hori entered Karnak	**322**
Piankhi	25	4	on/after II Akhet 14				Piankhi's travel to the north?	**207**
Piankhi	25	21?			III Akhet 2		Amun returns to Karnak	**300**
Psametik I	26	9	II Akhet 14 or later?				divine wife Nitocris was appointed at Thebes	**206**
Irike-Amannote	5 BC	2	II Akhet 30		III Akhet 23	24	appearance of Amun at Kawa	**279**
Ptolemy VI	Ptol.		II Akhet 2		III Akhet 1	30	Kom Ombo calendar ('Entering His Town')	**152**
Ptolemy X	Ptol.		II Akhet 19		III Akhet 3	15	Edfu calendar ('Appearance of Hathor')	**240**
Augustus/Nero?	Roman		II Akhet 19				Book of Traversing Eternity (P. Leiden T 32)	**241**
unknown	Roman		II Akhet 19				P. Boulaq III, 3, 22	**243**
unknown	Roman		II Akhet 19				Esna calendar ('Opet Feast')	**242**
Christian period			II Akhet 13				Triadon	**196**

Table 10. Entries for the Opet Festival in the Medinet Habu calendar.

18 (0) **eve**	bread 295 beer 25 *kꜣ*-cattle 1 living *r*-goose 1 ꜥ*šꜣ*-goose 5 wine 1
19 (1)	bread 355 beer 20 *iwꜣ*-cattle 1 slaughtered *r*-goose 1 ꜥ*šꜣ*-goose 5 wine 1
20 (2)	bread 375 beer 20 slaughtered *r*-goose 1 ꜥ*šꜣ*-goose 5 wine 1
21 (3)	bread 375 beer 20 *wnḏw*-cattle 1 ꜥ*šꜣ*-goose 5 wine 1
22 (4)	bread 375 beer 20 living *r*-goose 1 ꜥ*šꜣ*-goose 5 wine 1
23 (5)	bread 225 beer 6 *kꜣ*-cattle 1 ꜥ*šꜣ*-goose 5 wine 1
24 (6)	living *r*-goose 1, (bread 225/d hereafter?)
25 (7)	*rnn-iwꜣ*-cattle 1
26 (8)	living *r*-goose 1
clothing	bread 190, beer 25, living *r*-goose 1, ꜥ*šꜣ*-goose 5, wine 1
27 (9)	*kꜣ*-cattle 1, (beer 1?)
28 (10)	living *r*-goose 1, (beer 1, wine 1?)
29 (11)	*kꜣ*-cattle 1, (beer 1?)
30 (12)	living *r*-goose 1, (beer 1, wine 1?)
1 (13)	*kꜣ*-cattle 1, (beer 1?)
2 (14)	living *r*-goose 1, (beer 1?)
3 (15)	*kꜣ*-cattle 1, (beer 1?)
4 (16)	living *r*-goose 1, (beer 1, wine 1?)
5 (17)	*kꜣ*-cattle 1, (beer 1?)
6 (18)	living *r*-goose 1, (beer 1, wine 1?)
7 (19)	*kꜣ*-cattle 1, (beer 1?)
8 (20)	living *r*-goose 1, (beer 1, wine 1?)
9 (21)	*kꜣ*-cattle 1, (beer 1?)
10 (22)	living *r*-goose 1, (beer 1, wine 1?)
11 (23)	*kꜣ*-cattle 1, slaughtered *r*-goose 1, good wine 1
12 (*nṯr*) *s*ꜥ*ḳ n Ỉmn* **'Amun's entrance'**	*iwꜣ*-cattle 1, slaughtered *r*-goose 1, (good wine 1?)
total:	bread 6505, beer 150, *iwꜣ*-cattle 2, *rnn-iwꜣ*-cattle 1, *wnḏw*-cattle 1, *kꜣ*-cattle 10, slaughtered *r*-goose 4, living *r*-goose 12, ꜥ*šꜣ*-goose 35, good wine 2, wine 13

Table 11. Dates of the Valley Festival: activities at western Thebes.

source	date	year	reign [conjectured or debated]	event	remark	Appendix 1
O. Turin 57034	II Shemu 12	22	R III (Lopez 1978; Helck 2002; Krauss 1985, 145)	river procession (*pꜣ ḏꜣy*)		**1099**
Graffito DB 32	II Shemu 20	3	[R VI] (Krauss 2006b, 416) [Merenptah] (Dolińska 2007)	Amun's stay at R II's memorial temple		**1133**
Graffito DB 31	II Shemu 22	22	[R XI] (Krauss 2006b, 416) [R II] (Dolińska 2007) [R III] (*KRI* V, 417–8; Peden 2001, 122, n. 392)	*ḥb nfr n in.t*	offering to Hathor	**1141**
O. Cairo 25538	II Shemu 25	6	Seti II	Amun's river procession (*ḏꜣy n Ỉmn r niw.t*)		**1149**
O. Gardiner 11	II Shemu 25	2	[R V] (*KRI* VI, 249; Krauss 1985, 145) [R VI] (Helck 2002)	Amun's river procession (*ḏꜣy Ỉmn*)	work free day	**1150**
Graffito DB 3	II Shemu 28	7	[Tausret] (Peden 2001, 107, n. 292; Krauss 2006, 416)	Amun's stay at Tausret's memorial temple		**1160**
O. Turin 57044	II Shemu 28	26	R III (Lopez 1978; *KRI* V, 510; Helck 2002; Krauss 1985, 145)	night of the river procession (*ḫꜣ pꜣ ḏꜣy*)	work free day	**1161**
O. DeM 354	III Shemu 1	11	[R II] (*KRI* III, 508; Helck 2002)	Festival of Amenopet		**1184**
Graffito DB 9	III Shemu 9	6	[Siptah] (Krauss 2006b, 416) R IV (*KRI* VI, 102; Peden 2001, 122, n. 395) [R VII] (Dolińska 2007, 70)	Amun's stay at R IV's memorial temple?		**1217**
Graffito DB 10	III Shemu 9	7	[R III] (Peden 2001, 121, n. 388; Krauss 2006, 416)	Amun's stay at R III's memorial temple?		**1218**
O. Cairo 25794	III Shemu 25	4	[Siptah] (*KRI* IV, 361; Helck 2002; Krauss 1985, 148) [R III] (Janssen 1997, 155, n. 49)	Amun's river procession?	Emended to II Shemu by Helck (1964, 159) to be related to the Valley Feast.	**1273**
O. Cairo 25265	IV Shemu 1	5	[R IV] (Gutgesell 1983, vol. 2, 423–5; Krauss 1985, 145)	*ḏꜣy r imn.tt niw.t in Ỉmn-rꜥ* and *wꜣḥ-mw*	Emended to II Shemu by Černý (Notebook), Krauss (1985, 146), and McDowell (1999, 96–7) to be related to the Valley Feast.	**1311**
	IV Shemu 10			*ḏꜣy r niw.t in pꜣ nṯr*		**1337**

Table 12. Dates of the Wag Festival falling in the Shemu season.

source	date	year	reign	provenance	remark	Appendix 1
P. Berlin 10007	II Shemu 1	–	–	Lahun		**1066**
P. Berlin 10016	II Shemu 17	18	–	Lahun	'the second of the full moon'	**1121**
P. Berlin 10165	II Shemu 22	–	–	Lahun	close to the full moon	**1139**
P. Cairo 58065	II Shemu 29	9	–	Lahun		**1165**
P. Berlin 10419 a	III Shemu	38	–	Lahun		**1299**

Table 13. Dates of graffiti on the roof of the Khonsu temple, Karnak.

no.*	date	year	reign [conjectural]
100	I Akhet 20	6	[Sheshonq IV]
8	II Akhet 2	1?	[Osorkon II]
245 A	II Shemu 2	9	[Iuput]
101	II Shemu 2	1	[Osorkon III]
145	II Shemu 26	4	[Sheshonq III]
146	III Shemu 10	5	Iny
44	III Shemu 11 (or 2)	2	–
43	III Shemu 20	1?	–
135	III Shemu	10	–
244	III Shemu	9	Iuput I
147	III [ ]	2	–
190	IV Shemu 22	14	[Osorkon III]

*Numbering based on Jacquet-Gordon 2004.

Table 14. Dates of the *w3ḥ-mw* performed at western Thebes.

source	date	year	reign [conjectural]	provenance	remark	Appendix 1
O. Cairo 25779 recto	II Akhet 12	1	[Amenmes]	KV		**183**
O. Cairo 25779 verso	III Akhet 17	1	[Amenmes]	KV		**362**
O. BM 5634	I Peret 24–5	40	R II	–	performed by three different families	**670**
O. Cairo 25786	III Peret 28	–	[Amenmes]	KV		**863**
O. BM 50744	IV Peret 26	5	R IV	–	performed by the vizier Neferrenpet	**939**
O. BM 5634	II Shemu 8	40	R II	–		**1087**
O. Turin 57034	II Shemu 8	22	R III	QV		**1088**
P. Geneva MAH 15274+P. Turin 54063	III Shemu 16	6	[R IV]	–	performed for kings	**1248**
O. Cairo 25290	III Shemu 16	6	R IV	KV	performed by the vizier Neferrenpet for a goddess	**1249**
O. Cairo 25784	III Shemu 21	4	[Amenmes]	KV		**1265**
O. Cairo 25265	IV Shemu 1	5	[R IV]	KV	performed by Amun-Re for kings	**1311**

Table 15. Dates of graffiti at Thutmose III's valley temple at Deir el-Bahari.

no.*	date	year	reign [conjectural]	remark
65	II Akhet 10	2	Ramesside	petition to a deity
119	II Akhet 14	23	[R III]	petition to a deity
79	III Akhet 20	10	Ramesside	offering to Hathor
17	IV Akhet 1	32	R II	Sed Feast; offering to Amun and Hathor
63	IV Akhet 1	–	Ramesside	petition to Hathor
114	IV Akhet 1	–	Ramesside	visit to Hathor
58	[IV] Akhet 1	–	Ramesside	petition to Hathor
7	IV Akhet [1?]	20	Ramesside	following Khonsu
1	IV Akhet 4	20	[R II/III]	offering to Hathor
23 & 24	IV Akhet 23	18	[R III]	petition to Hathor
67	III Peret 10	8	Ramesside	curse for those who obliterate the text
96	III Peret 13	2	[R IV]	context unknown
39	IV Peret 16	6	Ramesside	petition to Hathor
105	II Shemu 10	8	Ramesside	context unknown
29	II Shemu 16	7	[R VI]	petition to Hathor
70	II Shemu 18	3	Ramesside	petition to a deity
28	II Shemu 19	4	Ramesside	petition to Hathor
60	II Shemu 20	1	Ramesside	petition to a deity
32	II Shemu 20	3	[R IV/Merenptah]	Amun at R II's memorial temple
31	II Shemu 22	22	[R II/III/XI]	Valley Festival
3	II Shemu 28	7	[Tausret]	Amun at Tausret's memorial temple
125	II Shemu [ ]	–	Ramesside	Hathor
36	III Shemu 1	21	[R III]	petition to Hathor
9	III Shemu 9	6	[Siptah/R IV]	Amun at R IV(?)'s memorial temple
10	III Shemu 9	7	[R III]	Amun at R III(?)'s memorial temple
71	III Shemu 3	2	Ramesside	offering to Hathor
2	[ ] Shemu 4	1	[R V][1]	petition to Amun-Re and Hathor
4	II [ ] 23	2	[R VI][2]	offering to Hathor
134	II [ ]	–	Ramesside	Theban triad; offering to Hathor

* Numbering based on Marciniak 1974, 41–2, Table 1.

[1] *KRI* VI, 235: 15; Peden 2001, 122, n. 396; Ullmann 2002, 531.
[2] *KRI* VI, 361: 15; Peden 2001, 122, n. 397.

Table 16. Offerings from various Theban temples.*

no.	reign	source	textual references (examples not explicitly associated with the Valley Feast are indicated in brackets)
1	Hatshepsut	Deir el-Bahari[1]	Amun rested at *ẖnm.t-ꜥnḫ* at the Valley Feast
2	later years of T III	TT 84 (7, 10, and 14)[2]	(7 and 14) (bouquet of Amun of Thutmose I from *ẖnm.t-ꜥnḫ*); (10) (every thing on the altar of Amun when he rests at *ḥnḳ.t-ꜥnḫ*)
3	later years of T III	TT 343 (11 and 13)[3]	(every thing on the altar of Amun-Re when he rests at *ḥnḳ.t-ꜥnḫ*)
4	T III–A II	TT 79 (8)[4]	(Amun's bouquet from *ḥnḳ.t-ꜥnḫ*)
5	T III–A II	TT 86 (1)[5]	Userhat barge being navigated towards *ḏsr-ꜣḫ.t*; sistrum and menit of Amun from *ḏsr-ꜣḫ*.t; bouquet of Amun from *ḥnḳ.t-ꜥnḫ*; bouquet of Amun from *ḏsr-ꜣḫ.t*; bouquet from [ ]*-s.t*)
6	T III–A II	TT 112 (3)[6]	(Amun's bouquet when he rests at *ḥnḳ.t-ꜥnḫ*; Amun's sistra and menits from *ḏsr-ḏsr.w*)
7	T III–A II	TT 129 (1)[7]	offerings of Amun-Re when he rests at *ḥnḳt-ꜥnḫ*
8	T III–T IV	TT 56 (4 and 5)[8]	(4) (when he rests at *ḥnḳ.t-ꜥnḫ*); (5) when he (Amun-Re) rests at *ꜥb-ꜣḫ.t*
9	T III–T IV	TT 74 (3)[9]	bouquets of Amun-Re, Mut, Amun of Karnak, and Khonsu
10	A II	TT 17 (2 and 5)[10]	(2) (Amun's bouquet when he rests at his western horizon) (5) (every thing on the altar of Amun when he rests at *ḏsr-ꜣḫ.t*)
11	A II	TT 95 (A, c)[11]	(offerings from the altar of Amun of *ꜥb-ꜣḫ.t*)
12	A II–T IV	TT 75 (7)[12]	(in the morning to see Amun when he appears from *ḏsr-ḏsr.w*)
13	A II–T IV	TT 98 (1)[13]	(Amun's bouquet when the god rests at His Beautiful Festival to the West)
14	T IV	TT 38 (6)[14]	(Amun's bouquet from *ḏsr-ḏsr.w*)
15	Tutankhamen–Horemheb	TT 49 (3; 9; 23; C, c)[15]	(3) offerings from *ḥnḳ.t-ꜥnḫ*; (9) (to see Amun-Re when he is at *ḥnḳ.t-ꜥnḫ*); (23) things coming from *ẖnm.t-ꜥnḫ*; (C, c) to see Amun resting at *ẖnm.t-ꜥnḫ*
16	R I–R II	TT 19 (3–4)[16]	*ḥnḳ.t-ꜥnḫ*
17	S I–R II	TT 106 (D, d)[17]	when you visit the West *ḥft-ḥr-nb=s*
18	R II (first half)	TT 263 (7)[18]	(he (Amun) goes to *ḏsr.w*)
19	R II	TT 217 (3)[19]	(bouquets from the temple of Amun at Karnak)
20	Merenptah/RVI	Graffito DB 32[20]	Amun stayed at Ramses II's memorial temple
21	Tausret?	Graffito DB 3	Amun stayed at Tausret's memorial temple
22	R III?	Graffito DB 10	Amun stayed at Ramses III's(?) memorial temple
23	R IV	Graffito DB 9	Amun stayed at Ramses IV's(?) memorial temple

**ẖnm.t-ꜥnḫ* (memorial temple of Thutmose I); *ḏsr-ḏsr.w* (valley temple of Hatshepsut at Deir el-Bahari); *ḏsr-ꜣḫ.t* (valley temple of Thutmose III at Deir el-Bahari); *ḥnḳ.t-ꜥnḫ* (memorial temple of Thutmose III); *ꜥb-ꜣḫ.t* (memorial temple of Amenhotep II).

1 See 3.4.3.
2 PM I-1^2, 169–70 (7, 10, and 14); *Urk.* IV, 136: 14 and 955: 4, 8.
3 PM I-1^2, 412 (11 and 13); Schott 1953, 122; Guksch 1979, 29 and 34.
4 PM I-1^2, 157 (8); Schott 1953, 118; Guksch 1995, 158, pl. 36.
5 PM I-1^2, 175 (1). Davies (1933b, 14, pl. 17) and Schott (1953, 118) regarded the last bouquet as coming from *ḏsr-s.t*, the Eighteenth Dynasty temple at Medinet Habu. If so, the delivery is unusual because offerings from temples close to the southern border of the Theban West is not attested elsewhere.
6 PM I-1^2, 229 (3); Davies 1933b, 21, pl. 24; Schott 1953, 118.
7 PM I-1^2, 244 (1); Schott 1953, 122.
8 PM I-1^2, 111–2 (4 left and 5); *Urk.* IV, 1479: 8–9; Beinlich-Seeber 1987, 55–6, 72, pls 1 and 8.
9 PM I-1^2, 144 (3); *Urk.* IV, 1012: 5–6.
10 PM I-1^2, 29 (2 and 5); Schott 1953, 122; Säve-Söderbergh 1957, 23, pl. 28 (2)
11 PM I-1^2, 197 (A, c); Schott 1953, 108.
12 PM I-1^2, 149 (7); *Urk.* IV, 1216: 6; Schott 1953, 109.
13 PM I-1^2, 204 (1); *Urk.* IV, 1500: 5.
14 PM I-1^2, 70 (6); *Urk.* IV, 1640: 10; Schott 1953, 118.
15 PM I-1^2, 91–4 (3, 9, 23, and C, c); Davies 1933a, pls 28, 36, 53 (c), and 55 (A); Schott 1953, 95.
16 PM I-1^2, 33 (3–4); Foucart 1928, pls 6–8, 13–4, and 16.
17 PM I-1^2, 223 (D, d).
18 PM I-1^2, 345 (7).
19 PM I-1^2, 316 (3); *KRI* III, 663: 3; Davies 1927, pl. 25; Schott 1953, 118–9.
20 For references to the graffiti at Deir el-Bahari, see Table 15.

Table 17. Attestations of bouquets of Amun and Amun-Re. (1/2)

TT	dedicator	title/appearance of dedicator	recipient	Amun	Amun-Re	specification	event/remark
39 (7)	man		deceased couple	○			fishing & fowling
39 (21)	son	T III's priest	-		○		
39 (22)	men		deceased couple	○		*nb=k*	
45 (8)	son?		deceased & mother?	○			
50 (2)	brother	lector-priest of Amun	deceased couple	○			
55 (7)	deceased	vizier	king	?	?	*it*; from Karnak	bouquets of the Theban triad
56 (4)	man		couple		○	when resting at *ḥnk.t-ʿnḫ*	
64 (3)	man		father of the deceased	?	?	when resting at his temple	Valley Feast
72 (5)	deceased	HPA at T III's temple	king & queen mother		○	*it*; from *ḥnk.t-ʿnḫ*	
74 (6)	deceased	royal scribe	king	?	?		
75 (3)	deceased	2PA	king	?	?	from Karnak	
76 (3)	man		deceased	?	?	when resting at his temple	
79 (8)	son	scribe at T III's temple	deceased couple	?	?	from *ḥnk.t-ʿnḫ*	offering list; musicians
80 (6)	brother?	[ ] of Amun	deceased couple		○		musicians
84 (7)	brother	4th lector at T I's temple	deceased	○		Amun-*ʿ3-ḫpr-k3-rʿ* from *ḫnm.t-ʿnḫ*	musicians
84 (14)	brother	4th lector at T I's temple	deceased couple	○		Amun-*ʿ3-ḫpr-k3-rʿ* from *ḫnm.t-ʿnḫ*	list
84 (16)	brother	4th lector at T I's temple	deceased couple	○?			inspection
85 (9)	wife	chief royal nurse	king	?	?	*it*	
85 (11)	son	child of the nursery	deceased couple	○		when son followed the king	musicians
85 (13)	man	HPA at Heriheramen	deceased	○			
85 (C, a)	deceased	lieutenant-commander of soldiers	wife		○		New Year Feast; wife suckling a prince
86 (1)	men		(destroyed)	○		from *ḥnk.t-ʿnḫ*, *ḏsr-s.t*, and *s.t-*[ ]	Userhat barge; sistra & menits from *ḏsr-3ḫ.t*
86 (8)	deceased	HPA	king		○?	from Karnak	Feast of *ḏsr-3ḫ.t*

Table 17. Attestations of bouquets of Amun and Amun-Re. (2/2)

TT	dedicator	title/appearance of dedicator	recipient	Amun	Amun-Re	specification	event/remark
88 (4)	deceased	lieutenant of the king	king		○	after a praise was made on king's behalf	
	wife	great royal nurse					
88 (6)	man	2PA	deceased couple	○			
88 (D, a)	son	wab-priest	deceased couple	?	?		
93 (23)	two sons	wab-priest of Amun	deceased couple	○		when resting at his western temple	list
93 (24)	son		deceased couple	○		when the god rests	list
96 (12)	deceased	mayor of Thebes	brother & wife	?	?		
96 (22)	grandson		deceased couple	?	?	after his praise was made at the temple	musicians
98 (1)	two daughters	singer of Amun	deceased couple	○			Feast of the West
112 (3)	man		deceased & (mother?)	○		Amun of Karnak; when resting at *ḥnk.t-ʿnḫ*	sistra & menits from *ḏsr-ḏsr.w*
130 (3)	two men		deceased couple	?	?	when resting at his temple	
139 (3)	son	wab-priest	deceased couple	○		*nb=k*	
145 (1)	man		deceased couple	?	?		
147 (14)	son?		deceased couple	?	?		funeral
161 (3)	son	gardener of the divine offerings of Amun	deceased couple	○		when he rests at his temple	
217 (3)	son & daughter	son as a sem-priest	deceased couple	○		from Karnak	
253 (3)	man		deceased couple	?	?		
253 (4)	man		deceased couple	?	?		
295 (1)	son & daughter	sem-priest	deceased couple	?	?	*nb=k*	
Stela OI 8798	man	wab-priest of Amun	deceased couple & daughter	○			together with a bouquet of Hathor

Table 18. Locations of private tomb scenes depicting the Festivals of the Valley and the New Year. (1/9)

reign	TT	title	Valley	New Year	Valley (with probability)	New Year (with probability)	uncertain	remark
Senusret I	60	vizier		(11) deceased inspects NY gifts including an obelisk				
T 1–Hat/T III	345	eldest prince of T I		(3 and 5) banquet at the *nḥb-k3.w*			(1) *ḥb.w nb.w* [ ] *ẖn.t=f nfr.t n.t tp rnp.t*	
Hatshepsut	73	overseer of obelisks		(2–3) NY gifts to the king, including obelisks & Opet bulls				
Hat–T III	39	2PA		(14) *ḫ3.t-rnp.t*		(23, II) five tapers	(7) *ʿnḫ n ỉmn* [ ] (21) *ʿnḫ ỉmn-rʿ* (23, I) bouquet of the lord	three chapels dedicated to the celebrations of the NY, Valley, and Osiris respectively? (12) T III's obelisks
Hat–T III	82	overseer of the viziorate office		(5) banquet at *wpy-rnp.t* (17) epag., *wpy-rnp.t*, and *nḥb-k3.w*				
Hat–T III	127	royal scribe		(5, II) epag.		(1) five tapers (16) five men with tapers (18) torch, linen, and five bottles		(13) Wag Feast (18) NY bottles?
T III	24	steward of the royal wife Nebtu					(9) *šms=i nṯr imy-niw.t=i r ḏsr.w r 3ḫ.t imnt.t pr.tw n=i ḫr ʿnḫ pn ḥtp m 3ḫ.t=f*	(9) Schott related to Valley Feast
T III	61	vizier (same as the owner of TT 131)		(7) *hrw n wpy-rnp.t*				

Table 18. Locations of private tomb scenes depicting the Festivals of the Valley and the New Year. (2/9)

reign	TT	title	Valley	New Year	Valley (with probability)	New Year (with probability)	uncertain	remark
T III	86	HPA			(1, I–II) Userhat barge at the *ẖn.t r ḏsr-ꜣḫ.t*; bouquets from some memorial temples	(8) bouquet of [Amun] from Karnak to the king (*ḥb=f n dsr-ꜣḫ.t; ẖn.t=f n.t tpy-rnp.t*)		(1, III–IV) harvest
T III	99	overseer of the seal		(A, a) *hrw n wpy-rnp.t nḥb-kꜣ.w hrw tpy-rnp.t pr.t spd.t*				(3 and 5) commission from the king
T III	131	vizier		(8–9) appointment of the vizier				
late T III	343	overseer of works			(11 and 13) offering of Amun-Re when resting at *ḥnk.t-ꜥnḫ*		(2 and 6) [*wdn n ꞽmn-rꜥ nb ns.wt tꜣ.wy*] *m ḥw.t-nṯr=f n.t imnt.t*	
late T III	84	1st royal herald				(5 and 9) king in a kiosk at *s.t-wr.t*	(7 and 14) banquets with Amun's bouquets from *ẖnm.t-ꜥnḫ* (10) offering of Amun of *ḥnk.t-ꜥnḫ*	
T III–A II	42	captain of troops					(2) *ꜥnḫ n nb=k ꞽmn*	
T III–A II	79	overseer of granary					(8) bouquet [of Amun] from *ḥnk.t-ꜥnḫ; ḫft ḥtp nṯr hr ḥ.t*	

Table 18. Locations of private tomb scenes depicting the Festivals of the Valley and the New Year. (3/9)

reign	TT	title	Valley	New Year	Valley (with probability)	New Year (with probability)	uncertain	remark
T III–A II	85	lieutenant-commander of the army; captain of Userhat barge	(D, d) menit at *ḥb=f n ḏsr-ḏsr.w*	(C, a) Amun's bouquet at *ḥb=f n wpy-rnp.t*			(9) [*ʿnḫ ꞽImn nb nsw.t tꜣ.wy ḫnty ip.t-s.wt*] (11) *ʿnḫ* [*ꞽImn*]	(9 and 17) king in a kiosk
T III–A II	96	mayor of Thebes		(6) *inḏ-ḥr n wpy-rnp.t ḥꜣ.t nḥḥ pḥ ḏt*		(25) taper and linen (39) tapers, list, sem-priest (G, c) cloth	(12) *ʿnḫ ꞽ*[*mn*] (22) *ʿnḫ n* [*ꞽImn*]	(10) harvest
T III–A II	112	HPA		(6, III) banquet on epag.	(3, I) banquet: *ʿnḫ n ꞽImn nb ns.wt tꜣ.wy ḫnty ip.t-s.wt niw.t ḫft ḥtp=f m ḥnk.t-ʿnḫ*	(3, II) banquet		
T III–A II	129	unknown	(1) [*ḥ*]*b=f n* [*i*]*n.t imnt.t*; at *ḥnk.t-ʿnḫ*					
T III–A II	172	royal butler		(9) deceased inspects NY gifts ordered by the king				(8–9) harvest
T III–T IV	56	royal scribe	(5) *ḫft ḥtp=f m ʿb-ꜣḫ.t m ḥb=f n in.t imnt.t*				(4) *ʿnḫ n ꞽImn … ḫft ḥtp=f m ḥnk.t-ʿnḫ m ḥb=f* [*n in.t imnt.t*]	(9) king in a kiosk

Table 18. Locations of private tomb scenes depicting the Festivals of the Valley and the New Year. (4/9)

reign	TT	title	Valley	New Year	Valley (with probability)	New Year (with probability)	uncertain	remark
T III–T IV	74	royal scribe	(2) *ḫn.t=f n.t imnt.t m ḥb=f nfr n [in.t]* (7) *ḫ[n.t]=f n.t imnt.t m ḥb=f [n]fr* [ ]				(1) *ḫn.t=f n.t imnt.t* (6) *ʿnḫ [n it=k ꞽImn]*	(6 and 11) king in a kiosk
A II	17	royal scribe					(2) *ḥtp=f m ʿnḫ m ꜣḫ.t=f n.t imnt.t* (5) offerings of [Amun] when he rests at *ḏsr-ꜣḫ.t*	
A II	45	steward of the HPA					(8, II) banquet with *ʿnḫ ꞽImn* and every offering of Amun from Karnak	(3, I and 7, I) ceremony of Sokar
A II	93	chief royal steward		(9) NY gifts to the king: *hrw tpy; inḏ.t-ḥr n wpy-rnp.t* (G, a) *inḏ-ḥr n nḥb-kꜣ.w*		(C, I) two tapers, linen paint	(3) *ḏꜣ.t … r imnt.t niw.t rsy.t* (16) king in a kiosk, as in (9) (23) *ʿnḫ n ꞽImn ḫft ḥtp pꜣ nṯr m ḥw.t-nṯr=f n.t imnt.t*	
A II	95	HPA					(A, c) Amun at *ʿb-ꜣḫ.t*	(B, d) NY candles? (C, b) *nṯry.t* (Sokar Feast)
A II–T IV	75	2PA	(7) *ḫft ḫʿ=f m ḏsr-ḏsr.w* in the morning			(8, II) four tapers, two candles	(3) [*ʿnḫ n ꞽImn nb ns.wt tꜣ.wy m*] *ip.t-s.wt*	(3) king in a kiosk
A II–T IV	98	3PA					(1) *ʿnḫ n ꞽImn ḫft pꜣ nṯr m ḥb=f nfr n imnt.t*	
A II–T IV	176	servant				(7, right II) two tapers, vase		

Table 18. Locations of private tomb scenes depicting the Festivals of the Valley and the New Year. (5/9)

reign	TT	title	Valley	New Year	Valley (with probability)	New Year (with probability)	uncertain	remark
T IV	38	counter of grain in the granary of Amun					(6, II) *ꜥnḫ [n ꞽImn] m ḏsr-ḏsr.w*	
T IV	76	fan-bearer on the right of the king					(3) *[ꜥnḫ n ꞽImn-rꜥ nb ns.wt tꜣ.wy] ḫft ḥtp=f m ḥw.t-nṯr=f* (B, b) *ḫn.t=f tp rnp.t m ḥb.w=f nfr n ḏsr*	(5) king in a kiosk
T IV–A III	52	astronomer of Amun				(5, I) four tapers, sem-priest		
T IV–A III	64	nurse of prince	(2) *ḫn.t n.t imnt.t [m ḥ] b=f n i[n.t]*		(3) *ꜥnḫ n ꞽImn ḫft ḥtp=f m ḥw.t-nṯr=f*		(7) *ꜥnḫ [ ] ḫft ḥtp=f [m] ḥw.t-nṯr=f*	
T IV–A III	69	scribe of the filed of the lord of the Two Lands	(1) *ḫn.t n ḏsr-ḏsr.w* (8) *ḥb=f nfr n in.t**			(7, II) sem-priest, two candles, list		
T IV–A III	90	standard-bearer of the royal barge				(7) two tapers	(3) sailing *r imnt.t; r pr ꞽImn* (continued to (4))	(4) appointment before the king (8) harvest
T IV–A III	147	head of the masters of ceremonies(?) of Amun	(2) *ḥb=k n [in.t]* (8) *ḥb=f nfr in.t m ḫn.t=f n.t imnt.t*				(14) *ꜥnḫ n [ꞽImn] pri m-bꜣḥ nb [nṯr.w]*	
T IV–A III	247	counter of the cattle of Amun	(1) *ḥb=f nfr n ḏsr.w*			(4, I) candle, cloths, Opening-of-the-Mouth		

* Only Schott's translations are available (Schott 1953, 109 (71).

Table 18. Locations of private tomb scenes depicting the Festivals of the Valley and the New Year. (6/9)

reign	TT	title	Valley	New Year	Valley (with probability)	New Year (with probability)	uncertain	remark
T IV–A III	253	counter of grain in the granary of Amun					(3) *ꜥnḫ* [*Imn*] (4) *ꜥnḫ* [*Imn*]	
T IV–A III	295	head of secrets in the chest of Anubis				(6, I) purification		
A III	89	steward in the Southern City				(13) candles, four tapers (B, a) T III in a kiosk (*s.t-wr.t*)		(15) king in a kiosk
A III	107	royal scribe		(2, I-1) *ms.wt tpy-rnp.t*				
A III	161	bearer of floral offerings of Amun					(4) *ḥb=f nfr m ḫꜥ.w=f* [ ] *wꜣ ꜥꜣ m ḫn.t=f n tpy-rnp.t*	(5, II) Wag Feast
A III	415 (C 1)	chamberlain		(1, II) *tkꜣ.w n wpy-rnp.t r di.t wꜥb*				
A III–A IV	46	overseer of the granaries of Upper and Lower Egypt		(1) *inḏ ḥr in ḥm.t=f hrw n wpy-rnp.t; msw n Rꜥ wpy-rnp.t hrw nḥb-kꜣ.w hrw tpy-rnp.t hrw pr.t spd.t*				
A III–A IV	181	head sculptor of the king				(3 sub-scene) candle, taper, sem-priest		

Table 18. Locations of private tomb scenes depicting the Festivals of the Valley and the New Year. (7/9)

reign	TT	title	Valley	New Year	Valley (with probability)	New Year (with probability)	uncertain	remark
late A III–A IV	55	vizier			(9–10, I) sistra and menits of Amun-Re	(9–10, II) Opening-of-the-Mouth and offering list	(7) bouquets of the Theban triad to the king in a kiosk	(12) rewarded by the king at a balcony
A IV	188	royal butler					(12) *ꜥnḫ n it=k* to the king in a kiosk	(3–5) harvest; (9) reward; (10) king offering
Tutankhamen–Horemheb	49	chief scribe of Amun	(3 thickness) *ḥb=f nfr n in.t; ḥnḳ.t-ꜥnḫ* (23) *ḥb=f n in.t; ẖnm.t-ꜥnḫ* (C, c) *ḥb=f n in.t; ẖnm.t-ꜥnḫ*				(3 jamb) *šms nṯr r nmt.t=f m ḥb=f n tp rnp.t* (9) Anubis, *ḥnḳ.t-ꜥnḫ*, and bouquet	(6–7) reward
Ay	271	royal scribe				(1) taper		
Horemheb	50	divine father of Amun		(9–10, I and IV) *msy grḥ* on IV Shemu 30, followed by *wpy-rnp.t*				(9–10) Feasts of Wag, Khoiak, Two Goddesses, and Bastet (2) reward
18 Dyn.	254	scribe of the treasury				(1, I) candle		
18 Dyn.	348	chief steward		(1?)				
R I–Seti I	51	HP of T I					(8, III) tapers, candles, sem-priest, and female mourners	(8, I) onions
R I–R II	19	HP of A I	(3, I) *ḥb=f nfr n in.t*		(4, I) continued from (3, I)			(7) Feast of A I

Table 18. Locations of private tomb scenes depicting the Festivals of the Valley and the New Year. (8/9)

reign	TT	title	Valley	New Year	Valley (with probability)	New Year (with probability)	uncertain	remark
Seti I–R II	106	vizier	(D, d) *ḥb=k nfr n in.t*				(H, c) *ḥb=f n tp rnp.t*	(M, b) Sokar barque; (5) reward; (8) appointment
early R II	4	chiseller of the Necropolis		(5, II) *msy* on IV Shemu 30				
early R II	263	scribe of the granary of Amun's temple					(7 left) *wḏꜣ=f r ḏsr.w m ḥb=f n tpy-rnp.t*	(3, II) *ḥb=f nfr nšm.t* (7 right) Khoiak Feast
R II	10	servants in the Necropolis				(1, II) candles (4, II) candles		
R II	189	head of the gold workers of Amun's temple			(3) deceased adoring to see Amun*			
R II	217	sculptor					(3) *ꜥnḫ pr m-bꜣḥ m hw.t-nṯr n.t ꜣImn m ip.t-s.wt*	(2, I) reward
late R II	2	servant of the Necropolis		(10, III) *msy* on IV Shemu 30				Feasts of (5) Mut; (9, I; 11, I; and 12, I) Amenhotep I; (9, II) Bastet; (9, II) Khoiak; and (10, II) Two Goddesses
late R II	31	HP of T III				(4–5 sub-scene) two candles, three tapers, and a sem-priest		(4–5) Mentu Feast
late R II	138	overseer of the garden of the Ramesseum					(8) *hrw ḥtp ꜣImn m tꜣ ḥw.t ꜥꜣ-ḫpr-kꜣ-rꜥ*	
late R II	409	counter of the cattle of Amun's temple				(6–7, II) list, candle, and sem-priest		(7, II) onions?

* Only Schott's translations are available (Schott 1953, 96 (11)).

Table 18. Locations of private tomb scenes depicting the Festivals of the Valley and the New Year. (9/9)

reign	TT	title	Valley	New Year	Valley (with probability)	New Year (with probability)	uncertain	remark
late R II–Merenptah	16	HP of A I				(5) large vases of Amun		
Merenptah	23	royal scribe		(8) [*ms*]*y*[.*t*] *n.t wpy-rnp.t*		(21, III) candle, two tapers		(31–2, I) Sokar barque; (18) reward
19 Dyn.	159	4PA					(4, II) two candles	
R III– R IV	359					(11, III) four candles, *ḥs*-vases, and a sem-priest		
after R III	9	servant of the Necropolis		(6, II) *msy* on IV Shemu [30]				(6, I) Khoiak Feast
R IX	65	head of the scribes of Amun's temple					(3–4 and 7–9) procession of the Theban triad	(11) Sokar barque
20 Dyn.	259	wab-priest				(2, I) candle (*tkA*) and libation		
20 Dyn.	277	divine father of the mansion of A III				(3, IV) candle and four (or five?) tapers		
20 Dyn.	278	herdsman of Amun-Re				(5) candle, two tapers, and sem-priest		
Psametik I	36	chief steward of divine adoratice	(23) *ḥb=f nfr n in.t*					

Table 19. Characteristics of private tomb scenes depicting the Festivals of the Valley and the New Year. (1/3)

no.	element		Valley Festival	New Year Festival	Khoiak Festival	others
1	location	thickness of doorway	36 (23); 49 (3); 69 (8)			
2		south east wall	64 (2); 74 (2); 147 (2)		148 (2)	
3		south wall	19 (3)	345 (3)		
4		south west wall	19 (4); 56 (5)	82 (5); 93 (9); 96 (6); 127 (5)		
5		north west wall		73 (3); 86 (8)		
6		north wall		2 (10); 4 (5); 9 (6); 73 (2)	9 (6)	
7		north east wall	147 (8)	112 (6); 131 (8–9); 345 (5)		
8		pillar (north)	49 (C, c)	85 (C, a); 93 (G, d)		
9		pillar (south)	106 (D, d)	99 (A, a)		
10		inner room		39 (14); 50 (9–10); 61 (7); 82 (17); 172 (9)	50 (9–10)	
11	topographical term	*ꜥḥ wr*		73 (3); 93 (9)		
12		*ḥw.t ꜥꜣ*				
13		*imnt.t*	56 (5); 64 (2); 74 (2 and 7); 106 (D, d); 129 (1); 147 (2 and 8)			
14		*s.t wr.t/imy wr.t*		131 (8–9)		
15		*ḏsr-ḏsr.w* or *ḏsr*				
16	temporal term	*m-ḫt ir.t ḥssw.t*		86 (8)		
17		*ḥꜣ.t-rnp.t*		39 (14)		
18		*ḫft ḥtp=f, ḫft ḫꜥ=f, ẖnm=f*	49 (C, c); 56 (5); 106 (D, d); 129 (1)			
19		*ẖr.t hrw n.t rꜥ nb*				
20		*sp tpy*		93 (9); 415 (1)		
21		*tpy-rnp.t*		46 (1); 99 (A, a)	2 (9)	
22		*dwꜣ.t* (morning)	129 (1)	9 (6); 50 (9–10)	50 (9–10)	
23	offering items	beer		99 (A, a)		
24		bouquet (of Amun)	49 (C, c)	85 (C, a)		
25		boxes of coloured cloths			23 (31–2); 41 (16); 157 (6)	
26		bull (brought)		60 (11); 73 (3); 82 (5 and 17)		
27		bull (slaughtered)	74 (2)			
28		bull (fighting)		82 (5)		

Table 19. Characteristics of private tomb scenes depicting the Festivals of the Valley and the New Year. (2/3)

no.	element		Valley Festival	New Year Festival	Khoiak Festival	others
29		candles/tapers		9 (6); 23 (8); 50 (9–10); 82 (17); 112 (6); 127 (5); 415 (1)		
30		cloth (pure linen *wꜥb* or *wnḫw*)	49 (3); 106 (D, d)	50 (9–10); 60 (11); 61 (7); 112 (6); 127 (5); 345 (3); 415 (1)		
31		eye paint		112 (6)		
32		menit				
33		New Year gifts to the king		73 (3); 86 (8); 93 (9); 96 (6)		
34		New Year gifts to the deceased		39 (14); 61 (7); 82 (5 and 17); 99 (A, a); 107 (2); 112 (6); 127 (5); 345 (5)		
35	offering items	New Year gifts inspected		60 (11); 172 (9)		
36		obelisk		60 (11); 73 (2)		
37		offering list		82 (17); 107 (2); 112 (6); 415 (1)	158 (3)	
38		offering bringers	56 (5); 74 (2); 147 (2)	82 (5 and 17); 415 (1)		
39		offerings on braziers	64 (2); 74 (2); 147 (2 and 8)			
40		oil (*ꜥḏ/ꜥntyw/wrḥ/mḏ.t/nwd/ḥknw*)	64 (2); 147 (2)	2 (10); 4 (5); 9 (6); 23 (8, II); 39 (14); 46 (1); 50 (9–10); 60 (11); 61 (7); 82 (17); 93 (G, d); 99 (A, a); 112 (6); 345 (3)		
41		onions			9 (6); 50 (9–10)	
42		sistrum				
43		vase		23 (8); 50 (9–10)		
44		banquet	56 (5); 74 (2); 129 (1); 147 (8)	82 (5 and 17)		
45		-ancestors as offering recipients				
46		-evening meal (*msy*)		2 (10); 4 (5); 9 (6); 23 (8); 50 (9–10); 82 (5); 107 (2); 112 (6)		
47	iconography	-guests seated on the ground	56 (5); 74 (2)	82 (17); 345 (5)		
48		-servicing figures	56 (5)			
49		carpenters		172 (9)		
50		female as main offering bringer	56 (5); 129 (1)	4 (5); 46 (1); 61 (7); 93 (G, d); 99 (A, a); 345 (3 and 5)		
51		foreigners		86 (8)		

Table 19. Characteristics of private tomb scenes depicting the Festivals of the Valley and the New Year. (3/3)

no.	element		Valley Festival	New Year Festival	Khoiak Festival	others
52	iconography (continued)	Heliopolitan gods		23 (8); 112 (6)		
53		king in a kiosk (*ḫ*ʿ*.t-nsw.t*)		73 (3); 86 (8); 93 (9); 96 (6); 131 (8)		
54		lector-priests		82 (17); 107 (2)		
55		musicians/singers	56 (5); 72 (2); 129 (1)	82 (5); 345 (5)	157 (6); 158 (3); 341 (9)	harvest: 39 (6)
56		Opening-of-the-Mouth ritual		23 (8); 50 (9–10); 82 (17); 107 (2); 415 (1)		
57		Osiris/Ptah/Sokar (incl. texts)	49 (3)			
58		priest in a panther skin		23 (8); 50 (9–10); 60 (11); 82 (5 and 17); 112 (6); 415 (1)		Feast of the Two Goddesses: 50 (9–10); Bastet Feast: 50 (9–10)
59		troops		93 (9)		
60		Userhat barge	19 (3)			
61		young prince	64 (2)	85 (C, a)		
62	phraseology	*ind ḥr* (*m33/sšp/ms*)	49 (3)	23 (8); 39 (14); 46 (1); 50 (9–10); 60 (11); 93 (9 and G, d); 96 (6); 99 (A, a); 345 (5)		Opet Feast: *Opet*, pl. 95
63		*ir hrw nfr*	49 (C, c); 56 (5); 129 (1)		50 (9–10)	
64		*bw nfr*	129 (1)	93 (9)		
65		*pr.t m dw3.t R*ʿ				
66		*m33 Ỉmn*				
67		*mskt.t*- and *m*ʿ*nḏ.t*-barque		23 (8)		
68		*ms in n wpy-rnp.t*		172 (9)		
69		*R*ʿ*/R*ʿ*-Ḥr-3ḫ.ty*	49 (3); 69 (8); 74 (2)			
70		*rnpy.t* (floral offerings)		112 (6)		
71		*rnpy* (water)		50 (9–10)	50 (9–10)	
72		*ḥtp-di-nsw.t* formula		82 (5 and 17)		
73		*iḫ.t nb.*t (*inn/wdn*)	74 (2)	82 (5)		
74		*ḫ3 pn n rnp.t*		61 (7); 99 (A, a)		
75		*sḫmḫ-ib*	129 (1)	39 (14); 73 (3); 93 (G, d)		
76		*sm3 iḫ.t nb.t*	129 (1); 74 (3)	415 (1)		harvest: 256 (2)
77		*šms nṯr*	36 (23); 49 (3 and C, c); 56 (5); 106 (D, d)		50 (3 and 9–10)	

Table 20. Occurrence of private tomb festival scenes in two registers (Ramesside tombs underlined).

1st reg. / 2nd reg.	New Year	Khoiak	Two Goddesses	Bastet	harvest	Min	Valley	inspection	funer-al	unknown
New Year	39 (22–3) 55 (9–10) 63 (13) 69 (7) 107 (2) 139 (3) 295 (3)	9 (6) 51 (8–9) 148 (2) 296 (4)	2 (10) 4 (5)	45 (8)			112 (3)	127 (5–6)		23 (8) 139 (6) 415 (1)
Khoiak										45 (7) 219 (5)
Two God-desses										
Bastet		341 (8–9)								
harvest	256 (2)									
Min		A 26								
Valley							98 (1) 295 (1)			
inspection							C4			
funeral		23 (31–2) 45 (3)		45 (2)						
unknown	145 (1) 217 (3) 259 (2)						129 (1)			

Table 21. *ḫꜥ.t-nsw.t* scenes in the Theban private tombs. (1/2)

reign	TT	wall	accompanied by	remark
Senusret I	60	3		
Hatshepsut	73	3	ka	New Year gifts
Hatshepsut	125	9		
Hat–T III	110	4 9		Thutmose III Hatshepsut
T III	86	2 8		 'His Feast of Djeser-akhet' in (8)
T III	99	3 5		royal decree to send the tomb owner to Lebanon return from Lebanon
T III	123	2		
T III	131	8–9	ka	appointment of vizier (on I Akhet 1, year 5, as attested in P. Turin 1878)
late T III	84	5 9		 *ḫꜥ.t-nsw.t* in (9)
T III–A II	42	5		
T III–A II	85	9 17		[bouquet of Amun, foremost of Karnak] from wife reward
T III–A II	88	4		bouquet of Amun
T III–A II	96	6		New Year gifts
T III–A II	100	5	ka	appointment of vizier
T III–A II	143	6		
T III–A II	200	3		two kings in kiosk (T III and A II)
T III–A II	256	3 5		Amenhotep II Thutmose III
T III–T IV	56	9		
T III–T IV	74	6 11		bouquet of [Amun]
T III–A III	78	4 8	unknown goddess unknown goddess	inspection foreigners
A II	72	5	mother queen	bouquets of [Amun from *ḥnk.t-ꜥnḫ*?]
A II	93	9 16–7	Maat	as matured king, New Year gifts at *ꜥḥ-wr* as young king, *ḫꜥ-nsw.t* and appointment
A II	101	5 7	Hathor	offering bringers, including a decorated bull
A II	367	5		bouquet
A II–T IV	43	3 4		
A II–T IV	75	3	ka	[bouquet of Amun] from Karnak; *ḫꜥ.t-nsw.t*
A II–T IV	116	2		
A II–T IV	239	2–3		
T IV	66	6		appointment of vizier
T IV	76	5	Hathor	New Year gifts?
T IV	C 6	non		
T IV–A III	63	5 10	ka in (5)	

Table 21. *ḫꜥ.t-nsw.t* scenes in the Theban private tombs. (2/2)

reign	TT	wall	accompanied by	remark
T IV–A III	64	5 8	ka ka	
T IV–A III	77	4 7		inspection at the quay of the memorial temple of T IV in (4)
T IV–A III	90	3–4 9		reward and appointment, and king's travel to the West in year 6 in (3–4)
T IV–A III	91	3 5	Hathor Hathor	
A III	47		queen	
A III	48	4 7		 New Year gifts in (7)
A III	58	5	Hathor	
A III	89	15 B, a	Hathor in (15)	 *ḫꜥ.t-nsw.t* in (B, a)
A III	120	3	queen	
A III	162	4		
A III	226	4	queen	[*s.t*]-*wr.t*
late A III	57	11 15		(11) report of harvest for 1st Sed Feast; *ḫꜥ.t-nsw.t* (15) reward ceremony in year 30
A III–A IV	55	7 13	Maat queen	bouquets of Re-Horakhety, Mut, and Khonsu reward ceremony
A III–A IV	192	5–6 7–8	Hathor and queen queen	1st Sed Feast in year 30 and reward ceremony 3rd Sed Feast in year 36
A IV	188	3 5 9 12	 queen queen	balcony kiosk kiosk; reward ceremony bouquet of Aten
Tutankhamen	40	7 8 11		 appointment of viceroy in (8)
Tut–Horemheb	49	6–7	queen	reward ceremonies
Horemheb	50	2		reward ceremony in year 3
S I–R II	106	5 B, a	Maat; souls of Pe & Nekhen	reward ceremony at West Thebes; king clad in Osiride dress
R II	157	8	queen	appointment of HPA in year 1 (after the Opet Feast)
R II	217	2, I		reward ceremony at balcony
R II	341	7	Ptah-Sokar-Osiris	
R II–S II	216	13		
Merenptah	23	18	goddess; souls of Pe & Nekhen	reward ceremony
19 Dyn.	368	3		deceased accompanied by a vizier
late 19 Dyn.	13	2–3, II	queen	
R III–R IV	222	2 3		Ramses IV Ramses III
R III–R V	148	4–5		reward ceremony in year 27 of R III
Ramesside	206	2		

Table 22. Dates of the *ihhy*.

date	year	reign	provenance	remark	Appendix 1
IV Shemu 21	year after 10th counting	Djedkare-Isesi	Abusir	*wdn.t ihy*	**1363**
I Akhet 1	35	Amenemhat III	Lahun	*wpy-rnp.t ihhy*	**2**
(I Akhet 9)	24	Middle Kingdom	Lahun	event missing in the original text	**56**
I Akhet 13	–	Amenhotep I	Karnak	*ihhy n ḥ3.t rnp.t*	**70**
I Akhet 13	–	Ptolemaic-Roman	Edfu	*hrw tpy n ihhy ḥ3.t rnp.t*	**73**
[I Akhet 1]8	–	Middle Kingdom	Lahun	*ihhy [w3]gi*	**97**
I Akhet 24+	–	Middle Kingdom	Lahun		**129**
I Akhet	–	Middle Kingdom	Lahun	new moon day	**147**
before II Akhet 6[1]	–	Middle Kingdom	Lahun	*ihhy rnpw.t rnp.t* 'rejuvenation of the year'	–
after *šsp-itrw*[2]	–	18 or early 19 Dyn.	unknown	*ihhy* [ ]	–
at Wag Feast[3]	–	18 Dyn.	unknown	*ihhy in t3.wy*	–

Table 23. Dates of *ḥ3.t nḥḥ*.

date	year	reign	provenance	remark	Appendix 1
I Akhet 1	year after 23	Thutmose III	Akh-menu, Karnak	*wpy[-rnp.t] ḥ3.t nḥḥ*	**5**
wpy-rnp.t[4]	–	Amenhotep II	TT 96	*pḥ ḏ.t*	–
–[5]	1	Seti I	Speos Artemidos	*rnp.wt ḥtp.wt*	–
I Peret 1	4	Seti I	Nauri	*rnp.wt ḥtp.wt*	**566**
III Akhet 8 (or 7)	9	Ramses II	Deir el-Medina		**330**
III Shemu	40	Ramses II	Heliopolis		**1301**
Thoth Festival[6]	–	Merenptah	Hermopolis		–

1 P. Berlin 10079 recto (Luft 1992, 86). Phraseology parallel to this is attested at the Akh-menu (PM II[2], 110 (332, 1); Barguet 1962a, 173; Pécoil 2000, pl. 82).

2 Relief BMFA 1972.651 (Simpson 1972, 77). Spalinger (1996, 65) restores as *ihhy [ḥ3.t rnp.t]*.

3 Stela Louvre C 286 (Moret 1931, 735, l. 8 for full publication; Lichtheim 1973, vol. 2, 82 for translation).

4 Tomb of Sennefer (PM I-1[2], 198 (6); *Urk.* IV, 1417: 5). *wpy-rnp.t ḥ3.t nḥḥ pḥw ḏ.t* 'opening of the year, front of eternity, ending of everlastingness'.

5 *KRI* I, 41: 10; Fairman and Grdseloff 1947, 21.

6 Dedicatory stela carved on the pylon of the temple of Thoth at Hermopolis (PM IV, 167; *KRI* IV, 29: 7; Roeder 1954, 338, pls 1–4).

Table 24. Duration of the New Year celebrations.*

	L	A	El	TT 82	TT 50	O. 209	B	Ko	E1	E2	D1	D2	Es
IV Shemu 23					↑								
IV Shemu 29					|	↑							
IV Shemu 30	↑				↓	|		↑	↑	⋮			↕
Epagomenal 1	⋮			↑	⋮	|	↑	|	⋮	⋮	⋮		
Epagomenal 2	⋮			|	⋮	|	|	|	|	⋮	⋮		
Epagomenal 3	⋮			|	⋮	|	|	|	⋮	⋮	⋮		
Epagomenal 4	⋮			|	⋮	|	|	|	|	|	⋮		
Epagomenal 5	⋮	↑		|	⋮	|	↓	|	⋮	⋮	⋮		
I Akhet 1	↓	↓	↑	↓	↓	|	↑	|	↓	↓	↓		↑
I Akhet 2			|			|	⋮	|					⋮
I Akhet 3			↓			↓	⋮	|					⋮
I Akhet 4							⋮	↓					⋮
I Akhet 5							↓						⋮
I Akhet 6							↑						⋮
I Akhet 7							|						⋮
I Akhet 8							|						⋮
I Akhet 9							↓						↓
I Akhet 10													
I Akhet 11													
I Akhet 12													
I Akhet 13										↕			
I Akhet 14													
I Akhet 15													
I Akhet 16													
I Akhet 17		↑			↑								
I Akhet 18		↓			↓					↑	↑		
I Akhet 19										|	|		
I Akhet 20										|	|	↑	
I Akhet 21										|	|	|	
I Akhet 22										↓	↓	|	
I Akhet 23												|	
I Akhet 24												|	
I Akhet 25												|	
I Akhet 26												|	
I Akhet 27												|	
I Akhet 28												|	
I Akhet 29												|	
I Akhet 30												|	
II Akhet 5												↓	

*L=P. Berlin 10007 from Lahun; A=tomb of Hepdjef at Asyut (Senusret I); El=Elephantine (Thutmose III); O. 209=O. DeM 209 (Amenmes); B=P. Brooklyn 47.218.50 (5–4 century BC); Ko=Kom Ombo (Ptolemy VI); E1=Edfu calendar for Horus (Ptolemy X); E2=Edfu calendar for Hathor (Ptolemy X); D1=Dendera calendar (Ptolemy XII); D2=Dendera outer hypostyle hall (Nero); Es=Esna calendar (Roman).

Table 25. Notable events during the reign of Thutmose III.*

year	date	event	building project
7		Hatshepsut assumes the *de facto* kingship[1]	construction of Djeser-djeseru began[2]
7–22			construction of Henqet-ankh began[3]
22	unknown	supposed Hatshepsut's death[4]	
22[5]	II Peret 10		Thutmose III's stela was erected at Armant (beginning of his sole reign?)
22	IV Peret 25	king leaves Egypt (stayed at Sile) on the 1st campaign	
23	I Shemu 21 to II Akhet 14	king returns to Thebes from the 1st campaign to celebrate feasts	
23	unknown		construction of the Userhat barge of Amun
(24)	(I Shemu 4)	(accession anniversary)	
24	I Peret?[6]	2nd campaign (king was in the country of Retenu)[7]	
24	II Peret 30		foundation ceremony taking place at the Akh-menu[8]
'year after 23'	I Shemu 2		royal decree to announce building plans and endowment, issued at West Thebes[9]
25	unknown	3rd campaign (king was in Upper Retenu, finding foreign plants to be brought back to Egypt)[10]	
after 42		proscription of Hatshepsut first attested[11]	
43–9			construction of Djeser-akhet began[12]

*Also compare with a similar table presented by Laboury (2006, 281).

[1] Dorman 2006, 49.
[2] Ćwiek 2007, 23. Brovarski (1976, 67) dated to year 3.
[3] Construction began during the coregency with Hatshepsut (Ullmann 2002, 87).
[4] See Dorman 2006, 57–8, fig. 2.4 for the date of her death on the basis of a stela from Serabit el-Khadim.
[5] *Urk.* IV, 1244: 14; Mond and Myers 1940, pl. 103. Hornung (2006, 201) relates this date to the beginning of Thutmose III's sole reign.
[6] Redford 2003, 211.
[7] Redford 2003, 55.
[8] Redford (2003, 212) assumed that the king was in Thebes.
[9] Redford 2003, 127. In this year the eldest prince Amenemhat was promoted to the position of the overseer of the cattle of Amun (*Urk.* IV, 1262: 1; der Manuelian 1987, 172). For the reading the 'year after 23' as year 24 in the archaic style, see Gardiner 1945, 16.
[10] The so-called Botanic Garden at the Akh-menu (PM II^2, 121 (407); Redford 2003, 213, n. 20).
[11] Nims 1966, 100; Dorman 2006, 58.
[12] Laskowski 2006, 208.

Table 26. The number of temple offerings and their quality value (yearly amount). (1/3)

	celebration	source	date	A. number of grain products	B. grain sacks (Haring 1997)	quality value (A/B)	(d)ḳw t-ḥḏ	t-ḥḏ	iwꜣ	rnn iwꜣ	wnḏw	kꜣ	mꜣ ḥḏ	gḥs	snṯr	linen
1	daily evening (addition in year 4)	MHC, list 1		1,225,305	24,911 ¼+	49.19–	6205+	147,460							7300 sacks + 1460 deben	
2	daily morning (addition in year 4)	MHC, list 2		43,435	182½	238.00		6570							1095 sacks	
3	daily	MHC, list 6		811,030+	11,140	72.80+	7300	14,600							2190 sacks	
4	daily (royal standard)	MHC, list 16		unspecified	91¼			2920							73 deben	
5	New Moon Festival	MHC, list 9		3840	60	64.00	48	48	12						120 sacks + 24 deben	
6	2nd Moon Festival	MHC, list 10		1200	12	100.00	48									
7	6th Moon Festival	MHC, list 12		4212	60	70.20	[48]	[48]			12	12			144 sacks	
8	Full Moon Festival	MHC, list 14		960	12	80.00	48									
9	30th Moon Festival	MHC, list 8		996	12	83.00	48									
10	Rising of Sothis	MHC, list 23	I Akhet 1	112	1½	74.67	4	20				1			2 sacks	
11	Wag Festival	MHC, lists 24–5	I Akhet 17–8	580	20	29.00	10					2			7 sacks	
12	Thoth Festival	MHC, list 26	I Akhet 19	160	5	32.00	5	65				1			2 sacks	
13	Victory over the Meshwesh	MHC, lists 53–5	I Akhet 28	1933+	69	28.01+	50	510	1	1	1	5			20 sacks + 6 deben	
14	Opet Festival	MHC, lists 28–38	II Akhet 19–III Akhet 12	11,341	316¼	35.86	146	3835	2	1	1	10			135 sacks	

Table 26. The number of temple offerings and their quality value (yearly amount). (2/3)

	celebration	source	date	A. number of grain products	B. grain sacks (Haring 1997)	quality value (A/B)	*(d)ḳw t-ḥḏ*	*t-ḥḏ*	*iwꜣ*	*rnn iwꜣ*	*wnḏw*	*kꜣ*	*mꜣ ḥḏ*	*gḥs*	*snṯr*	linen
15	drinking party at the Opet Feast	MHC, list 37	every day during the feast	2400	72	33.33										
16	Sokar Festival	MHC, lists 41–52	IV Akhet 20–I Peret 1	11,534+	239¾+	48.11	540	1712	1		1	5	1	1	110 sacks + 20 deben	lost
17	Writing King's Name on the *išd*-Tree	MHC, list 56	I Peret 6	640	25	25.60	20	450			1	1			10 sacks	
18	Lifting-Up the Sky	MHC, list 60	II Peret 28–III Peret 1	1150	126¾	9.07	8	320	1	1		1			5 sacks	
19	Chewing the Onions	MHC, list 62	IV Peret 4	320	12½	25.60	10	225							5 sacks	
20	Renenutet Festival	MHC, list 64	I Shemu 1	293	10	29.30	5					1			10 sacks	
21	Min Festival	MHC, list 66	I Shemu 11	299	6¼	47.84	30	20							5 sacks	
22	Accession anniversary	MHC, lists 19–21	I Shemu 26	4860+	46	105.65+	212	434	2	2					27 sacks	
23	drinking party at the accession anniversary	MHC, list 22		3000	70½	42.55										
24	Festival of I Shemu	MHC, list 67	I Shemu	256	50	5.12	8	180		1		2	1	1	5 sacks	
25	Valley Festival	MHC, lists 3–4	II Shemu	1150	21	54.76	8									
26	yearly (or monthly?) supply to Karnak (Ineni in the time of A I–T III)	TT 81 (*Urk.* IV, 171)													440 deben	

Table 26. The number of temple offerings and their quality value (yearly amount). (3/3)

	celebration	source	date	A. number of grain products	B. grain sacks (Haring 1997)	quality value (A/B)	*(d)ḳw t-ḥḏ*	*t-ḥḏ*	*iwꜣ*	*rnn iwꜣ*	*wnḏw*	*kꜣ*	*mꜣ ḥḏ*	*gḥs*	*snṯr*	linen
27	daily at Karnak (year 6 of R III)	Karnak (*RIK* II, pl. 108)		unspecified				13,140							1460 sacks	
28	daily at Karnak (year 7 of R III)	Karnak (*RIK* II, pl. 108)		11,315												
29	daily at Karnak (year 16 of R III)	Karnak (*RIK* II, pl. 108)		367,920			1460								lost	
30	Festivals of Opet & the accession anniversary (R III)	P. Harris I, XVII–XXI	II Akhet 19–III Akhet 15 I Shemu 26–II Shemu 14	(113,773)			(6076)	(19,742)	(20)	(16)	(24)	(36)				
31	unknown feast at Karnak (year 1 of R IV)	Karnak (K*RI* VI, 8)	II Shemu 23	5533			40?	2100+	2	2	4	4				
32	daily at Karnak (Imiseba in the time of R IX)	TT 65 (K*RI* VI, 544: 2)						29,200								

Text 1. New Year formula.

T= Tjay (TT 23)[1]; N=Neferhotep (TT 50)[2]; M=Mery (TT 95)[3]; Ke=Kenamun (TT 93)[4]; K1 and K2=Karnak[5].

T 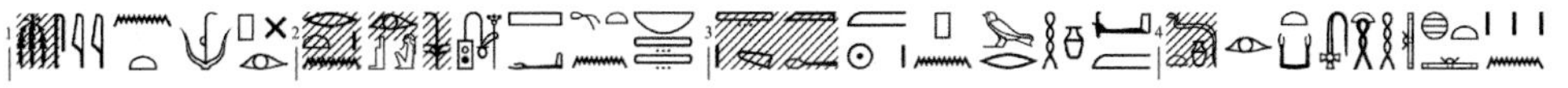

(1) *[ms]y(.t) n.t wpy-rnp.t* (2) *i[r.t n W]sir sš [nsw.t] šʿ.t n nb t3.wy* (3) *[T3 m3ʿ ḫrw] m hrw pn wrḥ* (4) *m[d.t] ir tk3 w3ḥ iḫ.wt n*

N 

[tpy 3ḫ.t sw 1 dw3y.t n wpy-rnp.t ir.t n Wsir it nṯr Nfr-ḥtp] m hrw pn wr[ḥ md.t ir.t ir.t tk3 wḏb iḫ.t n]

T 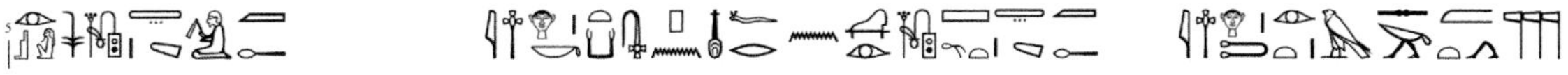

(5) *Wsir sš nsw.t T3 m3ʿ ḫrw inḏ ḥr=k tk3 pn nfr n Wsir sš šʿ.t T3 m3ʿ ḫrw inḏ ḥr=t ir.t Ḥr ssm.t nṯr.w*

N 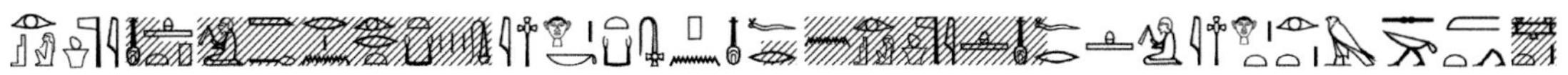

Wsir it nṯr [Nfr]-ḥtp [m3ʿ ḫrw r3 n ir.t tk3.w] inḏ ḥr=k tk3 pn nf[r n Wsir it nṯr N]fr-ḥtp inḏ ḥr=t ir.t Ḥr ssm.t [w3.t

K1 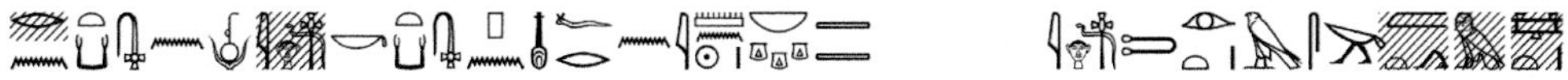

[r3] n tk3 n wpy-rnp.t [inḏ ḥr]=k tk3 pn nfr n Imn-rʿ nb ns.wt t3.wy inḏ ḥr=t ir.t Ḥr ss[m.t m w3.t]

T 

(6) *m kkw ssm.t Wsir sš nsw.t T3 m3ʿ ḫrw m s.t=f nb [r] bw nb m[rr]=f wnn=f [im iw ḥtp tk]3 p-*

N 

m k]kw [ssm.t] Wsir it nṯr Nfr-ḥtp m3ʿ ḫrw r bw nb mrr k3=f im iw ḥtp tk3 pn

K1 

kkw ssm.t Imn nb ns.wt t3.wy m bw nb mrr k3=k im ʿnḫ ḏ.t [one group lost] *ḥtp tk3*

T 

(7) *-n nfr n Wsir sš šʿ.t T3 m3ʿ ḫrw m ʿḏ m3w [ḥbs.w rḥty.w] m [dd n=k it]=k Gb mw.t=k Nw.t*

N 

nfr n Wsir it nṯr n Imn Nfr-ḥtp m3ʿ ḫrw m ʿḏ.w m3w.t ḥbs rḥty m dd n=k it=k Gb mw.t=k Nw.t

K1 

n Imn nb ns.wt t3.wy m ʿḏ m3w ḥbs.w rḥty.w m dd n=k it=k Gb mw.t=k Nw.t

---

[1] PM I-1², 39 (8, II); Davies 1924, 13; Haikal 1985.
[2] PM I-1², 96 (9–10, I); Hari 1985, 42, pl. 28; Assmann 2005, 412–4.
[3] PM I-1², 197 (pillar B, d); Gnirs 1995, 245.
[4] PM I-1², 191 (14, I); Davies 1930, pl. 45 B.
[5] K1: PM II², 45 (155, III, 2–3); Nelson 1949, 336 for translation; Nelson 1981, pls 211–2; Goyon 1986, 334 for partial translation. K2: PM II², 45 (155, I, 1); Nelson 1981, pl. 202.

T 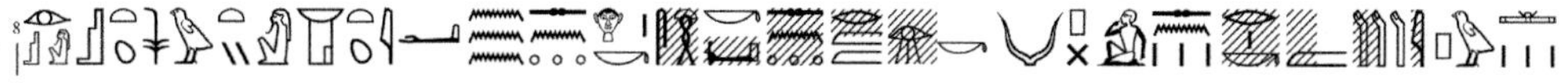

(8) *Wsir ꜣs.t Swty Nb-ḥw.t iꜥi=sn ḥr=k [s]k[=sn r]my=k wp=sn [rꜣ=k m ḏbꜥ.w i]p.w*

N 

Wsir ꜣs.t Swty Nb-ḥw.t iꜥi ḥr=k sk=sn r rmy=k wp=sn rꜣ=k m ḏbꜥ.w ip.w

K1 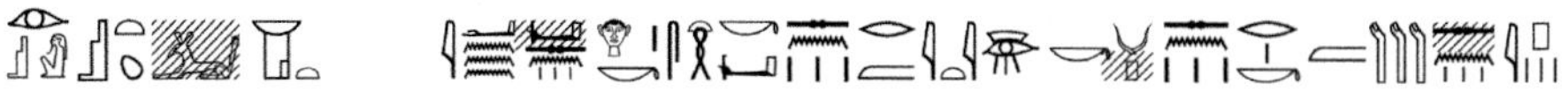

Wsir ꜣs.t [Stẖ] Nb-ḥw.t iꜥi[=s]n ḥr=k sk=sn rmy.t=k w[p]=sn rꜣ=k m ḏbꜥ.w[=s]n ip.w

---

T 

(9) *bꜣk.w wp rꜣ n n*[sic] *nṯr.w im=sn iw rd[i.tw n=k m p.t iw] rdi.tw n=k m tꜣ iw rdi.tw n=k m sẖ.t*

N 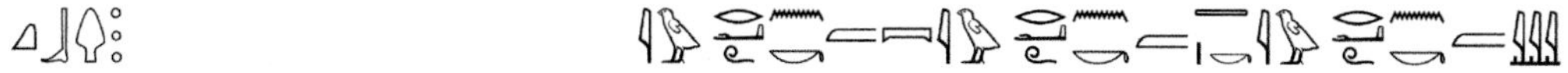

bꜣk.w iw rdi.w n=k m p.t iw rdi.w n=k m tꜣ=k[sic] *iw rdi.w n=k m sẖ.t*

M (transcription from the original text unavailable)

iw rdi(.w) n=k p.t iw rdi(.w) n=k tꜣ iw rdi(.w) n=k sẖ.t iꜣrw

K1 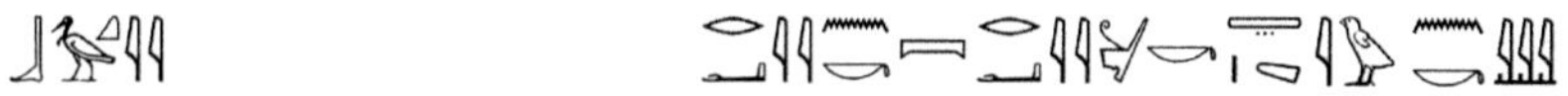

bꜣk.w rdy n=k p.t rdy n=k tꜣ iw (rdy) n=k sẖ.t

T 

(10) *iꜣrw m grḥ hrw pn nfr n w[py-rnp.t] r sm[n ꜣbd.w] iw rdi.tw n=k mw rnpi n nṯr iw*

N 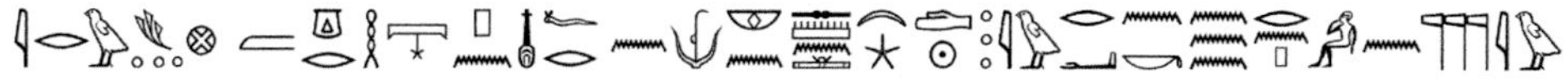

iꜣrw m grḥ pn nfr n wpy-rnp.t n smn ꜣbd.w iw rdi n=k mw rnpi n nṯr.w iw

K1 

iꜣrw m grḥ pn n [one group lost] *smn ꜣbd nb rdi hrw rdi mw rnpi n nṯr.w*

T 

(11) *rdi.tw n=k mw rnpi nṯry m mit.t m* [one group lost] *iḫm.w-wrḏ.w-m-ꜥb.w*

N 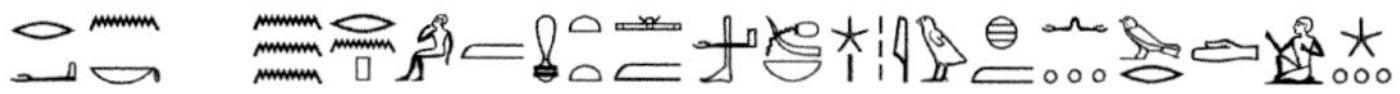

rdi n=k mw rnpi m mit.t m ꜥb nb sbꜣ.w iḫm.w-wrḏ.w

K1 

[rdi n=k nṯ]r.w mw rnpi m mit.t m ꜥb n[b sbꜣ.]w

T 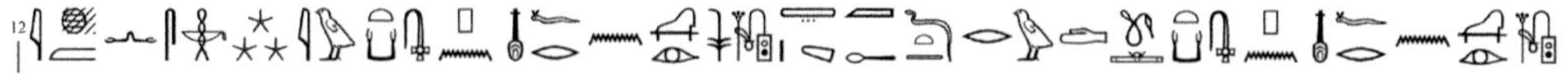

(12) *i[ḫ]m.w-sk.w iw tkꜣ pn nfr n Wsir sš nsw.t Tꜣ mꜣꜥ ḫrw ḏ.t rwd tkꜣ pn nfr n Wsir sš*

N 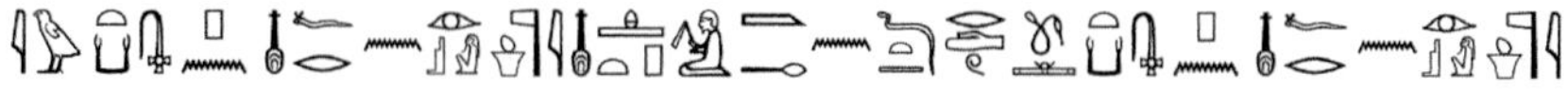

iw tkꜣ pn nfr n Wsir it nṯr Nfr-ḥtp mꜣꜥ ḫrw n ḏ.t rwd tkꜣ pn nfr n Wsir it nṯr

K1 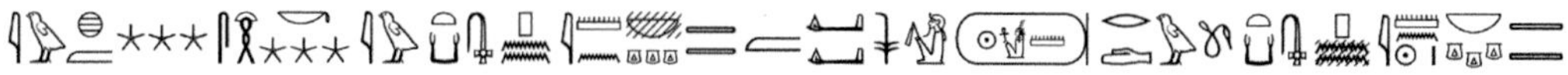

iḫm.w-sk.w iw tkꜣ pn n Imn [nb] ns.wt tꜣ.wy m dd nsw.t Mn-mꜣꜥ.t-rꜥ rwd tkꜣ p[n n] Imn-rꜥ nb ns.wt tꜣ.wy

T 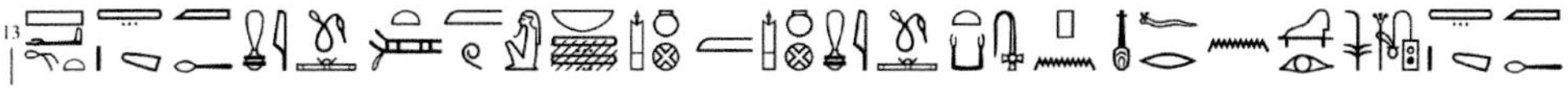

(13) *šʿ.t T3 m3ʿ ḫrw mi rwd Itm nb [t3.wy] iwn m iwn mi*[sic] *rwd tk3 pn nfr n Wsir sš nsw.t T3 m3ʿ ḫrw*

N 

Nfr-ḥtp m3ʿ ḫrw mi rwd rn n Itm nb t3.wy iwn m iwn

Ke 

rwd rn n Itm nb t3 m iwn rwd mnw pn [three or more groups lost] *ḏ.t ḏ.t*

K1 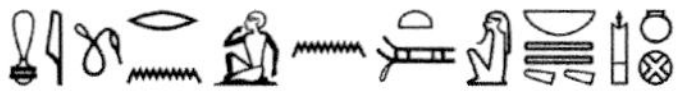

mi rwd rn n Itm nb t3.wy iwn

K2 

rwd rn n Itm nb t3.wy m iwn mi ḥtp nṯr pn m dd s3-Rʿ Sthy-mr-n-imn n Imn ḥnʿ psḏ.t=f

---

T 

(14) *mi rwd rn n Šw mn-s.t ḥry m iw[n] mi*[sic] *rwd tk3 pn nfr n Wsir sš šʿ.t T3 m3ʿ ḫrw mi*

N 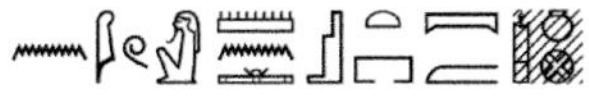

n Šw mn-s.t ḥry m [iwn

Ke 

rwd rn n Šw nb mn-s.t ḥry.t m iwn rwd mnw pn [three or more groups lost] *ḏ.t ḏ.t*

K1 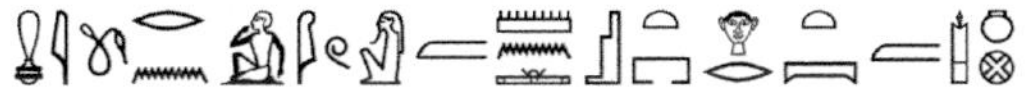

mi rwd rn Šw m mn-s.t ḥry.t m iwn

K2 

rwd [n] ḏ.t rwd rn n Šw m mn-s.t ḥry.t m iwn rwd n ḏ.t

T 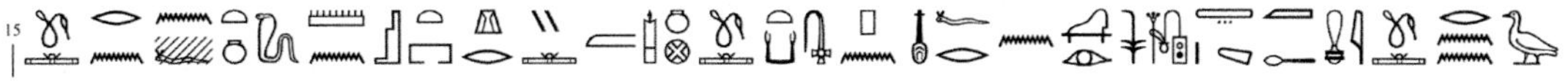

(15) *rwd rn n T[f]n.t mn-s.t ḥry m iwn rwd tk3 pn nfr n Wsir sš nsw.t T3 m3ʿ ḫrw mi rwd rn n G-*

N 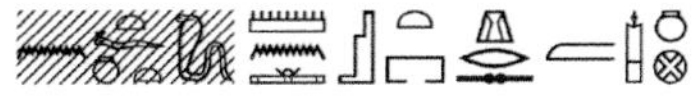

n Tfn.t] mn-s.t ḥry=s[sic] *m iwn*

Ke 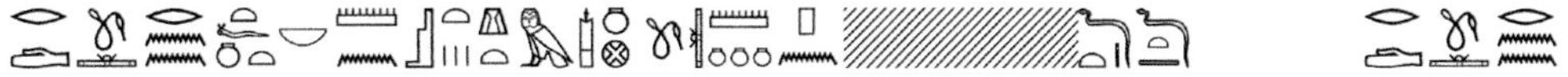

rwd rn n Tfn.t nb(.t) mn-s.t ḥry.t m iwn rwd mnw pn [three or more groups lost] *ḏ.t ḏ.t rwd rn n*

K1 

mi rwd rn n Tfn.t m mn-s.t ḥry.t m iwn mi rwd rn n

K2 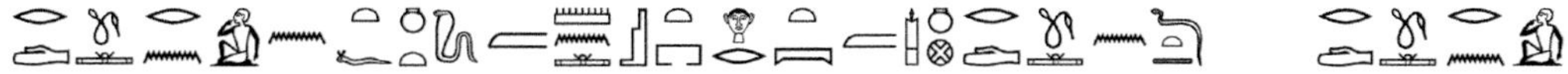

rwd rn n Tfn.t m mn-s.t ḥry.t[sic] *m iwn rwd n ḏ.t rwd rn*

T 16 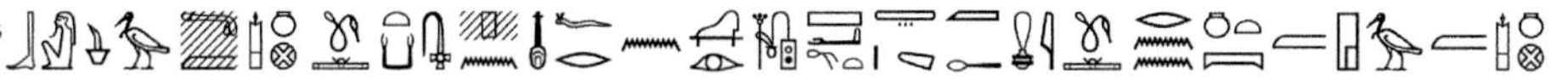

(16) *-b b3 [t3y m] iwn rwd tk3 [p]n nfr n Wsir sš šʿ.t T3 m3ʿ ḫrw mi rwd rn n Nw.t m ḥw.t b3 m iwn*

N 

n Gb [b3 t3y m iwn n Nw.t m ḥw.t b3 m iwn]

Ke 

Gb b3 t3 m iwn rwd mnw pn [three or more groups lost] *ḏ.t ḏ.t rwd rn n Nw.t m ḥw.t šnw m iwn*

K1 

n Gb b3 t3y m iwn mi rwd rn n Nw.t m ḥw.t šnw m iwn

K2 

Gb m b3 t3 mry m iwn rwd n ḏ.t [r]wd rn [Nw].t m ḥw.t šnw m iwn rwd [n] ḏ.t

---

T 17 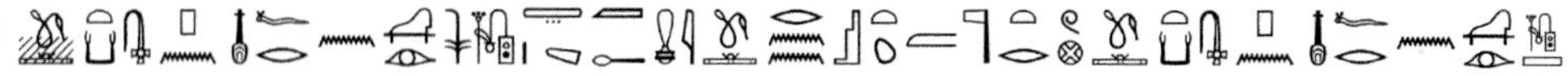

(17) *rw[d] tk3 pn nfr n Wsir sš nsw.t T3 m3ʿ ḫrw mi rwd rn n 3s.t m nṯrw rwd tk3 pn nfr n Wsir sš š-*

N 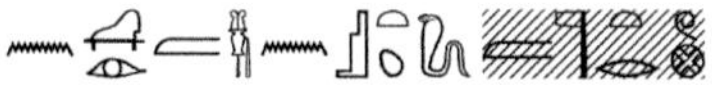

n Wsir m 3bḏw n 3s.t [m nṯrw]

Ke 

rwd mnw pn [three or more groups lost] *ḏ.t ḏ.t rwd rn n Wsir m t3-wr rwd mnw pn* [three or more groups lost] *ḏ.t ḏ.t*

rwd rn n ḫnty-imntyw m 3bḏw rwd mnw pn [three or more groups lost] *ḏ.t ḏ.t rwd rn n 3s.t m nṯrw*

rwd mnw pn [three or more groups lost] *ḏ.t ḏ.t rwd rn n Stḫ m nb.t rwd mnw pn* [three or more groups lost] *ḏ.t ḏ.t*

K1 

mi rwd rn n Wsir ḫnty imnt.t m 3bḏw mi rwd rn n 3s.t m nṯry mi rwd rn n Stḫ

K2 

rwd rn n Wsir ḫnty imnt.t m 3bḏw [r]wd n ḏ.t rn n 3s.t m nṯr rwd n ḏ.t rwd rn n Stḫ

T 18 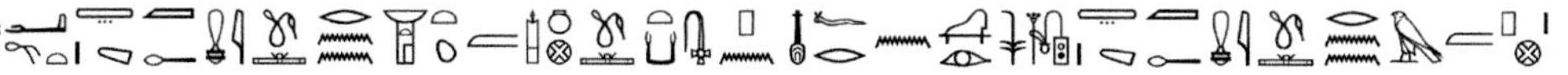

(18) *-ʿ.t T3 m3ʿ ḫrw mi rwd rn n Nb-ḥw.t m iwn rwd tk3 pn nfr n Wsir sš nsw.t T3 m3ʿ ḫrw mi rwd rn n Ḥr m p*

N 

[one column lost]

Ke 

rwd rn n Nb-ḥw.t m ḥw.t [ ] *rwd mnw pn* [three or more groups lost] *ḏ.t ḏ.t rwd rn n Ḥr m* [ ] *rwd mnw pn* [three or more groups lost] *ḏ.t ḏ.t*

K1 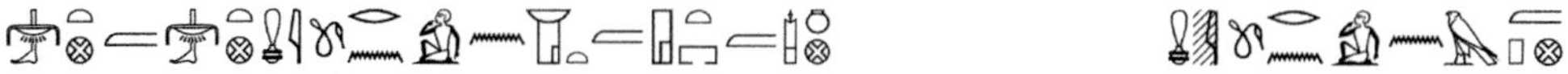

nb.t m nb.t mi rwd rn n Nb-ḥw.t m ḥw.t m iwn m[i] rwd rn n Ḥr m p

K2 

nb nb.t rwd n ḏ.t rwd rn n Nb-ḥw.t m ḥw.t [m] iwn rwd n ḏ.t

T 19

(19) [*rwd*] *tkꜣ p*[*n*] *n*[*f*]*r Wsir sš šꜥ.t Tꜣ mꜣꜥ ẖrw mi rwd rn n Wꜣḏy m dp rwd tkꜣ pn nfr n Wsir sš nsw.t Tꜣ*

N

[one column lost]

K1

mi rwd rn n [*Wꜣḏy.t m dp*

T 20

(20) [*mꜣꜥ*] *ẖrw mi rwd* [*rn n bꜣ*] *m ḏ*[*d*] *rwd tkꜣ p*[*n*] *n*[*f*]*r n Wsir sš šꜥ.t Tꜣ mꜣꜥ ẖrw mi rwd rn*

N

[one column lost]

Ke

rwd rn n bꜣ m ḏd.t rwd mnw pn [three or more groups lost] *ḏ.t ḏ.t rwd rn n*

K1

mi rwd rn] *n bꜣ m ḏdw* [*mi rwd rn*

K2

rwd rn n bꜣ nb ḏ[*dw rwd*] *n ḏ.t rwd rn*

T 21

(21) *n Ḏḥwty m ḫmnw* [*iw*] *tkꜣ pn nfr n Wsir sš* [*nsw.t š*]*ꜥ.t n nb tꜣ.wy Ṯꜣy mꜣꜥ ẖrw*

N

[*n Ḏḥwty ḫmnw hꜣy Wsir it nṯr Nfr-ḥtp mꜣꜥ ẖrw*]

Ke

N.t sꜣw rwd mnw pn [three or more groups lost] *ḏ.t ḏ.t rwd rn n* [four groups lost] *rwd mnw pn* [three or more groups lost] *ḏ.t ḏ.t*

rwd rn n Ḫnty-n-ir.ty m ḫm rwd mnw pn [three or more groups lost] *ḏ.t ḏ.t*

rwd rn n Ḥr m p rwd mnw pn [three or more groups lost] *ḏ.t ḏ.t*

rwd rn n Wꜣḏy.t m dp rwd mnw pn [three or more groups lost] *ḏ.t ḏ.t*

wḏꜣ.t=f [ ] *n Ḥr ir* [ ] *ḫfty.w*(?)

K1

n Ḏḥwty] *m ḫmnw*

K2

[*n*] *Ḏḥwty* [*m ḫmnw rwd n ḏ.t ḥtp-di-nsw.t* (*n*) *Gb st*]*p.w* [*n nṯr.w iptn ntsn bꜣ=sn ntsn*] *wꜣš*[*=sn*

ntsn di=sn di.tw(?) *n=sn ḥtp-di-nsw.t*] *m ḥtp-nṯr m d*[*d*] *nsw.t Mn-mꜣꜥ.t-rꜥ di ꜥnḫ* [*ḏ.t*]

T 

(22) (*m*) *mskt.t mꜥnḏ.t nn sk.tw=f nn sḥtm.tw=f m ḏ.t ḏ.t wꜥb wꜥb Wsir sš nsw.t šꜥ.t n nb tꜣ.wy*

K1 

iw [four groups lost *mskt.t*] *mꜥnḏ.t n sḥtm.tw=f* [one group lost] *nsw.t Mn-mꜣꜥ.t-rꜥ di ꜥnḫ ḏd* [*wꜣs*] *mi Rꜥ*

T 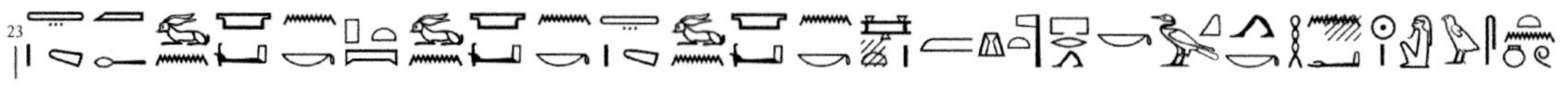

(23) *Tꜣ mꜣꜥ ḫrw wn n=k p.t wn n=k tꜣ wn n=k wꜣ[.t] m ḫr.t-nṯr pr=k ꜥḳ=k ḫ[n]ꜥ Rꜥ wstn*

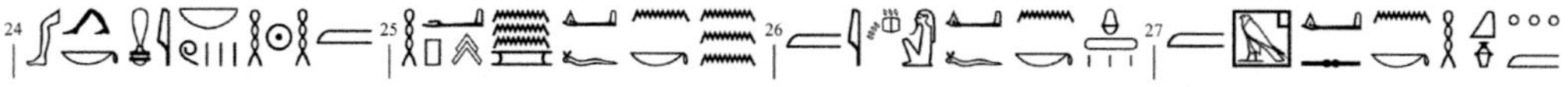

(24) *rd=k mi nb.w nḥḥ m* (25) *ḥꜥpy di=f n=k mw* (26) *m it di=f n=k t* (27) *m Ḥw.t-ḥr di=s n=k ḥnḳ.wt m*

(28) *Ḥsꜣ.t di=s n=k ir.wt* (29) *wꜥb wꜥb Wsir* (30) *sš nsw.t Tꜣy*

List of references

Abd el-Razik, M. 1967. Some remarks on the great pylon of the Luxor temple. *Mitteilungen der Deutschen Archäologischen Instituts, Abteilung Kairo* 22: 68–70.

Abd el-Razik, M. 1974. The dedicatory and building texts of Ramesses II in Luxor temple: I. The texts. *Journal of Egyptian Archaeology* 60: 142–60.

Abd el-Razik, M. 1975. The dedicatory and building texts of Ramesses II in Luxor temple: II. Interpretation. *Journal of Egyptian Archaeology* 61: 125–36.

el-Aguizy, O. 1996. Two new demotic temple oaths on ostraca. *Bulletin de l'Institut Français d'Archéologie Orientale* 96: 1–11.

Aksamit, J. 2007. Room C in the temple of Tuthmosis III at Deir el-Bahari, in B. Haring and A. Klug (eds), *6. ägyptologische Tempeltagung: Funktion und Gebrauch altägyptischer Tempelräume: Leiden, 4.-7. September 2002* (Königtum, Staat und Gesellschaft früher Hochkulturen 3): 1–10. Wiesbaden: Harrassowitz.

Aldred, C. 1969. The 'New Year' gifts to the pharaoh. *Journal of Egyptian Archaeology* 55: 73–81.

Allam, S. 1963. *Beiträge zum Hathorkult (bis zum Ende des Mittleren Reiches)* (Münchner ägyptologische Studien 4). Berlin: B. Hessling.

Allam, S. 1973. *Hieratische Ostraka und Papyri aus der Ramessidenzeit* (Urkunden zum Rechtsleben im alten Ägypten 1), 2 vols. Tübingen.

Allen, J.P. 2002a. The Speos Artemidos inscription of Hatshepsut. *Bulletin of the Egyptological Seminar* 16: 1–17.

Allen, J.P. 2002b. *The Heqanakht papyri* (Publications of the Metropolitan Museum of Art, Egyptian Expedition 27). New York: Metropolitan Museum of Art.

Allen, J.P. 2005. *The ancient Egyptian Pyramid Texts* (Writings from the ancient world 23). Atlanta: Society of Biblical Literature.

Allen, T.G. 1950. *Occurrences of Pyramid Texts, with cross indexes of these and other Egyptian mortuary texts* (Studies in ancient Oriental civilization 27). Chicago: University of Chicago Press.

1974. *The Book of the Dead or Going Forth by Day: Ideas of the ancient Egyptians concerning the hereafter as expressed in their own terms* (Studies in ancient Oriental civilization 37). Chicago: Oriental Institute of the University of Chicago.

Alliot, M.M. 1932. Fouilles de Deir el-Médineh 1930–1931: Un puits funéraire à Qournet-Mora'i. *Bulletin de l'Institut Français d'Archéologie Orientale* 32: 65–81.

Alliot, M.M. 1949. *Le culte d'Horus à Edfou au temps des Ptolémées* (Bibliothèque d'étude 20), 2 vols. Cairo: Imprimerie de l'Institut Français d'Archéologie Orientale.

Altenmüller, B. 1975: Anubis, in E. Otto and W. Helck (eds), *Lexikon der Ägyptologie*, vol. 1: 327–33. Wiesbaden: Harrassowitz.

Altenmüller, H. 1979. Ein Zauberspruch zum 'Schutz des Leibes'. *Göttinger Miszellen* 33: 7–12.

Altenmüller, H. 1982. Tausret und Sethnacht. *Journal of Egyptian Archaeology* 68: 107–15.

Altenmüller, H. 1984. Der Begräbnistag Sethos' II. *Studien zur Altägyptischen Kultur* 11: 38–47.

Altenmüller, H. 1994. Das Graffito 551 aus der thebanischen Nekropole. *Studien zur Altägyptischen Kultur* 21: 19–28.

Altenmüller, H. 1998a. Die Fahrt der Hathor nach Edfu und die heilige Hochzeit, in W. Clarysse, A. Schoors, and H. Willems (eds), *Egyptian religion: The last thousand years: Studies dedicated to the memory of Jan Quaegebeur*, vol. 2: 753–65. Leuven: Peeters.

Altenmüller, H. 1998b. *Die Wanddarstellungen im Grab des Mehu in Saqqara* (Archäologische Veröffentlichungen (Deutsches Archäologisches Institut, Abteilung Kairo) 42). Mainz: Philipp von Zabern.

Altenmüller, H. and Moussa, A.M. 1991. Die Inschrift Amenemhets II. aus dem Ptah-Tempel von Memphis: Ein Vorbericht. *Studien zur Altägyptischen Kultur* 18: 1–48.

Amer, A.A.M.A. 1981. A unique Theban tomb inscription under Ramesses VIII. *Göttinger Miszellen* 49: 9–12.

Amer, A.A.M.A. 1985a. Tutankhamun's decree for the chief treasurer Maya. *Revue d'Égyptologie* 36: 18–20.

Amer, A.A.M.A. 1985b. Reflections on the reign of Ramesses VI. *Journal of Egyptian Archaeology* 71: 66–70.

Amer, A.A.M.A. 1999. *The gateway of Ramesses IX in the temple of Amun at Karnak.* Warminster: Aris & Phillips.

Amer, H.I. and Morardet, B. 1983. Les dates de la construction du temple majeur d'Hathor à Dendara à l'époque gréco-romaine. *Annales du Service des Antiquités de l'Égypte* 69: 255–8.

Andrews, C.A.R. 1978. A family for Anhai? *Journal of Egyptian Archaeology* 64: 88–98.

Andrews, C.A.R. 1994. *Amulets of ancient Egypt.* London: British Museum Press.

Anthes, R. 1928. *Die Felseninschriften von Hatnub, nach den Aufnahmen Georg Möllers* (Untersuchungen zur Geschichte und Altertumskunde Aegyptens 9). Leipzig: J.C. Hinrichs.

Anthes, R 1939. Hieratic graffiti on statue fragments, in U. Hölscher (ed.), *The excavations of Medinet Habu II: The temples of the Eighteenth Dynasty* (Oriental Institute publications 41): 106–8. Chicago: University of Chicago.

Arnold, D. 1962. *Wandrelief und Raumfunktion in ägyptischen Tempeln des Neuen Reiches* (Münchner ägyptologische Studien 2). Berlin: B. Hessling.

Arnold, D. 1974. *Der Tempel des Königs Mentuhotep von Deir el-Bahari* (Archäologische Veröffentlichungen (Deutsches Archäologisches Institut, Abteilung Kairo) 8, 11, and 23), 3 vols. Mainz am Rhein: Philipp von Zabern.

Arnold, D. 1976. *Gräber des Alten und Mittleren Reiches in El-Tarif* (Archäologische Veröffentlichungen (Deutsches Archäologisches Institut, Abteilung Kairo) 17). Mainz am Rhein: Philipp von Zabern.

Arnold, D. 1997. Royal cult complexes of the Old and Middle Kingdoms, in B.E. Shafer (ed.), *Temples of ancient Egypt*: 31–85. Ithaca: Cornell University Press.

Arnold, F. 2004. Pharaonische Prozessionsstraßen: Mittel der Machtdarstellung unter Königin Hatshepsut, in E.-L. Schwandner and K. Rheidt (eds), *Macht der Architektur-Architektur der Macht: Bauforschungskolloquium in Berlin vom 30. Oktober bis 2. November 2002, veranstaltet vom Architektur-Referat des DAI* (Diskussionen zur archäologischen Bauforschung 8): 13–23. Mainz am Rhein: Philipp von Zabern.

Assmann, J. 1969. *Liturgische Lieder an den Sonnengott: Untersuchungen zur altägyptischen Hymnik. I* (Münchner ägyptologische Studien 19). Berlin: B. Hessling.

Assmann, J. 1983a. *Sonnenhymnen in thebanischen Gräbern*. Mainz am Rhein: Philipp von Zabern.

Assmann, J. 1983b. *Re und Amun: Die Krise des polytheistischen Weltbilds im Ägypten der 18.-20. Dynastie* (Orbis Biblicus et Orientalis 51). Freiburg and Göttingen: Universitätverlag, trans. by A. Alcock as *Egyptian solar religion in the New Kingdom: Re, Amun and the crisis of polytheism*. London and New York: Kegan Paul International, 1995.

Assmann, J. 1984. *Ägypten: Theologie und Frömmigkeit einer frühen Hochkultur* (Kohlhammer Urban-Taschenbücher 366). Stuttgart: Kohlhammer, trans. by D. Lorton as *The search for god in ancient Egypt*. Ithaca and London: Cornell University Press, 2001.

Assmann, J. 2001. *Tod und Jenseits im alten Ägypten*. München: Beck.

Assmann, J. 2002. *Altägyptische Totenliturgien I: Totenliturgien in den Sargtexten des Mittleren Reiches* (Supplemente zu den Schriften der heidelberger Akademie der Wissenschaften: Philosophisch-historische Klasse 14). Heidelberg: Universitätsverlag Winter.

Assmann, J. 2005. *Altägyptische Totenliturgien II: Totenliturgien und Totensprüche in Grabinschriften des Neuen Reiches* (Supplemente zu den Schriften der heidelberger Akademie der Wissenschaften: Philosophisch-historische Klasse 17). Heidelberg: Universitätsverlag Winter.

Assmann, J. 2008. *Altägyptische Totenliturgien III: Osirisliturgien in Papyri der Spätzeit* (Supplemente zu den Schriften der heidelberger Akademie der Wissenschaften: Philosophisch-historische Klasse 20). Heidelberg: Universitätsverlag Winter.

Assmann, J., Dziobek, E., Guksch, H., and Kampp, F. 1995. *Thebanische Beamtennekropolen: Neue Perspektiven archäologischer Forschung: Internationales Symposion, Heidelberg, 9.-13. Juni 1993* (Studien zur Archäologie und Geschichte Altägyptens 12). Heidelberg: Heidelberger Orientverlag.

Aston, D.A. and Aston, B.G. 2003. The dating of Late Period Bes vases, in C.A. Redmount and C.A. Keller (eds), *Egyptian pottery: Proceedings of the 1990 Pottery Symposium at the University of California, Berkeley* (University of California publications in Egyptian archaeology 8): 95–113. Berkeley: Regents of the University of California.

Aufrère, S. 1997. *Description de l'Égypte, ou recueil des observations et des recherches qui ont été faites en Égypte pendant l'expédition de l'armée française: Publié sous les ordres de Napoléon Bonaparte*. Paris: Bibliothèque de l'Image.

Aune, D.E. 1987: Oracles, in M. Eliade (ed.), *The encyclopedia of religion*, vol. 11: 81–7. New York and London: Macmillan and Collier Macmillan.

Awad, K. 2002. Untersuchungen zum Schatzhaus in Neuen Reich: Administrative und ökonomische Aspekte. Unpublished PhD dissertation, Universität Göttingen.

Bács, T.A. 1990. Two calendars of lucky and unlucky days. *Studien zur Altägyptischen Kultur* 17: 41–64.

Bács, T.A. 2001. Art as material for later art: The case of Theban tomb 65, in W.V. Davies (ed.), *Colour and painting in ancient Egypt*: 94–100. London: British Museum Press.

Bács, T.A. 2004. A royal litany in a private context. *Mitteilungen der Deutschen Archäologischen Instituts, Abteilung Kairo* 60: 1–16.

Badawi, A.M. 1943. Die neue historische Stele Amenophis' II. *Annales du Service des Antiquités de l'Égypte* 42: 1–23.

Badawy, A. 1964. The stellar destiny of pharaoh and the so-called air-shafts of Cheops' pyramid. *Mitteilungen des Instituts für Orientforschung* 10: 189–206.

Bailey, E. 1996. Circumcision in ancient Egypt. *Bulletin of the Australian Centre for Egyptology* 7: 15–28.

Baines, J. 1970. *Bnbn*: Mythological and linguistic notes. *Orientalia* 39: 389–404.

Baines, J. 1974. The inundation stela of Sobekhotpe VIII. *Acta Orientalia* 36: 39–54.

Baines, J. 1976. The Sobekhotpe VIII inundation stela: An additional fragment. *Acta Orientalia* 37: 11–20.

Baines, J. 1987. Practical religion and piety. *Journal of Egyptian Archaeology* 73: 79–98.

Baines, J. 1991. Society, morality, and religious practice, in B.E. Shafer (ed.), *Religion in ancient Egypt: Gods, myths, and personal practice*: 123–200. London: Routledge.

Baines, J. 2001. *Fecundity figures: Egyptian personification and the iconology of a genre*. Oxford: Griffith Institute.

Baines, J. 2006. Public ceremonial performance in ancient Egypt: Exclusion and integration, in T. Inomata and L.S. Coben (eds), *Archaeology of performance: Theaters of power, community, and politics* (Archaeology in society series): 261–302. Lanham and Oxford: Altamira.

Baines, J. 2013. *High culture and experience in ancient Egypt* (Studies in Egyptology and the ancient Near East). Sheffield and Bristol: Equinox.

Baines, J. and Frood, E. 2011. Piety, change and display in the New Kingdom, in M. Collier and S.R. Snape (eds), *Ramesside studies in honour of K. A. Kitchen*: 1–17. Bolton: Rutherford.

Baines, J. and Málek, J. 1980. *Atlas of ancient Egypt*. Oxford: Phaidon.

Baines, J. and Parkinson, R. 1997. An Old Kingdom record of an oracle? Sinai inscription 13, in J. van Dijk (ed.), *Essays on ancient Egypt in honour of Herman te Velde* (Egyptological memoirs 1): 9–27. Groningen: STYX Publications.

Baines, J. and Yoffee, N. 1998. Order, legitimacy, and wealth in ancient Egypt and Mesopotamia, in G.M. Feinman and J. Marcus (eds), *Archaic states*: 199–260. Santa Fe: School of American Research Press.

Bakir, A.e.-M. 1966. *The Cairo calendar no. 86637*. Cairo: General Organisation for Government Printing Offices.

Balcz, H. 1939. Zu den Szenen der Jagdfahrten im Papyrosdickicht. *Zeitschrift für Ägyptische Sprache und Altertumskunde* 75: 32–8.

Barguet, P. 1952a. Le rituel archaïque de fondation des temples de Medinet-Habou et de Louxor. *Revue d'Égyptologie* 9: 1–22.

Barguet, P. 1952b. Tôd: rapport de fouilles de la saison février-avil 1950. *Bulletin de l'Institut Français d'Archéologie Orientale* 51: 80–110.

Barguet, P. 1953. *La stèle de la famine à Séhel* (Bibliothèque d'étude 24). Cairo: Imprimerie de l'Institut Français d'Archéologie Orientale.

Barguet, P. 1962a. *Le temple d'Amon-Rê à Karnak: Essai d'exégèse* (Recherches d'archéologie, de philologie et d'histoire 21). Cairo: Imprimerie de l'Institut Français d'Archéologie Orientale.

Barguet, P. 1962b. *Le papyrus N. 3176 (S) du Musée du Louvre* (Bibliothèque d'étude 37). Cairo: Imprimerie de l'Institut Français d'Archéologie Orientale.

Barguet, P. 1980: Luxor, in E. Otto and W. Helck (eds), *Lexikon der Ägyptologie*, vol. 3: 1103–7. Wiesbaden: Harrassowitz.

Barguet, P. and Dewachter, M. 1967. *Le temple d'Amada II* (Collection scientifique). Cairo: Centre de Documentation et d'Études sur l'Ancienne Égypte.

Barta, W. 1963. *Die altägyptische Opferliste von der Frühzeit bis zur griechisch-römischen Epoche* (Münchner ägyptologische Studien 3). Berlin: B. Hessling.

Barta, W. 1968. *Aufbau und Bedeutung der altägyptischen Opferformel* (Ägyptologische Forschungen 24). Glückstadt: J.J. Augustin.

Barta, W. 1969. Zur Bedeutung des *snwt*-Festes. *Zeitschrift für Ägyptische Sprache und Altertumskunde* 95: 73–80.

Barta, W. 1975. *Untersuchungen zur Göttlichkeit des regierenden Königs* (Münchner ägyptologische Studien 32). München and Berlin: Deutscher Kunstverlag.

Barta, W. 1981. Der ägyptische Mondkalender und seine Schaltregulierung. *Göttinger Miszellen* 47: 7–13.

Barta, W. 1983. Zur Lokalisierung und Bedeutung der *mrt*-Bauten. *Zeitschrift für Ägyptische Sprache und Altertumskunde* 110: 98–104.

Barta, W. 1984. Zur Bedeutung des Stirnband-Diadems *sSd*. *Göttinger Miszellen* 72: 7–8.

Barta, W. 1985. Bemerkungen zur Existenz der Rituale für Geburt und Krönung. *Zeitschrift für Ägyptische Sprache und Altertumskunde* 112: 1–13.

Barthelmess, P. 1992. *Der Übergang ins Jenseits in den thebanischen Beamtengräbern der Ramessidenzeit* (Studien zur Archäologie und Geschichte Altägyptens 2). Heidelberg: Heidelberger Orientverlag.

Barwik, M. 2010. Sanctuary of the Hatshepsut temple at Deir el-Bahari, in M. Dolińska and H. Beinlich (eds), *8. ägyptologische Tempeltagung: Interconnections between temples, Warschau, 22.-25. September 2008* (Königtum, Staat und Gesellschaft früher Hochkulturen 3 (3)): 1–12. Wiesbaden: Harrassowitz.

Bataille, A. 1951. *Les inscriptions grecques du temple de Hatshepsout à Deir el-Bahari* (Publications de la Société Fouad I de Papyrologie: Textes et documents 10). Cairo: Imprimerie de l'Institut Français d'Archéologie Orientale.

Bataille, A. 1952. *Les Memnonia: Recherches de papyrologie et d'épigraphie grecques sur la nécropole de la Thèbes d'Égypte aux époques hellénistique et romaine* (Recherches d'archéologie, de philologie et d'histoire 23). Cairo: Imprimerie de l'Institut Français d'Archéologie Orientale.

Baud, M. 1935. *Les dessins ébauchés de la nécropole thébaine: Au temps du Nouvel Empire: Ouvrage publié avec le concours de l'Académie des Inscriptions et Belles Lettres, Fondation Catenacci*. Cairo: Imprimerie de l'Institut Français d'Archéologie Orientale.

Baud, M. 2006. The relative chronology of Dynasties 6 and 8, in E. Hornung, R. Krauss, D. Warburton, and M. Eaton-Krauss (eds), *Ancient Egyptian chronology* (Handbook of Oriental studies. Section 1, The Near and Middle East 83): 144–58. Leiden: Brill.

Baud, M. and Drioton, É. 1932a. Le tombeau de Roÿ, in G.M. Foucart (ed.), *Tombes thébaines: Nécropole de Dirâ' Abû'n-Nága* (Mémoires publiés par les membres de l'Institut Français d'Archéologie Orientale du Caire 57), vol. 1: 1–51. Cairo: Imprimerie de l'Institut Français d'Archéologie Orientale.

Baud, M. and Drioton, É. 1932b. Le tombeau de Panehsy (tombeau N 16), in G.M. Foucart (ed.), *Tombes thébaines: Nécropole de Dirâ' Abû'n-Nága* (Mémoires publiés par les membres de l'Institut Français d'Archéologie Orientale du Caire 57), vol. 2: 1–50. Cairo: Imprimerie de l'Institut Français d'Archéologie Orientale.

von Beckerath, J. 1968. Die 'Stele der Verbannten' im Museum des Louvre. *Revue d'Égyptologie* 20: 7–36.

von Beckerath, J. 1993. Bemerkungen zum ägyptischen Kalender. *Zeitschrift für Ägyptische Sprache und Altertumskunde* 120: 7–22.

von Beckerath, J. 1994. *Chronologie des ägyptischen Neuen Reiches* (Hildesheimer ägyptologische Beiträge 39). Hildesheim: Gerstenberg.

von Beckerath, J. 1997. *Chronologie des pharaonischen Ägypten: Die Zeitbestimmung der ägyptischen Geschichte von der Vorzeit bis 332. v. Chr* (Münchner ägyptologische Studien 46). Mainz am Rhein: Philipp von Zabern.

Bedier, S. 1994a. Ein Stiftungsdekret Thutmosis III. *Bulletin of the Center of Papyrological Studies* 10: 1–23.

Bedier, S. 1994b. Ein Stiftungsdekret Thutmosis' III. aus Buto, in M. Minas and J. Zeidler (eds), *Aspekte spätägyptischer Kultur: Festschrift für Erich Winter zum 65. Geburtstag* (Aegyptiaca Treverensia 7): 35–50. Mainz am Rhein: Philipp von Zabern.

Beinlich-Seeber, C. 1987. *Das Grab des Userhat (TT 56)* (Archäologische Veröffentlichungen (Deutsches Archäologisches Institut. Abteilung Kairo) 50). Mainz am Rhein: Philipp von Zabern.

Bell, B. 1975. Climate and the history of Egypt: The Middle Kingdom. *American Journal of Archaeology* 79: 223–69.

Bell, L. 1985. Luxor temple and the cult of the royal ka. *Journal of Near Eastern Studies* 44: 251–94.

Bell, L. 1987. The Epigraphic Survey: The philosophy of Egyptian epigraphy after sixty years' practical experience, in J. Assmann, G. Burkard, and W.V. Davies (eds), *Problems and priorities in Egyptian archaeology* (Studies in Egyptology: 43–55. London: Kegan Paul International.

Bell, L. 1997. The New Kingdom divine temple: The example of Luxor, in B.E. Shafer (ed.), *Temples of ancient Egypt*: 127–84. Ithaca: Cornell University Press.

Bell, L. 2002. Divine kingship and the theology of the obelisk cult in the temples of Thebes, in H. Beinlich (ed.), *5. ägyptologische Tempeltagung: Würzburg, 23.-26. September 1999* (Ägypten und Altes Testament 33 (3)): 17–46. Wiesbaden: Harrassowitz.

Belmonte Avilés, J.A. 2003. Some open questions on the Egyptian calendar: An astronomer's view, in *Trabajos de Egiptología: Paper on ancient Egypt*: 7–56. Tenerife: Puerto de la Cruz.

Belmonte Avilés, J.A. 2009. The Egyptian calendar: Keeping ma'at on earth, in J.A. Belmonte Avilés and M. Shaltout (eds), *In search of cosmic order: Selected essays on Egyptian archaeoastronomy*: 77–131. Cairo: Supreme Council of Antiquities.

Bénédite, G. 1893. Le tombeau de Neferhotpou, in U. Bouriant (ed.), (Mémoires publiés par les membres de la mission archéologique française au Caire 5 (3)): 489–540. Paris: Ernest Leroux.

Bénédite, G. 1893. *Le temple de Philae: Description et histoire de l'Ile de Philae* (Mémoires publiés par les membres de l'Institut Français d'Archéologie Orientale du Caire 13). Paris: Ernest Leroux.

Berlandini-Grenier, J. 1982: Meretkästen, in E. Otto and W. Helck (eds), *Lexikon der Ägyptologie*, vol. 4: 91–3. Wiesbaden: Harrassowitz.

Berlandini-Grenier, J. 1994. Un ankh/djed/ouas pour le nouvel an de Montouemhat. *Bulletin de la Société d'Égyptologie de Genève* 18: 5–22.

Berlandini-Grenier, J. 1995. Ptah-demiurge et l'exaltation du ciel. *Revue d'Égyptologie* 46: 9–41.

Berman, L.M. 1998. Overview of Amenhotep III and his reign, in D.B. O'Connor and E.H. Cline (eds), *Amenhotep III: Perspectives on his reign*: 1–25. Ann Arbor: University of Michigan Press.

Białostocka, O. 2010. Hatshepsut's regeneration in the royal cult complex of her temple at Deir el-Bahari, in M. Dolińska and H. Beinlich (eds), *8. ägyptologische Tempeltagung: Interconnections between temples, Warschau, 22.-25. September 2008* (Königtum, Staat und Gesellschaft früher Hochkulturen 3 (3)): 13–24. Wiesbaden: Harrassowitz.

Bianchi, R.S. 1998. The oracle at the temple of Dendur, in W. Clarysse, A. Schoors, and H. Willems (eds), *Egyptian religion: The last thousand years: Studies dedicated to the memory of Jan Quaegebeur*, vol. 2: 773–80. Leuven: Peeters.

Bickel, S. 1998. Changes in the image of the creator god during the Middle and New Kingdoms, in C. Eyre (ed.), *Proceedings of the Seventh International Congress of Egyptologists, Cambridge, 3-9 September 1995* (Orientalia Lovaniensia Analecta 82): 165–72. Leuven: Peeters.

Bickel, S. 2003. 'Ich spreche ständig zu Aton...': zur Mensch-Gott-Beziehung in der Amarna Religion. *Journal of Ancient Near Eastern Religions* 3: 23–45.

Bidoli, D. 1972. Stele des Königs Sethnacht. *Mitteilungen der Deutschen Archäologischen Instituts, Abteilung Kairo* 28: 193–200.

Bierbrier, M.L. 1975. *The late New Kingdom in Egypt: A genealogical and chronological investigation.* Warminster: Aris & Phillips.

Bierbrier, M.L. 1980. Review of *Ancient Egyptian coregencies* by W. Murnane. *Orientalia* 49: 107–9.

Bierbrier, M.L. 1986. *Papyrus: Structure and usage* (Occasional Paper (British Museum) 60). London: British Museum.

Bietak, M. and Reiser-Haslauer, E. 1978. *Das Grab des 'Anch-Hor, Obersthofmeister der Gottesgemahlin Nitokris* (Denkschriften der Gesamtakademie,

Österreichischen Akademie der Wissenschaften 6). Wien: Verlag der Österreichischen Akademie der Wissenschaften.

Bigler, R.R. and Geiger, B. 1994. Eine Schenkungsstele Thutmosis' IV. *Zeitschrift für Ägyptische Sprache und Altertumskunde* 121: 11–7.

Birch, S. 1864. On the sepulchral figures. *Zeitschrift für Ägyptische Sprache und Altertumskunde* 2: 89–96.

Bissing, F.W. 1941. *Zeit und Herkunft der in Cerveteri gefundenen Gefässe aus ägyptischer Fayence und glasiertem Ton* (Sitzungsberichte der Bayerischen Akademie der Wissenschaften 2 (7)). München: Bayerische Akademie der Wissenschaften.

Bissing, F.W. and Kees, H. 1922. *Untersuchungen zu den Reliefs aus dem Re-Heiligtum des Rathures. I. Teil* (Abhandlungen der Bayerischen Akademie der Wissenschaften: Philosophisch-philologische und historische Klasse 32 (1)). München: Verlag der Bayerischen Akademie der Wissenschaften.

Bisson de la Roque, M.F. and Drioton, E. 1927. *Rapport sur les fouilles de Médamoud (1926)* (Fouilles de l'Institut Français d'Archéologie Orientale du Caire 4), 2 vols. Cairo: Imprimerie de l'Institut Français d'Archéologie Orientale.

Black, J.A. 1981. The New Year ceremonies in ancient Babylon: 'Taking Bel by the Hand' and a cultic picnic. *Religion* 11: 39–59.

Blackman, A.M. 1908: Righteousness (Egyptian), in J. Hastings and J.A. Selbie (eds), *Encyclopedia of religion and ethics*, vol. 10: 792–800. Edinburgh: T. & T. Clark.

Blackman, A.M. 1911. *The temple of Dendûr* (Service des antiq. de l'Égypte. Temples immergés de la Nubie). Cairo: Imprimerie de l'Institut Français d'Archéologie Orientale.

Blackman, A.M. 1914. *The rock tombs of Meir* (Archaeological survey of Egypt 22–5 and 28–9), 6 vols. London and Boston: Egypt Exploration Fund.

Blackman, A.M. 1925. Oracles in ancient Egypt I. *Journal of Egyptian Archaeology* 11: 249–55.

Blackman, A.M. 1926. Oracles in ancient Egypt II. *Journal of Egyptian Archaeology* 12: 176–85.

Blackman, A.M. and Fairman, H.W. 1942. The myth of Horus at Edfu II: C. The triumph of Horus over his enemies: A sacred drama. *Journal of Egyptian Archaeology* 28: 32–8.

Blackman, A.M. and Fairman, H.W. 1943. The myth of Horus at Edfu II: C. The triumph of Horus over his enemies: A sacred drama (continued). *Journal of Egyptian Archaeology* 29: 2–36.

Blackman, A.M. and Fairman, H.W. 1944. The myth of Horus at Edfu II: C. The triumph of Horus over his enemies: A sacred drama (concluded). *Journal of Egyptian Archaeology* 30: 5–22.

Blackman, A.M. and Fairman, H.W. 1946. The consecration of an Egyptian temple according to the use of Edfu. *Journal of Egyptian Archaeology* 32: 75–91.

Blackman, W.S. 1922. Some occurrences of the corn-'arūseh in ancient Egyptian tomb paintings. *Journal of Egyptian Archaeology* 8: 235–40.

Blanquet, C.-H. 1991. Typologie de la bouteille de nouvel an, in C. Obsomer and A.-L. Oosthoek (eds), *Amosiadès: Mélanges offerets au professeur Claude Vandersleyen par ses anciens étudiants*: 49–54. Louvain-la-Neuve: Université Catholique de Louvain.

Bleeker, C.J. 1956. *Die Geburt eines Gottes: Eine Studie über den ägyptischen Gott Min und sein Fest* (Studies in the history of religions 3). Leiden: Brill.

Bleeker, C.J. 1967. *Egyptian festivals: Enactments of religious renewal* (Studies in the history of religions 13). Leiden: Brill.

Bleiberg, E. 1984. The king's privy purse during the New Kingdom: An examination of *inw*. *Journal of American Research Center in Egypt* 21: 155–67.

Bleiberg, E. 1988. The redistributive economy in New Kingdom Egypt: An examination of *bAkw(t)*. *Journal of American Research Center in Egypt* 25: 157–68.

Bleiberg, E. 1995. The economy of ancient Egypt, in J.M. Sasson (ed.), *Civilizations of the ancient Near East*, vol. 3: 1373–85. New York: Scribner.

Bleiberg, E. 1999: Taxation and conscription, in K.A. Bard (ed.), *Encyclopedia of the archaeology of ancient Egypt*: 761–3. London: Routledge.

Blumenthal, E. 1976. Die Datierung der *NHri*-Grafiiti von Hatnub. *Altorientalische Forschungen* 4: 35–62.

Blyth, E. 2006. *Karnak: Evolution of a temple*. London: Routledge.

Bohleke, B. 1997. An oracular amuletic decree of Khonsu in the Cleveland Museum of Art. *Journal of Egyptian Archaeology* 83: 155–67.

Bomann, A.H. 1991. *The private chapel in ancient Egypt: A study of the chapels in the workmen's village at El Amarna with special reference to Deir el Medina and other sites*. London: Kegan Paul International.

Bommas, M. 1999. *Die Mythisierung der Zeit: Die beiden Bücher über die altägyptischen Schalttage des magischen pLeiden I 346* (Göttinger Orientforschungen. IV. Reihe, Ägypten 37). Wiesbaden: Harrassowitz.

Bommas, M. 2000. Der Tempel des Chnum der 18. Dyn. auf Elephantine. Unpublished PhD dissertation, Universität Heidelberg.

Bonhême, M.-A. 1994. Appétit de roi, in C. Berger, G. Clerc, J. Leclant, and N.-C. Grimal (eds), *Hommages à Jean Leclant* (Bibliothèque d'étude 106), vol. 2: 45–53. Cairo: Institut Français d'Archéologie Orientale.

van den Boorn, G.P.F. 1988. *The duties of the vizier: Civil administration in the early New Kingdom* (Studies in Egyptology). London and New York: Kegan Paul International.

Borchardt, L. 1899. Der zweite Papyrusfund von Kahun und die zeitliche Festlegung des Mittleren Reiches der ägyptischen Geschichte. *Zeitschrift für Ägyptische Sprache und Altertumskunde* 37: 89–103.

Borchardt, L. 1907. Das Dienstgebäude des auswärtigen Amts unter den Ramessiden. *Zeitschrift für Ägyptische Sprache und Altertumskunde* 44: 59–61.

Borchardt, L. 1910. *Das Grabdenkmal des Königs S'a3ḥu-Re'* (Ausgrabungen der Deutschen Orient-Gesellschaft in Abusir 1902–1908 6–7), 2 vols. Leipzig: J.C. Hinrichs.

Borchardt, L. 1911. *Statuen und Statuetten von Königen und Privatleuten im Museum von Kairo* (Catalogue général des antiquités égyptiennes du Musée du Caire 53, 77, 88, 94, and 96), 5 vols. Berlin: Reichsdruckerei.

Borchardt, L. 1934. Einige astronomisch festgelegte Punkte zweiter Ordnung im Neuen Reiche. *Zeitschrift für Ägyptische Sprache und Altertumskunde* 70: 97–103.

Borchardt, L. 1935. *Die Mittel zur zeitlichen Festlegung von Punkten der ägyptischen Geschichte und ihre Anwendung* (Quellen und Forschungen zur Zeitbestimmung der ägyptischen Geschichte 2). Cairo.

Borchardt, L. 1936. Jahre und Tage der Krönungs-Jubiläen. *Zeitschrift für Ägyptische Sprache und Altertumskunde* 72: 52–9.

Borchardt, L. 1937. *Denkmäler des Alten Reiches (ausser den Statuen) im Museum von Kairo, Nr. 1295–1808*, 2 vols. Berlin: Reichsdruckerei.

Borchardt, L. and Ricke, H. 1938. *Ägyptische Tempel mit Umgang* (Beiträge zur ägyptischen Bauforschung und Altertumskunde 2). Cairo.

Boreux, C. 1933. La statue du serviteur royal Nofirronpit. *Monuments et Mémoires. Fondation Eugène Piot* 33: 11–26.

Borghouts, J.F. 1982. Divine intervention in ancient Egypt and its manifestation (*bAw*), in R.J. Demarée and J.J. Janssen (eds), *Gleanings from Deir el-Medîna*: 1–70. Leiden: Nederlands Instituut voor het Nabije Oosten.

Bothmer, B.V. 1952. Ptolemaic reliefs I: A granite block of Philip Arrhidaeus. *Bulletin of the Museum of Fine Arts, Boston* 50: 19–27.

Botti, G. and Peet, E.T. 1928. *Il giornale della necropoli de Tebe* (I papiri ieratici del Museo di Torino). Torino: Fratelli Bocca.

Bouriant, U. 1889. Notes de voyage (1–6). *Recueil de Travaux* 11: 131–59.

Bouriant, U. 1890. Notes de voyage (7–12). *Recueil de Travaux* 13: 153–79.

Boussac, H. 1896. *Tombeaux thébains: Le tombeau d'Anna* (Mémoires publiés par les membres de la mission archéologique française au Caire 18). Paris: Ernest Leroux.

Brack, A. and Brack, A. 1977. *Das Grab des Tjanuni: Theben Nr. 74* (Archäologische Veröffentlichungen (Deutsches Archäologisches Institut. Abteilung Kairo) 19). Mainz am Rhein: Philipp von Zabern.

Brand, P.J. 2000. *The monuments of Seti I: Epigraphic, historical and art historical analysis*. Leiden, Boston, and Köln: Brill.

Brand, P.J. 2004. A graffito of Amen-Re in Luxor temple restored by the high priest Menkheperre, in G.N. Knoppers and A. Hirsch (eds), *Egypt, Israel, and the ancient Mediterranean world: Studies in honor of Donald B. Redford* (Probleme der Ägyptologie 20): 257–66. Leiden and Boston: Brill.

Breasted, J.H. 1902. A new chapter in the life of Thutmose III, in Untersuchungen zur Geschichte und Altertumskunde Aegyptens 2: 1–31. Leipzig: J.C. Hinrichs.

Breasted, J.H. 1906. *Ancient records of Egypt: historical documents from the earliest times to the Persian conquest* (Ancient records (2nd series)), 5 vols. Chicago: University of Chicago Press.

Breasted, J.H. 1912. *Development of religion and thought in ancient Egypt: Lectures delivered on the Morse Foundation at Union Theological Seminary* (Morse lectures). New York: Charles Scribner's Sons.

Breasted, J.H. 1930. *The Edwin Smith surgical papyrus* (Oriental Institute publications 3–4), 2 vols. Chicago: University of Chicago Press.

The British Museum 1911. *Hieroglyphic texts from Egyptian stelae, etc., in the British Museum*. London: Trustees of the British Museum.

Brock, L.P. and Shaw, R.L. 1997. The Royal Ontario Museum epigraphic project: Theban tomb 89 preliminary report. *Journal of American Research Center in Egypt* 34: 167–77.

Brovarski, E. 1976. Senenu, high priest of Amūn at Deir el-Baḥri. *Journal of Egyptian Archaeology* 62: 57–73.

Brugsch, H.K. 1862. *Recueil de monuments égyptiens dessinés sur lieux et publiés sous les auspices de son altesse le vice-roi d'Égypte Mohammed-Saïd-Pasha*. Leipzig: J.C. Hinrichs.

Brugsch, H.K. 1864a. Ein geographischer Kalender. *Zeitschrift für Ägyptische Sprache und Altertumskunde* 2: 50–6.

Brugsch, H.K. 1864b. Über Aussprache und Bedeutung des Knotens und seiner Variante. *Zeitschrift für Ägyptische Sprache und Altertumskunde* 2: 13–9.

Brugsch, H.K. 1864c. *Matériaux pour servir à la reconstruction du calendrier des anciens égyptiens: Partie théorique*. Leipzig: J.C. Heinrichs.

Brugsch, H.K. 1867. *Hieroglyphisch-demotisches Wörterbuch*, 7 vols. Leipzig: J.C. Hinrichs.

Brugsch, H.K. 1870. Ein neues Sothis-Datum. *Zeitschrift für Ägyptische Sprache und Altertumskunde* 8: 108–12.

Brugsch, H.K. 1879. *Dictionnaire géographique de l'ancienne Égypte: Contenant par ordre alphabétique la nomenclature comparée des noms propres géographiques qui se rencontrent sur les monuments et dans les papyrus*. Leipzig: J.C. Hinrichs.

Brugsch, H.K. 1883. *Thesaurus inscriptionum aegyptiacarum: Altaegyptische Inschriften*. Leipzig: J.C. Hinrichs.

Brugsch, H.K. 1884. Der Apis-Kreis aus den Zeiten der Ptolemäer nach den hieroglyphischen und demotischen Weihinschriften des Serapeums von Memphis. *Zeitschrift für Ägyptische Sprache und Altertumskunde* 22: 110–36.

Brunner, H. 1937. *Die Texte aus den Gräbern der Herakleopolitenzeit von Siut mit Übersetzung und Erläuterungen* (Ägyptologische Forschungen 5). Glückstadt and New York: J.J. Augustin.

Brunner, H. 1964. *Die Geburt des Gottkönigs: Studien zur Überlieferung eines altägyptischen Mythos* (Ägyptologische Abhandlungen 10). Wiesbaden: Harrassowitz.

Brunner, H. 1965. *Hieroglyphische Chrestomathie.* Wiesbaden: Harrassowitz.

Brunner, H. 1977. *Die südlichen Räume des Tempels von Luxor* (Archäologische Veröffentlichungen (Deutsches Archäologisches Institut. Abteilung Kairo) 18). Mainz am Rhein: Philipp von Zabern.

Brunton, G. 1947. The oracle of Kôm el-Wist. *Annales du Service des Antiquités de l'Égypte* 47: 293–5.

Bruyère, B. and Nagel, G. 1924. *Rapport sur les fouilles de Deir el Médineh* (Fouilles de l'Institut Français d'Archéologie Orientale du Caire 1–26), 26 vols. Cairo: Imprimerie de l'Institut Français d'Archéologie Orientale.

Bryan, B.M. 1991. *The reign of Thutmose IV.* Baltimore: Johns Hopkins University Press.

de Buck, A. 1935. *The Egyptian Coffin Texts* (Oriental Institute publications 34, 49, 64, 67, 73, 81, 87, and 132), 8 vols. Chicago: University of Chicago Press.

de Buck, A. 1938. The building inscription of the Berlin Leather Roll. *Studia Aegyptiaca* 1: 48–57.

Budge, W.E.A. 1896. *Some account of the collection of Egyptian antiquities in the possession of Lady Meux, of Theobalds Park, Waltham Cross*, 2nd ed. London: Harrison & Sons.

Budge, W.E.A. 1904. *The decrees of Memphis and Canopus* (Books on Egypt and Chaldaea 17–9), 3 vols. London: Kegan Paul, Trench, and Trübner & Co.

Budge, W.E.A. 1909. *The Book of Opening the Mouth: The Egyptian texts with English translations* (Books on Egypt and Chaldaea 36–7), 2 vols. London: Kegan Paul, Trench, and Trübner & Co.

Budge, W.E.A. 1922. *Facsimiles of the Egyptian hieratic papyri in the British Museum: with descriptions, summaries of contents, etc.* (Hieratic papyri in the British Museum. Second series), 2 vols. London: British Museum.

Burgos, F. and Larché, F. 2006. *La Chapelle Rouge: Le sanctuaire de barque d'Hatshepsout*, 2 vols. Paris: Culturesfrance, éditions recherche sur les civilisations.

Burkard, G. 2000. Spätzeitliche Osirisliturgien, in M. Görg and G. Hölbl (eds), *Ägypten und der östliche Mittelmeerraum im 1. Jahrtausend v. Chr.: Akten des Interdisziplinären Symposions am Institut für Ägyptologie der Universität München 25.-27. 10. 1996* (Ägypten und Altes Testament 44): 1–21. Wiesbaden: Harrassowitz.

Burkard, G. 2006. Das *xtm n pA xr* von Deir el-Medine: Seine Funktion und die Frage seiner Lokalisierung, in A. Dorn and T. Hofmann (eds), *Living and writing in Deir el-Medine: Socio-historical embodiment of Deir el-Medine texts*: 31–42. Basel: Schwabe.

Burton, A. 1972. *Diodorus Siculus. Book 1: A commentary.* Leiden: Brill.

Cabrol, A. 1993. Remarques au sujet d'une scéne de la tombe de Neferhotep (TT 49): Les fonctions de Neferhotep, la représentation des abords ouest de Karnak et son contexte. *Cahier de Recherches de l'Institut de Papyrologie et d'Égyptologie de Lille* 15: 19–30.

Cabrol, A. 1995. Une represéntation de la tombe de Khâbekhenet et les dromos de Karnak-sud: Nouvelles hypothèses, in *Cahiers de Karnak 10: 1992–1994*: 33–64. Paris: Centre Franco-Égyptien d'Étude des Temples de Karnak.

Cabrol, A. 1999. Les bœufs gras de la fête d'Opet: Remarques complémentaires sur des animaux. *Cahier de Recherches de l'Institut de Papyrologie et d'Égyptologie de Lille* 20: 15–27.

Cabrol, A. 2001. *Les voies processionnelles de Thèbes* (Orientalia Lovaniensia Analecta 97). Leuven: Peeters.

Callender, V.G. 2002. The innovations of Hatshepsut's reign. *Bulletin of the Australian Centre for Egyptology* 13: 29–46.

Calverley, A.M. 1933. *The temple of king Sethos I at Abydos*, 4 vols. London and Chicago: Egypt Exploration Society and University of Chicago Press.

Caminos, R.A. 1952. Gebel es-Silsilah no. 100. *Journal of Egyptian Archaeology* 38: 46–61.

Caminos, R.A. 1954. *Late-Egyptian miscellanies* (Brown Egyptological Studies 1). London: Oxford University Press.

Caminos, R.A. 1958. *The chronicle of prince Osorkon* (Analecta Orientalia 37). Roma: Pontificium Institutum Biblicum.

Caminos, R.A. 1964. The Nitocris adoption stela. *Journal of Egyptian Archaeology* 50: 71–100.

Capart, J. 1940. *Fouilles de El Kab: Documents.* Bruxelles: Parc du cinquantenaire.

Capart, J. and Gardiner, A.H. 1939. *Le Papyrus Léopold II aux Musées Royaux d'Art et d'Histoire de Bruxelles et le Papyrus Amherst à la Pierpont Morgan Library de New York.* Bruxelles: Patrimoine des Musées Royaux d'Art et d'Histoire.

Capart, J. and Spiegelberg, W. 1902. Une statuette du temple de Wazmose à Thèbes. *Annales de la Société d'Archéologie de Bruxelles* 16: 160–9.

Carlotti, J.-F. 2000. Modifications architecturales du 'grand château d'Amon' de Sésostris Ier à Karnak. *Égypte Afrique & Orient* 16: 37–46.

Carlotti, J.-F. 2001. *L'Akh-menou de Thoutmosis III à Karnak: Étude architecturale.* Paris: Recherche sur les civilisations.

Carlotti, J.-F. 2003. Essai de datation de l'agrandissement à cinq barres de portage du pavois de la barque processionnelle d'Amon-Rê, in *Cahiers de Karnak 11*: 235–54. Cairo: Centre Franco-Égyptien d'Étude des Temples de Karnak.

Carrier, C. 2010. *Le papyrus de Nouou (BM EA 10477)* (Série des papyrus du Livre des Morts de l'Égypte ancienne 1). Paris: Cybele.

Casperson, L.W. 1986. The lunar dates of Thutmose III. *Journal of Near Eastern Studies* 45: 139–50.

Casperson, L.W. 1988. The lunar date of Ramesses II. *Journal of Near Eastern Studies* 47: 181–4.

Cauville, S. 1983. Une règle de la grammaire du temple. *Bulletin de l'Institut Français d'Archéologie Orientale* 83: 51–84.

Cauville, S. 1987. *Essai sur la théologie du temple d'Horus à Edfou* (Bibliothèque d'étude 102), 2 vols. Cairo: Institut Français d'Archéologie Orientale.

Cauville, S. 2001. *Dendara IV: Traduction* (Orientalia Lovaniensia Analecta 101). Leuven: Peeters.

Cauville, S. 2002. *Dendara: Les fêtes d'Hathor* (Orientalia Lovaniensia Analecta 105). Leuven: Peeters.

de Cenival, F. 1972. *Les associations religieuses en Égypte d'après les documents démotiques* (Bibliothèque d'étude 46). Cairo: Institut Français d'Archéologie Orientale.

Censorinus: *De die natali liber.*

Černý, J. 1927. Le culte d'Amenophis Ier chez les ouvriers de la nécropole thébaine. *Bulletin de l'Institut Français d'Archéologie Orientale* 27: 159–97.

Černý, J. 1935a. *Catalogue des ostraca hiératiques non littéraires de Deir el Médineh* (Publications de l'Institut Français d'Archéologie Orientale du Caire 3–14), 8 vols. Cairo: Imprimerie de l'Institut Français d'Archéologie Orientale.

Černý, J. 1935b. *Ostraca hiératiques: Nos. 25501-25832* (Catalogue général des antiquités égyptiennes du Musée du Caire 93 and 95), 2 vols. Cairo: Imprimerie de l'Institut Français d'Archéologie Orientale.

Černý, J. 1939. *Late Ramesside letters* (Bibliotheca Aegyptiaca 9). Bruxelles: Édition de la Fondation Égyptologique Reine Élizabeth.

Černý, J. 1942a. Nouvelle série des questions adressées aux oracles. *Bulletin de l'Institut Français d'Archéologie Orientale* 41: 13–24.

Černý, J. 1942b. Le caractère des ouchebtis d'après les idée du Nouvel Empire. *Bulletin de l'Institut Français d'Archéologie Orientale* 41: 105–33.

Černý, J. 1945. The will of Naunakhte and the related documents. *Journal of Egyptian Archaeology* 31: 29–53.

Černý, J. 1946. Studies in the chronology of the Twenty-First Dynasty. *Journal of Egyptian Archaeology* 32: 24–30.

Černý, J. 1949. *Répertoire onomastique de Deir el-Médineh* (Documents de Fouilles de l'Institut Français d'Archéologie Orientale du Caire 12). Cairo: Imprimerie de l'Institut Français d'Archéologie Orientale.

Černý, J. 1952a. *Ancient Egyptian religion* (Hutchinson's university library. World religions). London: Hutchinson's University Library.

Černý, J. 1952b. *Paper and books in ancient Egypt: An inaugural lecture delivered at University College, London, 29 May, 1947*. London: H.K. Lewis.

Černý, J. 1956. *Graffiti hiéroglyphiques et hiératiques de la nécropole thébaine nos 1060 à 1405* (Documents de Fouilles de l'Institut Français d'Archéologie Orientale du Caire 9). Cairo: Institut Français d'Archéologie Orientale.

Černý, J. 1958a. A hieroglyphic ostracon in the Museum of Fine Arts at Boston. *Journal of Egyptian Archaeology* 44: 23–5.

Černý, J. 1958b. Queen Ēse of the Twentieth Dynasty and her mother. *Journal of Egyptian Archaeology* 44: 31–7.

Černý, J. 1961. Brief communications: Note on the supposed beginning of a Sothic period unter Sethos I. *Journal of Egyptian Archaeology* 47: 150–2.

Černý, J. 1962. Egyptian oracles, in R.A. Parker (ed.), *A Saite oracle papyrus from Thebes in the Brooklyn Museum (Papyrus Brooklyn 47.218.3)* (Brown Egyptological Studies 4): 35–48. Providence: Brown University Press.

Černý, J. 1973. *A community of workmen at Thebes in the Ramesside Period* (Bibliothèque d'étude 50). Cairo: Institut Français d'Archéologie Orientale.

Černý, J. and Gardiner, A.H. 1957. *Hieratic ostraca*. Oxford: Charles Batey.

Černý, J. and Sadek, A.e.-A. 1969. *Graffiti de la montagne thébaine* (Collection scientifique), 4 vols. Cairo: Centre de Documentation et d'Études sur l'Ancienne Égypte.

Champdor, A. 1955. *Thèbes aux cent portes* (Collection hauts lieux de l'histoire 5), 3rd ed. Paris: A. Guillot.

Champollion, J.-F. 1844. *Monuments de l'Égypte et de la Nubie: Notices descriptives conformes aux manuscrits autographes*, 2 vols. Paris: Firmin Didot Frères.

Chappaz, J.-L. 1983. Un contrepoids de collier menat au Musée d'Art et d'Histoire. *Genava, nouvelle série* 31: 9–16.

Chassinat, É. 1897. *Le temple d'Edfou* (Mémoires publiés par les membres de la mission archéologique française au Caire 10–1 and 20–31), 14 vols. Paris: Ernest Leroux.

Chassinat, É. 1900. Textes provenant du Sérapéum de Memphis. *Recueil de Travaux* 22: 9–26.

Chassinat, É. 1930. Quelques parfums et onguents en usage dans les temples de l'Égypte ancienne. *Revue de l'Égypte Ancienne* 3: 117–67.

Chassinat, É. 1934. *Le temple de Dendara* (Publications de l'Institut Français d'Archéologie Orientale du Caire), 9 vols. Cairo: Institut Français d'Archéologie Orientale.

Chassinat, É. 1966. *Le mystère d'Osiris au mois de Khoiak* (Publications de l'Institut Français d'Archéologie Orientale du Caire), 2 vols. Cairo: Institut Français d'Archéologie Orientale.

Cherpion, N. and Corteggiani, J.P. 2010. *La tombe d'Inherkhâouy (TT 359) à Deir el-Medina* (Mémoires publiés par les membres de l'Institut Français d'Archéologie Orientale du Caire 128), 2 vols. Cairo: Institut Français d'Archéologie Orientale.

Cherpion, N., Kruchten, J.-M., and Ménassa, L. 1999. *Deux tombes de la XVIIIe Dynastie à Deir el-Medina: Nos 340 (Amenemhat) et 354 (anonyme)* (Mémoires publiés par les membres de l'Institut Français d'Archéologie Orientale du Caire 114). Cairo: Institut Français d'Archéologie Orientale.

Chevrier, H. 1947. Rapport sur les travaux de Karnak (1947–1948). *Annales du Service des Antiquités de l'Égypte* 47: 161–83.

Chevrier, H. 1956. Rapport sur les travaux de Karnak (1952–1953). *Annales du Service des Antiquités de l'Égypte* 53: 7–19.

Christophe, L.-A. 1951. *Karnak-nord III (1945-1949): Fouilles conduites par C. Robichon* (Fouilles de l'Institut Français d'Archéologie Orientale du Caire 23). Cairo: Imprimerie de l'Institut Français d'Archéologie Orientale.

Christophe, L.-A. 1954. Note à propos du rapport de M. Chevrier: Ramsès IV et la 'Salle des Fêtes' de Thoutmosis III à Karnak. *Annales du Service des Antiquités de l'Égypte* 52: 253–66.

Clagett, M. 1995. *Ancient Egyptian science II: Calendars, clocks, and astronomy* (Memoirs of the American Philosophical Society 214). Philadelphia: American Philosophical Society.

Clark, R.T.R. 1959. *Myth and symbol in ancient Egypt* (Myth and man). London: Thames and Hudson.

Clère, J.J. 1975. Un monument de la religion populaire de l' époque ramesside. *Revue d'Égyptologie* 27: 70–7.

Clère, P. 1961. *La porte d'Évergète à Karnak* (Mémoires publiés par les membres de l'Institut Français d'Archéologie Orientale du Caire 84). Cairo: Imprimerie de l'Institut Français d'Archéologie Orientale du Caire.

Cline, E.H. and O'Connor, D.B. 2006. *Thutmose III: A new biography*. Ann Arbor: University of Michigan Press.

Cline, E.H. and O'Connor, D.B. 2012. *Ramesses III: The life and times of Egypt's last hero*. Ann Arbor: University of Michigan Press.

Collier, M. 2004. *Dating late XIXth Dynasty ostraca* (Egyptologische uitgaven 18). Leiden: Nederlands Instituut voor het Nabije Oosten.

Collier, M. 2011. More on late Nineteenth Dynasty ostraca dates, and remarks on Paneb, in M. Collier and S.R. Snape (eds), *Ramesside studies in honour of K. A. Kitchen*: 111–22. Bolton: Rutherford.

Collier, M. and Quirke, S. 2002. *The UCL Lahun papyri: Letters* (British Archaeological Reports. International Series 1083). Oxford: Archaeopress.

Collier, M. and Quirke, S. 2004. *The UCL Lahun papyri: Religious, literary, legal, mathematical and medical* (British Archaeological Reports. International Series 1209). Oxford: Archaeopress.

Collier, M. and Quirke, S. 2006. *The UCL Lahun Papyri: Accounts* (British Archaeological Reports. International Series 1471). Oxford: Archaeopress.

Collier, S.A. 1996. The crowns of pharaoh: Their development and significance in ancient Egyptian kingship. Unpublished PhD dissertation, University of California.

Condon, V. 1978. *Seven royal hymns of the Ramesside Period: Papyrus Turin CG 54031* (Münchner ägyptologische Studien 37). München: Deutscher Kunstverlag.

Cooney, K.M. 2000. Edifice of Taharqa by the sacred lake: Ritual function and the role of the king. *Journal of the American Research Center in Egypt* 37: 15–47.

Coppens, F. 2008. *The wabet: Tradition and innovation in temples of the Ptolemaic and Roman Period*. Praha and Oxford: Czech Institute of Egyptology and Oxbow.

Coppens, F. 2010. Linen, unguents, pectorals, in M. Dolińska and H. Beinlich (eds), *8. ägyptologische Tempeltagung: Interconnections between temples, Warschau, 22.-25. September 2008* (Königtum, Staat und Gesellschaft früher Hochkulturen 3 (3)): 39–55. Wiesbaden: Harrassowitz.

Coppens, F. and Vymazalová, H. 2010. Long live the king!: Notes on the renewal of divine kingship in the temple, in L. Bareš, F. Coppens, and K. Smoláriková (eds), *Egypt in transition: Social and religious development of Egypt in the first millennium BCE: Proceedings of an international conference, Prague, September 1-4, 2009*: 73–101. Praha: Gardners Books.

Corthals, A. 2004. The New Year Festival in the Ptolemaic temples of Upper Egypt. Unpublished PhD dissertation, University of Oxford.

Corthals, A. 2005. The procession of the New Year in the staircases at Edfu, in A. Amenta, M.M. Luiselli, and M. Novella Sordi (eds), *L'acqua nell'antico Egitto: Vita, rigenerazione, incantesimo, medicamento: proceedings of the first International conference for young egyptologists: Italy, Chianciano Terme, October 15-18, 2003* (Egitto antico 3): 211–9. Roma: L'Erma di Bretschneider.

Cotelle-Michel, L. 2003. Présentation préliminaire des blocs de la chapelle de Sésostris Ier découverte dans le IXe pylône de Karnak, in *Cahiers de Karnak 11*: 339–63. Cairo: Centre Franco-Égyptien d'Étude des Temples de Karnak.

Coulon, L., Leclère, F., and Marchand, S. 1995. 'Catacombes' osiriennes de Ptolémée IV à Karnak, in *Cahiers de Karnak 10: 1992-1994*: 205–51. Paris: Centre Franco-Égyptien d'Étude des Temples de Karnak.

Couyat, J. and Montet, P. 1912. *Les inscriptions hiéroglyphiques et hiératiques du Ouadi Hammamat*

(Mémoires publiés par les membres de l'Institut Français d'Archéologie Orientale du Caire 34). Cairo: Imprimerie de l'Institut Français d'Archéologie Orientale.

Cumming, B. and Davies, B.G. 1982. *Egyptian historical records of the later Eighteenth Dynasty*, 6 vols. Warminster: Aris & Phillips.

Curran, B.A., Grafton, A., Long, P.O., and Weiss, B. 2009. *Obelisk: A history* (Burndy Library Publications, New Series 2). Cambridge and Massachusetts: MIT Press.

Ćwiek, A. 2007. Red, yellow and pink. Ideology of skin hues at Deir el-Bahari. *Fontes Archaeologici Posnanienses* 43: 23–50.

Ćwiek, A. 2008. Fate of Seth in the temple of Hatshepsut at Deir el-Bahari. *Études et Travaux* 22: 37–60.

Dąbrowska-Smektała, E. 1968. Remarks on the restoration of the eastern wall on the 3rd terrace of Hatshepsut temple. *Études et Travaux* 2: 65–78.

Dąbrowska-Smektała, E. and Gartkiewicz, P.M. 1968. Preliminary report concerning the restoration of the wall on the 3rd terrace of the Hatshepsut temple at Deir el-Bahari during the season 1965–1966. *Annales du Service des Antiquités de l'Égypte* 60: 213–9.

Daressy, G. 1892. La procession d'Ammom dans le temple de Louxor, in U. Bouriant (ed.), (Mémoires publiés par les membres de la mission archéologie française au Caire 8 (3)): 380–91. Paris: Ernest Leroux.

Daressy, G. 1893. *Notice explicative des ruines du temple de Louxor*. Cairo: Imprimerie Nationale.

Daressy, G. 1896. Une inondation à Thèbes sous le règne d'Osorkon II. *Recueil de Travaux* 18: 181–6.

Daressy, G. 1900. La chapelle d'Uazmès. *Annales du Service des antiquités de l'Égypte* 1: 97–108.

Daressy, G. 1901. *Ostraca* (Catalogue général des antiquités égyptiennes du Musée du Caire 1). Cairo: Imprimerie de l'Institut Français d'Archéologie Orientale.

Daressy, G. 1905. *Statues de divinités* (Catalogue général des antiquités égyptiennes du Musée du Caire 28–9), 2 vols. Cairo: Imprimerie de l'Institut Français d'Archéologie Orientale.

Daressy, G. 1909. *Cercueils des cachettes royales* (Catalogue général des antiquités égyptiennes du Musée du Caire 50). Cairo: Imprimerie de l'Institut Français d'Archéologie Orientale.

Daressy, G. 1913. Notes sur les XXII, XXIII et XXIV Dynasties. *Recueil de Travaux* 35: 129–50.

Daressy, G. 1926. Le voyage d'inscription de M. Grébaut en 1889. *Annales du Service des Antiquités de l'Égypte* 26: 1–22.

Darnell, D. 2000. Oasis ware flasks and kegs from the Theban desert. *Cahiers de la Céramique Égyptienne* 6: 227–34.

Darnell, J.C. 1991. Two sieges in the Aethiopic stelae, in D. Mendel and U. Claudi (eds), *Ägypten im afro-orientalischen Kontext: Aufsätze zur Archäologie, Geschichte und Sprache eines unbegrenzten Raumes: Gedenkschrift Peter Behrens* (Afrikanistische Arbeitspapiere. Sondernummer): 73–93. Köln: Institut für Afrikanistik, Universität Köln.

Darnell, J.C. 1994. Two notes on marginal inscriptions at Medinet Habu, in B.M. Bryan and D. Lorton (eds), *Essays in Egyptology in honor of Hans Goedicke*: 35–55. San Antonio: van Siclen Books.

Darnell, J.C. 1995. Hathor returns to Medamûd. *Studien zur Altägyptischen Kultur* 22: 47–94.

Darnell, J.C. 1997. The apotropaic goddess in the eye. *Studien zur Altägyptischen Kultur* 24: 35–48.

Darnell, J.C. 2002. *Theban desert road survey in the Egyptian western desert I: Gebel Tjauti rock inscriptions 1-45 and Wadi el-Hôl rock inscriptions 1-45* (Oriental Institute publications 119). Chicago: United Graphics Incorporated.

Darnell, J.C. 2010a: Opet Festival, in J. Dieleman and W. Wendrich (eds), *UCLA encyclopedia of Egyptology*: 1–15. Los Angeles.

Darnell, J.C. 2010b. A midsummer night's succubus: The herdsman's encounters in P. Berlin 3024, the pleasures of fishing and fowling, the songs of the drinking place, and the ancient Egyptian love poetry, in E. Frahm, W.R. Garr, B. Halpern, T.P.J. van den Hout, and I.J. Winter (eds), *Opening the tablet box: Near Eastern studies in honor of Benjamin R. Foster* (Culture and history of the ancient Near East 42): 99–140. Leiden and Boston: Brill.

Darnell, J.C. 2011. A stela of Seti I from the region of Kurkur Oasis, in M. Collier and S.R. Snape (eds), *Ramesside studies in honour of K. A. Kitchen*: 127–44. Bolton: Rutherford.

Darnell, J.C. and Manassa, C. 2007. *Tutankhamun's armies: Battle and conquest during ancient Egypt's late Eighteenth Dynasty*. Hoboken: John Wiley & Sons.

Daumas, F. 1967. L'origine d'Amon de Karnak. *Bulletin de l'Institut Français d'Archéologie Orientale* 65: 201–14.

Daumas, F. 1979. Sur un scarabée portant une inscription curieuse, in *Hommages à la mémoire de Serge Sauneron, 1927-1976* (Bibliothèque d'étude 81), vol. 1: 155–66. Cairo: Institut Français d'Archéologie Orientale.

Daumas, F. 1980. L'interprétation des temples égyptiens anciens à la lumière des temples gréco-romains, in *Cahiers de Karnak 6: 1973-1977*: 261–84. Cairo: Centre Franco-Égyptien d'Étude des Temples de Karnak.

Davies, B.G. 1997a. *Egyptian historical inscriptions of the Nineteenth Dynasty* (Documenta mundi. Aegyptiaca 2). Jonsered: Paul Åströms Förlag.

Davies, B.G. 1997b. Two many Butehamuns?: Additional observations on their identity. *Studien zur Altägyptischen Kultur* 24: 49–68.

Davies, N. and Davies, N.d.G. 1941. Syrians in the tomb of Amunedjeh. *Journal of Egyptian Archaeology* 27: 96–8.

Davies, N. and Davies, N.d.G 1963. *Scenes from some Theban tombs (nos. 38, 66, 162, with excerpts from 81)* (Private tombs at Thebes 4). Oxford: Vivian Ridler.

Davies, N. and Gardiner, A.H. 1915. *The tomb of Amenemhēt (no. 82)* (Theban tombs series 1). London: Egypt Exploration Fund.

Davies, N. and Gardiner, A.H. 1926. *The tomb of Huy, viceroy of Nubia in the reign of Tut'ankhamun (no. 40)* (Theban tombs series 4). London: Egypt Exploration Society.

Davies, N.d.G. 1900. *The mastaba of Ptahhetep and Akhethetep at Saqqareh* (Archaeological survey of Egypt 8–9), 2 vols. London: Egypt Exploration Fund.

Davies, N.d.G. 1903. *The rock tombs of El Amarna* (Archaeological survey of Egypt 13–8), 6 vols. London: Egypt Exploration Fund.

Davies, N.d.G. 1913. *Five Theban tombs* (Archaeological survey of Egypt 21). London: Egypt Exploration Fund.

Davies, N.d.G. 1917. *The tomb of Nakht at Thebes* (Publications of the Metropolitan Museum of Art, Egyptian expedition, Robb de Peyster Tytus memorial series 1). New York: Metropolitan Museum of Art.

Davies, N.d.G. 1922. *The tomb of Puyemrê at Thebes* (Publications of the Metropolitan Museum of Art, Egyptian expedition, Robb de Peyster Tytus memorial series 2–3), 2 vols. New York: Metropolitan Museum of Art.

Davies, N.d.G. 1923. *The tombs of two officials of Tuthmosis the Fourth (nos. 75 and 90)* (Theban tombs series 3). London: Egypt Exploration Society.

Davies, N.d.G. 1924. A peculiar form of New Kingdom lamp. *Journal of Egyptian Archaeology* 10: 9–14.

Davies, N.d.G. 1927. *Two Ramesside tombs at Thebes* (Publications of the Metropolitan Museum of Art, Egyptian expedition, Robb de Peyster Tytus memorial series 5). New York: Metropolitan Museum of Art.

Davies, N.d.G. 1928a. The town house in ancient Egypt. *Metropolitan Museum Studies* 1: 233–55.

Davies, N.d.G. 1928b. The graphic work of the expedition at Thebes. *The Metropolitan Museum of Art Bulletin* 23: 37–49.

Davies, N.d.G. 1929. The graphic work of the expedition. *The Metropolitan Museum of Art Bulletin* 24: 35–49.

Davies, N.d.G. 1930. *The tomb of Ḳen-Amūn at Thebes* (Publications of the Metropolitan Museum of Art, Egyptian expedition 5), 2 vols. New York: Metropolitan Museum of Art.

Davies, N.d.G. 1932. Tehuti: owner of tomb 110 at Thebes, in Egypt Exploration Society (ed.), *Studies presented to F. Ll. Griffith*: 279–90. London: Oxford University Press.

Davies, N.d.G. 1933a. *The tomb of Nefer-ḥotep at Thebes* (Publications of the Metropolitan Museum of Art, Egyptian expedition 9), 2 vols. New York: Metropolitan Museum of Art.

Davies, N.d.G. 1933b. *The tombs of Menkheperrasonb, Amenmose, and another (nos. 86, 112, 42, 226)* (Theban tombs series 5). London: Egypt Exploration Society.

Davies, N.d.G. 1941. *The tomb of the vizier Ramose* (Mond excavations at Thebes 1). London: Egypt Exploration Society.

Davies, N.d.G. 1943. *The tomb of Rekh-mi-rē' at Thebes* (Publications of the Metropolitan Museum of Art, Egyptian expedition 11), 2 vols. New York: The Plantin press.

Davies, N.d.G. and Davies, N. 1939. Harvest rites in a Theban tomb. *Journal of Egyptian Archaeology* 25: 154–6.

Davies, N.d.G. and Gardiner, A.H. 1920. *The tomb of Antefoker, vizier of Sesostris I, and of his wife, Senet (no. 60)* (Theban tombs series 2). London: G. Allen & Unwin.

Davies, N.d.G. and Gardiner, A.H. 1948. *Seven private tombs at Ḳurnah* (Mond exavations at Thebes 2). London: Egypt Exploration Society.

Davies, S. and Smith, H.S. 1997. Sacred animal temples at Saqqara, in S. Quirke (ed.), *The temple in ancient Egypt: New discoveries and recent research*: 112–31. London: British Museum Press.

Decker, W. and Herb, M. 1994. *Bildatlas zum Sport im alten Ägypten: Corpus der bildlichen Quellen zu Leibesübungen, Spiel, Jagd, Tanz und verwandten Themen*, 2 vols. Leiden, New York, and Köln: Brill.

Defossez, M. 1985. Les laitues de Min. *Studien zur Altägyptischen Kultur* 12: 1–4.

Dégardin, J.-C. 1984. Procession de barques dans la temple de Khonsou. *Revue d'Égyptologie* 35: 191–5.

Delange, E. 1987. *Catalogue des statues égyptiennes du Moyen Empire: 2060–1560 avant J.-C.* Paris: Editions de la Réunion des Musées Nationaux.

Delvaux, L. 2010. La statue de Thoutmosis Ier offerte à Qenamon (TT 93), in E. Warmenbol and V. Angenot (eds), *Thèbes aux 101 portes: Mélanges à la mémoire de Roland Tefnin* (Monumenta aegyptiaca 12): 63–77. Turnhout: Brepols.

Demarée, R.J. 2002. *Ramesside ostraca*. London: British Museum Press.

Depauw, M. and Smith, M.J. 2004. Visions of ecstasy: Cultic revelry before the goddess Ai/Nehemanit, Ostraca Faculteit Letteren (K.U. Leuven) dem. 1–2, in K.-T. Zauzich, F. Hoffmann, and H.-J. Thissen (eds), *Res severa verum gaudium: Festschrift für Karl-Theodor Zauzich zum 65. Geburtstag am 8. Juni 2004* (Studia demotica 6): 67–93. Leuven and Dudley: Peeters.

Depuydt, L. 1995. On the consistency of the wandering year as backbone of Egyptian chronology. *Journal of American Research Center in Egypt* 32: 43–58.

Depuydt, L. 1997. *Civil calendar and lunar calendar in ancient Egypt* (Orientalia Lovaniensia Analecta 77). Leuven: Peeters.

Depuydt, L. 2000. Sothic chronology and the Old Kingdom. *Journal of the American Research Center in Egypt* 37: 167–86.

Depuydt, L. 2003. Esna's triple New Year. *Journal of American Research Center in Egypt* 40: 55–67.

Derchain, P. 1965. *Le Papyrus Salt 825 (B.M. 10051): Rituel pour la conservátion de la vie en Égypte* (Mémoires de la classe des lettres 58), 2 vols. Bruxelles: Palais des académies.

Desplancques, S. 1999. Étude paléographique des termes *pr-HD, prwy-HD* et *prwy-nbw* de l'Ancien Empire à la fin du Moyen Empire. *Cahier de Recherches de l'Institut de Papyrologie et d'Égyptologie de Lille* 20: 29–40.

2006. *L'institution du trésor en Égypte des origines à la fin du Moyen Empire* (Les institutions dans l'Égypte ancienne 2). Paris: Presses de l'Université de Paris-Sorbonne.

Desroches-Noblecourt, C. and Kuentz, C.M. 1968. *Le petit temple d'Abou Simbel: Nofretari pour qui se lève le dieu-soleil* (Mémoire, Centre de Documentation et d'Études sur l'Ancienne Égypte 1–2), 2 vols. Cairo: Centre de Documentation et d'Études sur l'Ancienne Égypte.

van Dijk, J. 2000: The Amarna Period and the later New Kingdom, in I. Show (ed.), *The Oxford history of ancient Egypt*: 272–313. Oxford: Oxford University Press

Dittmar, J. 1986. *Blumen und Blumensträuße als Opfergabe im alten Ägypten* (Münchner ägyptologische Studien 43). München: Deutscher Kunstverlag.

Dodson, A. 2002. The problem of Amenirdis II and the heirs to the office of god's wife of Amun during the Twenty-Sixth Dynasty. *Journal of Egyptian Archaeology* 88: 179–86.

Dodson, A. and Janssen, J.J. 1989. A Theban tomb and its tenants. *Journal of Egyptian Archaeology* 75: 125–38.

Dolińska, M. 1994. Some remarks about the function of the Thutmosis III temple at Deir el-Bahari, in R. Gundlach and M. Rochholz (eds), *Ägyptische Tempel: Struktur, Funktion und Programm (Akten der ägyptologischen Tempeltagungen in Gosen 1990 und in Mainz 1992)* (Hildesheimer ägyptologische Beiträge 37): 33–45. Hildesheim: Gerstenberg Verlag.

Dolińska, M. 2007. Temples at Deir el-Bahari in the New Kingdom, in B. Haring and A. Klug (eds), *6. ägyptologische Tempeltagung: Funktion und Gebrauch altägyptischer Tempelräume: Leiden, 4.–7. September 2002* (Königtum, Staat und Gesellschaft früher Hochkulturen 3): 67–82. Wiesbaden: Harrassowitz.

Donker van Heel, K. 1992. Use and meaning of the Egyptian term *wAH-mw*, in R.J. Demarée and A. Egberts (eds), *Village voices: Proceedings of the symposium "Texts from Deir el-Medîna and their interpretation", Leiden, May 31–June 1, 1991* (Centre of non-Western studies publications 13): 19–30. Leiden: Centre of Non-Western Studies, Leiden University.

Donker van Heel, K 1996. Abnormal hieratic and early demotic texts collected by the Theban choachytes in the reign of Amasis: Papyri from the Louvre Eisenlohr lot. Unpublished PhD dissertation, Rijksuniversiteit te Leiden.

Doresse, M. 1971. Le dieu voilé dans sa châsse et la fête su début de la décade (I). *Revue d'Égyptologie* 23: 113–36.

Doresse, M. 1973. Le dieu voilé dans sa châsse et la fête su début de la décade (II). *Revue d'Égyptologie* 25: 92–135.

Doresse, M. 1979. Le dieu voilé dans sa châsse et la fête su début de la décade (III). *Revue d'Égyptologie* 31: 36–65.

Dorman, P.F. 1988. *The monuments of Senenmut: Problems in historical methodology*. London: Kegan Paul International.

Dorman, P.F. 1995. Two tombs and one owner, in J. Assmann, E. Dziobek, H. Guksch, and F. Kampp (eds), *Thebanische Beamtennekropolen: Neue Perspektiven archäologischer Forschung: Internationales Symposion, Heidelberg, 9.–13. Juni 1993* (Studien zur Archäologie und Geschichte Altägyptens 12): 141–54. Heidelberg: Heidelberger Orientverlag.

Dorman, P.F. 2006. The early reign of Thutmose III: An unorthodox mantle of coregency, in E.H. Cline and D.B. O'Connor (eds), *Thutmose III: A new biography*: 39–68. Ann Arbor: University of Michigan Press.

Dorman, P.F. and Bryan, B.M. 2007. *Sacred space and sacred function in ancient Thebes* (Studies in ancient Oriental civilization 61). Chicago: Oriental Institute of the University of Chicago.

Dorn, A. 2011. The provenance and context of the accession ostracon of Ramesses VI, in M. Collier and S.R. Snape (eds), *Ramesside studies in honour of K. A. Kitchen*: 159–68. Bolton: Rutherford.

Dresbach, G. 2012. *Zur Verwaltung in der 20. Dynastie: Das Wesirat* (Königtum, Staat und Gesellschaft früher Hochkulturen 9). Wiesbaden: Harrassowitz.

Dümichen, J. 1865. *Bauurkunde der Tempelanlagen von Dendera in einem der geheimen Corridore im Innern der Tempelmauer aufgefunden und erläuternd mitgetheilt*. Leipzig: J.C. Hindrichs.

Dümichen, J. 1866. *Altaegyptische Kalenderinschriften*. Leipzig: J.C. Hinrichs.

Dümichen, J. 1869. *Historische Inschriften altägyptischer Denkmäler. Zweite Folge: Nebst einigen geographischen und mythologischen Inschriften*. Leipzig: J.C. Hinrichs.

Dümichen, J. 1884. *Der Grabpalast des Patuamenap in der thebanischen Nekropolis: In vollständiger Copie seiner Inschriften und bildlichen Darstellungen, und mit Uebersetzung und Erläuterungen derselben*. Leipzig: J.C. Hinrichs.

Dunham, D. 1938. The biographical inscriptions of Nekhebu in Boston and Cario. *Journal of Egyptian Archaeology* 24: 1–8.

Dušan, M. 2000. On the orientation of Old Kingdom royal tombs, in J. Krejčí and M. Bárta (eds), *Abusir and Saqqara in the year 2000* (Archív orientální. Supplementa 9): 491–8. Praha: Academy of Sciences of the Czech Republic, Oriental Institute.

Dziobek, E. 1992. *Das Grab des Ineni: Theben Nr. 81* (Archäologische Veröffentlichungen (Deutsches Archäologisches Institut, Abteilung Kairo) 68). Mainz am Rhein: Philipp von Zabern.

Dziobek, E. 1994. *Die Gräber des Vezirs User-Amun: Theben Nr. 61 und 131* (Archäologische Veröffentlichungen (Deutsches Archäologisches Institut. Abteilung Kairo) 84). Mainz: Philipp von Zabern.

Dziobek, E. 1995. Theban tombs as a source for historical and biographical evaluation: The case of User-Amun, in J. Assmann, E. Dziobek, H. Guksch, and F. Kampp (eds), *Thebanische Beamtennekropolen: Neue Perspektiven archäologischer Forschung: Internationales Symposion, Heidelberg, 9.-13. Juni 1993* (Studien zur Archäologie und Geschichte Altägyptens 12): 129–40. Heidelberg: Heidelberger Orientverlag.

Dziobek, E. 1998. *Denkmäler des Vezirs User-Amun* (Studien zur Archäologie und Geschichte Altägyptens 18). Heidelberg: Heidelberger Orientverlag.

Dziobek, E. and Abd el-Razik, M. 1990. *Das Grab des Sobekhotep: Theben Nr. 63* (Archäologische Veröffentlichungen (Deutsches Archäologisches Institut. Abteilung Kairo) 71). Mainz: Philipp von Zabern.

Eaton-Krauss, M. 1999. The fate of Sennefer and Senetnay at Karnak temple and in the Valley of the King. *Journal of Egyptian Archaeology* 85: 113–29.

Edel, E. 1949. Zur Lesung von 'Regierungsjahr'. *Journal of Near Eastern Studies* 8: 35–9.

Edel, E. 1953. Die Stelen Amenophis' II. aus Karnak und Memphis mit dem Bericht über die asiatischen Feldzüge des Königs. *Zeitschrift des Deutschen Palästina-Vereins* 69: 97–176.

Edgerton, W.F. 1937a. Critical note on the chronology of the early Eighteenth Dynasty (Amenhotep I to Thutmose III). *The American Journal of Semitic Languages and Literatures* 53: 188–97.

Edgerton, W.F. 1937b. *Medinet Habu graffiti facsimiles* (Oriental Institute publications 36). Chicago: University of Chicago Press.

Edwards, I.E.S. 1939. *Hieroglyphic texts from Egyptian stelae, etc., in the British Museum VIII*. London: Trustees of the British Museum.

Edwards, I.E.S. 1960. *Oracular amuletic decrees of the late New Kingdom* (Hieratic papyri in the British Museum. Fourth series), 2 vols. London: Trustees of the British Museum.

Edwards, I.E.S. 1971. Bill of sale for a set of ushabtis. *Journal of Egyptian Archaeology* 57: 120–4.

Egberts, A. 1995. *In quest of meaning: A study of the ancient Egyptian rites of consecrating the meret-chests and driving the calves* (Egyptologische uitgaven 8), 2 vols. Leiden: Nederlands Instituut voor het Nabije Oosten.

Egberts, A. 1997. The chronology of the Horus myth of Edfu, in J. van Dijk (ed.), *Essays on ancient Egypt in honour of Herman te Velde* (Egyptological memoirs 1): 47–54. Groningen: STYX Publications.

Egli, E. 1959. *Geschichte des Städtebaues*, 3 vols. Erlenbach: E. Rentsch.

Eichler, E. 1993. *Untersuchungen zum Expeditionswesen des ägyptischen Alten Reiches* (Göttinger Orientforschungen 26). Wiesbaden: Harrassowitz.

Eichler, S.S. 2000. *Die Verwaltung des 'Hauses des Amun' in der 18. Dynastie* (Studien zur Altägyptischen Kultur Beihefte 7). Hamburg: Helmut Buske.

Eide, T., Hägg, T., and Pierce, R.H. 1994. *Fontes historiae nubiorum: Textual sources for the history of the middle Nile region between the eighth century BC and the sixth century AD*, 4 vols. Bergen: University of Bergen.

Engelbach, R. 1921. Report on the inspectorate of Upper Egypt from April 1920 to March 1921. *Annales du Service des Antiquités de l'Égypte* 21: 61–76.

Engelmann-von Carnap, B. 1995. Soziale Stellung und Grabanlage: Zur Struktur des Friedhofs der ersten Hälfte der 18. Dynastie in Scheich Abd el-Qurna und Chocha, in J. Assmann, E. Dziobek, H. Guksch, and F. Kampp (eds), *Thebanische Beamtennekropolen: Neue Perspektiven archäologischer Forschung: Internationales Symposion, Heidelberg, 9.-13. Juni 1993* (Studien zur Archäologie und Geschichte Altägyptens 12): 107–28. Heidelberg: Heidelberger Orientverlag.

Engelmann-von Carnap, B. 1999. *Die Struktur des thebanischen Beamtenfriedhofs in der ersten Hälfte der 18. Dynastie: Analyse von Position, Grundrißgestaltung und Bildprogramm der Gräber* (Abhandlungen des deutschen archäologischen Instituts Kairo, ägyptologische Reihe 15). Berlin: Achet Verlag.

Enmarch, R. 2005. *The Dialogue of Ipuwer and the Lord of All*. Oxford: Alden Press.

Enmarch, R. 2008. *A world upturned: Commentary on and analysis of the Dialogue of Ipuwer and the Lord of All*. Oxford and New York: Oxford University Press.

Epigraphic Survey 1932. *Medinet Habu II: Later historical records of Ramses III* (Oriental Institute publications 9). Chicago: University of Chicago Press.

Epigraphic Survey 1934. *Medinet Habu III: The calendar, the "slaughter house", and minor records of Ramses III* (Oriental Institute publications 23). Chicago: University of Chicago Press.

Epigraphic Survey 1936a. *Reliefs and inscriptions at Karnak I: Ramses III's temple within the great enclosure of Amon, part 1* (Oriental Institute publications 25). Chicago: University of Chicago Press.

Epigraphic Survey 1936b. *Reliefs and inscriptions at Karnak II: Ramses III's temple within the great inclosure of Amon, part 2: Ramses III's temple in the precinct of Mut* (Oriental Institute publications 35). Chicago: University of Chicago Press.

Epigraphic Survey 1940. *Medinet Habu IV: Festival scenes of Ramses III* (Oriental Institute publications 51). Chicago: University of Chicago Press.

Epigraphic Survey 1954. *Reliefs and inscriptions at Karnak III: Bubastite portal* (Oriental Institute publications 74). Chicago: University of Chicago Press.

Epigraphic Survey 1979. *The temple of Khonsu I: Scenes of king Herihor in the court* (Oriental Institute publications 100). Chicago: University of Chicago Press.

Epigraphic Survey 1980. *The tomb of Kheruef: Theban tomb 192* (Oriental Institute publications 102). Chicago: University of Chicago Press.

Epigraphic Survey 1981. *The temple of Khonsu II: Scenes and inscriptions in the court and the first hypostyle hall* (Oriental Institute publications 103). Chicago: University of Chicago Press.

Epigraphic Survey 1994. *The festival procession of Opet in the colonnade hall: with translations of texts, commentary and glossary* (Oriental Institute publications 112). Chicago: University of Chicago Press.

Epigraphic Survey 1998. *The façade, portals, upper register scenes, columns, marginalia, and statuary in the colonnade hall* (Oriental Institute publications 116). Chicago: University of Chicago Press.

Erichsen, W.C. 1933. *Papyrus Harris I: Hieroglyphische Transkription* (Bibliotheca Aegyptiaca 5). Bruxelles: Édition de la Fondation Égyptologique Reine Élizabeth.

Erman, A. 1901. Monatsnamen aus dem Neuen Reich. *Zeitschrift für Ägyptische Sprache und Altertumskunde* 39: 128–30.

Erman, A. 1911. Denksteine aus der thebanischen Gräberstadt. *Sitzungsberichte der Königlich preussischen Akademie der Wissenschaften* 49: 1086–110.

Erman, A. 1934. *Die Religion der Ägypter: Ihr Werden und Vergehen in vier Jahrtausenden.* Berlin: de Gruyter.

Erman, A. and Grapow, H. 1926. *Wörterbuch der aegyptischen Sprache*, 7 vols. Leipzig: J.C. Hinrichs.

Exell, K. 2009. *Soldiers, sailors and sandalmakers: A social reading of Ramesside Period votive stelae.* London: Golden House Publications.

Eyre, C.J. 1987a. Papyrus Deir el-Meîna XXIV: An appeal for wages? *Göttinger Miszellen* 98: 11–21.

Eyre, C.J. 1987b. Work and the organisation of work in the New Kingdom, in M.A. Powell (ed.), *Labor in the ancient Near East* (American Oriental Series 68): 167–221. New Haven: Amenrican Oriental Society.

Eyre, C.J. 2009. Again the *xtm* of the Tomb: Public space and social access, in D. Kessler, R. Schulz, M. Ullmann, A. Verbovsek, and S. Wimmer (eds), *Texte, Theben, Tonfragmente: Festschrift für Günter Burkard* (Ägypten und Altes Testament 76): 107–17. Wiesbaden: Harrassowitz.

Fairman, H.W. 1934. A statue from the Karnak cache. *Journal of Egyptian Archaeology* 20: 1–4.

Fairman, H.W. 1935. The myth of Horus at Edfu I. *Journal of Egyptian Archaeology* 21: 26–36.

Fairman, H.W. 1954/1955. Worship and festivals in an Egyptian temple. *Bulletin of the John Rylands Library* 37: 165–203.

Fairman, H.W. and Grdseloff, B. 1947. Texts of Hatshepsut and Sethos I inside Speos Artemidos. *Journal of Egyptian Archaeology* 33: 12–33.

Fakhry, A. 1943a. The tomb of Nebamun, captain of troops (no. 145 at Thebes). *Annales du Service des Antiquités de l'Égypte* 43: 369–79.

Fakhry, A. 1943b. Tomb of Paser (no. 367 at Thebes). *Annales du Service des Antiquités de l'Égypte* 43: 389–414.

Fakhry, A. 1944. *Siwa Oasis: Its history and antiquities* (Egyptian deserts). Cairo: Government Press.

Fakhry, A. 1959. *The monuments of Sneferu at Dahshur*, 2 vols. Cairo: General Organization for Government Printing Office

Fakhry, A. 1971. Recent excavation at the temple of the oracle at Siwa Oasis, in *Aufsätze zum 70. Geburtstag von Herbert Ricke* (Beiträge zur ägyptischen Bauforschung und Altertumskunde 12): 17–33. Wiesbaden: Franz Steiner.

Faulkner, R.O. 1936. The Bremner-Rhind papyrus I: A. The song of Isis and Nephthys. *Journal of Egyptian Archaeology* 22: 121–40.

Faulkner, R.O. 1937. The Bremner-Rhind papyrus II: B. The 'colophon'; C. The ritual of Bringing in Sokar. *Journal of Egyptian Archaeology* 23: 10–16.

Faulkner, R.O. 1942. The battle of Megiddo. *Journal of Egyptian Archaeology* 28: 2–15.

Faulkner, R.O. 1972. *The ancient Egyptian Book of the Dead.* London: British Museum Press.

Fecht, G. 1965. *Literarische Zeugnisse zur 'Persönlichen Frömmigkeit' in Ägypten: Analyse der Beispiele aus den ramessidischen Schulpapyri* (Abhandlungen der Heidelberger Akademie der Wissenschaften: Philosophisch-historische Klasse 1965/1). Heidelberg: Carl Winter.

Fecht, G. 1968. Zu den Inschriften des ersten Pfeilers im Grab des Anchtifi (Mo'alla), in W. Helck (ed.), *Festschrift für Siegfried Schott zu seinem 70. Geburtstag am 20. August 1967*: 50–60. Wiesbaden: Harrassowitz.

Fecht, G. 1985. Die Lesung von 'Regierungsjahr' als *rnpt-zp*, in *Ägypten: Dauer und Wandel, Symposium anlässlich des 75 jährigen Bestehens des Deutschen Archäologischen Instituts Kairo, am 10. und 11. Oktober 1982* (Sonderschrift, Deutsches Archäologisches Institut Abteilung Kairo): 85–96. Mainz am Rhein: Philipp von Zabern.

Feder, F. 1998. Das Ritual *saHa kA sHn.t* als Tempelfest des Gottes Min, in R. Gundlach and M. Rochholz (eds), *4. ägyptologische Tempeltagung, Köln 10.–12. Oktober 1996: Feste im Tempel* (Ägypten und Altes Testament 33 (2)): 31–54. Wiesbaden: Harrassowitz.

Feder, F. 2001. 'Gruss dir, Min-Amun, Herr der Sehnet-Kapelle!': Eine Hymne auf ihrem Weg durch die 'Kultgeschichte', in C.-B. Arnst, I. Hafemann, and

A. Lohwasser (eds), *Begegnungen: Antike Kulturen im Niltal: Festgabe für Erika Endesfelder, Karl-Heinz Priese, Walter Friedrich Reineke und Steffen Wenig*: 111–22. Leipzig: Wodtke und Stegbauer.

Felber, H. 1997. Die Daten in den demotischen Ackerpachtverträgen der Ptolemäerzeit und das landwirtschaftliche Jahr, in B. Kramer, W. Luppe, and H. Maehler (eds), *Akten des 21. Internationalen Papyrologenkongresses, Berlin, 13.-19. 8. 1995* (Archiv für Papyrusforschung und verwandte Gebiete 3), vol. 1: 281–9. Stuttgart and Leipzig: B.G. Teubner.

Feucht, E. 1992. Fishing and fowling with the spear and the throw-stick reconsidered, in U. Luft (ed.), *The intellectual heritage of Egypt: Studies presented to László Kákosy by friends and colleagues on the occasion of his 60th birthday* (Studia Aegyptiaca 14): 157–69. Budapest: Korrekt Nyomda Ipari.

Feucht, E. 2006. *Die Gräber des Nedjemger (TT 138) und des Hori (TT 259)* (Theben 15). Mainz am Rhein: Philipp von Zabern.

Feucht, E. and Assmann, J. 1985. *Das Grab des Nefersecheru (TT 296)* (Theben 2). Mainz am Rhein: Philipp von Zabern.

Firth, C.M. and Quibell, J.E. 1935. *The Step Pyramid* (Excavations at Saqqara), 2 vols. Cairo: Imprimerie de l'Institut Français d'Archéologie Orientale.

Fischer-Elfert, H.W. 1996. Two oracle petitions addressed to Horus-Khau with some notes on the oracular amuletic decrees. *Journal of Egyptian Archaeology* 82: 129–44.

Fitzenreiter, M. 1995. Totenverehrung und soziale Repräsentation im thebanischen Beamtengrab der 18. Dynastie. *Studien zur Altägyptischen Kultur* 22: 95–130.

Fitzenreiter, M. 2007. Statuenstifutung und religiöses Stiftungswesen im pharaonischen Ägypten: Notizen zum Grab des Pennut (Teil V), in M. Fitzenreiter (ed.), *Das Heilige und die Ware: Zum Spannungsfeld von Religion und Ökonomie* (Internet-Beiträge zur Ägyptologie und Sudanarchäologie 7): 233–64. London: Golden House Publications.

Foucart, G.M. 1924. Études thébaines: La Belle Fête de la Vallée. *Bulletin de l'Institut Français d'Archéologie Orientale* 24: 1–209.

Foucart, G.M. 1928. *Tombes thébaines: Nécropole de Dirâ Abû'n-Nága: Le tombeau d'Amonmos* (Mémoires publiés par les membres de l'Institut Français d'Archéologie Orientale du Caire 57). Cairo: Imprimerie de l'Institut Français d'Archéologie Orientale.

Fox, M.V. 1982. The entertainment song genre in Egyptian literature, in S. Israelit-Groll (ed.), *Egyptological studies* (Scripta hierosolymitana 28): 268–316. Jerusalem: Magnes Press, Hebrew University.

Fox, M.V. 1985. *The song of songs and the ancient Egyptian love songs*. Madison: University of Wisconsin Press.

Frandsen, P.J. 1998. On the avoidance of certain forms of loud voices and access to the sacred, in W. Clarysse, A. Schoors, and H. Willems (eds), *Egyptian religion: The last thousand years: Studies dedicated to the memory of Jan Quaegebeur*, vol. 2: 975–1000. Leuven: Peeters.

von Frank-Kamenetzky, J. 1914. Der Papyrus Nr. 3162 des Berl. Museum. *Orientalistische Literaturzeitung* 17: 145–53.

Franke, D. 1990. Erste und Zweite Zwischenzeit. *Zeitschrift für Ägyptische Sprache und Altertumskunde* 117: 119–29.

Frankfort, H. 1933. *The cenotaph of Seti I at Abydos* (Memoir of the Egypt Exploration Society 39), 2 vols. London: William Clowes and Sons.

Friedman, F.D. 1998. *Gifts of the Nile: Ancient Egyptian faience*. London: Thames and Hudson.

Friedman, F.D. 2011. Reading the Menkaure triads, part 1, in R. Gundlach and K. Spence (eds), *5. Symposium zur ägyptischen Königsideologie: Palace and temple, architecture-decoration-ritutal, Cambridge, July, 16th-17th, 2007* (Königtum, Staat und Gesellschaft früher Hochkulturen 4 (2)): 23–55. Wiesbaden: Harrassowitz.

Fritz, W. 1991. Bemerkungen zum Datierungsvermerk auf der Amarnatafel KN 27. *Studien zur Altägyptischen Kultur* 18: 207–14.

Frood, E. 2007. *Biographical texts from Ramessid Egypt* (Writings from the ancient world 26). Atlanta: Society of Biblical Literature.

Frood, E. 2010a. Horkhebi's decree and the development of priestly inscriptional practices in Karnak, in L. Bareš, F. Coppens, and K. Smoláriková (eds), *Egypt in transition: Social and religious development of Egypt in the first millennium BCE: Proceedings of an international conference, Prague, September 1-4, 2009*: 103–28. Praha: Gardners Books.

Frood, E. 2010b. Social structure and daily life: Pharaonic, in A.B. Lloyd (ed.), *A companion to ancient Egypt* (Blackwell companions to the ancient world), vol. 1: 469–90. Chichester: Wiley-Blackwell.

Frood, E. 2013. Egyptian temple graffiti and the gods: Appropriation and ritualization in Karnak and Luxor, in D. Ragavan (ed.), *Heaven on earth: Temples, ritual, and cosmic symbolism in the ancient world* (Oriental Institute Seminars 9): 285–318. Chicago: Oriental Institute of the University of Chicago.

Fukaya, M. 2007. Distribution of life force in the Festival of the Valley: A comparative study with the Opet Festival. *Orient* 42: 95–124.

Fukaya, M. 2012. Oracular sessions and the installations of priests and officials at the Opet Festival. *Orient* 47: 191–211.

Gaballa, G.A. 1973. Three documents from the reign of Ramesses III. *Journal of Egyptian Archaeology* 59: 109–13.

Gaballa, G.A. 1976. *Narrative in Egyptian art*. Mainz am Rhein: Philipp von Zabern.

Gaballa, G.A. and Kitchen, K.A. 1969. The Festival of Sokar. *Orientalia, nova series* 38: 2–76.

Gabolde, L. 1989. Les temples mémoriaux de Toutmosis II et Toutânkhamon: Un ritual destiné des statues sur barques. *Bulletin de l'Institut Français d'Archéologie Orientale* 89: 127–78.

Gabolde, L. 1993. La cour de fêtes de Thoutmosis II à Karnak, in *Cahiers de Karnak 9: 1989–1992*: 1–100. Cairo: Centre Franco-Égyptien d'Étude des Temples de Karnak.

Gabolde, L. 1998. *Le 'grand château d'Amon' de Sésostris 1er à Karnak: La décoration du temple d'Amon-Rê au Moyen Empire* (Mémoires de l'Académie des Inscriptions et Belles-Lettres 17). Paris: Diff. de Boccard.

Gabolde, L., Carlotti, J.-F., and Czerny, E. 1999. Aux origines de Karnak: Les recherches récentes dans la 'cour du Moyen Empire'. *Bulletin de la Société d'Égyptologie de Genève* 23: 31–49.

Gabolde, M. 1995. L'inondation sous les pieds d'Amon. *Bulletin de l'Institut Français d'Archéologie Orientale* 95: 235–58.

Galán, J.M. 2000. The ancient Egyptian Sed-Festival and the exemption from corvée. *Journal of Near Eastern Studies* 59: 255–64.

Gardiner, A.H. 1904. The installation of a vizier. *Recueil de Travaux* 24: 1–19.

Gardiner, A.H. 1905. Hymns to Amon from a Leiden papyrus. *Zeitschrift für Ägyptische Sprache und Altertumskunde* 42: 12–42.

Gardiner, A.H. 1906a. Mesore as first month of the Egyptian year. *Zeitschrift für Ägyptische Sprache und Altertumskunde* 43: 136–44.

Gardiner, A.H. 1906b. Four papyri of the 18 Dynasty from Kahun. *Zeitschrift für Ägyptische Sprache und Altertumskunde* 43: 27–47.

Gardiner, A.H. 1908. Inscriptions from the tomb of Sirenpowet I: Prince of Elephantine. *Zeitschrift für Ägyptische Sprache und Altertumskunde* 45: 123–40.

Gardiner, A.H. 1910. The goddess Nekhbet at the Jubilee Festival of Rameses III. *Zeitschrift für Ägyptische Sprache und Altertumskunde* 48: 47–51.

Gardiner, A.H. 1917. Professional magicians in ancient Egypt. *Proceedings of the Society of Biblical Archaeology* 39: 31–44.

Gardiner, A.H. 1925. The secret chambers of the sanctuary of Thoth. *Journal of Egyptian Archaeology* 11: 2–5.

Gardiner, A.H. 1927. *Egyptian grammar: Being an introduction to the study of hieroglyphs.* Oxford: The Clarendon Press.

Gardiner, A.H. 1928. The graffito from the tomb of Pere. *Journal of Egyptian Archaeology* 14: 10–1.

Gardiner, A.H. 1932. *Late-Egyptian stories* (Bibliotheca Aegyptiaca 1). Bruxelles: Édition de la Fondation Égyptologique Reine Élizabeth.

Gardiner, A.H. 1933. The Dakhleh stela. *Journal of Egyptian Archaeology* 19: 19–30.

Gardiner, A.H. 1935. *Hieratic papyri in the British Museum. Third series: Chester Beatty gift*, 2 vols. London: British Museum.

Gardiner, A.H. 1937. *Late-Egyptian miscellanies* (Bibliotheca Aegyptiaca 7). Bruxelles: Édition de la Fondation Égyptologique Reine Élizabeth.

Gardiner, A.H. 1940. Adoption extraordinary. *Journal of Egyptian Archaeology* 26: 23–9.

Gardiner, A.H. 1941. Ramesside texts relating to the taxation and transport of corn. *Journal of Egyptian Archaeology* 27: 19–73.

Gardiner, A.H. 1945. Regnal years and civil calendar in pharaonic Egypt. *Journal of Egyptian Archaeology* 31: 11–28.

Gardiner, A.H. 1946. Davies's copy of the great Speos Artemidos inscription. *Journal of Egyptian Archaeology* 32: 43–56.

Gardiner, A.H. 1947. *Ancient Egyptian onomastica*, 3 vols. London: Oxford University Press.

Gardiner, A.H. 1948. *Ramesside administrative documents.* London: Oxford University Press.

Gardiner, A.H. 1950. The baptism of pharaoh. *Journal of Egyptian Archaeology* 36: 3–12.

Gardiner, A.H. 1952. Tuthmosis III returns thanks to Amun. *Journal of Egyptian Archaeology* 38: 6–23.

Gardiner, A.H. 1953. The coronation of king Haremhab. *Journal of Egyptian Archaeology* 39: 13–31.

Gardiner, A.H. 1955a. A pharaonic encomium. *Journal of Egyptian Archaeology* 41: 30–5.

Gardiner, A.H. 1955b. The problem of the month-names. *Revue d'Égyptologie* 10: 9–31.

Gardiner, A.H. 1955c. *The Ramesseum papyri: Plates.* Oxford: Charles Batey.

Gardiner, A.H. 1956. A pharaonic encomium (II). *Journal of Egyptian Archaeology* 42: 8–20.

Gardiner, A.H. 1962. The gods of Thebes as guarantors of personal property. *Journal of Egyptian Archaeology* 48: 57–69.

Gardiner, A.H., Peet, E.T., and Černý, J. 1952. *The inscriptions of Sinai* (Memoir of the Egypt Exploration Society 45), 2 vols, 2nd ed. London: Egypt Exploration Society.

Gauthier, H.M. 1907. *Le livre des rois d'Égypte: Recueil de titres et protocoles royaux, noms propres de rois, reines, princes et princesses, noms de pyramides et de temples solaires, suivi d'un index alphabétique* (Mémoires publiés par les membres de l'Institut Français d'Archéologie Orientale du Caire 17–21), 5 vols. Cairo: Imprimerie de l'Institut Français d'Archéologie Orientale.

Gauthier, H.M. 1910. La grande inscription dédicatoire d'Abydos. *Zeitschrift für Ägyptische Sprache und Altertumskunde* 48: 52–66.

Gauthier, H.M. 1918. Un nouveau monument du dieu Imhotep. *Bulletin de l'Institut Français d'Archéologie Orientale* 14: 33–49.

Gauthier, H.M. 1931. *Les fêtes du dieu Min* (Recherches d'archéologie, de philologie et d'histoire 2). Cairo: Imprimerie de l'Institut Français d'Archéologie Orientale.

Gautschy, R. 2011. Der Stern Sirius im alten Ägypten. *Zeitschrift für Ägyptische Sprache und Altertumskunde* 138: 116–31.

Gawlikowski, M. 2001. Kazimierz Michałowski and his school, in Z.E. Szafrański (ed.), *Queen Hatshepsut and her temple 3500 years later*: 17–37. Warszawa: Agencja Reklamowo-Wydawnicza A. Grzegorczyk.

Gayet, A.J. 1894. *Le temple de Louxor* (Mémoires publiés par les membres de la mission archéologique française au Caire 15). Paris: Ernest Leroux.

Gayet, M.A. 1908. *Le destin, la divination égyptienne et l'oracle d'Antinoüs*. Paris: Ernest Leroux.

Germond, P. 1981. *Sekhmet et la protection du monde* (Ægyptiaca helvetica 9). Genève: Belles-Lettres.

Germond, P. 1986. *Les invocations à la bonne année au temple d'Edfou* (Ægyptiaca helvetica 11). Genève: Belles-Lettres.

Ginter, B. and Kammerer-Grothaus, H. 1998. *Frühe Keramik und Kleinfunde aus El-Târif* (Archaeologische Veroffentlichungen 40). Mainz: Philipp von Zabern.

Gitton, M. 1974. Le palais de Karnak. *Bulletin de l'Institut Français d'Archéologie Orientale* 74: 63–73.

Gitton, M. 1975. *L'épouse du dieu, Ahmes Néfertary: Documents sur sa vie et son culte posthume*. Paris: Belles Lettres.

Gitton, M. and Leclant, J. 1977: Gottesgemahlin, in E. Otto and W. Helck (eds), *Lexikon der Ägyptologie*, vol. 2: 792–812. Wiesbaden: Harrassowitz.

Glanville, S.R.K. 1930. Working plan for a shrine. *Journal of Egyptian Archaeology* 16: 237–9.

Gnirs, A.M. 1995. Das Pfeilerdekorationprogramm in Grab des Meri, Theben Nr. 95: Ein Beitrag zu den Totenkultpraktiken der 18. Dynastie, in J. Assmann, E. Dziobek, H. Guksch, and F. Kampp (eds), *Thebanische Beamtennekropolen: Neue Perspektiven archäologischer Forschung: Internationales Symposion, Heidelberg, 9.-13. Juni 1993* (Studien zur Archäologie und Geschichte Altägyptens 12): 233–54. Heidelberg: Heidelberger Orientverlag.

Gnirs, A.M. 2009. In the king's house: Audiences and receptions at court, in R. Gundlach and J.H. Taylor (eds), *4. Symposium zur ägyptischen Königsideologie: Egyptian royal residences: London, June, 1st-5th 2004* (Königtum, Staat und Gesellschaft früher Hochkulturen 4 (1)): 13–43. Wiesbaden: Harrassowitz.

Gnirs, A.M., Grothe, E., and Guksch, H. 1997. Zweiter Vorbericht über die Aufnahme und Publikation von Gräbern der 18. Dynastie der thebanischen Beamtennekropole. *Mitteilungen der Deutschen Archäologischen Instituts, Abteilung Kairo* 53: 57–83.

Godley, A.D. 1920. *Herodotus* (Loeb classical library 117–20), 4 vols. Cambridge and London: Harvard University Press.

Goebs, K. 2003. *xftj nTr* as euphemism: The case of the Antef decree. *Journal of Egyptian Archaeology* 89: 27–37.

Goebs, K. 2008. *Crowns in Egyptian funerary literature: Royalty, rebirth, and destruction*. Oxford: Griffith Institute.

Goebs, K. 2011. King as god and god as king: Colour, light and transformation in Egyptian ritual, in R. Gundlach and K. Spence (eds), *5. Symposium zur ägyptischen Königsideologie: Palace and temple, architecture-decoration-ritual, Cambridge, July, 16th-17th, 2007* (Königtum, Staat und Gesellschaft früher Hochkulturen 4 (2)): 57–101. Wiesbaden: Harrassowitz.

Goedicke, H. 1963. Was magic used in the harem conspiracy against Ramses III? (P. Rollin and P. Lee). *Journal of Egyptian Archaeology* 49: 71–92.

Goedicke, H. 1967. *Königliche Dokumente aus dem Alten Reich* (Ägyptologische Abhandlungen 14). Wiesbaden: Harrassowitz.

Goedicke, H. 1981. The '400-Year Stela' reconsidered. *Bulletin of the Egyptological Seminar* 3: 25–42.

Goedicke, H. 1994. A cult inventory of the Eighth Dynasty from Coptos (Cairo JE 43290). *Mitteilungen der Deutschen Archäologischen Instituts, Abteilung Kairo* 50: 71-84.

Goedicke, H. 2004. *The Speos Artemidos inscription of Hatshepsut and related discussions*. Oakville: Halgo.

Goedicke, H. and Wente, E.F. 1962. *Ostraka Michaelides*. Wiesbaden: Harrassowitz.

Goldbrunner, L. 2004. *Buchis: Eine Untersuchung zur Theologie des heiligen Stieres in Theben zur griechisch-römischen Zeit* (Monographies reine Élisabeth 11). Turnhout: Brepols.

Golénischeff, W.S. 1913. *Les papyrus hiératiques nos. 1115, 1116A et 1116B de l'Ermitage Impérial à St.-Pétersbourg*. St. Petersburg: Imprimerie de l'Institut Français d'Archéologie Orientale.

Golénischeff, W.S. 1927. *Papyrus hiératiques nos. 58001-58036* (Catalogue général des antiquités égyptiennes du Musée du Caire 83). Cairo: Imprimerie de l'Institut Français d'Archéologie Orientale.

Goyon, J.-C. 1967. Le cérémonial de glorification d'Osiris du papyrus du Louvre I. 3079. *Bulletin de l'Institut Français d'Archéologie Orientale* 65: 89–156.

Goyon, J.-C. 1972a. *Confirmation du pouvoir royal au nouvel an: Brooklyn Museum papyrus 47.218.50* (Bibliothèque d'étude 52). Cairo: Institut Français d'Archéologie Orientale.

Goyon, J.-C. 1972b. *Rituels funéraires de l'ancienne Égypte: Le rituel de l'embaumement, le rituel de l'Ouverture de la Bouche, les Livres des Respirations* (Littératures anciennes du Proche-Orient 4). Paris: Éditions du Cerf.

Goyon, J.-C. 1974. Sur une formule des rituels de conjuration des dangers de l'année. *Bulletin de l'Institut Français d'Archéologie Orientale* 74: 75–83.

Goyon, J.-C. 1976. Essai d'interpretation, in *Le Ramesseum X: Les annexes nord-ouest*: 196–223. Cairo: Centre d'Études et de Documentation sur l'Ancienne Égypte.

Goyon, J.-C. 1977. Un phylactère tardif: Le papyrus 3233 A et B du Musée du Louvre. *Bulletin de l'Institut Français d'Archéologie Orientale* 77: 45–54.

Goyon, J.-C. 1986. Le feu nouveau du jour de l'an à Dendara et Karnak, in *Hommages à François Daumas*, vol. 2: 331–44. Montpellier: Université de Montpellier.

Goyon, J.-C. 1987. Nombre et univers: Réflexions sur quelques données numériques de l'arsenal magique de l'Égypte pharaonique, in A. Roccati and A. Siliotti (eds), *La magia in Egitto ai tempi dei faraoni: Atti, Convegno Internazionale di Studi, Milano, 29-31 Ottobre 1985*: 57–76. Verona: Rassegna internazionale di cinematografia archeologica.

Goyon, J.-C. 2006. *Le rituel du sHtp sxmt au changement de cycle annuel: D'aprés les architraves du temple d'Edfou et textes parallèles, du Nouvel Empire à époque ptolémaïque et romaine.* Cairo: Institut Français d'Archéologie Orientale.

Graefe, E. 1986: Talfest, in E. Otto and W. Helck (eds), *Lexikon der Ägyptologie*, vol. 6: 187–9. Wiesbaden: Harrassowitz.

Graefe, E. 1994. Der autobiographische Text des Ibi, Obervermögensverwalter der Gottesgemahlin Nitokris, auf Kairo JE 36158. *Mitteilungen der Deutschen Archäologischen Instituts, Abteilung Kairo* 50: 85–99.

Graham, A. 2010. Ancient landscapes around the Opet temple, Karnak. *Egyptian Archaeology* 36: 25–8.

Graham, A. 2011. Ancient Theban waterways. *Egyptian Archaeology* 38: 3.

Graham, A. and Bunbury, J.M. 2005. The ancient landscapes and waterscapes of Karnak. *Egyptian Archaeology* 27: 17–9.

Graindorge-Héreil, C. 1992. Le oignons de Sokar. *Revue d'Égyptologie* 43: 87–105.

Graindorge-Héreil, C. 1994. *Le dieu Sokar à Thèbes au Nouvel Empire* (Göttinger Orientforschungen. IV. Reihe, Ägypten 28), 2 vols. Wiesbaden: Harrassowitz.

Graindorge-Héreil, C. 1996. La quête de la lumière au mois de Khoiak: Une histoire d'oies. *Journal of Egyptian Archaeology* 82: 83–105.

Graindorge-Héreil, C. 2002. Der Tempel des Amun-Re von Karnak zu Beginn der 18. Dynastie, in H. Beinlich (ed.), *5. ägyptologische Tempeltagung: Würzburg, 23.-26. September 1999* (Ägypten und Altes Testament 33 (3)): 83–90. Wiesbaden: Harrassowitz.

Graindorge-Héreil, C. and Martinez, P. 1999. Programme architectual et iconographique des monuments d'Amenophis I à Karnak. *Annales du Service des Antiquités de l'Égypte* 74: 169–82.

Grandet, P. 1994. *Papyrus Harris I: BM 9999* (Bibliothèque d'étude 109 and 129), 3 vols. Cairo: Institut Français d'Archéologie Orientale.

Grandet, P. 2000a. *Catalogue des ostraca hiératiques non littéraires de Deir el-Médineh VIII (no. 706-830)* (Documents de Fouilles de l'Institut Français d'Archéologie Orientale du Caire 39). Cairo: Imprimerie de l'Institut Français d'Archéologie Orientale.

Grandet, P. 2000b. L'exécution du chancelier Bay. *Bulletin de l'Institut Français d'Archéologie Orientale* 100: 339–45.

Grandet, P. 2002. Ostracon: Notes pour le journal de l'an 16 et de l'an 17 de Ramsès III, in G. Andreu and C. Barbotin (eds), *Les artistes de pharaon: Deir el-Médineh et la Vallée des Rois*: 205. Paris: Musée du Louvre.

Grandet, P. 2006a. *Catalogue des ostraca hiératiques non littéraires de Deir el-Médineh X (no. 10001-123)* (Documents de Fouilles de l'Institut Français d'Archéologie Orientale du Caire 46). Cairo: Imprimerie de l'Institut Français d'Archéologie Orientale.

Grandet, P. 2006b. KY JNR SRY 'un autre petit caillou': Ostraca hiératiques documentaires inédits de l'IFAO, in A. Dorn and T. Hofmann (eds), *Living and writing in Deir el-Medine: Socio-historical embodiment of Deir el-Medine texts* (Ægyptiaca helvetica 19): 93–105. Basel: Schwabe.

Gregorios, B. 1991: Feasts, minor, in A.S. Atiya (ed.), *The Coptic encyclopedia*, vol. 4: 1106–9. New York and Toronto: Macmillan and Maxwell Macmillan International.

Gregory, S.R.W. 2012. The obelisks of Augustus: The significance of a symbolic element of the architectural landscape in the transmission of ideology from Egypt to Rome. *Journal of Ancient Egyptian Interconnections* 4: 9–130.

Grenfell, A. 1908. *Amuletic scarabs etc. for the deceased* (Recueil de travaux relatifs à la philologie et à l'archéologie égyptiennes et assyriennes 30). Paris: Honoré Champion.

Grenfell, B.P. and Hunt, A.S. 1906. *The Hibeh papyri.* London: Kegan Paul.

Griffith, F.L. 1889. *The inscriptions of Siût and Der Rîfeh.* London: Trübner & Co.

Griffith, F.L. 1891. The account papyrus no. 18 of Boulaq. *Zeitschrift für Ägyptische Sprache und Altertumskunde* 29: 102–16.

Griffith, F.L. 1898. *The Petrie papyri: Hieratic papyri from Kahun and Gurob (principally of the Middle Kingdom)*, 2 vols. London: Bernard Quaritch.

Griffith, F.L. 1908. A contract of the fifth year of Amenhotp IV. *Proceedings of the Society of Biblical Archaeology* 30: 272–5.

Griffith, F.L. 1927. The Abydos decree of Seti I at Nauri. *Journal of Egyptian Archaeology* 13: 193–208.

Griffith, F.L. and Petrie, W.M.F. 1889. *Two hieroglyphic papyri from Tanis* (Memoir of the Egypt Exploration Fund). London: Trübner.

Grimal, N.-C. 1981a. *La stèle triomphale de Pi('ankh)y au Musée du Caire, JE 48862 et 47086-47089* (Études sur la propagande royale égyptienne 1). Cairo: Institut Français d›Archéologie Orientale.

Grimal, N.-C. 1981b. *Quatre stèles napatéennes au Musée du Caire: JE 48863-48866 textes et indices* (Études sur la propagande royale égyptienne 2). Paris: Institut Français d›Archéologie Orientale.

Grimal, N.-C. and Larché, F. 1995. Karnak, 1992–1994, in *Cahiers de Karnak 10: 1992-1994*: VII–XXXII. Paris: Centre Franco-Égyptien d'Étude des Temples de Karnak.

Grimm, A. 1994a. *Die altägyptischen Festkalender in den Tempeln der griechisch-römischen Epoche* (Ägypten und Altes Testament 15). Wiesbaden: Münchener Ludwig-Maximilians Universität.

1994b. Zur kalendarischen Fixierung des *ihhj*-(Freuden-)Festes nach dem Festkalender des Königs Amenophis I. aus Karnak. *Göttinger Miszellen* 143: 73–6.

Guermeur, I. 2004. Le group familial de Pachéryentaisouy: Caire JE 36576. *Bulletin de l'Institut Français d'Archéologie Orientale* 104: 245–88.

Guksch, H. 1979. *Das Grab des Benja, gen. Paheqamen: Theben Nr. 343* (Archäologische Veröffentlichungen (Deutsches Archäologisches Institut. Abteilung Kairo) 7). Mainz am Rhein: Philipp von Zabern.

Guksch, H. 1995. *Die Gräber des Nacht-Min und des Men-Cheper-Ra-Seneb: Theben Nr. 87 und 79* (Archäologische Veröffentlichungen (Deutsches Archäologisches Institut, Abteilung Kairo) 34). Mainz: Philipp von Zabern.

Gundel, W. 1936. *Dekane und Dekansternbilder: Ein Beitrag zur Geschichte der Sternbilder der Kulturvölker* (Studien der Bibliothek Warburg 19). Glückstadt and Hamburg: J.J. Augustin.

Gundlach, R. 1998. Tempelfeste und Etappen der Königsherrschaft in der 18. Dynastie, in R. Gundlach and M. Rochholz (eds), *4. ägyptologische Tempeltagung, Köln 10.-12. Oktober 1996: Feste im Tempel* (Ägypten und Altes Testament 33 (2)): 55–75. Wiesbaden: Harrassowitz.

Gundlach, R. 2006. Hof–Hofgesellschaft–Hofkultur im pharaonischen Ägypten, in R. Gundlach and A. Klug (eds), *Der ägyptische Hof des Neuen Reiches: Seine Gesellschaft und Kultur im Spannungsfeld zwischen Innen- und Aussenpolitik: Akten des internationalen Kolloquiums vom 27.-29. Mai 2002 an der Johannes Gutenberg-Universität Mainz* (Königtum, Staat und Gesellschaft früher Hochkulturen 2): 1–38. Wiesbaden: Harrassowitz.

Gundlach, R. 2010. Die Chapelle Blanche und das Tempelbauprogramm Sesostris' I. in Theben, in M. Dolińska and H. Beinlich (eds), *8. ägyptologische Tempeltagung: Interconnections between temples, Warschau, 22.-25. September 2008* (Königtum, Staat und Gesellschaft früher Hochkulturen 3 (3)): 81–109. Wiesbaden: Harrassowitz.

Gundlach, R. 2011. The Berlin Leather Roll (pBerlin 3029), in R. Gundlach and K. Spence (eds), *5. Symposium zur ägyptischen Königsideologie: Palace and temple, architecture-decoration-ritutal, Cambridge, July, 16th-17th, 2007* (Königtum, Staat und Gesellschaft früher Hochkulturen 4 (2)): 103–14. Wiesbaden: Harrassowitz.

Gunn, B. 1916. The religion of the poor in ancient Egypt. *Journal of Egyptian Archaeology* 3: 81–94.

Gutbub, A. 1961. Un emprunt aux textes des pyramides dans l'hymne à Hathor, dame de l'ivresse, in *Mélanges Maspero I: Orient ancien* (Mémoires publiés par les membres de l'Institut Français d'Archéologie Orientale du Caire 66), vol. 4: 31–72. Cairo: Imprimerie de l'Institut Français d'Archéologie Orientale.

Gutgesell, M. 1983. *Die Datierung der Ostraka und Papyri aus Deir el-Medineh und ihre ökonomische Interpretation. Teil I, die 20. Dynastie* (Hildesheimer ägyptologische Beiträge 18–9), 2 vols. Hildesheim: Gerstenberg.

Gutgesell, M. 2002. *Die Datierung der Ostraka und Papyri aus Deir el Medineh. Teil II, Die Ostraka der 19. Dynastie* (Hildesheimer ägyptologische Beiträge 44). Hildesheim: Gerstenberg Verlag.

Győri, H. 1989. Une amulette-ouadj aurmonteé d'une figure de chatte, in *Studia in honorem L. Fóti* (Studia Aegyptiaca 12): 129–41. Budapest: Chaire d'Égyptologie, l'Université Eötvös Loránd de Budapest.

Habachi, L. 1947. Finds at Kôm el-Wist. *Annales du Service des Antiquités de l'Égypte* 47: 285–7.

Habachi, L. 1950. An inscription at Aswan referring to six obelisks. *Journal of Egyptian Archaeology* 36: 13–8.

Habachi, L. 1957. Two graffiti at Sehēl from the reign of queen Hatshepsut. *Journal of Near Eastern Studies* 16: 88–104.

Habachi, L. 1965a. The triple shrine of the Theban triad in Luxor temple. *Mitteilungen der Deutschen Archäologischen Instituts, Abteilung Kairo* 20: 93–7.

Habachi, L. 1965b. A family from Armant in Aswan and in Thebes. *Journal of Egyptian Archaeology* 51: 123–36.

Habachi, L. 1972. Nia, the *wab*-priest and doorkeeper of Amun-of-the-hearing-ear. *Bulletin de l'Institut Français d'Archéologie Orientale* 71: 67–85.

Habachi, L. 1974. A high Inundation in the temple of Amenre at Karnak in the Thirteenth Dynasty. *Studien zur Altägyptischen Kultur* 1: 207–14.

Habachi, L. 1978. *The obelisks of Egypt: Skyscrapers of the past*. London, Toronto, and Melbourne: J.M. Dent & Sons.

Haeny, G. 1981. Die Stele aus dem Jahr 6 des Könings Horemheb, in G. Haeny, H. Ricke, and L. Habachi (eds), *Untersuchungen im Totentempel Amenophis'*

III. (Beiträge zur ägyptischen Bauforschung und Altertumskunde 11): 65–70. Wiesbaden: Franz Steiner.

Haeny, G. 1997. New Kingdom 'mortuary templs' and 'mansions of millions of years', in B.E. Shafer (ed.), *Temples of ancient Egypt*: 86–126. Ithaca: Cornell University Press.

Haikal, F.M.H. 1970. *Two hieratic funerary papyri of Nesmin* (Bibliotheca Aegyptiaca 14), 2 vols. Bruxelles: Édition de la Fondation Égyptologique Reine Élizabeth.

Haikal, F.M.H. 1985. Preliminary studies on the tomb of Thay in Thebes: The hymn to the light, in P. Posener-Kriéger (ed.), *Mélanges Gamal Eddin Mokhtar*, vol. 1: 361–72. Cairo: Institute Français d'Archéologie Orientale.

Hall, R. 1985. 'The cast-off garment of yesterday': Dresses reserved in life and death. *Bulletin de l'Institut Français d'Archéologie Orientale* 85: 235–41.

Hammerton, J.A. 1927. *Universal history of the world*, 2 vols. London: The Amalgamated Press.

Hamza, M. 1930. Excavations of the department antiquities at Qantîr (Faqûs District): Season, May 21st–July 7th, 1928. *Annales du Service des Antiquités de l'Égypte* 30: 31–68.

Hannig, R. 2003. *Ägyptisches Wörterbuch I: Altes Reich und Erste Zwischenzeit* (Kulturgeschichte der antiken Welt 98). Mainz am Rhein: Philipp von Zabern.

Hannig, R. 2006. *Ägyptisches Wörterbuch II: Mittleres Reich und Zweite Zwischenziet* (Kulturgeschichte der antiken Welt 112), 2 vols. Mainz am Rhein: Philipp von Zabern.

Harari, I. 1959. Nature de la stèle de donation de fonction du roi Ahmôsis à la reine Ahmès-Nefertari. *Annales du Service des Antiquités de l'Égypte* 56: 139–201.

Hari, R. 1964. Horemheb et la reine Moutnedjemet ou la fin d'une dynastie. Unpublished PhD dissertation, Université de Genève.

Hari, R. 1985. *La tombe thébaine du père divin Neferhotep (TT 50)* (Epigraphica). Genève: Belles-Lettres.

Haring, B.J. 1993. The economic aspects of royal funerary temples: A preliminary survey. *Göttinger Miszellen* 132: 39–48.

Haring, B.J. 1997. *Divine households: Administrative and economic aspects of the New Kingdom royal memorial temples in western Thebes* (Egyptologische uitgaven 12). Leiden: Nederlands Instituut voor het Nabije Oosten.

Haring, B.J. 2004. Hieratic varia. *Journal of Egyptian Archaeology* 90: 215–21.

Haring, B.J. 2007. Ramesside temples and the economic interests of the state: Crossroads of the sacred and the profane, in M. Fitzenreiter (ed.), *Das Heilige und die Ware: Zum Spannungsfeld von Religion und Ökonomie* (Internet-Beiträge zur Ägyptologie und Sudanarchäologie 7): 165–70. London: Golden House Publications.

Harpur, Y. and Scremin, P.J. 2006. *The chapel of Kagemni: Scene details* (Egypt in miniature 1). Reading: Oxford Expedition to Egypt.

Harpur, Y. and Scremin, P.J. 2008. *Chapel of Ptahhotep: Scene details* (Egypt in miniature 2). Reading: Oxford Expedition to Egypt.

Hartwig, M.K. 2001. The tomb of Menna, in K.R. Weeks and A. de Luca (eds), *Valley of the Kings: The tombs and the funerary temples of Thebes West*: 398–407. Vercelli: White Star.

Hartwig, M.K. 2004. *Tomb painting and identity in ancient Thebes, 1419-1372 BCE* (Monumenta aegyptiaca 10). Turnhout: Brepols.

Hartwig, M.K. 2013. *The tomb chapel of Menna (TT 69): The art, culture and, science of painting in an Egyptian tomb* (American Research Center in Egypt. Coservation series 5). Cairo and New York: The American University in Cairo Press.

Hassan, S. 1932. *Excavations at Gîza*, 10 vols. Oxford: Oxford University Press.

Hayes, W.C. 1942. *Ostraka and name stones from the tomb of Sen-Mūt (no. 71) at Thebes* (Publications of the Metropolitan Museum of Art, Egyptian expedition 15). New York: Metropolitan Museum of Art.

Hayes, W.C. 1946. Royal decree from the temple of Min at Coptos. *Journal of Egyptian Archaeology* 32: 3–23.

Hayes, W.C. 1947. Ḥoremkha'uef of Nekhen and his trip to It̠-Towe. *Journal of Egyptian Archaeology* 33: 3–11.

Hayes, W.C. 1951. Inscriptions from the palace of Amenhotep III. *Journal of Near Eastern Studies* 10: 35–56, 82–104, 156–83, and 231–42.

Hayes, W.C. 1960. A selection of Tuthmoside ostraca from Der el-Baḥri. *Journal of Egyptian Archaeology* 46: 29–52.

Hegazy, e.-S.A. and Tosi, M. 1983. *A Theban private tomb: Tomb no. 295* (Archäologische Veröffentlichungen (Deutsches Archäologisches Institut. Abteilung Kairo) 45). Mainz am Rhein: Philipp von Zabern.

Helck, W. 1955a. Das Dekret des Königs Haremheb. *Zeitschrift für Ägyptische Sprache und Altertumskunde* 80: 125–6.

Helck, W. 1955b. Eine Stele des Vizekönigs *Wśr-Śt.t*. *Journal of Near Eastern Studies* 14: 22–31.

Helck, W. 1956a. *Untersuchungen zu Manetho und den ägyptischen Königslisten* (Untersuchungen zur Geschichte und Altertumskunde Aegyptens 18). Berlin: Akademie-Verlag.

Helck, W. 1956b. Inhaber und Bauleiter des thebanischen Grabs 107. *Mitteilungen des Instituts für Orientforschung* 4: 11–26.

Helck, W. 1957. Ramessidische Inschriften aus Karnak. *Zeitschrift für Ägyptische Sprache und Altertumskunde* 82: 98–140.

Helck, W. 1958. *Zur Verwaltung des Mittleren und Neuen Reichs* (Probleme der Ägyptologie 3). Leiden: Brill.

Helck, W. 1959. Bemerkungen zu den Thronbesteigungsdaten im Neuen Reich, in *Studia biblica et orientalia III: Oriens antiquus* (Analecta biblica 12): Roma: Pontificio Istituto Biblico.

Helck, W. 1961. *Materialien zur Wirtschaftsgeschichte des Neuen Reiches* (Abhandlungen der Geistes- und Sozialwissenschaftlichen Klasse), 6 vols. Wiesbaden: Franz Steiner.

Helck, W. 1963. Der Papyrus Berlin P 3047. *Journal of American Research Center in Egypt* 2: 65–73.

Helck, W. 1964. Feiertage und Arbeitstage in der Ramessidenzeit. *Journal of the Economic and Social History of the Orient* 7: 136–66.

Helck, W. 1966a. Chronologische Kleinigkeiten. *Chronique d'Égypte* 41: 233–4.

Helck, W. 1966b. Zum Kult an Königsstatuen. *Journal of Near Eastern Studies* 25: 32–41.

Helck, W. 1968. *Die Ritualszenen auf der Umfassungsmauer Ramses' II. in Karnak* (Ägyptologische Abhandlungen 18), 2 vols. Wiesbaden: Harrassowitz.

Helck, W. 1975. *Historisch-biographische Texte der 2. Zwischenzeit und neue Texte der 18. Dynastie* (Kleine Ägyptische Texte 6 (2)). Wiesbaden: Harrassowitz.

Helck, W. 1977. Die Weihinschrift aus dem Taltempel des Sonnenheiligtums des Königs Neuserre bei Abu Grob. *Studien zur Altägyptischen Kultur* 5: 47–77.

Helck, W. 1980. Ein 'Feldzug' unter Amenophis IV. gegen Nubien. *Studien zur Altägyptischen Kultur* 8: 117–26.

Helck, W. 1984. Schamane und Zauberer, in *Mélanges Adolphe Gutbub*: 103–8. Montpellier: Université de Montpellier.

Helck, W. 1990. Drei ramessidische Daten. *Studien zur Altägyptischen Kultur* 17: 205–14.

Helck, W. 2002. *Die datierten und datierbaren Ostraka, Papyri und Graffiti von Deir el-Medineh* (Ägyptologische Abhandlungen 63). Wiesbaden: Harrassowitz.

Henrichs, A. 1973. Zwei Orakelfragen. *Zeitschrift für Papyrologie und Epigraphik* 11: 115–9.

Herbin, F.-R. 1984. Une liturgie des rites décadaires de Djemê: Papyrus Vienne 3865. *Revue d'Égyptologie* 35: 105–27.

Herbin, F.-R. 1994. *Le Livre de Parcourir l'Éternité* (Orientalia Lovaniensia Analecta 58). Leuven: Peeters.

Herbin, F.-R. 1999. Trois manuscrits originaux du Louvre porteurs du Livre des Respirations Fait par Isis (P. Louvre N 3121, N 3083 et N 3166). *Revue d'Égyptologie* 50: 149–223.

Herbin, F.-R. 2008. *Books of Breathing and related texts* (Catalogue of the books of the dead and other religious texts in the British Museum 4). London: British Museum Press.

Hermann, A. 1940. *Die Stelen der thebanischen Felsgräber der 18. Dynastie* (Ägyptologische Forschungen 11). Glückstadt and New York: J.J. Augustin.

Higazy, e.-S. and Bryan, B.M. 1986. A new stela of Thutmose IV from the Luxor temple. *Varia Aegyptiaca* 2: 93–100.

Hillier, J.K., Bunbury, J.M., and Graham, A. 2007. Monuments on a migrating Nile. *Journal of Archaeological Science* 34: 1011–5.

Hintze, F. and Reineke, W.F. 1989. *Felsinschriften aus dem sudanesischen Nubien* (Publikation der Nubien-Expedition 1), 2 vols. Berlin: Akademie-Verlag.

Hirsch, E. 2004. *Kultpolitik und Tempelbauprogramme der 12. Dynastie: Untersuchungen zu den Göttertempeln im alten Ägypten* (Achet A 3). Berlin: Achet Verlag.

Hodjash, S.I. and Berlev, O.D. 1982. *The Egyptian reliefs and stelae in the Pushkin Museum of Fine Arts, Moscow.* Leningrad: Aurora Art Publishers.

Hofmann, E. 2004. *Bilder im Wandel: Die Kunst der ramessidischen Privatgräber.* Mainz am Rhein: Philipp von Zabern.

Hölscher, U. 1934. *The excavation of Medinet Habu I: General plans and views* (Oriental Institute publications 21). Chicago: University of Chicago Press.

Hopfner, T. 1940. *Plutarch über Isis und Osiris* (Monographien des Archiv Orientální 9), 2 vols. Praha: Orientalisches Institut.

Hornung, E. 1964. *Untersuchungen zur Chronologie und Geschichte des Neuen Reiches* (Ägyptologische Abhandlungen 11). Wiesbaden: Harrassowitz.

Hornung, E. 1982. *Der ägyptische Mythos von der Himmelskuh: Eine Ätiologie des Unvollkommenen* (Orbis biblicus et orientalis 46). Freiburg and Göttingen: Vandenhoeck & Ruprecht.

Hornung, E. 2006. New Kingdom, in E. Hornung, R. Krauss, D. Warburton, and M. Eaton-Krauss (eds), *Ancient Egyptian chronology* (Handbook of Oriental studies. Section 1, The Near and Middle East 83): 197–217. Leiden: Brill.

Hornung, E., Krauss, R., Warburton, D., and Eaton-Krauss, M. 2006. *Ancient Egyptian chronology* (Handbook of Oriental studies. Section 1, The Near and Middle East 83). Leiden and Boston: Brill.

Hornung, E. and Staehelin, E. 1974. *Studien zum Sedfest* (Ægyptiaca helvetica 1). Genève: Belles-Lettres.

Hornung, E. and Staehelin, E. 2006. *Neue Studien zum Sedfest* (Ægyptiaca helvetica 20). Basel: Schwabe.

Hornung, E., Staehelin, E., and Brack, A. 1976. *Skarabäen und andere Siegelamulette aus Basler Sammlungen* (Ägyptische Denkmäler in der Schweiz 1). Mainz: Philipp von Zabern.

Hovestreydt, W. 1997. Secret doors and hidden treasure: Some aspects of Egyptian temple treasuries from the New Kingdom, in J. van Dijk (ed.), *Essays on ancient Egypt in honour of Herman te Velde*: 187–206. Groningen: STYX Publications.

Ibrahim, M.E.A. 1975. *The chapel of the throne of Re of Edfu* (Bibliotheca Aegyptiaca 16). Bruxelles: Édition de la Fondation Égyptologique Reine Élizabeth.

Ikram, S. 1995. *Choice cuts: Meat production in ancient Egypt* (Orientalia Lovaniensia Analecta 69). Leuven: Peeters.

Institute d'Égypte 1809–28. *Description de l'Égypte: Recueil des observations et des recherches qui ont et faites en Égypte pendant l'expedition de l'armee française*, 19 vols. Paris: L'imprimerie impériale.

Iskander, J.M. 2011. The Haker Feast and the transformation. *Studien zur Altägyptischen Kultur* 40: 137–42.

Iversen, E. 1941. *Two inscriptions concerning private donations to temples* (Historisk-filologiske meddelelser 27 (5)). København: I kommission hos E. Munksgaard.

Jacobsohn, H. 1939. *Die dogmatische Stellung des Königs in der Theologie der alten Ägypter* (Ägyptologische Forschungen 8). Glückstadt and New York: J.J. Augustin.

Jacq, C. 1993. *Recherches sur les paradis de l'autre monde d'apres les Textes des Pyramides et les Textes des Sarcophages*. Paris: Institut Ramses.

Jacquet-Gordon, H. 1988. *Karnak-nord VI: Le trésor de Thoutmosis Ier: La décoration* (Fouilles de l'Institut Français d'Archéologie Orientale du Caire 32), 2 vols. Cairo: Institut Français d'Archéologie Orientale.

Jacquet-Gordon, H. 2004. *Temple of Khonsu III: The graffiti on the Khonsu temple roof at Karnak: A manifestation of personal piety* (Oriental Institute publications 123). Chicago: Oriental Institute of the University of Chicago.

Jacquet-Gordon, H. 2009. The festival on which Amun went out to the treasury, in P.J. Brand and L. Cooper (eds), *Causing his name to live: Studies in Egyptian epigraphy and history in memory of William J. Murnane* (Culture and history of the ancient Near East 37): 121–3. Leiden and Boston: Brill.

Jaggi, R. 2002. Gegenkapellen in der Thebaïs. *Kemet* 3: 57–64.

James, T.G.H. 1955. The date of the month *rkh wr*. *Journal of Egyptian Archaeology* 41: 123.

James, T.G.H. 1962. *The Ḥeḳanakhte papers and other early Middle Kingdom documents* (Publications of the Metropolitan Museum of Art Egyptian Expedition 19). New York: Metropolitan Museum of Art.

Janák, J., Vymazalová, H., and Coppens, F. 2011. The Fifth Dynasty 'sun temples' in a broader context, in M. Bárta, F. Coppens, and J. Krejčí (eds), *Abusir and Saqqara in the year 2010/1*: 430–42. Praha: Czech Institute of Egyptology.

Jankuhn, D. 1972. *Das Buch 'Schutz des Hauses' (s3-pr)* (Habelts Dissertationsdrucke. Reihe klassische Philologie 12). Bonn: R. Habelt.

Janot, F. and Vezie, P. 1999. Les charmes de la galène. *Bulletin de l'Institut Français d'Archéologie Orientale* 99: 217–32.

Jansen-Winkeln, K. 1985. *Ägyptische Biographien der 22. und 23. Dynastie* (Ägypten und Altes Testament 8), 2 vols. Wiesbaden: Harrassowitz.

Jansen-Winkeln, K. 1989. Zwei Bemerkungen zu Gebel es-Silsila Nr. 100. *Journal of Egyptian Archaeology* 75: 237–9.

Jansen-Winkeln, K. 1993. Ein politisches Orakel. *Varia Aegyptiaca* 9: 7–18.

Jansen-Winkeln, K. 1995. Die Plünderung der Königsgräber des Neuen Reiches. *Zeitschrift für Ägyptische Sprache und Altertumskunde* 122: 62–78.

Jansen-Winkeln, K. 1996. *Spätmittelägyptische Grammatik der Texte der 3. Zwischenzeit* (Ägypten und Altes Testament 34). Wiesbaden: Harrassowitz.

Jansen-Winkeln, K. 1999. Die Wahl des Königs durch Orakel in der 20. Dynastie. *Bulletin de la Société d'Égyptologie de Genève* 23: 51–61.

Jansen-Winkeln, K. 2004. Zu einer Sekundärbestattung der 21. Dynastie in Kom Ombo. *Göttinger Miszellen* 202: 71–8.

Jansen-Winkeln, K. 2007. *Inschriften der Spätzeit, Teil I: Die 21. Dynastie*. Wiesbaden: Harrassowitz.

Jansen-Winkeln, K. 2008. *Inschriften der Spätzeit, Teil II: Die 22.-24. Dynastie*. Wiesbaden: Harrassowitz.

Jansen-Winkeln, K. 2009. *Inschriften der Spätzeit, Teil III: Die 25. Dynastie*. Wiesbaden: Harrassowitz.

Jansen-Winkeln, K. 2014. *Inschriften der Spätzeit, Teil IV: Die 26. Dynastie*, 2 vols. Wiesbaden: Harrassowitz.

Janssen, J.J. 1961. Two ancient Egyptian ship's logs: Papyrus Leiden I 350 verso and papyrus Turin 2008+2016. *Oudheidkundige Mededelingen uit het Rijksmuseum van Oudheden te Leiden* 42 (supplement): 1–114.

Janssen, J.J. 1963. An unusual donation stela of the Twentieth Dynasty. *Journal of Egyptian Archaeology* 49: 64–70.

Janssen, J.J. 1966. A Twentieth-Dynasty account papyrus (Pap. Turin no. Cat. 1907/8). *Journal of Egyptian Archaeology* 52: 81–94.

Janssen, J.J. 1967. Vizier Menteḥetef. *Journal of Egyptian Archaeology* 53: 163–4.

Janssen, J.J. 1968. The smaller Dakhla stela (Ashmolean Museum no. 1894.107 b). *Journal of Egyptian Archaeology* 54: 165–72.

Janssen, J.J. 1975a. *Commodity prices from the Ramessid Period: An economic study of the village of necropolis workmen at Thebes*. Leiden: Brill.

Janssen, J.J. 1975b. Prolegomena to the study of Egypt's economic history during the New Kingdom. *Studien zur Altägyptischen Kultur* 3: 127–85.

Janssen, J.J. 1979. The role of the temple in the Egyptian economy during the New Kingdom, in E. Lipinski (ed.), *State and temple economy in the ancient Near East: Proceedings of the international conference organized by the Katholieke Universiteit Leuven from the 10th to the 14th of April, 1978* (Orientalia Lovaniensia Analecta 5–6), vol. 2: 505–15. Leuven: Departement Oriëntalistiek.

Janssen, J.J. 1980. Absence from work by the necropolis workmen of Thebes. *Studien zur Altägyptischen Kultur* 8: 127–50.

Janssen, J.J. 1984. A curious error (O. IFAO. 1254). *Bulletin de l'Institut Français d'Archéologie Orientale* 84: 303–6.

Janssen, J.J. 1987. The day the inundation began. *Journal of Near Eastern Studies* 46: 129–36.

Janssen, J.J. 1991. Requisitions from Upper Egyptian temples (P. BM 10401). *Journal of Egyptian Archaeology* 77: 79–94.

Janssen, J.J. 1992a. Gear for the tombs (O. Turin 57366 and O. BM. 57033 + O. Petrie 30). *Revue d'Égyptologie* 43: 107–22.

Janssen, J.J. 1992b. A New Kingdom settlement: The verso of pap. BM. 10068. *Altorientalische Forschungen* 19: 8–23.

Janssen, J.J. 1994. An exceptional event at Deir el-Medina (P. Turin 1879, verso II). *Journal of the American Research Center in Egypt* 31: 91–7.

Janssen, J.J. 1997. *Village varia: Ten studies on the history and administration of Deir el-Medina* (Egyptologische uitgaven 11). Leiden: Nederlands Instituut voor het Nabije Oosten.

Janssen, J.J. 2005. *Donkeys at Deir el-Medina* (Egyptologische uitgaven 19). Leiden: Nederlands Instituut voor het Nabije Oosten.

Janssen, J.J. and Pestman, P.W. 1968. Burial and inheritance in the community of the necropolis workmen at Thebes (Pap. Bulaq X and O. Petrie 16). *Journal of the Economic and Social History of the Orient* 11: 137–70.

Jasnow, R.L. and Zauzich, K.-T. 2005. *The ancient Egyptian Book of Thoth: A demotic discourse on knowledge and pendant to the classical Hermetica*, 2 vols. Wiesbaden: Harrassowitz.

Jauhiainen, H. 2009. "Do not celebrate your feast without your neighbours": A study of references to feasts and festivals in non-literary documents from Ramesside Period Deir el-Medina. Unpublished PhD dissertation, Helsingin yliopisto.

Jéquier, G.M. 1921. *Les frises d'objets des sarcophages du Moyen Empire* (Mémoires publiés par les membres de l'Institut Français d'Archéologie Orientale du Caire 47). Cairo: Imprimerie de l'Institut Français d'Archéologie Orientale.

Jéquier, G.M. 1933. *Fouilles à Saqqarah: Deux pyramides du Moyen Empire*. Cairo: Imprimerie de l'Institut Français d'Archéologie Orientale.

Jéquier, G.M. 1936. *Fouilles à Saqqarah: Le monument funéraire de Pepi II*, 3 vols. Cairo: Imprimerie de l'Institut Français d'Archéologie Orientale.

Jin, S. 2001. Ein Gottesurteil im p.Boulaq X: Ein Fall von 'balance of power' bei dem Gottesorakel? *Journal of the Economic and Social History of the Orient* 44: 95–102.

Johnson, R.W. 1990. Images of Amenhotep III in Thebes: Style and intensions, in L.M. Berman (ed.), *The art of Amenhotep III: Art historical analysis: Papers presented at the international symposium held at the Cleveland Museum of Art, Cleveland, Ohio, 20-21 November 1987*: 29–32. Cleveland: Indiana University Press.

Jéquier, G.M. 1994. Honorific figures of Amenhotep III in the Luxor temple colonnade hall, in D.P. Silverman (ed.), *For his ka: Essays offered in memory of Klaus Baer* (Studies in ancient Oriental civilization 55): 133–44. Chicago: Oriental Institute of the University of Chicago.

Jéquier, G.M. 1998. Monuments and monumental art under Amenhotep III: Evolution and meaning, in D.B. O'Connor and E.H. Cline (eds), *Amenhotep III: Perspectives on his reign*: 63–94. Ann Arbor: University of Michigan Press.

Jéquier, G.M. 2009. A sandstone relief of Tutankhamun in the Liverpool Museum from the Luxor temple colonnade hall, in P.J. Brand and L. Cooper (eds), *Causing his name to live: Studies in Egyptian epigraphy and history in memory of William J. Murnane* (Culture and history of the ancient Near East 37): 125–8. Leiden and Boston: Brill.

Jonckheere, F. 1958. *Les médecins de l' Égypte pharaonique: Essai de prosopographie* (La médecine égyptienne 3). Bruxelles: Édition de la Fondation Égyptologique Reine Élizabeth.

Junker, H. 1910. *Die Stundenwachen in den Osirismysterien: Nach den Inschriften von Dendera, Edfu und Philae* (Denkschriften der kaiserlichen Akademie der Wissenschaften in Wien: Philosophisch-historische Klasse 54). Wien: Buchhändler der kaiserlichen Akademie der Wissenschaften.

Junker, H. 1913. *Das Götterdekret über das Abaton* (Denkschriften der kaiserlichen Akademie der Wissenschaften in Wien: Philosophisch-historische Klasse 56). Wien: Kommission bei A. Holder.

Junker, H. 1929. *Gîza: Bericht über die von der Akademie der Wissenschaften in Wien auf gemeinsame Kosten mit Dr. Wilhelm Pelizaeus unternommenen Grabungen auf dem Friedhof des Alten Reiches bei den Pyramiden von Gîza* (Denkschriften der kaiserlichen Akademie der Wissenschaften in Wien: Philosophisch-historische Klasse 69–73), 12 vols. Wien: Hölder-Pichler-Tempsky.

Junker, H. 1958. *Der grosse Pylon des Tempels der Isis in Philä*. Wien: R.M. Rohrer.

Jurman, C. 2010. Running with Apis: The Memphite Apis cult as a point of reference for social and religious practice in Late Period elite culture, in L. Bareš, F. Coppens, and K. Smoláriková (eds), *Egypt in transition: Social and religious development of Egypt in the first millennium BCE: Proceedings of an international conference, Prague, September 1-4, 2009*: 224–67. Praha: Gardners Books.

Kákosy, L. 1982: Orakel, in E. Otto and W. Helck (eds), *Lexikon der Ägyptologie*, vol. 4: 600–6. Wiesbaden: Harrassowitz.

Kammerzell, F. 2001. '... within the alter of the sun,' an unidentified hieroglyph and the construction of the sun temple *nxn-raw*. *Lingua Aegyptia* 9: 153–64.

Kampp, F. 1996. *Die thebanische Nekropole: Zum Wandel des Grabgedankens von der XVIII. bis zur XX. Dynastie* (Theben 13), 2 vols. Mainz: Philipp von Zabern.

Kanawati, N. 1980. *The rock tombs of El-Hawawish: The cemetery of Akhmim*. Sydney and Warminster: Aris & Phillips.

Kanawati, N. 2000. A new *HAt/rnpt-zp* for Teti and its implication for Old Kingdom chronology. *Göttinger Miszellen* 177: 25–32.

Kanawati, N. and Woods, A. 2010. *Beni Hassan: Art and daily life in an Egyptian province*. Cairo: Supreme Council of Antiquities.

von Känel, F. 1984. *Les prêtres-ouâb de Sekhmet et les conjurateurs de Serket* (Bibliothèque de l'École des Hautes Études. Section des sciences religieuses 87). Paris: Presses Universitaires de France.

Kaper, O.E. and Demarée, R.J. 2005. A donation stela in the name of Takeloth III from Amheida, Dakhleh Oasis. *Jaarbericht van het Vooraziatisch-Egyptisch Genootschap "Ex Oriente Lux"* 39: 19–37.

Kaplony-Heckel, U. 1971. *Ägyptische Handschriften*, 3 vols. Stuttgart: Franz Steiner.

Karkowski, J. 1976. Deir el-Bahari 1972–1973. *Études et Travaux* 9: 251–60.

Karkowski, J. 1979a. The question of the Beautiful Feast of the Valley representations in Hatshepsut's temple at Deir el-Bahari, in W.F. Reineke (ed.), *Acts. First International Congress of Egyptology* (Schriften zur Geschichte und Kultur des alten Orients 14): 359–64. Berlin: Akademie-Verlag.

Karkowski, J. 1979b. Deir el-Bahari 1974–1975. *Études et Travaux* 11: 217–20.

Karkowski, J. 1990. Deir el-Bahari, temple of Hatshepsut: Egyptological studies 1977–1980. *Études et Travaux* 14: 349–63.

Karkowski, J. 1992. Notes on the Beautiful Feast of the Valley as represented in Hatshepsut's temple at Deir el-Bahari, in *50 years of Polish excavations in Egypt and the Near East: Acts of the symposium at the Warsaw University, 1986*: 155–66. Warszawa: PAM.

Karkowski, J. 1997. Könihliche Schiffe, in *Geheimnisvolle Königin Hatschepsut: Ägyptische Kunst des 15. Jahrhunderts v. Chr.*: 106–7. Warszawa: Nationalmuseum in Warschau.

Karkowski, J. 2001. The decoration of the temple of Hatshepsut at Deir el-Bahari, in Z.E. Szafrański (ed.), *Queen Hatshepsut and her temple 3500 years later*: 99–157. Warszawa: Agencja Reklamowo-Wydawnicza A. Grzegorczyk.

Karkowski, J. 2003. *The temple of Hatshepsut, the solar complex* (Deir el-Bahari 6). Warszawa: Éditions Neriton.

Karlshausen, C. 1995. L'évolution de la barque processionnelle d'Amon à la 18e Dynastie. *Revue d'Égyptologie* 46: 119–37.

Katary, S.L.D. 2011: Taxation (until the end of the Third Intermediate Period), in J.C. Moreno García and W. Wendrich (eds), *UCLA encyclopedia of Egyptology*: 1–25. Los Angeles.

Kawai, N. 2010. Theban tomb 46 and its owner, Ramose, in S. D'Auria (ed.), *Offerings to the discerning eye: An Egyptological medley in honor of Jack A. Josephson* (Culture and history of the ancient Near East 38): 209–15. Leiden and Boston: Brill.

Kees, H. 1949. Ein Sonnenheiligtum im Amonstempel von Karnak. *Orientalia* 18: 427–42.

Kees, H. 1953. *Das Priestertum im ägyptischen Staat vom Neuen Reich bis zur Spätzeit* (Probleme der Ägyptologie 1). Leiden: Brill.

Kees, H. 1955. Zur Organisation des Ptahtempels in Karnak und seiner Priesterschaft. *Mitteilungen des Instituts für Orientforschung* 3: 329–44.

Kees, H. 1956. *Der Götterglaube im alten Ägypten* (Mitteilungen der Vorderasiatisch-ägyptsichen Geselschaft 45), 2nd ed. Berlin: Akademie-Verlag.

Keimer, L. 1933. Materialien zum altägyptischen Zwiebelkult. *Egyptian Religion* 1: 52–60.

Keller, C.A. 2005. The joint reign of Hatshepsut and Thutmose III, in C.H. Roehrig, R. Dreyfus, and C.A. Keller (eds), *Hatshepsut: From queen to pharaoh*: 96–8. New York and New Haven: Yale University Press.

Kemp, B.J. 1989. *Ancient Egypt: Anatomy of a civilization*. London: Routledge.

Kessler, D. 1987. Zur Bedeutung der Szenen des täglichen Lebens in den Privatgräbern (I): Die Szenen des Schiffsbaues und der Schiffahrt. *Zeitschrift für Ägyptische Sprache und Altertumskunde* 114: 59–88.

Kessler, D. 1988. Der satirisch-erotische Papyrus Turin 55001 und das 'Verbringen des schönen Tages'. *Studien zur Altägyptischen Kultur* 15: 171–96.

Kitchen, K.A. 1972. Ramesses VII and the Twentieth Dynasty. *Journal of Egyptian Archaeology* 58: 182–94.

Kitchen, K.A. 1973a. *The Third Intermediate Period in Egypt (1100–650 B.C.)*. Warminster: Aris & Phillips.

Kitchen, K.A. 1973b. A donation stela of Ramesses III from Medamūd. *Bulletin de l'Institut Français d'Archéologie Orientale* 73: 193–200.

Kitchen, K.A. 1975. *Ramesside inscriptions: Historical and biographical*, 8 vols. Oxford: Blackwell.

Kitchen, K.A. 1981. Review of *The edifice of Taharqa by the sacred lake of Karnak* by R. Parker, J. Leclant, and J-C Goyon. *Journal of American Oriental Society* 101: 438–9.

Kitchen, K.A. 1982. *Pharaoh triumphant: The life and times of Ramesses II, king of Egypt*. Warminster: Aris & Phillips.

Klebs, L. 1934. *Die Reliefs und Malereien des Neuen Reiches, Teil 1: Szenen aus dem Leben des Volkes* (Abhandlungen der Heidelberger Akademie der Wissenschaften:

Philosophisch-historische Klasse 9). Heidelberg: Carl Winters Universitätsbuchhandlung.

Klotz, D. 2008. Kneph: The religion of Roman Thebes. Unpublished PhD dissertation, Yale University.

Klotz, D. 2012. *Caesar in the city of Amun: Egyptian temple construction and theology in Roman Thebes* (Monographies reine Élisabeth 15). Turnhout: Brepols.

Klug, A. 2002. *Königliche Stelen in der Zeit von Ahmose bis Amenophis III.* (Monumenta aegyptiaca 8). Bruxelles: Brepols.

Knudsen, J. 2003. Manufacturing methods of pilgrims flasks and related vessels from cemetery 500 at El-Ahaiwa, in C.A. Redmount and C.A. Keller (eds), *Egyptian pottery: Proceedings of the 1990 Pottery Symposium at the University of California, Berkeley* (University of California publications in Egyptian archaeology 8): 87–94. Berkeley: Regents of the University of California.

Knudtzon, J.A., Ebeling, E., and Weber, O. 1915. *Die El-Amarna-Tafeln: Mit Einleitung und Erläuterungen* (Vorderasiatische Bibliothek), 2 vols. Leipzig: J.C. Hinrichs.

Koenig, Y. 1979. Livraisons d'or at de galène au trésor du temple d'Amon sous la XXe Dynastie, in *Hommages à la mémoire de Serge Sauneron, 1927-1976* (Bibliothèque d'étude 81), vol. 1: 185–220. Cairo: Institut Français d'Archéologie Orientale.

Koh, A.J. 2005/2006. Locating the *xtm n pA xr* of the workmen's village at Deir el-Medina. *Journal of American Research Center in Egypt* 42: 95–101.

Kondo, J. 1995. The re-clearance of tombs of WV-22 and WV-A in the western Valley of the Kings, in R.H. Wilkinson (ed.), *Valley of the sun kings: New explorations in the tombs of the pharaohs: Papers from the University of Arizona International Conference on the Valley of the Kings*: 25–33. Tucson: University of Arizona Egyptian Expedition.

Kondo, J. 1997. The re-use of the private tombs on the western bank of Thebes and its chronological problem: The cases of the tomb of *Xnsw* (no. 31) and the tomb of *Wsr-HAt* (no. 51). *Orient* 32: 50–68.

Kondo, J. 1999. The formation of the Theban necropolis: Historical changes and the conceptual architecture of the city of Thebes. *Orient* 34: 89–105.

Konrad, K. 2006. *Architektur und Theologie: Pharaonische Tempelterminologie unter Berücksichtigung königsideologischer Aspekte* (Königtum, Staat und Gesellschaft früher Hochkulturen 5). Wiesbaden: Harrassowitz.

el-Kordy, Z. 1984. Le bandeau du nouvel an, in *Mélanges Adolphe Gutbub*: 125–33. Montpellier: Université de Montpellier.

Kormyscheva, E. 1998. Festkalender im Kawa-Tempel, in R. Gundlach and M. Rochholz (eds), *4. ägyptologische Tempeltagung, Köln 10.-12. Oktober 1996: Feste im Tempel* (Ägypten und Altes Testament 33 (2)): 77–89. Wiesbaden: Harrassowitz.

Kozloff, A.P. and Bryan, B.M. 1992. *Egypt's dazzling sun: Amenhotep III and his world.* Bloomington: Indiana University Press.

Krauss, R. 1977. Untersuchungen zu König Amenmesse (2. Teil). *Studien zur Altägyptischen Kultur* 5: 131–74.

Krauss, R. 1980: Isis (Gottesgemahlin), in E. Otto and W. Helck (eds), *Lexikon der Ägyptologie*, vol. 3: 203–4. Wiesbaden: Harrassowitz.

Krauss, R. 1981. Zur historischen Einordnung Amenmesses und zur Chronologie der 19./20. Dynastie. *Göttinger Miszellen* 45: 27–33.

Krauss, R. 1982. Talfestdaten: Eine Korrektur. *Göttinger Miszellen* 54: 53.

Krauss, R. 1985. *Sothis- und Monddaten: Studien zur astronomischen und technischen Chronologie Altägyptens* (Hildesheimer ägyptologische Beiträge 20). Hildesheim: Gerstenberg.

Krauss, R. 1994. Fällt im Illahun-Archiv der 15. Mondmonatstag auf den 16. Mondmonatstag? *Göttinger Miszellen* 138: 81–92.

Krauss, R. 1996. Nochmals die Bestattungszeit Tutanchamuns und ein Exkurs über das Problem der Perseareife. *Studien zur Altägyptischen Kultur* 23: 227–54.

Krauss, R. 1998. Wenn und aber: Das Wag-Fest und die Chronologie des Alten Reiches. *Göttinger Miszellen* 162: 53–63.

Krauss, R. 2006a. Lunar days, lunar months, and the question of the 'civil-based' lunar calendar, in E. Hornung, R. Krauss, D. Warburton, and M. Eaton-Krauss (eds), *Ancient Egyptian chronology* (Handbook of Oriental studies. Section 1, The Near and Middle East 83): 386–91. Leiden: Brill.

Krauss, R. 2006b. Lunar dates, in E. Hornung, R. Krauss, D. Warburton, and M. Eaton-Krauss (eds), *Ancient Egyptian chronology* (Handbook of Oriental studies. Section 1, The Near and Middle East 83): 395–431. Leiden: Brill.

Krauss, R. 2006c. Egyptian Sirius/Sothic dates, and the question of the Sothis-based lunar calendar, in E. Hornung, R. Krauss, D. Warburton, and M. Eaton-Krauss (eds), *Ancient Egyptian chronology* (Handbook of Oriental studies. Section 1, The Near and Middle East 83): 439–57. Leiden: Brill.

Krejčí, J. and Bárta, M. 2000. *Abusir and Saqqara in the year 2000* (Archív orientální. Supplementa 9). Praha: Academy of Sciences of the Czech Republic, Oriental Institute.

Kruchten, J.-M. 1981. *Le décret d'Horemheb.* Bruxelles: Editions de l'Université de Bruxelles.

Kruchten, J.-M. 1982. Rétribution de l'armée d'après le décret d'Horemheb, in *L'Égyptologie en 1979: Axes prioritaires de recherches* (Colloques internationaux du Centre National de la Recherche Scientifique

595), vol. 2: 143–8. Paris: Éditions du Centre National de la Recherche Scientifique.

Kruchten, J.-M. 1985. Un instrument politique original: La belle fête de *pḥ-nṯr* des rois-pretres de la XXI Dynastie. *Bulletin de la Société Française d'Égyptologie* 103: 6–26.

Kruchten, J.-M. 1986. *Le grand texte oraculaire de Djéhoutymose, intendant du domaine d'Amon sous le pontificat de Pinedjem II* (Monographies reine Élisabeth 5). Bruxelles: Édition de la Fondation Égyptologique Reine Élizabeth.

Kruchten, J.-M. 1989. *Les annales des prêtres de Karnak (XXI-XXIIImes Dynasties) et autres textes contemporains relatifs à l'initiation des prêtres d'Amon* (Orientalia Lovaniensia Analecta 32). Leuven: Departement Oriëntalistiek.

Kruchten, J.-M. 1991. Le 'maître des dieux' de Karnak, in U. Verhoeven and E. Graefe (eds), *Religion und Philosophie im alten Ägypten: Festgabe für Philippe Derchain zu seinem 65. Geburtstag am 24. Juli 1991* (Orientalia Lovaniensia Analecta 39): 179–87. Leuven: Departement Oriëntalistiek.

Kruchten, J.-M. 2000. Un oracle d'Amenhotep du village sous Ramsès III: Ostracon Gardiner 103, in R.J. Demarée and A. Egberts (eds), *Deir el-Medina in the third millennium AD: A tribute to Jac. J. Janssen* (Egyptologische uitgaven 14): 209–16. Leiden: Nederlands Instituut voor het Nabije Oosten.

Kruchten, J.-M. 2001: Oracles, in D.B. Redford (ed.), *The Oxford encyclopedia of ancient Egypt*, vol. 2: 609–12. Oxford: Oxford University Press.

Kruchten, J.-M. and Delvaux, L. 2010. *La tombe de Sétaou* (Publication du Comité des Fouilles Belges en Égypte 8). Bruxelles: Brepols.

Krzyżanowski, L. 1992. *The temple of queen Hatshepsut IV: The report of the Polish-Egyptian archaeological and preservation mission Deir el-Bahari 1980-1988* (Reports of the research and preservation missions of P. K. Z. 14). Warszawa: Ateliers for Conservation of Cultural Property (P. K. Z.).

Kuentz, C.M. 1925. *Deux stèles d'Aménophis II (stèles d'Amada et d'Éléphantine)* (Bibliothèque d'étude 10). Cairo: Institut Français d'Archéologie Orientale.

Kuhlmann, K.P. and Schenkel, W. 1983. *Das Grab des Ibi, Obergutsverwalters der Gottesgemahlin des Amun (thebanisches Grab Nr. 36)* (Archäologische Veröffentlichungen (Deutsches Archäologisches Institut. Abteilung Kairo) 15), 2 vols. Mainz am Rhein: Philipp von Zabern.

Kurth, D. 1983. *Die Dekoration der Säulen im Pronaos des Tempels von Edfu* (Göttinger Orientforschungen. IV. Reihe, Ägypten 11). Wiesbaden: Harrassowitz.

Kurth, D. 1994a. Die Reise der Hathor von Dendera nach Edfu, in R. Gundlach and M. Rochholz (eds), *Ägyptische Tempel: Struktur, Funktion und Programm (Akten der ägyptologischen Tempeltagungen in Gosen 1990 und in Mainz 1992)* (Hildesheimer ägyptologische Beiträge 37): 211–6. Hildesheim: Gerstenberg Verlag.

Kurth, D. 1994b. *Treffpunkt der Götter: Inschriften aus dem Tempel des Horus von Edfu*. Zürich: Artemis.

Kurth, D. 2007. *Einführung ins ptolemäische: Eine Grammatik mit Zeichenliste und Übungsstücken*, 2 vols. Hützel: Backe.

Kurth, D. 2010. *A Ptolemaic sign-list: Hierogylphs used in the temples of the Graeco-Roman Period of Egypt and their meanings*. Hützel: Backe-Verlag.

Kurth, D. and Behrmann, A. 2004. *Edfou VII* (Inschriften des Tempels von Edfu. Begleithefte 2). Wiesbaden: Harrassowitz.

Kurth, D. and Waitkus, W. 1994. 'Der Tag des Nacht des Kindes in seinem Nest': Zur Lesung von Dendara IV, 60, 11–13. *Göttinger Miszellen* 140: 49–51.

Kwaśnica, A. 2001. Reconstructing the architectural layout of the upper courtyard, in Z.E. Szafrański (ed.), *Queen Hatshepsut and her temple 3500 years later*: 81–97. Warszawa: Agencja Reklamowo-Wydawnicza A. Grzegorczyk.

Laboury, D. 2006. Royal portrait and ideology: Evolution and signification of the statuary of Thutmose III, in E.H. Cline and D.B. O'Connor (eds), *Thutmose III: A new biography*: 260–91. Ann Arbor: University of Michigan Press.

Lacau, P. 1909. *Stèles du Nouvel Empire* (Catalogue général des antiquités égyptiennes du Musée du Caire). Cairo: Imprimerie de l'Institut Français d'Archéologie Orientale.

Lacau, P. 1953. L'érection du môt devant Amon-Min. *Chronique d'Égypte* 55: 13–22.

Lacau, P. and Chevrier, H. 1977. *Une chapelle d'Hatshepsout à Karnak* (Publications de l'Institut Français d'Archéologie Orientale du Caire 2), 2 vols. Cairo: Institut Français d'Archéologie Orientale.

Lacau, P. and Lauer, J.P. 1936. *La Pyramide à Degrés* (Fouilles à Saqqarah). Cairo: Imprimerie de l'Institut Français d'Archéologie Orientale.

Lagarce, E. and Leclant, J. 1976. Vase plastique en faïence KIT. 1747: Une fiole pour eau jouvence, in G. Clerc, V. Karageorghis, E. Lagarce, and J. Leclant (eds), *Fouilles de Kition II: Objets égyptiens et égyptisants: Scarabées, amulettes et figurines en pâte de verre et en faïence, vase plastique en faïence*: 183–290. Nicosia: Zavallis Press.

Łajtar, A. 1991. Proskynema inscriptions of a corporation of iron-workers from Hermonthis in the temple of Hatshepsut in Deir el-Bahari: New evidence for pagan cults in Egypt in the 4th cent. A.D. *Journal of Juristic Papyrology* 21: 53–70.

Łajtar, A. 2006. *Deir el-Bahari in the Hellenistic and Roman periods: A study of an Egyptian temple based on Greek sources* (Journal of Juristic Papyrology. Supplement 4). Warszawa: Uniwersytet Warszawski.

Lalouette, C. 1984. *Textes sacrés et textes profanes de l'ancienne Égypte* (Collection UNESCO d'œuvres représentatives. Série Égypte ancienne 54), 2 vols. Paris: Gallimard.

Lange, H.O. and Schäfer, H. 1902. *Grab- und Denksteine des Mittleren Reichs im Museum von Kairo* (Catalogue général des antiquités égyptiennes du Musée du Caire 5, 7, 36, and 78), 4 vols. Berlin: Reichsdruckerei.

Larché, F. 2009. A reconstruction of Senwosret's portico and of some structures of Amenhotep I at Karnak, in P.J. Brand and L. Cooper (eds), *Causing his name to live: Studies in Egyptian epigraphy and history in memory of William J. Murnane* (Culture and history of the ancient Near East 37): 37–73. Leiden and Boston: Brill.

Laskowska-Kusztal, E. 1984. *Le sanctuaire ptolémaïque de Deir el-Bahari* (Deir el-Bahari 3). Warszawa: PWN-Éditions scientifiques de Pologne.

Laskowski, P. 2006. Monumental architecture and the royal building program of Thutmose III, in E.H. Cline and D.B. O'Connor (eds), *Thutmose III: A new biography*: 183–237. Ann Arbor: University of Michigan Press.

Lauffray, J. 1980. Les 'talatat' du IXe pylône de Karnak et le Teny-menou, in *Cahiers de Karnak 6: 1973-1977*: 67–89. Cairo: Centre Franco-Égyptien d'Étude des Temples de Karnak.

Leahy, A. 1996. The adoption of Ankhnesneferibre at Karnak. *Journal of Egyptian Archaeology* 82: 145–65.

Leclant, J. 1961. *Montouemhat: Quatrième prophète d'Amon, prince de la ville* (Bibliothèque d'étude 35). Cairo: Institut Français d'Archéologie Orientale.

Leclant, J. 1965. *Recherches sur les monuments thébains de la XXVe Dynastie dite éthiopienne* (Bibliothèque d'étude 36). Cairo: Imprimerie de l'Institut Français d'Archéologie Orientale.

Leclère, F. and Coulon, L. 1998. La nécropole osirienne de la 'grande place' à Karnak: Fouilles dans le secteur nord-est du temple d'Amon, in C. Eyre (ed.), *Proceedings of the Seventh International Congress of Egyptologists, Cambridge, 3-9 September 1995* (Orientalia Lovaniensia Analecta 82): 649–59. Leuven: Peeters.

Leeuwenburg, L.G. 1940. Overzichten van de Geschiedenis en de Opgravingen in het Nabije Oosten III: Het Tempelcomplex van Medinet Haboe II: De Feestkalender. *Jaarbericht van het Vooraziatisch-Egyptisch Gezelschap "Ex Oriente Lux"* 7: 327–40.

Lefébure, M.E. 1889. *Les hypogées royaux de Thèbes* (Mémoires publiés par les membres de la mission archéologique française au Caire 3 (1–2)). Paris: Ernest Leroux.

Legrain, G. 1900. Notes prises à Karnak. *Recueil de Travaux* 22: 51–65.

Legrain, G. 1902. Le temple de Ptah Rîs-anbou-f dans Thèbes (suite). *Annales du Service des Antiquités de l'Égypte* 3: 97–114.

Legrain, G. 1905. Notes d'inspection. *Annales du Service des Antiquités de l'Égypte* 6: 130–40.

Legrain, G. 1906. *Statues et statuettes de rois et de particuliers* (Catalogue général des antiquités égyptiennes du Musée du Caire 71), 4 vols. Cairo: Imprimerie de l'Institut Français d'Archéologie Orientale.

Legrain, G. 1908. Sur une stèle de Senousrit IV. *Recueil de Travaux* 30: 15–6.

Legrain, G. 1917. Le logement et transport des baruques sacrées et des statues des dieux dans quelques temples égyptiens. *Bulletin de l'Institut Français d'Archéologie Orientale* 13: 1–140.

Legrain, G. 1929. *Les temples de Karnak*. Bruxelles and Paris: Vromant.

Leibovitch, J. 1953. Gods of agriculture and welfare in ancient Egypt. *Journal of Near Eastern Studies* 12: 73–113.

Leitz, C. 1989. *Studien zur ägyptischen Astronomie* (Ägyptologische Abhandlungen 49). Wiesbaden: Harrassowitz.

Leitz, C. 1993. Die Nacht des Kindes in seinem Nest in Dendera. *Zeitschrift für Ägyptische Sprache und Altertumskunde* 120: 136–65.

Leitz, C. 1994a. *Tagewählerei: Das Buch ḥ3t nḥḥ pḥ.wy ḏt und verwandte Texte* (Ägyptologische Abhandlungen 55), 2 vols. Wiesbaden: Harrassowitz.

Leitz, C. 1994b. Der Mondkalender und der Beginn des ägyptischen Kalendertages. *Bulletin de la Société d'Égyptologie de Genève* 18: 49–60.

Leitz, C. 1999. *Magical and medical papyri of the New Kingdom* (Hieratic papyri in the British Museum. Seventh series). London: British Museum Press.

Leitz, C. 2002a. *Lexikon der ägyptischen Götter und Götterbezeichnungen* (Orientalia Lovaniensia Analecta 110–6 and 129), 8 vols. Leuven: Peeters.

Leitz, C. 2002b. *Kurzbibliographie zu den übersetzten Tempeltexten der griechisch-römischen Zeit* (Bibliothèque d'étude 136). Cairo: Institut Français d'Archéologie Orientale.

Lello, G. 1978. Thutmose III's first lunar date. *Journal of Near Eastern Studies* 37: 327–30.

Lepsius, R. 1849. *Denkmaeler aus Aegypten und Aethiopien: Nach den Zeichnungen der von seiner Majestaet dem Koenige von Preussen Friedrich Wilhelm IV nach diesen Laendern gesendeten und in den Jahren 1842-1845 ausgefuehrten wissenschaftlichen Expedition*, 12 vols. Berlin: Nicolai.

Lichtheim, M. 1945. The songs of the harpers. *Journal of Near Eastern Studies* 4: 178–212.

Lichtheim, M. 1973. *Ancient Egyptian literature: A book of readings*, 3 vols. Berkeley and London: University of California Press.

Lichtheim, M. 1992. *Maat in Egyptian autobiographies and related studies*. Freiburg and Göttingen: Vandenhoeck & Ruprecht.

Lichtheim, M. 1997. *Moral values in ancient Egypt* (Orbis biblicus et orientalis 155). Fribourg and Göttingen: Vandenhoeck & Ruprecht.

von Lieven, A. 2001. Kleine Beiträge zur Vergöttlichung Amenophis' I. *Zeitschrift für Ägyptische Sprache und Altertumskunde* 128: 41–64.

von Lieven, A. 2007. *Grundriss des Laufes der Sterne: Das sogenannte Nutbuch* (CNI publications 31), 2 vols. København: Museum Tusculanum Press.

Lipińska, J. 1967. Names and history of the sanctuaries built by Tuthmosis III at Deir el-Baḥri. *Journal of Egyptian Archaeology* 53: 25–33.

Lipińska, J. 1968. The granite doorway in the temple of Thutmosis III at Deir el-Bahari. *Études et Travaux* 2: 79–97.

Lipińska, J. 1974. Studies on reconstruction of the Hatshepsut temple at Deir el-Bahari: A collection of the temple fragments in the Egyptian Museum, Berlin, in *Festschrift zum 150 jährigen Bestehen des Berliner Ägyptischen Museums* (Mitteilungen aus der ägyptischen Sammlung, Staatliche Museen zu Berlin 8): 18–23. Berlin: Akademie-Verlag.

Loeben, C.E. 1987. Amon à la place d'Aménophis I: Le relief de la porte des magasins nord de Thoutmosis III, in *Cahiers de Karnak 8: 1982–1985*: 233–43. Paris: Centre Franco-Égyptien d'Étude des Temples de Karnak.

Logan, T. 2000. The *jmyt-pr* document: Form, function, and significance. *Journal of American Research Center in Egypt* 37: 49–73.

Lohwasser, A. 1991. *Die Formel 'Öffnen des Gesichts'* (Veröffentlichungen der Institute für Afrikanistik und Ägyptologie der Universität Wien 58). Wien: Afro-Pub.

López, J. 1978. *Ostraca ieratici* (Catalogo del Museo Egizio di Torino. Serie seconda, Collezioni 3). Milano: Cisalpino-La Goliardica.

Loret, V. 1882. Les fêtes d'Osiris au mois de Khoiak. *Recueil de Travaux* 3: 43–57.

Loret, V. 1883. Les fêtes d'Osiris au mois de Khoiak. *Recueil de Travaux* 4: 21–33.

Loret, V. 1884. Les fêtes d'Osiris au mois de Khoiak. *Recueil de Travaux* 5: 85–103.

Loret, V. 1889. Le tombeau de l'Am-Xent Amen-hotep, in G. Maspero (ed.), (Mémoires publiés par les membres de la mission archéologie française au Caire 1 (1)): 23–32. Paris: Ernest Leroux.

Louant, E. 2000. *Comment Pouiemrê triompha de la mort: Analyse du programme iconographique de la tombe thébaine no. 39.* Leuven: Peeters.

Loukianoff, G. 1936. Une statue parlante ou oracle du dieu Ré-Harmakhis. *Annales du Service des Antiquités de l'Égypte* 36: 187–93.

Lowle, D.A. 1976. A remarkable family of draughtsmen-painters from early Nineteenth-Dynasty Thebes. *Oriens Antiquus* 15: 91–106.

Luft, U. 1986. Noch einmal zum Ebers-Kalender. *Göttinger Miszellen* 92: 69–77.

Luft, U. 1992. *Die chronologische Fixierung des ägyptischen Mittleren Reiches nach dem Tempelarchiv von Illahun* (Österreichische Akademie der Wissenschaften: Philosophisch-historische Klasse. Sitzungsberichte. Veröffentlichungen der Ägyptischen Kommission 2). Wien: Österreichische Akademie der Wissenschaften.

Luft, U. 1994. The date of the Wagy Feast: Considerations on the chronology of the Old Kingdom, in A.J. Spalinger (ed.), *Revolutions in time: Studies in ancient Egyptian calendrics* (Varia Aegyptiaca. Supplement 6): 39–44. San Antonio: van Siclen Books.

Luft, U. 2006. *Urkunden zur Chronologie der späten 12. Dynastie: Briefe aus Illahun* (Denkschriften der Gesamtakademie, Österreichischen Akademie der Wissenschaften 34). Wien: Verlag der Österreichischen Akademie der Wissenschaften.

Macadam, L.M.F. 1949. *The temples of Kawa: I. The inscriptions; II. History and archaeology of the site* (Oxford University excavations in Nubia), 4 vols. London: Oxford University Press.

Malek, J. 1980. Theban tomb tracings made by Norman and Nina de Garis Davies. *Göttinger Miszellen* 37: 31–6.

Malek, J. 1985. The tomb-chapel of Hekamaetre-neheh at Northern Saqqara. *Studien zur Altägyptischen Kultur* 12: 43–60.

Malek, J. 1988. The royal butler Hori at northern Saqqara. *Journal of Egyptian Archaeology* 74: 125–36.

Malek, J. 1995. Book review of *L'Égypte et la vallée du Nil II: De la fin de l'Ancien Empire à la fin du Nouvel Empire* by C. Vandersleyen. *Discussions in Egyptology* 32: 101–6.

Malek, J. 2000. Old-Kingdom rulers as 'local saints' in the Memphite area during the Middle Kingdom, in J. Krejčí and M. Bárta (eds), *Abusir and Saqqara in the year 2000* (Archív orientální 9): 241–58. Praha: Academy of Sciences of the Czech Republic, Oriental Institute.

Malek, J., Fleming, E., and Hobby, A. 2005. Two destroyed scenes in the burial chamber of the Tombeau des Vignes (TT 96). *Discussions in Egyptology* 62: 49–54.

Malinine, M. 1951. Un jugement rendu à Thèbes sous la XXVe Dynastie (pap. Louvre E. 3228 c). *Revue d'Égyptologie* 6: 157–78.

Malinine, M., Posener, G., and Vercoutter, J. 1968. *Catalogue des stèles du Sérapéum de Memphis*, 2 vols. Paris: Éditions des Musées Nationaux, Imprimerie Nationale.

Manniche, L. 1982. The Maru built by Amenophis III: Its significance and possible location, in *L'égyptologie en 1979: Axes prioritaires de recherches* (Colloques internationaux du Centre National de la Recherche Scientifique 595), vol. 2: 271–4. Paris: Éditions du Centre National de la Recherche Scientifique.

Manniche, L. 1986. The tomb of Nakht, the gardener, at Thebes (no. 161) as copied by Robert Hay. *Journal of Egyptian Archaeology* 72: 55–78.

Manniche, L. 1987. *City of the dead: Thebes in Egypt.* London: British Museum Publications.

Manniche, L. 1991. *Music and musicians in ancient Egypt.* London: British Museum Press.

Manniche, L. 2011. *Lost Ramessid and post-Ramessid private tombs in the Theban necropolis* (CNI Publications 33). København: Museum Tusculanum Press.

Manning, J.G., Greig, G., and Uchida, S. 1989. Chicago Oriental Institute Ostracon 12073 once again. *Journal of Near Eastern Studies* 48: 117–24.

der Manuelian, P. 1987. *Studies in the reign of Amenophis II* (Hildesheimer ägyptologische Beiträge 26). Hildesheim: Gerstenberg Verlag.

Marciniak, M. 1971. Encore sur la Belle Fête de la Vallée. *Études et Travaux* 5: 53–64.

Marciniak, M. 1974. *Les inscriptions hiératiques du temple de Thoutmosis III* (Deir el-Bahari 1). Warszawa: PWN-Editions scientifiques de Pologne.

Mariette, A. 1870. *Dendérah: Description générale du grand temple de cette ville*, 6 vols. Paris: A. Franck.

Mariette, A. 1871. *Les papyrus égyptiens du Musée de Boulaq*, 3 vols. Paris: A. Franck.

Mariette, A. 1875. *Karnak: Étude topographique et archéologique avec un appendice comprenant les principaux textes hiéroglyphiques découverts ou recuillis pendant les fouilles exécutées à Karnak*, 2 vols. Leipzig: J.C. Hinrichs.

Martin, G.T. 2005. *Stelae from Egypt and Nubia in the Fitzwilliam Museum, Cambridge, c. 3000 BC–AD 1150.* Cambridge: Cambridge University Press.

Marucchi, O. 1898. *Gli obelischi egiziani di Roma*, Edizioni riveduta ed ampliati. Roma: E. Loescher.

Maspero, G. 1880. Sur une tablette appartenant à M. Rogers. *Recueil de Travaux* 2: 13–8.

Maspero, G. 1893. Le double et les statues prophétiques, in G. Maspero (ed.), *Études de mythologie et d›archéologie égyptiennes* (Bibliothéque égyptologique), vol. 1: 77–91. Paris: Ernest Leroux.

Maspero, G. 1907. *Causeries d'Égypte* (Librairie orientale & américaine). Paris: E. Guilmoto.

Maspero, G. 1910. Varia. *Recueil de Travaux* 32: 88.

Masson, A. 2007. Le quartier des prêtres du temple de Karnak: Rapport préliminaire de la fouille de la Maison VII, 2001–2003, in *Cahiers de Karnak 12: 1982–1985*, vol. 2: 593–655. Paris: Centre Franco-Égyptien d'Étude des Temples de Karnak.

Mattha, G. 1962. The value *Hsb.t* for the dating group in Egyptian documents instead of *HA.t-sp*. *Bulletin of the Faculty of Arts, Cairo* 20: 17–20.

Maystre, C. 1936. *Tombes de Deir el-Médineh: La tombe de Nebenmât (no 219)* (Mémoires publiés par les membres de l'Institut Français d'Archéologie Orientale du Caire 61). Cairo: Imprimerie de l'Institut Français d'Archéologie Orientale.

Maystre, C. 1941. Le Livre de la Vache du Ciel dans les tombeaux de la Vallée des Rois. *Bulletin de l'Institut Français d'Archéologie Orientale* 40: 53–115.

McDowell, A.G. 1990. *Jurisdiction in the workmen's community of Deir el-Medîna* (Egyptologische uitgaven 5). Leiden: Nederlands Instituut voor het Nabije Oosten.

Maystre, C. 1999. *Village life in ancient Egypt: Laundry lists and love songs*. Oxford: Oxford University Press.

Meeks, D. 1979. Les donations aux temples dans l'Égypte du Ier millénaire avant J.-C., in E. Lipiński (ed.), *State and temple economy in the ancient Near East: Proceedings of the international conference organized by the Katholieke Universiteit Leuven from the 10th to 14th of April 1978* (Orientalia Lovaniensia Analecta 6), vol. 2: 605–87. Leuven: Departement Oriëntalistiek.

el-Menshawy, S. 2000. Pictorial evidence depicting the interaction between the king and his people in ancient Egypt, in A. McDonald and C. Riggs (eds), *Current research in Egyptology 2000* (British Archaeological Reports. International Series 909): 83–9. Oxford: Archaeopress.

Menu, B. 1985. Cessions de services et engagements pour dette sous les rois kouchites et saïtes. *Revue d'Égyptologie* 36: 73–87.

Mercer, S.A.B. 1952. *The Pyramid Texts in translation and commentary*, 4 vols. New York, London, and Toronto: van Rees Press.

el-Metwally, E. 1992. *Entwicklung der Grabdekoration in den altägyptischen Privatgräbern: Ikonographische Analyse der Totenkultdarstellungen von der Vorgeschichte bis zum Ende der 4. Dynastie* (Göttinger Orientforschungen. IV. Reihe, Ägypten 24). Wiesbaden: Harrassowitz.

Meyer, E. 1904. *Aegyptische Chronologie* (Abhandlungen der Königlich Preussischen Akademie der Wissenschaften, 1904). Berlin: Verlag der Königlichen Akadamie der Wissenschaften.

Meyer, E. 1913. *Fremdvölkerdarstellungen altägyptischer Denkmäler: Sammlung photographischer Aufnahmen aus den Jahren 1912-1913*. Berlin: Reichsdruckerei.

Meyer, E. 1928. *Gottesstaat, Militärherrschaft und Ständewesen in Ägypten: Zur Geschichte der 21. und 22. Dynastie*. Berlin: Verlag der Akademie der Wissenschaften.

Meyer, S. 1998. Festlieder zum Auszug Gottes, in R. Gundlach and M. Rochholz (eds), *4. ägyptologische Tempeltagung, Köln 10.-12. Oktober 1996: Feste im Tempel* (Ägypten und Altes Testament 33 (2)): 135–42. Wiesbaden: Harrassowitz.

Meyer-Dietrich, E. 2010. Die Opetprozession–mehr als nur eine rituelle Verbindung von Karnak mit Luxor: Die Verwendung von Schall zur Erzeugung eines symbolischen Raumes bei der Opetprozession, in M. Dolińska and H. Beinlich (eds), *8. ägyptologische Tempeltagung: Interconnections between temples, Warschau, 22.-25. September 2008* (Königtum, Staat und Gesellschaft früher Hochkulturen 3 (3)): 123–36. Wiesbaden: Harrassowitz.

Mikhail, L.B. 1983. Dramatic aspects of the Osirian Khoiak Festival. Unpublished PhD dissertation, Uppsala universitet.

Moens, M.-F. 1985. The procession of the god Min to the *xtyw*-garden. *Studien zur Altägyptischen Kultur* 12: 61–73.

Mojsov , B. 2012. The monuments of Ramesses III, in E.H. Cline and D.B. O'Connor (eds), *Ramesses III: The life and times of Egypt's last hero*: 271–304. Ann Arbor: University of Michigan Press.

Molen, R.V.D. 2000. *A hieroglyphic dictionary of Egyptian Coffin Texts* (Probleme der Ägyptologie 15). Leiden: Brill.

Möller, G. 1909. *Hieratische Paläographie: Die aegyptische Buchschrift in ihrer Entwicklung von der Fünften Dynastie bis zur römischen Kaiserzeit*, 3 vols. Leipzig: J.C. Hinrich.

Mond, R. and Emery, W.B. 1927. Excavations at Sheikh Abd el-Gurneh 1925–26. *Annals of Archaeology and Anthropology* 14: 13–34.

Mond, R. and Myers, O.H. 1934. *The Bucheum* (Memoir of the Egypt Exploration Society 41), 3 vols. London: Egypt Exploration Society.

Mond, R. and Myers, O.H. 1940. *Temples of Armant: A preliminary survey*, 2 vols. London: Egypt Exploration Society.

Montet, P. 1928. Les tombeaux de Siout et de Deir Rifeh (1). *Kêmi* 1: 53–68.

Montet, P. 1936. Les tombeaux de Siout et de Deir Rifeh (3). *Kêmi* 6: 131–63.

Montet, P. 1966. *Le lac sacré de Tanis* (Mémoires de l'Académie 44). Paris: Imprimerie Nationale.

Morenz, L.D. 2003a. Schamanismus in der Frühzeit Ägyptens? *Archiv für Religionsgeschichte* 5: 212–26.

Morenz, L.D. 2003b. Die thebanischen Potentaten und ihr Gott: Zur Konzeption des Gottes Amun und der (Vor-)Geschichte des Sakralzentrums Karnak in der XI. Dynastie. *Zeitschrift für Ägyptische Sprache und Altertumskunde* 130: 110–9.

Moret, A.M. 1931. La légende d'Osiris à l'époque thébaine d'après l'hymne à Osiris du Louvre. *Bulletin de l'Institut Français d'Archéologie Orientale* 30: 725–50.

Morgan, E.E. 2004. *Untersuchungen zu den Ohrenstelen aus Deir el Medine* (Ägypten und Altes Testament 61). Wiesbaden: Harrassowitz.

de Morgan, J., Bouriant, U., Legrain, G.A., Jéquier, G.M., and Barsanti, A. 1895. *Kom Ombos* (Catalogue des monuments et inscriptions de l'Égypte antique: Première série, Haute Égypte 2–3), 2 vols. Wien: Adolphe Holzhausen.

Morkot, R.G. 1990. *Nb-mAat-ra*-united-with-Ptah. *Journal of Near Eastern Studies* 49: 323–37.

Moursi, M. 1981. Die Stele des Vezirs Re-hotep (Kairo JdE 48845). *Mitteilungen der Deutschen Archäologischen Instituts, Abteilung Kairo* 37: 321–9.

Moussa, A.M. and Altenmüller, H. 1971. *The tomb of Nefer and Ka-hay* (Archäologische Veröffentlichungen (Deutsches Archäologisches Institut. Abteilung Kairo) 5). Mainz am Rhein: Philipp von Zabern.

Moussa, A.M. and Altenmüller, H. 1977. *Das Grab des Nianchchnum und Chnumhotep* (Archäologische Veröffentlichungen (Deutsches Archäologisches Institut. Abteilung Kairo) 21). Mainz am Rhein: Philipp von Zabern.

Muhs, B.P. 2005. *Tax receipts, taxpayers, and taxes in early Ptolemaic Thebes* (Oriental Institute publications 126). Chicago: Oriental Institute of the University of Chicago.

Muhs, B.P. 2016. *The ancient Egyptian economy*. Cambridge: Cambridge University Press.

Müller, K. 2006. *Settlements of the Ptolemies: City foundations and new settlements in the Hellenistic world* (Studia hellenistica 43). Leuven: Peeters.

Müller, W.M. 1906. The ceremony of pole-climbing by Nubians, in W.M. Müller and H.F. Lutz (eds), *Egyptological researches* (Carnegie Institution of Washington publications 53), vol. 1: 34–6. Washington D. C.: Carnegie Institution of Washington.

Munro, I. 1983. *Das Zelt-Heiligtum des Min: Rekonstruktion und Deutung eines fragmentarischen Modells (Kestner-Museum 1935.200.250)* (Münchner ägyptologische Studien 41). München: Deutscher Kunstverlag.

Murnane, W.J. 1971/1972. The 'king Ramesses' of the Medinet Habu procession of princes. *Journal of American Research Center in Egypt* 9: 121–31.

Murnane, W.J. 1975/1976. The accession date of Sethos I. *Serapis* 3: 23–33.

Murnane, W.J. 1976. On the accession date of Akhenaten, in *Studies in honor of George R. Hughes* (Studies in ancient Oriental civilization 39): 163–7. Chicago: University of Chicago Press.

Murnane, W.J. 1977. *Ancient Egyptian coregencies* (Studies in ancient Oriental civilization 40). Chicago: Oriental Institute of the University of Chicago.

Murnane, W.J. 1979. The bark of Amun on the third pylon at Karnak. *Journal of American Research Center in Egypt* 16: 11–27.

Murnane, W.J. 1982: Opetfest, in E. Otto and W. Helck (eds), *Lexikon der Ägyptologie*, vol. 4: 574–9. Wiesbaden: Harrassowitz.

Murnane, W.J. 1985. False doors and cult practices inside Luxor temple, in P. Posener-Kriéger (ed.), *Mélanges Gamal Eddin Mokhtar* (Bibliothèque d'étude 97), vol. 2: 135–48. Cairo: Institut Français d'Archéologie Orientale.

Murnane, W.J. 1986. La grand Fête d'Opet. *Dossiers d'Histoire et Archéologie* 101: 22–5.

Murnane, W.J. 1998. The organization of government under Amenhotep III, in D.B. O'Connor and E.H. Cline (eds), *Amenhotep III: perspectives on his reign*: 173–222. Ann Arbor: University of Michigan Press.

Murnane, W.J. and Meltzer, E.S. 1995. *Texts from the Amarna Period in Egypt* (Writings from the ancient world 5). Atlanta: Scholars Press.

Murnane, W.J. and van Siclen III, C.C. 1993. *The boundary stelae of Akhenaten*. London and New York: Kegan Paul International.

Murray, M.A. 1905. *Saqqara mastabas*, 2 vols. London: Bernard Quaritch.

Murray, M.A. 1934. Ritual masking, in *Mélanges Maspero I: Orient ancien* (Mémoires publiés par les membres de l'Institut Français d'Archéologie Orientale du Caire 66), vol. 1: 251–5. Cairo: Imprimerie de l'Institut Français d'Archéologie Orientale.

Myśliwiec, K. 1985. *Eighteenth Dynasty before the Amarna Period*. Leiden: Brill.

Nagel, P. 1983. *Das Triadon: Ein sahidisches Lehrgedicht des 14. Jahrhunderts* (Wissenschaftliche Beiträge, Martin-Luther-Universität Halle-Wittenberg). Halle: Abt. Wissenschaftspublizistik der Martin-Luther-Universität Halle-Wittenberg.

Naguib, S.-A. 1990. The Festivals of Opet and Abul Haggag: Survival of an ancient tradition? *Temenos* 26: 67–84.

Naville, É.H. 1883. *Inscription historique de Pinodjem III, grand prêtre d'Ammon à Thèbes*. Paris: Maisonneuve & cie.

Naville, É.H. 1886. *Das aegyptische Todtenbuch der XVIII. bis XX. Dynastie: Aus verschiedenen Urkunden*, 3 vols. Berlin: A. Asher.

Naville, É.H. 1892. *The festival-hall of Osorkon II in the great temple of Bubastis (1887-1889)* (Memoir of the Egypt Exploration Fund 10). London: Egypt Exploration Fund.

Naville, É.H. 1895. *The temple of Deir el Bahari* (Memoir of the Egypt Exploration Fund 13, 14, 16, 19, 27, and 29), 6 vols. London: Egypt Exploration Fund.

Naville, É.H. 1896a. *Transport of obelisks: As illustrated by a bas-relief in the temple of Deir el Bahari*. London: Egypt Exploration Society.

Naville, É.H. 1896b. Trois inscriptions de la reine Hatshepsou. *Recueil de Travaux* 18: 91–105.

Naville, É.H. 1897. Additions et corrections aux trois inscriptions de la reine Hatshepsou. *Recueil de Travaux* 19: 209–15.

Naville, É.H. 1907. *The XIth Dynasty temple at Deir el-Bahari* (Memoir of the Egypt Exploration Fund 28, 30, and 32), 3 vols. London: Egypt Exploration Fund.

Navrátilová, H. 2007. *The visitors' graffiti of Dynasties XVIII and XIX in Abusir and northern Saqqara* (The visitors' graffiti 1). Praha: Czech Institute of Egyptology.

Negm, M. 1997. *The tomb of Simut called Kyky: Theban tomb 409 at Qurnah*. Warminster: Aris & Philips.

Nelson, H.H. 1936. Three decrees of Ramses III from Karnak. *Journal of the American Oriental Society* 56: 232–41.

Nelson, H.H. 1942. The identity of Amon-Re of United-with-Eternity. *Journal of Near Eastern Studies* 1: 127–55.

Nelson, H.H. 1949. Certain reliefs at Karnak and Medinet Habu and the ritual of Amenophis I. *Journal of Near Eastern Studies* 8: 201–32 and 310–45.

Nelson, H.H. 1981. *The great hypostyle hall at Karnak* (Oriental Institute publications 106). Chicago: Oriental Institute of the University of Chicago.

Nelson, H.H. and Hölscher, U. 1934. *Work in western Thebes, 1931-33* (Oriental Institute communications 18). Chicago: University of Chicago Press.

Neugebauer, O. and Parker, R.A. 1960. *Egyptian astronomical texts* (Brown Egyptological Studies 3-6), 3 vols. Providence and London: Brown University Press.

Neureiter, S. 2005. Schamanismus im alten Ägypten. *Studien zur Altägyptischen Kultur* 33: 281–330.

Newberry, P.E. 1893. *Beni Hasan I* (Archaeological survey of Egypt 1). London: Egypt Exploration Fund.

Nims, C.F. 1948. An oracle dated in 'the repeating of births'. *Journal of Near Eastern Studies* 7: 157–62.

Nims, C.F. 1955. Places about Thebes. *Journal of Near Eastern Studies* 14: 110–23.

Nims, C.F. 1965. *Thebes of the pharaohs: Pattern for every city*. London: Elek Books.

Nims, C.F. 1966. The date of the dishonoring of Hatshepsut. *Zeitschrift für Ägyptische Sprache und Altertumskunde* 93: 97–100.

Nims, C.F. 1969. Thutmose III's benefactions to Amon, in *Studies in honor of John A. Wilson, September 12, 1969* (Studies in ancient Oriental civilization 35): 69–74. Chicago: University of Chicago Press.

Nims, C.F. 1971. The eastern temple at Karnak, in *Aufsätze zum 70. Geburtstag von Herbert Ricke* (Beiträge zur ägyptischen Bauforschung und Altertumskunde 12): 107–11. Wiesbaden: Franz Steiner.

Nims, C.F. 1976. Ramesseum sources of Medinet Habu reliefs, in *Studies in honor of George R. Hughes* (Studies in ancient Oriental civilization 39): 169–75. Chicago: University of Chicago Press.

Niwiński, A. 1984. Butehamon: Schriber der Nekropolis. *Studien zur Altägyptischen Kultur* 11: 135–56.

Nolan, J.S. 2003. The original lunar calendar and cattle counts in Old Kingdom Egypt, in S. Bickel and A. Loprieno (eds), *Basel Egyptology Prize 1: Junior research in Egyptian history, archaeology, and philology*: 75–97. Basel: Schwabe.

Nolan, J.S. 2008. Lunar intercalations and 'cattle counts' during the Old Kingdom: The Hebsed in context, in H. Vymazalová and M. Bárta (eds), *Chronology and archaeology in ancient Egypt (the third millennium B.C.)*: 44–60. Praha: Czech Institute of Egyptology.

O'Connor, D.B. 1989. City and palace in New Kingdom Egypt. *Cahier de Recherches de l'Institut de Papyrologie et d'Égyptologie de Lille* 11: 73–87.

O'Connor, D.B. 1998. The city and the world: Worldview and built forms in the reign of Amenhotep III, in D.B. O'Connor and E.H. Cline (eds), *Amenhotep III: Perspectives on his reign*: 125–72. Ann Arbor: University of Michigan Press.

O'Connor, D.B. 2012. The mortuary temple of Ramesses III at Medinet Habu, in E.H. Cline and D.B. O'Connor (eds), *Ramesses III: The life and times of Egypt's last hero*: 209–70. Ann Arbor: University of Michigan Press.

O'Connor, D.B. and Cline, E.H. 1998. *Amenhotep III: Perspectives on his reign*. Ann Arbor: University of Michigan Press.

O'Mara, P.F. 1988a. Was the Sed Festival periodic in early Egyptian history? (I). *Discussions in Egyptology* 11: 21–30.

O'Mara, P.F. 1988b. Was the Sed Festival periodic in early Egyptian history? (II). *Discussions in Egyptology* 12: 55–62.

O'Mara, P.F. 1993. Dating the Sed Festival: Was there only a single model? *Göttinger Miszellen* 136: 57–70.

O'Mara, P.F. 2003. Censorinus, the Sothic cycle, and calendar year one in ancient Egypt: The epistemological problem. *Journal of Near Eastern Studies* 62: 17–26.

Ockinga, B.G. 2004. Theban tomb 147: Observations on its owners and erasures. *Bulletin of the Australian Centre for Egyptology* 15: 121–9.

Ockinga, B.G. 2008. Theban tomb 147: Its owners and erasures revisited. *Bulletin of the Australian Centre for Egyptology* 19: 139–44.

Oldfather, C.H. 1933. *Diodorus of Sicily* (The Loeb classical library 279, 303, 340, 375, 377, 384, 389–90, 399, 409, and 422–3), 12 vols. London and Cambridge (Mass): W. Heinemann and Harvard University Press.

van Oosterhout, G.W. 1992. The heliacal rising of Sirius. *Discussions in Egyptology* 24: 71–111.

Osing, J. 1992. Zu zwei literarischen Werken des Mittleren Reiches, in J. Osing and E.K. Nielsen (eds), *The heritage of ancient Egypt: Studies in honour of Erik Iversen* (CNI publications 13): 101–19. København: Museum Tusculanum Press.

Osing, J. 1998. *Hieratische papyri aus Tebtunis I* (Carlsberg papyri 2), 2 vols. København: Museum Tusculanum Press.

Osing, J. and Rosati, G. 1998. *Papiri geroglifici e ieratici da Tebtynis*. Firenze: Istituto papirologico G. Vitelli.

Otto, E. 1952. *Topographie des thebanischen Gaues* (Untersuchungen zur Geschichte und Altertumskunde Aegyptens 16). Leipzig: J.D. Hinrichs.

Otto, E. 1960. *Das ägyptische Mundöffnungsritual*, 2 vols. Wiesbaden: Harrassowitz.

Pamminger, P. 1992. Amun und Luxor: Der Widder und das Kultbild. *Beiträge zur Sudanforschung* 5: 93–140.

Pantalacci, L. and Traunecker, C. 1998. *Le temple d'El-Qal'a II: Relevés des scènes et des textes: Couloir mystérieux, cour du nouvel an, ouabet per-nou, per-our, petit vestibule, 113-294*. Cairo and Paris: Institut Français d'Archéologie Orientale.

Papazian, H. 2010. The temple of Ptah and economic contacts between Memphite cult centers in the Fifth Dynasty, in M. Dolińska and H. Beinlich (eds), *8. ägyptologische Tempeltagung: Interconnections between temples, Warschau, 22.-25. September 2008* (Königtum, Staat und Gesellschaft früher Hochkulturen 3 (3)): 137–53. Wiesbaden: Harrassowitz.

Park, R. 1998. Stretching of the cord, in C.J. Eyre (ed.), *Proceedings of the Seventh International Congress of Egyptologists, Cambridge, 3-9, September 1995*: 839–48. Leuven: Peeters.

Parker, H.N. 2007. *The Birthday Book*. Chicago and London: University of Chicago Press.

Parker, R.A. 1950. *The calendars of ancient Egypt* (Studies in ancient Oriental civilization 26). Chicago: University of Chicago Press.

Parker, R.A. 1957a. The problem of the month-names: A reply. *Revue d'Égyptologie* 11: 85–107.

Parker, R.A. 1957b. The length of reign of Amasis and the beginning of the Twenty-Sixth Dynasty. *Mitteilungen der Deutschen Archäologischen Instituts, Abteilung Kairo* 15: 208–12.

Parker, R.A. 1957c. The lunar dates of Thutmose III and Ramesses II. *Journal of Near Eastern Studies* 16: 39–43.

Parker, R.A. 1962. *A Saite oracle papyrus from Thebes in the Brooklyn Museum (papyrus Brooklyn 47.218.3)* (Brown Egyptological Studies 4). Providence: Brown University Press.

Parker, R.A. 1969. Once again the coregency of Thutmose III and Amenhotep II, in *Studies in honor of John A. Wilson, September 12, 1969* (Studies in ancient Oriental civilization 35): 75–82. Chicago: University of Chicago Press.

Parker, R.A., Leclant, J., and Goyon, J.-C. 1979. *The edifice of Taharqa by the sacred lake of Karnak* (Brown Egyptological Studies 8). Providence and London: Brown University Press and Lund Humphries.

Parkinson, R. 2008. *The painted tomb-chapel of Nebamun*. London: British Museum Press.

Patané, M. 1986. Les hymnes du matin. Unpublished PhD dissertation, Université de Genéve.

Pécoil, J.-F. 1993. Les sources mythiques du Nil et le cycle de la crue. *Bulletin de la Société d'Égyptologie de Genève* 17: 97–110.

Pécoil, J.-F. 2000. *L'Akh-menou de Thoutmosis III à Karnak: La Heret-ib et les chapelles attenantes, relevés épigraphiques*. Paris: Recherche sur les civilisations.

Pécoil, J.-F. and Maher-Taha, M. 1983. Quelques aspects du bandeau-seched. *Bulletin de la Société d'Égyptologie de Genève* 8: 67–79.

Peden, A.J. 1994a. *Egyptian historical inscriptions of the Twentieth Dynasty* (Documenta mundi. Aegyptiaca 3). Jonsered: Paul Åströms förlag.

Peden, A.J. 1994b. A note on the accession date of Merenptah. *Göttinger Miszellen* 140: 69.

Peden, A.J. 1994c. *The reign of Ramesses IV*. Warminster: Aris & Phillips.

Peden, A.J. 2000. Carter graffito no. 1450 and the last known attestation of the vizier To in year 32 of Ramesses III. *Göttinger Miszellen* 175: 13–5.

Peden, A.J. 2001. *The graffiti of pharaonic Egypt: Scope and roles of informal writings (c. 3100-332 B.C.)* (Probleme der Ägyptologie 17). Leiden and Boston: Brill.

Peet, E.T. 1920. *The Mayer papyri A & B: Nos. M. 11162 and M. 11186 of the Free Public Museums, Liverpool*. London: Egypt Exploration Society.

Peet, E.T. 1925a. A possible year date of king Ramesses VII. *Journal of Egyptian Archaeology* 11: 72–5.

Peet, E.T. 1925b. The legend of the capture of Joppa and the story of the foredoomed prince, being a translation of the verso of Papyrus Harris 500. *Journal of Egyptian Archaeology* 11: 225–9.

Peet, E.T. 1930a. An ancient Egyptian ship's log. *Bulletin de l'Institut Français d'Archéologie Orientale* 30: 481–90.

Peet, E.T. 1930b. *The great tomb-robberies of the Twentieth Egyptian Dynasty: Being a critical study, with translations and commentaries, of the papyri in which these are recorded*, 2 vols. Oxford: The Clarendon Press.

Pereyra de Fidanza, V. 2000. A queen rewarding a nobleman in TT 49, in *Civilisations du Bassin Méditerranéen: Hommages à Joachim Sliwa*: 173–84. Kraków: Université Jagaellonne, Institut d'Archéologie.

Pestman, P.W. 1982. The last will of Naunakhte and the accession of Ramesses V, in R.J. Demarée and J.J. Janssen (eds), *Gleanings from Deir el-Medîna* (Egyptologische uitgaven 1): 173–81. Leiden: Nederlands Instituut voor het Nabije Oosten.

Pestman, P.W. 1992. *Il Processo di Hermias e altri documenti dell'archivio dei choachiti (P. Tor. Choachiti): Papiri greci e demotici conservati a Torino e in altre collezioni d'Italia* (Catalogo del Museo Egizio di Torino. Serie prima, Monumenti e testi 6). Torino: Ministero per i Beni Cultruali e Ambientali.

Pestman, P.W. 1993. *The archive of the Theban choachytes (second century B.C.): A survey of the demotic and Greek papyri contained in the archive* (Studia demotica 2). Leuven: Peeters.

Petrie, W.M.F. 1891. *Illahun, Kahun and Gurob, 1889-90*. London: David Nutt.

Petrie, W.M.F. 1896. *Koptos*. London: Bernard Quaritch.

Petrie, W.M.F. 1897. *Six temples at Thebes*. London: Bernard Quaritch.

Petrie, W.M.F. 1902. *Abydos* (Memoir of the Egypt Exploration Fund 22, 24, and 25), 3 vols. London: Egypt Exploration Fund.

Petrie, W.M.F. 1907. *Gizeh and Rifeh* (British School of Archaeology in Egypt and Egyptian Research Account 13th year, 1907). London: School of Archaeology in Egypt.

Petrie, W.M.F. 1909. *Qurneh* (British School of Archaeology in Egypt and Egyptian Research Account 15th year, 1909). London: Bernard Quaritch.

Petrie, W.M.F. 1917. *Scarabs and cylinders with names: Illustrated by the Egyptian collection in University College, London* (British School of Archaeology in Egypt and Egyptian Research Account 21st year, 1915). London: Constable & Co. and Bernard Quaritch.

Petrie, W.M.F. and Walker, J.H. 1909. *Memphis I* (British School of Archaeology in Egypt and Egyptian research account 14th year, 1908). London: School of Archaeology in Egypt, University College.

Pflüger, K. 1946. The edict of king Horemhab. *Journal of Near Eastern Studies* 5: 260–76.

Piankoff, A. 1942. *Le Livre du Jour et de la Nuit* (Bibliothèque d'étude 13). Cairo: Imprimerie de l'Institut Français d'Archéologie Orientale.

Piehl, K. 1886. *Inscriptions hiéroglyphiques recueillies en Europe et en Égypte*, 3 vols. Stockholm: J.C. Hinrichs.

Pieper, M. 1929. *Die grosse Inschrift des Königs Neferhotep in Abydos: Ein Beitrag zur ägyptischen Religions- und Literaturgeschichte* (Mitteilungen der Vorderasiatisch-aegyptischen Gesellschaft 32 (1)). Leipzig: J.C. Hinrichs.

Pillet, M. 1939. Deux représentations inédites de portes ornées de pylônes, à Karnak. *Bulletin de l'Institut Français d'Archéologie Orientale* 38: 239–51.

Pinch, G. 1993. Votive offerings to Hathor. Unpublished PhD dissertation, University of Oxford.

Pinch, G. 1994. *Magic in ancient Egypt*. London: British Museum Press.

Plas, D.v.d. and Borghouts, J.F. 1998. *Coffin Texts word index*. Utrecht: U-CCER, Utrecht University.

Pleyte, W. 1881. *Chapitres supplémentaires du Livre des Morts, 162 à 174*, 3 vols. Leiden: Brill.

Pleyte, W. and Rossi, F. 1869. *Papyrus de Turin*, 2 vols. Leiden: Brill.

Plutarch: *De Iside et Osiride*.

Polz, D. 1991. Jamunedjeh, Meri, und Userhat. *Mitteilungen der Deutschen Archäologischen Instituts, Abteilung Kairo* 47: 281–91.

Polz, D. 1998. The Ramsesnakht dynasty and the fall of the New Kingdom: A new monuments in Thebes. *Studien zur Altägyptischen Kultur* 25: 257–93.

Polz, D., Klug, S., Kürschner, H., and Johannes, D. 1997. *Das Grab des Hui und des Kel: Theben Nr. 54* (Archäologische Veröffentlichungen (Deutsches Archäologisches Institut. Abteilung Kairo 74). Mainz am Rhein: Philipp von Zabern.

Popper, W. 1951. *The Cairo nilometer: Studies in Ibn Taghrî Birdî's chronicles of Egypt: I* (University of California publications in Semitic philology 12). Berkeley: University of California Press.

Porceddu, S., Jetsu, L., Markkanen, T., and Toivari-Viitala, J. 2008. Evidence of periodicity in ancient Egyptian calendars of lucky and unlucky days. *Cambridge Archaeological Journal* 18: 327–39.

Porter, B. and Moss, R.L.B. 1952. *Topographical bibliography of ancient Egyptian hieroglyphic texts, reliefs, and paintings VII: Nubia, the desserts, and outside Egypt*. Oxford: Oxford University Press.

Porter, B. and Moss, R.L.B. 1960. *Topographical bibliography of ancient Egyptian hieroglyphic texts, reliefs, and paintings I: The Theban necropolis 1: Private tombs*, 2nd ed. Oxford: Alden Press.

Porter, B. and Moss, R.L.B. 1970. *Topographical bibliography of ancient Egyptian hieroglyphic texts, reliefs, and paintings VI: Upper Egypt, chief temples*, 2nd ed. Oxford: Alden Press.

Porter, B. and Moss, R.L.B. 1972. *Topographical bibliography of ancient Egyptian hieroglyphic texts, reliefs, and paintings II: Theban temples*, 2nd ed. Oxford: Alden Press.

Porter, B. and Moss, R.L.B. 1974. *Topographical bibliography of ancient Egyptian hieroglyphic texts, reliefs, and paintings III: Memphis 1: Abû Rawâsh to Abûsîr*. Oxford: Oxford University Press.

Porter, B. and Moss, R.L.B. 1981. *Topographical bibliography of ancient Egyptian hieroglyphic texts, reliefs, and paintings III: Memphis 2: Saqqâra to Dahshûr*. Oxford: Oxford University Press.

Posener, G. 1938. *Catalogue des ostraca hiératiques littéraires de Deir el Médineh (nos. 1001-1108)* (Documents de Fouilles de l'Institut Français d'Archéologie Orientale du Caire 1). Cairo: Imprimerie de l'Institut Français d'Archéologie Orientale.

Posener, G. 1963. Aménémopé 21, 13 et *bjAj.t* au sens d''oracle'. *Zeitschrift für Ägyptische Sprache und Altertumskunde* 90: 98–102.

Posener-Kriéger, P. 1976. *Les archives du temple funéraire de Néferirkarê-Kakaï (les papyrus d'Abousir): traduction et commentaire* (Bibliothèque d'étude 65), 2 vols. Cairo: Institut Français d'Archéologie Orientale.

Posener-Kriéger, P. 1985. Remarques préliminaires sur les nouveaux papyrus d'Abousir, in *Ägypten: Dauer und Wandel, Symposium anlässlich des 75 jährigen Bestehens des Deutschen Archäologischen Instituts Kairo, am 10. und 11. Oktober 1982* (Sonderschrift, Deutsches Archäologisches Institut Abteilung Kairo 18): 35–43. Mainz am Rhein: Philipp von Zabern.

Posener-Kriéger, P. 1986: Wag-Fest, in E. Otto and W. Helck (eds), *Lexikon der Ägyptologie*, vol. 6: 1135–9. Wiesbaden: Harrassowitz.

Posener-Kriéger, P. 2004. *I papiri di Gebelein: Scavi G. Farina 1935* (Studi del Museo Egizio di Torino: Gebelein 1). Torino: Ministero per i Beni e le Attività Culturali.

Posener-Kriéger, P. and de Cenival, J.L. 1968. *The Abu Sir papyri* (Hieratic papyri in the British Museum. Fifth series). London: British Museum.

Posener-Kriéger, P., Verner, M., and Vymazalová, H. 2006. *The pyramid complex of Raneferef: The papyrus archive* (Abusir 10). Praha: Czech Institute of Egyptology.

Postel, L. and Régen, I. 2005. Annales héliopolitaines et fragments de Sésostris Ier réemployés dans la porte de Bâb al-Tawfiq au Caire. *Bulletin de l'Institut Français d'Archéologie Orientale* 105: 229–93.

Preys, R. 2007. La Fête de Paophi et le culte des ancêtres. *Revue d'Égyptologie* 58: 111–22.

Prisse, d.A. 1847. *Monuments égyptiens, bas-reliefs, peintures, inscriptions, etc*. Paris: Firmin-Didot fréres.

Quaegebeur, J. 1986. Amenophis, nom royal et nom divin: Questions méthodologiques. *Revue d'Égyptologie* 37: 97–106.

Quibell, J.E. 1898. *The Ramesseum and the tomb of Ptah-hetep*. London: Bernard Quaritch.

Quirke, S.G.J. 1986. The hieratic texts in the tomb of Nakht the gardener at Thebes (No. 161) as copied by Robert Hay. *Journal of Egyptian Archaeology* 72: 79–90.

Quirke, S.G.J. 1990a. *The administration of Egypt in the late Middle Kingdom: The hieratic documents*. New Malden: SIA.

Quirke, S.G.J. 1990b. Kerem in the Fitzwilliam Museum. *Journal of Egyptian Archaeology* 76: 170–4.

Quirke, S.G.J. 1992. *Ancient Egyptian religion*. London: British Museum Press.

Quirke, S.G.J. and Andrews, C. 1988. *The Rosetta Stone: Facsimile drawing*. London: British Museum Publications.

Rachewiltz, B.d. 1958. *Il libro dei morti degli antichi Egiziani*. Milano: All'Insegna del Pesce d'Oro.

Radwan, A. 1969. *Die Darstellungen des regierenden Königs und seiner Familienangehörigen in den Privatgräbern der 18. Dynastie* (Münchner ägyptologische Studien 21). Berlin: B. Hessling.

Ragazzoli, C. and Frood, E. 2013. Writing on the wall: Two graffiti projects in Luxor. *Egyptian Archaeology* 42: 30–3.

Ranke, H. 1950. The Egyptian collections of the University Museum. *University Museum Bulletin* 15 (2–3): 5–109.

Raven, M.J. 1997. Charms for protection during the epagomenal days, in J. van Dijk (ed.), *Essays on ancient Egypt in honour of Herman te Velde*: 275–91. Groningen: STYX Publications.

al-Rayah, S.A.R. 1981. The Napatan Kingdom 860 B.C. to 310 B.C. Unpublished PhD dissertation, University of Liverpool.

Read, J.G. 1996. Chronological placements for Thutmose III, Amenhotep II, Ramesses II and the Third Dynasty. *Discussions in Egyptology* 36: 103–17.

Redford, D.B. 1965. The coregency of Tuthmosis III and Amenophis II. *Journal of Egyptian Archaeology* 51: 107–22.

Redford, D.B. 1966. On the chronology of the Egyptian Eighteenth Dynasty. *Journal of Near Eastern Studies* 25: 113–24.

Redford, D.B. 1967. *History and chronology of the Eighteenth Dynasty of Egypt: Seven studies* (Near and Middle East series 3). Toronto: University of Toronto Press.

Redford, D.B. 1971. The earliest years of Ramesses II, and the building of the Ramesside court at Luxor. *Journal of Egyptian Archaeology* 57: 110–9.

Redford, D.B. 1972. Studies in relations between Palestine and Egypt during the first millennium B.C., in J.W. Wevers and D.B. Redford (eds), *Studies on the ancient Palestinian world presented to professor F. V. Winnett on the occasion of his retirement 1 July 1971* (Toronto Semitic texts and studies 2): 141–56. Toronto: University of Toronto Press.

Redford, D.B. 1976. The palace of Akhenaten in the Karnak talatat, in R.W. Smith and D.B. Redford (eds), *The Akhenaten temple project I: Initial discoveries* (The Akhenaten temple project 1): 122–36. Warminster: Aris & Phillips.

Redford, D.B. 2001. *The Oxford encyclopedia of ancient Egypt*, 3 vols. Oxford: Oxford University Press.

Redford, D.B. 2003. *The wars in Syria and Palestine of Thutmose III* (Culture and history of the ancient Near East 16). Leiden: Brill.

Redmount, C.A. and Keller, C.A. 2003. *Egyptian pottery: Proceedings of the 1990 Pottery Symposium at the University of California, Berkeley* (University of California publications in Egyptian archaeology 8). Berkeley: Regents of the University of California.

Reeves, C.N. 1990. *Valley of the Kings: The decline of a royal necropolis* (Studies in Egyptology). London: Kegan Paul International.

Reisner, G.A. 1918. The tomb of Hepzefa, nomarch of Siût. *Journal of Egyptian Archaeology* 5: 79–98.

Reisner, G.A. 1920a. The viceroys of Ethiopia. *Journal of Egyptian Archaeology* 6: 28–55.

Reisner, G.A. 1920b. The viceroys of Ethiopia (continued). *Journal of Egyptian Archaeology* 6: 73–88.

Reisner, G.A. and Reisner, M.B. 1933. Inscribed monuments from Gebel Barkal: Part 2, The granite stela of Thutmosis III. *Zeitschrift für Ägyptische Sprache und Altertumskunde* 69: 24–39.

Renouf, P.l.P. 1880. *Lectures on the origin and growth of religion as illustrated by the religion of ancient Egypt: Delivered in May and June, 1879* (Hibbert lectures). London: Williams & Norgate.

Renouf, P.l.P. 1896. Book of the Dead: Chapter CXXVIII. *Proceedings of the Society of Biblical Archaeology* 18: 165–9.

Revez, J. 2003. Une stèle inédite de la Troisième Période Intermédiaire à Karnak: Une guerre civile en thébaïde? , in *Cahiers de Karnak 11*: 535–70. Cairo: Centre Franco-Égyptien d'Étude des Temples de Karnak.

Richards, J.E. 2000. Modified order, responsive legitimacy, redistributed wealth: Egypt, 2260–1650 B.C., in J.E. Richards and M. van Buren (eds), *Order, legitimacy, and wealth in ancient states*: 36–45. Cambridge: Cambridge University Press.

Richards, J.E. 2005. *Society and death in ancient Egypt: Mortuary landscapes of the Middle Kingdom*. Cambridge: Cambridge University Press.

Richter, B.A. 2010. On the heels of the wandering goddess: The myth and the festival at the temples of the Wadi el-Hallel and Dendera, in *8. ägyptologische Tempeltagung: Interconnections between temples, Warschau, 22.-25. September 2008* (Königtum, Staat und Gesellschaft früher Hochkulturen 3 (3)): 155–86. Wiesbaden: Harrassowitz.

Ricke, H. 1954. *Das Kamutef-Heiligtum Hatschepsuts und Thutmoses' III. in Karnak: Bericht über eine Ausgrabung vor dem Muttempelbezirk* (Beiträge zur ägyptischen Bauforschung und Altertumskunde 3). Cairo: Schweizerisches Institut.

Ritner, R.K. 2009. *The Libyan anarchy: Inscriptions from Egypt's Third Intermediate Period* (Writings from the ancient world 21). Leiden and Boston: Brill.

Robichon, C. and Varille, A. 1936. *Le temple du scribe royal Amenhotep, fils de Hapou* (Fouilles de l'Institut Français d'Archéologie Orientale du Caire 11). Cairo: Imprimerie de l'Institut Français d'Archéologie Orientale.

Rochholz, M. 1994. Sedfest, Sonnenheiligtum und Pyramidenbezirk, in R. Gundlach and M. Rochholz (eds), *Ägyptische Tempel: Struktur, Funktion und Programm (Akten der ägyptologischen Tempeltagungen in Gosen 1990 und in Mainz 1992)* (Hildesheimer ägyptologische Beiträge 37): 255–80. Hildesheim: Gerstenberg Verlag.

Roeder, G. 1913. *Aegyptische Inschriften aus den Königlichen Museen zu Berlin*, 2 vols. Leipzig: J.C. Hinrichs.

Roeder, G. 1954. Zwei hieroglyphische Inschriften aus Hermopolis (Ober-Ägypten). *Annales du Service des Antiquités de l'Égypte* 52: 315–442.

Roeder, G. 1960. *Kulte, Orakel und Naturverehrung im alten Ägypten* (Die ägyptische Religion in Texten und Bildern 3). Zürich and Stuttgart: Artemis-Verlag.

Roehrig, C.H. 1990. The Eighteenth Dynasty titles royal nurse (*mnat nswt*), royal tutor (*mna nswt*), and foster brother/sister of the lord of the Two Lands (*sn/ snt mna n nb t3wy*). Unpublished PhD dissertation, University of California.

Roehrig, C.H. 2012. Forgotten treasures: Tausret as seen in her monuments, in R.H. Wilkinson (ed.), *Tausret: Forgotten queen and pharaoh of Egypt*: 48–66. Oxford: Oxford University Press.

Rogge, E. 1990. *Statuen des Neuen Reiches und der Dritten Zwischenzeit* (Corpus Antiquitatum Aegyptiacarum 6). Mainz: Philipp von Zabern.

Rondot, V. 1997. *La grande salle hypostyle de Karnak: Les architraves*, 2 vols. Paris: Editions Recherche sur les Civilisations.

Rose, L.E. 1999. *Sun, moon, and Sothis: A study of calendars and calendar reforms in ancient Egypt*. Deerfield Beach: Kronos Press.

Rothe, R.D., Miller, W.K., and Rapp, G.R. 2008. *Pharaonic inscriptions from the southern eastern desert of Egypt*. Winona Lake: Eisenbrauns.

Rougé, E. and Rougé, J. 1877. *Inscriptions hiéroglyphiques copiées en Égypte pendant la mission scientifique de M. le vicomte Emmanuel de Rougé* (Études égyptologiques 9–12), 4 vols. Paris: F. Vieweg.

Roulin, G. 1998. The Book of the Night: A royal composition documenting the conceptions of the hereafter at the beginning of the Nineteenth Dynasty, in C. Eyre (ed.), *Proceedings of the Seventh International Congress of Egyptologists, Cambridge, 3-9 September 1995*: 1005–13. Leuven: Peeters.

Routledge, C.D. 2001. Ancient Egyotian ritual practice: *ir-xt* and *nt-a*. Unpublished PhD dissertation, University of Toronto.

Rummel, U. 2010. *Iunmutef: Konzeption und Wirkungsbereich eines altägyptischen Gottes* (Sonderschrift (Deutsches Archäologisches Institut. Abteilung Kairo) 33). Berlin and New York: de Gruyter.

Rummel, U. 2011. Two re-used blocks of the god's wife Isis at Deir el-Bakhit/Dra' Abu el-Naga (western Thebes), in M. Collier and S.R. Snape (eds), *Ramesside studies in honour of K. A. Kitchen*: 423–31. Bolton: Rutherford.

Ryhiner, M.-L. 1995. *La procession des étoffes et l'union avec Hathor* (Rites égyptiens 8). Bruxelles: Édition de la Fondation Égyptologique Reine Élizabeth.

Ryholt, K.S.B. 1993. A pair of oracle petitions addressed to Horus-of-the-camp. *Journal of Egyptian Archaeology* 79: 189–98.

Ryholt, K.S.B. 1997. *The political situation in Egypt during the Second Intermediate Period, c. 1800–1550 B.C.* (Carsten Niebuhr Institute of Ancient Near Eastern Studies Publications 20). København: Museum Tusculanum Press.

el-Saady, H. 1996. *The tomb of Amenemhab no. 44 at Qurnah: The tomb-chapel of a priest carrying the shrine of Amun.* Warminster: Aris & Phillips.

el-Sabban, S. 2000. *Temple festival calendars of ancient Egypt* (Liverpool monographs in archaeology & Oriental studies). Liverpool: Liverpool University Press.

Sackho-Autissier, A. 2003. Cinq fragments de statues de particuliers du magasin du Cheikh Labib, in *Cahiers de Karnak 11*: 571–9. Cairo: Centre Franco-Égyptien d'Étude des Temples de Karnak.

Sadek, A.A. 1984a. An attempt to translate the corpus of the Deir el-Bahri hieratic inscriptions (I). *Göttinger Miszellen* 71: 67–91.

Sadek, A.A. 1984b. An attempt to translate the corpus of the Deir el-Bahri hieratic inscriptions (II). *Göttinger Miszellen* 72: 65–86.

Sadek, A.I. 1979. Glimpse of popular religion in New Kingdom Egypt I: Mourning for Amenophis I at Deir el-Medina. *Göttinger Miszellen* 36: 51–6.

Sadek, A.I. 1987. *Popular religion in Egypt during the New Kingdom* (Hildesheimer ägyptologische Beiträge 27). Hildesheim: Gerstenberg.

Sadek, A.I. 1989. Les fêtes personnelles au Nouvel Empire, in S. Schoske (ed.), *Akten des Vierten Internationalen Ägyptologen Kongresses, München, 1985* (Studien zur altägyptischen Kultur): 353–68. Hamburg: Helmut Buske.

Sakkarah Expedition 1938. *The mastaba of Mereruka* (Oriental Institute publications 31 and 39), 2 vols. Chicago: University of Chicago Press.

Saleh, M. 1977. *Three Old-kingdom tombs at Thebes: I. The tomb of Unas-Ankh no 413; II. The tomb of Khenty no. 405; III. The tomb of Ihy no. 186* (Archäologische Veröffentlichungen (Deutsches Archäologisches Institut. Abteilung Kairo) 14). Mainz am Rhein: Philipp von Zabern.

Saleh, M. 1984. *Das Totenbuch in den thebanischen Beamtengräbern des Neuen Reiches: Texte und Vignetten* (Archäologische Veröffentlichungen (Deutsches Archäologisches Institut. Abteilung Kairo) 46). Mainz am Rhein: Philipp von Zabern.

Sander-Hansen, C.E. 1940. *Das Gottesweib des Amun* (Historisk-filosofiske meddelelser 1 (1)). København: E. Munksgaard.

Sandman, M. 1938. *Texts from the time of Akhenaten* (Bibliotheca Aegyptiaca 8). Bruxelles: Édition de la Fondation Égyptologique Reine Élizabeth.

Le Saout, F. 1982. Reconstitution des murs de la cour de la cahette, in *Cahiers de Karnak 7: 1978–1981*: 213–57. Paris: ADPF.

Le Saout, F. 1989. Une nouvelle fête d'Hathor à Karnak. *Cahier de Recherches de l'Institut de Papyrologie et d'Égyptologie de Lille* 11: 69–71.

Le Saout, F., Ma'arouf, A., and Zimmer, T. 1987. Le Moyen Empire à Karnak: Varia 1, in *Cahiers de Karnak 8: 1982–1985*: 293–323. Cairo: Centre Franco-Égyptien d'Étude des Temples de Karnak.

Satzinger, H. 1985. Zwei wiener Objekte mit bemerkenswerten Inschriften, in P. Posener-Kriéger (ed.), *Mélanges Gamal Eddin Mokhtar* (Bibliothèque d'étude 97), vol. 1: 249–59. Cairo: Institut Français d'Archéologie Orientale.

Sauneron, S. 1952. *Rituel de l'embaumement: Pap. Boulaq III, pap. Louvre 5.158.* Cairo: Imprimerie Nationale.

Sauneron, S. 1954. La justice à la porte des temples: À propos du nom égyptien des propylées. *Bulletin de l'Institut Français d'Archéologie Orientale* 54: 117–27.

Sauneron, S. 1962. *Esna V. Les fêtes religieuses d'Esna aux derniers siècles du paganisme* (Publications de l'Institut Français d'Archéologie Orientale du Caire 5). Cairo: Institut Français d'Archéologie Orientale.

Sauneron, S. 1963. *Le temple d'Esna* (Esna 2–4 and 6), 4 vols. Cairo: Institut Français d'Archéologie Orientale.

1983. *La porte ptolémaïque de l'enceinte de Mout à Karnak* (Mémoires publiés par les membres de l'Institut Français d'Archéologie Orientale du Caire 107). Cairo: Institut Français d'Archéologie Orientale.

Säve-Söderbergh, T. 1953. *On Egyptian representations of hippopotamus hunting as a religious motive* (Horae Soederblomianae 3). Uppsala: C.W.K. Gleerup.

Sauneron, S. 1957. *Four Eighteenth Dynasty tombs* (Private tombs at Thebes 1). Oxford: Oxford University Press.

Sayed Mohamed, Z. 2004. *Festvorbereitungen: Die administrativen und ökonomischen Grundlagen altägyptischer Feste* (Orbis biblicus et orientalis 202). Fribourg and Göttingen: Academic Press and Vandenhoeck & Ruprecht.

Schäfer, H. 1904. Die Mysterien des Osiris in Abydos unter Sesostris III: Nach dem Denkstein des Oberschatzmeisters I-Cher-

Nofret, in Untersuchungen zur Geschichte und Altertumskunde Aegyptens 4: 47–87. Leipzig: J.C. Hinrichs.

Schäfer, H. 1905. *Urkunden der älteren Äthiopenkönige* (Urkunden des ägyptischen Altertums 3). Leipzig: J.C. Hinrichs.

Scharff, A. 1922. Ein Rechnungsbuch des königlichen Hofes aus der 13. Dynastie. *Zeitschrift für Ägyptische Sprache und Altertumskunde* 57: 51–68.

Schiaparelli, E. 1882. *Il Libro dei funerali degli antichi egiziani*, 2 vols. Roma: Ermanno Loescher.

Schmidt, J.D. 1973. *Ramesses II: A chronological structure for his reign*. Baltimore: Johns Hopkins University Press.

Schmitz, F.-J. 1978. *Amenophis I.: Versuch einer Darstellung der Regierungszeit eines ägyptischen Herrschers der frühen 18. Dynastie*. Hildesheim: Gerstenberg.

Schneider, H.D. 1995. *Egyptisch Kunsthandwerk* (Reeks (Rijksmuseum van Oudheden te Leiden)). Amsterdam: de Bataafsche Leeuw.

Schott, E. 1970. Die heilige Vase des Amon. *Zeitschrift für Ägyptische Sprache und Altertumskunde* 98: 34–50.

Schott, S. 1934. The feasts of Thebes, in H.H. Nelson and U. Hölscher (eds), *Work in western Thebes* (Oriental Institute communications 18): 63–90. Chicago: University of Chicago Press.

Schott, S. 1937. Das Löschen von Fackeln in Milch. *Zeitschrift für Ägyptische Sprache und Altertumskunde* 73: 1–25.

Schott, S. 1950. *Altägyptische Festdaten* (Abhandlungen der Geistes- und Sozialwissenschaftlichen Klasse. Akademie der Wissenschaften und der Literatur 1950). Wiesbaden: Franz Steiner.

Schott, S. 1953. *Das schöne Fest vom Wüstentale: Festbräuche einer Totenstadt* (Abhandlungen der Geistes- und Sozialwissenschaftlichen Klasse. Akademie der Wissenschaften und der Literatur, 1952). Mainz: Franz Steiner.

Schubart, W. 1931. Orakelfragen. *Zeitschrift für Ägyptische Sprache und Altertumskunde* 67: 110–5.

Schulman, A.R. 1963. A cult of Ramesses III at Memphis. *Journal of Near Eastern Studies* 22: 177–84.

Schulman, A.R. 1967. Ex-votos of the poor. *Journal of American Research Center in Egypt* 6: 153–6.

Schulman, A.R. 1976. The royal butler Ramessesemperrē'. *Journal of American Research Center in Egypt* 13: 117–30.

Schulman, A.R. 1980. A Memphite stela, the bark of Ptaḥ, and some iconographic comments. *Bulletin of the Egyptological Seminar* 2: 83–109.

Schulman, A.R. 1984. The iconographic theme: 'Opening of the Mouth' on stelae. *Journal of American Research Center in Egypt* 21: 169–96.

Schulman, A.R. 1988. *Ceremonial execution and public rewards: Some historical scenes on New Kingdom private stelae* (Orbis biblicus et orientalis 75). Freiburg: Universitätsverlag.

Schwaller de Lubicz, R.A. 1957. *Le temple de l'homme: Apet du Sud à Louqsor*, 3 vols. Paris: Caractères.

Schwaller de Lubicz, R.A. 1982. *Les temples de Karnak: Contribution à l'étude de la pensée pharaonique* (Architecture et symboles sacrés), 2 vols. Paris: Dervy-livres.

Seele, K.C. 1935. A hymn to Amon-Re on a tablet from the temple of Karnak, in L.G. Leary (ed.), *From the pyramids to Paul: Studies in theology, archaeology and related subjects: Prepared in honor of the seventieth birthday of George Livingstone Robinson by former pupils, colleagues, and friends*: 224–41. New York: Nelson.

Seele, K.C. 1959. *The tomb of Tjanefer at Thebes* (Oriental Institute publications 86). Chicago: University of Chicago Press.

Seele, K.C. 1960. Ramesses VI and the Medinet Habu procession of the princes. *Journal of Near Eastern Studies* 19: 184–204.

Servajean, F. 2004. Le tissage de l'œil d'Horuset les trois registres de l'offrande: À propos de la fomule 608 des Textes des Sarcophages. *Bulletin de l'Institut Français d'Archéologie Orientale* 104: 523–52.

Sethe, K. 1896. *Die Thronwirren unter den Nachfolgern Königs Thutmosis' I.: Ihr Verlauf und ihre Bedeutung* (Untersuchungen zur Geschichte und Altertumskunde Aegyptens 1). Leipzig: J.C. Hinrichs.

Sethe, K. 1898. Altes und neues zur Geschichte der Thronstreitigkeiten unter den Nachfolgern Thutmosis' I. *Zeitschrift für Ägyptische Sprache und Altertumskunde* 36: 24–81.

Sethe, K. 1903. *Urkunden des Alten Reichs* (Urkunden des ägyptischen Altertums 1), 2 vols. Leipzig: J.C. Hinrichs.

Sethe, K. 1904. *Hieroglyphische Urkunden der griechisch-römischen Zeit* (Urkunden des ägyptischen Altertums 2). Leipzig: J.C. Hinrichs.

Sethe, K. 1905. *Beiträge zur ältesten Geschichte Ägyptens* (Untersuchungen zur Geschichte und Altertumskunde Aegyptens 3). Leipzig: J.C. Hinrichs.

Sethe, K. 1907a. Die Berufung eines Hohenpriesters des Amon unter Ramses II. *Zeitschrift für Ägyptische Sprache und Altertumskunde* 44: 30–5.

Sethe, K. 1907b. Mißverstandene Inschriften. *Zeitschrift für Ägyptische Sprache und Altertumskunde* 44: 35–41.

Sethe, K. 1908. *Die altaegyptischen Pyramidentexte nach den Papierabdrücken und Photographien des Berliner Museums*, 4 vols. Leipzig: J.C. Hinrichs.

Sethe, K. 1919. *Die Zeitrechnung der alten Aegypter im Verhältnis zu der der andern Völker: Eine entwicklungsgeschichtliche Studie* (Nachrichten der Königlichen Gesellschaft der Wissenschaften zu Göttingen: Philologisch-historische Klasse). Göttingen: Königliche Gesellschaft der Wissenschaften zu Göttingen.

Sethe, K. 1929a. *Amun und die acht Urgötter von Hermopolis: Eine Untersuchung über Ursprung und Wesen des ägyptischen Götterkönigs* (Abhandlungen der Preussischen Akademie der Wissenschaften: Philosophisch-historische Klasse 4). Berlin: Verlag der Akademie der Wissenschaften, in Kommission bei W. de Gruyter.

Sethe, K. 1929b. Die beiden alten Lieder von der Trinkstätte in den Darstellungen des Luksorfestzuges. *Zeitschrift für Ägyptische Sprache und Altertumskunde* 64: 1–5.

Sethe, K. 1930. Sethos I. und die Erneuerung der Hundssternperiode. *Zeitschrift für Ägyptische Sprache und Altertumskunde* 66: 1–7.

Sethe, K. 1936. *Übersetzung und Kommentar zu den altägyptischen Pyramidentexten*, 6 vols. Glückstadt and Hamburg: J.J. Augustin.

Sethe, K. and Helck, W. 1906. *Urkunden der 18. Dynastie: Übersetzung zu den Heften 1-22* (Urkunden des ägyptischen Altertums 4), 7 vols. Leipzig and Berlin: J.C. Hinrichs.

el-Sharkawy, A. 1997. Der Amun-Tempel von Karnak: Die Funktion der grossen Säulenhalle, erschlossen aus der Analyse der Dekoration ihrer Innenwände. Unpublished PhD dissertation, Universität Hamburg.

Shaw, R.L. 2006. The decorative scheme in TT 89 (Amenmose). *Journal of the Society of the Study of Egyptian Antiquities* 33: 205–33.

Shedid, A.G. and Seidel, M. 1991. *Das Grab des Nacht: Kunst und Geschichte eines Beamtengrabes der 18. Dynastie in Theben-West.* Mainz: Philipp von Zabern.

Sherrat, A. and Sherrat, S. 1991. From luxuries to commodities: The nature of Mediterranean bronze age trading systems, in N.H. Gale (ed.), *Bronze age trade in the Mediterranean: Papers presented at the conference held at Rewley House, Oxford, in December 1989*: 351–86. Jonsered: Åström.

Shirun-Grumach, I. 1989. On 'revelation' in ancient Egypt, in S. Schoske (ed.), *Akten des Vierten Internationalen Ägyptologen Kongresses, München, 1985* (Studien zur altägyptischen Kultur. Beihefte), vol. 3: 379–84. Hamburg: Helmut Buske.

Shirun-Grumach, I. 1993. *Offenbarung, Orakel und Königsnovelle* (Ägypten und Altes Testament 24). Wiesbaden: Harrassowitz.

Shorter, A.W. 1933. A stela of Seti I in the British Museum. *Journal of Egyptian Archaeology* 19: 60–1.

Shorter, A.W. 1934. Reliefs showing the coronation of Ramesses II. *Journal of Egyptian Archaeology* 20: 18–9.

Shorter, A.W. 1935. The god Neḥebkau. *Journal of Egyptian Archaeology* 21: 41–8.

van Siclen III, C.C. 1973. The accession date of Amenhotep III and the jubilee. *Journal of Near Eastern Studies* 32: 290–300.

van Siclen III, C.C. 1980. The temple of Meniset at Thebes. *Serapis* 6: 183–207.

van Siclen III, C.C. 1984. The date of the granite bark shrine of Thutmosis III. *Göttinger Miszellen* 79: 53.

van Siclen III, C.C. 1986. Amenhotep II's bark chapel for Amun at north Karnak. *Bulletin de l'Institut Français d'Archéologie Orientale* 86: 353–9.

Simonet, J.-L. 1994. *Le college des dieux, maitres d'autel: Nature et histoire d'une figure tardive de la religion égyptienne* (Orientalia Monspeliensia 7). Montpellier: Publications de la Recherche-Université Paul-Valéry.

Simpson, R.S. 1996. *Demotic grammar in the Ptolemaic sacerdotal decrees* (Griffith Institute monographs). Oxford: Griffith Institute.

Simpson, W.K. 1971. A Hours-of-Nekhen statue of Amenhotpe III from Soleb. *Bulletin of the Museum of Fine Arts, Boston* 69: 152–63.

Simpson, W.K. 1972. A relief of the royal cup-bearer Tja-wy. *Bulletin of the Museum of Fine Arts, Boston* 70: 68–82.

Simpson, W.K. 1974. *The mastaba of queen Mersyankh III, G7530-7540* (Giza mastabas 1). Boston: Department of Egyptian and Ancient Near Eastern Art, Museum of Fine Arts, Boston.

Simpson, W.K. 1976. *The mastabas of Qar and Idu, G7101 and 7102* (Giza mastabas 2). Boston: Department of Egyptian and Ancient Near Eastern Art, Museum of Fine Arts, Boston.

Simpson, W.K. 1999. The Nag'-ed-Deir papyri, in E. Teeter and J.A. Larson (eds), *Gold of praise: Studies on ancient Egypt in honor of Edward F. Wente* (Studies in ancient Oriental civilization 58): 387–96. Chicago: McNaughton & Gunn.

Simpson, W.K. 2003. *The literature of ancient Egypt: An anthology of stories, instructions, stelae autobiographies, and poetry*, 3rd ed. New Haven and London: Yale University Press.

Sist, L. 1976. Gli scavi dell'Università di Roma All'Asasif (1973–1974–1975): III. La presentazione dei sistri. *Oriens Antiquus* 15: 227–31.

Skeat, T.C. 1994. The beginning and the end of the καισαρος κρατησις era in Egypt. *Chronique d'Égypte* 69: 308–12.

Smith, H.S. 1976. *The fortress of Buhen: The inscriptions* (Excavations at Buhen 2). London: Egypt Exploration Society.

Smith, M. 1993. *The liturgy of Opening the Mouth for Breathing.* Oxford: Griffith Institute.

Smith, M. 2005. *Papyrus Harkness (MMA 31.9.7).* Oxford: Cambridge University Press.

Smith, M. 2009. *Traversing eternity: Texts for the afterlife from Ptolemaic and Roman Egypt.* Oxford: Oxford University Press.

Smith, R.W. and Redford, D.B. 1976. *The Akhenaten temple project I: Initial discoveries* (The Akhenaten Temple Project 1). Warminster: Aris & Phillips.

Smith, W.S. 1958. Review of *Das Kamutef-Heiligtum Hatshepsuts und Thutmoses' III.* by H. Ricke. *Journal of Near Eastern Studies* 17: 74–5.

Soliman, R. 2009. *Old and Middle Kingdom Theban tombs*. London: Golden House Publications.

Sotheby, C. 1964. *Catalogue of the Ernest Brummer collection of Egyptian and Near Eastern antiquities and works of art, which will be sold by auction by Messrs. Sotheby & Co.* London: Sotheby.

Spalinger, A.J. 1985. Notes on the day summary accounts of p. Bulaq 18 and the intradepartmental transfers. *Studien zur Altägyptischen Kultur* 12: 179–241.

Spalinger, A.J. 1990. A remark on renewal. *Studien zur Altägyptischen Kultur* 17: 289–94.

Spalinger, A.J. 1991. Some revisions of temple endowments in the New Kingdom. *Journal of American Research Center in Egypt* 28: 21–39.

Spalinger, A.J. 1992. *Three studies on Egyptian feasts and their chronological implications*. Baltimore: Halgo.

Spalinger, A.J. 1993a. A chronological analysis of the feast of *txy*. *Studien zur Altägyptischen Kultur* 20: 289–303.

Spalinger, A.J. 1993b. A religious calendar year in the Mut temple at Karnak. *Revue d'Égyptologie* 44: 161–84.

Spalinger, A.J. 1994a. *Revolutions in time: Studies in ancient Egyptian calendrics* (Varia Aegyptiaca. Supplement 6). San Antonio: van Siclen Books.

Spalinger, A.J. 1994b. Calendars: Real and ideal, in B.M. Bryan and D. Lorton (eds), *Essays in Egyptology in honor of Hans Goedicke*: 297–308. San Antonio: van Siclen Books.

Spalinger, A.J. 1994c. Dated texts of the Old Kingdom. *Studien zur Altägyptischen Kultur* 21: 275–319.

Spalinger, A.J. 1995a. The calendrical importance of the Tombos stela. *Studien zur Altägyptischen Kultur* 22: 271–81.

Spalinger, A.J. 1995b. The lunar system in festival calendars: From the New Kingdom onwards. *Bulletin de la Société d'Égyptologie de Genève* 19: 25–40.

Spalinger, A.J. 1996. *The private feast lists of ancient Egypt* (Ägyptologische Abhandlungen 57). Wiesbaden: Harrassowitz.

Spalinger, A.J. 1998a. The limitation of formal ancient Egyptian religion. *Journal of Near Eastern Studies* 57: 241–60.

Spalinger, A.J. 1998b. Chronological remarks. *Bulletin de la Société d'Égyptologie de Genève* 22: 51–8.

Spalinger, A.J. 2009. *The great dedicatory inscription of Ramesses II: A solar-Osirian tractate at Abydos*. Leiden and Boston: Brill.

Spalinger, A.J. 2011. The beginning of the civil calendar, in M. Bárta, F. Coppens, and J. Krejčí (eds), *Abusir and Saqqara in the year 2010*, vol. 2: 723–35. Praha: Czech Institute of Egyptology.

Speleers, L. 1917. *Le papyrus de Nefer Renpet: Un Livre des Morts de la XVIIIme Dynastie aux Musées Royaux du Cinquantenaire à Bruxelles*. Bruxelles: Vromant.

Spencer, A.J. 1989. *Excavations at El-Ashmunein II: The temple area* (Excavations at El-Ashmunein 2). London: British Museum Publications.

Spencer, P. 1984. *The Egyptian temple: A lexicographical study*. London: Kegan Paul Intertnational.

Spiegelberg, W. 1892. Studien und Materialien zum Rechtswesen des Pharaonenreiches der Dynastien XVIII–XXI (c. 1500–1000 v. Chr.). Unpublished PhD dissertation, Kaiser Wilhelms Universität.

Spiegelberg, W. 1895. Das Geschäftsjournal eines ägyptischen Beamten in der Ramsesstadt aus der Regierung Ramses' II. *Recueil de Travaux* 17: 143–60.

Spiegelberg, W. 1898. *Zwei Beiträge zur Geschichte und Topographie der thebanischen Necropolis im Neuen Reich*. Strasbourg: Schlesier & Schweikhardt.

Spiegelberg, W. 1921. *Ägyptische und andere Graffiti (Inschriften und Zeichnungen) aus der thebanischen Nekropolis*. Heidelberg: C. Winters Universitätsbuchhandlung.

Spiegelberg, W. 1922. *Der demotische Text der Priesterdekrete von Kanopus und Memphis (Rosettana): Mit den hieroglyphischen und griechischen Fassungen und deutscher Übersetzung nebst demotischem Glossar*. Heidelberg.

Spieß, H. 1991. Der Aufstieg eines Gottes: Untersuchungen zum Gott Thot bis zum Beginn des Neuen Reiches. Unpublished PhD dissertation, Universität Hamburg.

Stadelmann, R. 1965. Die 400-Jahr-Stele. *Chronique d'Égypte* 40: 46–60.

Stadelmann, R. 1994. Royal palaces of the late New Kingdom in Thebes, in B.M. Bryan and D. Lorton (eds), *Essays in Egyptology in honor of Hans Goedicke*: 309–16. San Antonio: van Siclen Books.

Stadelmann, R. 1996. Temple palace and residential palace, in M. Bietak (ed.), *Haus und Palast im alten Ägypten* (Denkschriften der Gesamtakademie, Österreichischen Akademie der Wissenschaften 14): 225–30. Wien: Verlag der Österreichischen Akademie der Wissenschaften.

Stadler, M. 2008: Procession, in J. Dieleman and W. Wendrich (eds), *UCLA encyclopedia of Egyptology*: 1–12. Los Angeles.

Steindorff, G. 1896. *Grabfunde des Mittleren Reichs in den Königlichen Museen zu Berlin* (Mitteilungen aus den orientalischen Sammlungen 8–9), 2 vols. Berlin: W. Spemann.

Stricker, B.H. 1948. Spreuken tot beveiliging gedurende de schrikkeldagen naar pap. I 346. *Oudheidkundige Mededelingen uit het Rijksmuseum van Oudheden te Leiden* 29: 55–70.

Stricker, B.H. 1950. De egyptische mysteriën: Pap. Leiden T 32 (1). *Oudheidkundige Mededelingen uit het Rijksmuseum van Oudheden te Leiden* 31: 45–63.

Stricker, B.H. 1953. De egyptische mysteriën: Pap. Leiden T 32 (2). *Oudheidkundige Mededelingen uit het Rijksmuseum van Oudheden te Leiden* 34: 13–31.

Stricker, B.H. 1956. De egyptische mysteriën: Pap. Leiden T 32 (3). *Oudheidkundige Mededelingen uit het Rijksmuseum van Oudheden te Leiden* 37: 49–67.

Stroot-Kiraly, E. 1989. L'offrande du pain blanc. *Bulletin de la Société d'Égyptologie de Genève* 13: 157–60.

Strudwick, N.C. 1995. The population of Thebes in the New Kingdom: Some preliminary thoughts, in J. Assmann, E. Dziobek, H. Guksch, and F. Kampp (eds), *Thebanische Beamtennekropolen: Neue Perspektiven archäologischer Forschung: Internationales Symposion, Heidelberg, 9.-13. Juni 1993* (Studien zur Archäologie und Geschichte Altägyptens 12): 97–105. Heidelberg: Heidelberger Orientverlag.

Strudwick, N.C. 2005. *Texts from the pyramid age* (Writings from the ancient world 16). Leiden and Boston: Brill.

Strudwick, N.C. and Strudwick, H. 1996. *The tombs of Amenhotep, Khnummose, and Amenmose at Thebes* (Griffith Institute monographs), 2 vols. Oxford: Griffith Institute.

Struve, V.V. 1925. *Zum Töpferorakel*. Milano: Aegyptus.

Sturtewagen, C. 1990. Studies in Ramesside administrative documents, in S. Israelit-Groll (ed.), *Studies in Egyptology: Presented to Miriam Lichtheim*, vol. 2: 933–42. Jerusalem: Magnes Press, Hebrew University.

Sugi, A. 2007. Iconography and usage of an *anx*-vessel in New Kingdom temple ritual, in B. Haring and A. Klug (eds), *6. ägyptologische Tempeltagung: Funktion und Gebrauch altägyptischer Tempelräume: Leiden, 4.-7. September 2002* (Königtum, Staat und Gesellschaft früher Hochkulturen 3): 237–55. Wiesbaden: Harrassowitz.

Sweeney, D. 1994. Henuttawy's guilty conscience: Gods and grain in late Ramesside letter no. 37. *Journal of Egyptian Archaeology* 80: 208–12.

Szpakowska, K.M. 2003. *Behind closed eyes: Dreams and nightmares in ancient Egypt*. Swansea and Oakville: Classical Press of Wales and David Brown Book.

Tawfik, S. 1979. Aton studies. *Mitteilungen der Deutschen Archäologischen Instituts, Abteilung Kairo* 35: 335–44.

Teeter, E. 1997. *The presentation of Maat: Ritual and legitimacy in ancient Egypt* (Studies in ancient Oriental civilization 57). Chicago: Oriental Institute of the University of Chicago.

Teeter, E. 2003. *Scarabs, scaraboids, seals and seal impressions from Medinet Habu* (Oriental Institute publications 118). Chicago: United Graphics.

Teeter, E. 2012. Change and continuity in religion and religious practices in Ramesside Egypt, in E.H. Cline and D.B. O'Connor (eds), *Ramesses III: The life and times of Egypt's last hero*: 27–65. Ann Arbor: University of Michigan Press.

Thissen, H.-J. 1989. *Die demotischen Graffiti von Medinet Habu: Zeugnisse zu Tempel und Kult im ptolemäischen Ägypten* (Demotische Studien 10). Sommerhausen: Zauzich.

Thomas, E. 1980. The tomb of queen Ahmose (?) Merytamen, Theban tomb 320. *Serapis* 6: 171–81.

Tiele, C.P. 1882. *History of the Egyptian religion* (Comparative history of the Egyptian and Mesopotamian religions 1). London: Trübner.

Török, L. 1997. *The kingdom of Kush: Handbook of the Napatan-Meriotic civilization* (Handbuch der Orientalistik. Erste Abteilung, Nahe und der Mittlere Osten 31). Leiden: Brill.

Traunecker, C. 1972. Les rites de l'eau à Karnak d'après les textes de la rampe de Taharqa. *Bulletin de l'Institut Français d'Archéologie Orientale* 72: 195–236.

Traunecker, C. 1982. Un vase dédié à Amon de Heriherimen, in *Cahiers de Karnak 7: 1978-1981*: 307–11. Paris: Centre Franco-Égyptien d'Étude des Temples de Karnak.

Traunecker, C. 1989. Le 'château de l'or' de Thoutmosis III et les magasins nord du temple d'Amon. *Cahier de Recherches de l'Institut de Papyrologie et d'Égyptologie de Lille* 11: 89–111.

Traunecker, C. 1992. *Coptos: Hommes et dieux sur le parvis de Geb* (Orientalia Lovaniensia Analecta 43). Leuven: Peeters.

Traunecker, C. 1995. Le Papyrus Spiegelberg et l'évolution des liturgies thébaines, in S.P. Vleeming (ed.), *Hundred-gated Thebes: Acts of a colloquium on Thebes and the Theban area in the Graeco-Roman Period* (Papyrologica Lugduno-Batava 27): 183–201. Leiden and New York: Brill.

Traunecker, C., Le Saout, F., and Masson, O. 1981. *La chapelle d'Achôris à Karnak. II* (Recherche sur les grandes civilisations. Synthèse 5), 2 vols. Paris: ADPF.

Tresson, P. 1961. L'inscription de Chechanq Ier au Musée du Caire: Un frappant exemple d'impôt progressif en matière religieuse, in *Mélanges Maspero I: Orient ancien* (Mémoires publiés par les membres de l'Institut Français d'Archéologie Orientale du Caire 66), vol. 2: 817–40. Cairo: Imprimerie de l'Institut Français d'Archéologie Orientale.

Tylor, J.J. 1895. *Wall drawings and monuments of El Kab: The tomb of Paheri*. London: Egypt Exploration Fund.

Tylor, J.J. and Griffith, F.L. 1894. *The tomb of Paheri at El Kab* (Memoir of the Egypt Exploration Fund 11). London: Egypt Exploration Fund.

Ullmann, M. 2002. *König für die Ewigkeit: Die Häuser der Millionen von Jahren: Eine Untersuchung zu Königskult und Tempeltypologie in Ägypten* (Ägypten und Altes Testament 51). Wiesbaden: Harrassowitz.

Ullmann, M. 2005. Zur Lesung der Inschrift auf der Säule Antefs II. aus Karnak. *Zeitschrift für Ägyptische Sprache und Altertumskunde* 132: 166–72.

Ullmann, M. 2007. Thebes: Origins of a ritual landscape, in P. Dorman and B.M. Bryan (eds), *Sacred space and sacred function in ancient Thebes* (Studies in ancient Oriental civilization 61): 3–25. Chicago: Oriental Institute of the University of Chicago.

Uphill, E.P. 1961. A joint Sed-Festival of Thutmose III and queen Hatshepsut. *Journal of Near Eastern Studies* 20: 248–51.

Uphill, E.P. 1963. The Sed-Festivals of Akhenaten. *Journal of Near Eastern Studies* 22: 123–7.

Valbelle, D. 1985. *Les ouvriers de la tombe: Deir-el-Médineh à l'époque ramesside* (Bibliothèque d'étude 96). Cairo: Institut Français d'Archéologie Orientale.

Valbelle, D. and Husson, G. 1998. Les questions oraculaires d'Égypte: Histoire de la rechercher, nouveautés et perspectives, in W. Clarysse, A. Schoors, and H. Willems (eds), *Egyptian religion: The last thousand years. Studies dedicated to the memory of Jan Quaegebeur*, vol. 2: 1055–71. Leuven: Peeters.

van der Valk, M.H.A.L.H. 1971. *Eustathii archiepiscopi Thessalonicensis commentarii ad Homeri Iliadem pertinentes ad fidem codicis Laurentiani editi*, 5 vols. Leiden: Brill.

Vandekerckhove, H. and Müller-Wollermann, R. 2001. *Elkab VI: Die Felsinschriften des Wadi Hilâl*, 2 vols. Turnhout: Brepols.

Vandier d'Abbadie, J. 1954. *Deux tombes ramessides à Gournet-Mourraï* (Mémoires publiés par les membres de la mission archéologique française au Caire 87). Cairo: Imprimerie de l'Institut Français d'Archéologie Orientale.

Vandier, J. 1950. *Mo'alla: La tombe d'Ankhtifi et la tombe de Sebekhotep* (Bibliothèque d'étude 18). Cairo: Imprimerie de l'Institut Français d'Archéologie Orientale.

Vandorpe, K. 1995. City of many a gate, harbour for many a rebel, in S.P. Vleeming (ed.), *Hundred-gated Thebes: Acts of a colloquium on Thebes and the Theban area in the Graeco-Roman Period* (Papyrologica Lugduno-Batava 27): 204–39. Leiden and New York: Brill.

Varille, A. 1968. *Inscriptions concernant l'architecte Amenhotep, fils de Hapou* (Bibliothèque d'étude 44). Cairo: Imprimerie de l'Institut Français d'Archéologie Orientale.

te Velde, H. 1982: Mut, in E. Otto and W. Helck (eds), *Lexikon der Ägyptologie*, vol. 4: 246–8. Wiesbaden: Harrassowitz.

Ventura, R. 1986. *Living in a city of the dead: A selection of topographical and administrative terms in the documents of the Theban necropolis*. Freiburg: Vandenhoeck & Ruprecht.

Ventura, R. 1987. On the location of the administrative outpost of the community of workmen in western Thebes. *Journal of Egyptian Archaeology* 73: 149–60.

Vercoutter, J. 1950. Les statues du général Hor, gouverneur d'Hérakléopolis, de Busiris et d'Héliopolis. *Bulletin de l'Institut Français d'Archéologie Orientale* 49: 85–114.

Verner, M. 1980. Die Königsmutter Chentkaus von Abusir und einige Bemerkungen zur Geschichte der 5. Dynastie. *Studien zur Altägyptischen Kultur* 8: 243–68.

Verner, M. 2006a. *The pyramid complex of Raneferef: The archaeology* (Abusir 9). Praha: Czech Institute of Egyptology.

Verner, M. 2006b. Contemporaneous evidence for the relative chronology of Dyns. 4 and 5, in E. Hornung, R. Krauss, D. Warburton, and M. Eaton-Krauss (eds), *Ancient Egyptian chronology* (Handbook of Oriental studies. Section 1, The Near and Middle East 83): 124–43. Leiden: Brill.

Verner, M. 2008. The system of dating in the Old Kingdom, in H. Vymazalová and M. Bárta (eds), *Chronology and archaeology in ancient Egypt (the third millennium B.C.)*: 23–43. Praha: Czech Institute of Egyptology.

Vernus, P. 1973. La stèle C 3 du Louvre. *Revue d'Égyptologie* 25: 217–34.

Vernus, P. 1975. Une texte oraculaire de Ramsès VI. *Bulletin de l'Institut Français d'Archéologie Orientale* 75: 103–10.

Vernus, P. 1978. Littérature et autobiographie: Les inscriptions de *s3-mwt* surnommé *kyky*. *Revue d'Égyptologie* 30: 115–46.

Vernus, P. 1980. Inscriptions de la Troisième Période Intermédiaire (IV): Le texte oraculaire réemployé dans le passage axial du IIIe pylône dans le temple de Karnak, in *Cahiers de Karnak 6: 1973-1977*: 215–33. Paris: Centre Franco-Égyptien d'Étude des Temples de Karnak.

Vernus, P. 1987. Études de philologie et de linguistique (VI). *Revue d'Égyptologie* 38: 163–81.

Versnel, H.S. 1970. *Triumphus: An inquiry into the origin, development and meaning of the Roman triumph*. Leiden: Brill.

Vinson, S. 2009. The demotic 'regnal year' group as *Hsb*, 'reckoning'. *Enchoria* 30: 151–4.

Virey, P. 1886. Le tombeau d'Am-n-teh et la fonction de *imy-r ry.t*. *Recueil de Travaux* 7: 32–46.

Virey, P. 1891. Le tombeau d'Amenemheb, in P. Virey (ed.), *Sept tombeaux thébains de la XVIIIe Dynastie* (Mémoires publiés par les membres de l'Institut Français d'Archéologie Orientale du Caire 5 (2)): 224–85. Paris: Ernest Leroux.

Virey, P. 1900. La Tombe des Vignes à Thèbes. *Recueil de Travaux* 22: 83–97.

Vittmann, G. 2001. Zwei Priestereinführungsinschriften der 25. Dynastie aus Luxor (Berlin 2096 und 2097). *Studien zur Altägyptischen Kultur* 29: 357–70.

Vleeming, S.P. 1980. The sale of a slave in the time of pharaoh Py. *Oudheidkundige Mededelingen uit het Rijksmuseum van Oudheden te Leiden* 61: 1–17.

Vleeming, S.P. 1982. The days on which the *qnbt* used to gather, in R.J. Demarée and J.J. Janssen (eds), *Gleanings from Deir el-Medîna* (Egyptologische uitgaven 1): 183–92. Leiden: Nederlands Instituut voor het Nabije Oosten.

Vogelsang-Eastwood, G. 1992. *The production of linen in pharaonic Egypt*. Leiden: Textile Research Centre.

Vörös, G. 1998. *Temple on the pyramid of Thebes: Hungarian excavations on Thoth Hill at the temple of pharaoh Montuhotep Sankhkara, 1995-1998*. Budapest: Százszorszép Kiadó és Nyomda.

Vörös, G. 2003. The ancient nest of Horus above Thebes: Hungarian excavations on Thoth Hill at the temple of king Sankhkara Montuhetep III (1995–1998), in Z.A. Hawass and L.P. Brock (eds), *Egyptology at the dawn of the twenty-first century: Proceedings of the Eighth International Congress of Egyptologists, Cairo, 2000*: 547–56. Cairo and New York: American University in Cairo Press.

Vos, R.L. 1998. Varius coloribus Apis: Some remarks on the colours of Apis and other sacred animals, in W. Clarysse, A. Schoors, and H. Willems (eds), *Egyptian religion: The last thousand years: Studies dedicated to the memory of Jan Quaegebeur*, vol. 1: 709–18. Leuven: Peeters.

Vymazalová, H. 2008. Some remarks on the *wAg*-Festival in the papyrus archive of Raneferef, in H. Vymazalová and M. Bárta (eds), *Chronology and archaeology in ancient Egypt (the third millennium B.C.)*: 137–43. Praha: Czech Institute of Egyptology.

Wagner, G. 1971. Inscriptions grecques du temple de Karnak (I). *Bulletin de l'Institut Français d'Archéologie Orientale* 70: 1–38.

Wagner, G. 1998. Le concept de *Hsy* à la lumière des inscriptions grecques, in W. Clarysse, A. Schoors, and H. Willems (eds), *Egyptian religion: The last thousand years: Studies dedicated to the memory of Jan Quaegebeur*, vol. 2: 1073–8. Leuven: Peeters.

Waitkus, W. 1997. *Die Texte in den unteren Krypten des Hathortempels von Dendera: Ihre Aussagen zur Funktion und Bedeutung dieser Räume*. Mainz: Philipp von Zabern.

Waitkus, W. 2008. *Untersuchungen zu Kult und Funktion des Luxortempels* (Aegyptiaca hamburgensia 2), 2 vols. Gladbeck: PeWe-Verlag.

van Walsem, R. 1982. Month-names and feasts at Deir el-Medina, in R.J. Demarée and J.J. Janssen (eds), *Gleanings from Deir el-Medîna* (Egyptologische uitgaven 1): 215–44. Leiden: Nederlands Instituut voor het Nabije Oosten.

Warburton, D. 1990. An hieratic graffito, in E. Hornung (ed.), *Zwei ramessidische Königsgräber: Ramses IV. und Ramses VII.* (Theben 11): 132–3. Mainz: Philipp von Zabern.

Warburton, D. 1997. *State and economy in ancient Egypt: Fiscal vocabulary of the New Kingdom* (Orbis biblicus et orientalis 151). Freiburg and Göttingen: University Press Fribourg and Vandenhoeck & Ruprecht.

Wasmuth, M. 2003. *Innovationen und Extravaganzen: Ein Beitrag zur Architektur der thebanischen Beamtengräber der 18. Dynastie* (British Archaeological Reports. International Series 1165). Oxford: Archaeopress.

Weeks, K.R. 2000. *Atlas of the Valley of the Kings* (Publications of the Theban Mapping Project 1). Cairo: American University in Cairo Press.

Weinstein, J.M. 1973. Foundation deposits in ancient Egypt. Unpublished PhD dissertation, University of Pennsylvania.

Wells, R.A. 1987. The Amarna M, X, K boundary stelae date: A modern calendar equivalent. *Studien zur Altägyptischen Kultur* 14: 313–33.

Wente, E.F. 1961. A letter of complaint to the vizier To. *Journal of Near Eastern Studies* 20: 252–7.

Wente, E.F. 1962. Egyptian 'Make merry' songs reconsidered. *Journal of Near Eastern Studies* 21: 118–28.

Wente, E.F. 1967. *Late Ramesside letters* (Studies in ancient Oriental civilization 33). Chicago: University of Chicago Press.

Wente, E.F. 1969. Hathor at the jubilee, in *Studies in honor of John A. Wilson, September 12, 1969* (Studies in ancient Oriental civilization 35): 83–91. Chicago: University of Chicago Press.

Wente, E.F. 1975. Thutmose III's accession and the beginning of the New Kingdom. *Journal of Near Eastern Studies* 34: 265–72.

Wente, E.F. 1980. The Gurob letter to Amenhotep IV. *Serapis* 6: 209–15.

Wente, E.F. 1990. *Letters from ancient Egypt* (Writings from the ancient world 1). Atlanta: Scholars Press.

Werbrouck, M. 1949. *Le temple d'Hatshepsout à Deir el Bahari*. Bruxelles: Édition de la Fondation Égyptologique Reine Élizabeth.

Werner, E.K. 1986. Montu and the 'falcon ships' of the Eighteenth Dynasty. *Journal of American Research Center in Egypt* 23: 107–23.

Wessetzky, V. 1984. Die Teilnahme von Nichtägyptern in einem ägyptischen Fest. *Annales Universitatis Scientiarum Budapestinensis de Rolando Eötvös nominatae, Sectio classica* 7: 15–22.

Westendorf, W. 1967. Bemerkungen zur 'Kammer der Wiedergeburt' im Tutanchamungrab. *Zeitschrift für Ägyptische Sprache und Altertumskunde* 94: 139–50.

Wiebach, S. 1986. Die Begegnung von Lebenden und Verstorbenen im Rahmen des thebanischen Talfestes. *Studien zur Altägyptischen Kultur* 13: 263–91.

Wiercińska, J. 1990. La procession d'Amon dans la décoration du temple de Thoutmosis III à Deir el-Bahari. *Études et Travaux* 14: 62–90.

Wiercińska, J. 2006. Fragment of a wall relief from the temple of Thutmosis III at Deir el-Bahari, in K.N. Sowada and B. Ockinga (eds), *Egyptian art in the Nicholson Museum, Sydney*: 303–12. Sydney: Meditarch Publishing.

Wilcken, U. 1927. *Urkunden der Ptolemäerzeit: Ältere Funde*, 2 vols. Berlin: de Gruyter.

Wildung, D. 1969. Zur Frühgeschichte des Amun-Tempels von Karnak. *Mitteilungen des Deutschen Archäologischen Instituts Kairo* 25: 212–9.

Wilkinson, J.G. and Birch, S. 1878. *The manners and customs of the ancient Egyptians*, 3 vols, new ed. London: J. Murray.

Wilkinson, R.H. 2000. *The complete temples of ancient Egypt*. London: Thames and Hudson.

Wilkinson, R.H. 2009. The Tausert Temple Project 2009 season. *The Ostracon: Journal of the Egyptian Study Society* 20: 3–13.

Wilkinson, T.A.H. 2000. *Royal annals of ancient Egypt: The Palermo Stone and its associated fragments*. London and New York: Kegan Paul International.

Willcocks, W. and Craig, J.I. 1913. *Egyptian irrigation*, 2 vols, 3rd ed. London and New York: E. & F.N. Spon and Spon & Chamberlain.

Willems, H. 1996. *The coffin of Heqata (Cairo JdE 36418): A case study of Egyptian funerary culture of the early Middle Kingdom* (Orientalia Lovaniensia Analecta 70). Leuven: Uitgeverij Peeters en Departement Oriëntalistiek.

Williams, R.J. 1977/1978. Piety and ethics in Ramessid age. *Journal of the Society of the Study of Egyptian Antiquities* 18: 131–7.

Wilson, H. 1989. Pot-baked bread in ancient Egypt. *Discussions in Egyptology* 13: 87–100.

Wilson, J.A. 1948. The oath in ancient Egypt. *Journal of Near Eastern Studies* 7: 129–56.

Wilson, J.A. 1969. The legend of the possessed princess, in J.B. Pritchard (ed.), *Ancient Near Eastern texts relating to the Old Testament*, 3rd ed.: 29–31. Princeton: Princeton University Press.

Wilson, J.A. 1970. The Theban tomb (no. 409) of Si-Mut, called Kiki. *Journal of Near Eastern Studies* 29: 187–92.

Wilson, P. 1997. *A Ptolemaic lexikon: A lexicographical study of the texts in the temple of Edfu* (Orientalia Lovaniensia Analecta 78). Leuven: Uitgeverij Peeters en Department Oosterse Studies.

Winand, J. 2003. Les décrets oraculaires pris en l'honneur d'Henouttaouy et de Maâtkarê (Xe et VIIe pylônes), in *Cahiers de Karnak 11*: 603–710. Cairo: Centre Franco-Égyptien d'Étude des Temples de Karnak.

Winlock, H.E. 1932. *The tomb of queen Meryet-Amun at Thebes*. New York: Metropolitan Museum of Art.

Winlock, H.E. 1947. *The rise and fall of the Middle Kingdom in Thebes*. New York: Macmillan.

Winter, E. 1951. Das ägyptische Wag-Fest. Unpublished PhD dissertation, Universität Wien.

Wissa-Wassef, C. 1991a: Calendar and agriculture, in A.S. Atiya (ed.), *The Coptic encyclopedia*, vol. 2: 440–3. New York and Toronto: Macmillan and Maxwell Macmillan International.

Wissa-Wassef, C. 1991b: Calendar, seasons, and Coptic liturgy, in A.S. Atiya (ed.), *The Coptic encyclopedia*, vol. 2: 443–4. New York and Toronto: Macmillan and Maxwell Macmillan International.

de Wit, C. 1958. *Les inscriptions du temple d'Opet à Karnak* (Bibliotheca Aegyptiaca 11–3), 3 vols. Bruxelles: Édition de la Fondation Égyptologique Reine Élizabeth.

de Wit, C. 1961a. Inscriptions dédicatoires du temple d'Edfou: I. E. IV, 1–16. *Chronique d'Égypte* 36: 56–97.

de Wit, C. 1961b. Inscriptions dédicatoires du temple d'Edfou: II. E. VII, 1–20. *Chronique d'Égypte* 36: 277–320.

Wohlgemuth, G. 1957. Das Sokarfest. Unpublished PhD dissertation, Universität Göttingen.

Wolf, W. 1931. *Das schöne Fest von Opet: Die Festzugsdarstellung im grossen Säulengange des Tempels von Luksor* (Veröffentlichungen der Ernst von Sieglin Expedition in Ägypten 5). Leipzig: J.C. Hinrichs.

Wolterman, C. 1996. A vizier of Ramses III visits an oracle of Amun and Deir el-Medina. *Revue d'Égyptologie* 47: 147–70.

Wreszinski, W. 1923. *Atlas zur altaegyptischen Kulturgeschichte*, 3 vols. Leipzig: J.C. Hinrichs.

Wreszinski, W. 1931. Die Statue eines hohen Verwaltungsbeamten. *Zeitschrift für Ägyptische Sprache und Altertumskunde* 67: 132–3.

Xekalaki, G. and el-Khodary, R. 2011. Aspects of the cultic role of queen Nefertari and the royal children during the reign of Ramesses II, in M. Collier and S.R. Snape (eds), *Ramesside studies in honour of K. A. Kitchen*: 561–71. Bolton: Rutherford.

Yamani, S. 2002. New Year's bottles from Tell Marqula (Dakhla Oasis). *Bulletin de l'Institut Français d'Archéologie Orientale* 102: 425–36.

Yoshimura, S., Kondo, J., and Sakurai, K. 1988. *Comparative studies of noble tombs in Theban necropolis (tomb nos. 8, 38, 39, 48, 54, 57, 63, 64, 66, 74, 78, 89, 90, 91, 107, 120, 139, 147, 151, 181, 201, 253, 295)*. Tokyo: Waseda University.

Young, E. 1963. Some notes on the chronology and genealogy of the Twenty-First Dynasty. *Journal of the American Research Center in Egypt* 2: 99–112.

Yoyotte, J. 1962. Études géographiques II. Les localités méridionales de la région memphite et le 'pehou d'Héracléopolis'. *Revue d'Égyptologie* 14: 75–111.

Yoyotte, J. 1983. Un souhait de bonne année en faveur du prince Nechao. *Revue d'Égyptologie* 34: 142–5.

Žába, Z. 1956. *Les Maximes de Ptaḥḥotep*. Praha: Éditions de l'Académie Tchécoslovaque des Sciences.

Žabkar, L.V. 1988. *Hymns to Isis in her temple at Philae*. Hanover and London: University Press of New England.

Zandee, J. 1947. *De hymnen aan Amon van Papyrus Leiden I 350* (Oudheidkundige Mededelingen uit het Rijksmuseum van Oudheden te Leiden 28). Leiden: Rijksmuseum van Oudheden.

Ziegler, C. 1982. Le calendar d'Éléphantine, in B. André-Leicknam and C. Ziegler (eds), *Naissance de l'écriture: Cunéiformes et hiéroglyphes: Galeries Nationales du Grand Palais, 7 mai–9 août 1982*: 264–5. Paris: Ministère de la Culture, Editions de la Réunion des Musées Nationaux.

Zinn, K. 2011. Temples, palaces and libraries: A search for an alliance between archaeological and textual evidence, in R. Gundlach and K. Spence (eds), *5. Symposium zur ägyptischen Königsideologie: Palace and temple, architecture-decoration-ritual, Cambridge, July, 16th-17th, 2007* (Königtum, Staat und Gesellschaft früher Hochkulturen 4 (2)): 181–202. Wiesbaden: Harrassowitz.

Zivie, C.M. 1976. *Giza au deuxième millénaire* (Bibliothèque d'étude 70). Cairo: Institut Français d'Archéologie Orientale.

Zivie, C.M. 1979. Les rites d'érection de l'obélisque et du pilier ioun, in *Hommages à la mémoire de Serge Sauneron, 1927-1976* (Bibliothèque d'étude 81), vol. 1: 477–98. Cairo: Institut Français d'Archéologie Orientale.

Zivie, C.M. 1982. *Le temple de Deir Chelouit*, 4 vols. Cairo: Institut Français d'Archéologie Orientale.